Lecture Notes in Computer Science 5143

Commenced Publication in 1973
Founding and Former Series Editors:
Gerhard Goos, Juris Hartmanis, and Jan van Leeuwen

T0223253

Gene Tsudik (Ed.)

Financial Cryptography and Data Security

12th International Conference, FC 2008
Cozumel, Mexico, January 28-31, 2008
Revised Selected Papers

 Springer

Volume Editor

Gene Tsudik
Computer Science Department
University of California
Irvine, CA, USA
E-mail: gts@ics.uci.edu

Library of Congress Control Number: Applied for

CR Subject Classification (1998): E.3, D.4.6, K.6.5, K.4.4, C.2, J.1, F.2.1-2

LNCS Sublibrary: SL 4 – Security and Cryptology

ISSN   0302-9743
ISBN-10   3-540-85229-8 Springer Berlin Heidelberg New York
ISBN-13   978-3-540-85229-2 Springer Berlin Heidelberg New York

Springer is a part of Springer Science+Business Media

springer.com

© Springer-Verlag Berlin Heidelberg 2008
Printed in Germany

Typesetting: Camera-ready by author, data conversion by Scientific Publishing Services, Chennai, India
Printed on acid-free paper   SPIN: 12443772   06/3180   5 4 3 2 1 0

Foreword

This volume contains the proceedings of the 12th Financial Cryptography and Data Security International Conference, held in Cozumel, Mexico, January 28–31 2008.

Financial cryptography (FC) and data security has been for years the main international forum for research, advanced development, education, exploration, and debate regarding information assurance in the context of finance and commerce.

Despite the strong competition from other top-tier related security conferences, the Program Committee received a significant number of submissions, indicating a growing acceptance of FC as the premier financial and data security forum. The Program Committee, led by the PC Chair Gene Tsudik, achieved an excellent program balance between research, practice, and panel sessions. This year the program included two new additions, namely, a short-paper track and a poster session, both extremely well received.

Intimate and colorful by tradition, the high-quality program was not the only attraction of FC. In the past, FC conferences have been held in highly research-synergistic locations such as Tobago, Anguilla, Dominica, Key West, Guadeloupe, Bermuda, and the Grand Cayman. In 2008 we continued this tradition and the conference was located in sunny Cozumel, Mexico. The ongoing carnival, sailing, submarine trips, and Mayan ruins were just a few of the numerous excitements.

Organizing a conference with such high standards was a true team effort. I would like to thank all those who made this possible: the International Financial Cryptography Association, the Program Committee for their careful reviews, the keynote speakers and panel members, the Local Arrangements Chair Ray Hirschfeld for finding such a great all-inclusive resort venue, Peter Williams for his help beyond the call of duty, and the authors and participants that made this such an exhilarating, intellectually rich experience. Last but not least, I am also thankful to our sponsors for their valuable support.

Ultimately, I hope this year's experience and quality research program will entice you to participate in Financial Cryptography 2009. I look forward to seeing you in Barbados in February.

May 2008   Radu Sion

Preface

I am are very happy to have taken part in the 12th Financial Cryptography and Data Security Conference (FC 2008). Due to the recent growth in the number of security and cryptography venues, the competition for high-quality submissions has been on the rise. Despite that, the continued success of FC is attested by the research community's enthusiastic support reflected in the number and the quality of submitted research papers.

FC 2008 received a total of 86 submissions. They were reviewed by a highly competent Program Committee and a set of qualified external reviewers. Each submission was reviewed by at least three reviewers. Following a rigorous selection, ranking and discussion process, 26 submissions were accepted, corresponding to 16 full and 9 short papers. In addition, the conference included two invited talks, two panels, a poster session and a rump session. All these components resulted in a very eclectic, engaging and interesting program.

A number of people contributed a great deal to FC 2008. First and foremost, I would like to thank the authors of all submissions. They are the key factor in making the conference successful and their confidence and support are hightly appreciated. I am also grateful to the dedicated, knowledgeable and hard-working Program Committee members who – despite tight deadlines and a less-than-perfect reviewing system – delivered excellent reviews on time and took part in lengthy deliberations. Their selfless dedication and community service spirit are highly appreciated! I am very much indebted to Radu Sion (General Chair), who oversaw a myriad of organizational aspects and made the conference run very smoothly (with valuable assistance by Peter Williams). A special word of thanks goes to Paul van Oorschot and Moti Yung for delivering two excellent invited talks, to Mary Ellen Zurko and Yvo Desmedt – for organizing two very exciting panels – and to Bogdan Carbunar for putting together a successful poster session. Last but not least, I thank Ray Hirschfeld and the IFCA directors for their guidance during the conference planning stages.

May 2008   Gene Tsudik

Organization

The 12th International Conference on Financial Cryptography and Data Security (FC 2008) was organized by the International Financial Cryptography Association (IFCA).

Executive Committee

General Chair	Radu Sion (Stony Brook University)
Program Chair	Gene Tsudik (University of California, Irvine)
Poster Chair	Bogdan Carbunar (Motorola Labs)
Local Arrangements Chair	Rafael Hirschfeld (Unipay)

Program Committee

N. Asokan	Nokia Research
Giuseppe Ateniese	Johns Hopkins University
Nikita Borisov	University of Illinois, Urbana-Champaign
George Danezis	Microsoft Research, Cambridge
Stefan Dziembowski	Università di Roma (La Sapienza)
Kevin Fu	University of Massachusetts, Amherst
Philippe Golle	PARC
Dieter Gollmann	Technische Universität Hamburg-Harburg
Stanislaw Jarecki	University of California, Irvine
Aggelos Kiayias	University of Connecticut
Javier Lopez	Universidad de Málaga
Arjen Lenstra	Ecole Polytechnique Fédérale de Lausanne
Ninghui Li	Purdue University
Patrick McDaniel	Pennsylvania State University
Alessandro Mei	Università di Roma (La Sapienza)
Refik Molva	Institut Eurecom
Pino Persiano	Università di Salerno
Ahmad-Reza Sadeghi	Ruhr-Universität Bochum
Diana Smetters	PARC
Michael Szydlo	Akamai Technologies
Suzanne Wetzel	Stevens Institute of Technology

External Referees

Krzysztof Pietrzak	Ali Bagherzandi
Rahul Savani	Josh Olsen
Bartosz Przydatek	Xiaomin Liu

Benessa Defend
Thomas Heydt-Benjamin
Mastooreh Salajegheh
Benjamin Ransford
David Molnar
Lisa Johansen
Will Enck
Patrick Traynor
Luke St. Clair
Kevin Butler
Vicente Benjumea
Jose Onieva
Melek Önen
Rahul Savani
Stefan Shiffner

Slim Trabelsi
Yves Roudier
Alessandro Sorniotti
John Solis
Ulrike Mayer
Jared Cordasco
David Galindo
Liu Yang
Berry Schoenmakers
Hong-Sheng Zhou
Alice
Bob
Eve
Elvis

Sponsors

PGP Corporation (Silver)
Google (Bronze)
Nokia (Bronze)

Bibit (In-kind)

Table of Contents

Attacks and Counter-Measures II

Signatures and Encryption

Anonymity and E-Cash

Miscellaneous

Quantifying Resistance to the Sybil Attack*

N. Boris Margolin and Brian Neil Levine

Dept. of Computer Science, Univ. of Massachusetts, Amherst, MA USA
{margolin,brian}@cs.umass.edu

Abstract. Sybil attacks have been shown to be unpreventable except under the protection of a vigilant central authority. We use an economic analysis to show quantitatively that some applications and protocols are more robust against the attack than others. In our approach, for each distributed application and an attacker objective, there is a critical value that determines the cost-effectiveness of the attack. A Sybil attack is worthwhile only when the critical value is exceeded by the ratio of the value of the attacker's goal to the cost of identities. We show that for many applications, successful Sybil attacks may be expensive even when the Sybil attack cannot be prevented. Specifically, we propose the use of a recurring fee as a deterrent against the Sybil attack. As a detailed example, we look at four variations of the Sybil attack against a recurring fee based onion routing anonymous routing network and quantify its vulnerability.

1 Introduction

Many distributed services and peer-to-peer (p2p) applications are vulnerable to *Sybil attacks* [17], where a single malicious *entity* masquerades as many counterfeit *identities* and uses them to launch a coordinated assault. The attack can be used to ruin the integrity of reputation systems [12,5], create false routes in mobile ad hoc networks [23], identify users of anonymous routing protocols [16], cheat p2p computing systems (e.g., SETI@home) [47], and free-ride cooperative file storage systems [15]. A form of the Sybil attack is commonly used to fool Google's PageRank algorithm [6]. In most situations it is not possible to prevent Sybil attacks using resource tests, and certificate systems generally do not guarantee no entity has two keys. The Sybil attack has been widely studied but remains unsolved in general. Several papers have evaluated formally the conditions under which applications are susceptible to the attack [17, 12], however this is a coarse-grained approach. It is not true that all applications are equally vulnerable.

In this paper, we quantify the threat of the Sybil attack using an economic model. For the first time, we show that the attack poses a different level of threat to different applications. We derive a concrete measure of attack resistance called the *Sybil valuation*. The valuation is the critical ratio of the value of the attacker's goal to the per-identity cost of the protocol — at the critical ratio or above the attacker can expect to profit from attacking the protocol. This measure allows us to quantitatively compare the threat as the number of peers in the system changes. Moreover, our analysis distinguishes applications not by what type of service they provide, but rather by the specific Sybil attack variations the applications allow.

* This work was supported in part by National Science Foundation award NSF-0133055.

G. Tsudik (Ed.): FC 2008, LNCS 5143, pp. 1–15, 2008.

Many have suggested addressing the Sybil attack by charging one-time resource costs per participating identity. As part of our analysis, we show that protocols that charge a *recurring fee per participating identity* are more effective as a disincentive against successful Sybil attacks. Our previous work on the Informant protocols is an example [26] of how recurring fees can also be used to detect Sybil attacks, and our work here is complementary. We show that recurring fee protocols are more secure because they require that the successful attacker's has resources that scale linearly with the number of other participants (instead of a constant amount). This linear requirement is synergistic with p2p applications that seek to increase the number of peers for other performance benefits. Moreover, in recurring fee protocols, two uncoordinated Sybil attackers will increase the resources required of each other without increasing costs to honest participants.

As a concrete example of protocol analysis using the Sybil valuation, we evaluate a Recurring Fee Onion Routing protocol, which we refer to as *RFOR* to distinguish it from Onion Routing or the deployed Tor protocol [16], which operates without explicit or implicit recurring fees. In Tor, as it is deployed now, an attacker will always find benefit from setting up just two identities no matter the population size, and the attacker can amortize all costs over time to a negligible amount. Evaluations of RFOR using the traces of participation of the actual Tor system show a sharp contrast. For example, as of September 2007, the traces show $n = 1373$ volunteer peers acting as proxy servers. With the recurring router entry fee charged by a RFOR protocol, a rational entity would have to value the knowledge of a single connection of a specific user at $4n$ times the router entry fee in order to launch a Sybil attack. For a fee set at $0.01, this value is $54.92 given the population in the traces, which may be enough to discourage only casual attackers; if RFOR was deployed to protect users that are more concerned about their anonymity, the fee could be set higher. Using these real traces in our evaluation, we are able to show that a RFOR system would grow less vulnerable to some Sybil attacks with increases popularity, but would still be susceptible to Sybil-based DoS attacks by resource-poor attackers.

For applications that cannot tolerate any entity with multiple identities, centralized manual identity certification is the only solution, but, as Douceur points out, few applications can bear the cost. For many applications, managing recurring payment of fees is a more reasonable solution. Several distributed, Internet-based micro-payment schemes can manage fees [8, 7, 42, 41]. For applications whose users may be unwilling to make monetary payments, fees can also be imposed less robustly, though perhaps more readily, through the use of non-monetary mechanisms such as CAPTCHAs [43] and SMS messages. Our approach is flexible in that peers in the system need to show only that a payment was made; the payment does not have to be to other peers in the system. Furthermore, in our approach identities are never asked to prove they are separate entities.

Outline. In Section 2, we state our model and assumptions regarding identity, protocols, and Sybils. In Section 3, we present a cost-benefit analysis for malicious attackers based on entry fees. In Section 4 we discuss different types of entry fees. In Section 5, we give an overview of approaches to the Sybil attack in the literature. To our knowledge, this is the first broad overview of research on this subject. We offer concluding remarks in Section 6.

2 Goals and Model

Our model is an extension of Douceur's [17] in which each peer participating in a network protocol is a unique *identity* that is controlled by a rational actor [34] known as an *entity*. A Sybil attack occurs when one entity secretly controls multiple identities. Identities send messages to each other through a *communications cloud* that precludes definite identification using direct observation. We assume that messages can be securely linked to identities, though not to entities. This can be accomplished, as in Douceur, by having identities choose public/private key pairs and signing their messages or by other methods [37]. The use of public keys does not imply a PKI because the keys are not linked securely to any real-world entity.

We model the applications running the network protocol as having an *entry phase* and a *service phase*. During the entry phase, each identity is charged an *entry fee*, and we assume the identity can later demonstrate to others that the fee has been paid. Recurring fee applications force peers to repeat the entry phase (and fee) after one or more service phases.

Below, we introduce a model that includes entity utility and strategy, the value of the Sybil attack in general, and then we define three specific types of Sybil attacks. First, we discuss the limitations of our approach.

Limitations. Our model applies to applications that involve weakly authenticated participants sharing resources. We show that such applications that charge recurring fees are more secure than those that pay a one-time fixed cost. We evaluate anonymous communication systems (and other applications) below as an example — yet, Tor charges no fees at all currently. It is not our intent to compare having no fees (and therefore no defense against the Sybil attack) against having fees. Moreover, our analysis does not indicate whether applications would be more or less popular if they charged (recurring) fees. On the one hand, some users might not find the increased cost worth the application's services; on the other hand, some users might find the application has added benefit since it is more secure. The answer to this financial question depends on the specific application and business model.

We do not investigate how to ensure fees are paid, though many others have done so [8, 7, 42, 41]). We do note that doing so is an easier task than requiring a trusted authority that can certify that each identity is an independent entity; the latter is difficult even with access to real-world documents [1]. Finally, we note that fees do not need to be monetary, and typically will not be. Instead, it may involve the use of CAPTCHAS [43], SMS messages, or other techniques, as discussed in Section 4. Given the prevalence of botnets, fees that can be paid by obtaining a computer and IP address are not satisfactory.

2.1 Entity Utility

Because our entities are rational actors, they have a specific utility for each possible protocol outcome, and they apply strategies that give them the highest possible expected utility. Rational actors perform a cost-benefit analysis to determine what action to take — including whether to launch a Sybil attack against a specific protocol.

Our model follows basic game theory [34]. Let E represent a set of entities participating in a protocol, controlling a set of identities I. Let S_e be the set of possible actions, called *strategies*, that an entity $e \in E$ can carry out. An entity must decide on a single strategy based on his knowledge and goals. An example strategy would be launching a Sybil attack with a certain number of identities. Since there are multiple entities participating, there is a set of outcomes for $n = |E|$ entities

$$O = S_{e_1} \times S_{e_2} \times \cdots \times S_{e_n} \tag{1}$$

The combination of the strategies of participating entities completely defines an *outcome*. An outcome $o \in O$ is a selection of one strategy from each of these n sets; that is o is tuple $(s_{e_1}, \ldots, s_{e_n})$ representing the strategy taken by all entities. For simplicity, we do not discuss non-deterministic (i.e., irrational) attackers, but they require only minor changes to our model.

Each entity's preferences are expressed using a utility function that maps outcomes to a utility score. The utility of an outcome o to an entity e is the sum of a *benefit utility* $\tau_e(o)$ and a *cost utility* $\pi_e(o)$ (normally negative) determined by payments made by e in outcome o:

$$u_e(o) \equiv \tau_e(o) + \pi_e(o). \tag{2}$$

When entry fees are used, the cost, $\pi_e(o)$, is the product of the entry fee and the number of identities controlled by the entity.

2.2   The General Sybil Objective

For an attacker entity m considering the wisdom of a Sybil attack, $\sigma_q \in S_m$ represents the strategy of entering q identities — and doing whatever else is necessary in order to reach some objective.

Let A be the set of the objectives that an attacker can attempt to achieve using Sybil attacks. We define an *objective success count* operator $\psi(o)$, which gives the number of successes by m in the outcome o. For example, one set of objectives is to control the entire path through an anonymity system, revealing the initiator of a packet. When participating as multiple Sybil identities, an attacker may control multiple paths, revealing multiple initiators, which increases the value of ψ accordingly.

We assume that the attacking entity $m \in E$ values attacks linearly, with the success of a single attack valued at v, so that

$$\tau_m(o) = v\psi(o). \tag{3}$$

In general, an attacker's expected benefit from a Sybil attack using q identities is

$$\mathrm{E}[\tau_m | s_m = \sigma_q] = \sum_{o \in O} v\psi(o)\Pr[o|\sigma_q]. \tag{4}$$

We restrict our analysis to protocols in which honest entities do not gain any benefit from Sybil attacks. That is, we assume honest users value most the protocol's objectives (e.g., anonymity) and that malicious users value outside objectives more (e.g., breaking anonymity).

2.3 Specific Sybil Objectives

The Sybil attack can be launched as one of several specific *objectives* that depend on the application being attacked. We distinguish these attacks by the way the application uses peers to offer service. In all cases, the application starts the service phase by selecting a subset of k peers (identities); typically, a subset k is selected for each of the n participating identities. For example, Crowds forms a path of k peers for anonymous routing for each peer that is a source of traffic. From here, we can distinguish several different Sybil attack objectives.

First, for any specific application, there is a **minimum number of identities** required for a successful attack. For example, to successfully launch the predecessor attack an attacker needs only $c = 1$ identities for the Crowds protocol but $c = 2$ identities to for the Onion Routing protocol [45].

Second, we distinguish **One-time fee objectives**, which are applicable to applications where the attacker can launch Sybil attacks repeatedly without additional cost — as when entry fees are charged only one time ever per identity. Since any attack with a non-zero probability of success is expected to succeed eventually, a given strategy has either no chance of success, or is guaranteed success. In this case, the only strategies that the attacker needs to consider are σ_0 (entering no identities) and σ_c (entering the minimum number of identities required for success). One-time fee attacks are denoted T_c. Onion Routing and the deployed Tor system are examples of one-time fee protocols.

Third, for applications that charge a **recurring entry fee** for one or more service phases, several attacks can be distinguished. For example, while most anonymous routing protocols create subgroups (paths) of k peers, choosing with replacement from a set I of peers, Pastiche [15] is a p2p application that stores backup data from each source node with k other peers, choosing without replacement (though Pastiche does not charge fees in reality). In both cases, the objective of the attacker is to control c of the k identities chosen each service phase for each of n sources. However, we distinguish the former case as a *binomial objective*, since k identities are chosen *with* replacement from I. And we refer to the latter case as a *hypergeometric objective*, since k identities are chosen *without* replacement from I. We further detail these cases below.

- **Binomial objectives.** For each identity in the application, a subgroup is chosen with replacement, and the attacker may try to target all subgroups, a specific victim's subgroup, or try to succeed against any (that is, no one specifically) victim's subgroup, as we detail below.
  - When attacking a **specific** subgroup, denoted $B_{c,k}^{\text{spec.}}$, the attacker's utility is proportional to the probability of success against the one identity.
  - When seeking success against **any one** subgroup, denoted $B_{c,k}^{\text{any}}$, the attacker's utility is proportional to the probability of success against at least one identity.
  - When attacking **all** n subgroups, denoted $B_{c,k}^{\text{all}}$, the attacker's utility is proportional to the total number of group control successes.

- **Hypergeometric objectives.** A subgroup of k identities are chosen without replacement. Such objectives are denoted $H_{c,k}$. SETI@home [38] and Pastiche [15] are subject to the hypergeometric objectives, since identities in peer groups are chosen without replacement, for redundancy. The notation $H_{c,k}$ represents the objective of controlling a specific peer group. There are a large number of natural subcases of the Hypergeometric objective (compared to just three for the Binomial objective), and to avoid complexity we omit them.

Commonly, p2p applications select identities for subgroups uniformly at random, and we assume so here for all objectives; our previous work [45] suggests that uniform random selection is the most attack-resistant approach for anonymous communications systems, and we conjecture that it is the most attack-resistant approach for many other p2p systems as well.

3   The Sybil Valuation

In this section, we use our model to determine when the benefits of a specific Sybil attack exceeds the costs, a point we call the *Sybil valuation. When an attacker's valuation of their objective, in terms of the entry fee cost, exceeds the Sybil valuation, it is in their interest to launch the attack.*

We denote the Sybil valuation for an objective a by γ_a, defined

$$\gamma_a \equiv \min_q \frac{q}{E[\psi_a|\sigma_q]} \tag{5}$$

where $E[\psi_a|\sigma_q]$ gives the expected number of successes for an attacker with the objective a launching a Sybil attack with q identities.

Using this measure, a protocol designer or user can determine how intrinsically resistant a protocol is to a Sybil attack, so she can independently evaluate the design of the protocol and the setting of entry fee. Once the design is fixed, she can use the measure to determine how to set the entry fee to discourage attackers with different valuations for success in reaching an objective.

First, we show that an attacker m only benefits from an attack when their objective valuation is at least γ_a times their per-identity cost. The attacker's expected utility for a Sybil attack with q identities must be non-negative for the attack to be rational. So an attack is rational if and only if

$$E[\tau_m|\sigma_q] - qf \geq 0 \tag{6}$$

$$vE[\psi_a|\sigma_q] \geq qf \tag{7}$$

$$v \geq \frac{qf}{E[\psi_a|\sigma_q]}. \tag{8}$$

Since the attacker is rational, she will choose the optimal number of identities q to include in the protocol. Therefore,

$$v \geq \min_q \frac{qf}{E[\psi_a|\sigma_q]} \tag{9}$$

$$v \geq \gamma_a f. \tag{10}$$

For clarity, we began this subsection by defining the Sybil valuation; note that Inequalities 6 through 9 are a template for deriving the ratio.

Table 1. Optimal number of identities, Sybil valuation, and asymptotic behavior as n grows large for different objectives. For derivations, see the Appendix. The Sybil valuations of the Binomial and Hypergeometric objectives have no closed-form representation for general c and k [11], and they are omitted for readability.

Objective Type	Example Applications	Specific objective	Optimal num identities	Sybil Valuation (γ_a^*)	γ_a^* as $n \to \infty$
One-time Fee	[13, 24, 17]	T_c	c	c	c
Binomial	RFOR denial of service, RFOR endpoints attack, and Predecessor attack [44]	$B_{1,k}^{\text{spec.}}$	1	$\left(1 - \left(\frac{n}{n+1}\right)^k\right)^{-1}$	$k^{-1}n$
		$B_{k,k}^{\text{spec.}}$	$(k-1)n$	$\left(\frac{k}{k-1}\right)^{k-1} kn$	ekn
		$B_{1,k}^{\text{any}}$	1	$\left(1 - \left(\frac{n}{n+1}\right)^{kn}\right)^{-1}$	e^{-k}
		$B_{k,k}^{\text{any}}$	$(k-1)n+k$		kn
		$B_{1,k}^{\text{all}}$	1	$1/n\left(1 - \left(\frac{n}{n+1}\right)^k\right)$	k^{-1}
		$B_{k,k}^{\text{all}}$	$(k-1)n$	$\left(\frac{k}{k-1}\right)^{k-1} k$	k
Hyper-geometric	SETI@Home [38], Pastiche [15]	$H_{1,k}$		*Same as $B_{1,k}^{\text{spec.}}$*	
		$H_{k,k}$	$(k-1)n+k$		kn

Inequality 10 says nothing about the *resources* available to a particular attacker. An attacker may value an objective highly, but not launch a Sybil attack if she does not have enough sufficient resources to achieve it. However, in this paper, we take the defender's point of view and conservatively assume that an attacker controls an unlimited amount of resources.

In some cases, the optimal number of identities q will be very small, so the attacker will only have a very small chance of success each round. By entering a larger number of identities, the attacker would decrease the expected number of rounds until success, but the expected total cost would be higher.

3.1 γ_a for Specific Objectives

We now quantify γ_a, the susceptibility of applications to Sybil attacks. Table 1 has results for each objective discussed in Section 2.3: the one-time fee, binomial, and hypergeometric objectives. While the derivation of γ_a is not difficult, the analysis of each protocol type is more involved, lengthy, and in some cases it has no closed form.

As an example, consider the objective $B_{1,k}^{\text{spec.}}$, where a specific identity's subgroup is targeted and the attacker needs to be selected as only 1 of k peers in the subgroup. The probability of success given q identities is $1 - \left(\frac{n}{q+n}\right)^k$. Therefore for this objective,

$$\gamma_a = \min_q \frac{q}{1 - \left(\frac{n}{q+n}\right)^k}. \qquad (11)$$

The minimizing q must be either 1 (the lowest possible value for q) or some root of the derivative of the minimized expression. It is possible to show that the derivative of the minimized expression is always positive for positive integer values q. The minimum must therefore be at 1, the lowest possible value for q, and therefore for this objective

$$\gamma_a = \frac{1}{1 - (\frac{n}{n+1})^k}. \tag{12}$$

As n grows large in this case, then γ_a approaches n/k, meaning that increasing popularity increases costs linearly for the attacker. Because of space limitations, details of the other γ_a calculations appear in our technical report [27]. We discuss the implications of the results that are summarized in Table 1 below.

• The **one-time fee objective**, T_c is easily achieved in most cases; regardless of the number of participants, it takes only c times the entry fee to achieve the objective. For example, the analysis applies to an onion-routing system requiring a one-time entry fee where the objective is the predecessor attack [44], which requires a minimum of two identities for success. Then an attacker only needs to value the attack at twice the entry fee and enter two identities into the protocol, which is a very inexpensive Sybil attack. One-time fees are not well-suited to discouraging Sybil attacks.

• The **binomial objective** varies in difficulty depending on the objective; the intended victim can be some specific user, any user, or all users.

Against specific users, the difficulty of achieving the binomial objective is linear in the n: a protocol is increasingly secure as more identities participate. This is true regardless of c and k, though c determines if γ_a is linear in k, linear in $1/k$, or somewhere in between[1].

In binomial objectives where the attacker wishes to succeed against any single user, c determines the difficulty of the attack. For $c = 1$, we find that γ_a converges to $\frac{e^k}{e^k-1}$ as n increases. Therefore, in this case, adding more honest identities has limited benefit. Conversely, when $c = k$ (and $k > 1$), we find γ_a asymptotically approaches $(k-1)n$ as n increases.

In binomial objectives including all users, γ_a is asymptotically constant with increasing n. For $c = 1$ it approaches $1/k$, while for $c = k$ it does not depend on n at all, but is asymptotically equal to ek.

• **Hypergeometric objectives** are those where an attacker attempts to control c of k peer group identities, chosen without replacement. They are similar to binomial objectives, but are more difficult for the attacker, since her identities cannot be reused; the difference is most pronounced when n and k are small.

3.2 Application: Recurring Fee Onion Routing (RFOR)

In this section, we apply our Sybil valuation measure to reveal properties of a recurring fee onion routing protocol. RFOR operates exactly according to the Onion Routing protocol definition with two exceptions; *(i)* routers pay a fee for every path reformation; *(ii)* paths are constructed by choosing proxies with replacement.

Our goal is to contrast RFOR's relative strength against the Sybil attack with standard Onion Routing, which provides free services to users through volunteer routers.

---

[1] There is no closed-form expression of γ_a for any binomial objective when c is not exactly 1 or k; see Casella and Berger [11].

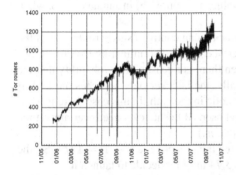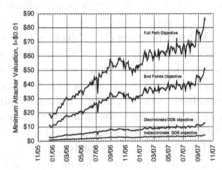

Fig. 1. (a) Tor router population over time. (b) Minimum valuation of four attacks against RFOR when f = \$0.01 (Population dips are smoothed out.)

There is no defense against the Sybil attack in Onion Routing in design or in various deployments; i.e., Sybil attacks can launch the attack successfully for a negligible cost.

Tor is an example of Onion Routing that is deployed with other defenses such as guard nodes. We note that Tor operators do pay a cost to operate a Tor node, but this cost is not one that would grow if those operators increased the number of Sybil identities they operate on the network from the same computer. For example, Murdoch discovered through clock skew analysis that 30 particular routers on the Tor network were actually just two real machines [30].

Our goal is not to ask if Onion Routing deployments such as Tor should charge users a fee, but rather *what is the cost that Sybil attackers should expect to pay in a recurring fee version of Onion Routing?* We are unaware of previous work that quantifies the threat posed by Sybil attacks (rather than collaborating entities) to Onion Routing.

As a simple example, we assume that RFOR routers are charged a fee of f =\$0.01 every path reformation. We assume that the *path* length (i.e., circuit length) remains at the default setting of three. Below, we analyze four objectives of RFOR Sybil attackers: two types of denial-of-service (DoS) attacks, capturing the endpoints of a path, and capturing the full path. We show that these objectives vary considerably in difficulty; some have asymptotically linear Sybil valuations with reasonable coefficients, while others have asymptotically constant, and sometimes very low, Sybil valuations.

In our evaluations, we use Tor's directory server's public advertisements of available proxies, which have been archived by Peter Palfrader, who generously shared the data with us. The 73,309 trace files cover December 2005 until September 2007. See Wright et al. [45] for characteristics of Tor measurements, including up- and down-time distributions. Note that each peer router supports services to hundreds of clients of Tor. To join the Tor network as a routing peer, a person needs only a computer and one IP address for each router they wish to control. We are specifically concerned with attacking the peer routers that service the clients.

Figure 1(a) shows the number of Tor routers over time from the traces and Figure 1(b), discussed below, shows the required valuations of the objectives over time when there is a \$0.01 per path reformation fee for routers in RFOR. In our examples, we make use of peak population value in the logs of $n = 1,373$ routers on September 23, 2007.

However, it is instructive to examine these values in Figure 1(b) in January 2006, when $n = 275$, approximately.

• **Discriminating DoS objective.** If an attacker can control a single router out of the three in a user's RFOR path, she can deny service. In the discriminating DoS objective, the attacker wants to limit DoS to cases when there is a reasonable probability that the targeted user is on the target path. Specifically, the attacker only launches the DoS if she observes the target node as the previous node in the path. In this case there is a 1/3 chance that the path was initiated by the target user. (If the attacker needs certainty, then the end-points objective, discussed below, applies.)

This objective corresponds to $B_{1,1}^{\text{spec.}}$. γ_a for the objective is $n + 1 = 1374$. So the attacker would need to value the attack at \$13.74 in order decide to launch it.

• **Indiscriminate DoS objective.** In this case, the attacker launches a DoS attacker even if the target is not observed as a predecessor, possibly causing collateral damage. This is the $B_{1,3}^{\text{spec.}}$ objective when she receives utility from victimizing only a specific user, and it is the $B_{1,3}^{\text{any}}$ and $B_{1,3}^{\text{all}}$ objectives otherwise.

For the $B_{1,3}^{\text{spec.}}$ objective, when the attacker has a specific targeted user, γ_a is $\frac{1}{1-(\frac{n}{n+1})^3}$. At 1373 routers $\gamma_a = 458$, requiring a valuation of \$4.58 for the attack at a \$0.01 per-identity fee.

The cost is even less for the other objectives. The objective when the attacker is content with denying service to any one user, $B_{1,3}^{\text{any}}$, has a $\gamma_a = 1.05$ at 370 identities, requiring a valuation of \$0.0105 at a \$0.01 per-identity fee. The objective when the attacker receives utility that is proportional to the total number of users it can deny service to, $B_{1,3}^{\text{all}}$, has a $\gamma_a = 0.334$, requiring a valuation of just \$0.0033 for a profitable attack when the per-identity fee is \$0.01.

• **Endpoints objective.** For this objective, the attacker uses its sybil identities to capture the two end points of a path. The two proxies then launch a timing attack [31] to determine if they are on the same path, thereby learning the initiator and responder. The endpoints objective is a $B_{2,2}$ objective.

When the fee is charged per path reformation, the results are as follows. For the binomial objective, when the attack profits only from a specific user $\gamma_a = 4n$, or 5492 at $n = 1373$, which gives an attacker Sybil valuation of \$54.92. When the attacker succeeds after revealing any one user as the initiator, we have $\gamma_a = \frac{n+2}{1-(1-(1-\frac{n}{2(n-1)})^2)^n}$, or about 1375 at $n = 1373$; so the Sybil valuation is \$13.75. When the attack profits from attacking all users, we have $\gamma_a = 4$. In this case the attacker only needs to value the objective at \$0.04.

• **Full-path objective.** Attackers attempt, in this case, to control all k nodes in the path, and can then know for certain that the endpoints are communicating without additional mechanisms. (We note that since RFOR makes no attempt to thwart timing attacks, and a more accurate analysis of RFOR's vulnerability when using fees is given by the endpoints objective.)

We first analyze the full-path objective considering a specific user. If the fee of \$0.01 is charged per path reformation, then the objective corresponds to $B_{3,3}^{\text{spec.}}$. We have $\gamma_a = 274n$, which is about 9268 when $n = 1373$. So a rational attacker would have to value breaking the specific user's anonymity at at least \$92.68 to receive positive utility from attacking the protocol. In comparison, in January, 2006, this value would have been just \$18.56 showing how a recurring fee strategy can leverage an increase in the system's popularity to deter attackers, while the current policy of a one-time fee remains constant.

An attacker who is satisfied by compromising any one user's anonymity — perhaps to try to show that RFOR's anonymity protection is limited — has a $B_{3,3}^{\text{any}}$ objective. We have $\gamma_a = \frac{2n+3}{(1-(1-(1-\frac{n}{3(n-1)})^3)^n}$, which at $n = 1373$ is about 2749. A rational attacker with the goal of simply breaking anyone's anonymity would need to value the goal at \$27.49 or more to profitably attack.

The attacker who values equally any information she receives about who is communicating with whom has the $B_{3,3}^{\text{all}}$ objective and has a far easier task. Here, $\gamma_a = \frac{27}{4}$, which does not depend on the number of participants at all. Such an attacker only needs to value the attack at about \$0.07 to profit from attacking, even if many more Tor routers join the network.

4   Entry Fees

We require only proof that each identity has paid a recurring fee, and we do not require proof that each identity is actually a separate entity. Moreover, the fee does not have to be paid to the administrator or other participant in the application. We need only ensure that some real cost has been provably paid before participating. Peers may pairwise prove to one another that they have paid the recurring fee each round; however, we expect in practice, a central trusted authority is likely to be used, just as Tor uses a trusted directory server to learn of other peers.

Micropayments [8, 7, 42, 41] can be used to purchase certificates valid for a certain number of minutes or rounds in one or more applications. The seller of such certificates has a much easier task than a certification authority: she does not have to verify the identity of the purchasers, prevent customers from purchasing multiple certificates, or prevent certificates from being transfered.

CAPTCHAs [43] are automated puzzles in widespread use that attempt to force human effort by using computer generate puzzles which are difficult for a computer to solve, but easy for a human to solve. It takes the author an average of three seconds to solve and enter the type of CAPTCHAs used on sites such as `mail.com` and `yahoo.com`; this is equivalent to a cost of about \$0.01 at the average US individual wage (see `http://factfinder.census.gov`). Wages in other countries and economies of scale could drive these costs down significantly.

Another option for recurring fees is to use SMS messages. To apply this recurring fee, an SMS message is sent to the phone every application round, and no two identities can share the same phone number. A survey of current US cell phone plans reveals that most charge \$0.05 to receive a text message; though some plans that allowed unlimited reception would break this approach, reducing granularity to a monthly recurring fee. The interesting aspect of this approach is that the large monthly charges for a phone line are a deterrent only if it is purchased specifically to enable Sybil attacks. Obtaining multiple phone lines has little utility for users, so Sybils incur an extra charge. This illustrates that the networked application itself does not need to receive payment; we require only that the application can generate a cost that is incurred by the identity.

For RFOR, SMS is the easiest solution to implement, while micropayments are the most robust. We realize that anonymous communication systems are all volunteer networks and these real, recurring costs would diminish participation in the network, but our goal is to show how to better defend the system against the Sybil attack.

Many schemes for charging of one-time fees cannot be converted to recurring fees. For example, many past works have suggested the use of computation or storage as methods of imposing one-time fees (e.g., Abadi et al [2]). The real costs of these schemes is a diminished availability of the user's CPU, disk, or memory resource — a one-time purchase of additional hardware can replace these costs.

5   Related Work

Prevention of the Sybil attack has been discussed as part of the design of many distributed applications and protocols. Many follow Douceur's work and suggest prevention using a central authority, but several other approaches have been proposed, which we review below. We believe our work is the first to consider the economics of Sybil attackers in a general context using an economic analysis and we offer the most detailed analysis of Tor's and RFOR's vulnerability.

Before this broad review, we note other work related to our contributions and context. We assume that participants in p2p networks are rational agents. Shneidman and Parkes [39] give evidence of self-interested behavior in p2p applications. We also use ideas from game theory; Osborne and Rubinstein [34] give a rigorous introduction. In our previous work [26], we suggested a method of Sybil detection based on recurring fees. Finally, we are not the first to apply a cost-benefit analysis to security problems; e.g., See Meadows [29].

• **Trusted certification** [17, 28, 32, 22] Trusted certification is the most popular response to the Sybil attack. It is the only approach that has the potential to completely eliminate Sybil attacks. However, the certifying authority must ensure that each identity corresponds to exactly one entity, which may be costly for large-scale systems. To prevent all Sybil attacks, the certifying authority must also ensure that no certificates are lost or stolen, which is probably impossible in almost all applications.

• **Reputation Systems** have often been suggested as a solution to the problem of Sybil attacks. Cheng and Friedman [12] classify reputation as symmetric or asymmetric. In symmetric reputation systems [33, 18, 33] an identity's reputation depends solely on the topology of the trust graph, not on the relative positions in the trust graph of the identity and its querier. Cheng and Friedman prove formally that such reputation systems are susceptible to Sybil attacks. In asymmetric reputation systems [20, 18, 9], a trusted node determines on the reputation of all other nodes and Cheng and Friedman show the limited conditions under which Sybils are prevented. Unfortunately, asymmetric reputation systems inevitably penalize newcomers, who must prove themselves by offering benefits before getting anything in return.

• **Resource testing** [19, 46, 25] Resource tests include checks for computing ability, storage ability, and network bandwidth, as well as IP addresses. Both Freedman and Morris [19] and Cornelli et al. [14] suggest that requiring heterogeneous IP address (i.e., addresses in separate autonomous systems) is more effective at preventing Sybils than just requiring an IP address. Similarly, the SybilGuard technique [46] probabilistically weeds out Sybil identities based on the structure of social network graphs. Edges between nodes are assumed to imply "strong trust" in the real-world, a much stronger implication than is typical in social networks. SybilGuard can be used when there is a significant overlap between real-world social networks and participants in an online application and when users can be trusted to follow edge trust rules. This limits its applicability. For example, the social networks captured by MySpace, Friendster, or the PGP key-signing tree would not contain valid edges.

- **Recurring fees** [4, 18, 21] These works are the closest to ours, in that they consider recurring, rather than one-time costs. Awerbuch and Scheidler [4] suggest the use of Turing tests such as CAPTCHAs to impose recurring fees, but do not do an economic analysis. Dragovic et al. [18] require certification of identities, but this certification is not trusted; rather, it is seen as a way of imposing identity creation costs. Gatti et al. [21] is the work most similar to ours; it uses an economic, game-theoretical approach to examine when attacks on censorship resistant networks are cost-effective.

Other approaches that we do not review here due to lack of space include the following: trusted devices [32, 36], which like PKIs must avoid duplication; verifiable auditing [40, 3], for example by asking for the factors of a large number; physical observation [10, 35], which are typically proposed for mobile computing and do not entail a recurring cost for the attacker.

6 Conclusions

In this paper, we evaluate Sybil attacks from an economic point of view. We define the Sybil valuation as a way of quantifying the relative strength of attackers and use it as a quantitative measure of the application robustness. Our results show that the susceptibility to Sybil attacks varies considerably, and can vary for different attacks, as we examined for the Tor network. We show that, in contrast to one-time fees, recurring per-identity entry fees can discourage Sybil attacks in many cases by ensuring a cost for the attacker that is linear with the number of participants. These results provide an more fine-grained understanding the attack and allow protocol designers to measure the effectiveness of defenses, which is important since the attack is difficult to prevent using standard computer security measures.

References

1. Department of state bureau of diplomatic security: Investigating passport and visa fraud, http://www.state.gov/m/ds/investigat
2. Abadi, M., Burrows, M., Manasse, M., Wobber, T.: Moderately Hard, Memory-Bound Functions. Trans. Inter. Tech. 5(2), 299–327 (2005)
3. Anagnostakis, K., Greenwald, M.: Exchange-Based Incentive Mechanisms for Peer-to-Peer File Sharing. In: Proc. ICDCS, pp. 524–533 (March 2004)
4. Awerbuch, B., Scheideler, C.: Group Spreading: A Protocol for Provably Secure Distributed Name Service. In: Díaz, J., Karhumäki, J., Lepistö, A., Sannella, D. (eds.) ICALP 2004. LNCS, vol. 3142, pp. 183–195. Springer, Heidelberg (2004)

5. Bhattacharjee, R., Goel, A.: Avoiding Ballot Stuffing in eBay-like Reputation Systems. In: Proc. Wkshp on Econ of P2P Systems, pp. 133–137 (August 2005)
6. Bianchini, M., Gori, M., Scarselli, F.: Inside PageRank. Trans. Inter. Tech. 5(1), 92–128 (2005)
7. Blaze, M., et al.: TAPI: Transactions for Accessing Public Infrastructure. In: Proc. IFIP-TC6 Intl. Conf. Personal Wireless Communications, pp. 90–100 (September 2003)
8. Blaze, M., Ioannidis, J., Keromytis, A.: Offline Micropayments without Trusted Hardware. In: Proc. Fin. Crypto., pp. 21–40 (February 2001)
9. Buchegger, S., Boudec, J.-Y.L.: A Robust Reputation System for P2P and Mobile Ad hoc Networks. In: Proc. Wkshp. on Econ. of P2P Systems (2004)
10. Capkun, S., Hubaux, J., Buttyan, L.: Mobility helps peer-to-peer security. IEEE Trans. Mobile Comp. 5(1) (January 2006)
11. Casella, G., Berger, R.: Statistical Inference. Wadsworth (2000)
12. Cheng, A., Friedman, E.: Sybilproof Reputation Mechanisms. In: Proc. Wkshp. on Econ. of P2P Systems, pp. 128–132 (August 2005)
13. Clausen, A.: Online Reputation Systems: The Cost of Attack of PageRank. Master's thesis, Univ. of Melbourne (2003)
14. Cornelli, F., Damiani, E., Samarati, S.: Implementing a Reputation-Aware Gnutella Servent. In: Proc. IPTPS, pp. 321–334 (March 2002)
15. Cox, L., Noble, B.: Pastiche: Making Backup Cheap and Easy. In: Proc. OSDI, pp. 285–298 (December 2002)
16. Dingledine, R., Mathewson, N., Syverson, P.: Tor: The Second-Generation Onion Router. In: Proc. USENIX Security Symp., pp. 303—320 (August 2004)
17. Douceur, J.: The Sybil Attack. In: Druschel, P., Kaashoek, M.F., Rowstron, A. (eds.) IPTPS 2002. LNCS, vol. 2429, pp. 251–260. Springer, Heidelberg (2002)
18. Dragovic, B., Kotsovinos, E., Hand, S., Pietzuch, P.R.: Xenotrust: Event-based Distributed Trust Management. In: Proc. Intl. Wkshp. on Database and Expert Systems Applications, p. 410 (2003)
19. Freedman, M.J., Morris, R.: Tarzan: A Peer-to-Peer Anonymizing Network Layer. In: Proc. CCS, pp. 193–206 (November 2002)
20. Fu, Y., Chase, J., Chun, B., Schwab, S., Vahdat, A.: SHARP: An Architecture for Secure Resource Peering. In: Proc. SOSP, pp. 133–148 (October 2003)
21. Gatti, R., Lewis, S., Ozment, A., Rayna, T., Serjantov, A.: Sufficiently Secure Peer-to-Peer Networks. In: Proc. Wkshp. on Econ. of P2P Systems (May 2004)
22. Hildrum, K., Kubiatowicz, J.: Asymptotically efficient approaches to fault-tolerance in peer-to-peer networks. In: Proc. Intl. Symp. on Distributed Computing, pp. 321–336 (2003)
23. Hu, Y.-C., Perrig, A., Johnson, D.: Ariadne: A Secure On-Demand Routing Protocol for Ad hoc Networks. Wireless Networks 11(1–2), 21–28 (2005)
24. Kamvar, S.D., Schlosser, M.T., Garcia-Molina, H.: The eigentrust algorithm for reputation management in p2p networks. In: Proc. Intl. Conf. on World Wide Web, pp. 640–651. Press (2003)
25. Maniatis, P., Rosenthal, D.S.H., Roussopoulos, M., Baker, M., Giuli, T., Muliadi, Y.: Preserving Peer Replicas by Rate-Limited Sampled Voting. In: Proc. SOSP, pp. 44–59 (2003)
26. Margolin, N.B., Levine, B.N.: Informant: Detecting Sybils Using Incentives. In: Proc. Fin. Crypto. (FC) (February 2007)
27. Margolin, N.B., Levine, B.N.: Quantifying resistance to the sybil attack. Computer Science Technical Report 2007-64, University of Massachusetts Amherst (December 2007)
28. Marti, S., Garcia-Molina, H.: Limited reputation sharing in p2p systems. In: Proc. 5th conference on Electronic commerce (2004)
29. Meadows, C.: A cost-based framework for analysis of denial of service in networks. J. Comput. Secur. 9(1-2), 143–164 (2001)

30. Murdoch, S.J.: Hot or Not: Revealing Hidden Services by their Clock Skew. In: ACM Conference on Computer and Communications Security (CCS), pp. 27–36 (October 2006), http://www.cl.cam.ac.uk/~sjm217/talks/ccs06hotornot.pdf

31. Murdoch, S.J., Danezis, G.: Low-Cost Traffic Analysis of Tor. In: Proc. IEEE Symp. on Security and Privacy, pp. 183–195 (May 2005)

32. Newsome, J., Shi, E., Song, D., Perrig, A.: The Sybil Attack in Sensor Networks: Analysis & Defenses. In: Proc. IPSN, pp. 259–268 (2004)

33. Ntarmos, N., Triantafillou, P.: SeAl: Managing Accesses and Data in Peer-to-Peer Sharing Networks. In: Proc. IPTPS, pp. 116–123 (2004)

34. Osborne, M.J., Rubinstein, A.: A Course In Game Theory. MIT Press, Cambridge (1994)

35. Piro, C., Shields, C., Levine, B.N.: Detecting the Sybil Attack in Ad hoc Networks. In: Proc. SecureComm., pp. 1–11 (August 2006)

36. Rodrigues, R., Liskov, B., Shrira, L.: The design of a robust peer-to-peer system. In: Proc. SIGOPS European Wkshp. (September 2002)

37. Schneier, B.: Applied Cryptography. John Wiley & Sons, Chichester (1996)

38. Seti@home, http://setiathome.ssl.berkeley.edu

39. Shneidman, J., Parkes, D.C.: Rationality and Self-Interest in Peer-to-Peer Networks. In: Proc. IPTPS, pp. 139–148 (2003)

40. Srivatsa, M., Liu, L.: Vulnerabilities and Security Threats in Structured Overlay Networks: A Quantitative Analysis. In: Proc. ACSAC, pp. 252–261 (December 2004)

41. Stavrou, A., Cook, D.L., Morein, W.G., Keromytis, A.D., Misra, V., Rubenstein, D.: Web-SOS: An overlay-based system for protecting web servers from denial of service attacks. J. Comm. Networks 48(5) (August 2005)

42. Stavrou, A., et al.: A Pay-Per-Use DOS Protection Mechanism for the Web. In: Jakobsson, M., Yung, M., Zhou, J. (eds.) ACNS 2004. LNCS, vol. 3089, pp. 120–134. Springer, Heidelberg (2004)

43. von Ahn, L., Blum, M., Hopper, N., Langford, J.: CAPTCHA: Using Hard AI Problems for Security. In: Proc. Eurocrypt, pp. 294–311 (2003)

44. Wright, M., Adler, M., Levine, B., Shields, C.: The predecessor attack: An analysis of a threat to anonymous communications systems. TISSEC 7(4), 489–522 (2004)

45. Wright, M., Adler, M., Levine, B.N., Shields, C.: Passive-Logging Attacks Against Anonymous Communications Systems. TISSEC 11(2) (May 2008)

46. Yu, H., Kaminsky, M., Gibbons, P.B., Flaxman, A.: SybilGuard: Defending Against Sybil Attacks via Social Networks. In: Proc. SIGCOMM, pp. 267–278 (September 2006)

47. Yurkewych, M., Levine, B.N., Rosenberg, A.L.: On the Cost-Ineffectiveness of Redundancy in Commercial P2P Computing. In: Proc. CCS, pp. 280–288 (2005)

Evaluating the Wisdom of Crowds in Assessing Phishing Websites

Tyler Moore and Richard Clayton

Computer Laboratory, University of Cambridge
15 JJ Thomson Avenue, Cambridge CB3 0FD, United Kingdom
firstname.lastname@cl.cam.ac.uk

Abstract. We examine the structure and outcomes of user participation in PhishTank, a phishing-report collator. Anyone who wishes may submit URLs of suspected phishing websites, and may vote on the accuracy of other submissions. We find that PhishTank is dominated by its most active users, and that participation follows a power-law distribution, and that this makes it particularly susceptible to manipulation. We compare PhishTank with a proprietary source of reports, finding Phish-Tank to be slightly less complete and significantly slower in reaching decisions. We also evaluate the accuracy of PhishTank's decisions and discuss cases where incorrect information has propagated. We find that users who participate less often are far more likely to make mistakes, and furthermore that users who commit many errors tend to have voted on the same URLs. Finally, we explain how the structure of participation in PhishTank leaves it susceptible to large-scale voting fraud which could undermine its credibility. We also discuss general lessons for leveraging the 'wisdom of crowds' in taking security decisions by mass participation.

1   Introduction

Phishing is the process of enticing people to visit fraudulent websites and persuading them to enter identity information such as usernames and passwords. The information is then used to impersonate victims in order to empty their bank accounts, run fraudulent auctions, launder money, and so on. Researchers have proposed many technical countermeasures, from mechanisms to detect phishing websites [17,28], through to schemes that prevent users from disclosing their secrets to them [20]. The primary response from the banks, in contrast, has been to initiate 'take-down' procedures, removing the offending content so that there is nothing there for a misled visitor to see [15].

Attackers remain an elusive target, setting up new websites as quickly as the existing ones are removed. So obtaining an updated feed of new websites requires constant vigilance and demands significant resources. Most banks and specialist take-down companies maintain their own feed. One group, called 'Phish-Tank' [18], has tried to leverage the 'wisdom of crowds' to generate an open source list that strives to be as complete and accurate as possible. Users are invited not only to provide the content but also to undertake the somewhat more menial task of verifying that entries are correctly classified.

G. Tsudik (Ed.): FC 2008, LNCS 5143, pp. 16–30, 2008.
© Springer-Verlag Berlin Heidelberg 2008

PhishTank is part of a growing trend in turning to web-based participation to implement security mechanisms, from aggregating spam to tracking malware. In this paper, we study participation in PhishTank in order to better understand the effectiveness of crowd-based security more generally. In doing so, we make several specific contributions:

- we find participation in PhishTank is distributed according to a power law;
- we compare PhishTank's open list to a proprietary (closed) list, finding the closed list slightly more comprehensive, and faster in verifying submissions;
- we identify miscategorizations made in PhishTank;
- we determine that inexperienced users are far more likely to make mistakes;
- we find evidence that 'bad' users vote together more often than randomly;
- we explain how the structure of participation in PhishTank makes it especially vulnerable to manipulation;
- we outline several general lessons for implementing more robust crowd-sourced security mechanisms.

2   Data Collection and Analysis

2.1   Phishing Website Reporting and Evaluation

We gathered phishing reports from PhishTank [18], one of the primary phishing-report collators. The PhishTank database records the URL for the suspected website that has been reported, the time of that report, and sometimes further detail such as whois data or screenshots of the website.

PhishTank has explicitly adopted an open system powered by end-user participation. Users can contribute in two ways. First, they submit reports of suspected phishing websites. Second, they examine suspected websites and vote on whether they believe them to be phishing. PhishTank relies on the so-called 'wisdom of crowds' [25] to pick out incorrect reports (perhaps pointing to a legitimate bank) and confirm malicious websites. Each report is only confirmed (and subsequently disseminated to anti-phishing mechanisms) following the vote of a number of registered users. The tally of as-yet undecided votes is not revealed to users until after casting a vote. This helps prevent information cascades where early opinions influence later ones [3].

Consistent with PhishTank's open policy, they publish a record of all completed votes. This includes the identifiers of the user who submitted the report, the result of the vote (is or is-not a phish), the users who voted, and the percentage of votes cast for and against categorizing the website as a phish. However, the records do not specify how each user voted.

We examined reports from 200 908 phishing URLs submitted between February and September 2007. Voting was suspended for 24 254 of these because the websites in question went offline before a conclusive vote could be reached. In these cases, we could only determine who submitted the record and not who voted on it. We gathered completed votes for the remaining 176 366 submissions. 3 798 users participated by submitting reports and/or voting.

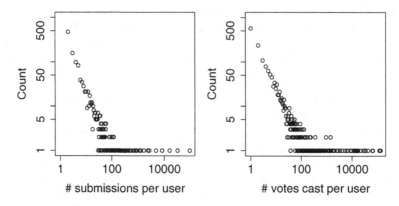

Fig. 1. Density of user submissions (left) and votes (right)

In all, 881 511 votes were cast, implying an average of 53 submissions and 232 votes per user. However, such averages are very misleading. Small numbers of users are responsible for the majority of submissions and votes. The top two submitters, adding 93 588 and 31 910 phishing records respectively, are actually two anti-phishing organizations that have contributed their own, unverified, feeds of suspect websites. However, neither verifies many submissions. The top verifiers have voted over 100 000 times, while most users only vote a few times.

Many of the leading verifiers have been invited to serve as one of 25 PhishTank moderators. Moderators are granted additional responsibilities such as cleaning up malformed URLs from submissions.[1] Collectively, moderators cast 652 625 votes, or 74% of the total. So while the moderators are doing the majority of the work, a significant contribution is made by the large number of normal users.

2.2 Power-Law Distribution of User Participation Rates

The wide range of user participation is captured in Figure 1. Noting the log-log axes, these plots show that most users submit and vote only a handful of times, while also indicating that a few users participate many times more.

In fact, the distribution of user submissions and votes in PhishTank are each characterized by a power law. Power-law distributions appear in many real-world contexts, from the distribution of city populations to the number of academic citations to BGP routing topologies (see [16] for a survey). More precisely, the probability density function of a power law corresponds to $p(x) \propto x^{-\alpha}$, where α is a positive constant greater than one. Power-law distributions have highly skewed populations with 'long tails', that is, a limited number of large values appear several orders of magnitude beyond the much-smaller median value.

The intuitive argument put forth in favor of the robustness of 'crowd-sourced' applications like PhishTank's phish verification mechanism is that the opinions of

---

[1] Moderators also, on some rare occasions, use their powers to pre-emptively remove obviously incorrect submissions.

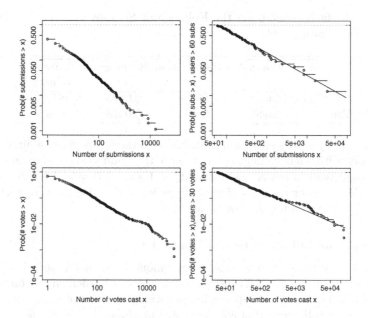

Fig. 2. Complementary CDF of user submissions (top left) and votes (bottom left). Tail of submission CDF with power-law curve fit (top right), $\alpha = 1.642$ and the number of submissions per user at least 60. Tail of vote CDF with power-law curve fit (bottom right), $\alpha = 1.646$ and the number of votes per user at least 30.

many users can outweigh the occasional mistake, or even the views of a malicious user. However, if the rate of participation follows a power-law distribution, then a single highly active user's actions can greatly impact a system's overall accuracy. This is why a power-law distribution invalidates the standard Byzantine Fault Tolerance view of reliability [11]: the subverting of even a single highly active participant could undermine the system. In Section 5, we study how the skewed structure of participation rates in PhishTank could cause trouble.

Figure 2 (top left) plots the complementary cumulative distribution function (CDF) of user submissions. Both axes are logarithmic in scale. Figure 2 (bottom left) plots the CDF for the number of votes. Power-law distributions appear as a straight line on log-log axes, so visual inspection suggests that PhishTank data is likely to be distributed in this way. We have examined the tails of the voting and submission distributions to determine whether the data are consistent with a power-law tail.

The CDF for a power-law distribution is given by:

$$Pr(X > x) = \left(\frac{x}{x_{\min}}\right)^{-\alpha+1}$$

For the submission data, we tested the tail by considering only those users who submit at least $x_{\min} = 60$ times, while we set $x_{\min} = 30$ for the voting data. We estimated the best fit for α using maximum-likelihood estimation. We then evaluated the fit by computing the Kolmogorov-Smirnov test. The results are given in the following table:

	Power-law distribution		Kolmogorov-Smirnov	
	α	x_{min}	D	p-value
Submissions	1.642	60	0.0533	0.9833
Votes	1.646	30	0.0368	0.7608

Given the large p-values and small D values from the Kolmogorov-Smirnov test, we can say with high confidence that both the submission and voting data are consistent with a power-law distribution. Figure 2 (top and bottom right) presents the CDF for the tails of the submission and voting data, respectively, along with a line showing the power-law fit.

2.3   Duplicate Submissions in Phishtank

PhishTank asks its users to vote on every unique URL that is submitted. Unfortunately, this imposes a very large and unnecessary burden on its volunteers. The 'rock-phish' gang is a group of criminals who perpetrate phishing attacks on a massive scale [14]. Instead of compromising machines for hosting fake HTML in an ad-hoc manner, the gang first purchases a number of domains with meaningless names like 1of80.info. They then send email spam with a long URL of the form http://www.bank.com.id123.1of80.info/vr. This URL includes a unique identifier; all variants are resolved to a particular IP address using 'wildcard DNS'. Up to 25 banks are impersonated within each domain. For a more complete description of rock-phish attacks see [15].

Transmitting unique URLs trips up spam filters looking for repeated links, and also fools collators like PhishTank into recording duplicate entries. Consequently, voting on rock-phish attacks becomes very repetitive. We observed 3 260 unique rock-phish domains in PhishTank. These domains appeared in 120 662 submissions, 60% of the overall total. Furthermore, 893 users voted a total of 550 851 times on these domains! This is a dreadfully inefficient allocation of user resources, which could instead be directed to speeding up verification times, for example.

Further duplication must also be addressed in the remaining 80 246 submissions. In many instances several URLs have been submitted that correspond to webpages from different stages within the same phishing attack. By ignoring any part of the URL following the right-most /, we arrive at 75 501 unique URLs. Of course, there may be a very small number of cases where this consolidation treats multiple distinct phishing websites as one. However, the benefits in reducing workload seem to outweigh this unlikely occurrence.

3   Comparing Open and Closed Phishing Feeds

PhishTank is not the only organization tracking and classifying phishing websites. Other organizations do not follow PhishTank's open submission and verification policy; instead, they gather their own proprietary lists of suspicious websites and employees determine whether they are indeed phishing. We have obtained a feed from one such company. In this section, we examine the feeds of PhishTank and the company to compare completeness and speed of verification.

3.1 Phishing Website Identification

We compared the feeds during a 4-week period in July and August 2007. We first examine ordinary phishing websites, excluding rock-phish URLs. PhishTank reported 10 924 phishing URLs, while the company identified 13 318. After removing duplicates, the numbers become much closer: 8 296 for PhishTank and 8 730 for the company. The two feeds shared 5 711 reports in common. This means that 3 019 reports were unique to the company's feed, while 2 585 reports only appeared in PhishTank. Hence, although neither feed is comprehensive, the company's feed contains a wider selection of websites than PhishTank achieves.

For rock-phish URLs the difference is starker. PhishTank identified 586 rock-phish domains during the sample, while the company detected 1 003, nearly twice as many. Furthermore, the company picked up on 459, or 78%, of the rock-phish domains found in PhishTank, and detected 544 that PhishTank had missed.

By examining the overlap between the feeds, we can gain some insight into the company's sources. The overlap for all phishing reports corresponded to 9 380 submissions to PhishTank. 5 881 of these submissions, 63% of the total overlap, came from a user called *PhishReporter*, that we understand to be an anti-phishing report collation organization in its own right. This certainly implies that the company and PhishTank both receive a feed from *PhishReporter*. However, the remaining reports are more widely distributed, coming from 316 users. Unfortunately, we cannot say with any certainty whether these reports were also given to the company or if they were independently rediscovered.

It is noteworthy that both feeds include many phishing websites which do not appear on the other. This observation motivates the case for a universal feed shared between the banks and the various anti-phishing organizations.

3.2 Phishing Website Verification

Given that prompt identification and removal of phishing websites is a priority, a feed's relevance depends upon the speed with which websites are reported and subsequently verified. Requiring several users to vote introduces significant delays. On average, PhishTank submissions take approximately 46 hours to be verified. A few instances take a very long time to be verified, which skews the average. The median, by contrast, is around 15 hours.

We also found that unanimous votes were verified slightly quicker than votes where there was disagreement on average, but that conflicting votes had a much shorter median (7 hrs). URLs confirmed to be phishing were verified a few hours faster than those determined not to be a phishing website. The precise values are given in the following table:

Verification time	All entries	Conflict	Unanimous	Is-phish	Not-phish
Mean (hours)	45.6	49.7	45.8	46.1	39.5
Median (hours)	14.9	6.6	27.8	14.1	20.6

We also compared the submission and verification times for both feeds during the four-week sample. On average, PhishTank saw submissions first, by around 11 minutes, but after an average delay of just 8 seconds the company had verified them.[2] However, PhishTank's voting-based verification meant that they did not verify the URLs (and therefore did not disseminate them) until 16 hours later. For the rock-phish URLs, we compared the earliest instance of each domain, finding that overlapping domains appeared in PhishTank's feed 12 hours *after* they appeared in the company's feed, and were not verified for another 12 hours. The time differences between feeds are summarized in the following table:

ΔPhishTank	Ordinary phishing URLs		Rock-phish domains	
− Company	Submission	Verification	Submission	Verification
Mean (hrs)	−0.188	15.9	12.4	24.7
Median (hrs)	−0.0481	10.9	9.37	20.8

To sum up, voting-based verification introduces a substantial delay when compared to a unilateral verification.

4   Testing the Accuracy of Phishtank's Crowd Decisions

Having compared the breadth and timeliness of PhishTank's reports to the closed source, we now examine the correctness of its users' contributions. Unfortunately, since the closed phishing feed does not provide a record of invalid submissions, we cannot compare its accuracy to PhishTank's. We first describe common causes of inaccuracy and discuss their prevalence. We then demonstrate that inexperienced users are far more likely to make mistakes than experienced ones. Finally, we show that users with bad voting records 'cluster' by often voting together.

4.1   Miscategorization in PhishTank

The vast majority of user submissions to PhishTank are indeed phishing URLs. Of 176 654 verified submissions, just 5 295, or 3%, are voted down as invalid. Most of these invalid submissions appear to be honest mistakes. Users who do not understand the definition of phishing submit URLs from their spam, while others add URLs for other types of malicious websites, such as those involved in advanced fee fraud (419 scams). However, a number of carefully-crafted phishing websites have also been miscategorized and 'foreign-language' websites are sometimes classified incorrectly. Most commonly, an obscure credit union or bank that uses a different domain name for its online banking may be marked as a phish.

---

[2] We suspect that verification of any particular URL is in the hands of an individual on-duty employee, who often submits and verifies in a single operation.

Yet there is even dissent among moderators as to what exactly constitutes a phish: 1.2% of their submissions are voted down as invalid. For example, some moderators take the view that so-called 'mule-recruitment' websites should be categorized phishing because they are used to recruit the gullible to launder the proceeds of phishing crime. Other mistakes may just be the result of fatigue, given that the moderators participate many thousands of times.

In addition to invalid submissions that are correctly voted down, submissions that are incorrectly classified present a significant worry. Identifying false positives and negatives is hard because PhishTank rewrites history without keeping any public record of changes. As soon as a submission has received enough votes to be verified, PhishTank publishes the decision. Sometimes, though, this decision is reversed if someone disputes the conclusion. In these cases, voting is restarted and the new decision eventually replaces the old one. Once we realized this was happening, we began rechecking all PhishTank records periodically for reversals. In all, we identified 42 reversals. We found 39 false positives – legitimate websites incorrectly classified as phishing – and 3 false negatives – phishing websites incorrectly classified as legitimate. 12 of these reversals were initially agreed upon unanimously!

We first discuss the false positives. 30 websites were legitimate banks, while the remaining 9 were other scams miscategorized as phishing. Sometimes these were legitimate companies using secondary domains or IP addresses in the URLs, which confused PhishTank's users for a time. However, several popular websites' primary domains were also voted as phish, including eBay (`ebay.com`, `ebay.de`), Fifth Third Bank (`53.com`) and National City (`nationalcity.com`). Minimizing these types of false positives is essential for PhishTank because even a small number of false categorizations could undermine its credibility.

Unsurprisingly, there are many more false positives than false negatives since the vast majority of submitted phishes are valid. However, we still observed 3 false negatives. Most noteworthy was incorrectly classifying as innocuous a URL for the rock-phish domain `eportid.ph`. Five other URLs for the same domain were submitted to PhishTank prior to the false negative, with each correctly identified as a phish. So in addition to the inefficiencies described in Section 2.3, requiring users to vote for the same rock-phish domain many times has enabled at least one rock-phish URL to earn PhishTank's (temporary) approval.

4.2 Does Experience Improve User Accuracy?

Where do these mistakes come from? It is reasonable to expect occasional users to commit more errors than those who contribute more often. Indeed, we find strong evidence for this in the data. The left-hand graph in Figure 3 plots the rates of inaccuracy for submissions and votes grouped by user participation rates. For instance, 44% of URLs from users who submit just once are voted down as invalid. This steadily improves (30% of submissions are invalid from users who submit between 2 and 10 URLs, 17% invalid for users with between 11 and 100 submissions), with the top submitters incorrect just 1.2% of the time.

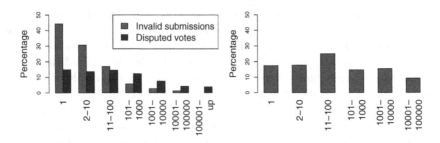

Fig. 3. Inaccuracy of user submissions and votes according to the total number of submissions and votes per user, respectively (left). Proportion of all invalid user submissions grouped by number of submissions (right).

A similar, albeit less drastic, difference can be observed for voting accuracy. Unfortunately, we cannot determine with certainty whether a user has voted incorrectly (i.e., voted a submission as a phish when the majority said otherwise, or vice versa). This is because PhishTank does not publicly disclose this information. So we are left to devise a proxy for incorrectness using votes where there is disagreement (i.e., a mixture of yes/no votes). This is a reasonable approximation given that nearly all submissions (97%) are decided unanimously.

Users voting fewer than 100 times are likely to disagree with their peers 14% of the time. This improves steadily for more active users, with the most active voters in conflict just 3.7% of the time, in line with the overall average.

These results suggest that the views of inexperienced users should perhaps be assigned less weight when compared to highly experienced users.[3] However, we must note that simply ignoring low-contribution users would not eradicate invalid submissions and votes. Since most contributions come from experienced users, many of the errors can be traced to them as well. The right-hand graph in Figure 3 groups user submissions together logarithmically, then plots the proportion of all invalid user submissions each group contributes. For instance, users submitting once contribute 17% of all invalid submissions. Users with fewer than 100 submissions collectively make 60% of the mistakes, despite submitting less than 7% of the phishing candidate URLs.

4.3   Do Users with Bad Voting Records Vote Together?

We now consider whether bad decisions reinforce themselves. More precisely, we ask whether users with bad voting records are likely to vote on the same phishing reports more often than randomly.

We define a *high-conflict user* as one where a large fraction of votes f_{HC} cast are in conflict. We denote the set of all high-conflict users as HC, and the set of votes for user A as V_A. T is the set of all phishing submissions, and $V_A \subset T$.

---

[3] Developers at PhishTank tell us that they have never treated users equally, but weigh their votes according to the user's accuracy over time.

For now, let's denote high-conflict users as those where the majority of their votes are in conflict ($f_{HC} = 0.5$). Of 3 786 users, 93 are in high conflict. We now explore the relationship between these users.

We can empirically measure the observed overlap between high-conflict votes using the following formula:

$$\text{overlap}(HC) = \sum_{A \in HC} \sum_{B \in HC, B \neq A} |V_A \cap V_B|$$

If there is no relationship between the users, then we would expect their interactions to be random chance. Hence, we can develop a measure of the expected overlap[4] in this case:

$$E(\text{overlap}) = \sum_{A \in HC} \sum_{B \in HC, B \neq A} \sum_{i=1}^{min(|V_A|,|V_B|)} i \times \frac{\binom{|V_A|}{i} \times \binom{|T|-|V_A|}{|V_B|-i}}{\binom{|T|}{|V_B|}}$$

If the overlap observed, overlap(HC), is greater than the overlap expected, E(overlap), then the high-conflict voters have tended to vote with each other more often than randomly. In our data, overlap(HC) = 254, while the expected overlap, E(overlap) = 0.225.

In other words, the rate of overlap in high-conflict voters is approximately one thousand times higher than would be the case if there was no connection between how high-conflict voters select their votes.

What are the implications? While it is possible that these high-conflict users are deliberately voting incorrectly together (or are the same person!), the more likely explanation is that incorrect decisions reinforce each other. When well-intentioned users vote incorrectly, they have apparently made the same mistakes.

5   Disrupting the PhishTank Verification System

We now consider whether PhishTank's open submission and voting policies may be exploited by attackers. Recently, a number of anti-phishing websites were targeted by a denial-of-service attack, severely hindering their work in removing malicious sites [12]. Hence, there is already evidence that phishermen are motivated to disrupt the operations of groups like PhishTank. But even if enough bandwidth is provisioned to counter these attacks, PhishTank remains susceptible to vote rigging that could undermine its credibility. Any crowd-based decision mechanism is susceptible to manipulation. However, as we will see, certain characteristics of user participation make PhishTank particularly vulnerable.

5.1   Attacks and Countermeasures

We anticipate three types of attacks on PhishTank:

1. Submitting invalid reports accusing legitimate websites.

---

[4] We are grateful to Jaeyeon Jung for correcting an earlier version of this formula.

2. Voting legitimate websites as phish.
3. Voting illegitimate websites as not-phish.

We can envision two scenarios where an attacker tries to manipulate Phish-Tank. The *selfish attacker* seeks to protect her own phishing websites by voting down any accusatory report as invalid. Such an attacker shares no empathy with other phishing attackers. The selfish attacker attempts to avoid unwanted attention by only allowing a few of her own websites through (attack type 3 above). The attacker's strong incentive to protect herself even when it causes harm to others is a novel property of PhishTank's voting system.

The *undermining attacker* does not bother with such subtleties. Instead, this attacker seeks to harm the credibility of PhishTank, which is best achieved by combining attacks 1 and 2: submitting URLs for legitimate websites and promptly voting them to be phish. This attacker may also increase the confusion by attempting to create false negatives, voting phishing websites as legitimate.

Detecting and defending against these attacks while maintaining an open submission and verification policy is hard. Many of the straightforward countermeasures can be sidestepped by a smart attacker. We consider a number of countermeasures in turn, demonstrating their inadequacy.

One simple countermeasure is to place an upper limit on the number of actions any user can take. This is unworkable for PhishTank due to its power-law distribution: some legitimate users participate many thousands of times. In any case, an enforced even distribution is easily defeated by a Sybil attack [7], where users register many identities. Given that many phishing attackers use botnets, even strict enforcement of 'one person, one vote' can probably be overcome.

The next obvious countermeasure is to impose voting requirements. For example, a user must have participated 'correctly' n times before weighing their opinion. This is ineffective for PhishTank, though the developers tell us that they do implement this countermeasure. First, since 97% of all submissions are valid, an attacker can quickly boost her reputation by voting for a phish slightly more than n times. Second, a savvy attacker can even minimize her implication of real phishing websites by only voting for rock-phish domains or duplicate URLs. Indeed the highly stylized format for rock-phish URLs makes it easy to automate correct voting at almost any desired scale.

Let us consider the complementary countermeasure. What about ignoring any user with more than n invalid submissions or incorrect votes? The idea here is that a malicious user is unlikely to force through all of his bad submissions and votes. Hence, a large number of deviating actions is a good proxy of misbehavior. Unfortunately, the power-law distribution of user participation causes another problem. Many heavily participating users who do a lot of good also make a lot of mistakes. For instance, the top submitter, *antiphishing*, is also the user with the highest number of invalid submissions, 578.

An improvement is to ban users who are wrong more than x% of the time. Nevertheless, attackers can simply pad their statistics by voting randomly, or by voting for duplicates and rock-phish URLs. Furthermore, many well-intentioned users might be excluded. Ignoring all users where more than 5% of their submissions are invalid would exclude 1 343 users, or 44% of all submitters. Ignoring them would also exclude 8 433 valid submissions, or 5% of all phishing URLs.

Moderators already participate in nearly every vote, so it would not be a stretch to insist that they were the submitter or voted with the majority. We do not know how often they vote incorrectly, but as discussed in Section 4.1, we know that even moderators make mistakes. One sign of fallibility is that just over 1% of moderator's submissions were voted down as invalid. Nonetheless, perhaps the best strategy for PhishTank is to use trusted moderators exclusively if they suspect they are under attack. Given that the 25 moderators already cast 74% of PhishTank's votes, silencing the whole crowd to root out the attackers may sometimes be wise, even if it contradicts principles of open participation.

5.2   Lessons for Secure Crowd-Sourcing

We can draw several general lessons about applying the open-participation model to security tools after examining the PhishTank data.

Lesson 1: The distribution of user participation matters. There is a natural tendency for highly skewed distributions, even power laws, in user participation rates. Power law-like distributions have also been observed in the interactions of online communities [27] and blogs [21]. While there may certainly be cases that are not as skewed as PhishTank, security engineers must check the distribution for wide variance when assessing the risk of leveraging user participation.

Skewed distributions can indeed create security problems. First, corruption of a few high-value participants can completely undermine the system. This is not a huge threat for PhishTank since attackers are probably too disorganized to buy off moderators. Nonetheless, the power-law distribution still means that the system could be in trouble if a highly active user stops participating.

Second, because good users can participate extensively, bad users can too. Simple rate-limiting countermeasures do not work here. Bad users may cause significant disruption under cover of a large body of innocuous behavior. Note that we do not take the view that all crowd-based security mechanisms should have balanced user participation. Enthusiastic users should be allowed to participate more, since their enthusiasm drives the success of crowd-based approaches. However, the distribution must be treated as a security consideration.

Lesson 2: Crowd-sourced decisions should be difficult to guess. Any decision that can be reliably guessed can be automated and exploited by an attacker. The underlying accuracy of PhishTank's raw data (97% phish) makes it easy for an attacker to improve her reputation by blindly voting all submissions as phish.

Lesson 3: Do not make users work harder than necessary. Requiring users to vote multiple times for duplicate URLs and rock-phish domains is not only an efficiency issue. It becomes a security liability since it allows an attacker to build up reputation without making a positive contribution.

6   Related Work

In earlier work, we have estimated the number and lifetimes of phishing websites using data from PhishTank [15] and demonstrated that timely removal reduced user exposure. Weaver and Collins computed the overlap between another two phishing feeds and applied capture-recapture analysis to estimate the number of overall phishing attacks [26].

In his book 'The Wisdom of Crowds', Surowiecki argued that under many circumstances the aggregation of a group's opinions can be more accurate than even the most expert individual [25]. He noted that web participation is particularly suited to crowd-based aggregation. Surowiecki listed a number of conditions where crowd-based intelligence may run into trouble: from overly homogeneous opinions to imitative users. We have highlighted how crowds may be manipulated if the distribution of participation is highly skewed and the correct decision can be reliably guessed.

Recently, user participation has been incorporated into security mechanisms, primarily as a data source rather than performing assessment as is done by PhishTank. Microsoft Internet Explorer and Mozilla Firefox both ask users to report suspicious websites, which are then aggregated to populate blacklists. 'StopBadware' collects reports from users describing malware and disseminates them after administrators have examined the submissions [23]. Herdict is a software tool which collects data from client machines to track malware [8]. Vipul's Razor, an open-source spam-filtering algorithm used by Cloudmark, solicits user spam emails as input [24]. NetTrust is a software application that shares information about the trustworthiness of websites via social networks [5].

Researchers have observed skewed distribution of user activity on the web in contexts other than security. Shirky argued that the influence of blogs (measured by the number of inbound links) naturally exhibited power-law distributions and discussed concerns about the effects of such inequality [22]. Adar et al. studied the structure of links between blogs to develop a ranking mechanism [1], while Shi et al. found blogs exhibited near-power-law distributions [21] in the number of inbound links. Meanwhile, Zhang et al. found power-law distributions in the participation rates of users in online communities [27].

Concerns over the manipulability of user-contributed web content have been raised before, most notably in the case of Wikipedia [6]. The SETI@Home distributed computational project was reported to have experienced widespread cheating [9]. More generally, Albert et al. found that networks whose connections between nodes are distributed according to a power law are vulnerable to targeted removal [2].

Countermeasures to voting manipulation where some users vote's are weighed more heavily than others share similarities to research in trust management [4]. Researchers have devised many different metrics which differentiate between good users and bad [19,13], often for use in reputation systems [10]. More sophisticated trust metrics like these might fare better than the simple countermeasures discussed in Section 5.1.

7   Conclusion

End-user participation is an increasingly popular resource for carrying out information security tasks. Having examined one such effort to gather and disseminate phishing information, we conclude that while such open approaches are promising, they are currently less effective overall than the more traditional closed methods. Compared to a data feed collected in a conventional manner, PhishTank is less complete and less timely. On the positive side, PhishTank's decisions appear mostly accurate: we identified only a few incorrect decisions, all of which were later reversed. However, we found that inexperienced users make many mistakes and that users with bad voting records tend to commit the same errors. So the 'wisdom' of crowds sometimes shades into folly.

We also found that user participation varies greatly, raising concerns about the ongoing reliability of PhishTank's decisions due to the risk of manipulation by small numbers of people. We have described how PhishTank can be undermined by a phishing attacker bent on corrupting its classifications, and furthermore how the power-law distribution of user participation simultaneously makes attacks easier to carry out and harder to defend against.

Despite these problems, we do not advocate against leveraging user participation in the design of all security mechanisms. Rather, we believe that the circumstances must be more carefully examined for each application, and furthermore that threat models must address the potential for manipulation.

Acknowledgments

Tyler Moore is supported by the UK Marshall Aid Commemoration Commission and by US National Science Foundation grant DGE-0636782. Richard Clayton is currently working on the spamHINTS project, funded by Intel Research.

References

1. Adar, E., Zhang, L., Adamic, L., Lukose, R.: Implicit structure and the dynamics of blogspace. In: Workshop on the Weblogging Ecosystem, 13th International World Wide Web Conference (WWW) (2004)
2. Albert, R., Jeong, H., Barabási, A.: Error and attack tolerance of complex networks. Nature 406, 378–382 (2000)
3. Anderson, L., Holt, C.: Information cascades in the laboratory. American Economic Review 87(5), 847–862 (1995)
4. Blaze, M., Feigenbaum, J., Lacy, J.: Decentralized trust management. In: IEEE Symposium on Security and Privacy (S&P), pp. 164–173. IEEE Computer Society, Los Alamitos (1996)
5. Camp, L.J.: Reliable, usable signaling to defeat masquerade attacks. In: Fifth Workshop on the Economics of Information Security (WEIS) (2006)
6. Denning, P., Horning, J., Parnas, D., Weinstein, L.: Wikipedia risks. Communications of the ACM 48(12), 152 (2005)

7. Douceur, J.R.: The Sybil Attack. In: Druschel, P., Kaashoek, M.F., Rowstron, A. (eds.) IPTPS 2002. LNCS, vol. 2429, pp. 251–260. Springer, Heidelberg (2002)
8. Hwang, T.: Herdict: a distributed model for threats online. In: Bradbury, D. (ed.) Network Security, pp. 15–18. Elsevier, Oxford (2007)
9. Kahney, L.: Cheaters bow to peer pressure. Wired (February 15, 2001), http://www.wired.com/news/technology/0,1282,41838,00.html
10. Kamvar, S., Schlosser, M., Garcia-Molina, H.: The EigenTrust algorithm for reputation management in P2P networks. In: 12th WWW, pp. 640–651. ACM Press, New York (2003)
11. Lamport, L., Shostak, R., Pease, M.: The Byzantine Generals Problem. ACM Transactions on Programming Languages and Systems 4(3), 382–401 (1982)
12. Larkin, E.: Online thugs assault sites that specialize in security help. PC World (September 11, 2007), http://www.pcworld.com/businesscenter/article/137084/ online_thugs_assault_sites_that_specialize_in_security_help_.html
13. Levien, R.: Attack resistant trust metrics. PhD thesis (draft), University of California at Berkeley (2004)
14. McMillan, R.: 'Rock Phish' blamed for surge in phishing. InfoWorld (December 12, 2006), http://www.infoworld.com/article/06/12/12/HNrockphish_1.html
15. Moore, T., Clayton, R.: Examining the impact of website take-down on phishing. In: Anti-Phishing Working Group eCrime Researcher's Summit (APWG eCrime), pp. 1–13. ACM Press, New York (2007)
16. Newman, M.: Power laws, Pareto distributions and Zipf's law. Contemporary Physics 46(5), 323–351 (2005)
17. Pan, Y., Ding, X.: Anomaly based web phishing page detection. In: 22nd Annual Computer Security Applications Conference (ACSAC 2006), pp. 381–392. IEEE Computer Society, Los Alamitos (2006)
18. PhishTank: http://www.phishtank.com/
19. Reiter, M., Stubblebine, S.: Toward acceptable metrics of authentication. In: IEEE S&P, pp. 10–20. IEEE Computer Society, Los Alamitos (1997)
20. Ross, B., Jackson, C., Miyake, N., Boneh, D., Mitchell, J.: Stronger password authentication using browser extensions. In: 14th USENIX Security Symposium, USENIX Association, Berkeley, p. 2 (2005)
21. Shi, X., Tseng, B., Adamic, L.: Looking at the blogosphere topology through different lenses. In: International Conference on Weblogs and Social Media (2007)
22. Shirky, C.: Power laws, weblogs, and inequality (2003), http://www.shirky.com/writings/powerlaw_weblog.html
23. Stop Badware: http://www.stopbadware.org
24. Vipul's Razor: http://razor.sourceforge.net
25. Surowiecki, J.: The wisdom of crowds: why the many are smarter than the few. Doubleday, New York (2004)
26. Weaver, R., Collins, M.: Fishing for phishes: applying capture-recapture to phishing. In: APWG eCrime, pp. 14–25. ACM Press, New York (2007)
27. Zhang, J., Ackerman, M., Adamic, L.: Expertise networks in online communities: structure and algorithms. In: 16th WWW, pp. 221–230. ACM Press, New York (2007)
28. Zhang, Y., Egelman, S., Cranor, L., Hong, J.: Phinding phish: evaluating anti-phishing tools. In: 14th Annual Network & Distributed System Security Symposium (NDSS 2007) (2007)

Don't Clog the Queue!
Circuit Clogging and Mitigation in P2P
Anonymity Schemes

Jon McLachlan and Nicholas Hopper

Computer Science & Engineering, University of Minnesota, Minneapolis MN 55455 USA
{hopper,jmcla}@cs.umn.edu

Abstract. At Oakland 2005, Murdoch and Danezis described an attack on the
Tor anonymity service that recovers the nodes in a Tor circuit, but not the client.
We observe that in a peer-to-peer anonymity scheme, the client is part of the
circuit and thus the technique can be of greater significance in this setting. We
experimentally validate this conclusion by showing that "circuit clogging" can
identify client nodes using the MorphMix peer-to-peer anonymity protocol. We
also propose and empirically validate the use of the Stochastic Fair Queueing discipline on outgoing connections as an efficient and low-cost mitigation technique.

1 Introduction

Anonymous communication schemes allow their users to communicate with others
while concealing who communicates with whom. Deployed anonymity schemes tend
to be either high-latency – they provide strong anonymity, but are unsuitably slow for
casual Internet browsing – or low-latency, aiming for anonymity against weaker adversaries, but better-suited for casual Internet browsing. The majority of these schemes
forward end-user traffic though redirecting relays, using multi-layered encryption between the source and every intermediate relay to ensure both end-to-end privacy and
message size unity. This layered encryption creates virtual "anonymous tunnels," or
circuits running through N relay nodes. The ultimate node in the anonymous tunnel
performs the traditional Internet communication on behalf of the end-user. Returning
messages then follow the reverse path through the same N relays, arriving at the source
of the anonymous tunnel.

Such low-latency anonymity schemes can be further categorized as either *centralized*
systems, in which a relatively small number of nodes act as "servers" that form the tunnels, or *peer-to-peer* systems, in which every end system may act as a relay for any other
user. Example centralized systems include AN.ON [1], where tunnels are further constrained to follow one of a few paths through the central relays, and Tor [7], where currently 1000 servers act as relays for an estimated 100,000 users. Example peer-to-peer
anonymity schemes include Crowds [22], Tarzan [10], Salsa [19] and Morph-Mix [23].
While peer-to-peer schemes offer the potential to scale more easily to a large user-base,
it is interesting to note that to date, only centralized schemes are widely deployed.

Despite having a relatively weak security goal, a variety of attacks against low-
latency anonymity schemes have been proposed [2,12,5,21,18,17]. Perhaps the simplest

G. Tsudik (Ed.): FC 2008, LNCS 5143, pp. 31–46, 2008.

is the "clogging" attack proposed by Back *et al.* [2], which we anachronistically call "relay clogging:" an adversary at one end of an anonymous tunnel can determine which nodes participate in the tunnel by sequentially "clogging" each of the possible relays (either within the protocol or at the network level) and looking for a corresponding drop in the throughput across the tunnel. This attack seems unavoidable under the current Internet architecture, but is also quite expensive in terms of the time and bandwidth required.

Murdoch and Danezis [17] proposed and empirically validated a dramatically lower-cost form of this attack, that we call "circuit clogging." In this attack, a malicious server alternately "clogs and unclogs" an anonymous tunnel, while measuring the latency of simple "timing" connections that run across all relays. The relays with latency functions most strongly correlated to the clogging periods are identified as the members of the tunnel. This attack works because in most low-latency schemes, relays divide their outgoing bandwidth among active tunnels, rather than across all tunnels.

In this paper, we present 3 significant contributions. First, we empirically corroborate the effectiveness of the circuit clogging attack against a prototype P2P scheme, MorphMix [23]. Second, building on the observation that in a P2P environment, the client is one of the relays, we empirically demonstrate that circuit clogging in a P2P system can be used to identify the client end of an anonymous tunnel. This makes the attack much more powerful, because it yields direct information about clients, and also because it allows a malicious server to take advantage of prior information about suspected clients: if 10 nodes are suspected as clients, the server can run timing connections across just those 10 nodes to confirm which one is the client. Finally, we propose and empirically validate a strategy for mitigating the circuit clogging attack while maintaining efficiency.

The problem of mitigating the circuit clogging attack represents an interesting optimization problem involving tradeoffs between efficient resource usage and vulnerability to several related attacks. The attack works because of interference between tunnels running through a relay, suggesting several possible mitigations. For example, one solution is for each relay to strictly divide its resources into N time slots or buckets, and map each circuit to a unique bucket; unused buckets represent wasted resources, while a relay with all buckets full would turn away additional circuits. With the possible exception of minor effects due to the scheduling code, this solution eliminates any interference between circuits, but uses system resources very inefficiently, and opens the way for new attacks. An adversary can essentially perform the $N - 1$ [24] attack by keeping all but one of the buckets in each relay full, then intermittently testing whether an additional circuit succeeds; or the adversary can simply deny service by filling all buckets in all relays.

Another seemingly obvious alternative is to let relays accept any number of circuits but to equally allocate resources between all circuits, busy-waiting when a given circuit is inactive. This solution is less resource-wasteful in a friendly environment than the previous, but makes the relay-clogging attack very simple: to test whether a relay is involved in a tunnel, we can build a few additional circuits through the relay and watch for a corresponding drop in circuit throughput.

Our proposed mitigation mechanism is based on an existing queueing discipline, *Stochastic Fair Queueing*, which assigns circuits randomly to one of a small number of queues, which each receive equal service. Service within a queue is divided equally

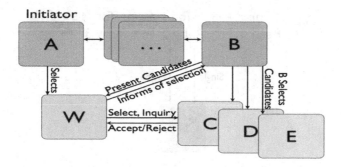

Fig. 1. Simplified MorphMix Next-Hop Selection

among just the active circuits. When the number of queues is set correctly, this scheme does not waste system resources and does not facilitate the $N-1$ or relay clogging attacks; and since any given circuit will intersect with a target circuit with small probability, it limits the amount of interference an attacker can cause with a single circuit. Our experiments show that while an attacker can still mount a circuit clogging attack using what we call an "N-probe" variant, the costs of mounting this attack are significantly increased, and can be controlled as a function of the number of queues in a relay.

In the remainder of this paper, we discuss the MorphMix P2P anonymity scheme and related work in section 2 and the results of our circuit clogging experiments on MorphMix in section 3. We then present our SFQ mitigation mechanism and experiments analyzing its effectiveness and efficiency in section 4, along with experimental analysis of a possible counterattack. Finally we discuss implications of these findings in section 5.

2 Background

Morphmix. Our experiments were conducted against the Java implementation of the MorphMix P2P layered encryption anonymity scheme [23], selected mainly for the existence of a working prototype. Abstracting away the details of encryption algorithms and packet formats, the main distinguishing characteristics of such schemes are the mechanisms for peer discovery and circuit construction.

In MorphMix, these mechanisms are closely related. A morphmix node joins the network by "bootstrapping" from any existing node by sending a request to initiate an encrypted link. The node responds with a list of the other nodes it is connected to. This process can be repeated to discover a small set of nodes. Thereafter an honest node learns about new nodes in the process of circuit construction, shown in Figure 1. When extending a circuit, the node currently at the end of the circuit provides a list of several of its neighbors to a "witness" node chosen by the initiator. The witness node chooses the next hop and also returns the list of neighbors through the tunnel. Thus, a node never needs to know about more than a few other peers, but through repeated connection attempts and tunnel building, can quickly learn many nodes.

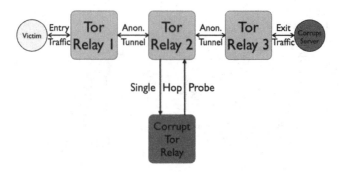

Fig. 2. Murdoch and Danezis Experiment

Since there is, by design, no admission control in MorphMix, a sybil attack [8] or other large-scale collusions are an obvious concern, especially given that random nodes assist in the construction of a circuit. Thus MorphMix includes a Collusion Detection System which attempts to identify nodes that seem to prefer selecting each other as next hops in anonymous tunnel creation. This scheme, which is essentially irrelevant to our paper, is based on locally collected statistics about the behavior of other nodes.

As with most low-latency anonymity schemes, MorphMix is mainly concerned with local active adversaries. In other words, they aim to provide anonymity against localized eavesdroppers, packet injections, packet replays, and most importantly against prying recipients of anonymous traffic. These adversaries are assumed to control only a few nodes within the MorphMix network. The circuit clogging attack (on Tor, and on MorphMix) falls within this threat model, motivating the need to mitigate this vulnerability in not only MorphMix, but in all low-latency schemes.

Related Work. As discussed above, Murdoch and Danezis [17] introduced the circuit clogging attack and measured its effectiveness against Tor. The basic setup of their experiment is illustrated in Figure 2: a "probe" machine, running a corrupt Tor node, initializes a circuit of length one – looping back to the probe machine – through each Tor node. The victim connects to the corrupt server through a circuit, and the server modulates its response in 30-60 second "on" periods of high data rate, followed by 30 second "off" periods with no outgoing data. The latency of packets sent through the "probe" tunnels was then correlated against the on/off period of the corrupt server. In their experiments, they correctly identified 11/13 true positives, with no false positives. Once the nodes in a Tor circuit are identified, they can be used to link two connections from the same exit node. Recently, another paper [12] discussed a way to extend this attack, using circuit latency measurements, to learn some information about the network location of the client.

Tabriz and Borisov [27] derived a way to model the statistical correlations used by victim nodes to detect collusion and simulated the same statistical tracking within the colluding nodes themselves. This way, the colluding nodes were able to intelligently select other colluding nodes without overstepping their statistically inferred node selection "canaries," avoiding the CDM on victimized MorphMix nodes while still undermining a substantial portion of the MorphMix network. This attack, however, requires several colluding morphmix nodes.

Several other timing-based attacks on low-latency anonymity schemes have been proposed. *Packet-counting* attacks [2,25,29,14,3] work by examining either the packet flux over several time periods or the inter-packet arrival times of a flow to find correlations between flows. This information can be used to identify flows where the adversary controls the first and last node in a circuit, or for a global observer to identify all flows. Several countermeasures have been performed, such as link padding and defensive dropping [14]; the extent to which these defeat an active adversary engaged in counting attacks is uncertain [5]. A similar attack can allow a local observer to identify anonymously downloaded websites by their packet-count fingerprints [11].

An explicitly stated goal of some P2P anonymity systems, such as Salsa [19], is to hide the complete list of participants in the scheme. This is to prevent *intersection attacks* [6,15], that work by observing the differences in network traffic based on a node's presence or absence in the anonymity protocol. Contrary to the suggestion of [28], we demonstrate that MorphMix does not effectively hide the list of participating nodes.

3 Attacking Morphmix

To evaluate the effectiveness of circuit-clogging against the MorphMix prototype, we ran a series of experiments against small MorphMix deployments. The first set, run against a small deployment on the PlanetLab [4] wide-area testbed, replicated the Murdoch and Danezis experiment and were used to measure the experiment's ability to distinguish between circuit relays, circuit initiators, and non-circuit nodes. The second set, conducted against a local lab deployment, measured the difficulty of finding the set of nodes in a morphmix network.

3.1 Wide-Area Experiments

Setup. In our first set of wide-area experiments, we performed two sets of twenty runs each using the setup shown in Figure 3. In this experiment, the *victim* node initiates

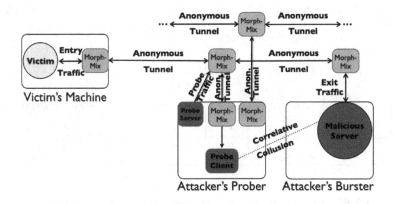

Fig. 3. Circuit clogging attack on MorphMix, probe targeting a middleman relay

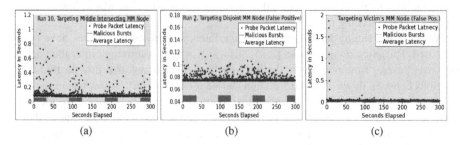

Fig. 4. Representative experiment results: (a) and (b) show probe latencies targeting a relay node, while (c) shows probe latencies targeting a disjoint node

a circuit of length three and connects to the (malicious) *burst server*. Meanwhile, the *probe server* builds two *probe circuits* that each run in a separate MorphMix instance and connect to one external MorphMix instance. The first circuit passes through an *intersecting* node in the victim's circuit, while the second passes through a *disjoint* node outside of the victim's circuit. These probe circuits then connect back to the probe server, which sends a short (64 byte) packet every 0.2 seconds to measure the latency of the probe circuits. In *middleman* runs, the intersecting morhpmix instance is the third relay in the circuit, while in *victim* runs, the intersecting instance runs on the victim node. Finally, the burst server alternates between 30 second "on periods," during which it sends a 10KB payload every 25ms, and 60 second "off periods," where it sends no data. Each run, testing two nodes, ran for 5 minutes.

Results and Analysis. Figure 4 shows the results of three runs. Fig. 4(a) shows the expected results — when targeting a relay in the circuit, latency increases dramatically during the burst server's "on" periods compared to the "off" periods. Fig. 4(b) shows a "false negative" run — latency remains quite high during the off periods. This may well be due to the fact that we selected the burst server load by measuring the average

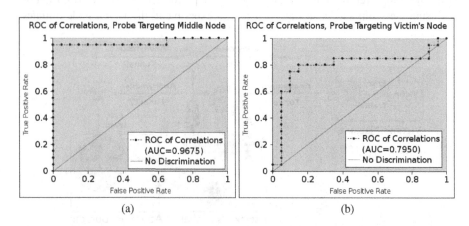

Fig. 5. ROC plots for MD correlation of (a) middleman and (b) victim relays

throughput capacity of morphmix instances on our planetlab nodes. Fig. 4(c) shows a "false positive", e.g. the probe latencies of a disjoint node that show high correlation to the burst signal. It seems clear that the high correlation here is due to an unrelated spike in the load of the "disjoint" planetlab node.

To determine whether a node was in a relay, Murdoch and Danezis computed the correlation of its normalized latency signal $L'(t)$ with the burst server's binary template signal $S(t)$, i.e. the correlation is calculated as $\frac{\sum_t S(t) \times L'(t)}{\sum_t S(t)}$, and nodes with "high" correlation are classified as intersecting the circuit. Setting different thresholds of classification will yield different rates of true and false positives; varying this threshold produces the receiver operating characteristic (ROC) curve for this correlation function. Figure 5 shows the resulting curves for the victim and middleman nodes. Following [9], we summarize an ROC curve by its AUC (Area Under Curve), where 0.5 indicates a non-distinguishing classifier and 1.0 indicates a perfect classifier. In our experiments, the MD correlation function had AUC 0.9675 when targeting a middleman node and 0.795 when targeting a victim node. This suggests that circuit clogging can be applied to effectively confirm suspected circuit initiators in MorphMix, and even more effectively to identify relays.

Motivated by several of the anomalies shown in figure 4, we also calculated the correlation when probe latencies are normalized with respect to the median probe latency, rather than the average. Figure 6 shows the impact of this change. The AUC for runs targeting the middleman node increases to 1.0, while the AUC for runs targeting the victim node increases to 0.87, with an equal error rate of 10%. Fig. 6 also shows that the magnitude of the median-normalized correlation is a good indicator of whether an intersecting node is a victim or middleman.

3.2   Node Discovery Attack

Although finding all nodes in a morphmix network is less critical given that suspected clients can be monitored directly, the full circuit clogging attack depends to some extent on building a list of currently participating nodes. Although it is not an explicit goal of MorphMix to hide the participant list, we performed a simple experiment to measure an attacker's ability to discover this information. In our experiment, we first start, and

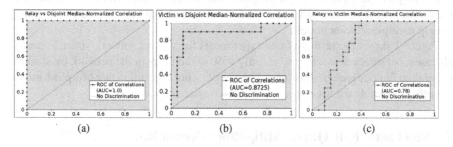

Fig. 6. ROC plots for median-normalized correlation of (a) middleman vs disjoint,(b) victim vs. disjoint, and (c) victim vs middleman morphmix instances

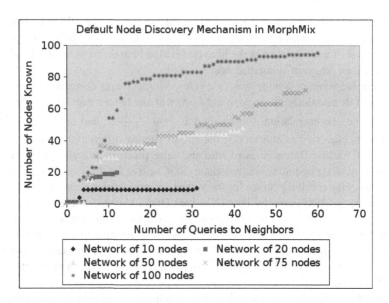

Fig. 7. Results of Node Discovery experiment for $N \in 10, 25, 50, 75, 100$: experiments halted when 95% of peers were found

allow to stabilize, a network of N nodes. Then we start our "attacker" node, which starts off with a list consisting of a single known node. The attacker node repeatedly picks a random node from its list, contacts that node with a link request, and adds any neighbors of that node to its list. Note that this search can be easily distributed to multiple nodes.

Using the default configuration of the MorphMix protocol, a stabilized client will always return at least four nodes in response to a link request. If we assume that the neighbor list of each MorphMix node is uniformly chosen, and that the initial node of the attacker is uniformly chosen, then the probability, over all choices of neighbors, initial nodes, and sequences of contacted nodes, of contacting a node at a given step is $1/N$. Thus, we heuristically estimate that the expected number of steps needed to contact all nodes is $N \ln N/4$. We note that the number of lookups needed could be further reduced by a factor of $\ln N/4$ by having the attacker implement a breadth-first search of the network, at the expense of a slight increase in the amount of coordination required among multiple attacker nodes.

Figure 7 shows the results of our experiments for various network sizes. In nearly all cases, our attacker was able to identify 95% of the peers in the network by sending fewer than N node request messages. This supports our contention that MorphMix does not effectively hide the list of peers from an adversarial node.

4   Stochastic Fair Queue Mitigation Mechanism

The main reason for the success of circuit clogging is the fact that in most low-latency anonymity schemes, circuits *interfere* with each other: the amount, and timing, of traffic in one circuit can influence the service received by another. In particular, the available throughput of a node is typically divided between active circuits, in order to make good use of this throughput. The side effect of this decision is that the activity of on circuit influences the queueing time for other circuits. As Murdoch and Danezis argue, this interference is effectively a covert channel between the circuits in a relay.

This covert channel can be mitigated to some extent by enforcing fairness among all circuits at the application layer - if each circuit has an equal share of resources regardless of activity, then from the application's point of view, the circuits do not interfere with each other. Unfortunately, this approach may not make efficient use of the resources available to the application: if we reserve service for circuits that do not use that service, we incur a performance penalty compared to servicing only active circuits. Furthermore, the use by the application of shared resources may results in exploitable "covert channels" at other levels. While we expect that the interference due to factors like shared operating system and processor time will be minimal, we note that relay clogging can exploit interference at the network level by denying service to a relay and checking whether service on the circuit improves or stays the same. This attack seems unavoidable at the application level, though we note that it is much more costly to mount this attack.

In the MorphMix prototype that we evaluated, messages for all circuits passing through a relay are processed through a single, central, first-in/first-out queue. Our mitigation technique is to simply change the scheduling policy for messages in this queue, reducing the extent to which circuits interfere. We replaced this FIFO outgoing queue with a Stochastic Fair Queue (SFQ) [16], a queueing discipline originally designed for routers to relieve network congestion due to ill-behaved UDP traffic. In the remainder of this section, we describe SFQ and its properties in more detail, give empirical evidence that SFQ reduces the effectiveness of circuit clogging while incurring only a small performance penalty, and consider alternative, more costly attacks on SFQ-enhanced morphmix.

4.1   Basic Properties of SFQ

The SFQ policy probabilistically fairly distributes resources over a set M of circuits passing through a relay. It randomly maps each $m \in M$ to one of q queues for the entire life-span of the circuit m. Each of these q queues receives exactly $\left(\frac{1}{q}\right)$ fraction of the available throughput. If a particular queue has no active circuits, it still receives $\left(\frac{1}{q}\right)$ of the available throughput; in our implementation this was accomplished through busy waiting for a time period determined by a running average for all live message processing times. Within a queue, messages were still processed in a first-in/first-out fashion, so that circuits received service within a queue proportionally to their level of activity.

The parameter q determines how effectively a SFQ-enabled morphmix node utilizes its resources. If there are active circuits in some number $n < q$ of queues, then performance is degraded by a factor of $\frac{q}{q-n}$ while servicing the $q - n$ inactive queues. If we set q to be about half the expected number of active circuits passing through a relay, then we find that the probability that a queue is inactive is $(1 - \frac{1}{q})^{2q} \approx e^{-2}$, so that the expected performance degradation is $\frac{e^2}{e^2-1} \approx 1.16$.

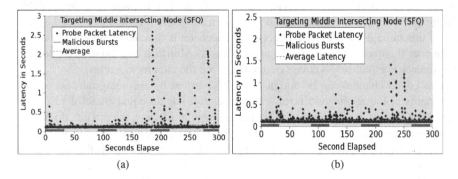

Fig. 8. Circuit clogging results for SFQ-enabled MorphMix: (a) a true positive experiment (b) a false negative experiment

The number q of queues also impacts the extent to which SFQ mitigates the circuit clogging attack. In particular, an attacker-controlled circuit interferes with a given circuit with probability $1/q$. Thus, in the circuit clogging attack, there is a $1/q$ probability that the probe circuit and the burst circuit will interfere. This gives the probe server a $1/q$ advantage in distinguishing nodes that intersect the circuit from disjoint nodes. In our experiments with SFQ-enhanced morphmix, we set $q = 8$, so we expect that a probe server should be able to correctly identify an intersecting node 62.5% of the time.

4.2 Circuit Clogging Mitigation

To test the effectivness of SFQ in mitigating the circuit clogging attack, we performed another series of 20 runs on a planetlab deployment identical to the experiments described in Section 3.1, replacing every MorphMix instance with an instance of SFQ-enabled MorphMix. Figure 8 shows two representative experimental results. In Fig. 8(a), we see the result of an experiment where the probe circuit collided with the burst circuit, resulting in a high correlation, while Fig. 8(b) shows the more common result,

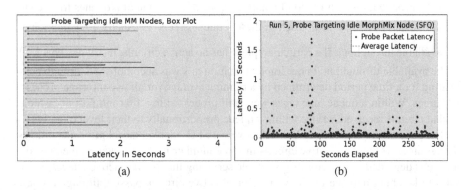

Fig. 9. Probe latencies with no burst server present: (a) Box Plot of all probe times, 20 probes total. (b) Typical run showing several latency spikes.

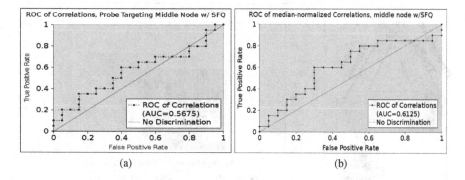

Fig. 10. SFQ circuit clogging: ROC plots for (a) MD correlation of relay vs disjoint nodes and (b) median-normalized correlation of relay vs disjoint nodes

when the probe circuit was mapped to a different queue than the burst circuit and so had effectively no interference.

One observation about both of the runs shown in Figure 8 is the "noise" caused by large latency peaks during off periods. We speculated that these spikes resulted from the interaction of MorphMix's Java implementation with the PlanetLab shared execution environment. To highlight this, we ran an extra set of 20 experiments with the probes targeting only idle MorphMix node with SFQ. This batch was identical to the other SFQ batch, except that there was no victim node or burst server. Figure 9 summarizes the variability in probe latencies present even with no burst server. This illustrates the need for robust normalization.

Results. When all nodes composing the P2P network (except for the two controlled by the probe server) utilized SFQ, we notice a significant mitigation of the attack. The average MD correlation with the probe targeting an node intersecting the victim's tunnel was 1.0154 with standard deviation of 0.1071 and the average MD correlation with the probe targeting a disjoint node was 0.9789 with standard deviation 0.16241. Using median-normalized correlations, we see an average correlation of 1.246 targeting intersecting nodes and 1.191 for disjoint nodes, with standard deviations of 0.218 and 0.170, respectively. ROC plots for both correlation figures are shown in figure 10. As expected, the AUC for these measures is only slightly better than the line of no discrimination: 0.5675 in the case of MD correlations, and 0.6125 when using median-normalized correlation.

4.3 Efficiency of SFQ Mitigation

To test the performance penalty of running SFQ on a morphmix relay, we performed a set runs on a small planetlab deployment of MorphMix. In each run of the experiment, shown in Figure 11(a), the "client" machine started 8 standard MorphMix instances, and the "server" machine started either a SFQ-enhanced MorphMix instance or a standard MorphMix instance. The client instances each built a one-hop circuit through the server instance, and connected back to the client machine to download a 52KB file. The time required for all 8 instances to complete the download (not including circuit

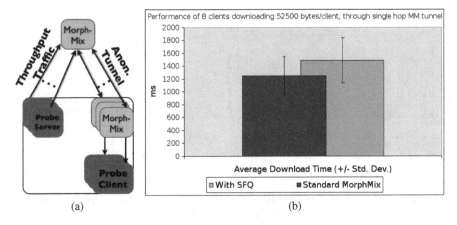

(a)   (b)

Fig. 11. Performance comparison for SFQ-enhanced and standard morphmix: (a) panetlab experimental setup, and (b) results for 3 runs of each type

construction) was recorded. In all, 3 runs with a standard MorphMix relay and 3 runs with a SFQ-enhanced relay were performed.

The results of the experiment are shown in Figure 11(b). With 8 queues and 8 active circuits, we expect to see performance degraded by a factor of $\frac{e}{e-1} \approx 1.6$. In our experiments, the performance was slightly better: average download time for standard MorphMix was 1250 ms with a standard error of 61ms, while average download time for SFQ was 1488ms, with a standard error of 71ms, giving an estimated performance penalty of 19%, rather than 60%. This suggests that, with the proper settings, SFQ can be an efficient mitigation technique for the basic circuit clogging attack.

4.4 N-Probe Attack

Given an anonymous network utilizing SFQ initialized to q slots, a clever adversary could initialize N probe circuits, rather than one, per relay. This increases the

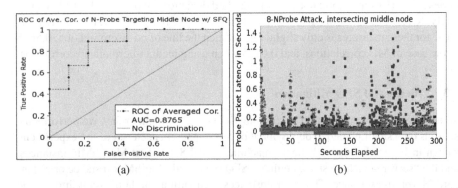

(a)   (b)

Fig. 12. Results of 8-probe attack on 8-queue SFQ: (a) ROC of maximum MD correlation, relay vs disjoint nodes; (b) typical result targeting a relay node, all 8 probes included.

probability that *some* probe circuit will intersect the queue supporting the the burst circuit. This way, the burst traffic and the probe traffic collide with each other as if they were sharing the same standard queue. Given q SFQ slots in neighboring MorphMix nodes, N probe connections into a single neighbor, and one "target" SFQ slot containing the modulating server's stream, the probability of an adversary intersecting the target SFQ slot with at least one of the N probe connections is $\rho(q, N) = 1 - \left(\frac{q-1}{q}\right)^N$. Thus an adversary running N probe circuits should ideally have advantage roughly $1/2 + \rho(q, N)/2$ at distinguishing relay intersecting from disjoint MorphMix nodes.[1]

To test the effectiveness of this attack, we performed another set of 9 runs each against our PlanetLab deployment of SFQ-enabled MorphMix. We used the same experimental setup as in section 4.2, including the use of 8 queues, except that the probe server ran 8 separate probing MorphMix instances (so that eight one-hop circuits ran through the targeted relay). Since the probe server had no way to determine a priori *which* of the 8 probe circuits intersected with the burst circuit, we calculated the MD correlation of the latencies of each circuit and took the maximum correlation as the summary statistic for a node. Figure 12(a) shows the ROC curve resulting from this experiment, while Fig 12(b) shows results of a typical run. The average max-MD correlation for an intersecting node was 2.99 with a standard error of 0.90, while the average max-MD correlation for a disjoint node was 1.16, with a standard error of 0.17. The AUC for the experiment was 0.8765.

These results suggest that the N-probe circuit clogging attack can potentially be effective against SFQ. We note, however, that the parameters $N = 8$, $q = 8$, were selected somewhat arbitrarily. In an active morphmix deployment, we might expect each node to initiate, e.g., 8 circuits (the default number of concurrent connections in Mozilla-based web browsers), each spanning 5 relays (the default circuit length), so that on average each MorphMix node would support 40 active circuits. In this case, using 20 queues would require the probe attacker to run 20 probes. In our experiments, the downstream bandwidth required per probe was 27Kbps, and the upstream bandwidth required per probe was 10Kbps. Thus the bandwidth cost of running 20 probes through a single relay would be 540Kbps downstream and 200Kbps upstream. Several measurement studies suggest that the average download capacity of an internet user is roughly 500Kbps [20,13]; thus enabling SFQ makes the cost of circuit clogging roughly comparable to the cost of relay clogging.

5   Discussion

In this paper, we have confirmed that the Murdoch and Danezis circuit clogging attack can be applied to identify circuit initiators in the MorphMix P2P anonymity scheme. This makes the attack much more powerful, for two reasons: first, by directly identifying victims, the attack obtains much more valuable information than when it is deployed

---

[1] This analysis assumes that an adversary cannot detect when two probes are in the same queue; an adversary who can do so can improve the probability $\rho(q, N)$ to N/q by ensuring that his probes are in disjoint buckets. Note that it is unclear how effectively this can be done in practice

against Tor; second, this enables confirmation attacks, where only a small set of suspect nodes need to be monitored, rather than all nodes in the network.

In response to this observation, we proposed a novel application of an existing queueing policy, Stochastic Fair Queueing, to mitigate circuit clogging attacks. We have demonstrated empirically that enforcing SFQ on outgoing circuit links effectively mitigates the basic circuit clogging attack, and significantly increases the cost of a more sophisticated approach. Combined with recent results of Shmatikov and Wang [26], we believe that this indicates that understanding the security implications of different queueing policies in low-delay anonymity schemes may be an interesting direction for further research.

One interesting question that we have not fully addressed is how the N-probe circuit clogging attack will be affected by the presence of multiple active circuits on a relay. In our experiments, both the intersecting and disjoint relays supported no active circuits other than those created by the attack - probe circuits in both cases and the burst circuit in the case of the intersecting relay. In a sense, this is a best-case scenario for the N-probe attack, since other than random delay spikes, probes passing through a disjoint node will never intersect another circuit, causing all probe latencies to be close to the average and median. When another active circuit intersects with a probe circuit, probes may have higher than average latencies during some on-periods, leading to greater maximum correlations in disjoint nodes. This in turn would likely imply a greater false positive rate for a given correlation threshold.

Another interesting direction for future work is to apply the SFQ scheduling policy to circuits in Tor, mitigating the original circuit clogging attack as proposed by Murdoch and Danezis. Since each Tor node supports many clients, the expected number of active circuits in a Tor node may be quite high, possibly allowing a relay to support hundreds of queues. This leads us to expect that stochastic fair queueing may in fact make relay clogging – via network-level denial of service – a more attractive option than circuit clogging in the Tor network.

Acknowledgements. The authors wish to thank Roger Dingledine, Yongdae Kim, Marc Rennhard, Eugene Vasserman, and the anonymous FC reviewers for helpful discussions and comments about this work. This work was supported by the University of Minnesota's Undergraduate Research Opportunities Program and by the NSF under grant CNS-0546162.

References

1. AN.ON: Anonymity online, http://anon.inf.tu-dresden.de/
2. Back, A., Möller, U., Stiglic, A.: Traffic analysis attacks and trade-offs in anonymity providing systems. In: Moskowitz, I.S. (ed.) IH 2001. LNCS, vol. 2137, pp. 245–257. Springer, Heidelberg (2001)
3. Blum, A., Song, D., Venkataraman, S.: Detection of Interactive Stepping Stones: Algorithms and Confidence Bounds. In: Jonsson, E., Valdes, A., Almgren, M. (eds.) RAID 2004. LNCS, vol. 3224, pp. 258–277. Springer, Heidelberg (2004)
4. Chun, B., Culler, D., Roscoe, T., Bavier, A., Peterson, L., Wawrzoniak, M., Bowman, M.: Planetlab: an overlay testbed for broad-coverage services. SIGCOMM Comput. Commun. Rev. 33(3), 3–12 (2003)

5. Dai, W.: Two attacks against freedom
6. Danezis, G.: Statistical disclosure attacks: Traffic confirmation in open environments. In: Gritzalis, Vimercati, Samarati, and Katsikas (eds.) Proceedings of Security and Privacy in the Age of Uncertainty (SEC 2003), IFIP TC11, pp. 421–426. Kluwer, Dordrecht (2003)
7. Dingledine, R., Mathewson, N., Syverson, P.F.: Tor: The second-generation onion router. In: 13th USENIX Security Symposium (August 2004)
8. Douceur, J.: The sybil attack (2002)
9. Fawcett, T.: An introduction to ROC analysis. Pattern Recognition Letters 27(8), 861–874 (2006)
10. Freedman, M.J., Morris, R.: Tarzan: a peer-to-peer anonymizing network layer. In: CCS 2002: Proceedings of the 9th ACM conference on Computer and communications security, pp. 193–206. ACM Press, New York (2002)
11. Hintz, A.: Fingerprinting websites using traffic analysis. In: Dingledine, R., Syverson, P.F. (eds.) PET 2002. LNCS, vol. 2482, pp. 171–178. Springer, Heidelberg (2003)
12. Hopper, N., Vasserman, E.Y., Chan-Tin, D.: How much anonymity does network latency leak? In: Proceedings of CCS 2007 (October 2007)
13. Izal, M., Urvoy-Keller, G., Biersack, E.W., Felber, P., Al Hamra, A., Garces-Erice, L.: Dissecting BitTorrent: Five Months in a Torrents Lifetime. Passive and Active Measurements 2004 (2004)
14. Levine, B.N., Reiter, M.K., Wang, C., Wright, M.K.: Timing attacks in low-latency mix-based systems. In: Juels, A. (ed.) FC 2004. LNCS, vol. 3110, pp. 251–265. Springer, Heidelberg (2004)
15. Mathewson, N., Dingledine, R.: Practical traffic analysis: Extending and resisting statistical disclosure. In: Martin, D., Serjantov, A. (eds.) PET 2004. LNCS, vol. 3424. Springer, Heidelberg (2005)
16. McKenney, P.: Stochastic fairness queuing (1990)
17. Murdoch, S.J., Danezis, G.: Low-cost traffic analysis of tor. IEEE SP 00, 183–195 (2005)
18. Murdoch, S.J., Zieliński, P.: Sampled traffic analysis by internet-exchange-level adversaries. In: Borisov, N., Golle, P. (eds.) PET 2007. LNCS, vol. 4776, pp. 167–183. Springer, Heidelberg (2007)
19. Nambiar, A., Wright, M.: Salsa: a structured approach to large-scale anonymity. In: Proceedings of the 13th ACM conference on Computer and communications security, pp. 17–26 (2006)
20. Pouwelse, J.A., Garbacki, P., Epema, D.H.J., Sips, H.J.: The bittorrent p2p file-sharing system: Measurements and analysis. In: Castro, M., van Renesse, R. (eds.) IPTPS 2005. LNCS, vol. 3640, pp. 205–216. Springer, Heidelberg (2005)
21. Raymond, J.-F.: Traffic Analysis: Protocols, Attacks, Design Issues, and Open Problems. In: Federrath, H. (ed.) Designing Privacy Enhancing Technologies. LNCS, vol. 2009, pp. 10–29. Springer, Heidelberg (2001)
22. Reiter, M., Rubin, A.: Crowds: Anonymity for web transactions. ACM Transactions on Information and System Security 1(1) (June 1998)
23. Rennhard, M., Plattner, B.: Introducing MorphMix: peer-to-peer based anonymous Internet usage with collusion detection. In: WPES 2002: Proceedings of the 2002 ACM workshop on Privacy in the Electronic Society, pp. 91–102. ACM Press, New York (2002)
24. Serjantov, A., Dingledine, R., Syverson, P.: From a trickle to a flood: Active attacks on several mix types. In: Petitcolas, F.A.P. (ed.) IH 2002. LNCS, vol. 2578, pp. 36–52. Springer, Heidelberg (2003)
25. Serjantov, A., Sewell, P.: Passive attack analysis for connection-based anonymity systems. In: Snekkenes, E., Gollmann, D. (eds.) ESORICS 2003. LNCS, vol. 2808, pp. 116–131. Springer, Heidelberg (2003)

26. Shmatikov, V., Wang, M.-H.: Timing analysis in low-latency mix networks: Attacks and defenses. In: Gollmann, D., Meier, J., Sabelfeld, A. (eds.) ESORICS 2006. LNCS, vol. 4189, pp. 18–33. Springer, Heidelberg (2006)
27. Tabriz, P., Borisov, N.: Breaking the collusion detection mechanism of morphmix. In: Danezis, G., Golle, P. (eds.) PET 2006. LNCS, vol. 4258, pp. 368–383. Springer, Heidelberg (2006)
28. Wiangsripanawan, R., Susilo, W., Safavi-Naini, R.: Design principles for low latency anonymous network systems secure against timing attacks. In: Proceedings of the fifth Australasian symposium on ACSW frontiers (ACSW 2007), pp. 183–191. Australian Computer Society, Inc., Darlinghurst (2007)
29. Wright, M., Adler, M., Levine, B.N., Shields, C.: Defending anonymous communication against passive logging attacks. In: Proceedings of the 2003 IEEE Symposium on Security and Privacy (May 2003)

An Efficient Deniable Key Exchange Protocol (Extended Abstract)

Shaoquan Jiang and Reihaneh Safavi-Naini

Department of Computer Science
University of Calgary, Calgary, T2N 1N4

Abstract. A deniable key exchange allows two parties to jointly share a secret key while neither of two nor an outsider can prove to a third party that the communication between the two happened. This is an important mechanism for realizing a deniably secure channel. In this paper, we propose an efficient key exchange protocol and prove its deniable security. We compare our construction with the best known protocol with the same property and show the advantages of the new construction.

1 Introduction

A subtle security property of communication over the Internet is *deniability* which allows communicants to deny their participation in the communication. Deniability provides privacy for communicants and allows them to freely discuss details that otherwise would be considered binding because of the communication traces. This is essential in many financial negotiations over the Internet, where there is a need for parties to remain uncommitted. Deniability is a desirable security property for protocols that secure IP layer in the Internet protocol stack [9]. Deniable authentication can be achieved by requiring parties to share a secret key, which can be achieved through a key exchange protocol. However, such a protocol may leave undeniable traces about the participant's communication. Thus, it is important to design a deniably secure key exchange protocol.

1.1 Our Work

In this work, we first formalize an adversarial model for a deniably secure key exchange protocol by adding deniability [8] to Bellare-Rogaway key exchange model [1]. We model deniability by requiring that the adversary's view of the exchanges be simulatable using only the adversary's knowledge. We then construct an efficient three round key exchange protocol that uses a trapdoor one-way permutation and a hash function, and prove its deniable security in a variant of random-oracle (RO) model. This variant of RO was first adopted by [12] for deniable zero knowledge. If the trapdoor permutation is instantiated by an RSA function, our protocol requires each party to perform only two modular exponentiations.

G. Tsudik (Ed.): FC 2008, LNCS 5143, pp. 47–52, 2008.

1.2   Related Work

Deniability was first introduced by Dolev et al. in [7] while the formal study was initiated by Dwork et al. in [8]. Dwork et al defined deniable authentication by requiring the message to be authentic and deniable in the sense that the receiver's view can be simulated by using his own knowledge and especially without the sender's secret. The tool used for achieving this property is concurrent zero knowledge proofs. This line of research was followed by a number of authors. Di Raimondo et al [6] considered deniable security for key exchange protocols, where deniability is formalized using the simulatability of [8]. They showed that SKEME [11], an IPsec protocol, is deniably secure. Jiang [10] formalized the deniable security in the real-ideal world model and gave a deniably secure key exchange protocol in this model. In this paper, we are interested in designing more efficient key exchange protocols with deniable security.

2   Security Model

We first recall the security model for key exchange due to Bellare and Rogaway [1] and then add deniability to this model following the approach in [8].

Consider a set of n parties $P_1, \cdots, P_n$. A key exchange protocol Ξ is a two-party protocol that might be executed between a pair P_i and P_j, at the end of which, P_i and P_j will share a secret key (called *a session key*). First, a trusted third party $\mathbb{T}$ executes an initialization function I with a random input r where $r \leftarrow \{0,1\}^*$, to generate a tuple $(I_0, I_1, \cdots, I_n)$. It then provides I_i to P_i as his secret key and publishes I_0 as the public information. Each P_i can concurrently execute multiple copies of Ξ with possibly distinct P_j. A copy of the protocol at P_i is called an *instance* and $\Pi_i^{l_i}$ denotes the instance labeled by l_i. A protocol Ξ consists of a number of messages exchanged between the two parties and $Flow_i$ denotes the ith message of the protocol. Let $\mathsf{sid}_i^{l_i}$ denote the *session identifier* of an instance $\Pi_i^{l_i}$. Let $\mathsf{pid}_i^{l_i}$ denote the party that $\Pi_i^{l_i}$ is presumably interacting with. If an instance $\Pi_i^{l_i}$ successfully completes, then it defines a session key $sk_i^{l_i}$. Two instances $\Pi_i^{l_i}$ and $\Pi_j^{l_j}$ are said to be *partnered* if (1) $\mathsf{pid}_i^{l_i} = P_j$ and $\mathsf{pid}_j^{l_j} = P_i$; (2) $\mathsf{sid}_i^{l_i} = \mathsf{sid}_j^{l_j}$. Intuitively, two instances are partnered if they are executing Ξ with each other.

Adversarial Model. An adversary $\mathcal{A}$ has full control over the external network and can corrupt some users to obtain their secret keys and internal states. Ξ is secure if the adversary can not obtain any information about an established session key unless it is compromised trivially (e.g., party corruption).

$\mathcal{A}$'s capabilities are modeled by allowing him access to a number of oracles. $\mathcal{A}$'s calls to the oracles are responded according to the specification of Ξ (see below).

–A query $\mathsf{Send}(d, i, l_i, M)$ sends a message M in $Flow_d$ of Ξ to $\Pi_i^{l_i}$. The oracle then processes M according to the specification of Ξ in $\Pi_i^{l_i}$.

–A query $\mathsf{Reveal}(i, l_i)$ returns the session key $sk_i^{l_i}$ (if defined).

–A query Corrupt(i) corrupts P_i. The oracle response is to provide I_i and internal states of P_i to $\mathcal{A}$.

To test the security of $\varXi$, $\mathcal{A}$ send a query to oracle Test(i, l_i). The response is a number α, which is either $sk_i^{l_i}$ or a random number. The task of $\mathcal{A}$ is to guess which is the case. For the test to be meaningful, $\varPi_i^{l_i}$ and its partnered session are not allowed to be exposed trivially via a Corrupt or Reveal query. Adversary *succeeds* if he guesses correctly in the test query.

The security is specified by four properties: correctness, secrecy, authentication and deniability.

Correctness. If two partnered instances $\varPi_i^{l_i}$ and $\varPi_j^{l_j}$ successfully complete, then $sk_i^{l_i} = sk_j^{l_j}$.

Secrecy. Let Succ($\mathcal{A}$) denote the success of $\mathcal{A}$ in the Test query. The secrecy is to require $\Pr[\mathsf{Succ}(\mathcal{A})] < \frac{1}{2} + negl(\kappa)$.

Authentication. Let Non-Auth denote the event that $\varPi_i^{l_i}$ successfully completes execution of $\varXi$ but does not have a unique partnered instance. Then $\varXi$ is said to be *authenticated* if $\Pr[\mathsf{Non\text{-}Auth}(\mathcal{A})]$ is negligible.

Deniability. Deniability [8] requires that the adversary $\mathcal{A}$'s view can be simulated using the adversary's knowledge only. In our setting, $\mathcal{A}$'s view consists of oracles' replies to the adversary's queries, and his own random coins. The *deniability* is to require that the adversary's view when interacting with the oracles which are implemented according to the real run of protocol $\varXi$, is indistinguishable from his view when interacting with the oracles that are simulated by a polynomial time simulator $\mathcal{S}$ that satisfies the following restrictions.

–Initially, $\mathbb{T}$ prepares $(I_0, I_1, \cdots, I_n)$. Then I_0 will be provided to $\mathcal{S}$ and an adversary $\mathcal{A}$.
–When $\mathcal{A}$ queries Corrupt(i) oracle, $\mathcal{S}$ forwards this query to $\mathbb{T}$, receives the response I_i and passes it to $\mathcal{A}$. $\mathcal{S}$ is allowed to issue Corrupt(i) to $\mathbb{T}$ if and only if P_i is corrupted by $\mathcal{A}$.

Definition 1. *A key exchange protocol $\varXi$ is said to be* deniably secure *if it satisfies correctness, secrecy, authentication and deniability.*

2.1 Deniability in Public Random Oracle Model

Our construction is proven deniably secure in the *public random oracle* (pRO) model where the random oracle is a public random function that is accessible by the adversary and the simulator by submitting inputs and receiving outputs. The simulator can see the input/ouput pairs for all random oracle queries. This type of random oracle is introduced by [12] for proving deniability. Note here the simulator has a weaker simulation power than a traditional simulator that can maintain the random oracle.

3   Our Protocol

Let T_i be a trapdoor permutation for party P_i and D_i be the trapdoor. In case of RSA function, T_i is the public key (e_i, N_i), and D_i is the decryption exponent d_i. The global public information I_0 is defined to $\{T_i\}_{i=1}^n$. D_i is the secret for P_i. Let $H : \{0,1\}^* \rightarrow \{0,1\}^\kappa$ be a hash function. The execution of pRO-KE between P_i and P_j can be described as follows.

1. P_i takes $s \leftarrow \{0,1\}^\kappa$, computes and sends out $P_i, T_j(s), H(s|P_i|P_j)$ to P_j.
2. Receiving (P_i, α, σ) from P_i, P_j uses D_j to compute $s = D_j(\alpha)$ and verifies whether $\sigma = H(s|P_i|P_j)$. If it fails, he rejects; otherwise, he takes $r \leftarrow \{0,1\}^\kappa$, and sends $T_i(r), H(s|r|P_i|P_j|0)$ to P_i.
3. Receiving (β, δ_1) from P_j, P_i uses D_i to compute $r = D_i(\beta)$ and verifies whether $\delta_1 = H(s|r|P_i|P_j|0)$. If it fails, he rejects; otherwise, he defines session key $sk = H(s|r|P_i|P_j|2)$ and sends out $H(s|r|P_i|P_j|1)$ to P_j.
4. Receiving δ_2 from P_i, P_j verifies whether $\delta_2 = H(s|r|P_i|P_j|1)$. If not, he rejects. Otherwise, he defines the session key $sk = H(s|r|P_i|P_j|2)$.

4   Security Analysis

We consider the security in pRO model. Define $\mathsf{sid}_i^{l_i}$ and $\mathsf{sid}_j^{l_j}$ as $s|r|P_i|P_j$. The correctness holds trivially since *partnered instances* see the same $s|r|P_i|P_j$.

4.1   Secrecy

Now we consider the secrecy. We need to show $\Pr[\mathsf{Succ}(\mathcal{A})] < 1/2 + negl(\kappa)$. Intuitively, if a test session is not *exposed*, then, by the difficulty to invert T, both s and r are unpredictable. Thus, adversary should not be able to query $s|r|P_i|P_j|2$ to H oracle. So $H(s|r|P_i|P_j|2)$ remains uniformly random to him.

Theorem 1. *If H is a random oracle and T is a trapdoor permutation, then pRO-KE satisfies secrecy property.*

4.2   Authentication

Authentication is to require that a test instance $\Pi_{i^*}^{l^*}$ must have a unique partnered instance in $\mathsf{pid}_{i^*}^{l^*}$. We can show the following.

Theorem 2. $\Pr[\mathsf{Non\text{-}Auth}(\mathcal{A})]$ *is negligible.*

4.3   Deniability

In order for pRO-KE to be deniable, we need to construct a simulator $\mathcal{S}$ to answer Send, Reveal, Test and Corrupt queries such that the adversary's view in the simulated game is indistinguishable from that in the real execution, while $\mathcal{S}$ should not use any of the uncorrupted secret keys. It is not hard to see that the only difficulty is to answer $\mathsf{Send}(t, *)$ query for $t = 1, 2$. We illustrate the idea for $\mathsf{Send}(1, j, l_j, Flow_1)$. If $Flow_1 = < P_i, T_j(s), \sigma >$ satisfies $\sigma = H(s|P_i|P_j)$, then $(s|P_i|P_j)$ must have been queried to H-oracle; otherwise since $H(s|P_i|P_j)$ is random, the consistency of $Flow_1$ happens negligibly. Ignoring this unlikely event, s can be found out by $\mathcal{S}$ from the history of H-oracle queries. So $\mathcal{S}$ can answer $\mathsf{Send}(1, j, l_j, Flow_1)$ without D_j. $\mathsf{Send}(2, *)$ can be answered similarly.

Theorem 3. *If H is a public random oracle, then* pRO-KE *is deniable.*

5 Performance

We compare our protocol with SKEME [6,11] and uROE-KE [10], which are proven deniably secure KE protocols. SKEME has 3 rounds and requires a CCA2-secure and plaintext-aware public-key cryptosystem. The best known scheme with these properties is Cramer-Shoup [4] (plaintext-awareness is proven in [5] under the *knowledge of exponent assumption* (KEA)). uROE-KE has 9 rounds and requires trapdoor permutation and a semantically secure public-key cryptosystem. The best known instantiations are respectively the RSA function and ElGamal cryptosystem. We require a trapdoor permutation that we instantiate with RSA function. Comparison of three protocols is shown in Table blow. It can see that our protocol is the most efficient. We note however that our security is obtained in pRO model while SKEME is in the standard model.

Scheme	Comput. Cost	Round Comp.	Worst Assum.	Instant. primit.
SKEME [11,6]	6 exps	3	KEA	Cramer-Shoup [4]
uROE-KE [10]	5 exps	9	pRO	ElGamal and RSA
pRO-KE (*ours*)	2 exps	3	pRO	RSA

Acknowledgement. S.Jiang has been supported as a postdoctoral fellow by two Informatics Circle of Research Excellence grants on Information Security, and Algorithmic Number Theory and Cryptography.

References

1. Bellare, M., Rogaway, P.: Entity Authentication and Key Distribution. In: Stinson, D.R. (ed.) CRYPTO 1993. LNCS, vol. 773, pp. 232–249. Springer, Heidelberg (1994)
2. Bellare, M., Rogaway, P.: Random Oracle is Practical: A Paradigm for Designing Efficient Protocols. In: ACM CCS 1993, pp. 62–73 (1993)
3. Bellare, M., Palacio, A.: Towards Plaintext-Aware Public-Key Encryption without Random Oracles. In: Lee, P.J. (ed.) ASIACRYPT 2004. LNCS, vol. 3329, pp. 48–62. Springer, Heidelberg (2004)
4. Cramer, R., Shoup, V.: A Practical Public Key Cryptosystem Provably Secure Against Adaptive Chosen Ciphertext Attack. In: Krawczyk, H. (ed.) CRYPTO 1998. LNCS, vol. 1462, pp. 13–25. Springer, Heidelberg (1998)

5. Dent, A.: The Cramer-Shoup Encryption Scheme is Plaintext Aware in the Standard Model. In: Vaudenay, S. (ed.) EUROCRYPT 2006. LNCS, vol. 4004, pp. 289–307. Springer, Heidelberg (2006)
6. Di Raimondo, M., Gennaro, R., Krawczyk, H.: Deniable Authentication and Key Exchange. In: ACM CCS 2006 (2006)
7. Dolev, D., Dwork, C., Naor, M.: Non-malleable Cryptography. In: STOC 1991 (1991)
8. Dwork, C., Naor, M., Sahai, A.: Concurrent Zero-Knowledge. In: STOC 1998 (1998)
9. Harkins, D., Kaufman, C., Kivinen, T., Kent, S., Perlman, R.: Design Rationale for IKEv2. Internet Draft (February 2002)
10. Jiang, S.: Deniable Authentication on the Internet. In: INSCRYPT 2007 (2007)
11. Krawczyk, H.: SKEME, a versatile secure key exchange mechanism for Internet. In: NDSS 1996, pp. 114–127 (1996)
12. Pass, R.: On the deniability in the common reference string and random oracle model. In: Boneh, D. (ed.) CRYPTO 2003. LNCS, vol. 2729, pp. 316–337. Springer, Heidelberg (2003)

Revisiting Pairing Based Group Key Exchange

Yvo Desmedt[1,*] and Tanja Lange[2,**]

[1] BT Chair of Information Security, Department of Computer Science,
University College London, UK
y.desmedt@cs.ucl.ac.uk
[2] Department of Mathematics and Computer Science
Technische Universiteit Eindhoven, Netherlands
tanja@hyperelliptic.org

Abstract. Secure communication within a large group of users such as participants in a phone or video conference relies on the availability of secure data and efficient data transmission. Group key exchange protocols allow a (large) group of n users to establish a joint secret key which can be used in symmetric systems to efficiently en- and decrypt messages to and from the group. To deal with varying constellations of the groups and to ensure key freshness it is essential that the group key exchange protocol is efficient.

Most protocols are generalizations of two-party protocols like Diffie-Hellman key exchange. The Burmester and Desmedt I protocol establishes a key in a constant number of rounds independent of the size of the group of users and in $O(n)$ complexity of computation per user.

After Joux's proposal to use pairings to enable a one-round tripartite key exchange (KE) several extensions of existing group KE and authenticated key exchange (AKE) protocols were published. However, quite a few turned out to be flawed and the complexity is often worse than for the original scheme. In this paper we propose a new constant round pairing based group AKE protocol which requires a lower computational complexity per user compared to previous proposals. Furthermore, the scheme is particularly interesting for groups in which some members enjoy more computational power than others. The protocol is most efficient if these members constitute roughly half of the group.

We also provide a pairing-based version of the Burmester-Desmedt II group key exchange which runs in 3 rounds and requires only $O(\log n)$ computation and communication.

Both protocols are faster than any published pairing-based key exchange protocols. If the parameters are chosen appropriately so that the pairing computations are fast the protocols can outperform the respective DL-based Burmester-Desmedt key exchange protocols.

Keywords: Pairings, Key Distribution, Group Key Exchange, Forward Security, Authentication.

* Part of this research was done while visiting the ITSC Bochum 2004. The work has been supported in part by EPSRC EP/C538285/1.
** The work has been supported in part by the European Commission through the IST Programme under Contract IST-2002-507932 ECRYPT.

G. Tsudik (Ed.): FC 2008, LNCS 5143, pp. 53–68, 2008.

1   Introduction

With the increasing use of databases and distributed computing, secure communication in networks is receiving more and more attention. Applications include secure phone and video conferencing or short term task forces for specific projects in different locations communicating by encrypted email. The scenarios for this paper assume no ranking of the participants but are most beneficial if some users have less computational resources. These could be users on the phone conference using a mobile and being without access to more computational power or users behind modem lines as opposed to users in their offices with powerful computers and high-speed ADSL connections.

An important feature of efficient secure communication is that the partners must share a common *secret key* which should be agreed upon in a key exchange (KE) protocol over an insecure channel. To avoid man-in-the-middle attacks these schemes must be equipped with authentication.

Several group key agreement protocols have been proposed [8,9,16,18,10]. Joux's tripartite KE [17] has led to further variants [1,2,12,14]. Unfortunately, some of the so far proposed group key agreement schemes are not very efficient, e. g. in some the number of rounds grows with the group size. A major problem with many of these schemes is the authenticity issue. To turn a secure group KE protocol into an authenticated group KE protocol, Katz and Yung [19] derived a compiler. The model used is a refinement of models proposed in [7]. The compiler can be applied under the condition that the secret key is indistinguishable from random. As an example they consider the Burmester-Desmedt I scheme (BD I) [8,10] which bases its security on the Decisional Diffie-Hellman problem (DDHP) and runs in a constant number of rounds and has complexity $O(n)$. The compiler has been adjusted to cover more efficient GKE protocols in [13].

At PKC 2004, Choi, Hwang, and Lee [12] proposed a pairing based group KE scheme. Their scheme requires a constant number of rounds, broadcast of n messages, multicast of n messages, and per participant 2 pairings and $4n$ modular exponentiations. They refer to Katz and Yung's results for an authenticated version. In fact, a few adaptations are necessary to prove security, in particular the security must be based on the Decisional Bilinear Diffie-Hellman problem (DBDHP). The DBDHP was introduced by Boneh and Franklin [3,4] as the equivalent to the DDHP for pairing and ID-based systems.

Barua, Dutta, and Sarkar recently proposed pairing based group KEs using a tree [1,2]. An advantage is that due to the tree structure only $O(\log n)$ operations are needed. However, the basic scheme has the disadvantage that it requires all parties to listen to the multicast at $O(\log n)$ sequential times and needs $O(\log n)$ rounds. So the number of rounds is not constant but grows logarithmically with n. An additional drawback is that their scheme relies on hashing for security; more precisely they need the DHBDH (Decisional Hash Bilinear Diffie-Hellman) assumption. For comparison, the first scheme in [12] requires only the DBDH assumption but has $O(n)$ computation.

Du, Wang, Ge, and Wang [14] propose an authenticated ID-based group KE scheme which attains a constant number of rounds. Their scheme and the second one in [12] involve the long term secret key associated with the identity and a trusted third party which can compute the secret joint key.

We prefer to avoid using long-term secret keys in KE protocols and to use only a PKI instead of a trusted third party. In a classical PKI it is possible to update keys regularly and the usual protocol flow of requesting a certificate before using a public key automatically deals with revocation. The main quoted advantage of ID-based settings is that no certificates are required. This automatically implies the main disadvantage of ID-based systems, namely that revocation is virtually impossible. For more discussion on the pitfalls of ID-based encryption we refer to Burmester and Desmedt [11].

Our first scheme is a modification of the BD I scheme using an approach different from [12]. The amount of computation in our first scheme is of the same order of magnitude as that of the first scheme in [12] but the constants are smaller. Additionally our scheme fits well to the situation of users with different levels of power – only half of them are required to broadcast. A typical scenario would be servers that are permanently online and play the roles of the odd nodes while home users have less bandwidth in particular in the upstream and thus prefer not to broadcast.

We first present a non-authenticated version of our first scheme and prove it secure under the DBDH assumption. To deal with man-in-the middle attacks it is necessary to add authenticity to the exchange. As mentioned earlier, Katz and Yung [19] showed how to turn a GKE into an authenticated GKE by signing every message. Their compiler was generalized in our paper with Burmester [13] to be applicable to any possible arrangement of users and to maintain the same complexity as the non-authenticated protocol. The motivating example in that paper was the BD II key exchange which uses a tree structure to arrange users and can run in a constant number of rounds needing $O(\log n)$ communication and computation. Applying the generalized compiler to our new protocol in this paper gives an authenticated version secure under BDHP.

Our second scheme is a pairing-based version of the Burmester-Desmedt II key exchange protocol [9,10,13]. The fixed costs are larger in the pairing-based version but the dominating computation is signature verification and multiplication in a group. For the DL-based version each of these is done $\log_2 n$ times while the pairing-based version needs $\log_4 n$, so only half as many steps. Therefore, for a large number of users the pairing based protocol is more efficient. On the other hand, the fixed costs per user are higher than in the traditional BD II protocol and both versions of the BD I protocol, so each protocol has its merits.

Dealing with malicious insiders as considered in [18] remains an open problem which we are *not* going to touch in this publication. In the Katz-Yung [19] model the advantage of an active adversary is defined to be the advantage of obtaining the common group key. So, it does *not* deal with active malicious insiders that attempt to prevent an honest party from obtaining the common group key or with impersonation attacks by collaborating insiders.

The remainder of this paper is organized as follows: we start with briefly introducing bilinear maps and then generalize the BD I scheme to this setting with the aim of achieving better performance. We compare our first scheme with the proposals in the literature. Then we briefly review the differences between the BD I and BD II schemes and present our generalization of BD II together with a performance comparison.

2 Bilinear Maps

Here we briefly define bilinear maps and state the properties we are going to use in the sequel. We use two groups G_1 and G_2 and to ease notation we assume that the first group is additive while the second one is written multiplicatively.

Definition 1. *Let G_1 and G_2 be two cyclic groups of prime order ℓ. A map $\hat{e} : G_1 \times G_1 \to G_2$ is called a* bilinear map *if it satisfies*

$$\hat{e}(aP, bQ) = (\hat{e}(P, Q))^{ab}.$$

Throughout this paper we assume the pairing to be non-degenerate, i. e. there is a pair $P, Q \in G_1$ such that $\hat{e}(P, Q) \neq 1$; in particular $\hat{e}(P, P) \neq 1$ As we want to use the groups in protocols we assume for both groups that the discrete logarithm problem is hard. An efficiently computable bilinear map has two immediate consequences:

1. It allows to transfer the DLP in G_1 to a DLP in G_2 as $\hat{e}(P, kP) = (\hat{e}(P, P))^k$.
2. The map makes the DDHP easy in G_1. Namely given P, aP, bP, and Q one can distinguish $Q = abP$ from $Q = rP$ by comparing

$$\hat{e}(aP, bP) = (\hat{e}(P, P))^{ab} \stackrel{?}{=} \hat{e}(P, Q).$$

Joux [17] observed that one can use $\hat{e}$ for tripartite key exchange using $(\hat{e}(P, P))^{abc} = (\hat{e}(cP, bP))^a = (\hat{e}(aP, cP))^b = (\hat{e}(aP, bP))^c$ as joint key.

Example 1. The most famous known instantiation consists in taking as G_1 a cyclic group of order ℓ of a supersingular elliptic curve E over a finite field $\mathbb{F}_q$. The bilinear map $\hat{e}$ is derived from the Tate-pairing on E [3,4,15] and maps into an extension field $\mathbb{F}_{q^k}$ of $\mathbb{F}_q$. The group G_2 is the group of l-th roots of unity in $\mathbb{F}_{q^k}$. Note that the pairing e obtained that way has $e(P, P) = 1$ and so $\hat{e}$ is a modified version of it, using e.g. distortion maps [22]. It is possible to construct non-supersingular curves with small k e.g., MNT curves [20].

There are no known subexponential algorithms against the DLP on elliptic curves and the size of G_1 is approximately q. In $\mathbb{F}_{q^k}$ index calculus attacks can be applied, so good choices have $k \geq 6$ for current security levels.

Boneh and Franklin [3,4] propose the following problems.

- The computational bilinear Diffie-Hellman (CBDH) problem, i. e. given P, aP, bP, and cP to compute $\hat{e}(P, P)^{abc}$.
- The decisional bilinear Diffie-Hellman (DBDH) problem, i. e. to decide upon input P, aP, bP, cP and an element $h \in \langle \hat{e}(P, P) \rangle$ whether $h \stackrel{?}{=} \hat{e}(P, P)^{abc}$.

3   The First Key Exchange Scheme

The aim of this section is to describe how to generalize the Burmester-Desmedt scheme I to the setting of pairings. We assume the description of G_1, G_2 and $\hat{e}$ to be public together with a base point $P \in G_1$. The following protocol allows n users $U_1, \ldots, U_n$ to jointly generate a common conference key K. Here we state the basic version omitting all checks of consistency and authenticity. To ease the understanding we first give a picture of how the participants are arranged[1].

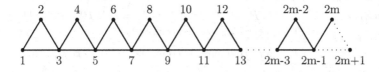

Fig. 1. Organization of the users in our tripartite variant of BD I

As the pairing allows a tripartite key exchange the building blocks of the graph connecting the users consist of triangles. The resulting group key will have the tripartite key of each triangle as a contribution, i.e. there will be a part $\hat{e}(P, P)^{r_1 r_2 r_3}$ from the triangle consisting of users U_1, U_2, and U_3. This corresponds to the appearance of the Diffie-Hellman keys in the original BD I scheme. A direct application of BD I to our idea, i.e. an arrangement of the users in a circle, where the n-participant is next to the first one, requires the number of members to be even. We break up the circle to allow any number of participants. Note that the users with odd index > 1 have a higher workload and that broadcast is only required from them; the other users need only be able to listen to broadcast and send messages to their direct neighbors. In case of an even number of participants vertex $2m + 1$ is omitted and identified with 1 (which corresponds to the circle mentioned above).

Protocol 1 (Pairing based GKE). *Let $U_1, \ldots, U_n$ be a (dynamic) subset of all users who want to generate a common key and put $n = 2m + a, a \in \{0, 1\}$.*

Step 1. *Each U_i, $i = 1, \ldots, n$, selects $r_i \in_R [1 \ldots \ell - 1]$, computes and sends to his direct neighbors $Z_i = r_i P$.*

Step 2. *Each U_i, $i = 3, 5 \ldots, 2m - 1$, odd, computes and broadcasts*

$$X_i = (\hat{e}(Z_{i+1}, Z_{i+2})/\hat{e}(Z_{i-2}, Z_{i-1}))^{r_i},$$

where the indices are taken modulo n if necessary.

Step 3. *Each U_i, $i = 1, \ldots, n$, computes the conference key,*

$$K_i = \begin{cases} (\hat{e}(Z_2, Z_3))^{(m-1)r_1} X_3^{m-2} X_5^{m-3} \cdots X_{2m-3}, & \text{when } i = 1, \\[2mm] T_i^{(m-1)r_i} (X_3 X_5^2 \cdots X_{2j-1}^{j-1})^{-1} (X_{2j+1}^{m-j-1} X_{2j+3}^{m-j-2} \cdots X_{2m-3}), & \text{else,} \end{cases}$$

---

[1] The arrangement resembles standard BD I where each edge is replaced by a triangle.

where $i = 2j + k, k \in \{0, 1\}$ and $T_i = \hat{e}(Z_{i-1}, Z_{i+1})$ for i even and $T_i = \hat{e}(Z_{i-2}, Z_{i-1})$ for odd i.

To see what is going on we now give an example:

Example 2. Let $n = 6$, i.e. $m = 3$. We show how the key is computed for the respective users.

$$K_1 = \hat{e}(Z_2, Z_3)^{2r_1} X_3 = \hat{e}(P, P)^{2r_1 r_2 r_3 - r_1 r_2 r_3 + r_3 r_4 r_5} = \hat{e}(P, P)^{r_1 r_2 r_3 + r_3 r_4 r_5}$$

$$K_2 = \hat{e}(Z_1, Z_3)^{2r_2} X_3 = \hat{e}(P, P)^{2r_1 r_2 r_3 - r_1 r_2 r_3 + r_3 r_4 r_5} = \hat{e}(P, P)^{r_1 r_2 r_3 + r_3 r_4 r_5}$$

$$K_3 = \hat{e}(Z_1, Z_2)^{2r_3} X_3 = \hat{e}(P, P)^{2r_1 r_2 r_3 - r_1 r_2 r_3 + r_3 r_4 r_5} = \hat{e}(P, P)^{r_1 r_2 r_3 + r_3 r_4 r_5}$$

$$K_4 = \hat{e}(Z_3, Z_5)^{2r_4} X_3^{-1} = \hat{e}(P, P)^{2r_3 r_4 r_5 - (-r_1 r_2 r_3 + r_3 r_4 r_5)} = \hat{e}(P, P)^{r_1 r_2 r_3 + r_3 r_4 r_5}$$

$$K_5 = \hat{e}(Z_3, Z_4)^{2r_5} X_3^{-1} = \hat{e}(P, P)^{2r_3 r_4 r_5 - (-r_1 r_2 r_3 + r_3 r_4 r_5)} = \hat{e}(P, P)^{r_1 r_2 r_3 + r_3 r_4 r_5}$$

$$K_6 = \hat{e}(Z_1, Z_5)^{2r_6} (X_3 X_5^2)^{-1} = \hat{e}(P, P)^{2r_1 r_5 r_6 - (-r_1 r_2 r_3 + r_3 r_4 r_5 + 2(-r_3 r_4 r_5 + r_5 r_6 r_1))}$$
$$= \hat{e}(P, P)^{r_1 r_2 r_3 + r_3 r_4 r_5}$$

Remark 1. All users compute the same key, $K = \hat{e}(P, P)^d$ for

$$d = r_1 r_2 r_3 + r_3 r_4 r_5 + r_5 r_6 r_7 + \cdots + r_{2m-3} r_{2m-2} r_{2m-1}.$$

Indeed, for $i = 1$ almost like in the usual BD I scheme one has

$$d_1 = (m-1)r_1 r_2 r_3 + (m-2)(-r_1 r_2 r_3 + r_3 r_4 r_5) + (m-3)(-r_3 r_4 r_5 + r_5 r_6 r_7)$$
$$+ \cdots\cdots + (-r_{2m-5} r_{2m-4} r_{2m-3} + r_{2m-3} r_{2m-2} r_{2m-1})$$
$$= r_1 r_2 r_3 + r_3 r_4 r_5 + r_5 r_6 r_7 + \cdots + r_{2m-3} r_{2m-2} r_{2m-1} = d.$$

For $i = 2j + 1$ we have the exponent

$$d_i = (m-1)r_{2j-1} r_{2j} r_{2j+1} - (-r_1 r_2 r_3 + r_3 r_4 r_5 + 2(-r_3 r_4 r_5 + r_5 r_6 r_7) + \cdots$$
$$\cdots + (j-1)(-r_{2j-3} r_{2j-2} r_{2j-1} + r_{2j-1} r_{2j} r_{2j+1})) +$$
$$+ (m-j-1)(-r_{2j-1} r_{2j} r_{2j+1} + r_{2j+1} r_{2j+2} r_{2j+3}) + \cdots$$
$$+ (-r_{2m-5} r_{2m-4} r_{2m-3} + r_{2m-3} r_{2m-2} r_{2m-1})$$
$$= (m-1-(j-1)-(m-j-1))r_{2j-1} r_{2j} r_{2j+1} + r_1 r_2 r_3 + r_3 r_4 r_5 + \cdots$$
$$\cdots + r_{2j-3} r_{2j-2} r_{2j-1} + r_{2j+1} r_{2j+2} r_{2j+3} + \cdots + r_{2m-3} r_{2m-2} r_{2m-1} = d.$$

The same equation holds for $i = 2j$ as T_i gives $r_{i-1} r_i r_{i+1} = r_{2j-1} r_{2j} r_{2j+1}$.

Remark 2. The respective powers should be computed using Horner's rule, e.g. for $i = 1$ initialize the loop with $t = (\hat{e}(Z_2, Z_3))^{r_1}$ and $s = (\hat{e}(Z_2, Z_3))^{r_1}$. For $j = 1$ to m in each round multiply $t \leftarrow tX_{2j-1}$ and then $s \leftarrow st$. The other users follow similar computations. This allows the computation of K in one exponentiation and $2m \approx n$ multiplications.

The protocol mentions several pairings. Note that an implementation using the Weil or Tate-pairing can always omit the final exponentiation. At the very end of Step 3 the whole value of K_i is raised to the respective power.

For more efficiency improvements we refer to Section 5.

To turn this GKE into an AGKE one can use the compilers in [19,13] which append a group identifier and fresh randomness for each round of GKE to each message. Then every message is signed and every user checks the signature of every message he uses. The security of the AGKE is based on the security of the GKE and that of the signature scheme and the underlying hash function. The next section gives a security proof showing that the GKE is secure under the DBDH assumption.

Our set-up requires efficient computations of pairings. This makes the use of the short BLS signatures [5,6] particularly attractive. This scheme requires the messages to be elements of G_1 which can be achieved using hash functions. Note that even though the messages sent out in Step 1 of Protocol 1 already are elements of G_1 one cannot avoid hash functions. First of all one needs to include the group identifier and the fresh randomness into the message but more importantly the BLS scheme is homomorphic and so would allow to combine two old signatures to create a fresh one. Alternatively, any signature scheme, e. g. ElGamal signatures, can be used with an appropriate hash function.

Remark 3. The key does not depend on r_{2m} (and r_{2m+1} for odd n) which might raise suspicion that the scheme could be vulnerable to replay attacks. Imagine the following scenario: an attacker has learned a previous session key, which has then has been revoked. He has also recorded all messages sent during the protocol execution, so he has valid signed messages for a GKE involving exactly the same users $U_1, \ldots, U_{2m}$. Since the compiler does not actually request to check for the freshness of the randomness (otherwise, storage would be problematic) U_{2m} would accept the replayed messages as part of a fresh key agreement with $U_1, \ldots, U_{2m-1}$. The $r_1, \ldots, r_{2m-1}$ have not changed, so from the attackers point of view, the old, compromised key is now the fresh key.

However, the message from U_{2m-1} sent in Step 2 depends on r_{2m}. Unless the attacker can fake a fresh signature from U_{2m-1} he can only repeat the recorded message. And U_{2m}'s computations do depend heavily on the fresh randomness chosen by him and so a replay would make U_{2m} compute a different key.

To show this we use the exponent ^{o} to refer to the old choice and ^{f} for the fresh. E.g. U_{2m}'s old secret scalar is r_{2m}^o while the new one is r_{2m}^f. Non-modified values have no superscript.

The attacker posing as U_{2m-1} receives $Z_{2m}^f = r_{2m}^f P$ and is supposed to use it to issue $X_{2m-1}^f = \left(\hat{e}(Z_{2m}^f, Z_{2m+1}) / \hat{e}(Z_{2m-3}, Z_{2m-2}) \right)^{r_{2m-1}}$ in Step 2. But he does not know r_{2m-1} and only has X_{2m-1}^o which differs in Z_{2m}^o. If he uses the old one then U_{2m} will compute the session key

$$K_{2m}^f = (\hat{e}(Z_{2m-1}, Z_{2m+1}))^{(m-1)r_{2m}^f} (X_3 X_5^2 \cdots X_{2m-1}^{m-1})^{-1}$$
$$= K_{2m}^o (\hat{e}(Z_{2m-1}, Z_{2m+1}))^{(m-1)(r_{2m}^f - r_{2m}^o)}$$

which is thus different by an unknown power from the key K_{2m}^o known to the attacker. So all the attacker did was make U_{2m} believe that he shares a fresh key with the other players but the attacker does not know this key and thus fails.

4 Proof of Security

The main idea of the proof of security is given in the following lemma which shows that an attacker who could compute the secret group key in Protocol 1 could be used to solve the computational bilinear Diffie-Hellman problem, i.e. it issues $\hat{e}(P, P)^{a_1 a_2 a_3}$ on input $P, a_1 P, a_2 P, a_3 P$.

Lemma 1. *Let $n \geq 5$. An adversary $\mathcal{A}$ obtaining the secret key in Protocol 1 with probability ε can be turned into an adversary $\mathcal{B}$ solving the CBDH problem with probability ε needing $5(m + 1) + a$ exponentiations in G_1, one computation of an $(m - 2)^{th}$ root in G_2, $m - 1$ multiplications and 1 division in G_2, $2m + 1$ computations of pairings, and one call to $\mathcal{A}$.*

Proof. $\mathcal{B}$ uses $\mathcal{A}$ to compute $\hat{e}(P, P)^{a_1 a_2 a_3}$ given $P, A_1 = a_1 P, A_2 = a_2 P$ and $A_3 = a_3 P$. We need to show how to construct a valid input to $\mathcal{A}$ and also prove that the distribution achieved is as random as in a usual key-exchange protocol.

Put $Z'_1 := A_1, Z'_2 := A_2$ and $Z'_3 := A_3$. For $i = 3j + k, k \in \{1, 2, 3\}$ put $Z'_i = A_k + c_i P$, where $c_i \in_R [0 \ldots \ell - 1]$ and break if $Z'_i = P_\infty$. If for one i we have $Z'_i = P_\infty$ then we know that $A_k = -c_i P$ and thus know that $a_k \equiv -c_i \bmod \ell$ which allows us to compute $\hat{e}(P, P)^{a_1 a_2 a_3}$. Otherwise the distribution of the Z'_i is identical to that of the $Z_i = r_i P$ in the real protocol since the c_i $(i \geq 4)$ are uniformly random. The computations need less than $2m + a + 1$ scalar multiplications in G_1 (we state one more to take into account the additions as $n \ll \ell$). From this $\mathcal{B}$ can compute valid X'_i, for odd $i \geq 3$ as follows: Put $c_1 = c_2 = c_3 = 0$ and let $k \equiv i \bmod 3$ with $k \in \{1, 2, 3\}$. To get valid X'_is $\mathcal{B}$ needs to obtain

$$
\begin{aligned}
X'_i &= \left(\frac{\hat{e}(Z'_{i+1}, Z'_{i+2})}{\hat{e}(Z'_{i-2}, Z'_{i-1})} \right)^{a_k + c_i} \\
&= \hat{e}(P, P)^{-(a_{k-2} + c_{i-2})(a_{k-1} + c_{i-1})(a_k + c_i) + (a_k + c_i)(a_{k+1} + c_{i+1})(a_{k+2} + c_{i+2})} \\
&= \hat{e}(A_k + c_i P, (c_{i+1} - c_{i-2})A_{k-1} + (c_{i+1} c_{i+2} - c_{i-2} c_{i-1})P) \cdot \\
&\quad \cdot \hat{e}(A_k + c_i P, (c_{i+2} - c_{i-1})A_{k+1}),
\end{aligned}
$$

where the indices of a_j and A_j are taken modulo 3 so that $A_{k-2} = A_{k+1}$ and $A_{k+2} = A_{k-1}$. This expression can be computed since the c_i are chosen by $\mathcal{B}$. Due to the randomness in the c_i, the distribution of the so obtained X'_i is identical to that in the Protocol 1. This computation needs $2(m - 1)$ pairings and $3(m - 1)$ exponentiations in G_1 and $m - 1$ multiplications in G_2.

Put $m_0 = \lfloor \frac{m}{3} \rfloor$ $m_1 = \lfloor \frac{m-1}{3} \rfloor$ $m_2 = \lfloor \frac{m-2}{3} \rfloor$ $m_3 = \lfloor \frac{m-3}{3} \rfloor$ $m_4 = \lfloor \frac{m-4}{3} \rfloor$ and let $2m - 3 \equiv k \bmod 3$, i.e., $Z'_{2m-3} = A_k + c_{2m-3} P$. Running $\mathcal{A}$ on input $Z'_i, 1 \leq i \leq n$ and $X'_{2j+1}, 1 \leq j \leq m - 1$ it outputs

$$
\begin{aligned}
K' &= \hat{e}(P, P)^{a_1 a_2 a_3 + a_3(a_1 + c_4)(a_2 + c_5) + \cdots + (a_k + c_{2m-3})(a_{k+1} + c_{2m-2})(a_{k+2} + c_{2m-1})} \\
&= \hat{e}(P, P)^{(m-2) a_1 a_2 a_3} \cdot \hat{e}(A_1, S_1) \cdot \hat{e}(A_2, S_2) \cdot \hat{e}(P, S_3)
\end{aligned}
$$

with probability ε, where

$$S_1 = \left(\sum_{i=1}^{m_1} c_{6i} + 2 \sum_{i=1}^{m_2} c_{6i+3} \right) A_2 + \left(2 \sum_{i=1}^{m_0} c_{6i-1} + \sum_{i=1}^{m_2} c_{6i+2} \right) A_3 +$$

$$+ \left(\sum_{i=0}^{m_2} c_{6i+2} c_{6i+3} + \sum_{i=0}^{m_3} c_{6i+3} c_{6i+5} + \sum_{i=0}^{m_4} c_{6i+5} c_{6i+6} \right) P,$$

$$S_2 = \left(\sum_{i=1}^{m_0} c_{6i-2} + 2 \sum_{i=1}^{m_1} c_{6i+1} \right) A_3 + \left(\sum_{i=1}^{m_1} c_{6i} c_{6i+1} + \sum_{i=1}^{m_2} c_{6i+1} c_{6i+3} + \sum_{i=1}^{m_3} c_{6i+3} c_{6i+4} \right) P,$$

$$S_3 = \left(\sum_{i=1}^{m_0} c_{6i-2} c_{6i-1} + \sum_{i=1}^{m_1} c_{6i-1} c_{6i+1} + \sum_{i=1}^{m_2} c_{6i+1} c_{6i+2} \right) A_3$$

$$+ \left(\sum_{i=1}^{m_0} c_{6i-3} c_{6i-2} c_{6i-1} \sum_{i=1}^{m_1} c_{6i-1} c_{6i} c_{6i+1} \sum_{i=1}^{m_2} c_{6i+1} c_{6i+2} c_{6i+3} \right) P.$$

Since S_1, S_2 and S_3 can be computed with a total of 7 scalar multiplications in G_1 we obtain $\hat{e}(P, P)^{a_1 a_2 a_3}$ by 3 more pairings, 1 division in G_2, and extracting an $(m-2)^{\text{th}}$ root in G_2 which is doable since ℓ is a known prime.   □

We omit the proof of the following theorem. It uses the methodology as in [19,13] combined with the construction given in the proof of Lemma 1.

For ease of notation we use $\mathcal{P}_1$ as an abbreviation for Protocol 1. The sizes and specific choices of G_1 and G_2 give the security of the cryptographic primitive behind the protocol and thereby dictate the security of the protocol. We model the different security levels by including a security parameter k. The advantage of attacker $\mathcal{A}$ against Protocol 1 running with security parameter k, short $\mathcal{P}_1(k)$, is defined as $\mathsf{Adv}_{\mathcal{A}, \mathcal{P}_1(k)} = |2 \cdot \mathrm{Pr}[\mathsf{Succ}] - 1|$, where event Succ occurs if the attacker is successful. In the attack game the attacker is allowed to issue $\mathsf{Execute}$ queries; these are queries to execute Protocol 1. A fresh transcript related to the same DBDHP is obtained by varying the c_i in the proof of Lemma 1. To also update the initial inputs one picks random c_1, c_2, c_3 and replaces A_1, A_2, A_3 and h by $A_1 + c_1 P, A_2 + c_2 P, A_3 + c_3 P$ and

$$h \cdot \hat{e}(A_1, c_3 A_2 + c_2(A_3 + c_3 P)) \cdot \hat{e}(A_2, c_1(A_3 + c_3 P)) \cdot \hat{e}(c_1 P, c_2(A_3 + c_3 P)).$$

Theorem 1. *Assuming the Decisional Bilinear Diffie-Hellman problem is hard, Protocol 1 is a secure GKE protocol. Namely*

$$\mathsf{Adv}^{\mathsf{GKE}}_{\mathcal{P}_1}(t, q_{\mathrm{ex}}) \leq \mathsf{Adv}^{\mathsf{ddh}}_{G}(t'),$$

where $t' = t + O(n q_{\mathrm{ex}}(t_{\mathrm{exp}} + t_{\mathrm{pair}}))$, n is the number of players, q_{ex} is the number of $\mathsf{Execute}$ queries, t_{exp} is the time required to perform exponentiations in G_1, and t_{pair} is the time required to compute a pairing.

The compilers from Katz and Yung [19] and Desmedt, Lange, and Burmester [13] turn Protocol 1 into an authenticated GKE protocol which is secure against active attacks. The game now also includes individual Send queries which allow the active attacker to prompt a user to execute Protocol 1.

Theorem 2. *The authenticated key agreement scheme* $\mathcal{P}'$ *obtained from* $\mathcal{P}_1$ *by applying the compiler is secure against active attacks.*

Namely, for q_s *the number of* Send *queries and* q_{ex} *the number of* Execute *queries we obtain*

$$\mathsf{Adv}^{\mathsf{AKE-fs}}_{\mathcal{P}'}(t, q_{ex}, q_s) \leq \frac{q_s}{2} \cdot \mathsf{Adv}^{\mathsf{KE}}_{\mathcal{P}_1}(t', 1) + \mathsf{Adv}^{\mathsf{KE}}_{\mathcal{P}_1}(t', q_{ex}) + n \cdot \mathsf{Succ}_{\Sigma}(t') + \frac{q_s^2 + q_{ex} q_s}{2^k},$$

where $t' = t + O(n q_{ex}(t_{exp} + t_{pair}) + q_s)$, n *is the number of players,* t_{exp} *is the time required to perform exponentiations in* G_1, t_{pair} *is the time required to compute a pairing, and* Succ_{Σ} *is the success probability against the signature scheme* Σ.

5   Efficiency Improvements

In this section we present alternative ways of computing the values mentioned in Protocol 1. We remind the reader that we are computing in two groups G_1 and G_2 of prime order ℓ and that the usual instantiation is via elliptic curves (see Remark 1). Then, by Remark 2, the final exponentiation in the pairing computation is postponed until the end of the computation of K_i.

For the odd users this implies in particular that instead of computing an inversion in G_2 they can compute an exponentiation of length $\log \ell$. More precisely, in Step 2 they first compute $\hat{e}(Z_{i+1}, Z_{i+2})$ and $\hat{e}(Z_{i-2}, Z_{i-1})$, where the latter value should be stored to be used as T_i in Step 3. To obtain X_i they compute $X_i = \left(\hat{e}(Z_{i+1}, Z_{i+2}) (\hat{e}(Z_{i-2}, Z_{i-1}))^{\ell-1} \right)^{r_i}$.

Unless the communication bandwidth is severely limited the odd users should not only send X_i but also X_i^{-1}. This removes the need for the even users to ever compute inversions while the number of inversions remains constant for the odd users. Note that like above an inversion can be replaced by the computation of the $(\ell - 1)$-th power. Note that this does not weaken the security since X_i is given. We thank Cristina Onete for the idea of having U_i also send X_i^{-1}.

If the groups G_1 and G_2 are optimally chosen, e.g. G_1 is a MNT curve [20] with embedding degree 6 or larger and if twists can be used for fast pairing evaluation, scalar multiplication in G_1 is faster than exponentiation in G_2.

In that case the odd users can just as well start by computing $\hat{e}(r_i Z_{i+1}, Z_{i+2})$ and $\hat{e}(r_i Z_{i-2}, Z_{i-1})$ and then obtain $X_i = \hat{e}(r_i Z_{i+1}, Z_{i+2}) (\hat{e}(r_i Z_{i-2}, Z_{i-1}))^{\ell-1}$. Note that $T_i^{r_i} = \hat{e}(r_i Z_{i-2}, Z_{i-1})$ is being computed here already.

In the unlikely case that exponentiation in G_2 is more expensive than a pairing computation U_i could also compute $X_i = \hat{e}(r_i Z_{i+1}, Z_{i+2})(\hat{e}(-r_i Z_{i-2}, Z_{i-1}))$ and then do an extra pairing computation to obtain $T_i^{r_i}$.

If the even users have enough computation power to compute pairings and if scalar multiplication in G_1 is faster than exponentiation in G_2, they should compute their $T_i^{(m-1)r_i}$ as $T_i^{(m-1)r_i} = \hat{e}((m-1)r_i Z_{i-1}, Z_{i+1})$.

If the even users are too weak to compute pairings more work is put on the odd users. User U_i for $i > 1$ odd computes X_i, X_i^{-1} as before and also $T_{i-1} = \hat{e}(Z_{i-2}, Z_i)$ for user U_{i-1}. This means an extra pairing computation for U_i and the extra bandwidth to send one more element of G_2. The even user U_{i-1}

still needs to compute the exponentiation using his secret r_{i-1}. Note that this does not weaken the security; any eavesdropper can compute this pairing value.

6   Comparison

For stating the comparison we assume that scalar multiplications in G_1 are faster than exponentiations in G_2. If this is not the case one can modify the computations. We further assume that all users are able to compute pairings. We do not point out the extra effects of delayed final exponentiation. Any value mentioned as exponent or scalar is of the size of ℓ, in particular the inversion is counted as an exponentiation in G_2 and mentioned only for the odd users.

In our scheme each even user computes two scalar multiplications in G_1 (one in Step 1 and one in Step 3), one pairing, and n multiplications in G_2.

The odd users compute three scalar multiplications in G_1 (one in Step 1 and two in Step 2), one exponentiation in G_2 (to obtain $X_i^{\ell-1}$), two pairing computations, and n multiplications in G_2.

Hence, half of the users have significantly lower workload, namely the even users save 1 scalar multiplication in G_1, one exponentiation in G_2, and one pairing computation. Additionally, they need not have broadcast facilities [2].

In the authenticated version each even user computes one signature on its contribution Z_i while the odd users additionally compute one signature on the message $m = X_i, X_i^{\ell-1}$. Each user needs to check the $\lfloor n/2 - 1 \rfloor$ signatures on the X_i and 2 signatures for the Z_i of their neighbors.

So far the most efficient pairing based scheme was proposed by Choi, Hwang, and Lee [12]. Like our Protocol 1 their AKE needs a constant number of rounds and $O(n)$ communication and computation.

The advantages of our scheme become clear by inspecting the exact computation costs. In their scheme *each* user is required to perform 3 scalar multiplications in G_1, compute two pairings and $2n$ multiplications in G_2. We point out an improvement: it is actually possible to reduce the number of scalar multiplications in G_1 to two by observing that both pairing computations have Z_{i+1} as second input and both are raised to the power of r_i, so one could use $r_i Z_{i+1}$ as second input to both pairings.

For the odd users our scheme is faster as soon as one scalar multiplication in G_1 and one exponentiation in G_2 are faster than n multiplications in G_2; this is the case if n is $\Omega(\log \ell)$.

The even users always profit from our scheme. In comparison with [12] they save one pairing computation and n multiplications in G_2.

In the authenticated version the savings become more striking. The number of signatures is equal to two in both protocols but the number of signature verifications is $n/2 + 1$ in our scheme while it is $n + 1$ in [12]. Note that for usual ElGamal signatures each verification consists of a double-exponentiation. Even with batch verification techniques the factor of two in the number of signatures is clearly noticeable.

---

[2] Note, however, that in case of an invalid signature a message should be broadcasted.

Protocol 1 is not only faster than previous pairing-based protocols but will also outperform standard GKE based on BD I [8,10]. The initial overhead of our pairing-based protocol is larger than in the standard BD I scheme but with a growing number of users the dominating costs are $2n$ multiplications and n signature verifications in BD I while our first scheme needs only about n multiplications and $n/2$ signature verifications.

Onete [21] reports on an implementation of our first scheme. She uses curves with embedding degree 2 which come with an easy distortion map but also with comparably slow arithmetic on the elliptic curve side. Her implementation does not include authentication. Nevertheless, for 10,000 users our pairing-based protocol almost reaches the speed of BD I; it should exceed the speed of BD I when authentication is used even for less than 10,000 users. Better curve choices lower the number of users required for the break even point.

7   Pairing-Based Version of BD II

The second Burmester Desmedt (BD II) protocol was introduced in [9]; a full proof of security can be found in [13] based on [10]. The advantage of BD II over BD I comes from arranging the users in a binary tree of logarithmic depth. Each edge corresponds to the computation of a Diffie-Hellman key. The final key computation looks very similar to the computation of K_i in Step 3 of Protocol 1 but the product runs only over $\log_2 n$ indices. Instead of using a tree in which each node has one incoming and 2 outgoing edges one could reduce the depth by having more outgoing edges at the expense of more computation per node. For details we refer to [13]. Note that in tree-based protocols leaves have a reduced workload and that there are $n/2$ leaves in the binary tree.

We now present a pairing-based version of the BD II protocol. Each node has higher degree since it participates in several tripartite key exchanges. So we start with a triangle and use a tree in which each node has degree 6. To simplify the notation we refer to the other child of parent(i) in the same triangle as sibling(i). The following picture shows only the first and second level. The structure around each triangle in the tree looks like the middle triangle (emphasized in bold).

According to Figure 2 we have parent(4) = 1, sibling(4) = 5, rightchild$_1$(1) = 4, rightchild$_2$(1) = 5, and leftchild$_1$(1) = 6, etc. For the vertices on the top level we put parent(1) = 2, parent(2) = 3, parent(3) = 1 and sibling(1) = 3,

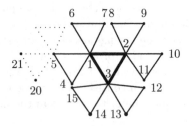

Fig. 2. Organization of the users in our tripartite variant of BD II

sibling(2) = 1, sibling(3) = 2. To ease notation let ancestors(i) be the set of indices of all ancestors of U_i, including i *but* having removed 1, 2 and 3, e.g., ancestors(20) = $\{20, 5\}$. If left child(i) or right child(i) is used without index then each user stores the value in its own ancestors line with respective index. As in Protocol 1 we first construct some Z_i and X_i and then compute the key.

Protocol 2. *Let $U_1, \ldots, U_n$ be a (dynamic) subset of all users who want to generate a common conference key.*

Step 1. *Each U_i, $i = 1, \ldots, n$, selects $r_i \in_R [1 \ldots \ell - 1]$, computes and sends $Z_i = r_i P$ to his parent, sibling, and children.*

Step 2. *Each U_i, except for leaves, computes and multicasts to its left resp. right descendants:*

$$X_{\text{left child}(i)} = \left(\hat{e}(Z_{\text{parent}(i)}, Z_{\text{sibling}(i)})/\hat{e}(Z_{\text{left child}_1(i)}, Z_{\text{left child}_2(i)})\right)^{r_i}.$$

$$X_{\text{right child}(i)} = \left(\hat{e}(Z_{\text{parent}(i)}, Z_{\text{sibling}(i)})/\hat{e}(Z_{\text{right child}_1(i)}, Z_{\text{right child}_2(i)})\right)^{r_i}.$$

Step 3. *Each U_i, $i = 1, \ldots, n$, computes the conference key,*

$$K_i = (\hat{e}(Z_{\text{parent}(i)}, Z_{\text{sibling}(i)}))^{r_i} \prod_{j \in \text{ancestors}(i)} X_j.$$

Remark 4. All users compute the same key $K = \hat{e}(P, P)^{r_1 r_2 r_3}$ (cf. [13]).

The leaves need to compute a total of 1 exponentiation in G_1, 1 exponentiation in either G_1 or G_2, 1 pairing and $2 \log_4 n - 1$ multiplications in G_2.

For the other nodes we note that the pairing used in Step 3 was already computed in Step 2. Accordingly, the protocol needs 3 pairings, 4 exponentiations in either G_1 or G_2, and $2 \log_4 n - 1$ multiplications in G_2.

Using the compiler from [13] the protocol leads to a secure authenticated group key exchange protocol which is secure provided that the signature scheme is secure and that the DBDH problem is hard. By the construction of the tree only $\log_4 n$ signatures need to be verified.

7.1   Comparison

For this protocol we can use the same techniques such as delayed final exponentiation of the pairing computation as for Protocol 1. The advantage of Protocol 2 lies in a higher efficiency for the same number of rounds. The bilinear map together with the tree structure makes it possible to compute the key in $\log_4 n$ multiplications. There are $3n/4$ leaves which need less computational power.

Compared to the DL-based BD II protocol this one needs only half as many multiplications in the final key computation at the expense of needing some pairings. Obviously one could have obtained the same lower number of multiplications by choosing a tree with 4 outgoing edges.

To give an overview, we present a cost comparison of the authenticated schemes for non-leaves. Pairings are denoted by P, scalar multiplications by

E, multiplications by M, signatures by S, and verifications by V. For the communication costs **p** denotes peer-to-peer messages and **b** denotes broadcast. Note that several **p** could be replaced by one multicast. The parameter d gives the number of outgoing edges in the classic BD II tree.

	rounds	messages	communication	computation
BD II ($d = 2$)	3	3**p**, 1**b**	6**p**, $(\log_2 n)$**b**	$2S, (\log_2 n)V, 4E, 2(\log_2 n)M$
BD II ($d = 4$)	3	5**p**, 1**b**	10**p**, $(\log_4 n)$**b**	$2S, (\log_4 n)V, 6E, 2(\log_4 n)M$
BD II, pair.	3	6**p**, 1**b**	12**p**, $(\log_4 n)$**b**	$2S, (\log_4 n)V, 4E, 3P, 2(\log_4 n)M$

The pairing-based version is faster than BD II with $d = 2$ for large n. The generalization to $d > 1$ was considered in [9] and [13] but has not received much attention; the case $d = 4$ is likely faster than the pairing-based version.

Remark 5. If authentication is not an issue one can also use a tree as in the following picture leading to only $3E, 2P, 2(\log_2 n)M$ and 3 rounds. In

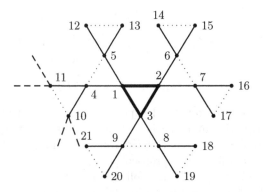

Fig. 3. Organization of the users in the alternative tripartite variant of BD II. "Siblings" are indicated using a dotted line.

this version user U_i computes $X_i = \left(\frac{\hat{e}(Z_{\text{parent}(i)}, Z_{\text{sibling}(i)})}{\hat{e}(Z_{\text{left child}(i)}, Z_{\text{right child}(i)})} \right)^{r_i}$ and $K_i = (\hat{e}(Z_{\text{parent}(i)}, Z_{\text{sibling}(i)}))^{r_i} \prod_{j \in \text{ancestors}(i)} X_j = (\hat{e}(P, P))^{r_1 r_2 r_3}$. This has the drawback that the authenticated version needs $(\log_2 n)V$ instead of $(\log_4 n)V$.

Acknowledgements. The authors would like to thank Igor Shparlinski for his encouragement to submit this result.

References

1. Barua, R., Dutta, R., Sarkar, P.: Extending Joux's protocol to multi party key agreement. In: Johansson, T., Maitra, S. (eds.) INDOCRYPT 2003. LNCS, vol. 2904, pp. 205–217. Springer, Heidelberg (2003)

2. Barua, R., Dutta, R., Sarkar, P.: Provably secure authenticated tree based group key agreement protocol using pairing. In: López, J., Qing, S., Okamoto, E. (eds.) ICICS 2004. LNCS, vol. 3269, pp. 92–104. Springer, Heidelberg (2004); (see also: ePrint archive, 2004/090)
3. Boneh, D., Franklin, M.: Identity based encryption from the Weil pairing. In: Kilian, J. (ed.) CRYPTO 2001. LNCS, vol. 2139, pp. 213–229. Springer, Heidelberg (2001)
4. Boneh, D., Franklin, M.: Identity based encryption from the Weil pairing. SIAM J. Comput. 32(3), 586–615 (2003)
5. Boneh, D., Lynn, B., Shacham, H.: Short signatures from the Weil pairing. In: Boyd, C. (ed.) ASIACRYPT 2001. LNCS, vol. 2248, pp. 514–532. Springer, Heidelberg (2001)
6. Boneh, D., Lynn, B., Shacham, H.: Short signatures from the Weil pairing. J. Cryptology 17, 297–319 (2004)
7. Bresson, E., Chevassut, O., Pointcheval, D., Quisquater, J.-J.: Provably authenticated group Diffie-Hellman key exchange. In: Proc. 8th Annual ACM Conference on Computer and Communications Security, pp. 255–264 (2001)
8. Burmester, M., Desmedt, Y.: A secure and efficient conference key distribution system. In: De Santis, A. (ed.) EUROCRYPT 1994. LNCS, vol. 950, pp. 275–286. Springer, Heidelberg (1995)
9. Burmester, M., Desmedt, Y.: Efficient and secure conference key distribution. In: Lomas, M. (ed.) Security Protocols 1996. LNCS, vol. 1189, pp. 119–130. Springer, Heidelberg (1997)
10. Burmester, M., Desmedt, Y.: A secure and scalable group key exchange system. Information Processing Letters 94(3), 137–143 (2005)
11. Burmester, M., Desmedt, Y.: Identity-based Key Infrastructures (IKI). In: Security and Protection in Information Processing Systems – SEC 2004, pp. 167–176. Kluwer, Dordrecht (2004)
12. Choi, K.Y., Hwang, J.Y., Lee, D.H.: Efficient ID-based group key agreement with bilinear maps. In: Bao, F., Deng, R., Zhou, J. (eds.) PKC 2004. LNCS, vol. 2947, pp. 130–144. Springer, Heidelberg (2004)
13. Desmedt, Y., Lange, T., Burmester, M.: Scalable Authenticated Tree Based Group Key Exchange for Ad-Hoc Groups. In: Financial Crypto 2007. LNCS, vol. 4886, pp. 104–118. Springer, Heidelberg (2007)
14. Du, X., Wang, Y., Ge, J., Wang, Y.: An improved ID-based authenticated group key agreement scheme. ePrint archive, 2003/260 (2003)
15. Frey, G., Müller, M., Rück, H.G.: The Tate pairing and the discrete logarithm applied to elliptic curve cryptosystems. IEEE Trans. Inform. Theory 45(5), 1717–1719 (1999)
16. Ingemarsson, I., Tang, D.T., Wong, C.W.: A conference key distribution system. IEEE Trans. Inform. Theory 28, 714–720 (1982)
17. Joux, A.: A one round protocol for tripartite Diffie-Hellman. In: Bosma, W. (ed.) ANTS 2000. LNCS, vol. 1838, pp. 385–394. Springer, Heidelberg (2000)
18. Just, M., Vaudenay, S.: Authenticated multi-party key agreement. In: Kim, K.-c., Matsumoto, T. (eds.) ASIACRYPT 1996. LNCS, vol. 1163, pp. 36–49. Springer, Heidelberg (1996)
19. Katz, J., Yung, M.: Scalable protocols for authenticated group key exchange. In: Boneh, D. (ed.) CRYPTO 2003. LNCS, vol. 2729, pp. 110–125. Springer, Heidelberg (2003), http://www.cs.umd.edu/~jkatz/research.html

20. Miyaji, A., Nakabayashi, M., Takano, S.: New Explicit Conditions of Elliptic Curve Traces for FR-Reduction. IEICE Trans. Fundamentals E84-A(5), 1234–1243 (2001)
21. Onete, C.: Elliptic Curves and Pairing Based Cryptosystems. Internship report, Technische Universiteit Eindhoven (2008)
22. Verheul, E.: Evidence that XTR Is More Secure than Supersingular Elliptic Curves Cryptosystems. J. Cryptology 17, 277–296 (2004)

Constant-Round Password-Based Authenticated Key Exchange Protocol for Dynamic Groups⋆

Shuhua Wu and Yuefei Zhu

Department of Networks Engineering,
Zhengzhou Information Science Technology Institute,
Zhengzhou 450002, China
wushuhua726@sina.com.cn

Abstract. In this paper, we extend the work of Abdalla et al. to take into account the notion of dynamicity in the membership and present an improved compiler that transforms any provably secure password-based authenticated 2-party key exchange into a more attractive password-based authenticated group key exchange. The resulting protocol is a provably secure and efficient dynamic password-based authenticated group key exchange protocol in a constant number of rounds. To the best of our knowledge, our proposal is the first solution to design constant-round password-based authenticated group key exchange protocols for dynamic groups. Furthermore, its security result does not assume the Random Oracle model or the ideal cipher model.

Keywords: password authenticated, key exchange, dynamic group, provably secure.

1 Introduction

A group key exchange protocol allows a group of users to exchange information over public network to agree upon a common secret key from which a session key can be derived. This common session key can later be used to achieve desirable security goals, such as authentication, confidentiality and data integrity. Due to the usefulness of such protocols, several papers have attempted to design secure group key exchange protocols. In order to protect against an active adversary who may inject messages, impersonate one or more of the parties, or otherwise control the communication in the network, these protocols need incorporate some authentication mechanism to be authenticated ones. The most classical way to add authentication to key exchange protocols is to sign critical message flows. Unfortunately, such techniques require the use of complex infrastructures to handle public keys and certificates. One way to avoid such infrastructures is to use passwords for authentication. Humans directly benefit from this approach since they only need to remember a low-quality string chosen from a relatively

---

⋆ This work was partially supported by the National Science Foundation of the Republic of China (No.60473021) and by a grant from the National High Technology Research and Development Program of China (863 Program) (No. 2007AA01Z471).

G. Tsudik (Ed.): FC 2008, LNCS 5143, pp. 69–82, 2008.

small dictionary (e.g. 4 decimal digits). However, since passwords are easily-guessed strings, many password-based systems are vulnerable to replay attack or dictionary attacks [1]. To design a secure password-based system is a precise task that has attracted many cryptographers.

During the last decades, the design of 2-party Password-based Authenticated Key Exchange(PAKE) has been explored intensively [2,3,4,5]. Nonetheless, very few group key exchange protocols have been proposed with password authentication. The situation for it is not very satisfying and there is a need for significant theoretical progress. In [6,7], Bresson et al. showed how to adapt their group Diffie-Hellman protocols to the password-based scenario. Both of the protocols allowed users to securely join and leave the wireless group at any time—the so-called dynamic case. However, as the original protocols on which they are based, the total number of rounds is linear in the number of players, making their schemes impractical for large groups. As noted in [8], even in the case of a group where only few members have a slow network connection, the efficiency of the protocol with n rounds for a group of n members can be severely degraded. Furthermore, it is clear that a scheme with n rounds is not scalable. More recently, several constant-round password-based group key exchange protocols have been proposed in the literature by Abdalla et al. [9,10,11], by Bohli et al. [12], by Dutta and Barua [13], and by Kim, Lee, and Lee [14]. All of these constructions are based on the Burmester and Desmedt protocol [15,16] and are attractive, but none of them allows dynamic membership as in [7]. However, dynamicity in the membership may be of critical concern in practical environment. For example, it is a feature of prime importance to the IEEE 802.11 standards since users join and leave a group as they move from one wireless realm to another [17]. We note that re-running the protocol from scratch is always possible, and hence the goal of such operations is to provide an efficient means to update the existing session key into a new one. To the best of our knowledge, none of constant-round password-based authenticated group key exchange schemes enjoys dynamicity in the membership. Other protocols, such as the protocols in [18,19], do consider dynamic group key exchange problem but not in the password-based scenario. Our goal is to present a constant-round Password-based Authenticated Group Key Exchange(PAGKE) protocol for dynamically changing groups in *ad hoc* networks, i.e., for environments such that a member of a group may join and/or leave at any given time and a group key is exchanged without the help of any central sever.

In this paper, we extend the work of Abdalla et al. [11] to take into account the notion of dynamicity in the membership and present an improved compiler that transforms any provably secure password-based authenticated 2-party key exchange into a more attractive password-based authenticated group key exchange. The resulting protocol is a provably secure and efficient dynamic password-based authenticated group key exchange protocol in a constant number of rounds and therefore well suited for *ad hoc* networks, i.e., absent fixed infrastructure. Difficulties in designing a secure and efficient dynamic password-based authenticated group key exchange scheme arise from the facts that a group key should be updated whenever a membership changes and exchanged without any trustee so that this value is only known to the members of the newly formed pool. Our goal is achieved by enhancing the framework with additional, atomic operations which enable the group to grow or decrease, and no more rounds of communication is needed in contrast with the original compiler. To the best of our knowledge, our proposal is the first solution to design constant-round password-based authenticated group key exchange protocol for dynamic groups. For dynamic group communications, we propose setup, join, and leave algorithms. All of them are quite efficient, only requiring a small amount of computation by each user. Furthermore, the security result does not assume the Random Oracle (RO) model [20] or the ideal cipher model.

The remainder of this paper is organized as follows. Section 2 recalls the security model for password-based key exchange. Section 3 then presents algorithmic assumptions to be used in this paper briefly. Section 4 gives a detailed description of our compiler along with the efficiency analysis and security proof. Finally, conclusion is presented in Section 5.

2   Security Models for Password-Based Key Exchange

A secure password-based key exchange is a key exchange protocol where the parties use their passwords in order to derive a common session key sk that will be used to build secure channels. Loosely speaking, such protocols are said to be secure against *dictionary attacks* if the advantage of an attacker in distinguishing a real session key from a random key is less than $O(q_s/|\mathcal{D}|) + \epsilon(l)$, where $|\mathcal{D}|$ is the size of the dictionary $\mathcal{D}$, q_s is the number of active sessions and $\epsilon(l)$ is a negligible function depending on the security parameter l.

In this section, we recall the security model we will use in the rest of the paper to define the execution of the protocol for password-based authenticated key exchange. We refer to the model newly introduced by Michel Abdalla, Pierre-Alain Fouque, and David Pointcheval(AFP) [21] as the Real-Or-Random (ROR) model and to the model introduced by Bellare, Pointcheval, and Rogaway (BPR) [22] as the Find-Then-Guess (FTG) model, following the terminology of Bellare et al. for symmetric encryption schemes [23]. As proved in [21], the Real-Or-Random (ROR) security model is actually stronger than the Find-Then-Guess (FTG) security model. In this paper, we prove our protocol is semantically secure in ROR model.

2.1   The Security Model

We denote by U_i a player that can participate in the key exchange protocol. The players belongs to a nonempty set $\mathcal{U}$ of n users who can participate in the key exchange protocol $\mathcal{P}$. A player U_i may have several instances called oracles involved in distinct, possibly concurrent, executions of the protocol. We denote by U_i^j the instance j of a player U_i . The players also share low-entropy secrets which are drawn from a small dictionary $\mathcal{D}$, according to the uniform distribution.

The key exchange algorithm $\mathcal{P}$ is an interactive protocol among a group users that provides the instances of them with a session key sk. The interaction between an adversary $\mathcal{A}$ and the protocol participants occurs only via oracle queries, which model the adversary capabilities in a real attack. The types of oracles available to the adversary are as follows:

- *Execute($\mathcal{U}$)*: This query models passive attacks in which the attacker eavesdrops on honest executions of the protocol. The output of this query consists of the messages that were exchanged during the honest execution of the protocol.
- *Send(U_i^j, m)*: This query models an active attack, in which the adversary may intercept a message and then either modify it, create a new one, or simply forward it to the intended participant. The output of this query is the message that the participant instance U_i^j would generate upon receipt of message m.

2.2 Security Definitions

The aim of the adversary is to break the privacy of the session key (a.k.a., semantic security). The security notions take place in the context of executing $\mathcal{P}$ in the presence of the adversary $\mathcal{A}$. One first draws passwords from $\mathcal{D}$ according to the uniform distribution, provides coin tosses to $\mathcal{A}$, all oracles, and then runs the adversary by letting it ask any number of queries as described above, in any order.

AKE Security. In order to model the privacy (semantic security) of the session key, we consider the game $\text{Game}_{\mathcal{P}}^{ake}$ in which an additional oracle is made available to the adversary: the $Test(U^i)$ oracle. Let b be a bit chosen uniformly at random at the beginning of the game defining the semantic security of session keys. The $Test$ oracle in the ROR model is defined as follows:.

- $Test(U^i)$:If no session key for instance U^i is defined, then return the undefined symbol $\perp$. Otherwise, return the session key for instance U^i if $b = 1$ or a random of key of the same size if $b = 0$. This query is only available to $\mathcal{A}$ if the attacked instance U is Fresh (which roughly means that the session key is not "obviously" known to the adversary.)

As in FTG models, the $Test$ oracle in the ROR model also tries to capture the adversary's ability (or inability) to tell apart a real session key from a random one. The main difference is that it does so not only for a single session but for all sessions. More precisely, the adversary in the ROR model is not restricted to ask a single $Test$ query, but it can in fact ask multiple ones. All $Test$ queries in this case will be answered using the same value for the hidden bit b that was chosen at the beginning of the game defining the semantic security of the session keys. That is, the keys returned by the $Test$ oracle are either all real or all random. However, in the random case, the same random key value is returned for $Test$ queries that are asked to he instances that belong to the same session. The goal of the adversary in the ROR model is still the same: to guess the value of the hidden bit.

Let SUCC denote the event in which the adversary is successful. The **ror-ake-advantage** of an adversary $\mathcal{A}$ in violating the semantic security of the protocol $\mathcal{P}$ in the ROR sense and the **advantage function** of the protocol $\mathcal{P}$, when passwords are drawn from a dictionary $\mathcal{D}$, are respectively

$$Adv_{\mathcal{P},\mathcal{D}}^{ror-ake}(\mathcal{A}) = 2 \cdot Pr[\text{SUCC}] - 1$$

and

$$Adv_{\mathcal{P},\mathcal{D}}^{ror-ake}(t, R) = \max_{\mathcal{A}}\{\mathbf{Adv}_{\mathcal{P},\mathcal{D}}^{ror-ake}(\mathcal{A})\},$$

where the maximum is over all $\mathcal{A}$ with time-complexity at most t and using resources at most R (such as the number of queries to its oracles). The definition of time-complexity that we use henceforth is the usual one, which includes the maximum of all execution times in the games defining the security plus the code size [24]. Note that the advantage of an adversary that simply guesses the bit b is 0 in the above definition due to the rescaling of the probabilities.

3   Algorithmic Assumptions

In this section, we will briefly introduce some algorithmic assumptions to be used later. The arithmetic is in a finite cyclic group $G = \langle g \rangle$ of order a l-bit prime number q, where the operation is denoted multiplicatively.

Computational Diffie-Hellman problem (CDH): On input g^x, g^y, computing g^{xy}. A variant to the classical computational Diffie-Hellman problem is the particular case where $y = x$: the computational square Diffie-Hellman problem. The square Diffie-Hellman problem is as hard as the basic computational Diffie-Hellman problem[25]. For simplicity, we do not distinguish them. An algorithm that solves the computational Diffie-Hellman problem is a probabilistic polynomial time Turing machine, on input g^x, g^y, outputs g^{xy} with non-negligible probability. Computational Diffie-Hellman assumption means that there is no such a probabilistic polynomial time Turing machine. This assumption is believed to be true over G.

Computational Diffie-Hellman inversion problem (CDHI): On input g^x, outputs $g^{x^{-1}}$. An algorithm that solves the inverse computational Diffie-Hellman problem is a probabilistic polynomial time Turing machine, on input g^x, outputs $g^{x^{-1}}$ with non-negligible probability. Computational Diffie-Hellman inversion assumption means that there is no such a probabilistic polynomial time Turing machine. Fortunately, the CDH assumption and CDHI assumption are equivalent [25].

This paper is interested in more generalized versions of them:

$s-$**Computational Diffie-Hellman problem (s-CDH):** On input Q, Q^x, $Q^{x^2}, Q^{x^3}, \cdots, Q^{x^s}$, computing $Q^{x^{s+1}}$, where Q is a random element in G.

$s-$**Computational Diffie-Hellman inversion problem (s-CDHI):** On input Q, Q^x, $Q^{x^2}, \cdots, Q^{x^s}$, computing $Q^{1/x}$,where Q is a random element in G.

The $s-$CDH problem and $s-$CDHI problem are proven equivalent in [26]. Similarly,we say that the $s-$CDH($s-$CDHI) assumption holds if no algorithm running in polynomial time can solve a random instance of the $s-$CDH($s-$CDHI, resp.) problem with non-negligible probability.

4   From Two to Group: An Improved Compiler

In this section, we introduce the improved compiler that transforms any 2-party PAKE protocol into an efficient constant-round PAGKE protocol for dynamic groups with 2 more rounds and then prove the security for the resulting PAGKE protocol based on the hardness of the s-CDH and s-CDHI problems and the security of the underlying primitives.

4.1   Description

Our compiler is based on the design of [11], in which the notion of dynamicity in the membership was not taken into account. We enhance the framework with additional, atomic operations which enable the group to grow or decrease. Once the pairwise key exchanges have been completed, each principal must commit to the XOR-value of the two transformed keys he shares with his neighbors. This value is disclosed in a subsequent round, allowing all principals to derive each of the transformed 2-party keys, from which the session key will be derived. The group key space belongs to $\{0,1\}^l$ where l is a security parameter. Let $G = \langle g \rangle$ be a cyclic group of prime order p. Let $\mathcal{F} : \{0,1\}^* \to \{0,1\}^l$ be a collision-resistant pseudorandom function, and $f: : G \to Z_q$ be an injective map function(not imposing one-way on it, can be instantiated with a collision-resistant pseudorandom function). For dynamic group communications, we propose **Setup, Join,** and **Leave** algorithms.

Setup. Let $G_0 = \{U_1, \cdots, U_n\}$ be an initial group. We consider a ring structure among the members of G_0, i.e., members indices could be considered on the circulation of $\{1, \cdots, n\}$. All indices are to be taken in a cycle, i. e., $U_{n+1} = U_1$, etc. Figure 1 shows the example of this algorithm with three members.

- **Round 1.** Each member U_i executes 2-party PAKE with U_{i-1} and U_{i+1}. Thus, each user U_i holds two keys K_i, K_{i+1} shared with U_{i-1} and U_{i+1} respectively.
- **Round 2.** Each U_i computes $X_i := f(g^{K_i}) \oplus f(g^{K_{i+1}})$ and broadcasts $M_i := (U_i, X_i)$.
- **Round 3.** Each U_i checks that $X_1 \oplus X_2 \oplus \cdots \oplus X_n = 0$. If the check fails, set $\mathrm{acc}_i :=$ false and terminate the protocol execution. Otherwise, he sets $K'_i := f(g^{K_i})$ and computes the $n-1$ values $K'_{i-j} := K'_i \oplus X_{i-1} \oplus \cdots \oplus X_{i-j}(j = 1, \cdots, n-1)$ and defines a master key $K := (K'_1, ..., K'_n, G_0)$, and sets $sk_i := \mathcal{F}(K)$ and $\mathrm{acc}_i :=$ true.

$$G_0 = \{U_1, U_2, U_3\}$$

U_1 $\qquad\qquad\qquad U_2$ $\qquad\qquad\qquad\qquad\qquad U_3$

ROUND 1:

$$K_1 \xleftarrow[\text{2-party PAKE}]{(U_3, U_1)} \qquad K_2 \xleftarrow[\text{2-party PAKE}]{(U_1, U_2)} \qquad K_3 \xleftarrow[\text{2-party PAKE}]{(U_2, U_3)}$$

$$\xrightarrow[\text{2-party PAKE}]{(U_1, U_2)} K_2 \qquad \xrightarrow[\text{2-party PAKE}]{(U_2, U_3)} K_3 \qquad \xrightarrow[\text{2-party PAKE}]{(U_3, U_1)} K_1$$

ROUND 2:

computes

$$X_1 = f(g^{K_1}) \oplus f(g^{K_2}) \quad X_2 = f(g^{K_2}) \oplus f(g^{K_3}) \quad X_3 = f(g^{K_3}) \oplus f(g^{K_1})$$

and broadcasts

$$M_1 = (U_1, X_1) \qquad M_2 = (U_2, X_2) \qquad M_3 = (U_3, X_3)$$

ROUND 3:

If $X_1 \oplus X_2 \oplus X_3 = 0$, then computes K_1', K_2', K_3'

defines $K := (K_1' = f(g^{K_1}), K_2' = f(g^{K_2}), K_3' = f(g^{K_3}), G_0)$, and sets

$sk_1 = \mathcal{F}(K)$ $\qquad\qquad sk_2 = \mathcal{F}(K)$ $\qquad\qquad sk_3 = \mathcal{F}(K)$

$acc_1 = $ true $\qquad\qquad acc_2 = $ true $\qquad\qquad acc_3 = $ true

Fig. 1. *Setup* algorithm $G_0 = \{U_1, U_2, U_3\}$

Join. Let $G_{v-1} = \{U_1, \cdots, U_n\}(v \geq 1)$ be the current group and $\mathcal{J} = \{U_{n+1}, \cdots, U_{n+n'}\}(n' \geq 1)$ be a set of new members. In this algorithm, we consider a ring structure among the members $\{U_1, \cdots, U_{n+n'}\}$ as above, i. e., $U_{n+n'+1} = U_1$, etc. Figure 2 shows the example of this algorithm.

- **Round 1.** Each member U_{n+i} of $\mathcal{J}$ executes 2-party PAKE with U_{n+i-1} and U_{n+i+1}. As a result, each of the keys $K_{n+1}, K_{n+2}, \cdots, K_{n+n'}, K_1$ will be generated freshly. As for the rest keys, i.e., $K_2, K_3, \cdots, K_n$, each of them will be updated to be its square by the holders.
- **Round 2.** Same as **Round 2.** of *Setup* with the new group size $n + n'$.
- **Round 3.** Same as **Round 3.** of *Setup* with the new group size $n + n'$.

Intuitively, if a joining member is unable to deduce g^x from g^{x^2} for an unknown random $x \in Z_q$(i.e., computational Diffie-Hellman inversion assumption), neither will he be able to retrieve any information about the previous group session key. We will argue it later.

Leave. Let $G_{v-1} = \{\overline{U}_1, \cdots, \overline{U}_n\}(v \geq 1)$ be the current group. For convenience of explanation, we assume and $\mathcal{R} = \{\overline{U}_{n-n''+1}, \cdots, \overline{U}_n\}(n'' \geq 1)$ be a set of revoked members. In this algorithm, we consider a ring structure among the members $\{U_1 = \overline{U}_1, \cdots, U_{n-n''} = \overline{U}_{n-n''}\}$ as above, i. e., $U_{n-n''+1} = U_1$, etc. Figure 3 shows the example of this algorithm.

- **Round 1.** The member $U_{n-n''}$ executes 2-party PAKE with U_1. As a result, the key K_1 will be generated freshly. At the same time, all of the keys $K_{n-n''+1}, \cdots, K_n$ will be expired . As for the rest keys, i.e., $K_2, K_3, \cdots, K_{n-n''}$, each of them will be updated to be its square by the holders.
- **Round 2.** Same as **Round 2.** of *Setup* with the new group size $n - n''$.
- **Round 3.** Same as **Round 3.** of *Setup* with the new group size $n - n''$.

$$G_{v-1} = \{U_1, U_2, U_3\}, \mathcal{J} = \{U_4\}$$

U_1	U_2	U_3	U_4

holds previously-generated keys

K_1, K_2   **K_2, K_3**   **K_3, K_1**

ROUND 1:

$$K_1 \xleftarrow{(U_4,U_1)}{2-partyPAKE} \qquad K_2 \leftarrow \mathbf{K_2}^2 \qquad K_3 \leftarrow \mathbf{K_3}^2 \qquad K_4 \xleftarrow{(U_3,U_4)}{2-partyPAKE}$$

$$\mathbf{K_2}^2 \to K_2 \qquad \mathbf{K_3}^2 \to K_3 \qquad \xrightarrow[2-partyPAKE]{(U_3,U_4)} K_4 \qquad \xrightarrow[2-partyPAKE]{(U_4,U_1)} K_1$$

ROUND 2:

computes

$$X_1 = f(g^{K_1}) \oplus f(g^{K_2}) \quad X_2 = f(g^{K_2}) \oplus f(g^{K_3}) \quad X_3 = f(g^{K_3}) \oplus f(g^{K_4}) \quad X_4 = f(g^{K_4}) \oplus f(g^{K_1})$$

and broadcasts

$$M_1 = (U_1, X_1) \qquad M_2 = (U_2, X_2) \qquad M_3 = (U_3, X_3) \qquad M_4 = (U_4, X_4)$$

ROUND 3:

If $X_1 \oplus X_2 \oplus X_3 \oplus X_4 = 0$, then computes K_1', K_2', K_3', K_4'

defines $K := (K_1' = f(g^{K_1}), K_2' = f(g^{K_2}), K_3' = f(g^{K_3}), K_4' = f(g^{K_4}), G_v)$, and sets

$$sk_1 = \mathcal{F}(K) \qquad sk_2 = \mathcal{F}(K) \qquad sk_3 = \mathcal{F}(K) \qquad sk_4 = \mathcal{F}(K)$$

$acc_1 =$ true $acc_2 =$ true $acc_3 =$ true $acc_4 =$ true

Fig. 2. *Join* algorithm $G_{v-1} = \{U_1, U_2, U_3\}$ and $\mathcal{J} = \{U_4\}$, where the previously-generated values are marked in bold

Intuitively, if a leaving member is unable to deduce g^{x^2} from g^x for an unknown random $x \in Z_q$ (i.e., computational Diffie-Hellman assumption), neither will he be able to retrieve any information about the previous group session key. We will argue it later.

Note 1. When compared with the design of [11], what is new here is in essence a simple trick – instead of using component 2-party AKE instantiations and then using the result to directly derive a shared group key using XOR, the parties base that shared group key on a derived value $f(g^{K_i})$, of their pairwise keys K_i. This allows the K_is to remain secret, allowing parties to be added to and removed from the group by having the new members perform 2-party AKEs among themselves, and then join the ring of existing members by doing one AKE at each edge of the join. Previous members of the group simulate having participated in a new round of key exchange by modifying their existing shared keys by squaring them. In essence, joins and leaves are handled by performing a new group key exchange, where $n - 2$ of the continuing group members can use a non-interactive protocol to move to the next round. In the algorithms, we use the injective map function f to transform the elements in G into bit strings for speedup. Actually, we can perform operations on the elements over G immediately but it seems less efficient than XOR-operation.

Note 2. Our proposal is the first solution to design constant-round password-based authenticated group key exchange protocol for dynamic groups. Other works may leverage our work to obtain dynamic group key exchange protocols as well.

$$G_{v-1} = \{U_1, U_2, U_3, U_4\}, \mathcal{R} = \{U_4\}$$

| U_1 | U_2 | U_3 | U_4 |

holds previously-generated keys

| $\mathbf{K_1, K_2}$ | $\mathbf{K_2, K_3}$ | $\mathbf{K_3, K_4}$ | $\mathbf{K_4, K_1}$ |

ROUND 1:

$$K_1 \xleftarrow[2-partyPAKE]{(U_3, U_1)} \qquad K_2 \leftarrow \mathbf{K_2}^2 \qquad K_3 \leftarrow \mathbf{K_3}^2$$

$$\mathbf{K_2}^2 \rightarrow K_2 \qquad \mathbf{K_3}^2 \rightarrow K_3 \qquad \xrightarrow[2-partyPAKE]{(U_3, U_1)} K_1$$

ROUND 2:

computes

$$X_1 = f(g^{K_1}) \oplus f(g^{K_2}) \quad X_2 = f(g^{K_2}) \oplus f(g^{K_3}) \quad X_3 = f(g^{K_3}) \oplus f(g^{K_1})$$

and broadcasts

$$M_1 = (U_1, X_1) \qquad M_2 = (U_2, X_2) \qquad M_3 = (U_3, X_3)$$

ROUND 3:

If $X_1 \oplus X_2 \oplus X_3 = 0$, then computes K_1', K_2', K_3'

defines $K := (K_1' = f(g^{K_1}), K_2' = f(g^{K_2}), K_3' = f(g^{K_3})), G_v)$, and sets

$$sk_1 = \mathcal{F}(K) \qquad sk_2 = \mathcal{F}(K) \qquad sk_3 = \mathcal{F}(K)$$

$$acc_1 = true \qquad acc_2 = true \qquad acc_3 = true$$

Fig. 3. *Leave* algorithm $G_{v-1} = \{U_1, U_2, U_3, U_4\}$ and $\mathcal{R} = \{U_4\}$, where the previously-generated values are marked in bold

4.2 Efficiency

Our protocol is quite efficient, only requiring a small amount of computation by each user. In the **Setup** algorithm, each group member performs two 2-party PAKEs, one modular exponentiation, two random permutation function operations, and at most $2n$ XOR operations. Since the operation dependent on the number of group members is the XOR operation, the total cost of computations can be highly reduced, compared to the previous protocols, e.g. [10]. The most expensive part of our protocol is the number of the 2-party key computation(established through 2-party PAKE). Fortunately, the number of such computations is only two per participant, independent of the group size n. Furthermore, such computations could be avoided if the 2-party key is reused for generations of a new group session key when group membership changes.

In addition, the three algorithms *Setup, Join* and *Leave* are very similar and only different in building 2-party keys. Thus we do not need three separate parts of programme code to support them respectively. Instead we can use a common programme to support them all, with a few line of branch codes to support the difference in building 2-party keys. Therefore, much storage resource can be saved. This is very attractive in resource constrained environments.

4.3 Security

Assume that we are given a secure authenticated 2-party PAKE protocol. Assume further that $\mathcal{F}$ is a collision-resistant pseudorandom function. In the following, we show that under these assumptions our compiler yields a secure PAGKE $\mathcal{P}_g$.

Theorem 1. *Let $\mathcal{P}_2$ be a secure 2-party password-based key exchange (in the ROR model), and $\mathcal{F}$ be a collision-resistant pseudorandom function. Let q_{exe}, q_{send} and q_{test} represent the number of queries to Execute, Send and Test oracles. Then*
$$Adv^{ror-ake}_{\mathcal{P}_g,\mathcal{D}}(t, q_{exe}, q_{test}, q_{send}) \le 4Adv^{ror-ake}_{\mathcal{P}_2,\mathcal{D}}(t, nq_{exe}, nq_{exe} + 2q_{test}, 2q_{send}) + \frac{q_{send}}{2^{l-1}} + \frac{(q_{send} + q_{exe})^2}{q} + \frac{(q_{send} + q_{exe})^2}{2^l}.$$

Proof. We prove it using Abdalla and Pointcheval et al.'s style [21]. Let $\mathcal{A}$ be an adversary against the semantic security of $\mathcal{P}_g$. The idea is to use $\mathcal{A}$ to build adversaries for each of the underlying primitives in such a way that if $\mathcal{A}$ succeeds in breaking the semantic security of $\mathcal{P}_g$, then at least one of these adversaries succeeds in breaking the security of an underlying primitive. Our proof consists of a sequence of hybrid games, starting with the real attack and ending in a game in which the adversary's advantage is 0, and for which we can bound the difference in the adversary's advantage between any two consecutive games. In the following games **Game$_n$**, we study the event S_n which occurs if the adversary correctly guesses the bit b involved in the $Test$-query.

Game$_0$: This game corresponds to the real attack. By definition, we have

$$Adv^{ror-ake}_{\mathcal{P}_g,\mathcal{D}}(\mathcal{A}) = 2Pr[S_0] - 1 \tag{1}$$

Game$_1$: In this game, we replace all the 2-party session keys $K_1, \cdots, K_n$ by n random session keys in our simulation. Therefore, we do no longer need to execute $\mathcal{P}_2$ to establish the 2-party session keys. By using a similar technique that is used in [21], we can prove that the difference between the success probability of the adversary $\mathcal{A}$ between the current and previous games is at most that of breaking the security of the underlying $\mathcal{P}_2$. Thus, we have

$$|Pr[S_1] - Pr[S_0]| \le 2Adv^{ror-ake}_{\mathcal{P}_2,\mathcal{D}}(t, nq_{exe}, nq_{exe} + 2q_{test}, 2q_{send}) \tag{2}$$

Game$_2$: In this game, we consider such a M_i is invalid if it is not previously generated in our simulation. As by now all keys are random values, the probability for any XOR sum of keys not consisting exactly of the keys in one session (thus canceling each other w.r.t. XOR) to be 0 is only $1/2^l$. The adversary $\mathcal{A}$ is at maximum capable of doing this q_{send} times, giving him a probability $q_{send}/2^l$ of distinguishing the games. Thus, we have

$$|Pr[S_2] - Pr[S_1]| \le \frac{q_{send}}{2^l} \tag{3}$$

Game$_3$: In this game, we change the simulation of the $Execute$ and $Send$ oracles at the point of computing the session key. We keep a list of assignments $(K'_1, \cdots, K'_n, U_1, \cdots, U_n)$. Once the adversary asks a $Send$ query on an instance that is in such an expecting state to receive $M_1, \cdots, M_n$ and the input message is also of that format, we compute $K'_1, \cdots, K'_n$ and checks if for this sequence a master key was already issued and assigns this key to the instance. If no such entry exists in the list, we choose a session key $sk_i \in \{0,1\}^l$ uniformly at random. It would let the probabilities unchanged.

$$|Pr[S_3] = |Pr[S_2] \tag{4}$$

At this moment, one can remark that the session key cannot be guessed by the adversary, better than at random for each attempt unless some (unlikely) collisions appear occurs.

- collisions on the records $(K_1', \cdots, K_n')$. Note that records involve at least one honest party, and thus one item is truly uniformly distributed;
- collisions on the output of $\mathcal{F}$.

Both probabilities are bounded by the birthday paradox and thus we have,

$$|Pr[S_3] - \frac{1}{2}| \leq \frac{(q_{send} + q_{exe})^2}{2q} + \frac{(q_{send} + q_{exe})^2}{2^{l+1}} \tag{5}$$

Finally, combining all the above equations, one gets the announced result as follows.
$$Adv_{\mathcal{P},\mathcal{D}}^{ror-ake}(\mathcal{A}) = 2Pr[S_0] - 1 = 2(Pr[S_0] - \frac{1}{2})$$
$$\leq 2(|Pr[S_0] - Pr[S_1]| + |Pr[S_1] - Pr[S_2]| + |Pr[S_3] - \frac{1}{2}|)$$
$$\leq 4Adv_{\mathcal{P}_1,\mathcal{D}}^{ror-ake}(t, nq_{exe}, nq_{exe} + 2q_{test}, 2q_{send}) + \frac{q_{send}}{2^{l-1}} + \frac{(q_{send}+q_{exe})^2}{q} + \frac{(q_{send}+q_{exe})^2}{2^l}.$$

$$\square$$

Now, we come to consider key privacy with respect to the joining or leaving member. Assume further that s-computational Diffie-Hellman assumption and s-computational Diffie-Hellman Inversion assumption hold over G. In the following, we show that under these assumptions our compiler yields a secure PAGKE that has key privacy with respect to the joining or leaving member.

Theorem 2. *Let $\mathcal{P}_2$ be a secure 2-party password-based key exchange (in the ROR model), and $\mathcal{F}$ be a collision-resistant pseudorandom function. Then the resulting PAGKE has key privacy with respect to the joining or leaving member as long as s-computational Diffie-Hellman assumption and s-computational Diffie-Hellman Inversion assumption hold over G.*

Proof. Let x be a 2-party key that is reused for $v + 1$ times to generate the session keys of the dynamic groups. Actually, $g^x, g^{x^2}, g^{x^{2^2}}, \cdots, g^{x^{2^v}}$ (in fact, $f(g^x), f(g^{x^2})$, $f(g^{x^{2^2}}), \cdots, f(g^{x^{2^v}})$) are immediate values used at the point of computing the group session keys. One can remark that x is unknown to the joining or leaving member in the throughout course. We firstly consider the joining case. We assume a user joins the group in the $(i+1)$-th key exchange process. Then we have in mind the joining member that knows $g^{x^{2^{i+1}}}$ possibly along with some subsequent items. We consider an extreme case in which he knows $Q, Q^x, Q^{x+1} \cdots, Q^{x^w}$ ($Q = g^{x^{2^{i+1}}}$, $w = v - 2^i - 1, 0 \leq i < v$) and attacks on the i-th group session. If s-computational Diffie-Hellman Inversion assumption holds over G(Let s be the maximum of all possible w), the joining member should not be able to compute $Q^{1/x} = g^{x^{2^i}}$. Since the target group session key is computed via a collision-resistant random function $\mathcal{F}$ using an unknown string as input, nor is the joining member able to retrieve any information about the target group session key, i.e., the resulting PAGKE has key privacy with respect to the joining member.

Next, we consider the leaving case. We assume a user leaves the group in the i-th key exchange process. Then we have in mind the leaving member that knows $g^{x^{2^{i-1}}}$ possibly along with some foregoing items. We consider an extreme case in which he knows $Q, Q^x, Q^{x+1} \cdots , Q^{x^s}(Q = g^x, w = 2^i - 2, 0 < i \le v)$ and attacks on the i-th group session. If $s-$computational Diffie-Hellman assumption holds over G(Let s be the maximum of all possible w), the leaving member should not be able to compute $Q^{x^{w+1}} = g^{x^{2^i}}$. Since the target group session key is computed via a collision-resistant random function $\mathcal{F}$ using an unknown string as input, nor is the leaving member able to retrieve any information about the target group session key,i.e., the resulting PAGKE has key privacy with respect to the leaving member.   □

Note 3. The security analysis does not assume the Random Oracle (RO) model [20]. That is, if the underlying primitives do not make use of the RO model, neither does our scheme. Hence, by using schemes whose security is in the standard model, one gets a password-based authenticated group key exchange protocol whose security is in the standard model.

5   Conclusion

We have presented the first solution to design constant-round password-based authenticated group key exchange protocols for dynamic groups. Our proposal is an improved compiler that transforms any provably secure password-based authenticated 2-party key exchange protocol into such an attractive protocols. The security result does not assume the Random Oracle model or the ideal cipher model.

Acknowledgement

The authors would like to thank anonymous reviewers for their valuable suggestions and comments that highly improve the readability and completeness of the paper. And we would give our special thanks to Man Ho Au for her great help at the conference.

References

1. Bellovin, S.M., Merritt, M.: Encrypted key exchange: password-based protocols secure against dictionary attacks. In: Proc. 1992 IEEE Computer Society Symp. on Research in security and Privacy, pp. 72–84 (May 1992)

2. Bresson, E., Chevassut, O., Pointcheval, D.: Security proofs for an efficient password-based key exchange. In: ACM CCS 2003, pp. 241–250. ACM Press, New York (2003)
3. Bresson, E., Chevassut, O., Pointcheval, D.: New security results on encrypted key exchange. In: Bao, F., Deng, R., Zhou, J. (eds.) PKC 2004. LNCS, vol. 2947, pp. 145–158. Springer, Heidelberg (2004)
4. Abdalla, M., Pointcheval, D.: Simple Password-Based Encrypted Key Exchange Protocols. In: Menezes, A. (ed.) CT-RSA 2005. LNCS, vol. 3376, pp. 191–208. Springer, Heidelberg (2005)
5. Abdalla, M., Chevassut, O., Pointcheval, D.: One-time verifier-based encrypted key exchange. In: Vaudenay, S. (ed.) PKC 2005. LNCS, vol. 3386, pp. 47–64. Springer, Heidelberg (2005)
6. Bresson, E., Chevassut, O., Pointcheval, D.: Group Diffie-Hellman key exchange secure against dictionary attacks. In: Zheng, Y. (ed.) ASIACRYPT 2002. LNCS, vol. 2501, pp. 497–514. Springer, Heidelberg (2002)
7. Bresson, E., Chevassut, O., Pointcheval, D.: A Security Solution for IEEE 802.11s Ad-hoc Mode: Password-Authentication and Group-Diffie-Hellman Key Exchange. International Journal of Wireless and Mobile Computing, Inderscience 2(1), 4–13 (2007)
8. Bresson, E., Catalano, D.: Constant Round Authenticated Group Key Agreement via Distributed Computation. In: Bao, F., Deng, R., Zhou, J. (eds.) PKC 2004. LNCS, vol. 2947, pp. 115–129. Springer, Heidelberg (2004)
9. Abdalla, M., Bresson, E., Chevassut, O., Pointcheval, D.: Password-based group key exchange in a constant number of rounds. In: Yung, M., Dodis, Y., Kiayias, A., Malkin, T.G. (eds.) PKC 2006. LNCS, vol. 3958, pp. 427–442. Springer, Heidelberg (2006)
10. Abdalla, M., Pointcheval, D.: A Scalable Password-based Group Key Exchange Protocol in the Standard Model. In: Lai, X., Chen, K. (eds.) ASIACRYPT 2006. LNCS, vol. 4284, pp. 332–347. Springer, Heidelberg (2006)
11. Abdalla, M., Bohli, J.-M., Vasco, M.I.G., Steinwandt, R. (Password) Authenticated Key Establishment: From 2-Party To Group. In: Vadhan, S.P. (ed.) TCC 2007. LNCS, vol. 4392, pp. 499–514. Springer, Heidelberg (2007)
12. Bohli, J.-M., Vasco, M.I.G., Steinwandt, R.: Password-authenticated constant-round group key establishment with a common reference string. Cryptology ePrint Archive, Report 2006/214 (2006), http://eprint.iacr.org/
13. Dutta, R., Barua, R.: Password-based encrypted group key agreement. International Journal of Network Security 3(1), 30–41 (2006), http://isrc.nchu.edu.tw/ijns
14. Kim, H.-J., Lee, S.-M., Lee, D.H.: Constant-round authenticated group key exchange for dynamic groups. In: Lee, P.J. (ed.) ASIACRYPT 2004. LNCS, vol. 3329, pp. 245–259. Springer, Heidelberg (2004)
15. Burmester, M., Desmedt, Y.: A secure and efficient conference key distribution system (extended abstract). In: De Santis, A. (ed.) EUROCRYPT 1994. LNCS, vol. 950, pp. 275–286. Springer, Heidelberg (1995)
16. Burmester, M., Desmedt, Y.: A secure and scalable group key exchange system. Information Processing Letters 94(3), 137–143 (2005)
17. IEEE Std 802.11. Wireless LAN Medium Access Control (MAC) and Physical Layer (PHY) specification (1999 edition)
18. Kim, H.-J., Lee, S.-M., Lee, D.H.: Constant-round authenticated group key exchange for dynamic groups. In: Lee, P.J. (ed.) ASIACRYPT 2004. LNCS, vol. 3329, pp. 245–259. Springer, Heidelberg (2004)

19. Dutta, R., Barua, R.: Dynamic Group Key Agreement in Tree-Based Setting. In: Boyd, C., González Nieto, J.M. (eds.) ACISP 2005. LNCS, vol. 3574, pp. 101–112. Springer, Heidelberg (2005)
20. Bellare, M., Rogaway, P.: Random oracles are practical: A paradigm for designing efficient protocols. In: ACM CCS 1993: 1st Conference on Computer and Communications Security, Fairfax, Virginia, USA, pp. 62–73. ACM Press, New York (1993)
21. Abdalla, M., Fouque, P.-A., Pointcheval, D.: Password-Based Authenticated Key Exchange in the Three-Party Setting. In: Vaudenay, S. (ed.) PKC 2005. LNCS, vol. 3386, pp. 65–84. Springer, Heidelberg (2005)
22. Bellare, M., Pointcheval, D., Rogaway, P.: Authenticated key exchange secure against dictionary attacks. In: Preneel, B. (ed.) EUROCRYPT 2000. LNCS, vol. 1807, pp. 139–155. Springer, Heidelberg (2000)
23. Bellare, M., Desai, A., Jokipii, E., Rogaway, P.: A concrete security treatment of symmetric encryption. In: 38th Annual Symposium on Foundations of Computer Science, Miami Beach, Florida, pp. 394–403. IEEE Computer Society Press, Los Alamitos (1997)
24. Abdalla, M., Bellare, M., Rogaway, P.: The oracle Diffie-Hellman assumptions and an analysis of DHIES. In: Naccache, D. (ed.) CT-RSA 2001. LNCS, vol. 2020, pp. 143–158. Springer, Heidelberg (2001)
25. Bao, F., Deng, R.H., Zhu, H.: Variations of diffie-hellman problem. In: Qing, S., Gollmann, D., Zhou, J. (eds.) ICICS 2003. LNCS, vol. 2836, pp. 301–312. Springer, Heidelberg (2003)
26. Zhang, F., Safavi-Naini, R., Susilo, W.: An efficient signature scheme from bilinear pairings and its applications. In: Bao, F., Deng, R., Zhou, J. (eds.) PKC 2004. LNCS, vol. 2947, pp. 277–290. Springer, Heidelberg (2004)

A Practical Universal Circuit Construction and Secure Evaluation of Private Functions

Vladimir Kolesnikov[1] and Thomas Schneider[2],*

[1] Bell Laboratories, 600 Mountain Ave. Murray Hill, NJ 07974, USA
`kolesnikov@research.bell-labs.com`
[2] Dept. of Comp. Sci., University of Erlangen-Nuremberg, Germany
`thomaschneider@gmail.com`

Abstract. We consider general secure function evaluation (SFE) of *private functions* (PF-SFE). Recall, privacy of functions is often most efficiently achieved by general SFE [18,19,10] of a Universal Circuit (UC).

Our main contribution is a new simple and efficient UC construction. Our circuit UC_k, universal for circuits of k gates, has size $\sim 1.5k \log^2 k$ and depth $\sim k \log k$. It is up to 50% smaller than the best UC (of Valiant [16], of size $\sim 19k \log k$) for circuits of size up to ≈ 5000 gates.

Our improvement results in corresponding performance improvement of SFE of (small) private functions. Since, due to cost, only small circuits (i.e. < 5000 gates) are practical for PF-SFE, our construction appears to be the best fit for many practical PF-SFE.

We implement PF-SFE based on our UC and Fairplay SFE system [11].

Keywords: SFE of private functions, universal circuit, privacy.

1 Introduction

We consider two-party secure function evaluation (SFE) of *private functions* (PF-SFE). Recall, "regular" SFE techniques allow two parties to evaluate any function on their respective inputs x and y, while keeping the inputs secret. SFE is a subject of immense amount of research, e.g. [18,19,10]. Efficient SFE algorithms enable a variety of electronic transactions, previously impossible due to mutual mistrust of participants. Examples include auctions [12,3,5,1], contract signing [4], distributed database mining [7,9], etc. As computation and communication resources have increased, SFE became practical for common use. Fairplay [11] is a full implementation of generic two-party SFE with malicious players. It demonstrates feasibility and efficiency of SFE of practical functions, represented as circuits of up to $\approx 10^6$ gates. Today, generic SFE is a relatively mature technology, and even small improvements are non-trivial and welcome.

In this work, we impose an additional restriction on SFE. Namely, we require that the evaluated function is known only by one party and needs to be kept secret (i.e. everything besides the size, the number of inputs and the number of

---

* The work was done while the author was visiting Bell Laboratories.

G. Tsudik (Ed.): FC 2008, LNCS 5143, pp. 83–97, 2008.
© Springer-Verlag Berlin Heidelberg 2008

outputs is hidden from the other party). Examples of real-life private functions include credit evaluation function, background- and medical history checking function, airport no-fly check function, etc. Full or even partial revelation of these functions opens vulnerabilities in the corresponding process, exploitable by dishonest participants (e.g. credit applicants), and should be prevented.

It is well known that the problem of PF-SFE can be reduced to the "regular" SFE [15,14]. This is done by parties evaluating a *Universal Circuit* (UC) instead of a circuit defining the evaluated function. UC can be thought of as a "program execution circuit", capable of simulating any circuit C of certain size, given the description of C as input. Therefore, disclosing the UC does not reveal anything about C, except its size. At the same time, the SFE computes output correctly and C remains private, since the player holding C simply treats description of C as additional (private) input to SFE. This reduction is the most common (and often the most efficient) way of securely evaluating private functions [15,14].

Our improvement of the UC construction directly results in improvements of PF-SFE for many practical private functions of interest. Indeed, circuit-based SFE (e.g. Yao's garbled circuit [18,19,10]) is still the most efficient SFE method for many important functions, such as the comparison function. The elegant and very efficient auction system of Naor, Pinkas and Sumner [12] implements auction function as a circuit, as well. Further, due to the size of UC constructions, PF-SFE is practical only for small circuits (UC for 5000-gate circuits has size 10^6, pushing the general SFE size limit). Therefore, improvements of circuit representation is particularly relevant for small circuits, and this is the focus and the result of our work.

1.1   Our Contributions

Our main contribution is a new elegant and efficient universal circuit UC_k construction of size $\sim 1.5k \log^2 k$ and depth $\sim k \log k$. For the circuits most relevant for PF-SFE (of size up to ≈ 5000), our approach results in up to 50% size reduction compared to asymptotically optimal construction of Valiant [16]. See Table 1 in Sect. 5 for detailed comparison. As described above, this immediately implies improvement in the practical PF-SFE. We expand this discussion and present additional applications below in Sect. 1.3.

Our constructions are simple and practical. We used them to implement PF-SFE as an extension of the Fairplay SFE system [11].

The basic building blocks we developed (such as the efficient S_v^u selection blocks of Sect. 4.2) may be of use in other circuit constructions as well.

1.2   Related Work

The most efficient known UC_k construction is the celebrated construction of Valiant [16]. With size $\sim 19k \log k$, it is asymptotically optimal, with a small constant factor. It relies on universal graphs. UC_k is derived from a universal graph UG_k; UC_k is universal for circuits of size k, if UG_k is universal for graphs of k nodes and in- and out-degrees 2. Embedding of the graph representation of a circuit C into UG_k defines the programming of UC_k to simulate C. As noted above, our construction produces smaller UC_k for circuits most relevant for PF-SFE. Further, we believe that implementation of our construction is more self-contained and straightforward.

Waksman [17] describes how to construct and program a permutation network, a circuit implementing an arbitrary permutation on n elements. Waksman's construction is asymptotically optimal (size $\sim 2n \log n$ and depth $\sim 2 \log n$). We use this work in an essential way – fundamental building blocks of our UC construction rely on [17].

1.3 Applications for Universal Circuits

As discussed above, UC is naturally used to extend the functionality or privacy in numerous practical SFE applications, in particular those based on Yao's garbled circuit [18,19,10]. Recall, Yao's approach views the evaluated function as a binary circuit known to both parties. The idea is to encrypt the signals on all wires of the circuit. Then the evaluator (one of the participants of the computation) uses clever setup and properties of encryption to compute (gate by gate) encryption of the output wires from the encryptions of input wires. The result of SFE is obtained by decrypting the values of the output wires of the circuit. We note that the cost of Yao's construction depends only on the size of the circuit, and not on its depth or fan-out. To perform PF-SFE, instead of evaluating the circuit directly, a UC that is programmed with the original circuit is evaluated. As UC can be programmed with any circuit, the evaluated function is entirely hidden from the evaluator.

We discuss natural applications that directly benefit from our improvements.

Frikken et. al [6] show a privacy-preserving credit checking scheme that is based on the evaluation of a garbled circuit. Their scheme is limited to the special class of credit-checking policies that can be expressed as the weighted sum of criteria. By evaluating a universal circuit their scheme can be extended to arbitrary, more complicated, private credit-checking policies.

Cachin et al. [2] describe autonomous mobile agents which migrate between several distrusting hosts. Garbled-circuit-based, their scheme ensures the privacy of the inputs of the visited hosts but not the structure of the mobile agent's code. The privacy of the executed code can be guaranteed by evaluating universal circuits instead.

Ostrovsky and Skeith [13] show how to filter remote streaming data (e.g airports' passenger lists, on-line news feeds or internet chat-rooms) using secret keywords and their combinations, such as no-fly lists. Their protocol allows Collector (e.g. airport) to obliviously filter out entries that match the (encrypted) query, which are then sent back for decryption. Their scheme can be naturally extended to allow a much finer private matching criteria, additionally preserving data privacy, as follows. The Collector encrypts each filtered stream element with a random pad. The querying party thus obtains the list of encrypted matches. In the second round, the querying party uses PF-SFE (e.g. using our UC_k) to search the matching data with an arbitrary, more detailed private search function.

2   Definitions and Preliminaries

In this section, we present basic notation and building blocks of our construction.

In the following, a *gate* is the implementation of a boolean function $\{0,1\}^2 \to \{0,1\}$ that has two *inputs* and one *output*. We consider acyclic *circuits* that consist of connected gates with arbitrary fanout, i.e. the (single) output of each gate can be used as input to an arbitrary number of gates. Further, each output of the circuit C is the output of a gate and not a redirected input of C.

A *block* B_v^u is a circuit that has u inputs $in_1, .., in_u$ and v outputs $out_1, .., out_v$ (we always associate variable u with inputs and v with outputs). B_v^u computes a function $f_B : \{0,1\}^u \to \{0,1\}^v$ that maps the input values to the output values. For simplicity, we identify B_v^u with f_B and write: $B(in_1, \ldots, in_u) = (out_1, \ldots, out_v)$. The *size* of a block B, $size(B)$, is the number of gates B consists of; its depth, $depth(B)$, is the maximum number of gates between any input and any output of B. A block can be a sub-block of a larger block. We construct a circuit as a collection of functional blocks, as this simplifies presentation.

A *programmable* block is a block that consists of connected programmable gates with unspecified function tables. *Programming* a programmable block is done by providing a specific function table for each of its gates.

A *Universal Circuit* $UC_{u,v,k}$ is a programmable block with u inputs and v outputs that can be programmed to simulate any circuit C with up to u inputs, v outputs and k gates. UC_C denotes UC that is programmed to simulate circuit C, that is $\forall(in_1, \ldots, in_u) : UC_C(in_1, \ldots, in_u) = C(in_1, \ldots, in_u)$.

A *one-output switching block* Y is a programmable block that computes $(in_1, in_2) \to in_1$ or in_2, as shown in Fig. 1(a). It is implemented by one gate programmed with the corresponding function table. $size(Y) = depth(Y) = 1$.

A *two-output switching block* X is a programmable block shown on Fig. 1(b) that computes $(in_1, in_2) \to (in_1, in_2)$ or (in_2, in_1). It is implemented by using (in parallel) two Y blocks: one for each of the outputs. $size(X) = 2; depth(X) = 1$.

(a) Y switching block   (b) X switching block

Fig. 1. Switching blocks

A *selection block* S_v^u is a programmable block that selects for each of its v outputs one of the u input values (with duplicates). S_v^u is programmed according to the selection mapping $(\sigma_i)_{i=1}^v, \sigma_i \in \{1..u\}$ that selects the σ_i-th input as the i-th output. That is, a programmed S_v^u computes $S(in_1, \ldots, in_u) = (in_{\sigma_1}, \ldots, in_{\sigma_v})$.

A S_1^u selection block can be implemented by $(u-1)$ Y blocks that are programmed to switch the desired input value in_{σ_1} to the output. Shallow S_1^u is obtained by arranging Y blocks in a tree. Thus, $size(S_1^u) = u-1; depth(S_1^u) = \log u$.

A naive implementation of S_v^u selection block uses a S_1^u selection block for each of the v outputs, resulting in $size(S_v^u) = v(u-1)$ and $depth(S_v^u) = \log u$. Selection blocks are crucial for our UC construction. We describe much more efficient S_v^u constructions in Sect. 4.2.

3 Our Universal Circuit Construction

In this section, we present our modular UC construction. All of the necessary building blocks were introduced in Sect. 2; here we show how to assemble them. Then, in Sect. 4, we design improved versions of some building blocks, which results in performance improvement of our UC.

In our UC construction, we simulate each gate G_i of the original circuit C. That is, for each G_i, $UC_{u,v,k}$ has a corresponding programmable G_i-simulation gate G_i^{Sim}. In our construction, we always ensure that inputs, outputs and semantics of G_i^{Sim} correspond to G_i. Additionally, we hide the wiring of C by ensuring that every possible wiring can be implemented in $UC_{u,v,k}$. This is the natural method of construction of UC, and is, in fact, employed by Valiant [16].

We design our UC construction recursively (we build a circuit from two circuits of smaller size). We first note that the input/output interface of $UC_{u,v,k}$ is different from that of the natural recursion step. This is why we introduce a *universal block* U_k. U_k can be viewed as a UC with specific input and output semantics. Namely, U_k has $2k$ inputs and k outputs, since this is a maximum $UC_{u,v,k}$ can have. Further, we restrict that U_k's inputs in_{2i-1}, in_{2i} are only delivered to the simulation gate G_i^{Sim}, and U_k's i-th output comes from G_i^{Sim}. (Of course, input of some gates G_i may come from any other gates' outputs, and not from in_{2i-1} or in_{2i}, which may not be used at all. U_k allows this; it only restricts that G_i's input cannot come from other in_j). U_k is thus a UC for the class of circuits of size k with the above input/output restrictions.

Now, given an implementation of U_k, it is easy to construct $UC_{u,v,k}$ (shown on Fig. 2). We need to provide the input selection block, which directs inputs of UC to the proper inputs of U_k. Finally, we need the output selection block, directing outputs of U_k to the proper outputs of UC, and discarding unused outputs. Both blocks are instances of selection blocks discussed above.

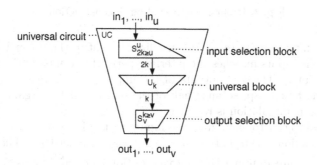

Fig. 2. Modular universal circuit construction

In the next section, we present our U_k construction. Plugged in the construction of Fig. 2, it gives a complete UC construction.

3.1   Recursive Universal Block Construction

In this section, we describe the natural divide-and-conquer procedure for constructing U_k, capable of simulating any circuit C_k of size k, with the input/output restrictions mentioned above.

In the following, we refer to the gates of the circuit C_k by their index. We choose a topological order of the gates $G_1, \ldots, G_k$, which ensures that the i-th gate G_i has no inputs that are outputs of a successive gate G_j, where $j > i$. Since we only consider acyclic circuits, we can always obtain this ordering by topological sorting with complexity $O(k)$.

Now, suppose we have two blocks $U_{k/2}$, universal for circuits $C_{k/2}$ of size $k/2$. We wish to combine them to obtain U_k. Clearly, because of their universality, one of $U_{k/2}$ could simulate the "upper" half of C_k (i.e. gates G_1 through $G_{k/2}$) , and the other $U_{k/2}$ could simulate the lower half (gates $G_{k/2+1}, \ldots, G_k$). Note, by the topological ordering, there is no data going into the upper $U_{k/2}$ from the lower one. Thus, U_k must only direct its inputs/outputs and allow implementation of all possible data paths from the upper $U_{k/2}$ to the lower one. This can be naturally done, as shown on Fig. 3(a). We describe this in detail below.

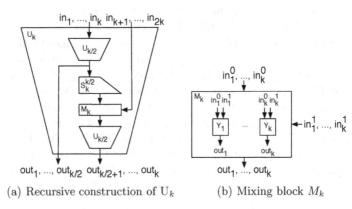

(a) Recursive construction of U_k (b) Mixing block M_k

Fig. 3. Recursive universal block construction

The first k inputs to U_k $in_1, .., in_k$ are directly sent to the upper $U_{k/2}$. Note, the order of the inputs matches the interface perfectly, so no additional manipulation is required. The $k/2$ outputs of the upper (resp. lower) $U_{k/2}$ are sent directly to the first (resp. second) half of the outputs of U_k. Again, interfaces match, and no manipulation is required.

We now only need to show how the inputs to the lower $U_{k/2}$ are provided. These inputs could come from (any G_i^{Sim} gate of) the upper $U_{k/2}$. Therefore, we also wire the outputs of upper $U_{k/2}$ into a selection block $S_k^{k/2}$. This allows to direct, with duplicates, the output of any gate of upper $U_{k/2}$ to any position of the input interface of lower $U_{k/2}$ (and thus to any gate of lower $U_{k/2}$). Additionally, (some of) lower $U_{k/2}$'s inputs could come from the U_k inputs $in_{k+1}, ... in_{2k}$. Since the lower $U_{k/2}$ simulates gates $G_{k/2+1}$ through G_k of C_k, inputs $in_{k+1}, ... in_{2k}$ are already ordered to match lower $U_{k/2}$'s interface. Now, for each input of lower $U_{k/2}$, we need to switch between the two input wires: one provided by upper $U_{k/2}$ via $S_k^{k/2}$, and the other coming from U_k's input directly. This is easily achieved by a Y switching block. On the diagram, for ease of presentation, we combine the k of these Y blocks into a *mixing block* M_k, shown on Fig. 3(b) with $size(M_k) = k \cdot size(Y) = k$ and $depth(M_k) = 1$.

The base case of the recursive construction is U_1, a universal block implementing a single gate. U_1 is implemented by a single programmable gate. This completes the description of the recursive U_k construction.

The above immediately implies efficient methods of UC programming, given the circuit C_k. In particular, if the first (resp. second) input of a gate G_j in the lower half of C_k ($k/2 < j \leq k$) is connected to an input of C_k, the mixing block M_k is programmed to select the corresponding input in_{2j-1} (resp. in_{2j}) of U_k by programming Y_{2j-k-1} (resp. Y_{2j-k}) of M_k correspondingly (see Fig. 3(b)). Otherwise, if G_j is connected to an output of a gate G_i in the upper half of C_k ($1 \leq i \leq k/2$), M_k and $S_k^{k/2}$ are programmed to select the corresponding output from the upper $U_{k/2}$ block by programming Y_{2j-k-1} (resp. Y_{2j-k}) correspondingly and programming $S_k^{k/2}$ with $\sigma_{2j-k-1} = i$ (resp. $\sigma_{2j-k} = i$).

We now compute the complexity of our constructions U_k and UC (using selection block constructions of Sect. 4.2). Recall, the cost of Yao's garbled circuit depends only on its size, and not on depth. Note, $size(U_1) = 1; depth(U_1) = 1$.

$$size(U_k) = 2size(U_{k/2}) + size(S_k^{k/2}) + size(M_k)$$

$$= k \cdot size(U_1) + \sum_{i=0}^{\log(k)-1} 2^i(size(S_{k/2^i}^{k/2^{i+1}}) + size(M_{k/2^i}))$$

$$= k + 3k\log^2 k - 2k\log k - 3k \sum_{i=0}^{\log(k)-1} i + 3 \sum_{i=0}^{\log(k)-1} 2^i$$

$$= 1.5k\log^2 k - 0.5k\log k + 4k - 3 ;$$

$$depth(U_k) = 2depth(U_{k/2}) + depth(S_k^{k/2}) + depth(M_k) = ...$$

$$= k\log k + k + 4\log k - 12 .$$

Using the optimization of Sect. 4.3, U_k has complexity $size(U_k) = 1.5k\log^2 k - 1.5k\log k + 6k - 5$ and $depth(U_k) = k\log k + 4\log k - 11$.

U_k combined with input- and output-selection blocks of Sect. 4.2 as shown in Fig. 2, results in a UC construction of complexity

$$size(UC) = 1.5k\log^2 k + 2.5k\log k + 9k + (u + 2k)\log u + (k + 3v)\log v$$
$$-2u - 4v + 1 ;$$

$$depth(UC) = k\log k + 2k + v + 7\log k + 2\log u + 3\log v - 14 .$$

4   Improved Selection Block Constructions

In this section, we present efficient selection block S_v^u constructions. They can be plugged directly in our UC construction. The size and depth computation of UC presented in Sect. 3.1, uses efficient constructions of this section.

We start the presentation with two useful generalizations of the permutation blocks of Waksman [17]. Based on these, we construct efficient selection blocks which are directly used in our UC construction.

4.1   Generalized Permutation Blocks

P_u^u permutation block. A *permutation block* P_u^u is a programmable block that can be programmed to output any permutation of the inputs. Formally, given a permutation $(\pi_i)_{i=1}^u, \pi_i \in \{1, \ldots, u\}, \forall i \neq j : \pi_i \neq \pi_j$ that selects for the i-th output a unique input π_i, P_u^u computes $P(in_1, .., in_u) = (in_{\pi_1}, .., in_{\pi_u})$.

When u is a power of 2, Waksman [17] describes an efficient recursive P_u^u construction built from X switching blocks. His P_u^u has $size(P_u^u) = 2u \log u - 2u + 2$ and $depth(P_u^u) = 2 \log u - 1$.

Waksman also gives an efficient recursive algorithm to program the X switching blocks of his construction. (Fig. 4 describes a slight generalization of Waksman's construction; fixing $u = v$ in Fig. 4 corresponds to Waksman's P_u^u.) The programming algorithm takes a $u \times u$ permutation matrix for the permutation (π_i) as input. It splits this $u \times u$ permutation matrix into two $u/2 \times u/2$ permutation matrices that are recursively implemented by the left and the right $P_{u/2}^{u/2}$ permutation sub-block and programs the X switching blocks correspondingly. Using a sparse matrix representation for the permutation matrices this algorithm can be efficiently implemented in $O(u \log u)$.

We note that Waksman's construction can be naturally generalized to the cases where $u \neq v$, i.e. the number of inputs and outputs differ. Below we define the resulting objects (which we call "truncated permutation" and "expanded permutation" blocks), and present their efficient constructions.

$TP_v^{u \geq v}$ truncated permutation block. A $TP_v^{u \geq v}$ truncated permutation block permutes a subset of v of the u inputs to the $v \leq u$ outputs. The remaining $u - v$ input values are discarded. Formally, an output mapping $(\mu_i)_{i=1}^v$, $\mu_i \in \{1, \ldots, u\}, \forall j \neq i : \mu_i \neq \mu_j$ selects the μ_i-th input as the i-ths output. The truncated permutation block computes $TP(in_1, \ldots, in_u) = (in_{\mu_1}, \ldots, in_{\mu_v})$.

The $TP_v^{u \geq v}$ block is recursively constructed analogous to Waksman's permutation network construction as seen in Fig. 4. W.l.o.g we assume u and v are even at each recursion step (otherwise we introduce an unused dummy input or output with small overhead). If $u \geq 2$ the $TP_v^{u \geq v}$ truncated permutation block is divided into two $TP_{v/2}^{u/2 \geq v/2}$ truncated permutation sub-blocks. The upper $u/2$ X switching blocks distribute the inputs of $TP_v^{u \geq v}$ to the two sub-blocks. The lower $(v/2 - 1)$ X switching blocks distribute the outputs of the two sub-blocks to the outputs of $TP_v^{u \geq v}$ as shown in Fig. 4. At the base of the recursion, if $v = 1$, a S_1^u selection block selects the intended input.

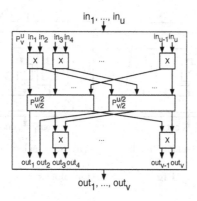

Fig. 4. Recursive construction of a P_v^u permutation block

The $TP_v^{u \geq v}$ block is programmed using a natural generalization of Waksman's recursive programming algorithm. The intended output mapping (μ_i) is expressed as a $u \times v$ truncated permutation matrix. In each recursion step the algorithm splits the $u \times v$ matrix into two $u/2 \times v/2$ truncated permutation matrices implemented by the left and right sub-block and programs the X switching blocks accordingly. In the end of the recursion, if the truncated permutation matrix is a $u \times 1$ matrix with a one in the i-th row, the S_1^u selection block is programmed to select the i-th input value as output: $\sigma_1 = i$. This algorithm can be implemented in $O((u + v) \log v)$ using sparse matrix representations.

The complexity of this construction is $size(TP_v^{u \geq v}) = (u+v) \log v + u - 3v + 2$ and $depth(TP_v^{u \geq v}) = \log u + \log v - 1$.

$EP_{v \geq u}^u$ expanded permutation block. An $EP_{v \geq u}^u$ expanded permutation block permutes the u inputs to a subset of u of the $v \geq u$ outputs. The remaining $v - u$ outputs are allowed to obtain any input value (they are intended to be later discarded and are called *dummy* outputs). Formally, an input mapping $(\mu_i)_{i=1}^u, \mu_i \in \{1, \ldots, v\}, \forall j \neq i : \mu_i \neq \mu_j$ specifies that the i-th input should be mapped to the μ_i-th distinct output. The expanded permutation block computes $EP(in_1, \ldots, in_u) = (out_1, \ldots, out_v)$ where $(out_s = in_r) \leftrightarrow (\mu_r = s), s \in \{1, \ldots, v\}, r \in \{1, \ldots, u\}$.

The construction of the $EP_{v \geq u}^u$ is analogous to the previously described $TP_v^{u \geq v}$ block. At the base of the recursion, if $u = 1$, the single input in_1 is connected to each of the v outputs. The programming algorithm of $EP_{v \geq u}^u$ is analogous to that of $TP_v^{u \geq v}$ as well. The input is a $u \times v$ matrix that corresponds to (μ_i) and it can be implemented in $O((u + v) \log u)$. The construction has complexity $size(EP_{v \geq u}^u) = (u+v) \log u - 2u + 2$ and $depth(EP_{v \geq u}^u) = 2 \log u$.

4.2 Efficient Selection Blocks

We use truncated and expanded permutation blocks of the previous section to build efficient selection blocks S_v^u, used directly in the UC construction.

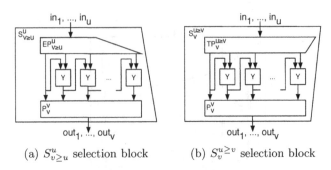

(a) $S^u_{v \geq u}$ selection block   (b) $S^{u \geq v}_v$ selection block

Fig. 5. S^u_v selection blocks

Efficient $S^u_{v \geq u}$ selection block. We obtain the $S^u_{v \geq u}$ selection block from one $EP^u_{v \geq u}$ expanded permutation block, one P^v_v permutation block, and $(v - 1)$ Y switching blocks as shown in Fig. 5(a).

It is not hard to see that the above $S^u_{v \geq u}$ is indeed a selection block, i.e. it can be programmed with any selection mapping $(\sigma_i)^v_{i=1}, \sigma_i \in \{1, \ldots, u\}$. To program $S^u_{v \geq u}$, first count the frequency of occurrence c_j of each input value in the output: $c_j = \#\{\sigma_i : \sigma_i = j; i \in \{1 \ldots v\}\}; j \in \{1 \ldots u\}$. Note, $0 \leq c_j \leq v$ and $\sum^u_{j=1} c_j = v$. The $EP^u_{v \geq u}$ expanded permutation block is programmed to

1) map the needed inputs ($c_j \neq 0$) to its $(\sum^{j-1}_{k=1} c_k)$-th output and
2) map the unused inputs ($c_j = 0$) to an unused (dummy) output.

The $(v - 1)$ Y switching blocks connected to the outputs of $EP^u_{v \geq u}$ duplicate the needed inputs as necessary and feed them to the P^v_v permutation block. They are programmed as follows. If the right input of a Y block is a needed output (produced by Step 1), then the Y block selects it as output. Otherwise, the output of the neighbor Y block is selected. For each j, this construction inputs c_j copies of in_j into the P^v_v permutation block. P^v_v then permutes these values to the corresponding outputs indicated by the selection mapping (σ_i). The complexity of this construction is $size(S^u_{v \geq u}) = (u + v) \log u + 2v \log v - 2u - v + 3$ and $depth(S^u_{v \geq u}) = 2 \log u + 2 \log v + v - 2$.

Efficient $S^{u \geq v}_v$ selection block. An efficient $S^{u \geq v}_v$ selection block can be constructed and programmed analogously, but using a $TP^{u \geq v}_v$ truncated permutation block instead as shown in Fig. 5(b). Its complexity is $size(S^{u \geq v}_v) = (u + 3v) \log v + u - 4v + 3$ and $depth(S^{u \geq v}_v) = \log u + 3 \log v + v - 3$.

Improved S^u_{2u} selection block. In this section, we optimize the $S^u_{v \geq u}$ selection block construction for the case $v = 2u$, most frequently used in our recursive construction of the universal block U_k. We improve by replacing the $EP^u_{v \geq u}$ expanded permutation block in the construction of $S^u_{v \geq u}$ in Fig. 5(a) with a smaller P^u_u permutation block and a different connection of the $(v - 1)$ Y blocks as shown in Fig. 6. Our construction achieves $size(S^u_{2u}) = 6u \log u + 3$ and $depth(S^u_{2u}) = 4 \log u + 2u - 1$.

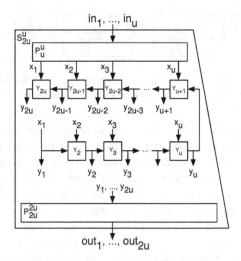

Fig. 6. Improved S_{2u}^u selection block

Lemma 1. *Construction of Fig. 6 is a S_{2u}^u selection block.*

Proof. To prove Lemma 1, we only need to show that the upper permutation block P_u^u together with the layer of Y blocks output the selected values (with the right number of duplicates each) in some order. (The rest, i.e. imposing the desired order, is done by the lower permutation block P_{2u}^{2u}.)

We use the network of Y blocks to duplicate (or omit) inputs as required by the selection block specification. The upper permutation block P_u^u can be programmed to deliver the desired input in_i to any Y-layer input x_j not already used by another input. For example, if input in_i needs to be duplicated c_i times, this can be achieved by programming the permutation to map in_i to x_j, and have blocks Y_j through Y_{j+c_i-1} to output x_j. This way, as required, the value in_i would be duplicated c_i times.

For efficiency reasons, the wiring of the Y-layer is limited. In particular, input x_i is delivered only to blocks Y_i and Y_{2u-i+1}, which are in column i. From there, x_i can be propagated "to the right" from Y_i (i.e. to blocks $Y_{i+1}, ...,$ in the lower row) and/or "to the left" from Y_{2u-i+1} (i.e. to blocks $Y_{2u-i+2}, ...,$ in the upper row). Note, blocks Y_i and Y_{2u-i+1} cannot receive different inputs from P_u^u. They, however, can produce different outputs, since one or both of them could be propagating the value of their neighbouring Y block.

It is not immediately clear that the inputs $in_1...in_u$ can be permuted such that the Y-layer can provide the right number of duplicates for each input. We show, that this in fact can be done. We observe that this permutation and the Y-layer programming can be reduced to the following box-packing problem.

Box-packing. (See Fig. 7 for illustration.) There are u rectangular boxes of sizes $c_1, ..., c_u$, where $c_i \in \{0, ..., 2u\}$ and $\sum_{i=1}^u c_i = 2u$. Each non-empty i-th box consists of a head cell (dark gray), and $c_i - 1$ trailing cells (light gray). There

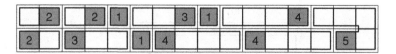

Fig. 7. Valid arrangement of boxes produced by Algorithm 1 for boxes of size $(c_j) = \{2, 3, 1, 4, 4, 5, 4, 1, 3, 1, 2, 2, 0, 0, 0, 0\}$. Dark gray head cells contain size.

is a rectangular $2 \times u$ grid of slots that consists of an upper row and a lower row. A box of size c_i occupies c_i consecutive slots in one row (one exception is that the right-most box might wrap around from the lower to the upper row, as seen on Fig. 7). The boxes in the upper row are oriented with heads to the right, and the boxes in the lower row are oriented with heads to the left. A *collision* occurs when two heads occupy slots in the same column. The arrangement of all u boxes is called *valid*, if it contains no collisions. (Note that a valid arrangement leaves no empty slots.) A solution to the box-packing problem is a valid arrangement.

A procedure for a valid arrangement of the boxes of sizes $c_1, \ldots, c_u$ gives the following natural programming of the P_u^u permutation block and the Y-layer. Associate (1-to-1) each input in_i of size c_i with a box of same size c_i and compute a valid arrangement. Then, input in_i is switched by P_u^u to x_j if the j-th column is occupied by the head of the box associated with in_i. Inputs in_i with $c_i = 0$ (unused inputs) are switched to the columns j which have no head boxes. Both switching blocks Y_i and Y_{2u-i+1} of each column i are programmed as follows. They select input x_i iff the corresponding slot in the valid arrangement is occupied by the head (otherwise, the output of the neighbored Y switching block is selected). It is not hard to see that this programming results in the desired output, given the corresponding valid arrangement of boxes.

Lemma 2 below shows an efficient box-packing procedure. This completes the proof of Lemma 1. □

Algorithm 1. *(Box-packing)*

0. Each box is always put in the leftmost unoccupied slots in the specified row.
1. Sort boxes by size in increasing order.
2. while there is at least one box of size 1, do
   (a) if there are at least two boxes of minimal sizes $s_2 \geq s_1 \geq 2$ left
      i. put the box of size s_1 in the upper row
      ii. put remaining (but no more than s_1-2) boxes of size 1 in lower row
      iii. put the box of size s_2 in the lower row (possibly wrap around)
      iv. put remaining (but no more than s_2-2) boxes of size 1 in upper row
   (b) else // there is only one box of size $s_1 \geq 2$ left
      i. put the remaining boxes of size 1 in the lower row
      ii. put the box of size $s_1 \geq 2$ in the lower row and wrap around
3. while there is at least one box of minimal size $s_3 \geq 2$ left, do
   (a) if there is another box of minimal size $s_4 \geq s_3 \geq 2$ left
      i. put the box of size s_3 in the upper row
      ii. put the box of size s_4 in the lower row (possibly wrap around)

(b) else // there is only one box of size $s_3 \geq 2$ left
  i. put the box of size $s_3 \geq 2$ in the lower row and wrap around

Lemma 2. *Algorithm 1 efficiently produces a valid arrangement for any given set of u boxes of sizes $c_1, \ldots, c_u; 0 \leq c_j \leq 2u; \sum_{j=1}^{u} c_j = 2u$.*

Proof. Note, since $\sum c_j = 2u$, for each box of size $2 + i$, there must be i boxes of size 1, or $i/2$ boxes of size 0, or a corresponding combination.

A) Algorithm 1 always puts all boxes and *terminates*. We first show that Step 2 eliminates all boxes of size 1. Indeed, suppose the contrary, a block of size 1 remains. Then, in each previous execution of Step 2a, we eliminated blocks of sizes $s_2 \geq s_1 \geq 2$ and $s_1 + s_2 - 4$ blocks of size 1, and in Step 2b we eliminated a block of size s_1 and $s_1 - 2$ blocks of size 1. Since $\sum c_j = 2u$, there could not have been more blocks of size 1 than we eliminated, and we arrive at contradiction. Further, Step 3 eliminates all remaining boxes of size ≥ 2. In each iteration, at least one box of size $s_3 \geq 2$ is eliminated either in Step 3(a)i or Step 3(b)i, until all boxes of size ≥ 2 are eliminated. (Observe, at each iteration, upper row "grows" not more than the lower. Thus, Algorithm's actions are always legal.)

B) Algorithm 1 produces a *valid* arrangement. We need to show that no step of Algorithm 1 causes a collision. It is easy to see that Step 2a and Step 2b never cause a collision. Further, once Step 2 has finished, the number of occupied slots in the upper row ω_{up} is less or equal to the number of occupied slots in the lower row ω_{down}, with $0 \leq \omega_{down} - \omega_{up} \leq s_2 - 2$ (here s_2 is the size of the most recently put block in Step 2(a)iv). Since the boxes are processed in increasing order, in Step 3, $s_3 \geq s_2 \geq 2$. If the box of size s_3 is the last remaining one, it is put in the lower row in Step 3(b)i and, as is easy to see, doesn't cause a collision. Otherwise, in Step 3(a)i, the box of size s_3 is put in the upper row. The number of occupied slots in the upper row is now $\omega'_{up} = \omega_{up} + s_3$, and the upper row has at least two more occupied slots than the lower row: $\omega'_{up} - \omega_{down} = (\omega_{up} + s_3) - \omega_{down} \geq 2$. This implies that the next Step 3(a)ii doesn't cause a collision when putting the box of length $s_4 \geq s_3$ into the lower row. After Step 3(a)ii, the number of occupied slots in the lower row is $\omega'_{down} = \omega_{down} + s_4$. In the end of the current iteration of Step 3, the number of occupied slots in the upper row is again less or equal to the number of occupied slots in the lower row: $\omega'_{down} - \omega'_{up} = (\omega_{down} + s_4) - (\omega_{up} + s_3) = (\omega_{down} - \omega_{up}) + (s_4 - s_3) \geq 0$ and hence the length relationship between the upper and lower rows ($0 \leq \omega'_{down} - \omega'_{up} \leq s_4 - 2$) is the invariant of Step 3. Therefore, no iteration of Step 3 causes a collision. As no step causes a collision, Algorithm 1 produces a valid arrangement.

C) Algorithm 1 is *efficient*. Sorting of the u boxes in Step 1 costs $O(u \log u)$. Steps 2 and 3 have a runtime of $O(u)$, as in every iteration at least one box is eliminated. Hence the runtime of Algorithm 1 is in $O(u \log u)$.   □

4.3   Optimization of the Universal Circuit Construction

As the order of the two inputs of a gate simulation block G can be swapped by swapping its function table, we can omit the last row of X blocks in the lower

P_k^k permutation block of the $S_k^{k/2}$ selection block in the construction of U_k (see Fig. 3(a), Fig. 6 and Fig. 4) and adapt the programming correspondingly. This results in a reduction of $\Delta size(U_k) = k \log k - 2k + 2$ and $\Delta depth(U_k) = k - 1$.

5   Comparison and Conclusion

We now compare our UC solution to the best previously known Valiant's UC [16]. Recall, we consider circuits $UC_{u,v,k}$, universal for circuits of k gates, u inputs and v outputs. Valiant's UC has $size(UC_{u,v,k}^{Valiant}) = (19k+9.5u+9.5v) \log k+O(k)$ and ours has $size(UC_{u,v,k}) = 1.5k \log^2 k + 2.5k \log k + (u+2k) \log u + (k+3v) \log v + O(k)$. To help visualize the relationship, Table 1 shows sample relative sizes of our UC compared to Valiant's: $size_{rel} = \frac{size(UC_{u,v,k})}{size(UC_{u,v,k}^{Valiant})}$. The break-even point $k_{eq} = k|_{size_{rel}=1}$ is the maximum size of circuits for which our UC is smaller.

Table 1. Comparison between our and Valiant's UC construction [16]

circuit inputs and outputs		break-even	relative size $size_{rel}$		
u	v	point k_{eq}	$k = 1,000$	$k = 5,000$	$k = 10,000$
few	$o(k)$	$o(k)$	2,048	91.8%	110.2%	118.1%
	$0.5k$	$0.1k$	5,000	86.0%	100.1%	106.2%
	$0.5k$	$0.25k$	8,000	83.1%	96.4%	102.1%
	$1k$	$0.5k$	117,000	69.0%	79.5%	84.0%
many	$2k$	$1k$	26,663,000	53.6%	60.9%	64.1%

While Valiant's construction is asymptotically better, our UC is up to 50% smaller for small circuits, due to much lower constant factors. For PF-SFE, small circuits are of most interest, since only they can be evaluated efficiently today (indeed, UC for 5000-gate circuits has size $\approx 10^6$). In addition, our construction is more detailed and seems to be much easier to implement than Valiant's. Thus, we think that our UC construction is a good fit for *practical* PF-SFE. In support of this, we have successfully implemented FairplayPF [8], an extension of the Fairplay SFE system [11] for general PF-SFE based on our UC construction.

Acknowledgements. We thank reviewers of FC'08 for helpful comments.

References

1. Blake, I.F., Kolesnikov, V.: Conditional encrypted mapping and comparing encrypted numbers. In: Di Crescenzo, G., Rubin, A. (eds.) FC 2006. LNCS, vol. 4107, pp. 206–220. Springer, Heidelberg (2006)
2. Cachin, C., Camenisch, J., Kilian, J., Müller, J.: One-round secure computation and secure autonomous mobile agents. In: Welzl, E., Montanari, U., Rolim, J.D.P. (eds.) ICALP 2000. LNCS, vol. 1853, pp. 512–523. Springer, Heidelberg (2000)

3. Di Crescenzo, G.: Private Selective Payment Protocols. In: Frankel, Y. (ed.) FC 2000. LNCS, vol. 1962. Springer, Heidelberg (2001)
4. Even, S., Goldreich, O., Lempel, A.: A randomized protocol for signing contracts. Commun. ACM 28(6), 637–647 (1985)
5. Fischlin, M.: A cost-effective pay-per-multiplication comparison method for millionaires. In: Naccache, D. (ed.) CT-RSA 2001. LNCS, vol. 2020, pp. 457–471. Springer, Heidelberg (2001)
6. Frikken, K., Atallah, M., Zhang, C.: Privacy-preserving credit checking. In: EC 2005: Proceedings of the 6th ACM conference on Electronic commerce, pp. 147–154. ACM Press, New York (2005)
7. Kantarcioglu, M., Clifton, C.: Privacy-preserving distributed mining of association rules on horizontally partitioned data. In: ACM SIGMOD Workshop on Research Issues on Data Mining and Knowledge Discovery (DMKD 2002) (2002)
8. Kolesnikov, V., Schneider, T.: FairplayPF, http://thomaschneider.de/FairplayPF
9. Lindell, Y., Pinkas, B.: Privacy preserving data mining. In: Bellare, M. (ed.) CRYPTO 2000. LNCS, vol. 1880, pp. 20–24. Springer, Heidelberg (2000)
10. Lindell, Y., Pinkas, B.: A proof of Yao's protocol for secure two-party computation. Cryptology ePrint Archive, Report 2004/175 (2004)
11. Malkhi, D., Nisan, N., Pinkas, B., Sella, Y.: Fairplay — a secure two-party computation system. In: USENIX (2004)
12. Naor, M., Pinkas, B., Sumner, R.: Privacy preserving auctions and mechanism design. In: 1st ACM Conf. on Electronic Commerce (1999)
13. Ostrovsky, R., Skeith III, W.E.: Private Searching on Streaming Data. In: Shoup, V. (ed.) CRYPTO 2005. LNCS, vol. 3621, pp. 223–240. Springer, Heidelberg (2005)
14. Pinkas, B.: Cryptographic techniques for privacy-preserving data mining. SIGKDD Explor. Newsl. 4(2), 12–19 (2002)
15. Sander, T., Young, A., Yung, M.: Non-interactive cryptocomputing for NC^1. In: Proc. 40th IEEE Symp. on Foundations of Comp. Science, New York, pp. 554–566. IEEE, Los Alamitos (1999)
16. Valiant, L.G.: Universal circuits (preliminary report). In: Proc. 8th ACM Symp. on Theory of Computing, pp. 196–203. ACM Press, New York (1976)
17. Waksman, A.: A permutation network. J. ACM 15(1), 159–163 (1968)
18. Yao, A.C.: Protocols for secure computations. In: Proc. 23rd IEEE Symp. on Foundations of Comp. Science, Chicago, pp. 160–164. IEEE, Los Alamitos (1982)
19. Yao, A.C.: How to generate and exchange secrets. In: Proc. 27th IEEE Symp. on Foundations of Comp. Science, Toronto, pp. 162–167. IEEE, Los Alamitos (1986)

Generalized Non-Interactive Oblivious Transfer Using Count-Limited Objects with Applications to Secure Mobile Agents*

Vandana Gunupudi[1] and Stephen R. Tate[2]

[1] Dept. of Computer Science and Engineering, University of North Texas, Denton, TX 76203
vgunupudi@gmail.com
[2] Dept. of Computer Science, University of North Carolina at Greensboro, Greensboro, NC 27402
srtate@uncg.edu

Abstract. Oblivious transfer (OT) is a fundamental primitive used in many cryptographic protocols, including general secure function evaluation (SFE) protocols. However, interaction is a primary feature of any OT protocol. In this paper, we show how to remove the interaction requirement in an OT protocol when parties participating in the protocol have access to slightly modified Trusted Platform Modules, as defined by Sarmenta *et al.* in proposing the notion of count-limited objects (clobs) [8]. Specifically, we construct a new cryptographic primitive called "generalized non-interactive oblivious transfer"(GNIOT). While it is possible to perform GNIOT using clobs in a straightforward manner, with multiple clobs, we show how to perform this *efficiently*, by using a single clob regardless of the number of values that need to be exchanged in an oblivious manner. Additionally, we provide clear definitions and a formal proof of the security of our construction. We apply this primitive to mobile agent applications and outline a new secure agent protocol called the GTX protocol which provides the same security guarantees as existing agent protocols while removing the need for interaction, thus improving efficiency.

1 Introduction

Oblivious Transfer (OT) was introduced by Rabin [7] as a fundamental cryptographic primitive, and subsequently many variants have been studied and used in a variety of cryptographic protocols such as secure multi-party computation. In a 1-out-of-2 OT protocol, Alice (the sender) has 2 values s_0 and s_1, and Bob (the receiver) has a selection bit c. At the end of the protocol, Bob learns the

---

* This work is supported by the National Science Foundation under grants CNS-0627754, CNS-0516807, CNS-061987 and CNS-0551694 . Any opinions, findings, conclusions or recommendations expressed in this material are those of the author(s) and do not necessarily reflect the views of the National Science Foundation.

G. Tsudik (Ed.): FC 2008, LNCS 5143, pp. 98–112, 2008.

value s_c while obtaining no information about s_{1-c}, and Alice cannot determine which value Bob received. While in some OT variants the selection bit c is random, in this paper we only consider variants in which Bob selects the value c. We call an OT protocol *interactive* if Bob must communicate with Alice or some other party after selecting c, and *non-interactive* otherwise.

In the standard model of computation, non-interactive OT is clearly impossible: Bob can take a "snapshot" of his state immediately before picking a value of c, and then run his computation with $c = 0$ to learn s_0. Since this computation was non-interactive, no state external to Bob is affected, so Bob can roll back his state to the snapshot and re-run his computation with $c = 1$, thus learning s_1 as well.

In this paper we consider a slightly augmented model of computation, reflecting changes happening in real systems with "Trusted Computing" technologies, and show that interactive OT is possible in such a model. We consider how to efficiently accomplish an expanded and generalized form of non-interactive oblivious transfer in such a model, define sensible security properties which we prove hold in our protocols, and explore how this non-interactive oblivious transfer can be used to improve the efficiency of secure function evaluation and secure mobile agent protocols.

Trusted Computing is an initiative of the Trusted Computing Group [12], an industry consortium of over 160 companies, to strengthen security in computing platforms through the use of trusted hardware. Key to Trusted Computing are devices, called Trusted Platform Modules (TPMs) [13], which are already appearing in many desktop PCs and laptops. Various researchers have begun to explore the capabilities of systems that use these hardware modules, utilizing their unique functionality for various real-world applications. Recent work at MIT by Sarmenta *et al.* [8] has introduced the idea of a *virtual monotonic counter* which can be used as a building block for various applications like digital cash, e-wallets, virtual trusted storage and digital rights management (DRM). A virtual monotonic counter is a trusted counter that can be incremented but not reset back to any previous value, thus removing the ability to roll the system back to a previous state as described above. This security property is enforced by the TPM alone and does not require a trusted OS for this purpose — in fact, the required capabilities can be provided by other system augmentations, including smartcards or other crypto processors that control key usage. In addition to having interesting applications, virtual monotonic counters allow us to realize *count-limited objects* or *clobs* which are tied to a particular virtual monotonic counter. Examples of these include *n-time use* decryption or signature keys. The use of each key is tied to a counter which enforces the condition that the key is not used more than n times.

In this paper, we show how to use count-limited objects to implement a useful generalized form of non-interactive oblivious transfer. This new primitive, which we call "Generalized Non-interactive Oblivious Transfer" (GNIOT), is a way of performing a collection of general (k-out-of-n) independent oblivious transfers with a single request. In Section 3 we present a formal definition with the desired security properties, along with our implementation and a security proof. GNIOT can be accomplished in an obvious and inefficient way by using a distinct clob for each value to be transferred, but this requires a significant number of expensive key generation steps (one RSA key generation per clob). In this paper, we show how to accomplish this in an *efficient* manner — by using a *single* clob, regardless of the number of values to be transmitted. As an example application of GNIOT, we show how this primitive can be directly applied to mobile agent computation, where strong security is often enforced by *interactive* oblivious transfer in various agent protocols. Removing the interaction from these agent protocols removes a significant bottleneck to their efficiency and practicality.

In summary, our contributions include

- Definition of a new primitive called "Generalized Non-interactive Oblivious Transfer", which is impossible to implement in standard computation models, but is possible in a realistically augmented model based on Trusted Computing technologies;
- An implementation of GNIOT which has significantly improved efficiency over the straightforward implementation;
- Careful security analysis and rigorous proofs of our implementation; and
- Use of the GNIOT primitive to create a new *non-interactive*, secure agent protocol called the *GTX* protocol.

2   Definitions and Preliminaries

In this section, we briefly present background information on the building blocks of GNIOT, namely, oblivious transfer and count-limited objects.

2.1   Virtual Monotonic Counters and Count-Limited Objects

Sarmenta *et al.* [8] outline how to create a potentially unlimited number of virtual monotonic counters from a physical monotonic counter or from other potential capabilities of TPMs. While this requires some changes in TPMs, the additional requirements are quite modest, as outlined in this section. They model a virtual monotonic counter as a mechanism that stores a value and provides 2 commands to access this value: a Read command that returns the current value of the counter, and an Increment command that increments the value of the counter and returns the updated value of the counter. A virtual monotonic counter must be *non-volatile*, i.e., the value of the counter must not change unless incremented in response to a command. It must also be *irreversible*, namely, it must be infeasible for any adversary (including the owner) to reset the counter to any previous value. Finally, the virtual counter must produce verifiable output. This is accomplished by using *unforgeable* execution certificates. First, the counter produces a verifiable output message in response to the Read or Increment commands. This output is then typically signed using an Attestation Identity Key (AIK)[1] and random nonces are used to prevent replay attacks.

---

[1] An AIK is a special type of signature key created on a TPM. The private portion of this key is non-migratable.

Building from these virtual counters, Sarmenta *et al.* have proposed count-limited objects, or clobs, as an interesting and important primitive. These are proposed objects that utilize the ability of a TPM to encrypt data or keys into "blobs" such that they can only be decrypted when the TPM is in a specified state, which in current TPMs is limited to conditions based on the PCRs. In Sarmenta's construction, these encrypted blobs are then linked to a virtual monotonic counter which is used to track/limit the usage of the blob. They also proposed an efficient hash-tree based scheme that allows the TPM to keep track of a large number of virtual monotonic counters, thereby enabling various count-limited objects, each having its own dedicated virtual monotonic counter. While this scheme requires a new command to be added to the TPM, the computations required are relatively simple and could easily be implemented on the microcontrollers that current TPMs are being built from.

2.2   Non-Interactive Oblivious Transfer

In this section we outline new ideas on how count-limited objects can be used to implement a non-interactive version of standard *oblivious transfer*. In an oblivious transfer protocol, two parties can exchange information without learning anything about each other's inputs.

1-out-of-2 Oblivious Transfer (OT): In the standard 1-out-of-2 OT, when Alice transmits one of s_0 or s_1 to Bob in an oblivious manner, interaction between Alice and Bob is typically required. In a common solution, Bob needs to supply Alice with keys to encrypt her strings and this is done only after he decides which value he requires. Therefore, Alice cannot encrypt the strings unless Bob sends her the keys, which he cannot do until he decides which string he wants. Using count-limited objects, Bob can compute keys before making a decision of which s_c he wants, and his later use of that key is restricted by the count-limited property.

   We point out that Bellare and Micali [3] have previously introduced a related but different notion of non-interactive oblivious transfer, but in their case Bob receives a randomly selected s_c (he doesn't get to choose which one). This is useful in some applications, but not in the Secure Function Evaluation problems that we are interested in, such as secure mobile agents.

Non-interactive OT using a count-limited decryption key: Alice has 2 values s_0 and s_1. Bob has a TPM and generates a one-time use non-migratable key pair, K_p, K_s and publishes the public key K_p, which is certified using an AIK I_b, which in turn is certified by a Privacy CA. This one-time use key pair is tied to a virtual monotonic counter which limits the private key K_s to being used no more than once. Alice encrypts both values s_0 and s_1 using K_p, having verified that the key is indeed Bob's via the accompanying certificate. At some later time, after receiving the ciphertexts, Bob can decide which value he wants. Then Bob decrypts only that value using K_s, being restricted to do so by the virtual monotonic counter, which is incremented as soon as one of the values is decrypted.

This clearly solves the non-interactive OT problem, but in applications which use multiple oblivious transfers, a separate key must be generated for each OT, which is very inefficient. In the following section, we will show how a *single* clob can control multiple oblivious transfers.

3   Generalized Non-Interactive Oblivious Transfer

We generalize the 1-out-of-2 OT concept to a form where multiple independent oblivious transfers (of the general k-out-of-n type) are defined as part of a single operation. In many applications (such as secure function evaluation) multiple instances of OT must be run, so by defining this as a single operation we have the flexibility of creating solutions which can exploit improvements possible by aggregating multiple requests. We call this combined operation *"generalized non-interactive oblivious transfer* (GNIOT)," which we formally define in the following section.

3.1   Problem Definition

We first define Generalized Oblivious Transfer (GOT), and we will subsequently define phases which will force this to be non-interactive, producing GNIOT.

Definition 1 (GOT). *Define λ as the security parameter and l_d as the length of the data items being sent by Alice to Bob. Assume that Alice has n data sets $S_1, S_2, \cdots, S_n$, with values $x_{i,j} \in \{0,1\}^{l_d}$ for $i \in \{1, 2, \cdots, n\}$ and $j \in \{1, 2, \cdots, m_i\}$, and parameters $k_1, k_2, \ldots, k_n$, where $1 \le k_i \le m_i$. At the end of the GOT execution, Bob will have either no result (represented by $\perp$) or a set of exactly k_i values of his choice from each set S_i, for $i \in \{1, 2, \cdots, n\}$.*

We will need to refer to sets of indices into the data set, so define index set $\mathcal{I}$ to be a set of indices (i, j), and define $\mathcal{I}(i) = \{j \mid (i, j) \in \mathcal{I}\}$. With respect to the parameters provided in an instance of GOT, we say that index set $\mathcal{I}$ is *well-formed* if $|\mathcal{I}(i)| = k_i$ for all $i \in \{1, \ldots, n\}$.

We define GNIOT as a set of operations which perform GOT, but accomplish this task without requiring any interaction between the receiver and another party after the receiver decides which values he wants. For maximum flexibility, allowing either batched or individual decryptions, we define the decryption operation as a stateful process which is called repeatedly — only at the very end are we required to have the actual plaintext values.

Definition 2 (GNIOT). *Generalized Non-Interactive Oblivious Transfer consists of the following phases, which provide a solution to the GOT problem.*

Setup Phase. *This phase involves key generation. Given security parameter λ, the key generation algorithm returns*

$$(\mathcal{K}_p, \mathcal{K}_s) \leftarrow Setup(1^\lambda)$$

where $\mathcal{K}_p$ is the public key information, and $\mathcal{K}_s$ is the secret key information.

Transmit Phase. *This phase transforms the set of values $x_{i,j} \in \{0,1\}^{l_d}$ for $i \in \{1,2,\cdots,n\}$ and $j \in \{1,2,\cdots,m_i\}$ into a data blob which can be transmitted to the receiver. Specifically,*

$$C \leftarrow Transmit_{\mathcal{K}_p} \begin{pmatrix} \langle k_1, x_{1,1}, x_{1,2}, \cdots, x_{1,m_1} \rangle, \\ \langle k_2, x_{2,1}, x_{2,2}, \cdots, x_{2,m_2} \rangle, \\ \vdots \\ \langle k_n, x_{n,1}, x_{n,2}, \cdots, x_{n,m_n} \rangle \end{pmatrix}.$$

Decrypt Phase. *In this phase, the receiver gives the indices (i,j) of the $x_{i,j}$ values that he wishes to receive. The state-based process begins by calculating the initial state $\mathcal{S}_0 \leftarrow InitialState(C)$, and then evolving the state and providing answers to queries as*

$$(t_k, \mathcal{S}_k) \leftarrow Decrypt_{\mathcal{K}_s}(\mathcal{S}_{k-1}, C, i_k, j_k),$$

for $k = 1, 2, \ldots, q$ for some number of queries q. We require that index information be embedded in t_k such that there is a function "ind" that extracts this information as

$$(i_k, j_k) \leftarrow ind(t_k).$$

PostProcess Phase. *This phase takes the results of the Decrypt calls and either fails (giving $\perp$ as the result) or produces q plaintext values as*

$$\langle v_1, v_2, \ldots, v_q \rangle \leftarrow PostProcess(t_1, t_2, \cdots, t_q)$$

3.2 Desired Security Properties

A secure GNIOT scheme must satisfy the following properties:

Correctness. If the Alice and Bob follow the above steps in the prescribed way, and the index set defined by $\mathcal{I} = \{(i,j) \mid ind(t_k) \text{ for } 1 \leq k \leq q\}$ is well-formed, then the values produced by *PostProcess* are exactly the requested plaintext values such that $v_k = x_{ind(t_k)}$ for $k = 1, \ldots, q$.

Sender's Privacy. Bob should not be able to obtain any information about the remaining $m_i - k_i$ elements in each set S_i.

Receiver's Privacy. Alice should not be able to determine which k_i values Bob received from each set.

In a non-interactive process, where there is no communication with the sender in the *Decrypt* or *PostProcess* phases, the Receiver's Privacy property is trivially met. For the Sender's privacy, we define a game played between a probabilistic, polynomial time (PPT) adversary $\mathcal{A}$ and an oracle, where the oracle runs the parts of the parts of the protocol associated with the Sender.

1. The adversary supplies a plaintext input to the GNIOT scheme where each
   input has two different possibilities:

$$\langle (x_{1,1}^0, x_{1,1}^1), (x_{1,2}^0, x_{1,2}^1) \cdots, (x_{1,m_1}^0, x_{1,m_1}^1) \rangle$$
$$\langle (x_{2,1}^0, x_{2,1}^1), (x_{2,2}^0, x_{2,2}^1) \cdots, (x_{2,m_2}^0, x_{2,m_2}^1) \rangle$$
$$\vdots$$
$$\langle (x_{n,1}^0, x_{n,1}^1), (x_{n,2}^0, x_{n,2}^1) \cdots, (x_{n,m_n}^0, x_{n,m_n}^1) \rangle$$

2. The oracle generates an independent random bit $r_{i,j} \in_R \{0,1\}$ for each
   pair. The oracle then creates a single GNIOT input by using inputs $x_{i,j}^{r_{i,j}}$
   for $i = 1, 2, \cdots, n$ and $j = 1, 2, \cdots, m_i$ and calls the *Transmit* function. The
   resulting C is sent back to the adversary.
3. (a) $\mathcal{A}$ makes a series of calls to *Decrypt*, receiving values $t_1, t_2, \ldots, t_q$.
   (b) The adversary is free to perform any computation using the information
       it obtained, possibly calling the *PostProcess* function of the GNIOT
       scheme.
   (c) The adversary finally outputs a guess g and an index (a, b).

The adversary wins this game if $g = r_{a,b}$, but we are only interested in when the
adversary wins to learn a value that it shouldn't. Therefore, if $\mathcal{I}$ is the index set
for the queries made in Step 3a, we define the "advantage" for adversary $\mathcal{A}$ as

$$Adv_{GNIOT,\mathcal{A}} = \left| Pr[g = r_{a,b} | (a, b) \notin \mathcal{I} \text{ or } \mathcal{I} \text{ not well-formed}] - \frac{1}{2} \right|.$$

The security of a GNIOT scheme is defined as the advantage of the best adversary,

$$Adv_{GNIOT} = \max_{\mathcal{A}}(Adv_{GNIOT,\mathcal{A}}),$$

and the scheme satisfies the Sender Privacy property if Adv_{GNIOT} is negligible.

3.3   TPM-Based Solution

Our TPM-based solution makes use of both a standard symmetric cipher and
a public key cryptosystem in which use of the private key is count-limited by
the TPM. Based on previously defined parameters λ and l_d we define several
additional parameters for our solution, as given below.

- l_b (Encrypted Data Length): Length of the data after encryption with the
  symmetric cipher.
- l_s (Symmetric Key Length): Length of the key for the symmetric cipher.
  Must be polynomial in λ.
- l_p (Public Key Payload Size): Length of data that can be encrypted with the
  public key scheme. Must be polynomial in λ, and must satisfy $l_p \geq l_b + l_s$.

The basic idea behind our GNIOT scheme is to doubly encrypt the values $x_{i,j}$
with the symmetric scheme and the public key scheme so that the count-limit
restriction ensures that not too many values are decrypted, and a secret sharing
scheme is used to make sure that at least k_i are decrypted from each set to allow

recovery of the symmetric key for the final plaintext decryption. As a result, exactly k_i values from each set must be decrypted. Our formal definition follows the phases defined in Section 3.1.

Setup Phase. Bob creates an N-time use count limited key pair [8] (K_p, K_s), where $N = (k_1 + k_2 + \cdots + k_n)$. For further assurance in subsequent key transfer, Bob can certify K_p using an Attestation Identity Key (AIK).

Transmit Phase. The plaintext values $x_{i,j}$ provided to the *Transmit* function will be first protected using a symmetric cipher (such as AES), using a session key R that is generated by selecting n partial keys $R_i \in_R \{0,1\}^{l_s}$ and letting $R = R_1 \oplus R_2 \oplus \cdots \oplus R_n$. Next, for each i we compute m_i shares of each R_i using a threshold-k_i secret sharing scheme, such as the polynomial interpolation based scheme due to Shamir [9], and we denote the shares of R_i by $f_i(j)$, for $j = 1, \ldots, m_i$. By using threshold k_i in the secret sharing scheme, we will be able to compute R_i given any k_i of the $f_i(j)$ values. Using $\mathcal{PKE}_{K_p}$ and $\mathcal{SKE}_R$ to denote the public key and symmetric encryption schemes with keys K_p and R, respectively, we doubly encrypt each $x_{i,j}$ along with a share of R_i to give

$$C_{i,j} = \mathcal{PKE}_{K_p}(\langle \mathcal{SKE}_R(x_{i,j}), f_i(j) \rangle). \tag{1}$$

The collection of ciphertexts $C_{i,j}$, for $i \in \{1, 2, \cdots, n\}$ and $j \in \{1, 2, \cdots, m_i\}$, is then the output of the *Transmit* function.

Decrypt Phase. The only state used in our implementation is in the virtual monotonic counter maintained by the TPM, so all state operations are implicit in the use of count-limited keys. $Decrypt_{K_s}(\mathcal{S}_{k-1}, C, i_k, j_k)$ then just uses $\mathcal{K}_s$ to decrypt C_{i_k, j_k}, and bundles the resulting values with the index (i_k, j_k) to give

$$t_k = \langle i_k, j_k, \mathcal{SKE}_R(x_{i_k, j_k}), f_{i_k}(j_k) \rangle.$$

PostProcess Phase. For the final *PostProcess* stage, let $\mathcal{I} = \{(i_k, j_k) | 1 \leq k \leq q\}$ be the index set of requests made in the Decrypt phase. Then Bob extracts the shares $f_{i_k}(j_k)$ from each t_k, and for each $i \in \{1, \ldots, n\}$ combines the shares corresponding to $\mathcal{I}(i)$ to recover each R_i. These values are then exclusive-ORed together to recover the symmetric key R, which is used to decrypt the plaintexts x_{i_k, j_k}.

3.4   Security Analysis

In this section, we formally prove that our scheme has the required security properties. We use standard security definitions of public key encryption and symmetric key encryption schemes (for example, see [1]).

Theorem 1. *If PKE is an IND-CCA2 secure public key scheme and SKE is a IND-CCA2 secure symmetric cipher, then a probabilistic, polynomial time adversary $\mathcal{A}$ can win the GNIOT game with non-negligible probability if and only if $\mathcal{I}$ is a well-formed index set and $(a, b) \in \mathcal{I}$.*

Proof

Case 0. $(a, b) \in \mathcal{I}$, and $\mathcal{I}$ is a well-formed index set.

It is easy to see that the PPT adversary $\mathcal{A}$ wins in this case: If $\mathcal{I}$ is a well-formed index set, $\mathcal{A}$ can obtain exactly k_i values from set S_i, by calling the decrypt function, which returns $t_{i,j}$ values as the decryption of the corresponding $C_{i,j}$ values in each set. If $(a, b) \in \mathcal{I}$, then $\mathcal{A}$ can call the PostProcess function to correctly obtain corresponding value $x_{a,b}$.

Case 1. $(a, b) \notin \mathcal{I}$, where $\mathcal{I}$ is a well-formed index set.

Let $\mathcal{A}$ be a PPT adversary that wins the GNIOT game with non-negligible probability, i.e. $\mathcal{A}$ distinguishes between the encryptions of $x_{i,j}^0$ and $x_{i,j}^1$ with non-negligible probability. We can use $\mathcal{A}$ to construct a PPT adversary $\mathcal{A}'$ that attacks the CCA security of the PKE as follows: $\mathcal{A}'$ obtains pk from the PKE oracle which it passes along to $\mathcal{A}$, and then receives the values $x_{i,j}^b$ from $\mathcal{A}$, where $i \in \{1, \ldots, n\}$, $j \in \{1, \ldots, m_i\}$, and $b \in \{0, 1\}$. $\mathcal{A}'$ picks values $R_1, \ldots, R_n$ and computes R and the shares $f_i(j)$ of each R_i as in the GNIOT.Transmit phase, and selects an index (a, b) at random. For each $(i, j) \neq (a, b)$, $\mathcal{A}'$ picks $r_{i,j}$ at random and computes $C_{i,j}$ according to (1). For index (a, b), $\mathcal{A}'$ submits $\langle \mathcal{SKE}_R(x_{a,b}^0), f_i(j) \rangle$ and $\langle \mathcal{SKE}_R(x_{a,b}^1), f_i(j) \rangle$ to the PKE oracle, which returns the encryption of one of these values, which $\mathcal{A}'$ uses for $C_{a,b}$. $\mathcal{A}'$ the sends all of the $C_{i,j}$ values to $\mathcal{A}$ as the output of GNIOT.Transmit.

In the next stage of the GNIOT game, $\mathcal{A}$ requests the decryption of values $C_{i,j}$, and as long as $(i, j) \neq (a, b)$, $\mathcal{A}'$ can answer these directly by providing $x_{i,j}^{r_{i,j}}$. If $\mathcal{A}$ requests the decryption of $C_{a,b}$, then $\mathcal{A}'$ outputs $\perp$, and quits the game. After q queries $\mathcal{A}$ outputs an index (a', b') and a guess g. If $(a', b') = (a, b)$ then $\mathcal{A}'$ outputs g as its own guess in the PKE game, and if $(a', b') \neq (a, b)$, $\mathcal{A}'$ outputs $\perp$ and quits the game.

For $\mathcal{A}'$ to win this game, $\mathcal{A}'$'s randomly chosen index (a, b) must be the same as $\mathcal{A}$'s selected index (a', b') (which occurs with probability $1/N$) and $\mathcal{A}$ must win the GNIOT game. Therefore

$$Pr[\mathcal{A} \; wins] = \frac{1}{N} Pr[\mathcal{A}' \; wins],$$

and so $Pr[\mathcal{A}' \; wins] = N \cdot Pr[\mathcal{A} \; wins] \leq N \cdot Adv_{PKE}$. Since PKE is an IND-CCA2 secure public key scheme, Adv_{PKE} is negligible, and therefore the probability that $\mathcal{A}$ wins the GNIOT game is also negligible (as required for this case).

Case 2. $(a, b) \in \mathcal{I}$ but $\mathcal{I}$ is *not* a well-formed index set.

Let $\mathcal{A}$ be a probabilistic, polynomial time (PPT) adversary that plays the GNIOT game and attacks the TPM-based scheme. The intuition behind this case is that in order for $\mathcal{A}$ to win the GNIOT game in this case, it must either break the SKE scheme to decrypt $\mathcal{SKE}_R(x_{a,b})$ without knowing R, or must break the PKE scheme to gain additional information about R.

Define game $\mathcal{G}_1$ as the GNIOT game as defined in definition 3, i.e., $\mathcal{A}$ tries to distinguish between the encryptions of $x_{i,j}^0$ and $x_{i,j}^1$ for some (i, j). Now let us define a modified game $\mathcal{G}_2$, where instead of using the real symmetric key R, the transmit oracle (in part 3 of the GNIOT game) uses a different, independent, random key, $\tilde{R}$, to encrypt the values in each set. Let T_1 be the event that $\mathcal{A}$ wins in game $\mathcal{G}_1$ and T_2 be the event that $\mathcal{A}$ wins in game $\mathcal{G}_2$.

We can use $\mathcal{A}$ to construct a PPT adversary $\mathcal{A}'$ that attacks the CCA security of the PKE scheme. In particular, since $\mathcal{I}$ is not well-formed, there must be some set i such that $|\mathcal{I}(i)| < k_i$, so R_i and hence R is independent of the decrypted shares of R_i. Therefore, unless $\mathcal{A}$ can get some information from the non-decrypted $C_{i,j}$ values it gets no information about R and so must break the SKE scheme.

$\mathcal{A}'$ gets public key K_p from the PKE game. $\mathcal{A}'$ picks random key R and computes all R_i values and shares $f_i(j)$. Next, $\mathcal{A}'$ picks a random index (a', b'), and for all $(i, j) \neq (a, b)$ computes $C_{i,j}$ for random selection $r_{i,j}$ exactly as our GNIOT algorithm. For index (a', b'), $\mathcal{A}'$ substitutes a random share $\tilde{f}_{a'}(b')$ in place of the real $f_{a'}(b')$ for one alternative:

$$P^0_{a',b'} = \langle \mathcal{SKE}_R(x^0_{a',b'}), f_{a'}(b') \rangle \qquad P^1_{a',b'} = \langle \mathcal{SKE}_R(x^1_{a',b'}), \tilde{f}_{a'}(b') \rangle .$$

These two plaintexts are then passed along to the PKE game as the challenge plaintexts, and we receive a ciphertext $C_{a',b'}$ back, which is the encryption of one of these. Note that if $P^0_{a',b'}$ is chosen, the key used is the correct key constructed from the share $f_{a'}(b')$, so we're perfectly simulating the GNIOT game (game $\mathcal{G}_1$). On the other hand, if $P^1_{a',b'}$ is chosen then the fake share $\tilde{f}_{a'}(b')$ makes the symmetric key R independent of the key reconstructed from the shares, and so we're perfectly simulating game $\mathcal{G}_2$. Let $\delta \in \{0, 1\}$ represent the choice made by the PKE game.

When $\mathcal{A}$ produces an index (a, b) and guess g, if $(a, b) = (a', b')$ we output "fail" and quit. When $(a, b) \neq (a', b')$, if $g = r_{a,b}$ (i.e., the guess is correct), we output $\hat{\delta} = 0$ as our guess in the PKE game; otherwise we output $\hat{\delta} = 1$. Analyzing the probability that output $\hat{\delta}$ is correct,

$$\begin{aligned} Pr[\hat{\delta} = \delta] &= Pr[g = r_{a,b} | \delta = 0] Pr[\delta = 0] + \\ &\quad (1 - Pr[g = r_{a,b} | \delta = 1]) \, Pr[\delta = 1] \\ &= \frac{1}{2} Pr[T_1] + \frac{1}{2} (1 - Pr[T_2]) \\ &= \frac{1}{2} (Pr[T_1] - Pr[T_2]) + \frac{1}{2} . \end{aligned}$$

Since $\hat{\delta} = \delta$ means $\mathcal{A}'$ wins the PKE game,

$$Pr[T_1] - Pr[T_2] = 2 \left(Pr[\hat{\delta} = \delta] - \frac{1}{2} \right) \leq 2 \, Adv_{PKE} . \qquad (2)$$

Next we use $\mathcal{A}$ to construct an adversary $\mathcal{A}''$ playing the standard SKE game. $\mathcal{A}''$ selects R_i values and computes R and the shares $f_i(j)$ as in the algorithm, and also generates a public keypair (K_p, K_s). $\mathcal{A}''$ initiates the SKE game, which causes the SKE oracle to select a symmetric key that is random and independent of R, and which will be used for all symmetric encryptions that are provided to $\mathcal{A}$ — this means that $\mathcal{A}$ is actually playing game $\mathcal{G}_2$. Next, $\mathcal{A}''$ selects a random index (a', b'), picks a random bit $r_{i,j}$ for each $(i,j) \neq (a', b')$, and uses the SKE encryption oracle to compute plaintexts $P_{i,j} = \langle SKE.Encrypt(x_{i,j}^{r_{i,j}}), f_i(j) \rangle$. $\mathcal{A}''$ then passes both $x_{a',b'}^0$ and $x_{a',b'}^1$ as the challenge plaintexts to the SKE game, and receives a ciphertext c back, which it uses to compute $P_{a',b'} = \langle c, f_{a'}(b') \rangle$. Now $\mathcal{A}''$ uses it's public key K_p to compute $C_{i,j} = \mathcal{PKE}_{K_p}(P_{i,j})$ for all (i, j).

Finally, $\mathcal{A}$ will produce index (a, b) and a guess bit g. If $(a, b) \neq (a', b')$ we output "fail" and quit; otherwise, we pass along the guess g as $\mathcal{A}''$'s guess in the SKE game. $\mathcal{A}''$ wins exactly when it's index (a, b) is correct and when $\mathcal{A}$ wins (in game $\mathcal{G}_2$), so

$$Adv_{SKE, \mathcal{A}''} = \frac{1}{N} Pr[T_2].$$

This means that $Pr[T_2] \leq N \cdot Adv_{SKE}$. Combining with equation (2), we get

$$Pr[T_1] - N \cdot Adv_{SKE} \leq 2\ Adv_{PKE}$$
$$Pr[T_1] \leq 2\ Adv_{PKE} + N \cdot Adv_{SKE}$$

Therefore, $Adv_{GNIOT} \leq 2\ Adv_{PKE} + N \cdot Adv_{SKE}$, and since PKE and SKE allow only negligible advantage, Adv_{GNIOT} is also negligible.   ∎

4   Non-interactive Secure Mobile Agents

In this section we give an example application of the GNIOT primitive, in which we significantly improve the efficiency of secure mobile agent protocols. In the mobile agent paradigm, an agent owner, also called the *originator*, creates software agents that can perform tasks on her behalf. After creating the agents for some specific purpose, the originator sends them out to visit various remote hosts, where the agents perform computations on behalf of the originator. When the agents return home, the originator retrieves the results of these computations from the agents. The utility of this paradigm is based on the ability of the originator to go *offline* after sending the agents out, and, ideally, no further interaction between the agent and the originator or the host should be required.

The agent and its state travel to potentially untrusted hosts, where it is at the mercy of the execution environment provided by that host, so the problem of protecting the agent's computation and state from malicious hosts is quite challenging. Secure Function Evaluation (SFE) provides a means to protect these computations, as described more carefully below, but requires interaction between the remote hosts and either the originator or proxies for the originator. Examining this interaction more closely, we will see that the only interaction required is for a set of oblivious transfers, and so by applying our GNIOT implementation we remove the interaction requirement for secure mobile agent computation. Since the oblivious transfer and the corresponding interaction is a major bottleneck in implementations of these protocols [6], the resulting non-interactive secure agent computations improve the practicality of these techniques significantly.

In the following sections, we review SFE concepts and techniques, explore the relation between SFE and secure mobile agent computation, and outline an improved agent protocol using the GNIOT primitive from the previous section.

4.1 Secure Function Evaluation

Two-party Secure Function Evaluation (SFE) is a cryptographic primitive that allows two parties, Alice and Bob (with inputs a and b respectively) to compute a function $(A, B) \leftarrow f(a, b)$ such that Alice learns output value A and Bob learns output B, and neither party learns anything more than what follows from its own values. Yao showed that for any polynomial-time computable function f, there exists a polynomial time SFE protocol [15]. The function is represented as an *encrypted circuit* where the values on the input wires are random strings (called signals) instead of the actual boolean values, and the mapping of the random signals to the real inputs is kept secret. Through carefully-specified truth tables that allow evaluation of gates without needing to know the semantics of the random signals, the encrypted circuit can be evaluated without any information being revealed to the evaluator. The result of the evaluation is in encoded form as well, and to decode the output, knowledge of the mapping of the random signals to the real outputs is required.

In this two-party protocol, Alice creates an encrypted circuit to evaluate the desired function. Then Alice sends the encrypted circuit (along with a proof that the circuit was constructed properly if Alice isn't trusted) along with the random signals corresponding to her input to Bob. She also sends a mapping which will allow Bob to decode his output (B) at the end of the computation. Bob must somehow learn the random signals for his input b, but he cannot be given the full input-to-signal mapping. To accomplish this, he engages in a 1-out-of-2 oblivious transfer protocol with Alice for *each bit* of his input, after which Bob knows the signals for his input bits while Alice learns nothing about which signals Bob received (i.e., Bob's input b). Bob now evaluates the encrypted circuit, having obtained random signals corresponding to both inputs a and b, and returns the resulting encrypted form of Alice's output A to her, which she can decode. Bob uses the previously-supplied mapping for his output signals to decrypt his output. Note that the only interaction required between Bob receiving the circuit and evaluating the circuit is the set of 1-out-of-2 OTs that he uses to receive the random signals for his input, and the form of this operation is exactly an instance of our GNIOT primitive.

4.2 Application of SFE to Mobile Agents

When an agent visits a host, it carries with it some state from previous computations, and performs a computation using this state and some input from the host being visited. Output of this computation consists of a new agent state, and possibly some output provided to the host. The agent state (both old and new) are "owned" by the agent, and should be protected from potentially malicious hosts, whereas the host input and output are "owned" by the host and should likewise be protected from potentially malicious agents. For the sake of efficiency, we also allow a host or the agent to provide some non-sensitive, unprotected data to the computation. We refer to this as the "Agent Data", and as a result we formalize an agent computation as the 3-input, 2-output computation illustrated in Figure 1.

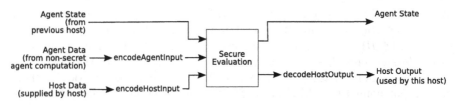

Fig. 1. Agent Computation at a Remote Host

In order to secure this computation we can use two-party Secure Function Evaluation, where one party (the originator) controls the top input and output in the figure, and the other party (the host) controls the bottom two inputs and the bottom output in the figure. Unfortunately, the standard SFE technique described in the previous section requires interaction between the parties, meaning the originator could not be offline, violating a basic property of mobile agent computation. Two existing solutions to the secure agent problem get around this in different ways: a protocol due to Algesheimer *et al.* [2] uses a trusted third party as a proxy for the originator in the oblivious transfer, and a protocol due to Tate and Xu [11,14] (the "TX protocol") uses threshold cryptography and collections of other agents to stand in for the originator. As noted in the previous section, the required oblivious transfer (a 1-out-of-2 transfer for each bit of the host's input) is exactly an instance of GNIOT, and by using our TPM-based implementation we can completely remove any need for interaction in the agent computation. Due to the similarity with the TX protocol, we call this new protocol the "GTX protocol."

4.3   The GTX Protocol

In this section we describe all of the steps required by our non-interactive secure agent protocol. We break down the required operations into three phases, initialization, evaluation, and finalization, corresponding to the three phases of the SAgent software framework for secure mobile agents [5]. While all steps are described here, space limits preclude a detailed descriptions and readers unfamiliar with previous work in secure agents may want to refer to earlier papers in this area [2,11,14].

1. *Initialization:* The originator creates an *encrypted circuit* for each sensitive computation to be carried out at a host — the square box in Figure 1. As outlined in section 4.1, encrypted circuits are special boolean circuits where the signals on the wires are random strings instead of 0 or 1. Since the encrypted circuit can be evaluated with encoded signals, the agent state and inputs must be encoded and incorporated into the agent.

   For the GTX protocol, the participating hosts are assumed to have TPMs, with unambiguous identities which can be verified by an agent originator. Each host willing to accept agents and supply n-bit inputs executes the *Setup* phase of GNIOT to generate n-time use keys that are made available to users wishing to send agents. When an originator wants to send out agents, the originator executes the *Transmit* phase of the TPM-based GNIOT scheme, where $m_i = 2$ and $k_i = 1$ for all $i \in \{1, \ldots, n\}$, and we let $x_{i,1}$ and $x_{i,2}$ be the two signals corresponding to boolean values 0 and 1 for host input bit i. Note that the output of the *Transmit* phase of GNIOT is exactly what the hosts will need to decrypt exactly one random signal for each of its n input bits. In creating the agent, the originator bundles together the encrypted circuit, the output C of the GNIOT *Transmit* phase, and the host's output-to-boolean mapping and includes all of this information in the agent. The originator keeps the final state signal-to-boolean mapping for use in decrypting the final agent state when it returns after having visited the hosts.

2. *Evaluation:* In the evaluation phase, the host has received an agent, which carries with it the values described above. If the host's input is made up of bits $\langle b_1, b_2, \ldots, b_n \rangle$, the host calls the GNIOT.*Decrypt* with indices $(i, b_i + 1)$ for $i = 1, \ldots, n$. Running *PostProcess* on the results of these *Decrypt* calls will provide $\langle x_{1,b_1+1}, x_{2,b_2+1}, \ldots, x_{n,b_n+1} \rangle$, which are exactly the random signals needed to evaluate the encrypted circuit. Note that if the host tries to cheat either by requesting both signals corresponding to a single input bit or by requesting more than the allowed number of decryptions, the GNIOT protocol guarantees that the host learns nothing at all about the random signals used by this encrypted circuit. After evaluation of the encrypted circuit, the host uses the output signal-to-boolean mapping supplied by the originator (and carried by the agent) in order to decrypt its input.

3. *Finalization:* When the agent returns to the originator, its final state will be decrypted by the originator.

5   Conclusion

In this paper, we have shown how to remove interaction requirements in the fundamental cryptographic primitive of oblivious transfer to create an expanded cryptographic primitive called "generalized non-interactive oblivious transfer" (GNIOT). Based on recent research which shows how to instantiate count-limited objects using the monotonic counter in trusted platform modules, we outline how to use count-limited objects to efficiently instantiate an oblivious transfer primitive while removing the interaction requirements necessary in such a protocol.

We provide rigorous proofs that under an assumption of secure TPMs (and standard complexity assumptions), our construction provides the same security properties as those of standard oblivious transfer. In addition, we show how to apply the GNIOT primitive to develop a secure mobile agent protocol (called the GTX protocol) where strong security guarantees can be achieved without the interaction requirements necessary in previous secure agent protocols.

References

1. Abe, M., Gennaro, R., Kurosawa, K., Shoup, V.: Tag-KEM/DEM:A New Framework for Hybrid Encryption and A New Analysis of Kurosawa-Desmedt KEM. In: Cramer, R.J.F. (ed.) EUROCRYPT 2005. LNCS, vol. 3494, pp. 128–146. Springer, Heidelberg (2005)
2. Algesheimer, J., Cachin, C., Camenisch, J., Karjoth, G.: Cryptographic security for mobile code. In: Proc. of the IEEE Symposium on Security and Privacy, pp. 2–11 (2001)
3. Bellare, M., Micali, S.: Non-interactive oblivious transfer and applications. In: Brassard, G. (ed.) CRYPTO 1989. LNCS, vol. 435, pp. 547–557. Springer, Heidelberg (1990)
4. Cramer, R., Shoup, V.: Design and analysis of practical public-key encryption schemes secure against adaptive chosen ciphertext attack. SIAM J. Comput. 33(1), 167–226 (2003)
5. Gunupudi, V., Tate, S.R.: SAgent: A Security Framework for JADE. In: AAMAS 2006: Proceedings of the fifth international joint conference on Autonomous agents and multiagent systems, pp. 1116–1118 (2006)
6. Gunupudi, V., Tate, S.R., Xu, K.: Experimental evaluation of security protocols in SAgent. In: Proceedings of the International Workshop on Privacy and Security in Agent-based Collaborative Environments (PSACE), pp. 60–74 (2006)
7. Rabin, M.O.: How to exchange secrets by oblivious transfer. Tech. Rep. TR-81, Harvard University (1981)
8. Sarmenta, L.F.G., van Dijk, M., O'Donnell, C.W., Rhodes, J., Devadas, S.: Virtual monotonic counters and count-limited objects using a TPM without a trusted OS. In: STC 2006: Proceedings of the First ACM Workshop on Scalable Trusted Computing, pp. 27–42 (2006)
9. Shamir, A.: How to share a secret. Communications of the ACM 22, 11 (1979)
10. Strasser, M., Sevnic, P.E.: A software-based TPM emulator for Linux. Master's thesis, Eidgenossische Technische Hochschule (ETH), Zurich, Project web page (2005), http://developer.berlios.de/projects/tpm-emulator/
11. Tate, S.R., Xu, K.: Mobile agent security through multi-agent cryptographic protocols. In: Proc. of the 4th International Conference on Internet Computing (IC), pp. 462–468 (2003)
12. Trusted Computing Group, http://www.trustedcomputinggroup.org
13. Trusted Computing Group. TPM main specification, version 1.2, revision 103, parts 1–3 (2007), http://www.trustedcomputinggroup.org
14. Xu, K., Tate, S.R.: Universally composable secure mobile agent computation. In: Zhang, K., Zheng, Y. (eds.) ISC 2004. LNCS, vol. 3225, pp. 304–317. Springer, Heidelberg (2004)
15. Yao, A.: How to generate and exchange secrets. In: Proc. of the 27th IEEE Symposium on Foundations of Computer Science(FOCS), pp. 162–167 (1986)

PBS: Private Bartering Systems

Keith Frikken and Lukasz Opyrchal

Department of Computer Science and Systems Analysis
Miami University, Oxford, OH 45056
{frikkekb, opyrchal}@muohio.edu

Abstract. Barter trade is a growing part of the world economy. Hundreds of thousands of companies in the US alone participate in barter. Barter is also used in other domains, such as resource management in distributed systems. Existing algorithms for finding barter trades require that values of goods are publicly known (whether they are set by a global function or individual utility functions for each user). The fact that each user must reveal her utility function in order to find barter trades is a potential disincentive to using bartering. We present a first step in the creation of a privacy-preserving bartering system. We present algorithms and privacy-preserving protocols in the honest but curious model for determining the existence of win-win trades (and algorithms and protocols for finding such trades). We discuss a number of remaining open problems and extensions for future work.

1 Introduction

Bartering is the act of transacting business through the exchange of commodities rather than currency. Countertrade is a generalization of bartering where the transaction consists of commodities and currency. There are many environments where bartering and countertrade lead to a win-win situation for both parties, including: business's exchanging surplus goods or services for other items that are needed [6], computers in a grid exchanging computational tasks (perhaps one has special hardware that can achieve a certain task more efficiently than another) [11], and nearby hospitals "exchanging" patients to help reduce costs (it may be that a hospital is understaffed in one unit but is overstaffed in another). The upcoming national kidney-exchange market is another example of barter exchange where kidney transplant patients can swap incompatible *living* donors [1].

As an example of bartering, in 2006 a man succesfully made a series of such win-win exchanges to trade a large red paper clip for a house [24]. In reality, many of the trades that could be expected from such a system will be less sensational than this. Much of the bartering done today is done in person, however various online countertrade systems exist. There are hundreds of barter trade exchanges in the US [16]. Many of them are members of barter organizations such as the International Reciprocal Trade Association (IRTA) [18] or the National Association of Trade Exchanges (NATE) [25]. Some of the biggest barter trade exchanges include ITEX, BizXchange, and Bartercard.com.

G. Tsudik (Ed.): FC 2008, LNCS 5143, pp. 113–127, 2008.

The International Reciprocal Trade Association estimated that the total value of products and services bartered by businesses through barter exchanges reached almost USD 8 billion in 2001 [18]. In North America, there were an estimated 719 trade companies (exchanges) and about 470,000 participating client businesses. IRTA estimates that the potential for barter trade is about USD 136 billion [18].

We believe that one roadblock to widely-used bartering system is the apparent need to exchange sensitive information. That is, in order to find win-win trades one needs to know each party's perceived values for the items. Current bartering sites use the trusted third party approach, however it would be better to avoid such an assumption. In this paper we make a first step in the creation of a privacy-preserving bartering system (without a third party). As this is a first step we make several simplifying assumptions, including: i) we focus on two-party trades, ii) we assume an honest-but-curious adversary model, iii) we assume that the barters are interested only in the existence of a win-win trade (we do extend our schemes to finding such a trade however), and iv) we assume trades are all-or-none (that is Alice cannot send half of an item to Bob).

The remainder of this paper is organized as follows, in section 2 we formally introduce our bartering framework and describe the contributions of this paper. In section 3 we introduce algorithms for bartering in the non-private case, and then in section 4 we convert these algorithms into privacy-preserving protocols. We discuss various extensions to our protocols in section 5. In section 6, related work is described, and finally in section 7 we summarize our results and describe future work.

2   Framework Definition/Our Contributions

2.1   Framework

Alice and Bob have respective item sets $A = \{a_1, \ldots, a_n\}$ and $B = \{b_1, \ldots, b_m\}$. In order to not clutter the notation, we assume that $m = n$; note that our protocols do not require this assumption. We also assume that A and B are disjoint, that they are public information, and that these are not multi-sets.

Alice associates a utility with each item in $A \cup B$; i.e., Alice defines a function $u_A : A \cup B \to [0, M]$ that maps each tradeable item to a monetary utility for Alice. Similarly, Bob defines a utility function u_B. We slightly abuse notation in that we also define the utility functions over sets. Furthermore, we make a simplifying assumption that the utility of a set of items is the sum of the utilities of all items in the set, that is for a set S, $u_A(S) = \sum_{s \in S} u_A(s)$ and $u_B(S) = \sum_{s \in S} u_B(s)$. Note that this implies that we are assuming that Alice's (Bob's) utility for an item is independent of what other items Alice (Bob) receives/gives up.

A trade is defined as a tuple (A', B') where $A' \subseteq A$ and $B' \subseteq B$; a trade (A', B') denotes that Alice sends the items in A' to Bob and that Bob sends the items in B' to Alice. Alice's profit from a trade (A', B') is denoted by $P_A(A', B') = \sum_{b \in B'} u_A(b) - \sum_{a \in A'} u_A(a)$. Similarly, Bob's profit from a trade (A', B') is denoted by $P_B(A', B')) = \sum_{a \in A'} u_B(a) - \sum_{b \in B'} u_B(b)$. A trade (A', B') is a win-win trade if and only if $P_A(A', B') > 0$ and $P_B(A', B') > 0$.

We consider three types of trades in this paper: i) $(1,1)$ where Alice and Bob exchange a single item, ii) $(1,n)$ where Alice sends a single item to Bob in exchange for one or more items, (Note that $(n,1)$ trades where Alice sends one or more items to Bob in exchange for a single item can be supported simply by flipping the roles of Alice and Bob), and iii) (n,n) where Alice sends one or more items to Bob in exchange for one or more items. Clearly, the most general form of trades is the (n,n) trade, however there is a tradeoff between efficiency and the generality of allowed trades.

Bartering Goals: Our initial goal is to create a privacy-preserving bartering system to find whether a win-win trade exists (EXIST). We also extend this to create a system that finds a win-win trade (FIND).

2.2   Example

We illustrate the above framework with an example. Assume that Alice wants to make a sculpture and needs some play-dough. She also wants to trade an old book she doesn't need anymore and she wants to get rid of some old computer parts. Bob is looking for an out-of-print book (same book Alice is trading), and he is also looking for some computer parts. He has a large stash of play-dough that he's willing to trade as well as some clay.

$$A = \{book, parts\} \quad B = \{play - dough, clay\}$$

Here are Alice's and Bob's utility functions:

$$u_A : \{book = 5, parts = 5, play - dough = 15, clay = 1\}$$
$$u_B : \{book = 20, parts = 7, play - dough = 5, clay = 10\}$$

A possible $(n,1)$ win-win trade is $(\{book, parts\}, \{play-dough\})$, which means that Alice trades her book and computer parts for play-dough. We note that Alice's profit is $P_A = 5$ and Bob's profit is $P_B = 22$. Even though Bob makes a bigger profit, both Alice and Bob are *happy* with the trade since both made a profit. It is important to note that if Alice knew Bob's utility function ahead of time, she could have increased her value of the book to get a better deal.

2.3   Our Contributions

In this paper we make a first step towards supporting a private bartering system. More specifically, the contributions of this paper include:

– We propose algorithms for checking the EXIST (see section 3) for $(1,1)$, $(1,n)$, and (n,n) trades. To the best of our knowledge these are novel algorithms. The difficult part of creating these algorithms was designing them so that they were convertible into privacy-preserving protocols.

- We modify the algorithms into privacy-preserving protocols in the honest but curious adversary model (see section 4). The communication and computation[1] of these protocols is shown in Table 1.
- We extend our protocols and algorithms to FIND.

Table 1. Communication/Computation Cost of Protocols

Trade type	Communication	Rounds
$(1,1)$	$O(n)$	$O(n)$
$(1,n)$	$O(Mn)$	$O(n)$
(n,n)	$O(Mn^2)$	$O(n)$

3   Non-private Bartering Systems

In this sections we introduce algorithms for finding the existence of each type of trade.

3.1   Algorithms for $(1,1)$ Trades

Before describing the details of our algorithms for EXIST for $(1,1)$ trades, we describe some other notation. First we will sort the items according to Alice's preference for the items; without loss of generality we will assume that these values are already sorted, that is:
$u_A(a_1) \geq u_A(a_2) \geq \cdots \geq u_A(a_n)$ and $u_A(b_1) \geq u_A(b_2) \geq \cdots \geq u_A(b_n)$.

We denote the number of Bob's items that Alice prefers to item a_j as c_j. More formally,

$$c_j = \begin{cases} 0 & : & u_A(a_j) > u_A(b_1) \\ \max_{1 \leq k \leq n} \{k | u_A(b_k) > u_A(a_j)\} & : & otherwise \end{cases}$$

We denote Bob's utility of the least valuable item in $b_1, \ldots, b_j$ from Bob's perspective as u_j and we denote the index of this item by i_j. More formally, $u_j = \min_{1 \leq k \leq j} \{u_B(b_k)\}$ and $i_j = \arg \min_{1 \leq k \leq j} \{u_B(b_k)\}$.

We are now ready to describe the primary observation that leads to our algorithms.

Theorem 1. *There exists a win-win $(1,1)$ trade if and only if $\exists j \in [1, n]$: $u_B(a_j) > u_{c_j}$. Furthermore, if such a j exists then the trade a_j and $b_{i_{c_j}}$ is a win-win trade.*

Proof: Suppose that $u_B(a_j) > u_{c_j}$, then we will show that a_j and $b_{i_{c_j}}$ is a win-win trade. First consider Alice's profit from the trade. We know that by definition of i that $i_{c_j} \leq c_j$, and for any index $\ell \leq c_j$ we know that $u_A(b_\ell) > u_A(a_j)$. Thus,

---

[1] We count only modular exponentiations as these are the most expensive operations.

$u_A(b_{i_{c_j}}) > u_A(a_j)$. Now consider Bob's profit from the trade. From the definition of u_{c_j}, we know that $u_B(b_{i_{c_j}}) = u_{c_j}$. Thus, $u_b(b_{i_{c_j}}) < u_B(a_j)$.

To show the other side of the statement, suppose that a_j and b_k is a win-win trade. Since this is a win-win trade, we know that: i) $u_A(a_j) < u_A(b_k)$ and ii) $u_B(b_k) < u_B(a_j)$. We will now show that $u_B(a_j) < u_{c_j}$ (which will establish our claim). First, since Alice profits from the trade, we know that $k \leq c_j$, and thus $u_k \geq u_{c_j}$. Now $u_B(a_j) > u_B(b_k) > u_B(b_{i_k}) = u_k \geq u_{c_j}$. $\square$

Algorithm: We are now ready to present our algorithm for checking for the existence of a $(1,1)$ trade. The basic idea of the algorithm is to compute the c-values and the u-values for each item. As a pre-computation phase we sort the lists according to Alice's preferences requiring $O(n \log n)$ time. We also add a dummy item to the end of Bob's list where Alice's preference is $-\infty$.

EXIST-$(1,1)$

```
 1: {Compute c values and u values}
 2: i ← 1
 3: u₀ ← ∞
 4: for j = 1 to n do
 5:     while u_A(b_i) > u_A(a_j) do
 6:         i ← i + 1
 7:     end while
 8:     c_j ← i − 1
 9:     if u_B(b_j) < u_{j−1} then
10:         u_j = u_B(b_j)
11:     else
12:         u_j = u_{j−1}
13:     end if
14: end for
15: {Determine if there is a trade}
16: for j = 1 to n do
17:     if u_B(a_j) > u_{c_j} then
18:         return true
19:     end if
20: end for
21: return false
```

Complexity analysis: It is easily verifiable that once the items are sorted that none of the above steps requires more than $O(n)$ time. Thus the total running time of the find algorithm is $O(n \log n)$.

3.2   Algorithms for $(1, n)$ Trades

In this section we introduce techniques for computing whether a win-win trade exists with Alice sending Bob a single item and Bob sending Alice one or more items exists. Recall that M is an upper bound on Alice and Bob's utility functions for their items. The first step is to compute $L(0, n), L(1, n), \ldots, L(M, n)$ where

$L(t,k) = \min_{S \subseteq [1,k]} \{ \sum_{i \in S} u_B(b_i) : \sum_{i \in S} u_A(b_i) \geq t \}$. That is, $L(t,k)$ is the minimum utility (from Bob's perspective) Bob needs to trade to Alice in order to give Alice at least t utility (from her perspective). This value can easily be computed with the following dynamic program:

1. $L(t,1) = u_B(b_1)$ if $u_A(b_1) \geq t$ and is ∞ otherwise.
2. $L(0,i) = 0$ for all i.
3. $L(t,i) = \min\{L(t,i-1), u_B(b_i)\}$ if $u_A(b_i) \geq t$
4. $L(t,i) = \min\{u_B(b_i) + L(t - u_A(b_i), i-1), L(t,i-1)\}$ otherwise.

Based on this value we prove the existence theorem for trades based on L.

Theorem 2. *There exists a win-win $(1,n)$ trade if and only if $\exists j \in [1,n]$:* $L(u_A(a_j) + 1, n) < u_B(a_j)$.

Proof: Suppose that $L(u_A(a_j) + 1, n) < u_B(a_j)$ for some value j. This means that there is a set of items $S \subseteq [1,n]$ where Bob's utility is smaller than $u_B(a_j)$ (by definition of L), and where Alice's utility is at least $u_A(a_j) + 1$. We claim that trading a_j for the items in S is a win-win trade. From Alice's perspective, the items she obtains are more valuable than a_j. From Bob's perspective, a_j is more valuable than all items in S.

To show the other direction, suppose that trading a_j for $S \subseteq \{b_1, \ldots, b_n\}$ is a win-win trade. Now $u_A(a_j) < \sum_{b_i \in S} u_A(b_i)$. Thus, $L(u_A(a_j) + 1, n) \leq \sum_{b_i \in S} u_B(b_i)$. However, we also know that $u_B(a_j) > \sum_{b_i \in S} u_B(b_i)$, and so $L(u_A(a_j + 1), n) < u_B(a_j)$. $\qquad \square$

Algorithm: EXIST-$(1,n)$

```
 1: {Compute L values}
 2: for t = 1 to M do
 3:    if u_A(b_1) ≥ t then
 4:       L(t,1) = u_B(b_1)
 5:    else
 6:       L(t,1) = ∞
 7:    end if
 8: end for
 9: for i = 1 to n do
10:    L(0,i) = 0
11: end for
12: for i = 1 to n do
13:    for t = 2 to M do
14:       if u_A(b_i) ≥ t then
15:          L(t,i) = min{L(t,i-1), u_B(b_i)}
16:       else
17:          L(t,i) = min{u_B(b_i) + L(t - u_A(b_i), i-1), L(t,i-1)}
18:       end if
19:    end for
```

20: **end for**
21: {Check for trade}
22: **for** $j = 1$ to n **do**
23:      **if** $u_B(a_j) > L(u_A(a_j), n)$ **then**
24:          **return** *true*
25:      **end if**
26: **end for**
27: **return** *false*

Complexity analysis: Note that the most expensive step is computing the L values which requires $O(Mn)$ time and thus this is a pseudopolynomial algorithm for EXIST.

3.3   Algorithms for (n, n) Trades

This case is similar to the $(1, n)$ situation. However, we define two functions this time: $L(t, m)$ and $K(t, m)$. $L(t, m)$ is defined exactly the same way as in the previous section. Meanwhile, $K(t, m) = \max_{S \subseteq [1,m]} \{ \sum_{i \in S} u_B(a_i) : \sum_{i \in S} u_A(a_i) \leq t \}$. In other words, $K(t, m)$ is the maximum utility (from Bob's perspective) that Alice can trade to Bob in a trade where her traded items have utility $\leq t$ (from her perspective). This value can be computed with the following dynamic program:

1. $K(t, 1) = 0$ if $u_A(a_1) > t$ and is $u_B(a_1)$ otherwise.
2. $K(0, i) = 0$ for all i.
3. $K(t, i) = K(t, i - 1)$ if $u_A(a_i) > t$
4. $K(t, i) = \max\{u_B(a_i) + K(t - u_A(a_i), i - 1), K(t, i - 1)\}$ otherwise.

Theorem 3. *There exists a win-win (n, n) trade if and only if $\exists q \in [1, Mn]$: $L(q + 1, n) < K(q, n)$.*

Proof: Omitted due to page constraints.

Algorithm: EXIST-(n, n)
1: {Compute L values for 1 to Mn as in EXIST-$(1, n)$}
2: {Compute K values for 1 to Mn with dynamic program}
3: {Check for trade}
4: **for** $j = 0$ to $Mn - 1$ **do**
5:      **if** $L(j + 1, n) < K(j, n)$ **then**
6:          **return** *true*
7:      **end if**
8: **end for**
9: **return** *false*

Complexity analysis: Note that the most expensive step is computing the L and K values which requires $O(Mn^2)$ time and thus this is a pseudopolynomial algorithm for EXIST.

4   Private Bartering Systems

4.1   Building Blocks

Homomorphic Encryption: In this paper we use an additively homomorphic encryption scheme. Recall that a homomorphic encryption scheme has the following properties: i) $E(x) * E(y) = E(x+y)$, ii) $E(x)^c = E(xc)$, iii) these are public key systems, and iv) an encryption $E(x)$ can be re-randomized by multiplying by $E(0)$. We also require the scheme to be semantically-secure [15], and examples of such a scheme include [26,7].

The protocols for privacy-preserving bartering require various operations to be performed on encrypted values (for details of how these can be achieved see [10,30]) in a provably secure manner. For these protocols assume that Bob has chosen a semantically-secure homomorphic encryption scheme E and has shared the parameters with Alice. Furthermore, in order to allow multiple invocations of the protocols with the same inputs we assume that these protocols all begin with a re-randomization of the encrypted values.

1. *GT* (and other types of comparisons): Suppose Alice has values $E(x)$ and $E(y)$, with Bob's help she would like to compute $E(c)$ where $c = 1$ if $x > y$ and $c = 0$ otherwise. This requires $O(\ell)$ communication and $O(1)$ rounds where ℓ is the number of bits in the upper bound of x and y.
2. *MAX/MIN*: Suppose Alice has two values $E(x)$ and $E(y)$ and with Bob's help would like to compute $E(\max\{x, y\})$; we denote this by $MAX(E(x), E(y))$. This can be computed using a slight variation of GT; this requires $O(\ell)$ communication and $O(1)$ rounds. Note that MIN can be computed in a similar fashion.
3. *OR*: If Alice is given $E(p_1), \ldots, E(p_m)$ where each p_i is either 0 or 1, then she can reveal $\vee_{i=1}^m p_i$ to Bob without revealing the individual values. This is done by sending $E(R * \sum_{i=1}^m p_i)$ to Bob where R is a randomly chosen non-zero value. Bob can decrypt this value and if it is 0, then the answer is 0 and otherwise the answer is 1.

4.2   Security Definitions

In this paper we consider the standard honest-but-curious (HBC) adversary model. Recall that in this model, participants will faithfully follow the protocol specification, but will try to learn additional information. Traditionally, to prove security in this model, one shows that the entire protocol can be simulated from the output of the protocol alone. However, due to page constraints we can only give a brief description of why these schemes are secure. In this paper we store all intermediate results of the protocol as a homomorphic encryption at Alice using Bob's key. Since the scheme being used is semantically-secure, these values are trivially simulateable. Furthermore, assuming that the building blocks from the previous section are secure (i.e., simulateable in the HBC adversary model), then using the composition theorem [5], the resulting protocols will be secure. It is easy to verify that the protocols described below are just compositions of the above building blocks, and that all of the above building blocks (except OR) only produce outputs that are encrypted with a homomorhpic encryption scheme. Furthermore, the OR protocol is only used to reveal a final output to Bob. Thus these protocols do not reveal intermediate outputs to Alice or Bob.

4.3   Protocols

In this section we convert the algorithms from the previous section into privacy-preserving protocols.

Common Setup. All of the protocols below, use the same setup, so we describe it here once. Assume that these two steps have already been completed below.

1. Bob chooses a semantically-secure homomorphic encryption scheme E, and sends the public parameters to Alice.
2. Bob sends $E(u_B(a_1)), \ldots, E(u_B(a_n)), E(u_B(b_1)), \ldots, E(u_B(b_n))$ to Alice.

EXIST $(1, 1)$ Trade Protocol

1. Alice builds tuples $(u_A(a_i), E(u_B(a_i)))$ and $(u_A(b_i), E(u_B(b_i)))$. She then sorts the two list of tuples according to her utility function. To avoid cluttering the notation, we will now assume that:
   $u_A(a_1) \geq u_A(a_2) \geq \cdots \geq u_A(a_n)$ and $u_A(b_1) \geq u_A(b_2) \geq \cdots \geq u_A(b_n)$.
2. Using only her input values, Alice computes the c values using lines 4-8 of EXIST-$(1, 1)$.
3. Alice creates $E(u_0) = E(\infty)^2$, and then her and Bob engage in several protocols where Alice learns: $E(u_j) = MIN(E(u_{j-1}), E(u_B(b_j))$ for $j \in [1, n]$.
4. Alice and Bob engage in n protocols in parallel to compute the predicate $E(p_j) = GT(E(u_B(a_j)), E(u_{c_j}))$.
5. Alice and Bob then compute $OR(E(p_1), \ldots, E(p_n))$ where Bob learns the result.

Complexity Analysis: Clearly, the communication and modular exponentiations in the above protocol is $O(n)$. Also because of Step 3 this protocol requires $O(n)$ rounds.

Computing $L(0, n), \ldots, L(Q, n)$ for some value Q. We now introduce how to compute the value L.

1. Alice can compute $L(t, 1)$ for all values t without interacting with Bob. That is, if $u_A(b_1) \geq t$, then she uses $E(u_B(b_1))$ and otherwise she uses $E(\infty)$.
2. To compute $E(L(q, j))$ when given $E(L(0, j-1)), \ldots, E(L(Q, j-1))$, Alice does the following:
   (a) For $q = 0$, she sets the result to $E(0)$.

---

[2] That is Alice encrypts a value that will be larger than any of Bob's possible utilities.

(b) For $q > 0$, Alice does one of two MIN protocols
  – If $u_A(b_i) \geq q$, $E(L(q,j)) = MIN(E(L(q,j-1)), E(u_B(b_j)))$.
  – Otherwise, $E(L(q,j)) = MIN(E(u_B(b_j) + L(q - u_A(b_j), j - 1)), E(L(q, j - 1)))$. Note that $E(u_B(b_j) + L(q - u_A(b_j), j - 1)) = E(u_B(b_j)) * E(L(q - u_A(b_j), j - 1))$.

3. Alice repeats the previous step until she has $E(L(0,n)), \ldots, E(L(Q,n))$.

Complexity Analysis: Clearly, the communication and modular exponentiations in the above protocol is $O(Qn)$ and the number of rounds is $O(n)$ (note that this requires that some of $L(0,i), \ldots, L(Q,i)$ are all computed in parallel)..

EXIST $(1,n)$ Trade Protocol

1. Alice and Bob engage in the protocol to compute the L values, where Alice learns, $E(L(0,n)), \ldots, E(L(M,n))$.
2. Alice and Bob engage in n protocols in parallel to compute the predicate $E(p_j) = GT(E(u_B(a_j)), E(L(u_A(a_j) + 1, n)))$.
3. Alice and Bob then compute $OR(E(p_1), \ldots, E(p_n))$ where Bob learns the result.

Complexity Analysis: Clearly, the communication and modular exponentiations in the above protocol is $O(Mn)$ and the number of rounds is $O(n)$.

Computing $K(0,n), \ldots, K(Q,n)$ for some value Q. We now introduce how to compute the value K.

1. Alice can compute $E(K(t,1))$ for all values t without interacting with Bob. That is, if $u_A(a_1) \leq t$, then she uses $E(u_B(a_1))$ and otherwise she uses $E(0)$.
2. To compute $E(K(q,j))$ when given $E(K(0,j-1)), \ldots, E(K(Q,j-1))$, Alice does the following:
  (a) For $q = 0$, she sets the result to $E(0)$.
  (b) For $q > 0$, Alice does one of two MAX protocols
    – If $u_A(a_j) > q$, $E(K(q,j)) = MAX(E(K(q,j-1)), E(0))$.
    – Otherwise, $E(K(q,j)) = MAX(E(u_B(a_j) + L(q - u_A(a_j), j - 1)), E(K(q, j - 1)))$. Note that $E(u_B(a_j) + L(q - u_A(a_j), j - 1)) = E(u_B(a_j)) * E(L(q - u_A(a_j), j - 1))$.
3. Alice does the above until the values $K(0,n), \ldots, K(Q,n)$ are reached.

Complexity Analysis: Clearly, the communication and modular exponentiations in the above protocol is $O(Qn)$ and it requires $O(n)$ rounds (note that this requires that some of $K(0,i), \ldots, K(Q,i)$ are all computed in parallel).

EXIST (n,n) Trade Protocol

1. Alice and Bob engage in the protocol to compute the L values, where Alice learns, $E(L(0,n)), \ldots, E(L(Mn,n))$.

2. Alice and Bob engage in the protocol to compute the K values, where Alice learns, $E(K(0, n)), \ldots, E(K(Mn, n))$.
3. Alice and Bob engage in $n - 1$ protocols in parallel to compute the predicate $E(p_j) = GT(E(K(j, n)), E(L(j + 1, n)))$.
4. Alice and Bob then compute $OR(E(p_1), \ldots, E(p_{Mn}))$ where Bob learns the result.

Complexity Analysis: Clearly, the communication and modular exponentiations in the above protocol is $O(Mn^2)$, and the protocol requires $O(n)$ rounds.

5   Extensions

In this section we briefly discuss how to extend our protocols to find a specific win-win trade. As a detailed description of such protocols would be redundant to previous section and due to page constraints, we outline only the major changes that need to be made for the protocols.

5.1   Finding a $(1, 1)$ Trade

To find a valid trade, the algorithm FIND-$(1, 1)$ must keep track of which item produces u_j, recall that this value is denoted by i_j. This is easily computable, if line 10 (from EXIST-$(1, 1)$) is executed this is j and otherwise it is i_{j-1}. Furthermore if $u_B(a_j) > u_{c_j}$ then trading a_j for b_{i_j} is a win-win trade.

To augment the secure protocol to compute the i values, one needs a slightly different primitive $SELECT(E(c), E(v_0), E(v_1))$ where $c \in \{0, 1\}$ and where Alice learns $E(v_c)$. This is achieved by computing $E((1 - c)v_0 + cv_1)$, which follows naturally from a protocol that multiplies two encrypted values.

To determine the valid trade, we choose the trade with the smallest j value (from line 16 of EXIST-$(1, 1)$). Now, we can reveal to Alice the predicate $u_B(a_j) > u_{c_j}$ for each j sequentially. Once the first of these values is true, Alice knows that a_j is her trade item, and then she reveals i_j to Bob so that he learns his value.

5.2   Finding a $(1, n)$ Trade

To augment the EXIST-$(1, n)$ algorithm to find a valid $(1, n)$ trade we use the standard backtracking technique from dynamic programming. Define $S_L(t, m)$ to be the largest item that helped produce the value $L(t, m)$. More specifically, this can be computed with the following dynamic program.

1. $S_L(t, 1) = 1$ if $u_A(b_1) \geq t$ and is 0 otherwise.
2. $S_L(0, i) = 0$ for all i.
3. $S_L(t, i) = S_L(t, i - 1)$ if $u_A(b_i) \geq t$ and $L(t, i - 1) \leq u_A(b_i)$.
4. $S_L(t, i) = i$ if $u_A(b_i) \geq t$ and $L(t, i - 1) > u_A(b_i)$.
5. $S_L(t, i) = S_L(t, i-1)$ if $u_A(b_i) < t$ and $L(t, i-1) \leq u_A(b_i) + L(t - u_A(b_i), i-1)$.
6. $S_L(t, i) = i$ $u_A(b_i) < t$ and $L(t, i - 1) > u_A(b_i) + L(t - u_A(b_i), i - 1)$.

Note that using the SELECT primitive this can easily be computed in the secure protocol. Furthermore, the backtracking can be achieved by revealing one index to Alice at a time.

5.3 Finding an (n, n) Trade

All that must be done is to compute a similar backtracking technique for $K(i, m)$, which we denote by $S_K(i, n)$. This is achieved with a similar dynamic program as in the previous section (we omit the details due to page constraints).

6 Related Work

As described in Section 1, barter trade is a growing phenomenon in the US and world economy. Originally, researchers assumed that barter develops during economic downturns or in countries with weak currencies. The examination of US barter and counter-trade shows that barter trade has a place in strong economies as well [6]. Barter is also often preferred in international trade due to import/export restrictions, shortages of currency, etc.[22].

In addition to retail or corporate barter used by companies, barter is popular among individuals as well. A number of websites exist to help users exchange unneeded items. Examples of such exchanges include Peerflix (DVDs) [27], Read It Swap It (books) [28], and Intervac (holiday homes) [17].

The growing popularity of web-based barter portals has led to research on algorithms to help find suitable trades or to find such trades automatically [21,16,23]. These algorithms are typically designed for multi-agent environments where automated agents work negotiate trades on users' behalf. In order for this approach to succeed, agents must know their users' preferences (what they need and what they want to trade) and their value function which assigns values to different goods.

A common thread of the above barter exchange techniques is the fact that the value assigned to goods by each user is public. Agent systems typically use a per-agent utility function which is known to all agents. Commercial barter exchanges assign values based on market prices of different goods and services. Other systems, such as the kidney-exchange, use constants as values of goods [1].

Commercial or corporate barter exchanges use internal currency called *trade credit*. Each member company gets a set sum of trade credits and can immediately use it to obtain goods and services they require. Each company can increase its credit balance by "selling" some of their goods or services [6]. This approach reduces the problem of finding matches to finding a seller for a good we need and removes the need for finding *win-win* bilateral trades. Since barter exchanges receive a percentage of each transaction, automated algorithm typically try to maximize the trade volume [16]. It is also important to keep the trade balance of each company close to zero (the value of purchased goods should be close to the value of goods sold). Haddawy *et.al.*, for example, formulate the problem as an integer program and reduce it to a minimum-cost circulation problem on an appropriate network. Once a balanced trade set is found, matching buyers and sellers is trivial. The authors present a greedy algorithm that attempts to minimize the average number of sellers matched to a buyer per good.

An *e-barter* system for multi-agent systems can be formally defined as in [20]. Such systems involve agents which, acting on the behalf of users, look for trades which make their users *happy*. Such systems often depend on a particular data representation such as node-labeled, arc-labeled weighted trees [4,23]. A tree similarity algorithm developed for a traditional buyer-seller scenario was extended to barter trades by Mathieu [23]. The algorithm supports barter trades among more than two users and defines the value of risk which indicates how likely a particular ring of barter trades is.

Barter approaches are also used to manage resources, such as upload/download bandwidth, storage space, and CPU time, in distributed systems [11,12,2]. The matching problem in such environments is typically simpler due to domain restrictions.

Clearly, this work is related to the area of Secure Multi-Party Computation. While general results [29,14] state that any function can be computed in a secure-manner (under various adversary assumptions), these schemes usually involve building some type of circuit for the problem at hand. At least the straight-forward circuit implementation of the bartering algorithms would be prohibitively expensive. For example, the FIND-$(1, 1)$ algorithm would require some type of sort (which can be done in $O(n \log n)$ gates [3], but this hides a very large constant). However, using the arithmetic properties of homomorphic encryption to achieve a domain-specific solution has been used in other situations including: scalar product [13], set operations [8,19,9], and trust negotiation [30]. The most related of these is the dynamic programs that were used in private point-based trust negotiation [30].

7   Summary

In this paper we made a first step in the direction of a private bartering system. This system allowed two users to determine if they had a win-win trade (and to find such a trade) between them while protecting their individual utility of their items. There are many potential avenues for future work, including:

1. Partial item trades: To generalize our system, we need to extend the scheme to allow partial trades. This would be necessary in a countertrade situation where one of the items is monetary.
2. Choosing trades: Our current approach finds one specific trade. However, whenever multiple trades are possible, which one should be chosen.
3. More realistic adversary models: The honest-but-curious adversary model is a nice first step, but it is necessary to strengthen the adversary model. Another issue with our protocol is that participants may lie about their valuations to game the system.
4. More than two people: Extending the scheme to more than two people is also necessary. There are many complicated issues, including is it possible to

do better than to search all pairs of users. Also, is it possible to find a k-way trade between k users. We suspect many of these problems will be NP-hard, and so heuristic approaches will be necessary.

5. Prototype implementation: We are planning a prototype implementation of our protocols.

Acknowledgements

The authors would like to thank the anonymous reviewers for their comments and useful suggestions.

References

1. Abraham, D.J., Blum, A., Sandholm, T.: Clearing algorithms for barter exchange markets: enabling nationwide kidney exchanges. In: EC 2007: Proceedings of the 8th ACM Conference on Electronic Commerce, pp. 295–304. ACM Press, New York (2007)
2. Ackemann, T., Gold, R., Mascolo, C., Emmerich, W.: Incentives in peer-to-peer and grid networking. Technical report, University College London (2002)
3. Ajtai, M., Komlós, J., Szemerédi, E.: An 0(n log n) sorting network. In: STOC 1983: Proceedings of the fifteenth annual ACM symposium on Theory of computing, pp. 1–9. ACM Press, New York (1983)
4. Bhavsar, V.C., Boley, H., Yang, L.: A weighted tree similarity algorithm for multi-agent system in e-business environments. In: Workshop on Business Agents and the Semantic Web, pp. 53–72 (June 2003)
5. Canetti, R.: Security and composition of multiparty cryptographic protocols. Journal of Cryptology 13(1), 143–202 (2000)
6. Cresti, B.: US domestic barter: an empirical investigation. Applied Economics 37(17), 1953–1966 (2005)
7. Damgård, I., Jurik, M.: A length-flexible threshold cryptosystem with applications. In: Safavi-Naini, R., Seberry, J. (eds.) ACISP 2003. LNCS, vol. 2727, pp. 350–364. Springer, Heidelberg (2003)
8. Freedman, M., Nissim, K., Pinkas, B.: Efficient private matching and set intersection. In: Cachin, C., Camenisch, J.L. (eds.) EUROCRYPT 2004. LNCS, vol. 3027, pp. 1–19. Springer, Heidelberg (2004)
9. Frikken, K.: Privacy-preserving set union. In: Katz, J., Yung, M. (eds.) ACNS 2007. LNCS, vol. 4521, pp. 237–252. Springer, Heidelberg (to appear, 2007)
10. Frikken, K.B., Atallah, M.J.: Privacy preserving route planning. In: WPES 2004: Proceedings of the 2004 ACM workshop on Privacy in the electronic society, pp. 8–15. ACM Press, New York (2004)
11. Fu, Y., Chase, J., Chun, B., Schwab, S., Vahdat, A.: SHARP: an architecture for secure resource peering. In: SOSP 2003: Proceedings of the Nineteenth ACM Symposium on Operating Systems Principles, pp. 133–148. ACM Press, New York (2003)
12. Ganesan, P., Seshadri, M.: On cooperative content distribution and the price of barter. In: Proceedings of the 25th IEEE International Conference on Distributed Computing Systems (ICDCS 2005), pp. 81–90 (June 2005)

13. Goethals, B., Laur, S., Lipmaa, H., Mielikainen, T.: On private scalar product computation for privacy-prerving data mining. In: Park, C., Chee, S. (eds.) ICISC 2004. LNCS, vol. 3506, pp. 104–120. Springer, Heidelberg (2005)
14. Goldreich, O., Micali, S., Wigderson, A.: How to play any mental game. In: Proceedings of the nineteenth annual ACM conference on Theory of computing, pp. 218–229 (May 1987)
15. Goldwasser, S., Micali, S.: Probabilistic encryption. Journal of Computer and System Sciences 28(2), 270–299 (1984)
16. Haddawy, P., Rujikeadkumjorn, N., Dhananaiyapergse, K., Cheng, C.: Balanced matching of buyers and sellers in e-marketplaces: the barter trade exchange model. In: ICEC 2004, pp. 85–94. ACM Press, New York (2004)
17. Intervac international home exchange (Last viewed: 10-08-2007), http://www.intervac.com
18. International reciprocal trade association (Last viewed: 10-08-2007), www.irta.com
19. Kissner, L., Song, D.: Privacy-preserving set operations. In: Shoup, V. (ed.) CRYPTO 2005. LNCS, vol. 3621, pp. 241–257. Springer, Heidelberg (2005), http://www.cs.cmu.edu/~leak/
20. López, N., Núñez, M., Rodríguez, I., Rubio, F.: A formal framework for e-barter based on microeconomic theory and process algebras. In: Unger, H., Böhme, T., Mikler, A.R. (eds.) IICS 2002. LNCS, vol. 2346, pp. 217–228. Springer, Heidelberg (2002)
21. López, N., Núñez, M., Rodríguez, I., Rubio, F.: A multi-agent system for e-barter including transaction and shipping costs. In: Matsui, M., Zuccherato, R.J. (eds.) SAC 2003. LNCS, vol. 3006, pp. 587–594. Springer, Heidelberg (2004)
22. Marin, D., Schnitzer, M.: The economic institution of international barter. The Economic Journal 112(479), 293–316 (2002)
23. Mathieu, S.: Match-making in bartering scenarios. Master's thesis, The University of New Brunswick (December 2005)
24. Muir, D.: Man trades up from paper clip to house (July 9, 2006), http://www.abcnews.go.com/wnt/story?id=2171378
25. National association of trade exchanges (Last viewed: 10-08-2007), www.nate.org
26. Paillier, P.: Public-key cryptosystems based on composite degree residuosity classes. In: Stern, J. (ed.) EUROCRYPT 1999. LNCS, vol. 1592, pp. 223–238. Springer, Heidelberg (1999)
27. Peerflix (Lastviewed: 10-08-2007), www.peerflix.com
28. Read it swap it (Last viewed: 10-08-2007), www.readitswapit.co.uk
29. Yao, A.C.: How to generate and exchange secrets. In: Proceedings of the 27th Annual IEEE Symposium on Foundations of Computer Science, pp. 162–167 (1986)
30. Yao, D., Frikken, K.B., Atallah, M.J., Tamassia, R.: Point-based trust: Define how much privacy is worth. In: Ning, P., Qing, S., Li, N. (eds.) ICICS 2006. LNCS, vol. 4307, pp. 190–209. Springer, Heidelberg (2006)

Breaking Legacy Banking Standards with Special-Purpose Hardware

Tim Güneysu and Christof Paar

Horst Görtz Institute for IT Security, Ruhr University Bochum, Germany

Abstract. In the field of eCommerce, online-banking is one of the major application requiring the usage of modern cryptography to protect the confidentiality and integrity of financial transactions between users and the banking system. In banking applications of some countries, the authorization of user transactions is performed with support of cryptographic One-Time-Password (OTP) tokens implementing ANSI X9.9-based challenge-response protocols.

The legacy ANSI X9.9 standard is a DES-based authentication method on which we will demonstrate an attack based on a special-purpose hardware cluster. In this work we show how to break such an OTP-token with little effort in terms of costs and time. With an investment of about US $ 10,000 we are able to perform an attack which computes the key of a DES-based OTP token in less than a week having only three challenge-response pairs. Our attack can even be scaled linearly according to the budget of the attacker resulting in even faster breaking times. With this work, we want to point out once more that the immediate migration from legacy products using the DES algorithm is absolutely mandatory for security critical applications.

Keywords: ANSI X9.9, Banking, Cryptanalysis, Special-Purpose Hardware.

1 Introduction

With the rise of the Internet during the last decades, this new communication medium has become increasingly relevant for financial transactions with respect to eCommerce and particularly, online-banking. At the same time, the Internet opens up new potential ways for digital criminals to attack banking applications what increases the demand for effective cryptography. Beside efficient data encryption schemes to protect the business transaction from being eavesdropped or altered by unauthorized parties, individuals need to authenticate themselves, e.g., for logging into an online-banking system of a financial institute. For this reason, several fundamentally different entity authentication techniques are in use worldwide. For instance, some banks make use of a combination of personal and transaction identification numbers (PIN/TAN), others employ single-use passwords which are generated by cryptographic tokens. In this contribution, we will focus

G. Tsudik (Ed.): FC 2008, LNCS 5143, pp. 128–140, 2008.

on the latter, token-based One-Time-Passwords[1] (OTP) used for authenticating users in financial applications. Note that in this work the tokens of interests are tokens which respond deterministically to a given ANSI X9.9 challenge without any further source of entropy like time or user events being involved.

In order to establish common methods for cryptography, worldwide standards for computer authentication have been developed since the 1980s. Financial security was historically one of the main motivation for such standards. Based on the Data Encryption Standard (DES) cipher [12,1], which was the most common cipher used for many years, several standards for authentication have been created, e.g., FIPS PUB 113 [11], ANSI X9.9 [2] and ISO 8730 [8]. In 1998, the Electronic Frontier Foundation (EFF) presented a hardware cracker called *Deep Crack* capable to break DES within 56 hours [7] due to its greatest weakness — the small key space. Deep Crack consisted of $1,536$ custom designed ASIC chips and was built for about US$ 250,000. As a response to cracking machines like this, it was agreed that new standards need be developed to replace the DES cipher, resulting in cipher schemes like Triple-DES [13] and the Advanced Encryption Standard (AES) [14] as a quick fix to the weak single-DES.

In 2004, the International Organization for Standardization (ISO) has withdrawn ISO 8730 for DES-based data authentication and replaced it with ISO 16609 [9] based on the AES. Similarly in 2004, the National Institute of Standards and Technology (NIST) has declared DES to be outdated and should be only used as a component of TDES [15]. Since 2005, DES is not recommended for use in any security-relevant application. Despite of this statement two years ago, it is known that there are still legacy DES-based systems which are also used in critical applications such as online-banking systems. We are aware of several banks in Europe, North and Central America[2] which are using OTP-tokens for banking systems to authorize financial transactions using a DES-based crypto-token according to ANSI X9.9. Although these DES-tokens partially support TDES operation, they still allow single DES operation as well as ANSI X9.9 authentication. We believe that such single DES-based systems are still in use in some banking applications due to compatibility reasons with legacy systems. One example of such crypto tokens which are still issued by banks for use in online-banking are the tokens by ActivIdentity [3], formerly ActivCard [20].

To emphasize the security weaknesses of legacy DES-based systems and, to hasten the replacement of unsecure crypto modules, we present the first hardware-based attack on single-DES tokens implementing a challenge-response protocol based on the common ANSI X9.9 standard. We would like to mention that we were able to actually break commercial on-line banking tokens in our lab. Again, we prefer not to name the manufacturer.

---

[1] Our abbreviation is not to be confused with *one time pad* or *one-time programmable*, which is also sometimes denoted by OTP.

[2] The names of respective institutions are known to the authors but will not be mentioned here. In fact, even large banks with about 2.5 million internet banking customers do not seem to have completely abandoned the use of single DES in their systems.

This contribution is structured as follows: in the next section, we briefly introduce relevant previous work related to DES. Next, we give a short introduction to the functionality of ANSI X9.9-based crypto tokens. Section 4 is dedicated to the development of attack scenarios against real-world protocols which are based on crypto tokens. The implementation of those are discussed in Section 6. Due to the fact that we can break ANSI X9.9-based tokens in about a week, we conclude our work with a strong recommendation for immediate replacement of obsolete crypto modules in security-sensitive environments.

2   Previous Work

Although the DES has been reaffirmed for use in (US government) security systems several times until 1998, the worries about the inherent threat of its short key space was already raised in 1977 [6] when it was first proposed. A first detailed hardware design description for a brute force attacker was presented by Michael Wiener at the rump session of CRYPTO'93, a printed version of which is available in [21]. It was estimated that the machine could be built for less than a million US dollars. The proposed machine consists of $57,000$ DES chips that could recover a key every three and half hours. The estimates were updated in 1998 due to the advances in hardware for a million dollar machine to 35 minutes for each key recovery [22]. Ian Goldberg and David Wagner estimated the cost for building a DES brute force attacker using FPGAs to US$ 45,000 for a key recovery within a year [7]. In 1997, a detailed cost estimate for three different approaches for DES key search: distributed computing, FPGAs and custom ASIC designs, was compiled by Blaze et al. [4]. The first actual DES attack (presumably outside government agencies) took place in 1998, and was based on the above mentioned *Deep Crack* [7]. To our knowledge, the latest step in the history of DES brute-force attacks took place in 2006, when the Cost Optimal Parallel Code Breaker (COPACOBANA) was built for less than US$ 10,000 [10]. COPACOBANA is capable of breaking DES in less than one week on average. We would like to stress that software-only attacks against DES still take more than 1,000 PC-years (worst case).

Most of these attacks assume that at least one complete plaintext-ciphertext pair is given. We will see that crypto tokens for bank applications typically do not provide such input, so that a smarter attack must be chosen to tackle this kind of systems. There are some theoretical contributions by Coppersmith et al. [5] as well as by Preneel and van Oorschot [16] considering the theoretical security of DES-based authentication methods (DES-MAC). But to our best knowledge an attack on an actually ANSI X9.9-based crypto system has not been proposed (or demonstrated) yet.

3   Basics of Token Based Data Authentication

We will now describe a OTP token-based data protocol according to FIPS 113 or ANSI X9.9 which is used for authentication in some real-world online-banking systems. Please note that in this work we assume that OTP tokens have a fixed, securely integrated static key inside and do not use additional entropy sources like time or events for computing the passwords. Indeed, there are tokens available which generate new passwords after a dedicated time interval (e.g., products like the RSA SecurID solution [18]) but those will not be the focus of this work. These type of tokens require additional assumptions concerning the unknown plaintext and thus are harder to attack. Thus, our contribution assumes fixed-key OTP tokens which can be used in combination with a challenge-response protocol. In such protocols, a decimal-digit challenge is manually entered into the token via an integrated keypad. The token in turn computes the corresponding response according to the ANSI X9.9 standard. Tokens implementing this standardized authentication scheme (incorporating ANSI 3.92 DES encryption) have a often a fixed size LCD allowing for displaying 8 decimal digits for input and output.

After the user has typed in eight decimal digits as input (challenge), the value is converted to binary representation using standard ASCII code notation according to the ANSI X9.9 standard. For instance, the typed number "12345678" is converted into the 64-bit challenge value in hexadecimal representation

$$c = (0x31, 0x32, 0x33, 0x34, 0x35, 0x36, 0x37, 0x38).$$

After recoding, c is used as plaintext to the DES encryption function $r = e_k(c)$ with the static key k stored securely in the token. The output of the encryption function is the 64-bit ciphertext $r = (r_1, r_0)$ where each r_i denotes a 32 bit word to be transformed using a mapping μ to fit the 8-digit display of the token. The mapping μ takes the 8 hexadecimal digits of r_1 (32 bits) of the DES encryption as input, and converts each digit individually from hexadecimal (binary) notation to decimal representation. Let $H = \{0, \ldots, 9, A, \ldots, F\}$ and $D = \{0, \ldots, 9\}$ be the alphabets of hexadecimal and decimal digits, respectively. Then μ is defined as:

$$\mu : H \to D : \{0_H \mapsto 0_D; \ldots; 9_H \mapsto 9_D; A_H \mapsto 0_D; \ldots; F_H \mapsto 5_D\}$$

Hence, the output after the mapping μ is an 8 decimal digit value which is displayed on the LCD of the token. Figure 1 shows how the response is generated on the token according to a given challenge. In several countries, this authentication method is used in banking applications whenever a customer needs to authenticate financial transactions. For this, each user of such an online-banking system possesses a personal token used to respond to challenges which are presented by the banking system on every security critical operation. In this context for example, a security critical operation can be the login to the banking system as well as the authorization of a money transfer. The central role in such a security-related application makes the secret token an interesting target for an attack.

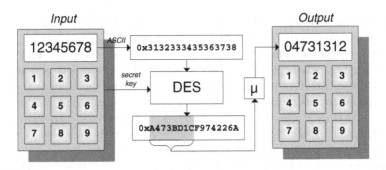

Fig. 1. Principle of the response generation on a ANSI X9.9-based crypto token

4   Cryptanalysis of the ANSI X9.9-Based Challenge-Response Authentication

With the knowledge of how an authenticator is computed in the challenge-response protocol, we will continue with identifying weaknesses to attack this authentication scheme. Firstly, ANSI X9.9 relies on the outdated DES algorithm for which we can build a low-cost special-purpose hardware machine to perform an exhaustive key search in under a week. Secondly, the output r of the DES encryption is only slightly modified. (Note that a more complex scrambling with additional dynamic input, like hash functions with salt, would make the attack considerably more complex.) The output r is only truncated to 32-bit and modified using the mapping μ to convert c_1 from hexadecimal to decimal notation. Due to the truncation to 32 bits, we need to acquire knowledge of at least two plaintext-ciphertext pairs when mounting an exhaustive key search returning only a single key candidate. The digit conversion in μ additionally reduces the information leaked by a single pair of plaintext-ciphertext which is addressed by Theorem 1.

Theorem 1. *Let $D = \{0, \ldots, 9\}$ be the alphabet of decimal digits. With a single challenge-response pair (c, r) of an ANSI X9.9-based authentication scheme where $c, r \in D^8$, on average 26 bits of a DES key can be determined (24 bits in the worst case, 32 bits in the best case).*

Proof: Since only 32 bits of the output c for a given challenge c are exposed, this is a trivial upper bound for the information leakage for a single pair. Assuming the DES encryption function to be a pseudo-random function with appropriate statistical properties, the 32 most significant bits of c form 8 hexadecimal digits uniformly distributed over $H^8 = \{0, \ldots, 9, A, \ldots, 8\}^8$. The surjective mapping μ has the domain $F = \{0, \ldots, 9\}$ of which $T = \{0, \ldots, 5\}$ are double assigned. Hence, we know that $\Delta = F\backslash T = \{6, \ldots, 9\}$ are four fixed points which directly correspond to output digits of c yielding four bit of key information (I). The six remaining decimal digits $\Omega = F \cap T$ can have two potential origins allowing for a potential deviation of one bit (II). According to a uniform distribution of the 8 hexadecimal output digits, the probability that (I) is given for an arbitrary digit

i of c is $Pr(i \in \Delta) = 1/4$. Thus, on average we can expect 2 out of 8 hexadecimal digits of c to be in Δ revealing four bits of the key whereas the remaining 6 digits introduce a possible variance of one unknown bit per digit. Averaged, this leads to knowledge of $R = 2 \cdot 4 + 6 \cdot 3 = 26$ bits of DES key material. Obviously, the best case with all 8 digits in Δ and worst case with no digits out of the set Δ provide 32 and 24 key bits, respectively.

According to Theorem 1, we can develop two distinguished attacks based on the knowledge of two and three known challenge-response pairs:

Corollary 1. *Given two known challenge-response pairs (c_i, r_i) for $i = \{0,1\}$ of the ANSI X9.9 authentication scheme, an exhaustive key search using both pairs will reveal $2^4 = 16$ potential key candidates on average (256 candidates in the worst case, in the best case the actual key is returned).*

Proof: Assuming independence of two different encrypted blocks related to the same key in block ciphers, we can use accumulated results from Theorem 1 for key determination using multiple pairs (p_i, c_i). Hence, on average we can expect to determine 52 bits of the key where each c_i has 2 digits from the set Δ. Given a full DES key of 56 bit size results in 2^4 possible variations for key candidates. Having at least 4 digits from Δ for each c_i, this will lead to the best case resulting in a single key candidate. In the worst case and with no Δ digits in any c_i, we will end up with 48 bits of determined key material and $2^8 = 256$ possible remaining key candidates. As a consequence, the number of potential key candidates is directly dependent on how many digits of a c_i are fixed points and out of the set Δ.

Corollary 2. *Given three known challenge-response pairs of the ANSI X9.9 authentication scheme, an exhaustive key search based on this information will uniquely reveal the DES key.*

Proof: This case can be directly derived from Corollary 1. For this attack, $3 \cdot 24 = 72 > 56$ bits of key material can directly determined (even in the worst case) resulting in the correct key to be definitely identified.

5   Possible Attack Scenarios on Banking Systems

With these theoretical means at hand, we can begin to develop two attack variants for two and three plaintext-ciphertext pairs. Since we need only few pairs of information, an attack is feasible in a real-world scenario. For instance, if we consider a phishing attack on an online-banking system, we can easily imagine that two or three (faked) challenges are presented to the user, who is likely to respond with the appropriate values generated by his token. Alternatively spying techniques, e.g., based on malicious software like key-loggers or hidden cameras, can be used to observe the user while responding to a challenge. It is important to state that the freshness of these values do not play a role since we use the information only for computing the secret key and not for an unauthorized login attempt. Figure 2 shows a possible attack scenario on ANSI X9.9 tokens and

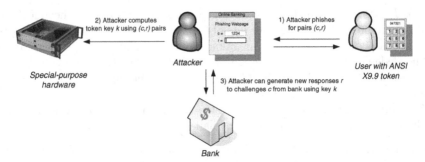

Fig. 2. Attack scenario for token-based banking applications using phishing techniques

associated banking applications based on phishing of challenge-response pairs (c, r). With at least two pairs of challenge-response data, we can perform an exhaustive key search on the DES key space implementing the specific features of ANSI X9.9 authentication. To cope with the DES key space of 2^{56} potential key candidates we will propose an implementation based on dedicated special-purpose hardware. In case that three pairs of challenge-responses pairs are given, we are definitely able to determine the key of the secret token using a single exhaustive key search. When only two pairs (c_i, r_i) are available to the attacker, then it is likely that several potential key candidates are returned from the key search (cf. Corollary 1). With 16 potential solutions on average, the attacker can attempt to guess the right solution by trial-and-error. Since most banking systems allow the user to enter up to three erroneous responds to a challenge in a row, two key candidates can be tried by the attacker at a time. Then, after a period of inactivity, the authorized user has probably logged into the banking application that resets the error counter and allows the attacker to start another trial session with further key candidates. On average, the attacker can expect to be successful after about four trial and error sessions, testing 8 out of the 16 keys from the candidate list. Hence, an attack on an ANSI X9.9-based token is very likely to be successful even with knowledge of only two given challenge-response pairs.

6   Implementing an Attack on ANSI X9.9-Based Systems

In this section we will discuss the implementation of an hardware attack on the ANSI X9.9 scheme with given two or three challenge-response pairs (c_i, r_i). Our hardware architecture will be designed for use with two pairs since data paths and multiplexers in hardware are less complex with only two inputs. For each potential key of the DES key space, the corresponding authenticator is computed for the given challenges and compared against the known responses. Potential key candidates satisfying the comparison for both (c_i, r_i) are transferred to a host computer. If even a third challenge-response pair is available, this is compared on the host computer to reduce hardware complexity.

Next, we will introduce our special-hardware cluster platform used to perform an exhaustive key search out of 2^{56} possible key candidates in about a week.

6.1 FPGA-Based Special-Purpose Hardware Cluster

Today low-cost Field Programmable Gate Arrays (FPGA) provide an interesting alternative to ASICs for the massive computational effort required for cryptanalytic applications and code breaking. Since FPGAs have evolved in gate complexity at reduced costs during the last years, their advantage of flexible configuration at runtime makes them competitive to ASIC devices which are designed for a single application only. Hence, a cluster system based on FPGAs can support a wide variety of applications providing a significant cost-performance advantage over PC-based machines.

6.2 Hardware Cluster Architecture

The COPACOBANA machine [10] is an existing FPGA cluster designed for parallel computations with only a minor demand on communication and volatile memory. It integrates 120 Xilinx Spartan-3 XC3S1000 FPGAs in a compact and modular design on a single backplane. Each FPGA consists of 1 million system gates providing 17280 equivalent logic cells which is sufficient for cost-optimized implementations of medium-scale circuits in reconfigurable hardware. The flexibility of our system platform has been achieved by 20 small and pluggable FPGA-modules (standard DIMM size) each populated with six FPGAs. The backplane hosts all FPGA-modules and a controller card which connects the COPACOBANA to a standard computer using a USB or Ethernet interface. All DIMM-modules are connected via the backplane by a 64-bit data bus and a 16-bit address bus. A detailed overview of the architecture is depicted in Figure 3. The COPACOBANA is an excellent platform for applications with very high computational requirements but low communication demands. A symmetric brute force attack is such a computational problem which can be hardly tackled with standard PCs. For example, an exhaustive key search on DES can be performed with the FPGAs clocked at 136 MHz, allowing for a total number of 544 million encryptions per second on *each* FPGA. Hence, the entire machine incorporating 120 FPGAs can compute about $2^{35.9}$ DES-encryptions per second resulting in an average key search duration of 6.4 days. A single standard PC performing 2 million DES encryptions per second, however, would take 585 years on average to complete this task [10]. Hence, a large number of PCs is required to achieve a equivalent computational power as provided by COPACOBANA. Due to the simple design of the COPACOBANA, its total material costs including manufacturing (but excluding initial design costs) are just about $ 10,000 which makes code breaking based on COPACOBANA affordable and realistic.

6.3 FPGA-Based Attack Architecture

Originally, the DES was designed to be optimal for hardware-based implementations. Therefore, an FPGA implementation of the DES can be more than a

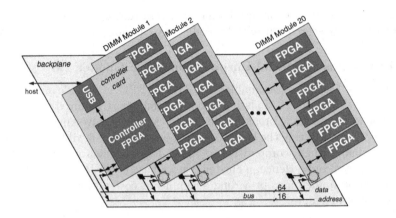

Fig. 3. The COPACOBANA cluster architecture provides 120 Spartan-3 FPGAs on a single backplane distributed over 20 DIMM-modules (each hosting 6 FPGA devices)

100 times faster than an implementation on a conventional PC. This allows a hardware-based key search engine to be much faster and more cost efficient compared to an approach using a comparable software cluster.

The main goal of our hardware design is a key search of the token to be done in a highly parallelized fashion by partitioning the key space among the available FPGAs on the COPACOBANA. This requires hardly any interprocess communication, as each of the DES engines can search for the right key within its allocated key subspace.

Within the FPGAs, we used an optimized version of the highly pipelined DES implementation of the Université Catholique de Louvain's Crypto Group [17], which computes one encryption per clock per engine. Thus, it is possible to test one potential key per clock cycle. This scales linearly with the number of available parallel engines. For breaking ANSI X9.9-based authentication, we can fit four such DES engines inside a single FPGA, and therefore allow for sharing of control circuitry and the key space as shown in Figure 4. The FPGA architecture comprises two 64-bit *plaintext* registers for the challenges and two 32-bit *ciphertext* registers for storing the corresponding responses which have been acquired from the OTP-token. The key space to be searched is allocated to each chip as the most-significant 14-bits of the key which is stored in the *Key* register. The counter (*CNT 1*) is used to run through the least significant 40 bits of the key. The remaining two bits of the 56-bit key for each of the DES engines is hardwired and dedicated to each of them. Thus, for every such FPGA, a task is assigned to search through all the keys with the 16 most-significant bits fixed, in total 2^{40} different keys. The key space is partitioned by a connected host-PC so that each chip takes around 150 minutes (at 120 MHz) to test all ANSI X9.9 authenticators in its allocated key subspace. During a single check of an authenticator, the DES engines use the first challenge (*plaintext 1*) as a primary input to the encryption function. Then, the upper 32-bits of the generated ciphertext is mapped digit-per-digit by the function μ and compared

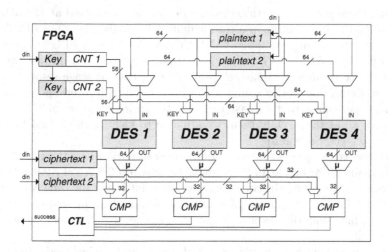

Fig. 4. Four ANSI X9.9 key search units based on fully pipelined DES cores in a Xilinx Spartan-3 FPGA

to the value of the response stored in the register *ciphertext 1*. If any of the DES engines provides a positive match, the corresponding engine switches its input to the second challenge encrypting it with the same key. To match the pipelined design of the DES engine, we are using a shadow counter (*CNT 2*) implementing a delay tracking the key position at the beginning of the pipeline. In case that the derived authenticator from the second encryption compares successfully to the second response, the controller *CTL* reports the counter value to the host-PC as a potential key candidate. The host-PC keeps track of the key range that is assigned to each of the FPGAs and, hence, can match the right key from a given counter value. If no match is found until the counter overflows, the FPGA reports completion of the task and remains idle until a new key space is assigned. In case that a third challenge-response pair has been specified, the host-PC performs a verification operation of the reported key candidate in software. In case the verification was successful, the search is aborted and the key returned as result of the search.

7 Implementation Results

We have implemented the FPGA architecture shown in Figure 4 using the Xilinx ISE 9.1 development platform. After synthesis of the design incorporating four DES engines and the additional logic for the derivation of the ANSI X9.9 authenticator, the usage of 8,729 flip flops (FF) and 12,813 Look-Up-Tables (LUT) has been reported by the tools (56% FF and 83% LUT utilization of the Spartan-3 device, respectively). Furthermore, we included FPGA specific optimizations like pipelined comparators since n-bit comparators are likely to introduce a long signal propagation path reducing the maximum clock frequency significantly. By removing these potential bottlenecks, the design can be clocked at 120MHz after place-and-route resulting in a throughput of 480 million keys per FPGA per second. In total, a fully equipped COPACOBANA with 120 FPGAs can compute 57.6 billion ANSI X9.9 authenticators per second. Based on this, we can present time estimates for an attack provided that two challenge-response pairs are given. Recall that in this scenario we will be faced with several potential key candidates per run so that we have to search the entire key space of 2^{56} to build a list with all of them. Only then, we are able to identify the actual key in a separate step (cf. Section 5).

Similarly, we can present figures for an attack scenario where three challenge-response pairs are available. In this attack, we must test 2^{55} ANSI X9.9 authenticators on average to find the corresponding key what is half the time complexity of an attack having two known pairs of data. Note that all presented figures of Table 1 include material costs only (not taking energy and development costs into account).

For comparison with our hardware-based cluster, we have included estimations for a Intel Pentium 4 processor operating at 3GHz. This microprocessor allows for a throughput of about 2 million DES computations a second and thus we assume this as throughput estimate for generating ANSI X9.9 authenticators.

Table 1. Cost-performance figures for attacking the ANSI X9.9 scheme with two and three known challenge-response pairs (c_i, r_i)

Hardware System	Cost	Attack using two pairs (c_i, r_i)	Attack using three pairs (c_i, r_i)
1 Pentium4 @ 3GHz	$ 50	1170 years	585 years
1 FPGA XC3S1000	$ 50	4.8 years	2.4 years
1 COPACOBANA	$ 10,000	14.5 days	7.2 days
100 COPACOBANAs	$ 1 million	3.5 hours	104 min

Summarizing, an investment of $ 1 million in COPACOBANA systems can break the ANSI X9.9-based security system of a bank account in less than 2 hours with only three given challenge-response pairs.

8   Conclusion

In this work we have presented a first hardware attack on the ANSI X9.9 authentication scheme as used in challenge-response protocols based on OTP-tokens in banking applications. Since legacy ANSI X9.9 employs the use of DES, it can be broken using a specialized brute-force attack based on special-purpose hardware. The key of OTP-token computing ANSI X9.9 responses to challenges issued by a banking application for user and transaction authentication can be broken for $ 10,000 using at most three challenge-response pairs in about a week. Even worse, the performance of the attack can be scaled linearly according the the attacker's budget.

In fact, our work shows that not only the DES encryption scheme is completely broken but also its related standards like ANSI X9.9 as used in banking use-cases. We like to enforce all affected institutes to migrate their systems as fast as possible to abandon DES-based cryptography when not already done.

We would like to point out that software-only attacks against DES still take more than $1,000$ PC-years (worst case), which is still a formidable hurdle even for determined attackers outside large organizations like government agencies. Thus, one lesson learned appears to be that it is not sufficient to only look at an attacker's available budget for computation, but also at the *type* of available computational platform.

Note: The attack architecture described in Section 6.3 has already been extensively tested using simulated challenge-response pairs. For an attack on existing devices, we acquired an off-the-shelf ANSI X9.9 OTP-token which is commercially available and currently used in real-world eCommerce systems. All upcoming results of this attack on an actual token will be presented on the project website of COPACOBANA available at [19].

References

1. Accredited Standards Committee X3. American National Standard X3.92: Data Encryption Algorithm (DEA) (1981)
2. Accredited Standards Committee X9. American National Standard X9.9: Financial Institution Message Authentication (1994)
3. ActivIdentity. Token-based Identity Systems (OTP Tokens) (2007), http://www.activeidentity.com
4. Blaze, M., Diffie, W., Rivest, R.L., Schneier, B., Shimomura, T., Thompson, E., Wiener, M.: Minimal Key Lengths for Symmetric Ciphers to Provide Adequate Commercial Security: A Report by an Ad Hoc Group of Cryptographers and Computer Scientists. Technical report (January 1996), http://www.counterpane.com/keylength.html
5. Coppersmith, D., Knudsen, L.R., Mitchell, C.J.: Key recovery and forgery attacks on the macDES MAC algorithm. In: Bellare, M. (ed.) CRYPTO 2000. LNCS, vol. 1880, p. 184. Springer, Heidelberg (2000)
6. Diffie, W., Hellman, M.E.: Exhaustive cryptanalysis of the NBS DES. Computer 10(6), 74–84 (1977)
7. Electronic Frontier Foundation. Cracking DES: Secrets of Encryption Research, Wiretap Politics & Chip Design. O'Reilly & Associates Inc. (July 1998)
8. International Organization for Standardization (ISO). ISO 8730/8731:1990 – Banking – Requirements for message authentication (1990)
9. International Organization for Standardization (ISO). ISO 16609:2004 – Banking – Requirements for message authentication using symmetric techniques (2004)
10. Kumar, S., Paar, C., Pelzl, J., Pfeiffer, G., Schimmler, M.: Breaking Ciphers with COPACOBANA - A Cost-Optimized Parallel Code Breaker. In: Goubin, L., Matsui, M. (eds.) CHES 2006. LNCS, vol. 4249, pp. 101–118. Springer, Heidelberg (2006)
11. National Institute for Standards and Technology (NIST). FIPS PUB 113: Standard for computer data authentication (May 1985)
12. National Institute for Standards and Technology (NIST). FIPS PUB 46-2: Data Encryption Standard (DES) (1993)

13. National Institute for Standards and Technology (NIST). FIPS PUB 46-3: Data Encryption Standard (DES) and Triple DES (TDES) (1999)
14. National Institute for Standards and Technology (NIST). FIPS 197: Advanced Encryption Standard (AES) (2001)
15. National Institute of Standards and Technology. Recommendation for the Triple Data Encryption Algorithm (TDEA) Block Cipher (May 2004), http://csrc.nist.gov/publications/nistpubs/800-67/SP800-67.pdf
16. Preneel, B., Van Oorschot, P.C.: Key recovery attack on ANSI X9.19 retail MAC. In: Electronics Letters, vol. 32(17), pp. 1568–1569. IEEE, Dept. of Electr. Eng., Katholieke Univ, Leuven (1996)
17. Rouvroy, G., Standaert, F.-X., Quisquater, J.-J., Legat, J.-D.: Design Strategies and Modified Descriptions to Optimize Cipher FPGA Implementations: Fast and Compact Results for DES and Triple-DES. In: Cheung, Y.K.P., Constantinides, G.A. (eds.) FPL 2003. LNCS, vol. 2778, pp. 181–193. Springer, Heidelberg (2003)
18. RSA - The Security Division of EMC^2. RSA SecurID (2007), http://www.rsa.com/
19. Sciengines GmbH. COPACOBANA - A Codebreaker for DES and other Ciphers. project and company website (2008), http://www.copacobana.org http://www.sciengines.de
20. Verisign. Activcard tokens. Data Sheet, http://www.verisign.com.au/guide/activcard/ActivCard_Tokens.pdf
21. Wiener, M.J.: Efficient DES Key Search. In: Stallings, W.R. (ed.) Practical Cryptography for Data Internetworks, pp. 31–79. IEEE Computer Society Press, Los Alamitos (1996)
22. Wiener, M.J.: Efficient DES Key Search: An Update. CRYPTOBYTES 3(2), 6–8 (1997)

ePassport: Securing International Contacts with Contactless Chips

Gildas Avoine, Kassem Kalach, and Jean-Jacques Quisquater

Université catholique de Louvain
Louvain-la-Neuve, Belgium

Abstract. Electronic passports (ePassports) have known a wide and fast deployment all around the world since the International Civil Aviation Organization published their specifications in 2004. Based on an integrated circuit, ePassports are significantly more secure than their predecessors. Forging an ePassport is definitely thwarted by the use of cryptographic means. In spite of their undeniable benefit, ePassports have raised questions about personal data protection, since attacks on the basic access control mechanism came into sight. Keys used for that purpose derive from the nothing but predictable machine readable zone data, and so suffer from weak entropy. We provide an in-depth evaluation of the basic access key entropy, and prove that Belgian passport, recipient of Interpol "World's most secure passport" award in 2003, provides the worst basic access key entropy one has ever seen. We also state that two-thirds of Belgian ePassports in circulation do not implement any data protection mechanism. We demonstrate our claims by means of practical attacks. We then provide recommendations to amend the ePassport security, and directions for further work.

1 Introduction

Malaysia was the first country in the world to issue electronic passports. It adopted this technology in March 1998, thus predating the standard [13, 14], aka Doc. 9303, elaborated by the *International Civil Aviation Organization* (ICAO). Belgium was the first country worldwide[1] to issue ICAO-compliant electronic passports (ePassports). Nowadays, more than 50 countries issue ePassports, for example USA, UK, Germany, France, Italy, Belgium, Australia, Singapore, Switzerland, etc.

The wide and fast deployment of ePassports has mainly been possible thanks to the ICAO efforts. In 1997, the ICAO commenced a comprehensive revision of its documents, and disclosed the first versions of ePassport specifications in 2004. The US Visa Waiver Program[2] has also considerably accelerated this wide spread. It enables citizens from about 27 countries to travel to the USA for

---

[1] http://judiciary.house.gov/OversightTestimony.aspx?ID=352
[2] http://travel.state.gov/visa/

G. Tsudik (Ed.): FC 2008, LNCS 5143, pp. 141–155, 2008.
© Springer-Verlag Berlin Heidelberg 2008

tourism or business for stays of 90 days or less without obtaining a visa. However, countries were required to have an ePassport issuing system in place by 26 October 2006, in order to continue as members of the program.

An ePassport (or biometric passport) is the same as a traditional passport combined with an *integrated circuit* (IC) embedded either in its cover pages or laminated over a data page. According to the ICAO, the IC must store as a minimum the duplicate of the *Machine Readable Zone* (MRZ) and a digital facial image of the passport's holder. The MRZ is the two optically readable encoded lines at the bottom of the passport first data page and includes the document type, full name, passport number, nationality, date of birth, gender, date of expiry, and the corresponding check digits. The IC may also contain lots of optional information such as handwritten signature, fingerprints, address, phone numbers, information about the persons to notify in case of emergency, etc.

Data stored in the IC is digitally signed by the issuing country using a highly protected private key. Consequently, one cannot modify or create from scratch a passport without being detected. Equipped with sufficient storage memory, the ePassport allows incorporating biometrics that add additional identification features, that is the name "biometric passport". Consequently, information stored in the IC, information available from the *Visual Inspection Zone*[3] (VIZ), and biometrics of the physical person can be compared. Finally, the IC may optionally prevent cloning or substitution since it has the ability to prove the possession of an asymmetric private key. A contactless or RFID (*Radio-Frequency Identification*) technology has been chosen due to its numerous advantages compared to the contact-based one. Incorporating the IC into the passport book is much easier and the inspection process becomes very handy. In particular, using this technology does not require to position the passport accurately on the reader.

However, based on a contactless technology, this IC has created many new security threats [1, 2]. Juels, Molnar, and Wagner [17] explored some of these threats in the context of the US passport. They mainly discussed the data leakage and biometric threats. Besides, they discussed the *Basic Access Control* (BAC) low entropy of the US passport. Kc and Karger [18] rewrote this work and discussed additional issues related to slice attacks (encountered in hotels and banks), fake fingers, and the BSI proposal for *Extended Access Control* (EAC). Hoepman *et al.* [12] discussed particularly the BAC in the context of Dutch passport, traceability, EAC, and threats of ePassport-based new applications. Monnerat, Vaudenay, and Vuagnoux [21] reviewed the ePassport privacy issues, and focused on the *Active Authentication* side effects. They proposed a GQ-based authentication protocol as a possible countermeasure. Lehtonen *et al.* [20] proposed combining RFID with optical memory devices in order to improve the security of machine readable documents. Witteman [27] established a practical attack against the BAC of the Dutch passport. Grunwald executed a similar attack on the German ePassport [7]. Laurie also successfully cloned a UK ePassport while it was hidden in an envelope [19]. All of them, however,

---

[3] Information on the passport's first data page.

assume some known information about the passport's owner. Recently, Halváč and Rosa [11] investigated the feasibility of performing a relay attack on Czech ePassport, and finally Ortiz-Yepes [22] supplied a short overview of security mechanisms recommended by ICAO.

In this work we go one step forward, proving that the real entropy of the BAC keys is much lower than what is stated in the previous analyzed passports. We operate a practical attack against the Belgian ePassport, and reveal that two-thirds of Belgian ePassports do not implement the BAC, which conflicts with the claims of the Belgian Minister for Foreign Affairs who declared in the Parliament [8] that Belgian ePassport benefits from the BAC. We then point out some further weaknesses, and provide heuristics that allow an adversary to guess the issuing country of a given passport while she is not able to pass the BAC. Finally, we present recommendations to enforce security in ePassports.

The remaining of this article is organized as follows. Section 2 provides a comprehensive introduction to the ICAO algorithms. Weaknesses in ICAO standard and practical attacks are presented in Section 3, and recommendations to improve ePassport security are presented in Section 4. Finally, Section 5 concludes our work.

2 ICAO Standard

ICAO began working on machine readable travel documents in 1968, in the interest of securing passports and accelerating the clearance of passengers. The MRZ concept was introduced in 1980 in Doc. 9303, published as "A Passport with Machine Readable Capability". That is only in 2004 that ICAO introduced a new direction in Doc. 9303, requiring passports to embed an electronic chip, an idea already suggested by Davida and Desmedt [4] in the eighties.

2.1 Embedded IC Specifications

The ICAO specifies that ICs are to conform to ISO/IEC 14443 Type A or Type B [16] and the onboard operating system shall conform to ISO/IEC 7816-4. The main difference between Type A and Type B is the modulation of the RF signals. As a consequence, the collision avoidance protocols are also different. In the world, Type A and Type B conforming ePassports are respectively 64% and 36% according to [26]. ISO/IEC 14443 also specifies that the reading range should be less than 10 cm (security feature), the frequency is 13.56 MHz, and the ICs are passive (power derived from the reader). Finally, the data storage capacity of the IC must be at least 32 kB in order to store the mandatory facial image and duplication of the MRZ data, but the common size is 70 kB. Besides, the passport chip contains a microprocessor with a coprocessor for the cryptographic functions in order to be able to use evolved cryptographic functions.

2.2 Data on the IC

First of all, to ensure global interoperability of ePassports, Doc. 9303 specifies a *Logical Data Structure* (LDS) compliant to ISO-7816. This LDS consists of 2 mandatory *Data Group*, DG1 and DG2, that respectively contain the facial image and a copy of the MRZ. It also consists of 17 optional DGs. For example, a handwritten signature may be stored in DG7 and DG15 is reserved for active authentication. Data groups DG17 to DG19 are reserved for future use to store electronic visa, automated border clearance, and travel record.

The IC also stores a file EF.COM that contains common information for the application, especially the list of DGs present on the IC. It stores as well a file named EF.SOD (*Document Security Object*) that contains security data that will be detailed later in this paper. Finally, the IC contains additional information whose storage and access are left to the developer discretion [6] (not accessible through the ICAO-standardized interface): BAC keys, active authentication private key, application identifier, life cycle status, etc.

2.3 Biometrics

Representing something you are, biometrics are used to identify uniquely a human being through the measurement of distinguishing physiological (face, fingerprint, iris, DNA) or behavioral (signature, keystroke dynamics, voice) characteristics. Biometrics can improve the security of the inspection process by increasing the strength of the link between the travel document and its owner. The ICAO only favored and classified three types of biometrics: face, fingerprint, and iris recognition. The facial image is not considered by the ICAO as sensitive (not confidential) information, contrarily to fingerprints and iris. The passport does not record a template of the biometrics, but a picture (JPEG or JPEG2000), enabling countries to choose their preferred facial recognition system.

2.4 Cryptographic Mechanisms

The ICAO has specified countermeasures to fulfill the ePassport security requirements. *Passive Authentication* proves that the passports content has not been modified. *Basic Access Control* (BAC) guarantees that the passport is open willingly and that the communication with the reader is secure. *Active Authentication* is to prevent chip cloning, and finally *Extended Access Control* (EAC) is to protect the confidentiality of additional biometrics.

Passive Authentication. The only countermeasure required by the ICAO is that data stored on the passport's IC be digitally signed by the issuing country in order to prevent data modification. To do so, each DG of the LDS is hashed using SHA-1 and all theses hashes together are signed by the *Document Signer Private Key*. The signature is stored in the IC's EF.SOD. Any inspection system needs the *Document Signer Public Key* to verify the LDS integrity. The appropriate certificate can be found either in the IC (EF.SOD) or from the ICAO dedicated repository accessible only for participants. The document signer public key certificate is in turn signed by the *Country Signing Private Key* and can be checked using a root certificate that is spread by diplomatic means.

Basic Access Control. In skimming the adversary queries the passport (without holder's consent), while in eavesdropping she passively intercepts communications between the reader and the passport. The ICAO recommends the BAC mechanism as a countermeasure against skimming and eavesdropping by (1) authenticating the reader and (2) encrypting the communication.

Authenticating the reader. When BAC is supported, the reader cannot get any information from the passport unless it goes through a challenge-response protocol (Fig. 1) based on the cryptographic functions here denoted ENC[4] and MAC[5]. In this protocol, C_P and C_R are two 8-byte random challenges respectively generated by the passport and the reader, and K_P and K_R are two 16-byte random values, again respectively generated by the passport and the reader. With this protocol, the reader proves to the passport the knowledge of the BAC keys (K_{ENC} and K_{MAC}) that are derived from some information of the MRZ (date of birth, date of expiry, and passport number) using SHA-1 (See Doc. 9303 for the description of the key derivation procedure). The exchanged values K_P and K_R are used afterwards by the reader and the ePassport to agree on session keys KS_{ENC} and KS_{MAC} for securing the communication. Note that this protocol does not ensure strong authentication. Instead it is intended to prove that the person has willingly opened his passport: anyone who knows the MRZ can successfully be authenticated. In other terms, the goal of BAC is to mitigate the security issue arisen from the contactless technology.

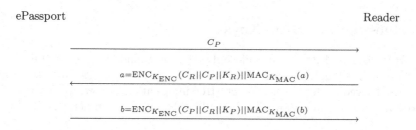

ePassport   Reader

$$C_P$$
———————————————————————————————→

$$a = \mathrm{ENC}_{K_{ENC}}(C_R \| C_P \| K_R) \| \mathrm{MAC}_{K_{MAC}}(a)$$
←———————————————————————————————

$$b = \mathrm{ENC}_{K_{ENC}}(C_P \| C_R \| K_P) \| \mathrm{MAC}_{K_{MAC}}(b)$$
———————————————————————————————→

Fig. 1. Basic Access Control

Encrypting the communication. After successful execution of BAC, both the reader and the IC compute session keys, KS_{ENC} and KS_{MAC}. Session keys are generated using the same key derivation procedure used for BAC keys but ($K_P \oplus K_R$) is used as seed instead of the hash of birth date, date of expiry, and passport number. These keys are used to encrypt all the subsequent communications using again the cryptographic functions ENC and MAC defined above. This

---

[4] ISO/IEC 11568-2, 3DES, CBC mode, zero IV (8 bytes).
[5] ISO/IEC 9797-1, MAC Algorithm 3, block cipher DES, zero IV, Padding Mode 2.

mechanism, known as *secure messaging*, provides confidentiality and integrity of the communication between the inspection system and the ePassport.

Active Authentication. BAC and Passive Authentication do not prevent chip cloning or substituting, an attack that may be particularly attractive in unattended identification systems[6]. Active Authentication is recommended to prevent these attacks using a challenge-response protocol in which the passport proves the possession of a private key. This private key is stored in a secure memory while the corresponding public key is stored in DG15. The procedure, which is depicted in Fig. 2, is that the reader sends a challenge C_R to the passport that signs it, and sends the signature back to the reader, which verifies it using the public key.

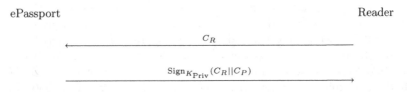

Fig. 2. Active Authentication

Extended Access Control. The ICAO has recommended EAC to guarantee the confidentiality of additional sensitive biometrics (fingerprint, iris) but it has not standardized any EAC protocol yet. The European Union pioneered this mechanism, and released a first version early in 2006 [24]. Security of EAC is still a work in progress, and several flaws have already been pointed out in [12, 21].

3   Guessing the BAC Keys

The BAC is founded on the philosophy that it cannot be passed unless the passport was willingly opened. This is not the case in practice since the BAC keys are derived from the easy-to-get MRZ information. Below, we describe the theoretical entropy and show that it really differs from the practical one.

3.1   Theoretical Entropy

Doc. 9303 [14] defines the structure of the date of birth as YYMMDD, implying an entropy of $\log_2(100 \times 365.25) \approx 15$. The date of expiry provides $\log_2(10 \times 365.25) \approx 12$ bits when the validity period is 10 years [14]. Only the first 9 characters of the passport number are involved to generate the BAC keys. Consequently, the relative entropy is $\log_2((26 + 10)^9) \approx 46$, leading to 73 bits in total. Unfortunately, the effective entropy is much lower. The ICAO itself estimates it to 56 bits, due to the weak passport numbering schemes.

---

[6] Automated border controls are already in use in airports, e.g., in Frankfurt, Paris, Amsterdam, and Sydney.

3.2   Effective Entropy

Doc. 9303 is flexible to take account the regulations of each participant. Especially, countries all have their own numbering schemes. US passport number consists of 9 digits where the first two digits are used to encode one of the 15 passport issuing agencies [17]. Thus, the entropy of this field decreases to $\log_2(15 \times 10^7) \approx 27$ and the total entropy becomes 54 at best.

German passport number consists of 9 digits where the first 4 digits are attributed to 5 700 local passport offices (in 16 Federal States) [5] and the remaining 5 digits for a serial number [3], so its entropy is $\log_2(5700 \times 10^5) \approx 29$. For 5-year passports, the total entropy is so 55 bits. Carluccio *et al.* [3] estimates it to 40 as realistic value, but they do not provide any explanation.

In the Netherlands, the passport number consists of a static letter "N" combined with 8-digit sequential number [23] and the passport is valid for 5 years. Moreover, the last digit is a predictable check digit [23, 27], reducing the total entropy to 50 bits according to Hoepman *et al.* [12]. They also report that this entropy can be reduced to 41 under certain assumptions (e.g., age can be guessed within a margin of 5 years).

In our case, that is the Belgian passport, the situation does not look worse: the passport number consists of 2-letter prefix and 6-digit suffix, providing an entropy of $\log_2(26^2 \times 10^6) \approx 29$ bits. Passports being valid during 5 years, the overall entropy is about 54 bits. The Belgian passport entropy is so fairly comparable to those of other countries. Unfortunately, our thorough analysis of the Belgian passport numbering scheme points out serious weaknesses. The main weakness is that numbers are chosen sequentially during the passport book *manufacturing* phase. Each blank passport has its unique identifier that becomes the passport number assigned during the *personalization* phase. Thus, there is a strong correlation between the date of issue (and so the date of expiry) and the passport number. For that reason, anyone can *roughly* guess the number of a passport given its issue date (or, equivalently, its date of expiry), that is to say, anyone is able to specify a range of passport numbers the target belongs to. The exact passport number cannot be guessed because (1) several thousand passports are issued every day; (2) the flow of issued passports is not constant and depends on several (more or less) predictable events, e.g., more passports are issued before the vacated months; (3) passports are not issued in exactly the same order as they have been manufactured, for some unclear logistic reasons. Consequently, given three pairs (d, n), (d', n'), and (d'', n''), where d, d', and d'' are three issue dates and n, n', and n'' are three passport numbers:

$$d \le d' \le d'' \not\Rightarrow n \le n' \le n''.$$

However, the observation of several pairs (issue date, passport number) allows calculating a value δ such that, for most of the passports:

$$d \le d' \le d'' \Rightarrow n - \delta \le n' \le n'' + \delta.$$

We recorded many Belgian passport numbers and respective issue dates. Each observed pair is represented by a cross in Fig. 3. On a given segment (the segmentation-effect will be explained later), the cross are not straight aligned due to the three above reasons. However, given an issue date of a targeted passport, it is possible to approximate its number with precision $\pm\delta$, and δ becomes tighter while new pairs of passport numbers and issue dates are recorded. Theoretically, 2δ can drop down to the number of daily-issued passports. That is however a theoretical bound that cannot be reached in practice due to reasons (2) and (3) stated above. Another reason is that some numbers are never assigned to blank passports, leaving some holes in the sequential numbering, in order to help detection of fake passports. In our case, we reached $\delta = 12\,000$ after only 40 observations, while about one thousand passports are issued every working day. One important phenomena in Fig. 3 is the segmentation-effect. These jumps in the numbering are due to a Belgian particularity: Belgium has several official languages, namely French, Dutch, and German. A Belgian citizen receives a passport such that its "reference" language is the one of the area he lives in or the one of his choice (ability to choose one's reference language is only available in a few bilingual areas, e.g., Brussels). This reference language does not only influence the personalization stage, but also the manufacturing process. Indeed, the passport cover and the on-page pre-printed information depends on the reference language. Consequently, the manufacturer provides language-dependent batches of blank passports to the authorities.

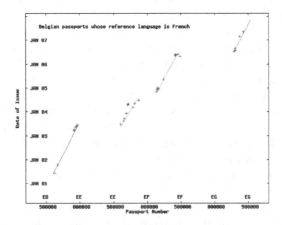

Fig. 3. Distribution of Belgian Passport Numbers

Figure 3 represents only passports whose reference language is French. The jumps correspond to the two other official languages. So, given the living place or the preferred language of a person, guessing his passport number[7] becomes much easier using the appropriate approximation.

Last but not least, ePassports are not issued during week-ends and holidays in Belgium, like in many other countries, meaning that ePassports are issued

---

[7] We did not consider official passports, as diplomatic, service, or politician passports.

roughly 250 days a year. Using all these heuristics, the entropy of the passport becomes $\log_2((250 \times 5) \times (100 \times 365.25) \times 2\delta) \approx 40$ bits, and the entropy still drops down with every new-known combination of passport number and date of expiry. Finally, second-generation Belgian passports have been issued since mid 2006 only and so the range of issue dates is today quarter of the theoretical range. This means that the entropy of todays Belgian passport is about 38 bits. Note that in case an adversary has a targeted victim, it is realistic to assume that his date of birth is known. This assumption, which is commonly done in the previous works, still lowers the entropy down to 23 bits (See Tab. 1).

Table 1. Effective Entropies of Selected Countries

Country	Effective	Birth date known
Germany [3]	55	40
USA [17]	54	39
Netherlands [23]	50	35
Belgium	38	23

3.3   Our Practical Attacks Against Belgian Passport

In this section, practical attack means successful reading of passport's digital content. In fact, two types of attacks can be distinguished, on-line and off-line. Off-line attack is when an adversary eavesdrops the communication, and later recovers the BAC keys by brute-force. On-line attack is trying to brute-force the keys in real time, by skimming.

On-line attack. This attack is definitely the most difficult to carry out due to (1) the response time of the IC and (2) the communication rate, which is between 106 kbit/s and 848 kbit/s according to ISO 14443.

Our equipment (low-cost reader that can reach 115 kbit/s baud, rather old laptop, and non-optimized implementation of Doc. 9303) was able to query the IC 400 times per minute. This is far below the limits. A high-performance system should be able to carry out few thousands queries per minute.

Using our heuristics, recovering the BAC keys should take a few weeks with our pretty non-optimal material, assuming only the date of birth is known (the issue date and passport number are not known). However, Sec. 3.2 considers that, for a given issue date, the passport number is uniformly distributed in a set of size 2δ, while this is not the case in practice. 2δ is the worst case for most of the passports, but a clever exhaustive search significantly decreases the cryptanalysis time: for a checked issue date, the cracking program looks for the corresponding expected passport number on the segment (Fig. 3), and tries every passport number from this point by positive and negative incremental steps.

Consequently, the average cryptanalysis time is far below the theoretical value. For instance, the last passport we cracked was issued on July 2007 (day not disclosed for security reason) and the corresponding passport number approximated by our program was EG473598, which was only about 4 000 numbers below the real value.

Off-line Attack. Off-line attacks are much more efficient. However, while on-line attacks use the passport as an oracle to test every BAC keys, off-line attacks require a ciphertext as material for the attack. Such a ciphertext is not provided by the IC till the BAC protocol succeeds. This means that an off-line attack is only possible if the adversary is able to eavesdrop a communication between a passport and a reader. Today, passports may be only read by immigration and police officers. However, tomorrow, they will be read by officer in banks, hotels, airlines companies, etc., and it will so become much easier to eavesdrop communications. With an entropy of 23 bits, carrying out an off-line attack takes about one second with any today's PC. An interesting point is that in the BAC protocol (Fig. 1), both messages $a = \text{ENC}_{K_{\text{ENC}}}(C_R||C_P||K_R)||\text{MAC}_{K_{\text{MAC}}}(a)$ (reader-to-passport message) and $b = \text{ENC}_{K_{\text{ENC}}}(C_P||C_R||K_P)||\text{MAC}_{K_{\text{MAC}}}(b)$ (passport-to-reader message) can be used as support of the off-line attack. Given that the reader-to-passport communication can be eavesdropped at a much larger distance than the passport-to-reader communication, an off-line attack does not require to be close to be performed. Of course, the adversary will have to approach the ePassport afterwards to download its content.

The Most Efficient Attack. Surprisingly, our attack initially failed when we sent to the first-experimented ePassport the command GET_CHALLENGE, which is required to execute the BAC. This failure meant that the interrogated ePassport was not able to generate the pseudo-random number C_P required in the first message of the BAC protocol (Fig. 1). Further investigations have shown that it did not implement BAC. In other words, the personal data were not protected. It turns out that Belgian ePassports are divided into two generations. The first generation that comprises passports issued from end 2004 till mid 2006 do not support BAC. Second generation passports have been issued since mid 2006 and implement BAC. Reading the content of a first generation passport (without the owner's knowledge) is obviously very simple since no authentication is required. A few seconds were needed with our low-performance system to download all the information from the passport. We put our attack into practice using a reader and a laptop hidden in an attaché-case.

Today[8], two-thirds of Belgian ePassports in circulation are 1st generation passports and some of these non-protected passports are valid until 2011. More precisely, there exist 1 500 000 valid Belgian passports in circulation. Among them, 430 000 are former non-electronic passports, 720 000 are 1st generation ePassports, and 350 000 are 2nd generation ePassports. Diplomats in some countries were among the first citizens to receive ePassports. It is so highly unlucky that Belgian diplomats hold or held 1st generation ePassports.

4   Recommendations

Ensuring that an adversary cannot impersonate someone else is a matter of the utmost importance. Ensuring that she cannot steal personal data is also a

---

[8] Mid 2007.

major concern. One may say that personal data available on an ePassport IC is nothing more than MRZ and VIZ. That is today's truth, but fingerprints and perhaps additional data will also be stored in ePassport ICs in the near future. Furthermore, even the remote disclosure of MRZ and VIZ can be felt as an intrusion in our personal lives. This theft can be done without the ePassport holders awareness, and stolen data can be used for further malicious exploits. For example, the Belgian passport stores, in addition to the mandatory data (DG1 and DG2), some optional data (DG7: handwritten signature; DG11: birth place and date; DG12: issue place and date). The passport does not record templates of the biometrics, but JPEG images. While today signed faxes or signed PDF files are accepted as an alternative to signed physical documents, the picture quality of the handwritten signature is good enough (800 × 265 pixels) to forge a fake fax or PDF file. Below, we provide recommendations and countermeasures to enforce security in ePassport. Some of them require modifications of the ICAO standard while some others only need modifications of the countries policy.

4.1   Delaying IC Answers

As we saw in the previous sections, one important security issue comes from skimming attacks. One possible way to thwart or mitigate these attacks is to delay the IC responses when several queries are received in a short period of time. If the response delay is progressively increased and upper-bounded, this protection cannot open the way to denial-of-service attacks. We know that this technique already exists but it is definitely not implemented on ePassport ICs. We do not see any technical issue to the implementation of such a protection in ePassports.

4.2   Random Passport Numbers

We have shown that the BAC keys suffer from very low entropy. In the Belgian case, the entropy can drop down to 23 bits if the date of birth is known. This issue can be mitigated without modifying the ICAO standard. Indeed, instead of using a deterministic passport numbering scheme, passport numbers should cover the full potential of ICAO standard. In other words, passport numbers should be randomly picked in $\{A - Z, 0 - 9\}^9$. The total entropy in that case would be about 57 bits when the date of birth is known and 73 otherwise (assuming passports are issued only 250 days a year).

To illustrate our recommendation, consider that an adversary writes down on the ground all the passport numbers she should check for each (issue date / date of birth) pair to break the BAC keys. Assuming that she is capable of writing one passport number every millimeter, she will have to walk 25 000 times around the World (along the equator) if the passport numbering scheme exploits the full passport number space. Using our (Evil) heuristics, writing Belgian passport numbers requires today walking only 24 meters. This clearly shows that using the full space of passport numbers is fundamental.

Using random passport numbers increases the entropy of the BAC keys up to 73 bits, but this remains insufficient, especially when the adversary knows some information, e.g., date of birth or date of expiry. This problem can be solved by modifying ICAO standard: BAC key generation should be randomized. Since there exists an optional 14-character field in the MRZ (whose purpose is at the discretion of the issuing countries, but usually never used), putting randomness in this field can be performed without modifying the MRZ structure.

4.3   Separate BAC Keys and Personal Data

Improving the effective entropy of BAC keys reduces the risk of remote access to the the ePassport without agreement of its holder. However this solution does not prevent inadvertent disclosure of BAC keys, e.g., in hotels, car rental shops, exchange office, etc. as they usually require a copy of the VIZ. Personal data are then digitalized and stored in databases, and they are eventually disclosed. The fundamental issue is that BAC keys are directly generated from the MRZ (and so from the VIZ). One way to avoid disclosure of the BAC keys is to generate them from random material that does not belong neither to the VIZ, nor to the MRZ. When the passport is shown up, and possibly photocopied for archives, the random material is not revealed if it is not printed on the same page as the VIZ. It can be printed on another page of the passport, e.g., on the last page in order to fasten the inspection, or it can be made available on another support (optically or electronically readable), e.g., a plastic card. This card should only be shown up to inspection officers.

4.4   Radio-Blocking Shield

Protecting personal data can be enforced using strongest BAC keys. Another palliative way to avoid IC access without the holder's awareness is to insert a radio-blocking shield in its cover, as it is done in the US passport. With such a shield, nobody can read a passport while it is closed. Surprisingly, this technique is only used in the US passport, up to our knowledge. We recommend to widely deploy this radio-blocking shield integrated in the cover.

4.5   Active Authentication

Active Authentication may allow an adversary to force an ePassport to sign some value [14]. Indeed, as depicted in Fig. 2, the adversary sends a value C_R she chose herself and the ePassport answers with $\text{Sign}_{K_{\text{Priv}}}(C_R || C_P)$, where C_P is a random value chosen by the passport. Sending an appropriate C_R, e.g., result of the lottery, an adversary can build a proof that the considered passport has been seen after a given date (she is then able to show this proof up in court). As suggested by Vaudenay and Vuagnoux in [25], a signature scheme without proof-transferability should be used instead of the current protocol. Later on, Monnerat, Vaudenay, and Vuagnoux [21] suggested a solution based on Guillou-Quisquater [9, 10] identification scheme. We consider that implementing a signature scheme that does not allow proof-transferability would constitute a step forward in securing ePassports. Our statement is also based on the fact that ePassports may also serve to secure external applications. In that direction, ICAO published a request for information [15] on the future specification development related to ePassport. Among the topics of interest, one could point out the category *Data chip partitioning* that concerns "effective methodology for securely partitioning data on e-Passport chips to allow for data and / or functions to be added by third parties"; and the category E-Commerce that deals with "electronic on-line systems that may be applied to secure Internet based passport and visa application processes".

4.6   Favorite Algorithms

Giving countries the ability to choose the BAC key generation procedure leads to weaknesses. Choice of other algorithms is also left to the discretion of the countries, although they must belong to a given cryptographic toolbox defined by ICAO. Unexpected security level may appear in case of non-appropriate choice. For instance, Tab. 2 and Tab. 3 show that Belgian ePassport uses SHA-1, which is not recommended, and absolutely not appropriate to be used with RSA-2048 and RSA-4096.

Table 2. ICAO-compliant Algorithms and Belgian Case

Algorithm	ICAO	Belgian ePassport
BAC (incl. secure messaging)	3DES/CBC Retail-MAC/DES	3DES/CBC Retail-MAC/DES
Hash for key derivation	SHA-1	SHA-1
Hash for signature	SHA-1*, SHA-224, SHA-256, SHA-384, SHA-512	SHA-1
Signature	RSA-PSS, RSA-PKCS1-v15, DSA, ECDSA (X9.62)	RSA-4096 (Country Signing Key), RSA-2048 (Document Signer Key), RSA-1024 (Active Auth.)

* ICAO [14] recommends not to use SHA-1 whenever hash collisions are of concern.

Table 3. ICAO Recommended Security Levels and Security Equivalence

Purpose	Security level	RSA modulus n	DSA modulus p,q	ECDSA base point ord	Hash function
Country Signing CA	128	3072	3072, 256	256	SHA-256
Document Signer	112	2048	2048, 224	224	SHA-224
Active Authentication	80	1024	1024, 160	160	SHA-1

Sizes are expressed in bits.

5 Conclusion

The ePassport is the most secure international identification document ever seen. It guarantees information integrity, authenticity, and confidentiality, based on well-known cryptographic tools. Security and safety are more than ever enforced by means of biometrics. Deploying a wide-range international trustful PKI was a prerequisite for this achievement. By doing so, the ICAO afforded to the ePassport a promising future in many domains as banking and trading to name a few. Nevertheless, some security and privacy issues still exist and must be addressed. Among them, the entropy of the BAC keys, which ensure privacy-protection, is not sufficient. We provided in this paper a thorough analysis of this issue and presented our investigations on the Belgian ePassport. We proved that the entropy can be as low as 23 bits under certain assumptions, and we revealed that two-thirds Belgian ePassports in circulation have no concern with privacy-protection. We then provided comprehensive security recommendations, for guiding countries in defining their policies and for amending future releases of Doc. 9303.

Acknowledgments

We would like to kindly thank people who helped us during this work. Among them, Danny De Cock and Elke Demulder for fruitful discussions about Belgian ePassport, and Serge Vaudenay and Martin Vuagnoux for providing us helpful information.

References

[1] Avoine, G.: Cryptography in Radio Frequency Identification and Fair Exchange Protocols. PhD thesis, EPFL, Lausanne, Switzerland (December 2005)

[2] Avoine, G.: Bibliography on security and privacy in RFID systems (2007)

[3] Carluccio, D., Lemke-Rust, K., Paar, C., Sadeghi, A.-R.: E-Passport: The Global Traceability Or How to Feel Like a UPS Package. In: Workshop on RFID Security (July 2006)

[4] Davida, G., Desmedt, Y.: Passports and Visas Versus IDs. In: Günther, C.G. (ed.) EUROCRYPT 1988. LNCS, vol. 330, pp. 183–188. Springer, Heidelberg (1988)

[5] Friedrich, E.: The Introduction of German Electronic Passports. In: Second Symposium on ICAO-Standard, MRTDs, Biometrics and Security (September 2006)

[6] Gemalto. e-Passport AXSEAL CC V2 36K – Common Criteria / ISO15408 EAL4+ – Security Target. Technical report, Gemalto (2004)

[7] Grunwald, L.: New Attacks against RFID-Systems. GmbH Germany

[8] Gucht, K.D.: Chambre des représentants de Belgique, compte rendu intégral avec compte rendu analytique traduit des interventions. Commission des relations extérieures (2007)

[9] Guillou, L., Quisquater, J.-J.: A Paradoxical Indentity-Based Signature Scheme Resulting from Zero-Knowledge. In: Pomerance, C. (ed.) CRYPTO 1987. LNCS, vol. 293. Springer, Heidelberg (1988)

[10] Guillou, L., Quisquater, J.-J.: A Practical Zero-Knowledge Protocol Fitted to Security Microprocessor Minimizing Both Trasmission and Memory. In: Günther, C.G. (ed.) EUROCRYPT 1988. LNCS, vol. 330, pp. 123–128. Springer, Heidelberg (1988)

[11] Halváč, M., Rosa, T.: A Note on the Relay Attacks on e-passports: The Case of Czech e-passports. Cryptology ePrint Archive, Report 2007/244 (2007)

[12] Hoepman, J.-H., Hubbers, E., Jacobs, B., Oostdijk, M., Schreur, R.W.: Crossing Borders: Security and Privacy Issues of the European e-Passport. In: Advances in Information and Computer Security. LNCS. Springer, Heidelberg (2006)

[13] ICAO. Machine Readable Travel Documents. Technical report, ICAO, Doc 9303 Part 1, 10th Draft, 6 ed. vol.1 (July 20, 2005)

[14] ICAO. Machine Readable Travel Documents. Technical report, ICAO, Doc 9303 Part 1, 9th Draft, vol. 2 (July 20, 2005)

[15] ICAO. Request For Information (RFI) 2007/2008. Technical report, Technical Advisory Group on Machine Readable Travel Documents, Canada (March 2007)

[16] ISO/IEC 14443. Proximity cards (PICCs) http://www.iso.org

[17] Juels, A., Molnar, D., Wagner, D.: Security and Privacy Issues in E-Passports. In: Conference on Security and Privacy for Emerging Areas in Communication Networks – SecureComm, Greece (2005)

[18] Kc, G., Karger, P.: Preventing Attacks on Machine Readable Travel Documents (MRTDs). Technical report, IBM Research Division, NY, USA (2006)

[19] Laurie, A.: RFIDIOt (May 2007), http://www.rfidiot.org/

[20] Lehtonen, M., Michahelles, F., Staake, T., Fleisch, E.: Strengthening the Security of Machine Readable Documents by Combining RFID and Optical Memory Devices. In: Int. Conf. on Ambient Intelligence Development – Amid 2006 (2006)

[21] Monnerat, J., Vaudenay, S., Vuagnoux, M.: About Machine-Readable Travel Documents: Privacy Enhacement Using (Weakly) Non-Transferable Data Authentication. In: Int. Conf. on RFID Security 2007. RFID Security (July 2007)

[22] Ortiz-Yepes, D.: ePassports: Authentication and Access Control Mechanisms. Technical report, Technische Univ. Eindhoven TU/e, Netherland (June 2007)

[23] Robroch, H.: ePassport Privacy Attack (2006), http://www.riscure.com

[24] Technical Guideline TR-03110. Advanced Security Mechanisms for Machine Readable Travel Documents, Extended Access Control (EAC), Version 1.00. Technical report, Bundesamt für Sicherheit in der Informationstechnik, Germany (2006)

[25] Vaudenay, S., Vuagnoux, M.: About Machine-Readable Travel Documents. Journal of Physics Conference Series 77 (July 2007)

[26] Wing, B.: e-Passport/MRTD Observations. In: Second Symposium on ICAO-Standard MRTDs, Biometrics and Security

[27] Witteman, M.: Attacks on Digital Passports. Riscure (July 2005)

Good Variants of HB$^+$ Are Hard to Find

Henri Gilbert, Matthew J.B. Robshaw, and Yannick Seurin

Orange Labs,
38–40 rue du General Leclerc, Issy les Moulineaux, France
{henri.gilbert,matt.robshaw,yannick.seurin}@orange-ftgroup.com

Abstract. The strikingly simple HB$^+$ protocol of Juels and Weis [11] has been proposed for the authentication of low-cost RFID tags. As well as being computationally efficient, the protocol is accompanied by an elegant proof of security. After its publication, Gilbert *et al.* [8] demonstrated a simple man-in-the-middle attack that allowed an attacker to recover the secret authentication keys. (The attack does not contradict the proof of security since the attacker lies outside the adversarial model.) Since then a range of schemes closely related to HB$^+$ have been proposed and these are intended to build on the security of HB$^+$ while offering resistance to the attack of [8]. In this paper we show that many of these variants can still be attacked using the techniques of [8] and the original HB$^+$ protocol remains the most attractive member of the HB$^+$ family.

Keywords: HB$^+$, RFID tags, authentication, LPN.

1   Introduction

The extension of cryptographic functions to low-cost RFID tags is an active area of research. The combination of novel security requirements and demanding physical environments provides a major incentive to the development of new designs and techniques.

Juels and Weis introduced HB$^+$ at Crypto 2005 [11]. The protocol is a multi-round symmetric key authentication protocol where each round consists of three communications between the reader and the tag. On the tag, HB$^+$ is computationally lightweight since it requires only simple bit-wise operations. Furthermore, the protocol is supported by a proof of security against an active attacker in what the HB$^+$ designers call the *detection-based* model. In this model adversaries can interrogate a tag in any way they wish, and then they must try and pass themselves off as an authentic tag to a legitimate reader. In loose terms, Juels and Weis show that for such an attack to succeed the attacker would be able to break an instance of the *Learning Parity with Noise (LPN)* problem which is believed to be hard.

However, if we allow the attacker to do a little more—*i.e.* if we leave the detection-based model—then HB$^+$ becomes susceptible to a simple attack. In particular, if an attacker can slightly modify messages from the reader and observe whether the legitimate reader still accepts the legitimate tag, then the

G. Tsudik (Ed.): FC 2008, LNCS 5143, pp. 156–170, 2008.
© Springer-Verlag Berlin Heidelberg 2008

attacker can recover secret key information. This is, in essence, the attack of Gilbert *et al.* [8] which we will refer to as the GRS attack in what follows. Some commentators suggest that interfering with the tag-reader communication would be technically difficult. Others claim that forbidding such manipulation during analysis ignores the full characteristics of a potential attack and makes potentially dangerous assumptions on the limitations of an attacker. However this is not the concern of this paper. Instead we will focus on the body of research that has evolved from both HB⁺ and the GRS attack.

In his paper introducing the block cipher RC5, Rivest states that " ... a simpler structure is perhaps more interesting to analyze and evaluate ... " [19]. This is now a well-established principle in cryptographic design and the simplicity of both the original HB⁺ proposal and the GRS attack have given rise to a number of HB-related protocols in the literature. The goal of these protocols is that they retain some of the successful properties of HB⁺ while also resisting the GRS attack. In this paper we will take a critical look at such variants. We can show that despite claims to the contrary, the GRS attack can often be applied or extended to these new variants. Thus the tolerance of the new schemes to the GRS attack is often equivalent to that of HB⁺ and yet, at the same time, they suffer from additional complexity and/or reduced practicality. In short, we show that HB⁺ variants that resist the GRS attack are not that easy to come by.

Our paper is organised as followed. After introducing the HB⁺ protocol we turn our attention to the variants HB⁺⁺, HB*, HB-MP′, and HB-MP. These are treated in the order they appear in the literature and in Sections 3, 4 and 5 we provide a description and security analysis of each. We then discuss the implications of our work in Section 6 and draw our conclusions. It should be noted that our work is not concerned with the proofs of security for HB⁺ or its variants. Instead our focus is on applications of the GRS attack.

Throughout we aim to use established notation. There will be some interplay between vectors $x \in \{0,1\}^k$ and scalars in $\mathbb{F}_2$ and we use bold type x to indicate a vector while scalars x are written in normal text. The *scalar product* of two vectors x and y will be written as $x \cdot y$ while their bitwise addition will be denoted using $\oplus$ just as for single bits. We denote the *Hamming weight* of x by $\mathrm{Hwt}(x)$. Several protocols require a rotation of x by i bit positions to the left; we denote this operation by $\mathrm{ROT}_i(x)$.

2   The HB⁺ Protocol and the GRS Attack

There are now several protocols based on HB⁺ and these offer a variable level of security and practicality. We start by reviewing the original protocol, though all depend for their security on the conjectured hardness of the *Learning Parity with Noise* (LPN) problem [11].

> **LPN Problem.** Let A be a random $(q \times k)$-binary matrix, let x be a random k-bit vector, let $\eta \in]0, \frac{1}{2}[$ be a noise parameter, and let ν be a random q-bit vector such that $\mathrm{Hwt}(\nu) \leq \eta q$. Given A, η, and $z = A \cdot x^t \oplus \nu^t$, find a k-bit vector y^t such that $\mathrm{Hwt}(A \cdot y^t \oplus z) \leq \eta q$.

Tag (secret x, y)		Reader (secret x, y)
$\nu \in_R \{0,1 \mid \text{Prob}(\nu = 1) = \eta\}$		
Choose $b \in_R \{0,1\}^k$	$\xrightarrow{\quad b \quad}$	
	$\xleftarrow{\quad a \quad}$	Choose $a \in_R \{0,1\}^k$
Let $z = (a \cdot x) \oplus (b \cdot y) \oplus \nu$	$\xrightarrow{\quad z \quad}$	Check $(a \cdot x) \oplus (b \cdot y) = z$

Fig. 1. One single round of HB$^+$ [11]. The entire authentication process requires r rounds and, in this basic form, each round consists of the three passes shown. Provided the tag fails less than some threshold t number of rounds, the tag is authenticated.

We will not consider the intractability of the LPN problem directly in this paper, though we observe that the problem is not as difficult as was originally thought [7,15]. This means that the parameters for HB$^+$ and its variants often need to be increased.

2.1   The HB$^+$ Protocol

The HB$^+$ protocol is outlined in Figure 1. The tag and the reader share two k-bit secrets x and y. One round of HB$^+$ is as follows: the tag selects a random k-bit blinding vector b and sends it to the reader. The reader challenges the tag with a random k-bit vector a. The tag computes the response $z = (a \cdot x) \oplus (b \cdot y) \oplus \nu$, where ν is a random noise bit taking the value 1 with probability $\eta \in]0, \frac{1}{2}[$. This is repeated for r rounds, and the tag is authenticated if the number of errors (*i.e.* z distinct from $(a \cdot x) \oplus (b \cdot y)$) is less than a threshold $t = ur$ where $u \in]\eta, \frac{1}{2}[$. The difficulty of the LPN problem [7,11,13,15] is related to both k and the parameter η which governs how much noise is added to the correct computations by a valid tag. In its original state HB$^+$ consists of multiple rounds each of three passes. The parallel version of HB$^+$—for which a proof of security also exists [13,14]—compresses the multiple rounds into one single three-pass round.

Immediately one can see that HB$^+$ requires very modest on-tag computation. Leaving aside generating b and the bit ν, computation on the tag is reduced to a dot-product, which can be computed bit-wise, and a single bit exclusive-or. The novelty and simplicity of HB$^+$ immediately generated considerable interest. Katz and Shin [13] closed gaps and extended the original proof of security while follow-on work by Katz and Smith [14] considered different noise levels.

2.2   An Active Attack on HB$^+$

A simple active attack on HB$^+$ is provided in [8]. The attack applies equally to the serial and the parallel versions of HB$^+$. For this attack it is assumed that an adversary can manipulate challenges sent by a legitimate reader to a legitimate tag during authentication. Further, we assume that the adversary learns whether such manipulation leads to an authentication failure or not.

Tag (secret $\boldsymbol{x}, \boldsymbol{y}$)	Reader (secret $\boldsymbol{x}, \boldsymbol{y}$)
$\nu \in \{0, 1 | \text{Prob}(\nu = 1) = \eta\}$	
Choose $\boldsymbol{b} \in_R \{0,1\}^k$	$\xrightarrow{\quad \boldsymbol{b} \quad}$
	$\xleftarrow{\boldsymbol{a}' = \boldsymbol{a} \oplus \boldsymbol{\delta}} \cdots \xleftarrow{\boldsymbol{a}}$ Choose $\boldsymbol{a} \in_R \{0,1\}^k$
Let $z' = (\boldsymbol{a}' \cdot \boldsymbol{x}) \oplus (\boldsymbol{b} \cdot \boldsymbol{y}) \oplus \nu$	$\xrightarrow{\quad z' \quad}$ Check $(\boldsymbol{a} \cdot \boldsymbol{x}) \oplus (\boldsymbol{b} \cdot \boldsymbol{y}) = z'$

Fig. 2. The attack of [8] on HB$^+$. The adversary modifies the communications between reader and tag (by adding some perturbation $\boldsymbol{\delta}$ and notes whether authentication is still successful. This reveals one bit of secret information.

The attack consists of choosing a constant k-bit vector $\boldsymbol{\delta}$ and using it to perturb the challenges sent by a legitimate reader to the tag; $\boldsymbol{\delta}$ is exclusive-or'ed to each authentication challenge for each of the r rounds of authentication. If the authentication process is successful then we must have that $\boldsymbol{\delta} \cdot \boldsymbol{x} = 0$ with overwhelming probability. Otherwise $\boldsymbol{\delta} \cdot \boldsymbol{x} = 1$ with overwhelming probability. Thus we gain one bit of secret information. The attack is illustrated in Figure 2 for one round of the HB$^+$ protocol.

To retrieve the k-bit secret $\boldsymbol{x}$ one can repeat the attack k times for linearly independent $\boldsymbol{\delta}$'s and solve the resulting system. Conveniently, an adversary can choose $\boldsymbol{\delta}$'s with a single non-zero bit. With $\boldsymbol{x}$ an attacker can impersonate the tag by setting $\boldsymbol{b} = \boldsymbol{0}$. Alternatively, an attacker can emulate a false tag using $\boldsymbol{x}$, send a chosen blinding factor $\boldsymbol{b}$ to a legitimate reader, and return $\boldsymbol{a} \cdot \boldsymbol{x}$ to the challenge $\boldsymbol{a}$. If successful $\boldsymbol{b} \cdot \boldsymbol{y} = 0$, otherwise $\boldsymbol{b} \cdot \boldsymbol{y} = 1$, with overwhelming probability. Thus $\boldsymbol{y}$ can be recovered with k linearly independent $\boldsymbol{b}$.

The attack is mathematically simple though it is not covered by the existing proof of security since the attacker needs to manipulate challenges and know whether authentication is successful [11]. Yet, despite the technical difficulties of interfering in a tag-reader exchange, the attack should be viewed as *certificational*. Certainly a variant of HB$^+$ that is both computationally simple and resistant to the GRS attack would be of some considerable interest.

All the variants to HB$^+$ we will consider in the following sections share some properties with HB$^+$. In particular, they all consist of the repetition of r basic rounds. An honest tag interacting with an honest reader may be rejected with a probability we denote P_{FR} (false rejection probability). An adversary answering randomly at each round will be authenticated with a probability we denote P_{FA} (false acceptance probability). For HB$^+$ these are given by $P_{\text{FR}} = \sum_{i=t+1}^{r} \binom{r}{i} \eta^i (1 - \eta)^{r-i}$ and $P_{\text{FA}} = \frac{1}{2^r} \sum_{i=0}^{t} \binom{r}{i}$.

3   The Variant HB^{++}

Description of HB^{++}. The protocol HB^{++} is proposed by Bringer *et al.* [3]. The complete proposal consists of two stages. In the first, illustrated in Figure 3, four k-bit secrets $\boldsymbol{x}, \boldsymbol{x}', \boldsymbol{y}, \boldsymbol{y}'$ are derived by the tag and the reader from a shared

Tag (secret Z)	Reader (secret Z)
Choose $B \in_R \{0,1\}^k$ $\xrightarrow{\quad B \quad}$	
$\xleftarrow{\quad A \quad}$	Choose $A \in_R \{0,1\}^k$
$(x, x', y, y') = h(Z, A, B)$	$(x, x', y, y') = h(Z, A, B)$

Tag (session x, x', y, y')	Reader (session x, x', y, y')
$\nu \in_R \{0,1 \| \mathrm{Prob}(\nu = 1) = \eta\}$ $\nu' \in_R \{0,1 \| \mathrm{Prob}(\nu' = 1) = \eta\}$	
Choose $b \in_R \{0,1\}^k$ $\xrightarrow{\quad b \quad}$	
$\xleftarrow{\quad a \quad}$	Choose $a \in_R \{0,1\}^k$
$\begin{cases} z = (a \cdot x) \oplus (b \cdot y) \oplus \nu \\ z' = (\mathrm{ROT}_i(f(a)) \cdot x') \\ \quad \oplus (\mathrm{ROT}_i(f(b)) \cdot y') \oplus \nu' \end{cases}$ $\xrightarrow{\quad (z, z') \quad}$	$\begin{cases} \text{Check } (a \cdot x) \oplus (b \cdot y) = z \\ \text{Check } (\mathrm{ROT}_i(f(a)) \cdot x') \\ \quad \oplus (\mathrm{ROT}_i(f(b)) \cdot y') = z' \end{cases}$

Fig. 3. The HB^{++} protocol. Above: At the start of each authentication, a preliminary exchange of $2k$ bits and the use of a universal hash function h are required to derive the session secrets x, x', y, y'. Below: One single round i of HB^{++}. The entire authentication process requires r rounds and, in this basic form, each round consists of the three passes shown. Provided the tag fails both tests less than some threshold t number of rounds, the tag is authenticated.

secret Z. These derived secrets might be viewed as session keys. Then HB^{++} consists of r rounds where each round consists of three passes, just as in HB^+.

A single round of HB^{++} is illustrated in Figure 3. We can see that things are slightly more complicated than in HB^+. In particular, once the blinding vector b and the challenge a have been sent, there are two on-tag computations. The first looks like the HB^+ on-tag computation and simply consists in computing $z = (a \cdot x) \oplus (b \cdot y) \oplus \nu$. The second involves a permutation f (which is in fact a layer of five-bit S-boxes) and also requires that k-bit quantities be rotated by i bit positions where i denotes the round (rounds are numbered from 0 to $r - 1$). The second response bit is given by $z' = (\mathrm{ROT}_i(f(a)) \cdot x') \oplus (\mathrm{ROT}_i(f(b)) \cdot y') \oplus \nu'$. Both noise bits ν and ν' are randomly chosen according to the noise parameter η. For the tag to be authenticated, the number of erroneous z answers *and* the number of erroneous z' answers must be less than some threshold $t = ur$, where $u \in]\eta, \frac{1}{2}[$. Consequently the false rejection and false acceptance probabilities are:

$$P_{\mathrm{FR}} = 1 - \left(\sum_{i=0}^{t} \binom{r}{i} \eta^i (1 - \eta)^{r-i} \right)^2 \quad \text{and} \quad P_{\mathrm{FA}} = \left(\frac{1}{2^r} \sum_{i=0}^{t} \binom{r}{i} \right)^2 .$$

The proposed number of rounds is not given, but the parameters in [3], in particular $k = 80$, give a much-reduced level of security when compared to HB^+.

Variant of Piramuthu. Piramuthu [18] proposes a modification to HB^{++} but the details are unclear. The main difference with HB^{++} appears to be the removal of the first on-tag computation. However this means that what remains is equivalent to HB$^+$ itself. Thus it will have all the characteristics of HB$^+$ while at the same time possessing a heavier on-tag computation. We do not consider this variant further.

Attacking HB^{++} without the renewed secrets. We first show how to attack HB^{++} when the preliminary phase to renew the secrets (x, x', y, y') is omitted. We note that Wagner described an attack on a preliminary version of HB^{++} where the rotations are omitted, which was described in the original paper [3]. In this attack, the attacker guesses a short portion of the secrets x and x' and then modifies the challenges sent by the reader but also the answer returned by the tag accordingly to his guess. If the tag is authenticated, the attacker knows that with high probability his guess was right. Bringer *et al.* introduced the rotations to counter this attack. The rationale is that this way, even if the perturbation of a is localized, the perturbation of $f(a)$ will affect all bits of the secret x'. It seems however that the following fact was overlooked: it is not necessary for the attacker to perturb *all* the rounds of the protocol but only a fixed fraction to be able to gain information through the decision of the reader. As we will show now, this leads to an efficient variant of the GRS attack.

Unlike the attack of Wagner, the attack we describe doesn't require that we modify the answers of the tag. As in the GRS attack, the attacker adds a fixed vector δ to the challenges a_i sent by the reader, *but only for a fixed number of rounds $s < r$* (say the first s rounds). Let σ_i and σ'_i denote the total error vectors on the answers z_i and z'_i of the tag at round i. For rounds $i = 0$ to $s - 1$, one has $\sigma_i = \nu_i \oplus \delta \cdot x$ and $\sigma'_i = \nu'_i \oplus \delta'_i \cdot x'$ where $\delta'_i = \text{ROT}_i(f(a_i \oplus \delta) \oplus f(a_i))$, whereas for rounds $i = s$ to $r - 1$, one simply has $\sigma_i = \nu_i$ and $\sigma'_i = \nu'_i$. Let N (resp. N') denote the number of answers z_i (resp. z'_i) in error. The function f was chosen to satisfy good differential properties, meaning that for a fixed δ and a fixed c, $\text{Pr}_a[f(a \oplus \delta) \oplus f(a) = c]$ is very small for most values of δ. Hence the noise bits σ'_i for rounds 0 to $s - 1$ are close to uniformly distributed and we may assume[1] that, whatever δ, N' is distributed as the sum of s Poisson trials taking the value 0 or 1 with probability $\frac{1}{2}$ and $r - s$ Poisson trials taking the value 0 with probability $1 - \eta$ and 1 with probability η. The expected value of N' is $\mu' = \frac{s}{2} + \eta(r - s) = \frac{1}{2}(1 - 2\eta)s + \eta r$. Unlike N', the distribution of N depends on the value of $\delta \cdot x$. When $\delta \cdot x = 0$, the answers z_i are undisturbed and N is distributed as the sum of r Poisson trials taking the value 0 with probability $1 - \eta$ and 1 with probability η. The expected value of N in this case is $\mu_0 = \eta r < t$. When $\delta \cdot x = 1$, the s first answers z_i are correct with probability η and incorrect with probability $1 - \eta$, while the $r - s$ remaining rounds are undisturbed. In that case, N' is distributed as the sum of s Poisson trials taking the value 0 with

---

[1] Note that this is strictly speaking an approximation and that in fact the distribution of $(\sigma'_0, \ldots, \sigma'_{s-1})$ will be nearly uniform for an overwhelming fraction of x' and δ. Concrete values will depend on the parameter Δ_f defined in [3].

probability η and 1 with probability $1 - \eta$ and $r - s$ Poisson trials taking the value 0 with probability $1 - \eta$ and 1 with probability η. The expected value of N is $\mu_1 = (1 - \eta)s + \eta(r - s) = (1 - 2\eta)s + \eta r$. Consequently, if we choose s such that $\mu' < t$, and $\mu_1 > t$, the number of errors on z' will be less than t with high probability, and the reader's decision will indicate whether the number of errors on z was less or more than t, which in turn will indicate whether $\boldsymbol{\delta} \cdot \boldsymbol{x} = 0$ or 1.

Going into details, we will compute the advantage of the attacker guessing $\boldsymbol{\delta} \cdot \boldsymbol{x} = 0$ when the reader accepts and $\boldsymbol{\delta} \cdot \boldsymbol{x} = 1$ when the reader rejects. Denoting WG the event that the guess is wrong, we will upper bound the probability of WG as follows:

$$
\begin{aligned}
\Pr[\text{WG}] &= \frac{1}{2} \left(\Pr[\text{WG} \,|\, \boldsymbol{\delta} \cdot \boldsymbol{x} = 0] + \Pr[\text{WG} \,|\, \boldsymbol{\delta} \cdot \boldsymbol{x} = 1] \right) \\
&= \frac{1}{2} \left(\Pr[\mathcal{R} \text{ rejects} \,|\, \boldsymbol{\delta} \cdot \boldsymbol{x} = 0] + \Pr[\mathcal{R} \text{ accepts} \,|\, \boldsymbol{\delta} \cdot \boldsymbol{x} = 1] \right) \\
&= \frac{1}{2} \big(\Pr[(N > t) \vee (N' > t) \,|\, \boldsymbol{\delta} \cdot \boldsymbol{x} = 0] \\
&\qquad\qquad + \Pr[(N \leq t) \wedge (N' \leq t) \,|\, \boldsymbol{\delta} \cdot \boldsymbol{x} = 1] \big) \\
&\leq \frac{1}{2} \left(\Pr[N' > t] + \Pr[N > t \,|\, \boldsymbol{\delta} \cdot \boldsymbol{x} = 0] + \Pr[(N \leq t) \,|\, \boldsymbol{\delta} \cdot \boldsymbol{x} = 1] \right) \\
&\leq \frac{1}{2} \left(e^{-\frac{(t-\mu')^2}{3\mu'}} + e^{-\frac{(t-\mu_0)^2}{3\mu_0}} + e^{-\frac{(\mu_1-t)^2}{2\mu_1}} \right)
\end{aligned}
$$

where the last inequalities come from the Chernoff bounds (see Appendix). According to the expressions of μ' and μ_1, the condition on s to have $\mu' < t$ and $\mu_1 > t$ is

$$
\frac{t - \eta r}{1 - 2\eta} < s < 2\frac{t - \eta r}{1 - 2\eta}.
$$

Whether such s exist will depend on the parameters of the scheme, however we note that in order for the protocol to have a low false rejection probability, t has to be sufficiently distinct from ηr. In particular, taking $t = \lceil \eta r \rceil$ yields $P_{\text{FR}} \simeq 0.4$ (see Section 6), which is unacceptable. Hence, it is arguable that such s will exist. However, concrete values in the formulae show that it is uncertain for the attacker to make a guess when the reader rejects, as the probability for this to happen when $\boldsymbol{\delta} \cdot \boldsymbol{x} = 0$ (due to $N' > t$) may be quite high when μ' is close to t. A much better strategy is to make a guess only when the reader accepts, guessing that $\boldsymbol{\delta} \cdot \boldsymbol{x} = 0$. In this case, the probability of a wrong guess is given by $\Pr[\text{WG}_{\text{a}}] = \Pr[\boldsymbol{\delta} \cdot \boldsymbol{x} = 1 \,|\, \mathcal{R} \text{ accepts}] = \frac{1}{2} P_{\text{a}}^{-1} \Pr[\mathcal{R} \text{ accepts} \,|\, \boldsymbol{\delta} \cdot \boldsymbol{x} = 1]$, where P_{a} is the probability that the reader accepts for a random $\boldsymbol{\delta}$. $\Pr[\text{WG}_{\text{a}}]$ decreases with s as the gap between t and μ_1 increases. The cost is that a higher number of attempts will be required to retrieve $\boldsymbol{x}$, namely $O(k \cdot P_{\text{a}}^{-1})$, which may become impractical as s tends to r since P_{a} becomes negligible. However, for $s = \left\lfloor 2\frac{t - \eta r}{1 - 2\eta} \right\rfloor$, $\mu' \simeq t$ so that N' is more or less than t with probability roughly $1/2$, and hence the reader accepts with probability roughly $1/4$. We computed concrete values for different set of parameters. For example, when $(r, t, \eta) = (80, 30, 0.25)$ we obtain, with $s = 40$, $\Pr[\text{WG}_{\text{a}}] \simeq 0.007$ and $P_{\text{a}}^{-1} \simeq 3.62$, whereas for $(r, t, \eta) = (160, 60, 0.25)$, we obtain, with $s = 80$, $\Pr[\mathrm{WG_a}] \simeq 0.0002$ and $P_a^{-1} \simeq 3.73$.

Once x has been retrieved with high confidence, x' can be obtained by adding to the i-th challenge a vector δ_i such that $\delta_i \cdot x = 0$ and $\mathrm{ROT}_i((f(a_i \oplus \delta_i) \oplus f(a_i))$ is constant, which will give linear equations on x'.

Attacking HB^{++} with renewed secrets. Let us now consider the situation where HB^{++} is operated with renewed secrets at each authentication, as recommended by the authors of [3]. We show that while secret renewal apparently protects HB^{++} against a simple application of the GRS attack, a slightly more complex attack remains.

To explain this attack, we need to introduce the function h that is used to derive the 320-bit temporary authentication key (x, x', y, y') from a permanent 768-bit secret Z. This function is derived from the hash functions family WH, a variant of the hash functions family NH on which the UMAC message authentication code is based [2] and which was proposed by Kaps et al. in [12].

The instance of WH used to construct h is defined as follows: given two 160-bit words $K = (K_1, \ldots, K_n) \in (\mathbb{F}_{2^{16}})^n$, and $M = (M_1, \ldots, M_n) \in (\mathbb{F}_{2^{16}})^n$, where $n = 10$, the 16-bit word $\mathrm{WH}_K(M)$ is defined as

$$\mathrm{WH}_K(M) = \sum_{i=1}^{n/2} (M_{2i-1} + K_{2i-1}) \cdot (M_{2i} + K_{2i}) \cdot c_i,$$

where the c_i are $\mathbb{F}_{2^{16}}$ constants defined in [12]. The function h results from $t = 20$ invocations of this instance of WH, according to the construction of a hash function family with a larger key and output size named WH^T proposed in [12]. Given $Z = (Z_1, \ldots, Z_{n+2(t-1)}) \in (\mathbb{F}_{2^{16}})^{n+2(t-1)} = (\mathbb{F}_{2^{16}})^{48}$, and $M = (M_1, \ldots, M_n) \in \mathbb{F}_{2^{16}}^n = (\mathbb{F}_{2^{16}})^{10}$, the t-uple $\mathrm{WH}_Z^T(M)$ of $\mathbb{F}_{2^{16}}$ words is defined as $\mathrm{WH}_Z^T(M) = (\mathrm{WH}_{Z_1 \ldots Z_n}(M), \mathrm{WH}_{Z_3 \ldots Z_{n+2}}(M), \cdots, \mathrm{WH}_{Z_{2t-1} \ldots Z_{n+2t-2}}(M))$. With the previous notation h is defined as $h(Z, A, B) = \mathrm{WH}_Z^T(M)$ where $M = (A \| B)$.

One can see from the former equations that given any fixed pair (A, B), $h(Z, A, B)$ is a known quadratic function of $(Z_1, \ldots, Z_{48})$. However, the security advantage that results from having a quadratic expression rather than a linear one is quite marginal for this particular function. This is due to the following property that immediately results from the definition of WH: for all (A, B) pairs, each of the t 16-bit words of $h(Z, A, B)$ can be expressed as a known affine function with $\mathbb{F}_{2^{16}}$ coefficients of only 15 unknown words, namely 10 consecutive values of the sequence $(Z_1, \cdots Z_{48})$ and 5 of the 24 products $Z_1 \cdot Z_2$, $Z_3 \cdot Z_4, \ldots, Z_{47} \cdot Z_{48}$. Equivalently, if we consider equations over $\mathbb{F}_2$ instead of $\mathbb{F}_{2^{16}}$, each bit of $h(Z, A, B)$ can be expressed for all (A, B) pairs as a known affine function of only 240 unknown bits, namely 160 Z bits and 80 quadratic functions of Z bits. We call hereafter such unknown bits *expanded key bits*.[2]

---

[2] Thus the function h involves 1152 expanded key bits in overall, namely 768 Z bits and 384 quadratic functions of the Z bits.

We now present the cryptanalysis of HB^{++}. We have shown in the former section that, by disturbing a subset of s rounds of an authentication and exploiting the authentication success or failure information for the disturbed protocol, an adversary is capable of getting approximate linear equations involving a subset of the bits of x, say the 16 first bits of x (which all linearly depends on the same 240 expanded key bits). If we collect a sufficient number m of such equations, relating to m temporary values x, we get an LPN problem in 240 expanded key bits. According to the previous analysis, the error parameter for this LPN problem will typically not be more than 0.01. Levieil and Fouque [15] estimate that such instances of the LPN problem can be solved with about 2^{30} noisy samples and 2^{41} steps of computation and bytes of memory. Thus 240 bits of the expanded key can be recovered by solving an LPN problem of medium complexity. The same method can be applied to recover 240-bit portions of the expanded key allowing the attacker to predict the other 16-bit words of x. Once this is done, x can be predicted by the adversary for each authentication. This renders the derivation of m approximate linear equations on x' bits even easier than the initial derivation of approximate equations on x bits and therefore the parts of the expanded key that allow the attacker to compute the value of x' at each authentication can now be derived.

At this stage, the adversary has enough information to impersonate the tag without having to derive the rest of the expanded key and derive y and y'. The adversary can re-use the masking vectors b used by the tag in a successful authentication along with its knowledge of x and x' to correct the z and z' values in an appropriate way. All in all, HB^{++} can be cryptanalyzed by solving 10 LPN problems of size 240 bits with small noise parameters. The total number of authentications needed is multiplied by $P_a^{-1} \simeq 4$ as only authentications where the reader accepts are used. For example, for $(r, t, \eta) = (80, 30, 0.25)$, the noise parameter of the LPN problem is roughly 0.01 so that the total number of authentications needed is $4 \times 10 \times 2^{30} \simeq 2^{35}$ and the total complexity is about 2^{44}. Moreover, it is possible to reduce the number of authentications needed at the expense of an increased complexity. Hence HB^{++} offers a much reduced level of security considering the complexity of the operations it requires.

4   The Variant HB*

Description of HB*. The variant HB* is proposed by Duc and Kim [5]. Again it consists of r rounds where each round consists of three passes. This is illustrated in Figure 4. There is an additional secret s which is used to secretly transmit from the tag to the reader a random bit γ, which is 1 with probability $\eta' \in]0, \frac{1}{2}]$, and which determines whether the right answer is computed as $(a \cdot x) \oplus (b \cdot y)$ or $(a \cdot y) \oplus (b \cdot x)$. As in HB$^+$, the tag is authenticated if the number of errors is less than some threshold $t = ur$, where $u \in]\eta, \frac{1}{2}[$. Note that the false rejection and false acceptance probabilities P_{FR} and P_{FA} are given by the same formulas as in the case of HB$^+$. In particular these probabilities are independent of η'. The on-tag computation is roughly twice that of HB$^+$

Tag (secret $\boldsymbol{x}, \boldsymbol{y}, \boldsymbol{s}$)		Reader (secret $\boldsymbol{x}, \boldsymbol{y}, \boldsymbol{s}$)
$\gamma \in_R \{0, 1 \| \text{Prob}(\nu = 1) = \eta'\}$		
$\nu \in_R \{0, 1 \| \text{Prob}(\nu = 1) = \eta\}$		
Choose $\boldsymbol{b} \in_R \{0,1\}^k$		
$w = (\boldsymbol{b} \cdot \boldsymbol{s}) \oplus \gamma$	$\xrightarrow{\quad b, w \quad}$	
	$\xleftarrow{\quad a \quad}$	Choose $\boldsymbol{a} \in_R \{0,1\}^k$
If $\gamma = 0$		
$\quad z = (\boldsymbol{a} \cdot \boldsymbol{x}) \oplus (\boldsymbol{b} \cdot \boldsymbol{y}) \oplus \nu$		
else		
$\quad z = (\boldsymbol{a} \cdot \boldsymbol{y}) \oplus (\boldsymbol{b} \cdot \boldsymbol{x}) \oplus \nu$	$\xrightarrow{\quad z \quad}$	If $(\boldsymbol{b} \cdot \boldsymbol{s}) = w$
		$\quad$ check $(\boldsymbol{a} \cdot \boldsymbol{x}) \oplus (\boldsymbol{b} \cdot \boldsymbol{y}) = z$
		else
		$\quad$ check $(\boldsymbol{a} \cdot \boldsymbol{y}) \oplus (\boldsymbol{b} \cdot \boldsymbol{x}) = z$

Fig. 4. One single round of HB*. The entire authentication process requires r rounds and, in this basic form, each round consists of the three passes shown. Provided the tag fails less than some threshold t number of rounds, the tag is authenticated.

(but less than that required in HB^{++}) while resistance to the GRS attack is claimed. In the next section we apply the GRS attack to HB* and show that HB* offers no advantage over HB$^+$.

Attacking HB*. We show that HB* remains vulnerable to an extremely close variant of the GRS attack. The first phase of the attack aims to gather information on $\boldsymbol{\delta} \cdot \boldsymbol{x}$ and $\boldsymbol{\delta} \cdot \boldsymbol{y}$ for independent vectors $\boldsymbol{\delta}$. For this, the adversary proceeds exactly as in the GRS attack and modifies the challenges sent by the reader by adding a vector $\boldsymbol{\delta}$ to $\boldsymbol{a}$. When $\boldsymbol{\delta} \cdot \boldsymbol{x} = 0$ and $\boldsymbol{\delta} \cdot \boldsymbol{y} = 0$, the protocol is undisturbed and the tag will be authenticated with high probability. In all other cases, the authentication will be less likely to succeed, so that the output of the reader gives information about $\boldsymbol{x}$ and $\boldsymbol{y}$. More precisely, depending on the values of $\boldsymbol{\delta} \cdot \boldsymbol{x}$ and $\boldsymbol{\delta} \cdot \boldsymbol{y}$, each round of the protocol will be successful or not with the following probabilities:

1. *if $\boldsymbol{\delta} \cdot \boldsymbol{x} = 0$ and $\boldsymbol{\delta} \cdot \boldsymbol{y} = 0$*, then none of the r rounds of the protocol are disturbed. The response of the tag is incorrect each time $\nu = 1$, hence with probability $\tau_1 = \eta$ and the reader accepts with probability $1 - P_{\text{FR}}$ and rejects with probability P_{FR}.
2. *if $\boldsymbol{\delta} \cdot \boldsymbol{x} = 0$ and $\boldsymbol{\delta} \cdot \boldsymbol{y} = 1$*, the response of the tag is incorrect each time $(\gamma = 0, \nu = 1)$ or $(\gamma = 1, \nu = 0)$, hence with probability

$$\tau_2 = (1 - \eta)\eta' + (1 - \eta')\eta = \eta + (1 - 2\eta)\eta' > \eta.$$

3. *if $\boldsymbol{\delta} \cdot \boldsymbol{x} = 1$ and $\boldsymbol{\delta} \cdot \boldsymbol{y} = 0$*, the response of the tag is incorrect each time $(\gamma = 0, \nu = 0)$ or $(\gamma = 1, \nu = 1)$, hence with probability

$$\tau_3 = (1 - \eta)(1 - \eta') + \eta\eta' = \eta + (1 - 2\eta)(1 - \eta') > \eta.$$

4. *if $\delta \cdot x = 1$ and $\delta \cdot y = 1$*, the response of the tag is incorrect each time $\nu = 0$, whatever γ, hence with probability $\tau_4 = 1 - \eta = \eta + (1 - 2\eta) > \eta$.

Note that $\tau_1 < \tau_2 \le \frac{1}{2} \le \tau_3 < \tau_4$. Note also that when $\eta' \to 0$ ($\eta' = 0$ corresponds to the classical HB$^+$ protocol), $\tau_2 \to \tau_1$ and $\tau_3 \to \tau_4$, whereas when $\eta' \to \frac{1}{2}$, $\tau_2 \to \frac{1}{2}$ and $\tau_3 \to \frac{1}{2}$. In each of the cases 2, 3 and 4, the reader will reject with probability greater than P_{FR}, namely $P_i^{\mathrm{rej}} = \Pr[\mathcal{R} \text{ rejects} \,|\, \text{case } i] = \sum_{j=t+1}^{r} \binom{r}{j} \tau_i^j (1 - \tau_i^{r-j})$.

According to the Chernoff bound (see Appendix), the adversary will be able to discriminate between case i and j as soon as $|P_i^{\mathrm{rej}} - P_j^{\mathrm{rej}}|$ is non-negligible. We have to distinguish two cases: either $\tau_2 \le u$, or $\tau_2 > u$.

When $\tau_2 \le u$, i.e. $\eta' \le \frac{u-\eta}{1-2\eta}$, we are "almost" in the HB$^+$ case: the reader will accept with overwhelming probability when $\delta \cdot x = 0$ and reject with overwhelming probability when $\delta \cdot x = 1$, independently of $\delta \cdot y$. The GRS attack applies as it is, meaning that the adversary can retrieve x with high probability in linear time. Once this is done, it can impersonate a tag by sending $(b, \omega) = (0, 0)$ as first message.

When $\tau_2 > u$, i.e. $\eta' > \frac{u-\eta}{1-2\eta}$, the attacker can only discriminate case 1 from cases 2, 3, and 4. Indeed the reader will accept with overwhelming probability when $\delta \cdot x = 0$ and $\delta \cdot y = 0$, and reject with overwhelming probability in the three other cases. However this does not prevent a slight variant of the GRS attack as follows.

We assume that x and y are linearly independent. For a random δ, case 1 happens with probability $\frac{1}{4}$, so that the adversary will be able to find with $\Theta(4k)$ attempts $k - 2$ independent vectors δ such that $\delta \cdot x = 0$ and $\delta \cdot y = 0$. Put a different way, he is able to learn the two-dimensional vectorial space $\langle x, y \rangle$. Let c_1, c_2 and c_3 denote the three non-null vectors in this vectorial space. Once they are found, the adversary can directly impersonate a valid tag with probability roughly $\frac{1}{8}$ by choosing at random two vectors among (c_1, c_2, c_3) (say c_1 and c_2), fixing two arbitrary values for (b, ω) that he will send at each round, and then answering $(c_1 \cdot a) \oplus (c_2 \cdot b)$ at each round. The adversary will be successfully authenticated when $(b \cdot s = \omega, c_1 = x, c_2 = y)$ or $(b \cdot s \neq \omega, c_1 = y, c_2 = x)$, which happens with probability $\frac{1}{8}$.

Alternatively, the adversary can do a little more work and identify from the three values (c_1, c_2, c_3) the one which is equal to $x \oplus y$. For this, the attacker queries the honest tag with challenges a systematically equal to the blinding vector b sent by the tag. That way, the answer of the tag is always equal to $b \cdot (x \oplus y) \oplus \nu$ and the attacker deduces that $x \oplus y$ is the value c_i such that the number of b's such that $b \cdot c_i$ is equal to the answer of the tag is maximal. Once this is done, the adversary knows the unordered set $\{x, y\}$. This is enough to impersonate the tag with probability $\frac{1}{2}$. Assume that the vector c_3 has been ruled out as being $x \oplus y$. The adversary randomly fixes values for (b, ω) that he will send at each round, and then answers $(c_1 \cdot a) \oplus (c_2 \cdot b)$ at each round. The adversary will be successfully authenticated when $(b \cdot s = \omega, c_1 = x, c_2 = y)$ or $(b \cdot s \neq \omega, c_1 = y, c_2 = x)$, which happens now with probability $\frac{1}{2}$. Note that whatever the outcome of this first attempt, the adversary will successfully pass

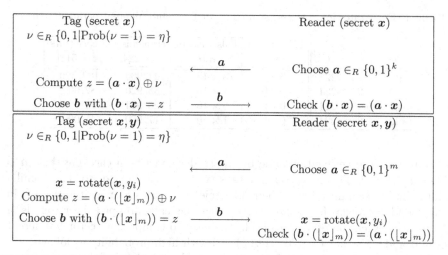

Fig. 5. Round i of HB-MP$'$ (above) and HB-MP (below). The entire authentication process requires r rounds and, in this basic form, each round consists of the two passes shown. Provided the tag fails less than some threshold t number of rounds, the tag is authenticated. For HB-MP $\lfloor x \rfloor_m$ denotes the m least significant bits of x and y_i is the ith bit of y which is used as the argument to a bitwise rotation.

the following attempt with probability 1. If the first attempt succeeded he can reuse the same (b, ω) and answer $(c_1 \cdot a) \oplus (c_2 \cdot b)$ at each round. If the first attempt failed, use the same (b, ω) but answer $(c_2 \cdot a) \oplus (c_1 \cdot b)$ at each round; the answer will always be correct and the tag will be successfully impersonated.

5   The Variants HB-MP$'$ and HB-MP

Description of HB-MP$'$ and HB-MP. Another prominent protocol due to Munilla and Peinado is HB-MP [17]. In a departure from the HB$^+$ approach, each of the r rounds consists of only a two-pass communication between the tag and the reader. This is illustrated in Figure 5 where two variants are depicted; the first variant HB-MP$'$ is claimed to be resistant to chosen challenges (presumably against the tag) while the second HB-MP is claimed to resist the GRS attack.

While HB-MP$'$ and HB-MP are reasonably lightweight, we show in the next section that both are less secure than HB$^+$ since they are vulnerable to a passive attack. These are the attacks that HB$^+$ provably resists and so HB-MP$'$ and HB-MP are not good alternatives.

Attacking HB-MP$'$ and HB-MP. In their paper, Munilla and Peinado claim that HB-MP is immune to passive attacks, but also active and man-in-the-middle attacks of the GRS type. However, there is a very simple passive attack which enables an adversary which simply eavesdrops the r rounds of one execution of the protocol to impersonate a valid tag with probability $1 - P_{\text{FR}}$.

Table 1. Error rates and transmission costs for HB$^+$ and different parameter choices

r	η	k	False reject rate	False accept rate	Transmission cost (bits) $[k = 224]$	$[k = 512]$
100	0.25	224	0.45	3×10^{-7}	44,900	102,500
80	0.25	224	0.44	4×10^{-6}	35,920	82,000
60	0.25	224	0.43	6×10^{-5}	26,984	61,500
40	0.25	224	0.42	1×10^{-3}	17,960	41,000

Note that the verification done by the reader consists in checking that $(a \oplus b) \cdot (\lfloor x \rfloor_m) = 0$. This equation is always verified when $b = a$, so that Munilla and Peinado recommend that the reader rejects a tag as soon as it answers a in any round. However, for an adversary which has eavesdropped the r rounds of a previous execution of the protocol, it is easy to compute a vector b different from a and such that $(a \oplus b) \cdot (\lfloor x \rfloor_m) = 0$ with high probability as follows.

The adversary simply records the r pairs (a_i, b_i) which are exchanged between the honest tag and the honest reader. Then we know that with probability $(1-\eta)$, $(a_i \oplus b_i) \cdot (\lfloor x \rfloor_m) = 0$. Hence, for any other challenge a_i', the answer $b_i' = a_i' \oplus a_i \oplus b_i$ is different from a_i' (because $b_i \neq a_i$) and $(a_i' \oplus b_i') \cdot (\lfloor x \rfloor_m) = (a_i \oplus b_i) \cdot (\lfloor x \rfloor_m)$. Hence the adversary is authenticated as soon as the tag was authenticated in the eavesdropped execution of the protocol. The attack works exactly in the same way against HB-MP'.

6   Discussion and Implications

The computational challenges posed by low-cost RFID tags have generated many cryptographic proposals which rely exclusively on the simplest (typically bitwise) operations. While some might express the view that some security is better than no security, even claims for "some security" need to be verified. Weaknesses in some of the simpler RFID protocols has already been demonstrated before, *e.g.* [4], and will undoubtedly be demonstrated in the future.

Those working in the field of RFID security are correct when claiming that one doesn't necessarily need full security for a deployment. This is why a proposal like HB$^+$ is actually rather successful: it doesn't claim to protect against all adversaries, but for adversaries with a minimum technical capability it provides a reasonable level of security. HB$^+$ does as claims and no more. The variants described in this note have attempted to do more and have, arguably, delivered less. It is difficult to do a lot with such basic operations.

This is not to say, however, that HB$^+$ is currently ideal. While the on-tag computation is low, the GRS attack may be practically important to some (*i.e.* it might be more than certificational). Furthermore, the communication overheads for HB$^+$ are substantial while the false acceptance and false rejection rates are not suitable for deployment. These are shown in Table 1 for the parameter $k = 224$ and acceptance threshold $r\eta$ proposed in HB$^+$ [11]. Based on the work of [15] we also consider the data transmission costs when $k = 512$ which is a more appropriate value to use if we are seeking 80-bit security.

These are unfortunate barriers for any practical deployment of HB$^+$. Nevertheless, the computational complexity and simplicity of HB$^+$ are very attractive and it nicely complements other work that seeks to extend more conventional forms of cryptography [1,6,10,16]. It is therefore an interesting challenge to find the right variant of HB$^+$ that simultaneously improves both security and efficiency: one such proposal has been named HB$^\#$ by the authors [9].

7 Conclusions

In this paper we have considered variants to HB$^+$. While they were designed with the sole intention of resisting the GRS attack on HB$^+$, all of HB^{++}, HB*, HB-MP$'$, and HB-MP are vulnerable to GRS-style attacks. In addition these variants sacrifice much of the simplicity and elegance of the original HB$^+$. Despite some questions on the practical implementation of HB$^+$ and the existence of the GRS attack, the computational efficiency and theoretical foundations of HB$^+$ are impressive. And while the work in this paper suggests that good variants to HB$^+$ are very hard to find, the right variant might offer a particularly interesting—and successful—solution to the problem of low-cost tag authentication.

Acknowledgements. We would like to thank Stanislaw Jarecki for his thoughtful feedback on a previous version of this paper.

References

1. Bogdanov, A., Knudsen, L.R., Leander, G., Paar, C., Poschmann, A., Robshaw, M.J.B., Seurin, Y., Vikkelsoe, C.: PRESENT: An Ultra-Lightweight Block Cipher. In: Paillier, P., Verbauwhede, I. (eds.) CHES 2007. LNCS, vol. 4727, pp. 450–466. Springer, Heidelberg (2007)
2. Black, J., Halevi, S., Krawczyk, H., Krovetz, T., Rogaway, P.: UMAC: Fast and Secure Message Authentication. In: Wiener, M.J. (ed.) CRYPTO 1999. LNCS, vol. 1666, pp. 216–233. Springer, Heidelberg (1999)
3. Bringer, J., Chabanne, H., Dottax, E.: HB^{++}: A Lightweight Authentication Protocol Secure Against Some Attacks. In: Georgiadis, P., Lopez, J., Gritzalis, S., Marias, G. (eds.) Proceedings of SecPerU 2006, pp. 28–33. IEEE Computer Society Press, Los Alamitos (2006)
4. Defend, B., Fu, K., Juels, A.: Cryptanalysis of Two Lightweight RFID Authentication Schemes. In: International Workshop on Pervasive Computing and Communication Security, PerSec 2007, pp. 211–216. IEEE Computer Society Press, Los Alamitos (2007)
5. Duc, D.N., Kim, K.: Securing HB$^+$Against GRS Man-in-the-Middle Attack. In: Institute of Electronics, Information and Communication Engineers, Symposium on Cryptography and Information Security, January 23–26 (2007)
6. Feldhofer, M., Dominikus, S., Wolkerstorfer, J.: Strong Authentication for RFID Systems Using the AES Algorithm. In: Joye, M., Quisquater, J.-J. (eds.) CHES 2004. LNCS, vol. 3156, pp. 357–370. Springer, Heidelberg (2004)

7. Fossorier, M.P.C., Mihaljevic, M.J., Imai, H., Cui, Y., Matsuura, K.: A Novel Algorithm for Solving the LPN Problem and its Application to Security Evaluation of the HB Protocol for RFID Authentication (2006), http://eprint.iacr.org/2006/197.pdf
8. Gilbert, H., Robshaw, M.J.B., Sibert, H.: An Active Attack Against HB$^+$: A Provably Secure Lightweight Authentication Protocol. IEE Electronics Letters 41(21), 1169–1170 (2005)
9. Gilbert, H., Robshaw, M.J.B., Seurin, Y.: HB$^\#$: Increasing the Security and Efficiency of HB$^+$. In: Proceedings of Eurocrypt (to appear, 2008), http://eprint.iacr.org/2008/028
10. Girault, M., Poupard, G., Stern, J.: On the Fly Authentication and Signature Schemes Based on Groups of Unknown Order. Journal of Cryptology 19(4), 463–488 (2006)
11. Juels, A., Weis, S.A.: Authenticating Pervasive Devices With Human Protocols. In: Shoup, V. (ed.) CRYPTO 2005. LNCS, vol. 3621, pp. 293–308. Springer, Heidelberg (2005)
12. Kaps, J.-P., Yüksel, K., Sunar, B.: Energy Scalable Universal Hashing. IEEE Trans. on Computers 54(12), 1484–1495 (2005)
13. Katz, J., Shin, J.: Parallel and Concurrent Security of the HB and HB$^+$Protocols. In: Vaudenay, S. (ed.) EUROCRYPT 2006. LNCS, vol. 4004, pp. 73–87. Springer, Heidelberg (2006)
14. Katz, J., Smith, A.: Analysing the HB and HB$^+$Protocols in the Large Error Case (2006), http://eprint.iacr.org/2006/326.pdf
15. Levieil, E., Fouque, P.-A.: An Improved LPN Algorithm. In: De Prisco, R., Yung, M. (eds.) SCN 2006. LNCS, vol. 4116, pp. 348–359. Springer, Heidelberg (2006)
16. McLoone, M., Robshaw, M.J.B.: Public Key Cryptography and RFID. In: Abe, M. (ed.) CT-RSA 2007. LNCS, vol. 4377, pp. 372–384. Springer, Heidelberg (2006)
17. Munilla, J., Peinado, A.: HB-MP: A Further Step in the HB-family of Lightweight Authentication Protocols. Computer Networks 51, 2262–2267 (2007)
18. Piramuthu, S.: HB and Related Lightweight Authentication Protocols for Secure RFID Tag/Reader Authentication. In: CollECTeR Europe Conference (June 2006)
19. Rivest, R.L.: The RC5 Encryption Algorithm. In: Preneel, B. (ed.) FSE 1994. LNCS, vol. 1008, pp. 86–96. Springer, Heidelberg (1995)

A   Chernoff Bounds

We recall here the classical Chernoff bounds. Let $X_1, \ldots, X_n$ be independent Poisson trials such that $\Pr[X_i = 1] = p_i$. Let $X = \sum_{i=1}^{n} X_i$ and μ be the expected value of X. Then for any $t < \mu$ and $t' > \mu$,

$$\Pr[X \leq t] \leq e^{-\frac{(\mu-t)^2}{2\mu}} \quad \text{and} \quad \Pr[X \geq t'] \leq e^{-\frac{(t'-\mu)^2}{3\mu}}.$$

Augmenting Internet-Based Card Not Present Transactions with Trusted Computing (Extended Abstract)

Shane Balfe and Kenneth G. Paterson

Inforamtion Security Group,
Royal Holloway, University of London,
Egham, Surrey, TW20 0EX, U.K.
{s.balfe,kenny.paterson}@rhul.ac.uk

Abstract. We demonstrate how Trusted Computing technology can be used to enhance the security of Internet-based Card Not Present (CNP) transactions. We focus on exploiting features of Trusted Computing as it is being deployed today, relying only on the presence of client-side Trusted Platform Modules. We discuss the threats to CNP transactions that remain even with our enhancements in place, focussing in particular on the threat of malware, and how it can be ameliorated.

1 Introduction

The Internet as an avenue for card-based payment transactions has seen a popularity explosion in recent years. However, this particular form of commerce, typically referred to as Card Not Present[1] (CNP) transactions is currently far from secure. A recent report on card fraud in the UK [1] showed that Internet-based CNP transactions accounted for 36% of all card fraud perpetrated in 2006 in the UK (up from 27% the previous year). This translated into £154.5 million in losses for card issuers and merchants. The vast majority of Internet-based payments are secured using a single protocol suite, namely SSL, to protect card account information. Unfortunately, SSL is not a panacea for enabling secure Internet-based CNP transactions. In particular SSL is used only to secure the payment channel – there is no guarantee that the customer owns the account number being proffered in a particular transaction. Demonstrating knowledge of a card's Personal Account Number (PAN) and corresponding Card Security Code (CSC) are deemed a sufficient form of transaction authorisation. 3-D Secure [2] is an optional adjunct to the SSL-based approach and attempts to provide cardholder authorisation for CNP transactions by requiring a separate customer authentication step prior to transaction processing. However, this approach has only limited security benefits in the face of the threat of malware such as trojans and keystroke loggers, a threat which is increasing at a frightening rate [3].

To address this issue there has been a recent development to strengthen 3-D Secure's authentication process through integration with EMV[2] chip cards.

---

[1] All references to CNP transactions herein refer to Internet-based CNP transactions.
[2] http://www.emvco.com/

G. Tsudik (Ed.): FC 2008, LNCS 5143, pp. 171–175, 2008.

This approach involves the use of "unconnected" card readers which, when interacting with a customer's physical card, generate a one-time passcode on a per-transaction basis. This passcode would then be used instead of a customer-supplied password for 3-D secure authentication. However, this approach suffers from the costs associated with distributing card readers to end-users.

In this paper, we operate from the sole assumption that client platforms are equipped with Trusted Platform Modules (TPMs) having limited but trusted cryptographic functionality. We use the TPM's trusted capabilities to build lightweight client-side enrollment and certification processes. These effectively bind a platform, and by extension its owner, to a particular card. The resulting public key certificates and TPM signing capabilities are then used to underpin authentication for CNP payments. We examine the malware/crimeware threat, explaining how it can be reasonably addressed within our architecture using the secure attention sequences that are a mandatory part of the TPM. For the remainder of this paper we use the terms user, client, cardholder and customer interchangeably.

Related Work: The idea of using Trusted Computing to enable client-side certification has previously been discussed in [4,5,6] as well as in the as-yet-unpublished Trusted Computing Group's TLS extensions for carrying attestations. However, none of this work takes into consideration the threat posed from malware nor the infrastructural requirements necessary to support client-side certification. The threat from malware is examined in greater detail in [7,8]. Other related work includes the use of Trusted Computing as an adjunct to securing connected card readers for generating digital signatures [9,10].

2   Applying Trusted Computing to CNP Transactions

We assume the reader is familiar with the generic four corner model used in card payment systems, the features of the SSL protocol, and the usage of 3-D Secure in enhancing Internet payments. We also assume the reader is familiar with the Trusted Computing (TC) specifications[3], as proposed by the Trusted Computing Group (TCG). We will make extensive use of the cryptographic keying infrastructure that is associated with these specifications, as well as the cryptographic processing capabilities of Trusted Platform Modules (TPMs). Further details on these background aspects can be found in the full version [11] of this extended abstract.

Enrollment: The goal is for a cardholder to engage in an enrollment process to obtain an X.509 certificate incorporating both card account details as well as a cardholder's public key (K_{i-pub}), with the corresponding private key (K_{i-priv}) being bound to the cardholder's TPM. This certification by the card issuer will effectively bind a cardholder's hardware platform to a particular card. The cardholder can later demonstrate this binding when authenticating himself to a merchant during a CNP transaction. Thus the TPM acts as both a secure storage

---

[3] https://www.trustedcomputinggroup.org/specs/

area for the cardholder's private key as well as providing a means by which the use of the private key can be controlled. In order for a card issuer to provide an enrollment facility for their customers' platforms, it is necessary for the card issuer to provide some form of CA functionality. This functionality may come in the form of a Privacy CA, an Subject Key Attestation Evidence (SKAE) CA or a hybrid CA. We defer discussion of the advantages and disadvantages of each of these three approaches to the full paper [11]. Additionally, the process by which a customer obtains an X.509 certificate for a TPM-bound non-migratable key in our system is specified in a 10 step process in the full paper [11]. The process requires minimal cardholder intervention, with users only needing to select and enter an authorisation string and a PIN/password during the process.

Client-Side Certification and Malware: In order for a cardholder to generate a signature using the private component of the key referenced in the X.509 certificate, the cardholder needs to send authorisation data to their TPM to activate their signature key. However, this authorisation information may be observed and replayed by malware to generate new transactions [8]. Moreover, malware may be capable of modifying transaction data that is sent to the TPM for signing. Our proposed mitigation for this malware problem is to use the TCG requirement that TPM-enabled platforms support a *secure attention sequence*, through which a user can demonstrate physical presence to a TPM. Here the design of a physical presence mechanism "should be difficult or impossible to spoof by rogue software" [12]. The combination of customer-provided card account details and evidence of the successful completion of a secure attention sequence can demonstrate that an authorised customer instigated a transaction. Malware on its own should be incapable of generating the required secure attention sequence.

The demonstration of physical presence on a TPM-enabled platform is typically associated with administrative functions of the TPM. However, physical presence may also be demonstrated ustilising the TPM_SetCapability and TPM_GetCapability commands [13]. These two commands can be used to set and retrieve bits in the Deferred Physical Presence Bit Map (DPPBM) that forms part of a TPM's TPM_STCLEAR_DATA structure [14].

In order for a cardholder (or more precisely an *untrusted* piece of software operating on a cardholder's behalf) to produce verifiable evidence of a (physical) commitment to a transaction, a cardholder needs to issue a series of commands to their TPM. A cardholder opens an *exclusive and logged transport session* [12] and calls the TPM_SetCapability to clear a single bit in the DPPBM. This command does not require a demonstration of physical presence and is used to prevent a bit from a previous transaction being reused by malicious software. Following this, a cardholder again calls TPM_SetCapability, but this time to set the newly cleared bit in the DPPBM (here the setting of the bit requires the cardholder to demonstrate physical presence). The cardholder next calls TPM_GetCapability to read the newly set bit indicating that physical presence has been demonstrated. Finally, a cardholder calls TPM_ReleaseTransportSigned to generate a *physical presence certificate*. The TPM_ReleaseTransportSigned produces a signature using K_{i-priv} over a data structure that includes a hash of the transport session log (consisting of the inputs, commands, and outputs encountered during the entire transport session) and a merchant-supplied anti-replay nonce. This nonce is constructed as a hash of the current transaction concatenated with a merchant-supplied random number. This physical presence certificate, together with the merchant's nonce and the transport session log, can be used to construct a *physical presence package* which a third party can verify. Note that, in order to load and use the key K_{i-priv}, the cardholder will need to input valid authorisation data. This is not intended to provide a defence against malware, but instead to prevent use of a stolen platform.

Unfortunately, user education now surfaces as a potential weak link in the security chain: malware may attempt to fool a user into providing a demonstration of physical presence. This is exacerbated by the fact that the manner in which physical presence functionality is presented to an end-user is entirely dependent on how a manufacturer chooses to implement it. Attesting to physical presence may be better suited to constrained devices such as mobile phones that conform to the Trusted Mobile specifications [15]. Here, the range of mechanisms available for this would be restricted by functional limitations. A second significant drawback is that the use of secure attention sequences will not prevent malware from modifying an on-going transaction (as opposed to generating multiple new transactions). Here we have to rely on the lack of a strong economic incentive for malware to behave in this way – we can assume that it will simply not be beneficial for malware to modify individual transactions, since this would lead to rapid detection for little benefit (from the malware's perspective).

Augmenting Existing Protocols with Trusted Computing: The full paper [11] describes how SSL can be augmented using a form of client-side authentication that is enabled using the enrollment and certification procedures outlined above. Our approach is an extension of that first described in [6] in the context of authentication in peer-to-peer networks.

The full paper also explains in detail how Trusted Computing can be used to enhance the security of the 3-D Secure system. With this approach, we can achieve the benefits of an unconnected card reading facility without the need for additional client-side security tokens, under the assumption of TPM ubiquity. This provides a lower cost approach and a more flexible deployment.

3   Conclusions

In the physical world, the introduction of EMV for card-based payments at point of sale terminals has seen a dramatic reduction in the fraud levels. Unfortunately, the benefits seen in the physical deployment of EMV for card payment transactions cannot be so easily gained in CNP scenarios. In this setting, knowledge of customer account information is all that is required to authorise a transaction. We have attempted to address this imbalance by using Trusted Computing to augment two different approaches for securing CNP transactions: SSL and 3-D Secure. In our approaches, knowledge of a customer's account details is no longer sufficient to complete a transaction; rather, a customer would need to demonstrate possession of a private key which is physically bound to a piece of hardware under their direct control. This approach can be easily adapted to other payment protocols such as SET, or indeed any protocol where it is important that a human presence be determined.

References

1. APACS: Fraud – The Facts 2007 (2007),
   http://www.apacs.org.uk/resources_publications/documents/
   FraudtheFacts2007.pdf
2. VISA: 3-D Secure Protocol Specification: Core Functions (2002),
   http://international.visa.com/fb/paytech/secure/main.jsp
3. Symantec: Symantec Internet Security Threat Report, vol. XI (2007),
   http://www.symantec.com/enterprise/theme.jsp?themeid=threatreport
4. TCG: TCG Infrastructure Workgroup Subject Key Attestation Evidence Extension. Version 1.0 (2005)
5. Alsaid, A., Mitchell, C.J.: Preventing Phishing Attacks Using Trusted Computing Technology. In: Proceedings of the 6th International Network Conference (INC 2006), Plymouth, UK, pp. 221–228 (2006)
6. Balfe, S., Lakhani, A., Paterson, K.G.: Securing Peer-to-Peer Networks Using Trusted Computing. In: Mitchell, C.J. (ed.) Trusted Computing, pp. 271–298. IEE Press, London (2005)
7. Gajek, S., Sadeghi, A.-R., Stüble, C., Winandy, M.: Compartmented Security for Browsers – or How to Thwart a Phisher with Trusted Computing. In: Proceedings of the 2nd International Conference on Availability, Reliability and Security (ARES 2007), Vienna, Austria, pp. 120–127. IEEE Computer Society, Washington (2007)
8. Jackson, C., Boneh, D., Mitchell, J.: Transaction Generators: Rootkits for the Web. In: Proceedings of the 2nd USENIX Workshop on Hot Topics in Security (HotSec 2007). The Advanced Computing Systems Association, Boston, MA, USA, USENIX (2007)
9. Balacheff, B., Chan, D., Chen, L., Pearson, S., Proudler, G.: Securing Intelligent Adjuncts Using Trusted Computing Platform Technology. In: Proceedings of the 4th Smart Card Research and Advanced Application (CARDIS 2001), pp. 177–195. Kluwer Academic Publishers, Norwell (2001)
10. Spalka, A., Cremers, A., Langweg, H.: Protecting the Creation of Digital Signatures with Trusted Computing Platform Technology Against Attacks by Trojan Horse Programs. In: Proceedings of the 16th International Conference on Information Security: Trusted information: the New Decade Challenge (IFIP SEC 2001), Paris, France. Kluwer International Federation For Information Processing Series, pp. 403–420 (2001)
11. Balfe, S., Paterson, K.G.: Augmenting Internet-based Card Not Present Transactions with Trusted Computing: An Analysis. Technical report, Royal Holloway, University of London (2006),
    http://www.ma.rhul.ac.uk/static/techrep/2006/RHUL-MA-2006-9.pdf
12. TCG: TPM Main: Part 1 Design Principles. Version 1.2, revision 103 (2007)
13. TCG: TPM Main: Part 3 Commands. Version 1.2, revision 103 (2007)
14. TCG: TPM Main: Part 2 Structures of the TPM. Version 1.2, revision 103 (2007)
15. TCG: The TCG Mobile Trusted Module Specification. Version 0.9, revision 1 (2006)

Weighing Down
"The Unbearable Lightness of PIN Cracking"*

Mohammad Mannan and P.C. van Oorschot

School of Computer Science, Carleton University
{mmannan, paulv}@scs.carleton.ca

Abstract. Responding to the PIN cracking attacks from Berkman and Ostrovsky (FC 2007), we outline a simple solution called *salted-PIN*. Instead of sending the regular user PIN, salted-PIN requires an ATM to generate a *Transport Final PIN* from a user PIN, account number, and a salt value (stored on the bank card) through, e.g., a pseudo-random function. We explore different attacks on this solution, and propose a variant of salted-PIN that can significantly restrict known attacks. Salted-PIN requires modifications to service points (e.g. ATMs), issuer/verification facilities, and bank cards; however, changes to intermediate switches are not required.

1 Introduction

Attacks on financial PIN processing APIs revealing customers' PINs have been known to banks and security researchers for years (see e.g. [5], [4], [3]). Apparently the most efficient of these 'PIN cracking' attacks are due to Berkman and Ostrovsky [2].[1] However, proposals to counter such attacks are almost non-existent in the literature, other than a few suggestions; for example, maintaining the secrecy (and integrity) of some data elements related to PIN processing (that are considered security insensitive according to current banking standards) such as the 'decimalization table' and 'PIN Verification Values (PVVs)/Offsets' has been emphasized [4], [2]. However, implementing these suggestions requires modifications to all involved parties' Hardware Security Modules (HSMs). Commercial solutions such as the `PrivateServer Switch-HSM` [1] rely mostly on 'tightly' controlling the key uploading process to a switch and removing 'unnecessary' APIs or weak PIN block formats. Even if the flawed APIs are fixed, or non-essential attack APIs are removed to prevent these attacks, it may be difficult in practice to ensure that all intermediate (third-party controlled) switches are updated accordingly. Thus banks rely mainly on protection mechanisms provided within banking standards, and *policy-based* solutions, e.g., mutual banking agreements to protect customer PINs.

---

* Version: June 13, 2008.
[1] We encourage readers unfamiliar with financial PIN processing APIs and PIN cracking attacks to consult the longer version of this work [6].

G. Tsudik (Ed.): FC 2008, LNCS 5143, pp. 176–181, 2008.

One primary reason that PIN cracking attacks are possible is that actual user PINs, although encrypted, travel from ATMs to a verification facility. We seek a solution that precludes real user PINs being extracted at verification facilities, and especially at switches (which are beyond the control of issuing banks), even in the presence of API flaws. While PIN cracking attacks get more expensive as the PIN length increases, it is unrealistic to consider larger (e.g. 12-digit) user PINs, for usability reasons. As part of our proposal, we assume that a unique random *salt* value of sufficient length (e.g. 128 bits) is stored on a user's bank card, and used along with the user's regular four-digit PIN ('Final PIN') to generate (e.g. through a pseudo-random function (PRF)) a larger (e.g. 12 digits) *Transport Final PIN* (TFP). This TFP is then encrypted and sent through the intermediate switches. We build our *salted-PIN* solution on this simple idea. We discuss several attacks on salted-PIN, and outline one variant of the original idea which is apparently resistant to currently known attacks. Our proposals require updating bank cards (magnetic-stripe/chip card), service-points (e.g. ATMs), and issuer/verification HSMs. However, our design goal is to avoid changing any intermediate switches, or requiring intermediate switches be trusted or compliant to anything beyond existing banking standards.

Salted-PIN provides the following benefits. (1) It does not depend on policy-based assumptions, and limits existing PIN cracking attacks even where intermediate switches are malicious. (2) It significantly increases the cost of launching known PIN cracking attacks; for example, the setup cost for the translate-only attack for building a complete Encrypted PIN Block (EPB) table now requires more than a trillion API calls in contrast to 10,000 calls as in Berkman and Ostrovsky [2]. (3) Incorporating service-point specific information such as 'card acceptor identification code' and 'card acceptor name/location' (as in ISO 8583) into a variant of salted-PIN, we further restrict attacks to be limited to a particular location/ATM.

2   Salted PIN

Here we present the salted-PIN proposal in its simplest form.

Threat model and notation. Our threat model assumes attackers have access to PIN processing APIs and transaction data (e.g. Encrypted PIN Blocks, account number) at switches or verification centers, but do not have direct access to keys inside an HSM, or modify HSMs in any way. Attackers can also create fake cards from information extracted at switches or verification centers and use those cards (perhaps through outsider accomplices). We primarily consider large scale attacks such as those that can extract millions of PINs in an hour [2]. We do not address attacks that are not scalable, such as *card skimming*, or cases where an accomplice steals a card and calls an insider at a switch or verification center for an appropriate PIN. The following notation is used:

PAN User's Primary Account Number (generally 14 or 16-digit).
PIN User's Final PIN (e.g. 4-digit, issued by the bank or chosen by the user).
PIN_t User's Transport Final PIN (TFP).
$Salt$ Long-term secret value shared between the user card and issuing bank.
$f_K(\cdot)$ A cryptographically secure Pseudo-Random Function (PRF).

Generating salted-PINs. A randomly generated salt value of adequate length (e.g. 128 bits) is selected by a bank for each customer. The salt is stored on a bank card in plaintext, and in an encrypted form at a verification facility under a bank-chosen *salt key*. API programmers (i.e. those who use HSM API) at the verification center have access to this encrypted salt (but do not know the salt key or plaintext salt values). Encrypted salt values also cannot be overwritten by API programmers. A user inputs her PIN at an ATM, and the ATM reads the plaintext salt value from the user's bank card, and generates a TFP as follows.

$$PIN_t = f_{Salt}(PAN, PIN) \tag{1}$$

The PRF output is interpreted as a number and divided by 10^{12}; the 12-digit remainder (i.e. PRF output modulo 10^{12}) is chosen as PIN_t and treated as the Final PIN from the user. Note that the maximum allowed PIN length by ISO standards is 12. The ATM encrypts PIN_t with the transport key shared with the adjacent switch, and forms an Encrypted PIN Block (EPB). An intermediate switch decrypts an EPB, (optionally) reformats the PIN block, and re-encrypts using the next switch's transport key. Additional functionalities are not required from these switches.

3   Attacks and Countermeasures

We now discuss attacks against the basic version of salted-PIN and outline one variant to limit these attacks.

3.1   Attacks on Salted-PIN

Enumerating EPBs through translate-only API call. Here the goal of an attacker is to create a table of EPBs, and then crack all user accounts. This attack in part follows an efficient variant of the translate attack as outlined by Berkman and Ostrovsky [2]. We assume an attacker M_i is an insider (e.g. application programmer) at a switch or verification center, and M_a is an outsider accomplice who helps M_i in carrying out user input at an ATM.

Assume that M_i extracts the salt value ($Salt_a$) and PAN from a card he possesses, and uses equation (1) to generate the 12-digit TFP PIN_{at} (through software or a hardware device, using any PIN PIN_a). Let PIN_{at} consist of $p_1p_2p_3 \ldots p_{12}$ where each p_i ($i = 1$ to 12) is a valid PIN digit. Then M_a inserts this card to an ATM, and enters PIN_a. Assume that the generated PIN_{at} is encrypted by the ATM to form an EPB, E_1. M_i captures E_1 at a switch. If E_1 is not in the ISO-1 format, M_i translates it into ISO-1 (to disconnect E_1 from the associated PAN). Let the translated (if needed) E_1 in the ISO-1 format be

E_1'. E_1' is then translated from ISO-1 to ISO-0 using $p_3 p_4 \ldots p_{12} 00$ as the input PAN. This special PAN is chosen so that the XOR of PIN positions 3 to 12 with PAN positions 1 to 10 removes $p_3 \ldots p_{12}$ when the translation API is called; i.e.,

$$
\begin{array}{rl}
\text{PIN block inside } E_1' = & 0 \ C \ p_1 \ p_2 \ p_3 \ p_4 \ p_5 \ p_6 \ p_7 \ p_8 \ p_9 \ p_{10} \ p_{11} \ p_{12} \ F \ F \\
\text{Input PAN} = & 0 \ 0 \ 0 \ 0 \ p_3 \ p_4 \ p_5 \ p_6 \ p_7 \ p_8 \ p_9 \ p_{10} \ p_{11} \ p_{12} \ 0 \ 0 \\
\text{Resulting ISO-0 PIN block} = & 0 \ C \ p_1 \ p_2 \ 0 \ 0 \ 0 \ 0 \ 0 \ 0 \ 0 \ 0 \ 0 \ 0 \ F \ F
\end{array}
$$

Assume the resulting EPB is $E_{p_1 p_2}$ which is the same as the one containing a TFP $p_1 p_2 0000000000$ with PAN 0. Now we can create all EPBs containing every 12 digit TFPs starting with $p_1 p_2$ from $E_{p_1 p_2}$. For example, an EPB with $p_1 p_2 q_3 q_4 \ldots q_{12}$ as the TFP can be generated through transforming $E_{p_1 p_2}$ using PAN $q_3 q_4 \ldots q_{12} 00$ (in ISO-0). Thus we can create all 10^{10} EPBs with TFPs from $p_1 p_2 0 \ldots 0$ to $p_1 p_2 9 \ldots 9$. Starting from a different $p_1 p_2$, all 10^{12} EPBs containing every 12 digit TFP can be generated.

To launch an attack, a valid EPB of a target customer is collected. The EPB is translated to ISO-1 (to decouple it from the target account, if not already in ISO-1), then to ISO-0 with PAN 0. The resulting EPB is then located on the EPB table (as created in the setup phase). The corresponding PIN from the table can now be used to exploit a card generated with the target's PAN, and the attacker's salt value (i.e. $Salt_a$). The cost of this attack is at most two API calls and a search of $O(10^{12})$, i.e., $O(2^{40})$.

In summary, the setup cost of this attack is about 10^{12} API calls with a per account cost of two API calls plus a search of $O(10^{12})$. The same translate-only attack by Berkman and Ostrovsky [2] on the current implementation of PIN processing requires only about 10,000 API calls as setup cost, and a per account cost of two API calls plus a search of $O(10^3)$. More on this attack is discussed in the longer version of this work [6].

Replay attack. In this attack, an adversary M_i at a switch or verification center collects a valid EPB E_c for a target PAN A_c, and then creates a fake card with the account number A_c (and any salt value). Note that M_i here does not know the actual salt value or PIN for the target account. An accomplice M_a uses the fake card with any PIN at an ATM, and the ATM generates a false EPB E_a. At the switch/verification center M_i locates E_a in transfer, and replaces E_a with the previously collected correct EPB E_c. Thus the fake card will be verified by the target bank, and M_a can access the victim's account. Note that this attack works against the basic variant of salted-PIN as well as current PIN implementations without requiring any API calls. Although quite intuitive, this attack has not been discussed elsewhere to our knowledge.

3.2 Service-Point Specific Salted-PIN

We now outline one variant of salted-PIN to practically restrict the above attacks by increasing the per account attack cost. If a fake bank card is created for a target account (e.g. through the attacks in Section 3.1), the card can be used from anywhere as long as it remains valid (i.e. the issuing bank does not cancel it). To restrict such attacks, we modify equation (1) as follows.

$$PIN_t = f_{Salt}(PAN, PIN, spsi) \qquad (2)$$

Here *spsi* stands for *service-point specific information* such as a 'card acceptor identification code' and 'card acceptor name/location' as in ISO 8583 (Data Elements fields). The verification center must receive *spsi* as used in equation (2). Although any PIN cracking attack can be used to learn a TFP or build an EPB table, the table is valid only for the particular values of *spsi*. Also, the replay attack may succeed only when the accomplice exploits a compromised card from a particular ATM. Thus this construct generates a localized TFP for each PIN verification, and thereby restricts the fake card to be used only from a particular location/ATM.

4   Conclusion

In the 30-year history of financial PIN processing APIs, several flaws have been uncovered. In this paper, we introduce a *salted-PIN* proposal to counter PIN cracking attacks from Berkman and Ostrovsky [2]. Our preliminary analysis indicates that salted-PIN can provide a higher barrier to these attacks in practice by making them considerably more expensive (computationally). Salted-PIN is motivated primarily by the realistic scenario in which an adversary may control switches, and use any standard API functions to reveal a user's PIN; i.e., an attacker has the ability to perform malicious API calls to HSMs, but cannot otherwise modify an HSM. Salted-PIN is intended to stimulate further research and solicit feedback from the banking community. Instead of relying, perhaps unrealistically, on honest intermediate parties (who diligently comply with mutual banking agreements), we strongly encourage the banking community to invest efforts in designing protocols that do not rely on such assumptions which end-users (among others) have no way of verifying.

Acknowledgements

This work benefited substantially from discussion and/or feedback from a number of individuals, including: Bernhard Esslinger of University of Siegen, Joerg-Cornelius Schneider and Henrik Koy of Deutsche Bank, especially regarding attacks on the simple version of salted-PIN; a reviewer from a large Canadian bank; Glenn Wurster; and anonymous reviewers. The first author is supported in part by an NSERC CGS. The second author is Canada Research Chair in Network and Software Security, and is supported in part by an NSERC Discovery Grant, and the Canada Research Chairs Program.

References

1. Algorithmic Research (ARX). PrivateServer Switch-HSM. White paper, http://www.arx.com/documents/Switch-HSM.pdf
2. Berkman, O., Ostrovsky, O.M.: The unbearable lightness of PIN cracking. In: Dietrich, S., Dhamija, R. (eds.) FC 2007. LNCS, vol. 4886. Springer, Heidelberg (2007)
3. Bond, M.: Attacks on cryptoprocessor transaction sets. In: Koç, Ç.K., Naccache, D., Paar, C. (eds.) CHES 2001. LNCS, vol. 2162. Springer, Heidelberg (2001)
4. Bond, M., Zielinski, P.: Decimalisation table attacks for PIN cracking. Technical report (UCAM-CL-TR-560), Computer Laboratory, University of Cambridge (2003)
5. Clulow, J.: The design and analysis of cryptographic APIs for security devices. Masters Thesis, University of Natal, Durban, South Africa (2003)
6. Mannan, M., van Oorschot, P.: Weighing down The Unbearable Lightness of PIN Cracking (extended version). Technical report, School of Computer Science, Carleton University (2008), http://www.scs.carleton.ca/research/tech_reports/

Phishwish: A Stateless Phishing Filter Using Minimal Rules

Debra L. Cook[1], Vijay K. Gurbani[2], and Michael Daniluk[3]

[1] dcook@cs.columbia.edu
[2] Alcatel-Lucent, Bell Labs
vkg@alcatel-lucent.com
[3] Polytechnic University
mikedaniluk@gmail.com

Abstract. We introduce *phishwish*, a phishing filter that offers advantages over existing filters: It does not need any training and does not consult centralized white or black lists. Furthermore, it is simple to configure, requiring only 11 rules to determine the veracity of an incoming email. We compare the performance of phishwish to SpamAssassin and to Google's browser-based phishing filter. Our results indicate that phishwish outperforms these filters and identifies zero days attacks that went undetected by existing filters.

Keywords: phishing, email, filters.

1 Introduction

We define *phishing* as the practice of directing unsuspecting users to fraudulent websites with the intent of obtaining personal information to be used for illicit purposes by a spammer. In August 2007, the Anti-Phishing Working Group (http://www.antiphishing.org) detected 32,079 unique phishing websites – an increase of more than 2,000 over the previous month – that hijacked a total of 129 brands. It does not appear that phishing will subside, so what can be done to dampen its effects?

The majority of literature surveyed on detecting phishing concerns techniques implemented through browser plugins (or toolbars) [4] [5]. This approach remains problematic; Zhang et. al [3] empirically analyzed ten toolbars and reported that the only toolbar able to consistently identify more than 90% of phishing URLs also incorrectly classified 42% of legitimate URLs as phishing. Wu et al. [2] determined that many users ignore toolbar warnings and instead chose to inspect the site's contents to determine whether or not it was a fraudulent site. But the average user visiting well-designed phishing websites is unable to tell them apart from genuine sites. Dhamija et al. [1] conducted a study on why phishing works by testing their hypothesis on 22 participants using 20 websites. They report that good phishing websites fooled 90% of the participants and that 23% of the participants in their study did not even bother looking at the address bar, status bar, or security indicators. Due to the inefficacy of the toolbar approach, we avoid such designs and instead focus on email content analysis in phishwish.

G. Tsudik (Ed.): FC 2008, LNCS 5143, pp. 182–186, 2008.

2   Phishwish Description

Our primary goals are to be able to identify zero-day attacks, minimize the complexity of the rule-base and configuration, and maximize the number of phishing emails detected while minimizing the number of false positives. Phishwish is applicable to emails that instruct the recipient to log into a web site. It processes text based and HTML formatted emails, although some rules are only applicable to HTML. Each rule is assigned a configurable weight, W_i and a flag X_i. Phishwish sets X_i to 1 if the rule is applicable to the email and to 0 otherwise. Each rule produces a value, P_i, ranging from 0.0 - 1.0. If the rule is not applicable, $P_i = 0$. The final score is $S = \frac{\sum W_i P_i}{\sum W_i X_i}$, with higher values of S indicating a greater probability of phishing.

When describing the rules, a **positive** result is indicative of phishing, in which case P_i is set to 1 except for rules 8 and 10 where it is set to a fraction. A **negative** result is indicative of a valid email, in which case P_i is set to 0. **Business** refers to the business from which the email supposedly has been sent. **Login URL** refers to the URL within the email that the recipient should use to access the business' login page. The rules fall into the following general categories: **(1)** identification and analysis of the login URL in the email, **(2)** analysis of the email headers, **(3)** analysis across URLs and images in the email, and **(4)** determining if the URL is accessible. Our rules are:

Rule 1: If the email appears (based on search engine results) to not be directing the recipient to the actual login page for the business, the result is positive.

Rule 2: In HTML formatted emails, if a URL displayed to the recipient uses TLS, it is compared to the URL in the HREF tag. If the URL in the tag does not use TLS , the result is positive.

Rule 3: If the login URL is referenced as a raw IP address instead of a domain name, the result is positive.

Rule 4: If the business name appears in the login URL, but not in the domain portion, the result is positive.

Rule 5: In HTML formatted emails, if a URL is displayed to the recipient, it is compared to the URL in the HREF tag. If their domains do not match, the result is positive.

Rule 6: The chain of "Received" SMTP headers is checked to determine if the path includes a server or a mail user agent in the same DNS domain as the business. The rule is positive if such a Received header is not present.

Rule 7: Rules 7 and 9 perform a case-insensitive byte-wise comparison of the domain of all URLs in the email message with the domain of the login URL. Rule 7 analyzes non-image URLs for such inconsistencies in their domains. If inconsistencies are detected, the rule is positive.

Rule 8: Rules 8 and 10 match the DNS registrant for the domain of each URL in the email with the DNS registrant for the domain in the login URL. Rule 8 analyzes non-image URLs for inconsistencies in their *whois* registrant information. P_8 is set to the percentage of URLs whose information differs from that of the login URL.

Rule 9: This rule analyzes image URLs for inconsistencies in their domains. If inconsistencies are detected, the rule is positive.

Rule 10: This rule analyzes image URLs for inconsistencies in their *whois* registrant information. P_{10} is set in the same manner as P_8 in Rule 8.

Rule 11: The rule is positive if the web page is inaccessible. The rule is considered not applicable otherwise.

3   Experiments and Observations

We collected 1,000 emails over a 6 month period from November 2006 to April 2007. From these emails, we culled and tested phishwish on 117 unique emails composed of 81 phishing attacks and 36 types of valid emails. We define a "unique email" to be a representative of a class of emails that essentially mount the same phishing attack with only slight variations in the email body (e.g., multiple emails from Chase Bank offering a small amount of money to the recipient that differed only in the dollar amount). Phishwish would produce the same score across emails within a class. The 36 valid emails consisted of legitimate emails that ask the recipient to access an account. These included emails from banks, brokerage firms, utilities, credit card companies, frequent traveler programs and online stores, among others.

We applied phishwish with all weights set to 1. The results are shown in Figure 1. Phishwish's scores for the 36 valid emails ranged from 0 to 55%, with an average of 25.6%. The scores for the 81 phishing emails ranged from 42.9% to 100%, with an average of 75.4%.

For comparison, we applied SpamAssassin version 3.1.8 using its default settings and no training (since phishwish was applied untrained with all weights set to 1). Its results are shown in Figure 2. SpamAssassin identifies spam emails in general so its rules are not specific to phishing emails. Since phishing is a subset of spam and it can generally cause more harm then general spam, we

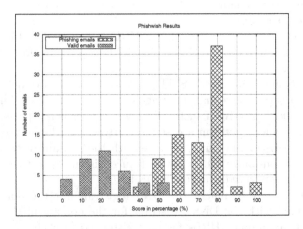

Fig. 1. Phishwish Results: x% indicates the score is in [x% to (x+10)%]

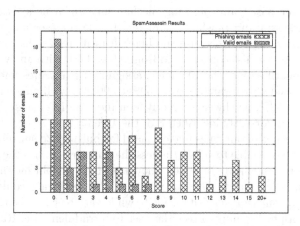

Fig. 2. Spamassassin Results: x indicates the score is in [x,x+1)

expected SpamAssassin to properly categorize the 117 emails. A score of 5 points
or higher is considered spam according to the default settings. SpamAssassin's
scores for the 36 valid emails ranged from 0 to 7 points, with an average score of
1.78 points. SpamAssassin's scores for the 81 phishing emails ranged from 0 to
23.1, with an average score of 6.62 points. While SpamAssassin performed well
on the valid emails, only misidentifying 3 of the 36 emails, it performed poorly
on the phishing emails, assigning less than 5 points to 37 of them.

Even with our basic method of treating all rules with equal weight, there is a
clear delineation between the scores phishwish assigned to valid emails and the
scores it assigned to phishing emails. Table 1 presents the summary of misdiag-
nosed emails for phishwish and SpamAssassin using varying thresholds for the
minimum score required to classify an email as phishing.

During our testing, we received ten zero-day attacks. The zero-day emails are
included in the set of 81 phishing emails. In each case, we immediately applied

Table 1. Comparing False Positives

Phishwish				
	Phishing Emails Score range: 42.9-100% Mean: 75.4%		**Valid Emails** Score range: 0-55% Mean: 25.6%	
Threshold	Correct Id	False Positive	Correct Id	False Positive
≥ 50%	79	2	33	3
≥ 60%	70	11	36	0
SpamAssassin				
	Phishing Emails Score range: 0.0-23.1 pts. Mean: 6.62 pts.		**Valid Emails** Score range: 0.0-7.0 pts Mean: 1.78 pts.	
Threshold	Correct Id	False Positive	Correct Id	False Positive
≥ 5 points	44	37	33	3

Google's browser based anti-phishing mechanism, which uses lists to classify email, SpamAssassin and phishwish. For all 10, the browser failed to identify the link as a phishing site because the black lists it utilizes had not yet been updated. SpamAssassin's scores ranged from 0.6 to 14.4, with an average of 5.92 points. It misidentified 5 of the 10 emails, assigning them scores under 5 points. Phishwish assigned scores ranging from 50% to 90.9%, with an average of 76%. Using a cutoff of 50%, phishwish correctly identified the 10 emails. With a cutoff of 60%, phishwish correctly identified 8 of the 10 emails.

Certain properties of our rules make it hard for phishers to subvert phishwish. Rule 2 (TLS) is impossible to subvert unless the phisher acquires the private keying material for a certificate of a well known business. If phishwish determines that the email is legitimate, the fingerprint of the certificate could be cached and compared on subsequent visits. Rule 5, while very basic, is also hard to subvert: after all, a phisher must direct the user to a fradulent site. Rule 6 (SMTP header analysis) is also difficult, but not impossible, to bypass. *Received* headers are added automatically by SMTP intermediaries. A *Received* header intentionally inserted by phishers will usually appear separate than those inserted by intermediaries, which are grouped together, providing an indication the header is spoofed. Rules 8 and 10 query *whois* servers outside the control of the phisher.

Phishwish does have limitations. Emails consisting of a text based form that the recipient is asked to fill in and email back to the sender are not processed by phishwish. Emails containing a large number of advertisements and links may create false positives if few rules other than rules 7 to 10 are applicable. This is due to different domains in the various links to the advertisements and images. Terse emails may also create false positives due to a low number of rules being applied. Finally, phishers have started to use images in lieu of the display string, allowing the user to click on an image composed of the bank's URL. To thwart such attacks, which are currently not detected by phishwish, we plan on building upon the work done by EZ-Gimpy [6] and other OCR-based CAPTCHAs [7].

References

1. Dhamija, R., Tygar, J.D., Hearst, M.: Why Phishing Works. In: Proceedings of the ACM Computer/Human Interaction (CHI 2006), pp. 581–590 (2006)
2. Wu, M., Miller, R.C., Garfinkel, S.: Do Security Toolbars Actually Prevent Phishing Attacks? In: Proceedings of the ACM Computer/Human Interaction (CHI), pp. 601–610. ACM, New York (2006)
3. Zhang, Y., Egelman, S., Cranor, L., Hong, J.: Phinding Phish: Evaluating Anti-Phishing Tools. In: Proceedings of NDSS (2007)
4. Zhang, Y., Hong, J., Cranor, L.: CANTINA: A Content-Based Approach to Detecting Phishing Web Sites. In: Proceedings of WWW, pp. 639–648 (2007)
5. Wu, M., Miller, R.C., Little, G.: Web Wallet: Preventing Phishing Attacks by Revealing User Intentions. In: Proceedings of SOUPS, pp. 102–113 (2006)
6. Mori, G., Malik, J.: Recognizing Objects in Adverserial Clutter: Breaking a Visual CAPTCHA. In: Proceedings of CVPR, pp. 1–8 (2003)
7. von Ahn, L., Blum, M., Langford, J.: Telling Humans and Computers Apart Automatically. Comm. of the ACM 47(2), 57–60 (2004)

Competition and Fraud in
Online Advertising Markets

Bob Mungamuru[1] and Stephen Weis[2]

[1] Stanford University, Stanford, CA, USA 94305
[2] Google Inc., Mountain View, CA, USA 94043

Abstract. An economic model of the online advertising market is presented, focusing on the effect of ad fraud. In the model, the market is comprised of three classes of players: publishers, advertising networks, and advertisers. The central question is whether ad networks have an incentive to aggressively combat fraud. The main outcome of the model is to answer this question in the affirmative.

1 Introduction

Advertising fraud, particularly click fraud, is a growing concern to the online advertising industry. At first glance, however, the incentives regarding fighting fraud seem somewhat perverse. If an advertiser is billed for clicks that are fraudulent, the ad network's revenues increase. As such, is it even in an ad network's interest to fight fraud at all? Would it make more sense for an ad network to just let fraud go unchecked? If not, can an advertising network actually gain a market advantage by aggressively combating fraud? In this paper, we address these questions by studying the economic incentives related to combating fraud, and how these incentives might translate into behavior.

An economic analysis of ad fraud is interesting because, unlike many online security threats, ad fraud is primarily motivated by financial gain. Successfully committing ad fraud yields direct monetary gains for attackers at the expense of the victims. The threat of fraud to the advertising business model and the technical challenge of detecting fraud have been topics of great concern in the industry (e.g., [5,6]). There have been many informal conjectures in online forums and the media attempting to answer the questions we have posed above. The arguments, while sometimes intuitive, generally are not backed by a sound economic analysis. Thus, the conclusions arrived at differ widely. To date, there has been little formal analysis of the economic issues related to fraud. This work attempts to fill this gap by performing just such an analysis.

Conducting an economic analysis of the online advertising market is difficult because faithful models of the market can quickly become intractable. For example, a content publisher's type includes, among other things, the volume of traffic they receive, the quality of their content, and their user demographics and interests. Advertisers can be differentiated by the size of their advertising budgets, their valuation of traffic that they receive through online ads, the quality of their campaign, and their relevance to particular demographics. Ad networks can differ in their ability to detect ad fraud, as well as the quality and relevance of their ad serving mechanisms. Our goal is to construct and analyze a simplified model that hones in on the effect of fighting fraud.

G. Tsudik (Ed.): FC 2008, LNCS 5143, pp. 187–191, 2008.

This paper will focus solely on *click fraud* in pay-per-click advertising systems. Click fraud refers to the act of clicking on advertisements, either by a human or a computer, in an attempt to gain value without having any actual interest in the advertiser's website. Click fraud is probably the most prevalent form of online advertising fraud today [2,3,4]. There are other forms of ad fraud[1] that will not be addressed here.

We begin by describing a simplified model of the pay-per-click online advertising market as a game between publishers, advertising networks and advertisers. We then predict the steady-state behaviour of the players in our model. Our conclusions can be summarized as follows:

1. It is not in an ad network's interest to let fraud go unchecked.
2. Ad networks can, indeed, gain a competitive edge by aggressively fighting fraud.
3. When ad networks fight fraud, it is the high-quality publishers that win.

For brevity's sake, we don't delve too deeply into the mathematical details of our model in this paper. We state the results and predictions of our model without proof, focusing instead on their intuitive content.

2 Model

In *pay-per-click advertising systems*, there are three classes of parties involved: publishers, ad networks and advertisers. *Publishers* create online content and display advertisements alongside their content. *Advertisers* design advertisements, as well as bid on *keywords* that summarize what their target market might be interested in. *Advertising networks* act as intermediaries between publishers and advertisers by first judging which keywords best describe each publisher's content, and then delivering ads to the publisher from the advertisers that have bid on those keywords. For example, an ad network might deduce that the keyword "automobile" is relevant to an online article about cars, and serve an ad for used car inspection reports.

When a user views the publisher's content and clicks on an ad related to a given keyword, she is redirected to the advertiser's site – we say that a *click-through* (or, *click* for short) has occurred on that keyword. The advertiser then pays a small amount to the ad network that delivered the ad. A fraction of this amount is in turn paid out to the publisher who displayed the ad. The exact amounts paid out to each party depend on several factors including the advertiser's bid and the auction mechanism being used. Advertisers are willing to pay for click-throughs because some of those clicks may turn into *conversions*[2], or "customer acquistions". The publishers and ad networks, of course, hope that users will click on ads because of the payment they would receive from the advertiser. The market for click-throughs on a single keyword can be thought of as a "pipeline", as illustrated in Figure 1 – click-throughs are generated on publishers' pages, which are distributed amongst advertisers via the ad networks, with the hope that some of the clicks turn into conversions.

---

[1] See [1] for a detailed discussion of the various types of ad fraud.

[2] The definition of a conversion depends on the agreement between the advertiser and the ad network, varying from an online purchase to joining a mailing list. In general, a conversion is some agreed-upon action taken by a user.

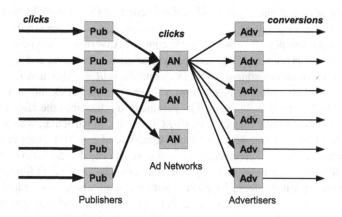

Fig. 1. The online advertising market

Apart from ad delivery, advertising networks serve a second important function, namely, trying to filter out invalid clicks. *Invalid clicks* can be loosely defined[3] as click-throughs that have zero probability of leading to a conversion. Invalid clicks include fraudulent click-throughs as well as *unintentional clicks*. For example, if a user unintentionally double-clicks on an ad, only one of the two clicks has a chance at becoming a conversion, so the other click is considered invalid. Going forward, we will speak of valid and invalid clicks, rather than "legitimate" and "fraudulent" clicks. In practice, advertisers are never billed for clicks that ad networks detect as invalid. Ad networks will, of course, make mistakes when trying to filter out invalid clicks. In particular, their filters may produce *false negatives* by identifying invalid clicks as valid, and *false positives* by identifying valid clicks as invalid. Ad networks differ in how effectively they are able to filter, as well as how aggressively they choose to filter. Our goal is to study how filtering effectiveness and aggressiveness affects an ad network in the market.

In some cases, a publisher and an ad network are owned by the same business entity. For example, major search engines often display ads next to their own search results. Similarly, a publisher and an advertiser can be owned by the same entity. Online newspapers are a common example. In our model, even if a publisher and an ad network are owned by the same entity, they will nevertheless both act independently. Consequently, the model may predict some behaviors that, while economically rational, are unlikely to occur in practice. For example, a real-world entity that owns both a publisher and an ad network is unlikely (for strategic reasons) to display ads from a rival ad network on its properties, even if it might yield an immediate economic advantage.

2.1 Player Types

We model the online advertising market as an infinite-horizon dynamic game between publishers, ad networks and advertisers. Publisher i's type is a triple (V_i, r_i, β_i) where $V_i \in [0, \infty)$ is the volume of clicks on i's site per period, $r_i \in [0, 1]$ is the fraction of

---

[3] It is still a topic of some debate what the exact definition of an invalid click should be.

i's clicks that are valid and $\beta_i \in [0,1]$ is the fraction of i's valid clicks that become conversions. For example, if $V_i = 10000$, $r_i = 0.7$ and $\beta_i = 0.2$, then publisher i has 7000 valid clicks per period of which 1400 convert. Advertiser k's type is (y_k, R_k), where $y_k \in [0, \infty)$ is the revenue generated by k on each conversion, and $R_k \in (0, \infty)$ is their target *return on investment* (ROI). For example, if $y_k = \$100$ and $R_k = 2$, then advertiser k would be willing to pay at most \$50 per converted click-through.

Ad network j's type is $\alpha_j \in [0,1]$. The parameter α_j describes the effectiveness of ad network j's invalid click filtering i.e., its *ROC curve*[4]. In particular, we assume that if ad network j is willing to tolerate a false positive rate of $x \in [0,1)$, they can achieve a true positive rate of x^{α_j}. Therefore, if $\alpha_1 < \alpha_2$, we can say that ad network 1 is more effective at filtering ad network 2. If $\alpha_j = 0$, it means j is "perfect" at filtering (i.e., j can achieve a true positive rate of 1 with an arbitrarily small false positive rate), whereas at the other extreme, $\alpha = 1$ means j is doing no better than randomly guessing. The parameter α_j captures the concave shape of typical real-world ROC curves.

2.2 Decision Variables

At the start of each period t, publishers decide which ad networks' ads to display, or equivalently, how to allocate their "inventory" of click-throughs across the ad networks. Publisher i chooses $c_{i,j,t} \in [0,1]\ \forall j$ such that $\sum_j c_{i,j,t} = 1$, where $c_{i,j,t}$ is the fraction of i's click-throughs that i allocates to j. In the earlier example with $V_i = 10000$, $c_{i,j,t} = 0.2$ means i sends 2000 clicks to j in period t. We assume that publisher i will choose $c_{i,j,t}$ such that their expected profit in period t is maximized.

Simultaneously, advertiser k chooses $v_{k,j,t} \in [0, \infty)\ \forall j$, which is their valuation of a click (on this keyword) coming from ad network j. If j is using a truthful auction mechanism to solicit bids on click-throughs, $v_{k,j,t}$ will also be k's bid for a click. We assume that advertisers submit bids on each ad network (i.e., they choose $v_{k,j,t}$) such that their period-t ROI on every ad network is R_k.

Having observed $c_{i,j,t}\ \forall j$ and $v_{k,j,t}\ \forall k$, ad network j then chooses $x_{j,t} \in [0,1)$, which is j's false positive rate for invalid click filtering. Recall that the true positive rate would then be $x_{j,t}^{\alpha_j}$. For example, if $\alpha_j = 0.5$ and $x_{j,t} = 0.25$, then j's period-t false positive rate would be 0.25 and the true positive rate would be $\sqrt{0.25} = 0.5$. There is a tradeoff involved here. If $x_{j,t}$ is high (i.e., filtering more aggressively), j will detect most invalid clicks, but the cost is that more valid clicks will be given to advertisers for "free". Conversely, if $x_{j,t}$ is low (i.e., filtering less aggressively), ad net j and its publishers will get paid for more clicks, but advertisers will be charged for more invalid clicks. Ad networks compete with each other through their choice of $x_{j,t}$. We assume that ad networks choose $x_{j,t}$ such that their infinite-horizon profits are maximized.

3 Equilibria

We now consider the *steady-state* behaviour of the players in our model i.e., $x_{j,t} = x_j$, $c_{i,j,t} = c_{i,j}$ and $v_{k,j,t} = v_{k,j}$.

---

[4] ROC is an acronym for *Receiver Operating Characteristic*.

Theorem 1. *Suppose there are $J \geq 2$ ad networks, and $\alpha_1 < \alpha_2 \leq \alpha_j \; \forall j \geq 2$. Then, the following is true in any subgame-perfect Nash equilibrium:*

1. *For every decision profile $\mathbf{x} \in [0,1)^J$, there exists a j^* such that $c_{i,j^*} = 1 \; \forall i$.*
2. *There exists an $x^* > 0$ such that if ad network 1 chooses any $x_1 > x^*$, then $c_{i,1} = 1 \; \forall i$, irrespective of what the other ad networks choose.*
3. *As $\alpha_1 - \alpha_2 \rightarrow 0$, $x^* \rightarrow 1$.*
4. *As $x^* \rightarrow 1$, low-quality publishers get a diminishing fraction of the total revenue.*

Thus, it is a dominant strategy for ad network 1 to filter at a level x_1 greater than x^*, and win over the entire market as a result.

The intuition behind Theorem 1 is as follows. Recall that $\alpha_1 < \alpha_2 \leq \alpha_j \; \forall j \geq 2$ implies that ad network 1 is the most effective at filtering invalid clicks, and ad network 2 is the second-most effective. Part 1 says that for any $\{x_1, \ldots, x_J\}$, all publishers (even the low-quality ones) will send their clicks to the same ad network. Part 2 says that since ad network 1 is the most effective at filtering, all publishers will choose ad network 1, as long as they filter more aggressively than than x^*. Ad network 1 will be indifferent between $x \in [x^*, 1)$. Part 3 says that as ad network 1's technology lead narrows, they must be increasingly aggressive in order to win over the market. Part 4 is intuitive, since filtering aggressively penalizes low-quality publishers most heavily.

4 Conclusion

Theorem 1 implies that, indeed, letting fraud go unchecked (i.e., choosing $x_j = 0$) is suboptimal. Moreover, the ad network that can filter most effectively (i.e., lowest α_j) does have a competitive advantage – a very dramatic one, in this simplified case. In the real world, obviously no ad network is earning 100% market share. On the other hand, publishers in the real world do often choose the most profitable ad network, and would switch to a different ad network if revenue prospects seemed higher and switching were frictionless. So, to the extent that players act purely rationally, we conjecture that our predictions would hold true in practice. Accounting for differences between ad networks in revenue sharing, ad targeting and "quality-based pricing" may explain deviations from Theorem 1, and would be a promising extension to our model.

References

1. Daswani, N., Mysen, C., Rao, V., Weis, S., Gharachorloo, K., Ghosemajumder, S.: Online Advertising Fraud. In: Crimeware: Understanding New Attacks and Defenses. Addison-Wesley Professional, Reading (2008)
2. Daswani, N., Stoppelman, M.: The anatomy of clickbot.A. In: Hot Topics in Understanding Botnets (HotBots), Usenix (April 2007)
3. Gandhi, M., Jakobsson, M., Ratkiewicz, J.: Badvertisements: Stealthy click-fraud with unwitting accessories. Journal of Digital Forensic Practice 1(2), 131–142 (2006)
4. Immorlica, N., Jain, K., Mahdian, M., Talwar, K.: Click fraud resistant methods for learning click-through rates. In: Deng, X., Ye, Y. (eds.) WINE 2005. LNCS, vol. 3828, pp. 34–45. Springer, Heidelberg (2005)
5. Penenberg, A.L.: Click fraud threatens web. In: Wired News (October 2004)
6. Schneier, B.: Google's click-fraud crackdown. In: Wired News (July 2006)

Identity Theft: Much Too Easy?
A Study of Online Systems in Norway

André N. Klingsheim and Kjell J. Hole

NoWires Research Group
Department of Informatics
University of Bergen, Norway
February 20, 2008
{klings,kjellh}@ii.uib.no

Abstract. Governments and commercial companies connect more and more computer systems to the Internet, giving people easier access to services. Many of these online services handle personal information. Leakage of such information can facilitate large-scale identity theft. This paper determines how personal information leaks from online systems of national importance, discusses proof of concept software to demonstrate the seriousness of the problem, and suggests how to improve the situation.

1 Introduction

Many companies and modern governments offer services through the Internet. Such online services often manage personal information. The services discussed in this paper are available on the Web, and users access them through their Web browser.

Adequate security and privacy are vital for online systems containing personal data. *Information privacy* refers to the individual's interest in controlling the flow of personal information [1, p. 63]. It can be difficult for a citizen to keep track of what information is available where, and to whom on the Internet. For example, a citizen might have an account in a governmental service without even knowing it.

A major problem is the information beyond the individual's control, which the individual cannot secure [2]. Large amounts of data leak from various systems, and governments seem to be struggling the most to keep the data safe [3], [4, p. 28]. During 2006, there were several news stories in Norway where various governmental institutions disclosed personal information on the Internet by accident. However, the amount of leaked information was insignificant compared to the scenarios described later in this paper.

Norwegian Birth Numbers (NBNs, no: fødselsnummer) are in widespread use in national computer systems in Norway. The NBNs are National Identification Numbers (NINs) comparable to the American Social Security numbers. Many countries have NINs, see [5] for pointers to governmental websites with information about NINs. NBNs have been used as tokens of authentication by

G. Tsudik (Ed.): FC 2008, LNCS 5143, pp. 192–196, 2008.

governmental institutions and companies in the private sector since long before the age of online services. This solution has worked well, still, identity theft has been possible with knowledge of a person's NBN and name for a long time. Because NBNs are still widely used as authenticators, they are of great value to an identity thief. The Norwegian Data Inspectorate has expressed concern over the use of NBNs as usernames in e.g. online banking systems. The problematic use of NBNs by a Norwegian pension fund was described in [6].

Identity theft occurs when someone uses another individual's personal information to pose as that individual [1, p. 99]. Useful information is e.g. credit card numbers and expiration dates, usernames/passwords, date of birth, NINs, name, and address of a victim. Successful impersonation of a victim lets the identity thief commit fraud.

This paper outlines the national identity system in Norway, and proof of concept software automating the collection of personal information from this system. Major privacy violations are highlighted and measures to reduce the problem are suggested. The paper focuses on the situation in Norway because of legal concerns. The authors are familiar with Norwegian laws and regulations, and our project was approved by Norwegian authorities. Still, our findings should be relevant to other countries using equivalent identifiers for their citizens. We leave it to the reader to apply our insights to domestic information systems.

The rest of this paper is organized as follows. Sect. 2 discusses personal identifiers, Sect. 3 determines why systems reveal personal information, and Sect. 4 describes software collecting such information. Sect. 5 makes suggestions on how to improve the current situation, and Sect. 6 concludes the paper.

2   The Norwegian Birth Number

An *identifier*, such as a name, NIN, or a customer number, points to an identity. The *identity* of an individual is the set of information associated with that individual in a particular computer system [1, p. 20]. Identifiers should be chosen with great care when designing a system. Certain identifiers can make the task easier for those who want to collect information about individuals.

All Norwegian citizens are assigned an NBN, containing the date of birth and reflecting the gender of an individual [7]. NBNs are assigned chronologically for a particular day, yielding a sub-range of used NBNs within the range of all valid NBNs for that day. NBNs are not secret by Norwegian law, but access to them is restricted.

The Norwegian National Identity Register (NNIR) (no: Folkeregisteret) contains the NBN, full name, full address, place of birth, and family relations for all Norwegian citizens. Approximately 7 million identities are kept in the registry, where 4.5 million people are residents in Norway and the rest are emigrants. The NNIR is often used to determine full name and address of an individual. Certain requirements defined by Norwegian law must be fulfilled to be allowed to interact with the NNIR. The Office of the National Registrar (no: Sentralkontoret for folkeregistrering) grants applicants access to the registry. Many governmental and commercial entities use information from the registry. In a 2005 press release, Skatteetaten stated that about 1 500 entities had access to the registry, and 30 million queries were executed.

3 Why Systems Leak

Many authentication schemes used by websites leak valid identifiers. This leakage has been considered bad design for decades [8]. Fig. 1 illustrates a popular solution in Norwegian systems where a user first enters his NBN, the system verifies that the NBN is used, and then asks for authentication information such as a password or Personal Identification Number (PIN). A software program can post candidate NBNs to such a website and log which NBNs are used. Online services in this category include e.g. governmental websites, online banks, and student portals at several universities.

Several mobile operators leak names and addresses corresponding to NBNs during their signup process, effectively publishing data from the NNIR on the Internet. Users select a subscription type and enter their NBN to sign up. The mobile operator will then conveniently present the full name and address associated with the NBN on the webpage for user confirmation. Since an NBN and a name suffice as authenticators in many online and offline systems, an identity thief can use these web services as a starting point before targeting other systems.

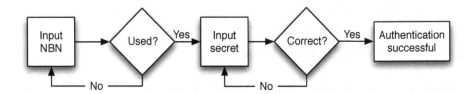

Fig. 1. Privacy violating authentication scheme

4 The Software

To establish how easy it is to automate harvesting of personal data, the first author developed a small graphical program in the Java programming language, called *NBNtool*. Two notable features are discussed here.

NBNtool was able to establish many of the customers in one of the largest banks in Norway, taking advantage of the bank's authentication scheme resembling Fig. 1. Furthermore, NBNtool used a particular mobile operator's signup procedure to extract full name and address for Norwegian citizens aged $\geq$ 18, by simply posting NBNs to the website. Hence, large parts of the NNIR could be mirrored through the mobile operator's website.

NBNtool communicated with the websites through The onion routing (Tor) network to avoid detection [9]. The bank is known to utilize intrusion detection technology, but NBNtool still ran uninterrupted on several occasions.

5 Improving the Situation

In the short-term, technical measures such as a Completely Automated Public Turing Test to Tell Computers and Humans Apart (CAPTCHA) would make it harder to automate the collection of personal data [10]. At least one Norwegian mobile operator has recently incorporated a CAPTCHA in its signup procedure. Traffic analysis can also be used to detect patterns indicating large-scale download of personal information. Most importantly, authentication schemes should be changed so they do not leak the validity of identifiers.

An important policy change that would improve the current situation is to enforce regulations on services with privacy implications so that users have to opt-in to access the service online. Today, individuals have to locate privacy violating services and try to invalidate their identities in these services.

In the long run, the NBN system must be changed. According to [11], an identity system should undergo a thorough analysis involving all stakeholders. Both the creators of the system and the users must be involved in the analysis. Scientists with expertise on privacy, and without commercial interests in the system, should also partake to ensure that citizens' privacy is well protected.

Authorities responsible for privacy in Norway need to find better ways to work in the future, enabling them to deal with privacy violators in a more efficient and swift manner. The findings described in this paper clearly show that the control of personal information is unsatisfactory. The authorities' shortcomings in this area have many explanations, including judicial limitations, lack of funding, shortage of staff, and unclear placement of liability.

6 Conclusions

Data harvesting is possible in Norwegian online systems. Large amounts of NBNs and corresponding personal information can be determined. Many websites use NBNs to identify, or even authenticate their users, facilitating creation of personal profiles. We conclude that large-scale identity theft is indeed possible in Norway. The risk of this happening is unclear, but it is definitely present as small-scale online identity theft is already a problem.

NBNs should not be used as authenticators anymore. They are in practice published on the Internet and can easily be collected. In addition, there are probably thousands of people with authorization to access the NNIR. NBNs must therefore be considered public information in the future. Privacy violating authentication schemes must be improved accordingly.

This paper highlights severe privacy issues, but the whole picture cannot be analyzed in a single short paper. A thorough analysis of the current NBN-based identity system in Norway is called for, and will lay the groundwork for the development of a new and improved identity system.

6.1   Final Remarks

Special thanks are due to the Norwegian Data Inspectorate for allowing us to demonstrate NBNtool at a meeting in January of 2007. The first author is very grateful to Senior Engineer Atle Årnes for several useful discussions on privacy issues. We also thank the FC'08 reviewers for thorough reviews and valuable feedback on this paper.

More information about our work can be found in a technical report [12].

References

1. Kent, S.T., Millett, L.I. (eds.): Who Goes There? Authentication Through the Lens of Privacy. National Academies Press, Washington (2003)
2. Schneier, B.: Risks of third-party data. Communications of the ACM 48(5), 136 (2005)
3. Privacy Rights Clearinghouse: A chronology of data breaches (Last checked February 20, 2008), http://www.privacyrights.org/ar/ChronDataBreaches.htm
4. Symantec Inc.: Symantec internet security threat report xi (Last checked February 20, 2008), http://www.symantec.com/threatreport/
5. Wikipedia: National identification number (Last checked February 20, 2008), http://en.wikipedia.org/wiki/National_identification_number
6. Moen, V., Klingsheim, A.N., Simonsen, K.I.F., Hole, K.J.: Vulnerabilities in e-governments. International Journal of Electronic Security and Digital Forensics 1(1), 89–100 (2007)
7. Selmer, E.S.: Personnummerering i norge: Litt anvendt tallteori og psykologi. Nordisk Matematisk Tidsskrift 12, 36–44 (1964); (in Norwegian)
8. Morris, R., Thompson, K.: Password security: a case history. Communications of the ACM 22(11), 594–597 (1979)
9. Tor: Anonymity online (Last checked February 20, 2008), http://tor.eff.org
10. von Ahn, L., Blum, M., Langford, J.: Telling humans and computers apart automatically. Communications of the ACM 47(2), 56–60 (2004)
11. Kent, S.T., Millett, L.I. (eds.): IDs—Not That Easy: Questions About Nationwide Identity Systems. National Academies Press, Washington (2002)
12. Klingsheim, A.N., Hole, K.J.: Personal information leakage: A study of online systems in norway. Technical Report 370, Department of Informatics, University of Bergen (2008)

A Proof of Concept Attack against Norwegian Internet Banking Systems*

Yngve Espelid, Lars–Helge Netland, André N. Klingsheim, and Kjell J. Hole

NoWires Research Group
Department of Informatics
University of Bergen, Norway
{yngvee,larshn,klings,kjellh}@ii.uib.no

Abstract. The banking industry in Norway has developed a new security infrastructure for conducting commerce on the Internet. The initiative, called BankID, aims to become a national ID infrastructure supporting services such as authentication and digital signatures for the entire Norwegian population. This paper describes a practical man-in-the-middle attack against online banking applications using BankID. The attack gives an adversary access to customer bank accounts in two different online banking systems. Proof of concept code has been developed and executed to demonstrate the seriousness of the problem.

1 Introduction

The Norwegian banking community has created a new infrastructure for secure e-commerce, called BankID.[1] As of October 2007, BankID has more than 700,000 end-users. This number is expected to exceed 1.5 million come 2008. At the time of writing, the infrastructure is mainly used for authentication of Internet banking customers, but BankID is extending into other markets, such as the government sector and e-commerce in general. It has also been used in conjunction with e-voting in some companies. BankID won a European prize, namely the *eema Award for Excellence in Secure Electronic Business* in 2006. The system is modeled after a Public-Key Infrastructure (PKI), where the banks themselves own and operate the central infrastructure. Within a few years, the Norwegian banking industry wants BankID to become a nationwide identity system.

No publicly available independent third party evaluation of the system confirms that BankID meets a minimum of security and privacy requirements. This is worrisome for several reasons: Firstly, a report by the US National Research Council [1] states that public review is essential when developing a nationwide identity system. The social costs of a poorly thought-out system are simply too high to justify. Secondly, the banking industry both owns the BankID infrastructure and provides financial services on top of the framework. It is not clear

---

* Short paper version, Feb. 21st, 2008.
[1] Not to be confused with the Swedish BankID initiative.

G. Tsudik (Ed.): FC 2008, LNCS 5143, pp. 197–201, 2008.

how potential conflicts of interest, involving the bank as a service provider and PKI operator, will be resolved. Uncontested, the combination of no trusted third party and a security-through-secrecy policy could undermine the legal protection of Norwegian bank customers. This issue was explored in depth in a previous report that performed a risk analysis of the BankID infrastructure [2]. Our work was done in parallel with the mentioned evaluation, and examines the therein suggested Man-in-the-Middle (MitM) attack in detail.

This paper is organized as follows: Section 2 looks at BankID from the attacker's point of view and describes a MitM attack against Norwegian online banks that use the security infrastructure; Section 3 provides improvement suggestions for BankID; Section 4 comments on related work; while Sect. 5 concludes the paper.

2   BankID through Adversarial Eyes

A rough sketch of BankID can be drawn after inspecting a white paper released by the BankID project [3]. The system is built around three entities: a central *infrastructure*, *customers*, and online *merchants*. Private keys and the corresponding public-key certificates issued to customers are stored and used by the central infrastructure. This design differs from a typical X.509 PKI, which requires private keys to be solely available to the entity identified in the matching certificate [4]. As a consequence, all customer authentication and digital signature services with PKI credentials are executed by the infrastructure. Merchants control their own cryptographic keys and rely on server software distributed by the BankID project.

A Java applet is central in the authentication procedure. The applet is readily available from the central infrastructure, and is provided to end-users by all affiliated merchants. This makes it a natural target for uncovering technical details about BankID.

2.1   Reverse Engineering

A common technique to understand undocumented software is *reverse engineering* [5]. The information gathered from public written sources was insufficient to understand the inner-workings of BankID protocols involving customers. Hence, we reverse engineered the applet to study the protocols in more detail. The process included studying input and output data, the communication flow, and representing the application as human-readable source code.

By inspecting merchant web pages we discovered that the applet is controlled through HTML parameters. Two parameters specify addresses to the infrastructure server running a two-factor authentication procedure and the merchant server carrying out a challenge-response protocol. Consequently, all merchants can use the same applet by configuring these initialization parameters.

2.2   The Attack

By changing the two parameters to the applet, it willingly communicates—over either HTTP or HTTPS—with the MitM proxy depicted in Fig. 1. We choose HTTP to avoid having to install a certificate on the MitM proxy. The decision to store the customers' cryptographic keys at the infrastructure results in a complex authentication protocol:

- The customer presents her birth number, one-time password (OTP), and fixed password to the central infrastructure. This action unlocks PKI functionality.
- The customer engages in a challenge-response protocol with the merchant. The infrastructure handles all PKI operations on behalf of the user.

The proxy learns the communication between the applet and the merchant, which is sufficient to obtain an authorized session to the merchant. However, the information flow between the customer and the infrastructure is encrypted, preventing the proxy from obtaining the customer credentials. The attack is carried out through the following steps:

1. Trick the user into visiting a webpage on the proxy, initializing the applet with malicious parameters.
2. Start the HTTPS session between the MitM proxy and the merchant to obtain session IDs.
3. Relay the traffic until the authentication completes.
4. Seize the HTTPS session to the merchant after the authentication is completed.

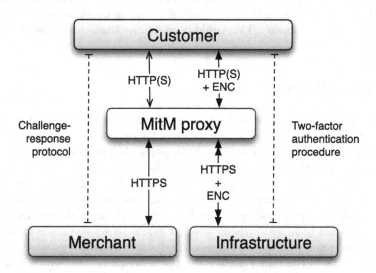

Fig. 1. The MitM proxy in the authentication protocol

Norwegian banks currently use OTPs and fixed passwords to authorize transactions. Therefore, the attacker must collect at least one OTP and the password to transfer money out of the account. This can be achieved by alerting the user at the end of the log-in procedure that the previously entered fixed password and OTP were incorrect, after which the attacker asks for them again.

Proof of Concept. The attack was tested against two randomly chosen Norwegian online banking systems. Both attempts gave access to a customer account in these banks. The vulnerability was first identified and tested in March 2007. The BankID community claims to have fixed the problem in November 2007.

3   Possible BankID Improvements

The MitM attack described herein must be addressed by the BankID community. The applet needs to properly authenticate its communication peers, enabling it to detect a MitM proxy. Also, the applet must require end-to-end encryption when communicating with both the infrastructure and the merchant.

In the long-term, the BankID community should evaluate the implications of moving to a traditional PKI where the clients possess their own credentials. This would improve the strength of the authentication, and yield a simpler design. Of course, such a change comes with a cost. However, a national security infrastructure must fulfill minimum security requirements, including resistance to MitM attacks.

As the system is now gaining serious momentum in Norway, its users need a better perception of the true level of security. In light of our attack, and the findings in [2], a thorough analysis of BankID is called for. The infrastructure and its documentation should be scrutinized by independent security experts to detect and resolve problems. This could increase the trustworthiness of BankID in the long run.

4   Related Work

A series of three articles analyze Norwegian banking systems [6,7,2]. Our attack builds on the above-mentioned article series and zooms in on weaknesses touched upon in the risk analysis of BankID [2]. In particular, our work further testify to the inefficacy of the banks' security-through-secrecy policy.

In [8], Anderson argues that a false threat model was accepted, due to the lack of feedback on why British retail banking systems failed. In doing so, the financial industry developed increasingly complex systems to protect against cryptanalysis and technical attacks, when it would have been wiser to focus on implementation and managerial failures. Analyses of banking systems published after Anderson's initial paper underscore the observation that systems fail not because of inadequate cryptographic primitives, but rather design flaws and implementation errors [9,10].

5   Conclusion

The new national security infrastructure for e-commerce in Norway, BankID, was vulnerable to a MitM attack in 2007. By changing initialization parameters to the BankID applet, an adversary could insert a proxy between a customer and a merchant. When BankID was used in Internet banking, an attacker could let a customer complete authentication, and later take over the banking session. The attack did not depend on malicious software being installed on the victim's computer. Proof of concept code was developed to demonstrate the attack.

The MitM vulnerability in BankID calls for immediate attention. The banks claim to have fixed the problem in November 2007. In the long run, the banks should carefully evaluate their development process, as their current methodology results in software that contradicts advice given in well-known security textbooks.

5.1   Final Remark

We would like to emphasize that *only* BankID accounts belonging to members of the NoWires Research Group were used to develop and demonstrate the MitM attack. No accounts belonging to others were involved in any way during our work with this paper.

References

1. Kent, S.T., Millett, L.I. (eds.): IDs—Not That Easy: Questions About Nationwide Identity Systems. National Academies Press, Washington (2002)
2. Hole, K.J.: Tjøstheim, T., Moen, V., Netland, L., Espelid, Y., Klingsheim, A.N.: Next generation internet banking in Norway. submitted to IEEE Security & Privacy (2007), http://www.nowires.org/Papers-PDF/BankIDevaluation.pdf
3. The Norwegian Banks' Payment and Clearing Centre: BankID FOI white paper (Release 2.0.0) (in Norwegian) (2006)
4. Adams, C., Lloyd, S.: Understanding PKI—Concepts, Standards, and Deployment Considerations, 2nd edn. Addison-Wesley, Reading (2003)
5. Chikofsky, E.J., Cross II, J.H.: Reverse engineering and design recovery: A taxonomy. IEEE Software 7(1), 13–17 (1990)
6. Hole, K.J., Moen, V., Tjøstheim, T.: Case study: Online banking security. IEEE Security & Privacy 4(2), 14–20 (2006)
7. Hole, K.J., Moen, V., Klingsheim, A.N., Tande, K.M.: Lessons from the Norwegian ATM system. IEEE Security & Privacy 5(6), 25–31 (2007)
8. Anderson, R.: Why cryptosystems fail. In: ACM 1st Conference on Computer and Communication Security, Fairfax, VA, USA (1993)
9. Berkman, O., Ostrovsky, O.M.: The unbearable lightness of pin cracking. In: Financial Cryptography and Data Security (FC), Lowlands, Scarborough, Trinidad/Tobago (2007)
10. Anderson, R., Bond, M., Clulow, J., Skorobogatov, S.: Cryptographic processors—a survey. Technical Report 641, University of Cambridge (2005)

Improvement of Efficiency in (Unconditional) Anonymous Transferable E-Cash[*]

Sébastien Canard[1], Aline Gouget[2], and Jacques Traoré[1]

[1] Orange Labs R&D, 42 rue des Coutures, F-14066 Caen, France
[2] Gemalto, 6, rue de la Verrerie, F-92190 Meudon, France

Abstract. The practical advantage expected from transferable e-cash compare to non-transferable is the significant reduction of the interaction number between the bank and the users. However, this property is not fulfilled by *anonymous* transferable e-cash schemes of the state-of-the art. In this paper, we first present a transferable e-cash scheme with a reduced number of communications between the bank and the users that fulfils the *computational anonymity* property. Next, we present a transferable e-cash scheme with a reduced interaction number that fulfils the *unconditional anonymity*. This latter scheme is quite less efficient.

Keywords: Electronic cash, anonymity, transferability.

1 Introduction

In regular cash systems, users withdraw coins from a bank, and then pay merchants using coins. Next, merchants can use the received coins to pay another merchant or deposit coins to the bank. Moreover, regular cash systems protect the anonymity of users.

Emulating regular cash in the electronic setting implies providing the user anonymity against both the bank and the merchant during a purchase, i.e., it must be impossible to link two spends and a spend to a withdrawal. Ideally, the anonymity of honest users must be protected and the identity of cheaters must be recovered without using a trusted third party. As it is easy to duplicate electronic data, an e-cash system must prevent a user from double-spending. An electronic coin system must also prevent a merchant from depositing the same coin twice.

The transferability property is another fundamental property of regular cash. However, it has received only little attention in the electronic setting. This may be explained by the impossibility to transfer a coin without increasing its size [6]. It is clearly a limitation but this apparent drawback is not unacceptable for some practical applications depending on the amount of available storage data and the growth of the coin size. The main expected advantage of the transferability property compare to non-transferability for e-cash is the decrease of the interaction

---

[*] This work has been partially financially supported by the European Commission through the IST Program under Contract IST-2002-507932 ECRYPT.

G. Tsudik (Ed.): FC 2008, LNCS 5143, pp. 202–214, 2008.
© Springer-Verlag Berlin Heidelberg 2008

number between the bank and the users. Thus, as on-line electronic payment systems require communications with a central authority during the payment transaction, then transferability is only an issue for off-line systems.

1.1 Related Works

As far as we know, the transferability property in e-cash schemes has received only little attention.

In 1989, Okamoto and Ohta [11] proposed a transferable e-cash scheme that does not provide the anonymity property since it is possible to link several spends of the same user. Next, van Antwerpen [15] proposed a method for transferring e-cash which was later sketched in [6]. This transferable e-cash scheme fulfils the user anonymity. However, at any time a user wants to act as a payee during a spending protocol, he has to beforehand interact with the bank in a protocol corresponding to the withdrawal of a coin with no monetary value. This drawback implies a significative increase of the number of transactions between the bank and users which make the scheme less attractive in the transferability setting where the aim is precisely to decrease these communications.

1.2 Our Contribution and Organization of the Paper

We present two anonymous transferable e-cash schemes that improve the state-of-the-art on anonymous transferable e-cash by addressing the problem of decreasing the interaction number between the bank and users. Indeed, it is no more necessary for a payee to beforehand interact with the bank for receiving a coin. Both schemes allow to withdraw efficiently a set of coins (a wallet) instead of a coin.

Section 2 introduces the security model and some useful tools. In Section 3, we present a first transferable scheme that fulfils a computational anonymity and in Section 4 we present a second transferable e-cash scheme that fulfils an unconditional anonymity at the cost of a less efficient result. We conclude in Section 5.

2 Definitions and Useful Tools

In this section, we first define transferable e-cash algorithms, global variables and oracles. Next, we describe the security properties.

2.1 Algorithms

A transferable e-cash system involves two types of player: a bank $\mathcal{B}$ and a user $\mathcal{U}$. A wallet W and a coin C are both represented by an identifier S and some values π needed to prove their validity.

– $\texttt{ParamGen}(k)$ is a probabilistic algorithm that outputs the parameters of the system Par (including the security parameter k).

- BKeyGen(Par) (resp. UKeyGen(Par)) is a probabilistic algorithm executed by $\mathcal{B}$ (resp. $\mathcal{U}$) that outputs its key pair $(sk_\mathcal{B}, pk_\mathcal{B})$ (resp. $(sk_\mathcal{U}, pk_\mathcal{U})$).

- Withdraw($\mathcal{B}(sk_\mathcal{B}, pk_\mathcal{B}, pk_\mathcal{U}, Par)$, $\mathcal{U}(sk_\mathcal{U}, pk_\mathcal{U}, pk_\mathcal{B}, Par)$) is an interactive protocol where $\mathcal{U}$ withdraws a wallet from $\mathcal{B}$. At the end, $\mathcal{U}$ either gets a wallet $W = (S, \pi)$ and outputs OK, or outputs $\perp$. The output of $\mathcal{B}$ is either its view $\mathcal{V}_\mathcal{B}^\mathsf{W}$ of the protocol (including $pk_\mathcal{U}$), or $\perp$.

- Spend $(\mathcal{U}_1(S, \pi, pk_{\mathcal{U}_2}, Par), \mathcal{U}_2(sk_{\mathcal{U}_2}, pk_\mathcal{B}, Par))$ is an interactive protocol where $\mathcal{U}_1$ gives a coin to $\mathcal{U}_2$. $\mathcal{U}_2$ outputs either $C = (S, \pi)$ or $\perp$, and $\mathcal{U}_1$ either saves that C is spent and outputs OK, or outputs $\perp$.

- Deposit $(\mathcal{U}(C, sk_\mathcal{U}, pk_\mathcal{U}, pk_\mathcal{B}, Par), \mathcal{B}(sk_\mathcal{B}, pk_\mathcal{B}, pk_\mathcal{U}, \mathcal{L}, Par))$ is an interactive protocol where $\mathcal{U}$ deposits a coin $C = (S, \pi)$ at the bank $\mathcal{B}$. If (S, π) is not consistent/fresh, then $\mathcal{B}$ outputs $\perp_1$. Else, if S belongs to $\mathcal{L}$, then there is an entry $(S, \tilde{\pi})$ and $\mathcal{B}$ outputs $(\perp_2, S, \pi, \tilde{\pi})$. Else, $\mathcal{B}$ adds (S, π) to $\mathcal{L}$, credits $\mathcal{U}$'s account, and returns $\mathcal{L}$. $\mathcal{U}$'s output is OK or $\perp$.

- Identify $(S, \pi, \tilde{\pi}, Par)$ is a deterministic algorithm executed by $\mathcal{B}$ that outputs a public key $pk_\mathcal{U}$ and a proof Π_G. If the users who had submitted π and $\tilde{\pi}$ are not malicious, then Π_G is evidence that $pk_\mathcal{U}$ is the registered public key of a user that double-spent a coin.

- VerifyGuilt($pk_\mathcal{U}, \Pi_G, Par$) is a deterministic algorithm that can be executed by any actor. It outputs 1 if Π_G is correct and 0 otherwise.

2.2 Global Variables and Oracles

The set of user's public (resp. secret) keys is denoted by $\mathcal{PK} = \{(i, pk_i) : i \in \mathbb{N}\}$ (resp. $\mathcal{SK} = \{(i, sk_i) : i \in \mathbb{N}\}$; $sk_i = \perp$ if user i is corrupted).

The oracle Create(i) creates a new honest user. Corrupt(i, pk_i) creates a new corrupted user with public key pk_i and Corrupt(i) corrupts user i by giving the secret key of user i to the caller.

The oracle Suppl() (resp. Withd(i)) plays the bank (resp. user i) side of a Withdraw protocol. The oracle Withd&Suppl(i) plays both sides of a Witdraw protocol and outputs the communications between $\mathcal{B}$ and $\mathcal{U}$.

The oracle Rcv(i) (resp. Spd(i)) plays the role of $\mathcal{U}_2$ (resp. $\mathcal{U}_1$) with secret keys of user i in the Spend protocol. The oracle Spd&Rcv(i_1, i_2, j) plays the role of both $\mathcal{U}_1$ with secret keys of user i_1 and $\mathcal{U}_2$ with secret keys of user i_2 during the spend protocol of the coin j and outputs the communications. We define four prototypes: Spd&Rcv($\perp, \perp, j$), Spd&Rcv($i_1, \perp, \perp$), Spd&Rcv($i_1, i_2, \perp$) and Spd&Rcv($\perp, i_2, j$), where $\perp$ denotes a random choice for a user or a coin.

The oracle CreditAccount() plays the role of $\mathcal{B}$ during a Deposit protocol. If the executed Deposit protocol outputs $(\perp_2, S, \pi, \tilde{\pi})$, then it runs the algorithm Identify on inputs $(S, \pi, \tilde{\pi})$ and outputs the result. The oracle Depo(i) plays the role of the user i during a Deposit protocol.

2.3 Security Properties

Unforgeability. Users cannot spend more coins than they honestly got.

Game. Let an adversary $\mathcal{A}$ be a p.p.t. Turing Machine with access to $\mathcal{PK}$.

1. $\mathcal{A}$ is given the public key $pk_\mathcal{B}$ and Par.
2. $\mathcal{A}$ can play as many times as he wants with the oracles: Create, Corrupt, Suppl, Withd&Suppl, Spd, Spd&Rcv, Rcv and CreditAccount.

Let q_W (resp. q_S, resp. q_C) denote the number of successful queries to Suppl (resp. Spd, resp. Corrupt). Let w_i denote the number of withdrawn coins of the i-th query and c_i denote the number of coins get back from the i-th corrupted user. Then, $\mathcal{A}$ wins if, at any time of the game, he makes $\sum_{i=1}^{q_W} w_i + q_S + \sum_{i=1}^{q_C} c_i + 1$ successful queries to the Rcv oracle.

Anonymity. The bank, even cooperating with users, cannot link spend and/or withdrawal transactions according to the underlying user identity.

Game. Let an adversary $\mathcal{A}$ be a p.p.t. Turing Machine with access to $\mathcal{PK}$.

1. $\mathcal{A}$ is given $(sk_\mathcal{B}, pk_\mathcal{B})$ and Par, and $\mathcal{A}$ can play with the oracles: Create, Corrupt, Withd, Spd, Spd&Rcv, Rcv and Depo.
2. At any time, $\mathcal{A}$ chooses two honest user public keys $pk_{i_0}, pk_{i_1} \in \mathcal{PK}$ such that users i_0 and i_1 own coins of the same size[1] and they have been manipulated only by the oracles: Create, Withd, Spd, Spd&Rcv$(i_1, \bot, \bot)$, Spd&Rcv$(\bot, \bot, j)$ and Depo.
3. A bit b is secretly and randomly chosen. Then $\mathcal{A}$ plays with Spd$(i_b, \bot)$.
4. $\mathcal{A}$ outputs a bit b'.

We require that, for every $\mathcal{A}$ playing this game, the probability that $b = b'$ differs from $1/2$ by a fraction that is at most negligible.

Identification of double-spenders. No collection of users can double-spend a coin twice without revealing one of their identities.

Game. Let an adversary $\mathcal{A}$ be a p.p.t. Turing Machine with access to $\mathcal{PK}$.

1. $\mathcal{A}$ is given the public key $pk_\mathcal{B}$ and Par.
2. $\mathcal{A}$ can play as many times as he wants with the oracles: Create, Corrupt, Suppl, Withd&Suppl, Spd, Spd&Rcv, Rcv and CreditAccount.

$\mathcal{A}$ wins if, at any time of the game, the oracle CreditAccount outputs $(\bot_2, S, \pi, \tilde{\pi})$ and the output of the oracle Identify on inputs $(S, \pi, \tilde{\pi})$ is not a registered user public key.

Exculpability. The bank, even cooperating with malicious users, cannot falsely accuse (with a proof) honest users from having double-spent a coin.

Game. Let an adversary $\mathcal{A}$ be a p.p.t. Turing Machine with access to $\mathcal{PK}$.

1. $\mathcal{A}$ is given the key pair $(pk_\mathcal{B}, sk_\mathcal{B})$ and Par.
2. $\mathcal{A}$ can play as many times as he wants with the oracles: Create, Corrupt, Withd, Spd, Spd&Rcv, Rcv and Depo.
3. At any time of the game, $\mathcal{A}$ outputs two spends (S, π) and $(S, \tilde{\pi})$.

$\mathcal{A}$ wins if the outputs of the algorithm Identify on inputs $(S, \pi, \tilde{\pi})$ is the public key pk of an honest user together with a valid proof Π_G, and the output of the algorithm VerifyGuilt on inputs (pk, Π_G) is 1.

---

[1] $\mathcal{A}$ is not allowed to use the coin size that necessary grows when transferred [6].

2.4   Useful Tools

Signature of knowledge. We consider zero-knowledge proofs of knowledge (ZKPK) constructed over a group $\mathcal{G}$ either of prime or unknown order. We use proofs of knowledge of a discrete logarithm [14,10] or of a representation, a proof of equality of two known representations [6], and a proof that a committed value is less than another committed value [5].

These proofs are three-move protocols between a prover and a verifier: a commitment t, a question c and an answer s. The soundness of these constructions ensures that given a single t, if someone is able to provide s and s' related to c and c' s.t. $c \neq c'$, then it is possible to compute the secret.

These interactive proofs can also be used non interactively (a.k.a. *signatures of knowledge*) by using the Fiat-Shamir heuristic [9]. Their security has been proven in [13], using the forking lemma.

Camenisch-Lysyanskaya Signature Scheme. These signature schemes are proposed in [3] with in addition some specific protocols:

- an efficient protocol between a user $\mathcal{U}$ and a signer $\mathcal{S}$ that permits $\mathcal{U}$ to obtain from $\mathcal{S}$ a signature σ of some commitment C on values $(x_1, \ldots, x_l)$ unknown from $\mathcal{S}$. $\mathcal{S}$ computes $\texttt{CLSign}(C)$ and $\mathcal{U}$ gets $\sigma = \texttt{Sign}(x_1, \ldots, x_l)$ that can be verified by $\texttt{Verif}(\sigma, (x_1, \ldots, x_l)) = 1$.
- an efficient proof of knowledge of a signature on committed values, denoted by $PK(\alpha_1, \ldots, \alpha_l, \beta : \beta = \texttt{Sign}(\alpha_1, \ldots, \alpha_l))$.

3   Transferable Compact E-Cash Scheme

In this section, we present a transferable e-cash scheme with a reduced number of communications between the bank and the users that fulfills the security properties given in Section 2.3. Moreover, the proposed construction allows to withdraw efficiently a wallet instead of a coin.

3.1   Overview of Our Construction

Our construction is based on the compact e-cash scheme [2]. More precisely, in the withdrawal, the user obtains from the bank a CL signature (see Section 2.4) on some data related to the withdrawn wallet. The spending of a withdrawn coin consists in the computation by the payer of a serial number S and a validity tag T used in case of double-spending.

The main modification comes from the possibility for the receiver to spend later a received coin. This is done by modifying the challenge sent by the receiver during a `Spend`: it should include a receiver identifier (here u_j), it should be verifiable (here using the Dodis-Yampolskiy pseudo-random function [8]) and it should be signed by the payer (here with the signature of knowledge of the payment validity) that permits the receiver to get a payer validation that he is allowed to spend later the coin.

Moreover, the security tag includes the serial number of the coin (so as to prevent double-spending) and the history of the coin (so as to prevent a fraud on the anonymity of the spenders done by the bank).

3.2   Description of the Scheme

Setup. Let k be a security parameter. Let $\mathcal{G}$ be a group of prime order p and $g, g_0, g_1, g_2, g_3, g_4, g_5$ are random generators in $\mathcal{G}$. These data constitute the public parameters Par. Let $\mathcal{H}$ be a cryptographic hash function. In the following, $a\|b$ denotes the concatenation of a and b.

In the BKeyGen algorithm, $\mathcal{B}$ computes two key pairs $(sk_{\mathcal{B},1}, pk_{\mathcal{B},1})$ and $(sk_{\mathcal{B},2}, pk_{\mathcal{B},2})$ of a CL signature scheme (see Section 2.4) that permit it to sign wallets and enroll users, respectively. Then, during the UKeyGen algorithm, each user $\mathcal{U}_i$ obtains a certificate C_i associated to his public key $pk_{\mathcal{U}_i} = g_0^{u_i}$ (related to $sk_{\mathcal{U}_i} = u_i \in_R \mathcal{G}$). The certificate is a CL (verifiable) signature done by $\mathcal{B}$: $C_i = \mathtt{Sign}(u_i, w_i)$ where w_i is a random value.

Withdrawal Protocol. A wallet is a signature under the bank's public key $pk_{\mathcal{B}}$ on the set of values (s, u_i, t, J, x) where u_i is the user secret key, s, t and x are random values and J is the number of coins contained in the wallet. The value s implicitly defines J unlinkable *serial numbers* and the value t implicitly defines J unlinkable *blinding values*.

A user $\mathcal{U}_i$ using $(u_i, g_0^{u_i})$ interacts with $\mathcal{B}$ using $(sk_{\mathcal{B}_1}, pk_{\mathcal{B}_1})$ as described in Figure 1 in a protocol close to the ones in [2,5]. At the end, $\mathcal{U}_i$ gets a wallet $W = (S, \pi) = (s, (u_i, t, J, x, \sigma))$ where σ is a CL signature on (s, u_i, t, J, x).

Spending a withdrawn coin. A user $\mathcal{U}_i$, owning $W = (s, (u_i, t, J, x, \sigma))$ withdrawn from $\mathcal{B}$, wants to spend a coin to a user $\mathcal{U}_j$. The protocol is similar to the one of the compact e-cash system, except that $\mathcal{U}_j$ computes the *random* value r using her secret key u_j and some data d'.

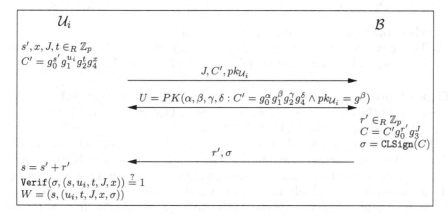

Fig. 1. Withdrawal protocol

1. $\mathcal{U}_j$ computes $r = g_0^{\overline{u_j + d'}}$ where d' represents some data related to the transaction. Next, $\mathcal{U}_j$ sends r and d' to $\mathcal{U}_i$.

2. $\mathcal{U}_i$ computes $R = \mathcal{H}(r\|d\|d')$ (where d represent some data related to the transaction) and chooses an unspent coin $j \in [1, J]$. Next, $\mathcal{U}_i$ computes $S = g_5^{\frac{1}{s+j+1}}$, $T = pk_{\mathcal{U}_i} g_5^{\frac{R}{\iota+j+1}}$ and a proof of validity:

$$V = PK(\alpha, \beta, \delta, \zeta, \eta, \iota, \theta : \alpha = \mathtt{Sign}(\iota, \beta, \delta, \zeta, \theta) \wedge \eta \in [1, \zeta] \wedge$$
$$\wedge S = g_5^{\frac{1}{\beta+\eta+1}} \wedge T = g_0^\delta g_5^{\frac{R}{\iota+\eta+1}})(S, T, r)$$

where the signature is the signature σ of the withdrawn wallet.

3. The spent coin is represented by $(S, \pi = (T, V, r, d, d'))$. Implicitly, a related variable $hist$ is initialized to $hist := S\|T$.

Spending a received coin. Assume that a user $\mathcal{U}_i$ owns a coin $C = (S, \pi = (\pi_1, \ldots, \pi_l))$, where π_k corresponds to T_k, V_k, r_k, d_k, d'_k, $1 \le k \le l$, that he legitimately received by another user. Since $\mathcal{U}_i$ legitimately received C, it is necessary that $r_l = g_0^{1/(u_i + d'_l)}$ and thus r_l involves u_i.

The spending of the coin C by user $\mathcal{U}_i$ to user $\mathcal{U}_j$ consists first in computing a security tag T implying the identifier u_i that is certified by the bank in order to be able to recover his identity in case of double-spending. Next, $\mathcal{U}_i$ proves that the same identifier u_i is embedded into T and in the challenge r_l of the previous spending (using the validity proof of the Dodis-Yampolskiy PRF and the signature of knowledge of the previous spending).

1. $\mathcal{U}_j$ computes $r = g_0^{\overline{u_j + d'}}$ where d' represents some data related to the transaction. Next $\mathcal{U}_j$ sends r and d' to $\mathcal{U}_i$.

2. $\mathcal{U}_i$ computes $R = \mathcal{H}(r\|d\|d')$, $h = \mathcal{H}(hist)$, $T = pk_{\mathcal{U}_i} g_5^{\frac{R}{u_i + S + h}}$ and a proof of validity:

$$V = PK(\alpha, \beta, \gamma : T = g^\alpha g_5^{\frac{R}{\alpha+S+h}} \wedge r_l = g_0^{\frac{1}{\alpha+d'_l}} \wedge \beta = \mathtt{Sign}(\alpha, \gamma))(S, T, r)$$

where the signature corresponds to the certificate of user $\mathcal{U}_i$.

3. The spent coin is $(S, \pi = (\pi_1, \ldots, \pi_l, \pi_{l+1}))$ where π_{l+1} corresponds to T, V, r, d, d'. The value $hist$ is updated by $hist := hist\|T$.

Deposit protocol. A coin may have been spent several times before being deposited at the bank. Then, a coin is represented by $(S, (\pi_1, \ldots, \pi_l))$ where π_k, $1 \le k \le l$, corresponds to T_k, V_k, r_k, d_k, d'_k.

The bank $\mathcal{B}$ first verifies the consistency of the coin (i.e. computes the values R using the hash function $\mathcal{H}$ and the values r and d to check the validity proofs). Next $\mathcal{B}$ verifies whether or not the coin has already been deposited by checking if the identifier S is already in the database of spent coins. If not, $\mathcal{B}$ credits the user account. Otherwise, $\mathcal{B}$ checks the freshness of the coin. If $R_l = \tilde{R}_l$ the depositer is a cheater. Else, the coin is fresh, there is a double-spending and $\mathcal{B}$ uses the identify protocol.

Identify protocol. In case of a double-spending detection, $\mathcal{B}$ has to retrieve the cheater identity from two deposited coins $(S, \pi = (\pi_1, \ldots, \pi_l))$ and $(S, \tilde{\pi} = (\tilde{\pi}_1, \ldots, \tilde{\pi}_{\tilde{l}}))$ with the same serial number S. Then, $\mathcal{B}$ looks for the minimal value k_{min} of k such that $\pi_k \neq \tilde{\pi}_k$ (this case always happens) and recovers the cheater's identity using the two double spending equations $T_{k_{min}}$ and $\tilde{T}_{k_{min}}$ included in $\pi_{k_{min}}$ and $\tilde{\pi}_{k_{min}}$. Then, $\mathcal{B}$ computes $R_{k_{min}} = \mathcal{H}(r_{k_{min}} \| d_{k_{min}} \| d'_{k_{min}})$ and $\tilde{R}_{k_{min}} = \mathcal{H}(\tilde{r}_{k_{min}} \| \tilde{d}_{k_{min}} \| \tilde{d}'_{k_{min}})$. Finally, $\mathcal{B}$ gets the public key of the cheater by computing:

$$pk_{\mathcal{U}} = (T_{k_{min}}^{\tilde{R}_{k_{min}}} / \tilde{T}_{k_{min}}^{R_{k_{min}}})^{\frac{1}{\tilde{R}_{k_{min}} - R_{k_{min}}}}$$

3.3   Security Proof

Theorem 1. *In the random oracle model, the transferable compact e-cash scheme fulfils:*

- *The unforgeability property under the unforgeability of the CL signature scheme.*
- *The anonymity property under the security of the Dodis-Yampolskiy PRF.*
- *The identification property under the unforgeability of the signatures of knowledge and the soundness of the underlying proofs of knowledge.*
- *The exculpability property under the DL assumption.*

Unforgeability. We want to show that if an adversary $\mathcal{A}$ is able to break the unforgeability of our construction, then it is possible to break the unforgeability of the CL signature scheme under adaptive chosen message attacks. More precisely, we have access to two signature oracles, both related to the CL signature scheme but with two different key pairs (one for the enrollment and one for the withdrawal). Our aim is to break the unforgeability of one among the two CL signature schemes involved in the construction. Let us consequently consider two different games with two adversaries.

In game 1, we play the role of an honest bank with access to a CL signature oracle for each enrollment, when $\mathcal{A}$ is active or not. In game 2, we play the role of an honest bank with access to a CL signature oracle for each withdrawal.

In both games, after each successful spending executed by $\mathcal{A}$, we extract, using standard techniques, all the values embedded into the valid proof of knowledge V of the last spending. For the CL signature, these values corresponds either to (s, u, t, J, x, σ) when a withdrawn coin is spent or to (u, w, C) when a received coin is spent. By assumption, at any time of both games, there are more spent coins than $\mathcal{A}$ can legitimately own, and there is no detection of double-spending.

In game 1, if $\mathcal{A}$ uses the spending of a received coin, then it is necessary that one signature C on a message $m = (u, w)$ does not come from the signature oracle. Thus, this one more signature is a forgery in the first CL's scheme on $m = (u, w)$. Otherwise, abort the game and output $\perp$.

In game 2, if $\mathcal{A}$ uses the spending of a withdrawn coin, it is necessary that one signature σ on a message $m = (s, u, t, J, x)$ is unknown and does not come from the signature oracle. Thus, this one more signature is a signature (forgery) in the second CL's scheme on the message $m = (s, u, t, J, x)$. Otherwise, abort the game and output $\perp$.

Consequently, by playing randomly one of the two above games until the result is not $\perp$, we can break the unforgeability of the CL signature scheme in expected running-time polynomial which is impossible.

Since our proof requires rewinding to extract the values, it is valid only against sequential attacks and not in a concurrent setting where $\mathcal{A}$ is allowed to interact with $\mathcal{B}$ in an arbitrarily interleaving manner. Indeed, our machine may be forced to rewind an exponential number of times. This drawback can be overcome by using well-know techniques [7] that require from the user the encryption of all values in a verifiable manner [4].

Anonymity. An adversary $\mathcal{A}$ can succeed in breaking the anonymity property using several ways:

1. $\mathcal{A}$ can succeed by linking a withdrawal and a (first) spending or two spends related to two withdrawn coins. This is impossible since if such an adversary exists, it would also break the anonymity property of the compact e-cash scheme [2].
2. $\mathcal{A}$ can succeed by linking the spending of a withdrawn coin and the spending of a received coin. That means that $\mathcal{A}$ succeeded in linking $T = pk_u g_5^{R/(t+j+1)}$ and $(\tilde{r} = g_0^{1/(u+\tilde{d})}, \tilde{T} = pk_u g_5^{\tilde{R}/(u+\tilde{S}+\tilde{h})})$. This comes to decide whether the two values $g^{1/(u+d)}$ and $g^u g_5^{1/(t+j+1)}$ embed the same u or not. This is impossible since even if $\mathcal{A}$ has access to the values g^u and $g^{\frac{1}{u+d}}$, he cannot decide whether this is the same u due to the security of the Dodis-Yampolskiy PRF [8].
3. $\mathcal{A}$ can succeed by linking two spends of two received coins. That means that $\mathcal{A}$ succeeded in linking $(r = g_0^{1/(u+d)}, T = pk_u g_5^{R/(u+S+h)})$ and $(\tilde{r} = g_0^{1/(u+\tilde{d})}, \tilde{T} = pk_u g_5^{\tilde{R}/(u+\tilde{S}+\tilde{h})})$. This comes to decide whether the two values $g^{\frac{1}{u+d}}$ and $g^{\frac{1}{u+d}}$ embed the same u or not. This is impossible since the Dodis-Yampoliskiy PRF is secure.

Note that a user can legitimately received twice the same coin without compromising his anonymity due to the h involved in the value T.

Remark 1. Assume that $\mathcal{A}$ is an unbounded adversary. Then $\mathcal{A}$ can break the unconditional anonymity. Indeed, given $T = pk_u g_5^{R/(u+S+h)}$, $\mathcal{A}$ knows or can compute S, $h = \mathcal{H}(hist)$ and $R = \mathcal{H}(r_2, d_2, d_2')$ and $\mathcal{A}$ is assumed to be able to compute $sk_v = v$ for every public key $pk_v = g_0^v$. Finally, $\mathcal{A}$ simply checks whether $T_2 \stackrel{?}{=} g_0^v g_5^{R_2/(v+S+h_2)}$.

Identification of Double-spenders. Suppose that an adversary $\mathcal{A}$ succeeds in breaking the identification of double-spender property. That means that there are two valid spends with the same serial number $S = g_5^{1/s+j+1}$ and two different proofs $\pi = (\pi_1, \cdots, \pi_l)$ and $\tilde{\pi} = (\tilde{\pi}_1, \cdots, \tilde{\pi}_{\tilde{l}})$. The double-spending has been detected at rank k, which means that for all $j < k$, $\pi_j = \tilde{\pi}_j$ and that $\pi_k \neq \tilde{\pi}_k$. Note that the receivers are honest, and thus the values R_k and $\tilde{R}_k$ are different and correctly computed.

1. Case $k = 1$: since the two spends are correct, R_1 and $\tilde{R}_1$ uniquely fixe $T_1 = pk_{\mathcal{U}} g_5^{R_1/(t+j+1)}$ and $\tilde{T}_1 = pk_{\mathcal{U}} g_5^{\tilde{R}_1/(t+j+1)}$ as the only security tags to accompany serial number S except if $\mathcal{A}$ has succeeded in faking the proof of knowledge V_1 (or $\tilde{V}_1$). Moreover, the embedded public key necessary belongs to a registered user, except if $\mathcal{A}$ has forged the CL signature scheme. Both cases only happens with negligible probability.

2. Case $k > 1$: since the two spends are correct, R_k and $\tilde{R}_k$ uniquely fixe $T_k = pk_{\mathcal{U}} g_5^{R_k/(u+S+1)}$ and $\tilde{T}_k = pk_{\mathcal{U}} g_5^{\tilde{R}_k/(u+S+1)}$ as the only possible security tags except if $\mathcal{A}$ has faked V_k (or $\tilde{V}_k$). Moreover, the public key belongs to a registered user, except if $\mathcal{A}$ has forged the CL signature scheme. Both cases only happens with negligible probability.

Exculpability. Suppose that an adversary $\mathcal{A}$ succeeded in breaking the exculpability property. That means that there are two valid spends with the same serial number $S = g_5^{1/s+j+1}$ and two different proofs $\pi = (\pi_1, \cdots, \pi_l)$ and $\tilde{\pi} = (\tilde{\pi}_1, \cdots, \tilde{\pi}_{\tilde{l}})$. The double-spending can be detected at rank k, which means that for all $j < k$, $\pi_j = \tilde{\pi}_j$ and $\pi_k \neq \tilde{\pi}_k$. The receivers are honest and thus the values R_k and $\tilde{R}_k$ are correct and different. As spends are correct, V_k (resp. $\tilde{V}_k$) includes a proof that T_k (resp. $\tilde{T}_k$) is well-formed. Thus, since the user is honest, $\mathcal{A}$ has faked T_k or $\tilde{T}_k$.

We now use $\mathcal{A}$ to break the one-more discrete logarithm problem [1]. Given $l+1$ values, we have to find the discrete logarithm of all these values, and we can ask a discrete logarithm oracle at most l times. We first associate each value to the public key of one user (assuming there are at most l users) and we ask the oracle each time $\mathcal{A}$ corrupt a user. It is moreover possible to simulate all withdrawals and spends using standard techniques (in the random oracle model). At the end, $\mathcal{A}$ outputs two correctly formed T_k and $\tilde{T}_k$ and the associated proofs of validity. Thus, T_k and $\tilde{T}_k$ are both formed from the same public key of a honest user.

From the two proofs of validity, we can extract the user secret key and thus break the one-more discrete logarithm. Indeed, since the user is honest, this discrete logarithm has not been requested to the oracle.

4 Unconditionally Anonymous Transferable Scheme

In this section, we present a transferable e-cash system providing the same features than the scheme presented in Section 3. In addition, the proposed scheme fulfils an unconditional anonymity. However, it necessitates a pre-computing phase before spending a withdrawn coin.

4.1   Overview of Our Construction

We adapt the scheme presented at Section 3 in order to get an unconditional anonymity of users. The withdrawal phase in unchanged and the spending phase also involves a challenge sent by the receiver including a receiver identifier u_j, that is verifiable and that is signed by the payer.

The main modification is the computation of the challenge sent by the receiver during the spending phase that will be used during the next spending. This challenge should provide an unconditional anonymity instead of a computational one. Then, the receiver computes the commitment t corresponding to the ZKPK of a representation (r, w) and that will be signed by the spender; t will necessary be used during the next spending. In case of double-spending, t will correspond to two different questions. Two different answers will thus permits to retrieve in particular r. This value r is moreover used in $T = g^u h^r = pk_{\mathcal{U}} h^r$ and thus $pk_{\mathcal{U}}$ can be retrieved. Finally, we introduce a pre-computation phase to achieve the unconditional anonymity.

4.2   Description of the Scheme

The setup and the withdrawal protocol are unchanged from Section 3.2.

Pre-computation phase. Before spending a withdrawn coin, a user $\mathcal{U}_i$ has to execute a *pre-computation* phase which is necessary to achieve the unconditional anonymity. This phase is similar to the spending protocol for a withdrawn coin defined in Section 3.2 with $\mathcal{U}_i = \mathcal{U}_j$. The main difference is the computation of the random value involving the receiver secret key; due to lack of space, this computation is only detailed in the spending protocol below.

Next, $\mathcal{U}_i$ takes at random a bit B. If $B = 0$, then the pre-computation phase is over. Else, $\mathcal{U}_i$ executes with himself the spending protocol.

Spending protocol. A user $\mathcal{U}_i$, owning a coin $(S, \pi = (\hat{T}, \pi_0, \pi_1, \ldots, \pi_l))$ where $\pi_k = (V_k, T_k, T'_k, t_k, d_k)$, $1 \leq k \leq l$ and l is the number of time this coin has been spent, can spend this coin to a user $\mathcal{U}_j$.

1. $\mathcal{U}_j$ chooses at random r, w, a, b, computes $T = g_0^{u_j} h^r$, $T' = g^r h^w$ and $t = g^a h^b$, and sends T, T' and t to $\mathcal{U}_i$.
2. Since $\mathcal{U}_i$ legitimately received this coin, it is necessary that $T_l = g^{u_i} h^{r_l}$, $T'_l = g^{r_l} h^{w_l}$ $t_l = g^{a_l} h^{b_l}$ and $\mathcal{U}_i$ knows the values of r_l, w_l, a_l and b_l. $\mathcal{U}_i$ first computes $R = \mathcal{H}(T\|T'\|t\|d)$ where d represents some data related to the spending and next computes a proof of validity of the spent coin, that is, the signature of knowledge:

$$V = PK(\alpha, \beta, \gamma, \delta, \zeta :$$
$$T_l = g_0^\alpha g_5^\beta \wedge T'_l = g_0^\beta g_5^\zeta \wedge \gamma = \text{Sign}(\alpha, \delta))(S, T_l, T'_l, t_l)$$

This proof is done by using as a commitment for T'_l the value t_l and as a challenge the value R. Consequently, to prove the knowledge of r_l and w_l

such that $T_l' = g_0^{r_l} g_5^{w_l}$, $\mathcal{U}_i$ uses $(t_l, R, (s_r = a_l - Ru_i, s_w = b_l - Rw_l))$ as a signature of knowledge (see Section 2.4).

3. The spent coin is represented by $(S, \pi = (\hat{T}, \pi_0, \ldots, \pi_{l+1})$ where $\pi_{l+1} = (V, T, T', t, d)$.

Deposit and Identify Protocol. The deposit phase of a coin $(S, \pi = (\hat{T}, \pi_0, \ldots, \pi_l))$, where $\pi_i = (V_i, T_i, T_i', d_i, t_i)$, $0 \leq i \leq l$, is similar to the one presented in Section 3.2 except that the value R is computed as $R = \mathcal{H}(T_l \| T_l' \| t_l \| d_l)$.

In case of a double-spending detection, the bank $\mathcal{B}$ has two deposited coins $C = (S, \pi = (\hat{T}, \pi_0, \pi_1, \ldots))$ and $\tilde{C} = (S, \tilde{\pi} = (\tilde{\hat{T}}, \tilde{\pi}_0, \tilde{\pi}_1, \ldots))$. If $\hat{T} \neq \tilde{\hat{T}}$, then $\mathcal{B}$ retrieves $pk_\mathcal{U}$ by computing $pk_\mathcal{U} = (\hat{T}^{\tilde{R}}/\tilde{\hat{T}}^R)^{1/(\tilde{R}-R)}$. Else, $\mathcal{B}$ looks for the minimum value k such that $\pi_k \neq \tilde{\pi}_k$; this case always happens. Both π_k and $\tilde{\pi}_k$ are correct and thus both V_k and $\tilde{V}_k$ include a proof that $T_k = \tilde{T}_k$ is well-formed. Moreover, both proofs necessary use the same commitment t. Using standard technique and the soundness of the proof of knowledge (see Section 2.4), $\mathcal{B}$ can easily retrieve $g_0^{u_{k-1}}$ by first retrieving r_{k-1} and thus, using T_{k-1}, the identity of the double-spender.

4.3   Achieving the Unconditional Anonymity

Due to lack of space, we only give security arguments for the unconditional anonymity property of our scheme. It is unconditionally impossible to learn anything about the user identity from a withdrawal due to the unconditional security of the Pedersen commitment. More precisely, the user identity is embedded twice during a spending protocol.

- In the Pedersen commitment $T = g^u h^r$ which is unconditionally hiding [12]. Thus, no Shannon information about u is revealed in T.
- In the zero-knowledge signature of knowledge V. The zero-knowledge property of the underlying proof of knowledge is also unconditional. Thus, no Shannon information about u is revealed in V.

During the pre-computation phase, the security tag $\hat{T} = pk_\mathcal{U} g_5^{R_0/(t+j+1)}$ (computed as in the first scheme) does not compromise the unconditional anonymity. Indeed, even if $\mathcal{A}$ knows $R_0 = \mathcal{H}(r_0, d_0, d_0')$, and that for every $pk_v = g_0^v$, $\mathcal{A}$ can compute $sk_v = v$, $\mathcal{A}$ does not know neither t_0 nor j_0 and thus $\mathcal{A}$ cannot determine which public key $pk_\mathcal{U}$ is embedded into $\hat{T}$.

This pre-computation phase may introduce some flaws for other security properties, such as the double-spender identification. Indeed, $\mathcal{A}$ can make the pre-computation twice, one with $R = \mathcal{H}(T_0 \| T_0' \| t_0 \| d_0)$ and the other with $\tilde{R} = \mathcal{H}(\tilde{T}_0 \| \tilde{T}_0' \| \tilde{t} \| \tilde{d})$, such that $R = \tilde{R}$. However, since the hash function is collision resistant, it is necessary that $T_0 = \tilde{T}_0$, $T_0' = \tilde{T}_0'$ and $t_0 = \tilde{t}_0$. The value T_0 will be necessary used during the first Spend protocol, i.e. either during the pre-computation phase or during an effective spending protocol. Thus, $\mathcal{A}$ necessary succeeded in faking a proof of knowledge or forged the CL signature scheme, which happens with negligible probability.

5   Conclusion

In this paper, we present two transferable e-cash schemes that improve the efficiency of anonymous transferable e-cash schemes by addressing the problem of decreasing the number of interaction between the bank and users. The first scheme fulfils the computational anonymity property whereas the second one fulfils an unconditional anonymity at the cost of a less efficient result. Moreover, both schemes allow to withdraw efficiently a wallet instead of a coin at a time.

References

1. Bellare, M., Namprempre, C., Pointcheval, D., Semanko, M.: The One-More-RSA-Inversion Problems and the Security of Chaum's Blind Signature Scheme. J. Cryptology 16(3), 185–215 (2003)
2. Camenisch, J., Hohenberger, S., Lysyanskaya, A.: Compact E-Cash. In: Cramer, R.J.F. (ed.) EUROCRYPT 2005. LNCS, vol. 3494, pp. 302–321. Springer, Heidelberg (2005)
3. Camenisch, J., Lysyanskaya, A.: Signature Schemes and Anonymous Credentials from Bilinear Maps. In: Franklin, M. (ed.) CRYPTO 2004. LNCS, vol. 3152, pp. 56–72. Springer, Heidelberg (2004)
4. Camenisch, J., Shoup, V.: Practical Verifiable Encryption and Decryption of Discrete Logarithms. In: Boneh, D. (ed.) CRYPTO 2003. LNCS, vol. 2729, pp. 126–144. Springer, Heidelberg (2003)
5. Canard, S., Gouget, A., Hufschmitt, E.: A Handy Multi-coupon System. In: Zhou, J., Yung, M., Bao, F. (eds.) ACNS 2006. LNCS, vol. 3989, pp. 66–81. Springer, Heidelberg (2006)
6. Chaum, D., Pedersen, T.P.: Transferred Cash Grows in Size. In: Rueppel, R.A. (ed.) EUROCRYPT 1992. LNCS, vol. 658, pp. 390–407. Springer, Heidelberg (1993)
7. Damgård, I.: Efficient Concurrent Zero-Knowledge in the Auxiliary String Model. In: Preneel, B. (ed.) EUROCRYPT 2000. LNCS, vol. 1807, pp. 418–430. Springer, Heidelberg (2000)
8. Dodis, Y., Yampolskiy, A.: A Verifiable Random Function with Short Proofs and Keys. In: Vaudenay, S. (ed.) PKC 2005. LNCS, vol. 3386, pp. 416–431. Springer, Heidelberg (2005)
9. Fiat, A., Shamir, A.: How to Prove Yourself: Practical Solutions to Identification and Signature Problems. In: Odlyzko, A.M. (ed.) CRYPTO 1986. LNCS, vol. 263, pp. 186–194. Springer, Heidelberg (1987)
10. Girault, M., Poupard, G., Stern, J.: On the Fly Authentication and Signature Schemes Based on Groups of Unknown Order. J. Cryptology 19(4), 463–487 (2006)
11. Okamoto, T., Ohta, K.: Disposable Zero-Knowledge Authentications and Their Applications to Untraceable Electronic Cash. In: Brassard, G. (ed.) CRYPTO 1989. LNCS, vol. 435, pp. 481–496. Springer, Heidelberg (1990)
12. Pedersen, T.P.: Non-Interactive and Information-Theoretic Secure Verifiable Secret Sharing. In: Feigenbaum, J. (ed.) CRYPTO 1991. LNCS, vol. 576, pp. 129–140. Springer, Heidelberg (1992)
13. Pointcheval, D., Stern, J.: Security Arguments for Digital Signatures and Blind Signatures. J. Cryptology 13(3), 361–396 (2000)
14. Schnorr, C.P.: Efficient Identification and Signatures for Smart Cards. In: Brassard, G. (ed.) CRYPTO 1989. LNCS, vol. 435, pp. 239–252. Springer, Heidelberg (1990)
15. van Antwerpen, H.: Electronic Cash. Master's thesis, CWI (1990)

Proactive RSA with Non-interactive Signing

Stanisław Jarecki and Josh Olsen

Department of Computer Science,
University of California, Irvine*
{stasio,jolsen}@ics.uci.edu

Abstract. We show the first proactive RSA scheme with a fully non-interactive signature protocol. The scheme is secure and robust with the optimal threshold of $t < n/2$ corruptions. Such protocol is very attractive in practice: When a party requesting a signature contacts $t' > t$ among n trustees which implement a proactive RSA scheme, the trustees do not need to communicate between each other, and simply respond with a single "partial signature" message to the requester, who can reconstruct the standard RSA signature from the first $t + 1$ responses he receives. The computation costs incurred by each party are comparable to standard RSA signature computation.

Such non-interactive signature protocol was known for threshold RSA [1], but previous proactive RSA schemes [2,3] required all trustees to participate in the signature generation, which made these schemes impractical in many networking environments. On the other hand, proactivity, i.e. an ability to refresh the secret-sharing of the signature key between the trustees, not only makes threshold cryptosystems more secure, but it is actually a crucial component for any threshold scheme in practice, since it allows for secure replacement of a trustee in case of repairs, hardware upgrades, etc. The proactive RSA scheme we present shows that it is possible to have the best of both worlds: A highly practical non-interactive signature protocol *and* an ability to refresh the secret-sharing of the signature key. This brings attack-resilient implementations of root sources of trust in any cryptographic scheme closer to practice.

1 Introduction

Threshold cryptosystems enable fault-tolerant distribution of a private key among a group of trustees in such a way that the trustees can compute the private-key operation via some distributed protocol, and the cryptosystem remains secure even if some threshold of the trustees becomes corrupted. A *threshold signature* scheme [4] is an example of this idea: It allows a group of n players to share the private signature key in such a way that the signature scheme remains *secure* in the sense of universal unforgeability under the chosen message attack, as long as no more than t of the players are corrupt. Simultaneously, as long as at least $n - t$ players are honest, the scheme remains *robust* in the sense that these players can efficiently produce correct signatures on any message even if the other t players act in an arbitrarily malicious way. Such schemes can be used for example to protect the root private keys of certification authorities, time-stamping services, or electronic commerce and electronic voting authorities.

---

* Research supported by NSF CyberTrust Grant #0430622.

G. Tsudik (Ed.): FC 2008, LNCS 5143, pp. 215–230, 2008.

Proactive signature schemes [6] are threshold schemes with an improved resilience in the face of player corruptions. Namely, security is maintained even in the presence of so-called *mobile* faults [7], where a potentially new group of up to t players becomes corrupted in each well-defined time period, e.g. each hour, day, week, etc. Technically, this is done by the players re-sharing the shared private key at the beginning of each period. Thus a proactive signature scheme offers stronger guarantees then a threshold scheme, which is important for long-lived applications which can come under repeated attacks, e.g. a certification authority or a timestamping service.

LIMITATIONS OF THRESHOLD CRYPTOSYSTEMS AND IMPORTANCE OF PROACTIVITY. Even though a proactive scheme offers strictly stronger security properties than a threshold scheme, it might seem at first glance that this additional level of security can be foregone in some applications to fault-tolerant computing, and that a threshold cryptosystem offers a good-enough level of resilience. We will argue that this is a misconception, and that fault-tolerant distributed cryptosystems which implement merely a threshold cryptosystem, but not a proactive one, have serious limitations in practice. For starters, it is not clear how to conduct repairs and hardware or software upgrades of a computing device which implements a trustee in a threshold cryptosystem, because conducting any such changes would make the data stored by this device vulnerable to exposure. It is even less clear how to ensure survival of a share stored by a trustee in case of unexpected break-downs, while at the same time protecting this share from exposure. This is an important consideration in practice. For example, the designers of Steward, a fault-tolerant distributed storage system which uses threshold (but not proactive!) RSA cryptosystem to assure database consistency in the presence of adversarial corruptions of the system components, had to resort to storing extra copies of key-shares in order to tolerate possible future upgrades and repairs of any component [8]. Even though these copies of key-shares can be kept off-line in some "secure" location, the necessity of storing them introduces unnecessary points of vulnerability and additional complexity to the management of such system.

Proactive cryptosystems solve all these problems in a natural way, because the same re-sharing protocol which is used in a proactive system to refresh the secret-sharing of the private key at the end of each time-period, can also be used after each repair of any of the trustees, to re-establish the proper secret-share at this trustee and eliminate the effects of potential exposure of the share which this trustee held previously. Proactive cryptosystems offer also additional benefits because they enable not just a secure removal of existing trustees and addition of new ones, but also enable modification to the secret-sharing threshold itself, thus allowing the system the flexibility to adjust the resilience level long after the system is created. Such ability is especially important in uses of threshold cryptosystems for peer-to-peer or ad-hoc groups, e.g. [9].

PRIOR WORK ON THRESHOLD AND PROACTIVE RSA SIGNATURES. Thresholdizing the RSA cryptosystem requires solving several difficulties posed by the fact that the private key d of an RSA cryptosystem "lives" in a group of order $\phi(N) = (p-1)(q-1)$, where $N = pq$ is the RSA modulus. Since knowledge of $\phi(N)$ implies ability to factor N, the players participating in a threshold scheme must be able to perform the threshold signature protocol without knowledge of this order. Thus the first threshold RSA scheme, proposed by Desmedt and Frankel [4], was not robust again malicious faults, and had only heuristic security. Frankel et al. [10,11] achieved provable security under the standard RSA assumption in the honest-but-curious model, and security against malicious faults was added in [12,13]. However, these schemes used secret shares which were elements of a polynomial extension field of $\mathbb{Z}_N$, which increased the cost of the signature operation by a factor of t. Finally, Victor Shoup [1] presented the most practical threshold RSA signature scheme for strong RSA moduli N, which is robust and provably secure with optimal adversarial threshold $t < n/2$, and which did away with the extension field representation of the shares, thus making the cost of the signature operation for each participating player comparable to the standard RSA signature generation. Shoup's threshold RSA scheme was then generalized by Damgard and Koprowski [14] and then Damgard and Dupont [15] to larger classes of RSA moduli.

Proactive RSA schemes have to deal with an additional difficulty of enabling the participating players to re-share the secret-sharing of the private key without knowledge of the modulus $\phi(N)$. The first proactive RSA scheme of Frankel et al. [16] solved this problem using additive secret sharing and combinatorial techniques, but the resulting scheme did not achieve optimal adversarial threshold $t < n/2$ and did not scale well with the group size n. These shortcomings were later overcome by the same authors [17], who showed how to use Shamir secret-sharing over integers using polynomials with specially chosen large integer coefficients. This enabled both interpolation of the secret d without knowing $\phi(N)$ and the secrecy of d given any t polynomial shares. However, in this solution, even though the underlying secret sharing was polynomial, the players needed to create a one-time additive sharing for every group of players participating in a threshold signature generation, which made the signature protocol cumbersome. A simpler and more efficient scheme was then given by Tal Rabin [2], who reversed the order of polynomial and additive sharing in the scheme of [17]: The primary sharing was additive (and over integers), and this sharing was used in a threshold signature protocol, but the additive shares were backed-up by a secondary level of polynomial secret sharing (also over integers), which enabled robustness. Subsequently, Jarecki and Saxena showed an alternative proactive RSA scheme which used polynomial sharing over a big-enough prime as a primary sharing [3]. (All the above schemes were shown secure only in the static model. See Almansa et al. [20] for extending the scheme of [2] to an adaptive adversary model.)

LIMITATIONS OF THE PROACTIVE RSA SCHEMES OF [2,3]: INTERACTIVE SIGNING. The most efficient existing proactive RSA schemes of [2,3] have a serious practical limitation compared to the most efficient threshold (but not proactive) RSA scheme of [1]. Namely, the signature protocol in these schemes requires participation of all n trustees in the protocol. For any player which is even temporarily not available, the remaining players not only have to engage in a round of interaction, but they have to reconstruct the shares of all unavailable players to create the signature. In effect, such protocol equates a benign fault, which causes temporary unavailability of a player, with a malicious fault, thus degrading, in practice, the resilience of the system to real malicious faults. Moreover, even if one player is not unavailable but merely slowed down due to traffic congestion, by requiring all n players to participate the protocol proceeds at the pace of the slowest player. Finally, such protocol is wholly impractical in networks which provide unreliable connectivity, like the wireless networks. By contrast, the threshold RSA scheme of [1] shows that without proactive update it is possible to share an RSA signing operation in a fully non-interactive way. Namely, when a party requesting a signature contacts any $t' > t$ among n trustees, each trustee independently responds with a single "partial signature" message to the requester, who can then reconstruct the standard RSA signature from any $t+1$ correct responses he receives. Almansa et al. [20] point out a related problem in the schemes of [2,3], namely that these schemes are not only interactive if any of the n players is unavailable during the signing protocol, but also that these schemes publicly reconstruct the shares of such players. This adversely affects security of the scheme because it equates common benign errors like temporary communication problem with active corruption of a player. In effect, in these schemes the adversary can learn the secret shares of some players by merely disrupting their communication links, which might be easier in practice than corrupting these players' private memories. The "no share exposure" variant of [2] proposed in [20] fixes this latter problem. However, the modified protocol remains interactive.

OUR CONTRIBUTION: PROACTIVE RSA WITH FULLY NON-INTERACTIVE SIGNING. We show that it is possible to create a threshold RSA scheme which offers both a fully non-interactive signing protocol as the protocol of [1] described above, and an ability to proactively re-fresh the secret-sharing of the private key. The key distribution and proactive re-sharing algorithms in a new scheme remain also highly practical. Technically, we do this by modifying the signature protocol in a proactive RSA scheme of [2] along the lines of the threshold RSA protocol of [1], and we prove that this modified way of signing does not endanger the security of the overall scheme. Using the terminology of the original scheme of [2] we sign using the back-up shares instead of the "first-layer" additive shares, although we keep the additive shares in the system to facilitate the proactive re-sharing protocol, keeping this part essentially unchanged from [2]. We note that we analyze the security of the proposed scheme assuming a strong RSA modulus N and a static adversarial model, and we leave open the issues of handling more general RSA moduli and adaptive adversaries.

Here we briefly sketch why our modification works: In Shoup's non-interactive signature protocol the players compute their partial signatures as m^{L*s_i}, where s_i's are shares of the private key d in a standard Shamir secret-sharing modulo $\phi(N)$, and $L = n!$ where n is the number of players. The reason for the L factor is that without the knowledge of modulus $\phi(N)$ it is not clear how the simulator could interpolate (in the exponent) the straightforward partial signatures m^{s_i} from t shares of the corrupt players and the final signature m^d, as that would seem to require computing inverses modulo $\phi(N)$ or roots modulo N. (Recall that interpolation of value $s_i = f(i)$ given set T of $f(j)$'s involves multiplication of each $f(j)$ by Lagrange coefficient $\lambda_{ij} = \prod_{k \in T} \frac{i-k}{j-k}$, which is not an integer.) Adding the L factor solves this problem because value $L * \lambda_{ij}$ is an integer. (Since $T \subseteq \{1, ..., n\}$, the denominator in the expression for λ_{ij} divides $n!$.) Another factor L is also added to the procedure that publicly interpolates the signature from the partial shares m^{s_i}, resulting in computation of $m^{L^2 d}$ instead of the standard RSA signature m^d. However, if e is high enough so that $gcd(e, L^2) = gcd(e, L) = 1$, value m^d can be computed from $m^{L^2 d}$ using the Euclidean algorithm. Even though this scheme assumes that secret d is shared polynomially modulo $\phi(N)$, a similar procedure can be used if d is secret-shared over integers as in Tal Rabin's proactive RSA. The only difference compared to Shoup's sharing which affects both the protocol and the simulation is that $f(0)$ for the secret-sharing polynomial f is no longer equal to the RSA private key d but to $L(d - d_{pub})$ where d_{pub} is a public value. This change affects only the public interpolation part of Shoup's signature protocol. Thus in our modification the players interpolate $m^{L^3 d}$ instead of $m^{L^2 d}$ as in Shoup's protocol, but m^d is computed via the same extended Euclidean algorithm because $gcd(e, L^3) = gcd(e, L) = 1$.

We should note that a related modification of [2] was proposed in the "no share exposure" variant of the protocol given by Almansa et al [20]. That variant uses a mixture of additive and polynomial shares in the signature protocol. The polynomial shares are used to interpolate in the exponent value $m^{L d_I}$, where d_I is the sum of the shares of the corrupt or non-participating players, thus known to the simulator. Together with d_{pub} and the m^{d_i} values of the honest players value $m^{L d_I}$ lets everyone locally interpolate signature m^d. This protocol modification takes two rounds: First players produce their partial signatures using additive shares, as in [2], and only then, when the missing set of indices I is identified, the players use polynomial shares to interpolate the missing piece $m^{L d_I}$. In contrast, we use polynomial shares directly and the protocol is non-interactive.

Apart from changing the signature protocol in Tal Rabin's proactive RSA scheme, we also show that the scheme remains secure with reduced sizes of both additive and polynomial shares. Note that since in the original scheme of [2] the back-up shares were used only in case of share reconstruction, their size was not crucial to the efficiency of the scheme. This, however, changes in our modification, where the size of the polynomial backup shares determines the efficiency of the signature generation. It was observed in [3] that the *additive* shares in [2] can be shortened, roughly, from $2|N|$ to $|N|+80$ bits. Here we extend the same observation to reducing also the sizes of the polynomial shares. In effect we shorten the polynomial shares from about $2n \log n + 3|N|$ bits in [2], where N is the RSA modulus, to just $2n \log n + |N| + 160$ bits. To give a concrete example, the cost of the signature generation per player in the new protocol is at most six times the cost of a standard RSA signature generation if $n = 50$, and it grows to twelve times the cost of a standard RSA signature for $n = 130$. Thus the per-player cost of our protocol should stay below 10 milliseconds on today's PCs, even for very large values of n like $n = 130$.

Organization. Section 2 recalls the standard model for proactive signature schemes. Section 3 contains the proposed scheme. The key generation and share update protocol are as in [2], except of shortened share-sizes, while the signature protocol is new. Section 4 argues that the new scheme is as secure as standard RSA.

2 Preliminaries

Adversarial Model. We prove our schemes secure in the standard model for threshold and proactive cryptography, namely a synchronous communication network with a reliable broadcast channel. Namely, we assume a set of n players $\{P_1, P_2, \ldots, P_n\}$ in a fully connected synchronous network in which each point-to-point connection is private, and each player has access to a (reliable) broadcast channel. As in all *proactive* cryptosystems, the lifetime of the system is evenly divided into rounds, so that upon the beginning of each round the players trigger a proactive update protocol. Since the scheme is designed to protect against a mobile adversary who might eventually corrupt all players (see below), we have to assume that the players have the ability to securely erase information at the beginning of every round. Finally, as in all practical threshold or proactive RSA schemes, we assume a trusted dealer in key generation.

We assume a computationally bounded *mobile* adversary, which may (statically) corrupt up to t players per update round. The adversary is mobile in the sense that it may corrupt a new and independent set of t players in each update round, while *static* means that the set of players to be corrupted is chosen at the beginning of the round (as opposed to an *adaptive* adversary who chooses which subset to corrupt on the basis of protocol execution). Upon corrupting a player, the adversary gains knowledge of the entire internal state of that player, and until the adversary leaves this player and corrupts some other one, this player can behave in an arbitrarily malicious way. This is a standard way of modeling an adversary in works on proactive cryptosystems, starting from [5] and including [2].

Proactive RSA. Recall that in a standard RSA signature scheme the public key is (N, e) where $N = pq$ for two large primes p, q, e is a (small) prime, and $d = e^{-1} \bmod \phi(N)$. An RSA signature on message $m \in \mathbb{Z}_N^*$ is $\sigma = m^d \bmod N$, where m is usually a special *encoding* of the real message, e.g., in the full-domain-hash version of RSA signature [22], element m is a hash of the real message. A *proactive* RSA signature scheme (with a trusted key generation) consists of a probabilistic algorithm TKeyDist and two distributed protocols TKeyDist and Update, with the following functionalities:

- TKeyDist is initiated by the trusted dealer on input (N, e, d) and security parameter τ, and generates a *sharing* Sh of the private key d among the n players, which is a distributed data structure consisting of public information and n private *shares*, handed to the n players.
- TSign is a distributed protocol followed by the players $P_1, ..., P_n$ on sharing Sh and message m. This protocol should output an RSA signature σ on m.
- Update is a distributed protocol followed by the players $P_1, ..., P_n$ on sharing Sh. The output of the protocol is another sharing Sh$'$ which should be a sharing of the same RSA private key d.

As in all work on threshold and proactive cryptosystems, e.g. [5], [18], [2], [3], we require two properties of this tuple of algorithms: First, the scheme must be *secure* in the sense of existential unforgeability under a Chosen Message Attack in the presence of a t-limited mobile adversary. Second, the scheme must be *robust* in the sense that no t-limited mobile adversary can prevent the uncorrupted players from successfully completing any instance of either the TSign or the Update protocol. We do not formally define either notion, since such definitions are both standard and cumbersome, but in section 4 we give formal arguments why both properties hold.

3   Proactive RSA with Non-interactive Signing: Protocols

Let $\tau, \hat{\tau}$ be security parameters. Let n denote the number of players, t denote the maximum number of corrupted players tolerated by the protocol, and r be the number of

---

Parameters: Range of the secret value R, statistical security parameter $\hat{\tau}$.
Input (to dealer): A secret value $s \in [R]$, modulus N, element $g \in Z_N^*$.

1. The dealer sets $a_0 \leftarrow Ls$, chooses $a_k \xleftarrow{\$} [tL^2R2^{\hat{\tau}}]$ for each $k \in [1 \ldots t]$. Define $f(x) \overset{\text{def}}{=} \sum_{k=0}^{t} a_k x^k$ (over integers), and let $b_k \leftarrow g^{a_k} \bmod N$ for each $k \in [0 \ldots t]$. The dealer broadcasts $\{b_k\}_{k \in [0\ldots t]}$.
2. For each i, the dealer sets $s_i \leftarrow f(i)$ (over integers), and sends s_i to P_i.
3. Each player P_i checks if $g^{s_i} = \prod_{k=0}^{t}(b_k)^{i^k} \bmod N$ holds. If not, P_i broadcasts a request that the dealer make $f(i)$ public.
4. The dealer broadcasts all requested values. Each player verifies that all values broadcast by the dealer satisfy the verification equation from step 3, and disqualifies the dealer if any of them fail.

Output of player P_i: If player P_i does not reject then it outputs a share s_i and a set of verification values $\{b_k\}_{k \in [0\ldots t]}$.

Fig. 1. Secret Sharing Procedure Feldman-Z_N-VSS [2]

proactive update rounds during the lifetime of the scheme. We define constant $L = n!$. We use $[x]$ to denote range of integer values $[-x, \ldots, x]$. We use notation $x \xleftarrow{\$} S$ to denote that random variable x is chosen uniformly in set S. For soundness of the efficient zero-knowledge proofs of discrete logarithm equality we assume the cryptographic setting of [2,1], i.e. a "safe RSA" modulus $N = pq$, where $p = 2p' + 1$, $q = 2q' + 1$, and p, q, p', q' are all primes, with $|q'| = |p'|$. We also require that the RSA public exponent e satisfies $gcd(e, L) = 1$, as in [1], e.g. e is any prime s.t. $e > n$.

VERIFIABLE SECRET SHARING FELDMAN-Z_N-VSS. We employ the Feldman-Z_N-VSS protocol of Rabin [2], generalized to accommodate any range of the secret-shared value and any desired level of statistical secrecy. The protocol is described in Figure 1. We omit the reconstruction part of this secret-sharing protocol since it is identical to [2], and it is used as a black-box in the proactive update procedure. Below we recall two lemmas from [2], which establish the secrecy of Feldman-Z_N-VSS. We state these lemmas in a slightly more general form compared to how they are stated in [2], to accommodate for a more flexible choice of range of the shared secret and a desired level of secrecy:

Lemma 1. [2] *For any R and $\hat{\tau}$, any N, g, any secrets $s, s' \in [R]$, and any set of t players $\mathcal{B}$ corrupted by an adversary, the statistical difference between the distribution of shares $\{s_i\}_{i \in \mathcal{B}}$ the adversary receives in the Feldman-Z_N-VSS sharing of secret s, and the distribution of the same shares in the Feldman-Z_N-VSS sharing of secret s', is at most $2^{-\hat{\tau}}$.*

Lemma 2. [2] *For any $g_0 \in \mathbb{Z}_N^*$ and $g = g_0^{L^2}$, for any set of t players $\mathcal{B}$ corrupted by an adversary, given shares $\{s_i\}_{i \in \mathcal{B}}$ and an additional value $g^s \bmod N$, it is possible to efficiently compute the verification values $\{b_k\}_{k \in [0\ldots t]}$, where $b_k = g^{a_k} \bmod N$ for all k, such that polynomial $f(x) = a_t x^t + a_{t-1} x^{t-1} + \ldots + a_1 x + sL$ satisfies $f(i) = s_i$ for all $i \in \mathcal{B}$.*

KEY DISTRIBUTION PROTOCOL. The protocol TKeyDist is presented in Figure 2. As in all practical threshold or proactive RSA schemes, we assume that it is executed by a trusted dealer. The dealer performs an additive sharing of the RSA secret d, and then performs a Feldman-Z_N-VSS sharing of each additive share. The purpose of the additive shares is Update, while the polynomial shares are primarily used in TSign, but also in Update in the case that a player is faulty. Our TKeyDist is essentially the same as in [2], but with reduced ranges for both additive and polynomial shares. In particular, [2] chooses additive shares that are roughly $2|N|$ bits long and polynomial shares that are $3|N| + 2|L|$ bits long, while our scheme uses $|N| + \tau$ bits for additive shares and $|N| + 2|L| + 2\tau$ bits for polynomial shares.

SIGNATURE PROTOCOL. The signature protocol TSign is described in Figure 3. It is non-interactive because players only need to send a single partial signature with an associated proof to complete the protocol. In particular, any entity that has received $t + 1$ such messages can compute the final signature. Note that in practice this protocol can be run optimistically, omitting the proofs (see below).

PROACTIVE UPDATE PROTOCOL. The proactive update procedure Update is shown in Figure 4. It is essentially same protocol as in [2] except for reduction in the ranges for the additive shares. In the protocol, each player P_i distributes its additive share d_i *additively*, similarly to the way the trusted dealer shared the top-level secret, the private key d, in the TKeyDist protocol. Then each player locally sums the additive shares received from all these sharings into its new single additive share, which it further shares using the Feldman-Z_N-VSS protocol. The additive shares are contained in the range $[R' = (r + 1)N2^\tau]$, as opposed to $[N^2]$ in [2].

EFFICIENCY OF THE SIGNING PROTOCOL. The computational costs incurred by our signing protocol are very practical. (As are the costs of the key distribution and the update protocols, although the cost of those protocols is less crucial.) Recall that $s_i = \sum_{k=0}^{t} a_k i^k$ (over integers), where $a_k \in [tL^2 R 2^{\hat{\tau}}]$ (see Figure 1), $R = n(r+1)N2^{\tau+1}$, and $\hat{\tau} = \tau + \log r + 2$ (see Figure 2). Therefore the length of s_i can be upper-bounded as follows:

$$|s_i| \leq |N| + 2\tau + (2n + 1)\log n + \log t + 2\log r + 5$$

As an example, let $|N| = 1024$, $n = 32$, $t = 8$, $r = 2^{10}$, and $\tau = 80$. This yields an approximate Feldman-Z_N-VSS share size of 1500 bits. (Note that the maximum number of update rounds r should always be upper-bounded given the intended life-time of the system. However, since even values of $r = 2^{40}$ add only 80 bits to the share size, this is not a significant cost factor.) Each player P_i first computes $\gamma_i \leftarrow m^{Ls_i} \mod N$. For parameters above, this is exponentiation to 1700 bit exponent. In general, the exponent length grows proportionally to $|L| = n \log n$, which is tolerable for groups of size up to few hundreds. (For example, with $n = 128$ the exponent size is approximately 4000 bits.) Regarding the zero-knowledge proofs of discrete log equality, in many applications one can execute the protocol "optimistically" and skip the computation of the zero-knowledge proof in the default case. Instead, the party that combines the partial signatures into a final signature checks if the final signature verifies, and if it does not then each trustee is then requested to provide the zero-knowledge proof

---

Input: RSA public key (N, e), private key d, security parameter τ.

1. The dealer creates an additive sharing of the private key $d \in [0, N]$:
   (a) Set $R = n(r + 1)N2^{\tau+1}$. Pick an element g of order $\phi(N)/4 = p'q'$ in $\mathbb{Z}_N^*$ (e.g. g can be a random square). For $i \in [1 \ldots n]$, pick $d_i \xleftarrow{\$} [R]$, and set $d_{pub} \leftarrow d - \sum_{i=1}^n d_i$ (over integers). For $i \in [1 \ldots n]$, set $w_i \leftarrow g^{d_i} \bmod N$.
   (b) Broadcast value d_{pub} together with the verification values $\{w_j\}_{j \in [1 \ldots n]}$, and for all i send an additive share d_i to player P_i.
2. For each $j \in [1 \ldots n]$, the dealer shares d_j using Feldman-Z_N-VSS on range R, parameter $\hat{\tau} = \tau + 2 + \log r$, and inputs $s = d_j$ and (N, g). Denote player P_i's outputs in the sharing of d_j as $s_i^{(j)}$ and $\{b_k^{(j)}\}_{k \in [0 \ldots t]}$.

Output of Player P_i: Value d_{pub}, element $g \in \mathbb{Z}_N^*$, an additive share d_i of d, a set of verification values $\{w_j\}_{j \in [1 \ldots n]}$, a set of polynomial shares $\{s_i^{(j)}\}_{j \in [1 \ldots n]}$, and another set of verification values $\{b_k^{(j)}\}_{k \in [0 \ldots t], j \in [1 \ldots n]}$.

Fig. 2. Key Distribution Protocol TKeyDist [2] with modified ranges

of partial signature correctness. Note that to slow this scheme down a corrupt player would have to reveal itself, so the adversary does not have much to gain from such active attack. Moreover, the computational cost of generating these proofs of partial signature correctness is similar to the cost of computing the partial signature itself. Finally, combining the partial signatures into the final signature σ may be carried out by any entity that has received $t + 1$ partial signatures. The cost of this operation is dominated by computation of $\gamma = m^{L^3 d_{pub}} \bmod N$, which has exponent length bounded by $(3n + 1) \log n + \log r + |N| + \tau$, which is in turn bounded by $|Ls_i|$. Therefore this computation has approximately the same cost as the generation of a partial signature. In addition, final signature computation requires computing two integers a, b s.t. $ae + bL^3 = 1$ and then performing a multiexponentiation $\sigma \leftarrow \gamma^b m^a \bmod N$. However, since a, b are independent of the message, they can be precomputed, and since $|a|, |b| \leq |L^3|$, the cost of this multiexponentiation is insignificant compared to computing $m^{L^3 d_{pub}} \bmod N$.

4 Security Arguments

We first note that *robustness* of the Update protocol follows from [2] because our proactive update protocol is the same as the protocol in [2] except for modified ranges, which does not change the robustness properties of this protocol. The robustness of the TSign protocol is also clear because it is achieved in the same way as in Rabin's proactive RSA scheme [2] or Shoup's threshold RSA scheme [1], namely through a zero-knowledge proof of discrete logarithm equality mod N, which shows that a player exponentiates the message with the proper share, to which he is committed. The assumption of safe RSA modulus plays a crucial role here, since several efficient proofs for discrete logarithm equality mod N are known, and these proofs are all generalizations of the proofs for discrete-logarithm equality on groups of known prime order, due to Chaum and Antwerpen [23,24,25] and Chaum and Pedersen [26], but such proofs are currently known to be

Input: Message $m \in Z_N^*$, public key (N, e), and outputs of the TKeyDist procedure: The private input of P_i is its polynomial share s_i, and the public input are d_{pub}, g, the verification values $\{b_k\}_{k \in [0...t]}$, where $s_i \leftarrow \sum_{j=0}^{n} s_i^{(j)}$, and $b_k \leftarrow \prod_{j=0}^{n} b_k^{(j)} \bmod N$ for all k.

1. Each player P_i broadcasts $\gamma_i \stackrel{\text{def}}{=} m^{Ls_i} \bmod N$. To enable robustness, P_i issues a (non-interactive in ROM) zero-knowledge proof (see section 4) for equality of discrete logarithms $DL[m^L, \gamma_i] = DL\left[g, \prod_{k=0}^{t}(b_k)^{(i^k)}\right]$.

2. Given values γ_i for any $(t+1)$-element set of indices T, one can compute

$$\gamma \stackrel{\text{def}}{=} (m^{L^3 d_{pub}}) \prod_{j \in T} (\gamma_j)^{L\lambda_{0,j}^T} \bmod N \text{ where } \lambda_{i,j}^T \stackrel{\text{def}}{=} \prod_{h \in T} \frac{i-h}{j-h}$$

Note that if all γ_i's are correct then $\gamma^e = m^{L^3} \bmod N$ because

$$\gamma = (m^{L^3 d_{pub}}) \prod_{j \in T} (m^{Ls_j})^{L\lambda_{0,j}^T} \bmod N$$

$$= (m^{L^3 d_{pub}})(m^{\sum_{j \in T} L^2 s_j \lambda_{0,j}^T}) \bmod N$$

$$= (m^{L^3 d_{pub}})(m^{L^3(d-d_{pub})}) = m^{L^3 d} \bmod N$$

3. From γ s.t. $\gamma^e = m^{L^3} \bmod N$ one can compute σ s.t. $\sigma^e = m \bmod N$ by the extended Euclidean algorithm, because $gcd(e, L) = 1$, which implies $gcd(e, L^3) = 1$. Specifically, compute integers a, b such that $ae + bL^3 = 1$, and set $\sigma \leftarrow \gamma^b m^a \bmod N$. Note that $\sigma^e = (m^{L^3 db + a})^e = m^{L^3 b + ae} = m \bmod N$.
   (Note that a proof of DL equality only shows that $\gamma_i = \pm m^{Ls_i} \bmod N$, but this leads to σ s.t. $\sigma^e = \pm m \bmod N$, and hence either σ or $-\sigma$ is output as a signature.)

Fig. 3. Threshold RSA signature protocol TSign

efficient only for safe RSA moduli, e.g. [13,1]. We note that these proofs actually only show that $\gamma_i = \pm m^{Ls_i}$ for the s_i committed in $\{b_k\}_{k \in [0...t]}$, but this is good enough for robust generation of RSA signatures, as we explain in step 3 of Figure 3.

We note that these proofs can be interactive in the standard model [13] or non-interactive and statistical zero-knowledge in the random-oracle model, using the Fiat-Shamir heuristic. For concreteness, we assume the second choice, since it seems more attractive in practice, and we denote by $2^{-\tau_{zk}}$ the statistical difference between the view of an execution and a simulation of this proof system. Note that in the random oracle model one can increase parameter τ_{zk} in such proofs to any desired value, e.g. 200, with only minuscule change in efficiency. This statistical difference enters into the following theorem, which states the *security* property of our scheme:

Theorem 1. (Security) *If there is a t-limited proactive adversary, for any $t < n/2$, which in time T succeeds with probability ϵ in a chosen-message attack against the proactive RSA scheme* (TKeyDist, TSign, Update), *after participating in q_s instances of the threshold signature protocol and r update rounds, then there is a Chosen Message Attack against the standard (full domain hash) RSA signature scheme, which succeeds*

Input: Public key (N, e), security parameter τ, element $g \in \mathbb{Z}_N^*$, value d_{pub}. Private input for player P_i: an additive share d_i of d, a set of verification values $\{w_j\}_{j \in [1...n]}$, a set of polynomial shares $\{s_i^{(j)}\}_{j \in [1...n]}$, and another set of verification values $\{b_k^{(j)}\}_{k \in [0...t], j \in [1...n]}$.

1. Set $R' \leftarrow \frac{R}{n} = (r + 1)N2^{\tau+1}$. Each P_i chooses $d_{i,j} \overset{\$}{\leftarrow} [R']$ for $j \in [1 \ldots n]$, and sets $d_{i,pub} \leftarrow d_i - \sum_{j=1}^{n} d_{i,j}$ (over integers). Each P_i broadcasts $d_{i,pub}$ and new d'_{pub} is set as $d'_{pub} \leftarrow d_{pub} + \sum_{i=1}^{n} d_{i,pub}$.
2. Each P_i sends $d_{i,j}$ to each P_j, sets $w_{i,j} \leftarrow g^{d_{i,j}} \bmod N$, and broadcasts $\{w_{i,j}\}_{j \in [1...n]}$. If $g^{d_{i,pub}} \prod_{j=1}^{n} w_{i,j} \neq w_i \bmod N$ then P_i is disqualified, his share d_i is reconstructed in public, and player P_i is ignored from here on.
3. Each P_j checks for all i that $d_{i,j} \in [R']$, and that $w_{i,j} = g^{d_{i,j}} \bmod N$. For all i for which either check fails, P_j requests that P_i make $d_{i,j}$ public. If any P_i fails to produce a correct $d_{i,j}$ then d_i is reconstructed and player P_i is ignored from here on.
4. Each player P_j replaces its additive share d_j as $d'_j \leftarrow \sum_{i=1}^{n} d_{i,j}$ and then shares d'_j via Feldman-Z_N-VSS with $R, \hat{\tau}$ as in TKeyDist. Let $b_0^{(j)}$ denote the verification value b_0 in the Feldman-Z_N-VSS instance with P_j as a dealer (see Figure 1). If the sharing protocol fails or if $b_0^{(j)} \neq (\prod_{j=1}^{n} w_{i,j})^L \bmod N$ then the original share d_j of P_j is reconstructed in public and P_j is thus disqualified.

Output of Player P_i: New value d'_{pub} and new additive share d'_i, a new set of verification values $\{w_j\}_{j \in [1...n]}$, where $w_j = \prod_{k=1}^{n} w_{k,j}$, new polynomial shares $\{s_i^{(j)}\}_{j \in [1...n]}$ (from n Feldman-Z_N-VSS instances in Step 4), and a corresponding new set of verification values $\{b_k^{(j)}\}_{k \in [0...t], j \in [1...n]}$.

Fig. 4. Proactive update protocol Update [2] with modified ranges

after making q_s signature queries, with probability $\epsilon - (2^{-\tau} + q_s n 2^{-\tau_{zk}})$, in time $T + (r + q_s) * p(n, \tau, |N|)$ for some small-degree polynomial p.

Proof. We show the above in the standard way, by exhibiting an efficient *simulation* of this proactive scheme, where the simulator plays the role of a CMA adversary against the standard FDH-RSA scheme on input (N, e), and it successfully translates an attack of any t-limited adversary against the proactive RSA scheme into an attack against the standard RSA scheme, except for probability upper-bounded by $2^{-\tau} + q_s n 2^{-\tau_{zk}}$. The simulation procedure we show below takes an additional time $p(n, \tau, |N|)$ to simulate the actions of the honest players in every instance of the signature and update protocol, where $p()$ is a small-degree polynomial. The exact value of $p(n, \tau, |N|)$ can be read off from the simulation procedure, but it's about the same as the time real players take to execute the scheme on such parameters, and therefore we view it as insignificant compared to the adversarial computational resources T.

We show the overall simulation procedure by showing three simulators, one for each of the three component algorithms of the scheme TKeyDist, TSign, and Update. These simulators pass information between them, which we denote as "simulated sharings" $\hat{\mathsf{Sh}}$, just like the protocols TKeyDist, TSign, and Update. More specifically, a simulator for TKeyDist outputs some initial simulated sharing $\hat{\mathsf{Sh}}_0$, and for every update round i, an execution of the simulator for Update changes $\hat{\mathsf{Sh}}_{i-1}$ to $\hat{\mathsf{Sh}}_i$. Every time the adversary triggers a threshold signature protocol on message m, the simulator asks its signature oracle for a signature σ on m under key (N, e) and simulates the signing procedure using the TSign simulator on current simulated shares Sh_i.

The theorem follows from two lemmas below, 4 and 3. By lemma 4 the statistical distance between the *simulation* of TKeyDist and r rounds of Update and the *execution* of these algorithms is at most $2^{-\tau}$, while by lemma 3 the difference between simulation and execution of all q_s instances of the TSign protocol is at most $q_s n 2^{-\tau_{zk}}$. Putting these two facts together implies the theorem.

In describing each simulator we let $\mathcal{B}$ be the set of corrupted ("bad") players, and $\mathcal{G}$ be the corresponding set of uncorrupted ("good") players. For simplicity of notation we also assume that $|\mathcal{B}| = t$ and that $n \in \mathcal{G}$. The simulation procedure does not depend on the identities of corrupted players, and we denote the index of one uncorrupted player as n purely for notational convenience. We show the simulation procedures $\mathsf{SIM}_{\mathsf{TKeyDist}}$, $\mathsf{SIM}_{\mathsf{TSign}}$, and $\mathsf{SIM}_{\mathsf{Update}}$ below, followed by the lemmas that describe the information-hiding quality of each simulation.

SECURITY OF KEY DISTRIBUTION. We start with the simulation for TKeyDist which is given in [2], with the exception of the minor modification to the generation of $\hat{d}_{pub}$, which we adopt from [3], and the fact that we are shortening the ranges in which all the values are chosen. The input to simulator $\mathsf{SIM}_{\mathsf{TKeyDist}}$ is the public key (N, e) and parameter τ. The simulator sets R and $\hat{\tau}$ as in the TKeyDist procedure, and chooses element g by picking a random square s in $\mathbb{Z}_N^*$, and setting $g_0 = s^e \bmod N$, $g = g_0^{L^2} \bmod N$, and $D = s^{L^2} \bmod N$. Note that $D = g^d \bmod N$. The simulator then simulates the sharing of d corresponding to the public key (N, e) as follows, where $\mathcal{B}$ is the set of t corrupted players:

1. Set $\hat{d} \leftarrow 0$, pick $\hat{d}_i \overset{\$}{\leftarrow} [R]$ for $1 \leq i \leq n$. Set $\hat{d}_{pub} \leftarrow \hat{d} - \sum_{i=1}^{n} \hat{d}_i$.
2. Let $\hat{w}_i \leftarrow g^{\hat{d}_i} \bmod N$ for $1 \leq i \leq n-1$, and $\hat{w}_n \leftarrow D/g^{\hat{d}_{pub}} \prod_{i=1}^{n-1} \hat{w}_i \bmod N$.
3. For $1 \leq j \leq n-1$, share $\hat{d}_j$ via Feldman-Z_N-VSS using $R, \hat{\tau}, N$, and g. Denote the resulting shares $\{\hat{s}_i^{(j)}\}_{i \in [0...n]}$ and verification values $\{\hat{b}_k^{(j)}\}_{k \in [0...t]}$.
4. Generate shares $\{\hat{s}_i^{(n)}\}_{i \in \mathcal{B}}$ by sharing any value in $[R]$ using Feldman-Z_N-VSS, and then use these shares together with values g_0, g and $\hat{w}_n$ (the last value playing the role of g^s), to generate the Feldman-Z_N-VSS verification values $\{\hat{b}_k^{(n)}\}_{k \in [0...t]}$ via the procedure from Lemma 2.
5. Denote $\hat{s}_i \leftarrow \sum_{j=0}^{n} \hat{s}_i^{(j)}$.

It is easy to see that since the difference between the values d in execution and $\hat{d}$ in the simulation is at most N, the difference between the distribution of values $\{d_1, ..., d_{n-1}, d_{pub}\}$ in the execution and the above simulation is at most N/R, essentially because the one unknown value d_n, is uniformly chosen over $[-R, R]$, and it acts as a one-time pad for the secret d (imperfect, because computed over integers, but statistically hiding). Next, by lemma 1, the difference between the view of Feldman-Z_N-VSS in the execution, where it shares value d_n, and in the simulation, where it shares value $\hat{d}_n$, is at most $2^{-\hat{\tau}}$. The rest of the simulation is perfect by lemma 2. Therefore the total distance is upper-bounded by $N/R + 2^{-\hat{\tau}} \leq 2^{-\tau - \log(r+1)}$.

SECURITY OF THRESHOLD SIGNATURE. We show a simulator $\mathsf{SIM}_{\mathsf{TSign}}$ of the TSign procedure. The input to the simulator is a message/signature pair (m, σ), the public key (N, e), and all information created in the simulation of TKeyDist, but most importantly $\hat{d}_{pub}$ and shares $\{\hat{s}_i\}_{i\in\mathcal{B}}$ issued to the set of corrupted players $\mathcal{B}$, defined in step 5 of the simulation of TKeyDist.

Let $\mathcal{G}$ be the set of uncorrupted players, and let $T = \{0\} \cup \mathcal{B}$. The information the adversary sees during an execution of TSign is γ_j's for all $j \in \mathcal{G}$, which $\mathsf{SIM}_{\mathsf{TSign}}$ creates, for all $j \in \mathcal{G}$, as follows:

$$\hat{\gamma}_j \leftarrow (\sigma/m^{\hat{d}_{pub}})^{L^2\lambda_{j,0}^T} \prod_{i\in\mathcal{B}} m^{L\lambda_{j,i}^T\hat{s}_i} \bmod N$$

where $\lambda_{j,i}^T$ is a Lagrange coefficient, defined in Figure 3. The adversary also sees the zero-knowledge proofs performed by players in $\mathcal{G}$, which $\mathsf{SIM}_{\mathsf{TSign}}$ simulates.

The values $\hat{\gamma}_j$ created by the simulator coincide exactly with the values created in the real execution on the same shares $\{s_i\}_{i\in\mathcal{B}}$, d_{pub}, and e (which defines d): Let $f(x)$ be the unique degree t polynomial such that (1) $f(0) = L(d - \hat{d}_{pub})$ where d is the secret key corresponding to the public key (N, e), and (2) $f(i) = \hat{s}_i$ for all $i \in \mathcal{B}$.

$$\hat{\gamma}_j = (m^{d-\hat{d}_{pub}})^{L^2\lambda_{j,0}^T} \prod_{i\in\mathcal{B}} m^{L\lambda_{j,i}^T\hat{s}_i} = \prod_{i\in T} m^{L\lambda_{j,i}^T f(i)} = m^{Lf(j)} \bmod N$$

The only difference between this simulation and the corresponding execution is at most $n2^{-\tau_{zk}}$ statistical difference between the adversarial view of, respectively, the executions and the simulations, of the zero-knowledge proofs of DL equality performed by the uncorrupted players. This implies the following lemma:

Lemma 3. *For any m, an RSA instance (N, e, d), any value d_{pub}, any set of t players $\mathcal{B}$ corrupted by an adversary, and any set of shares $S_\mathcal{B} = \{s_i\}_{i\in\mathcal{B}}$, the statistical difference between the adversary's view of the execution of the TSign protocol on m, N, e, d_{pub}, and shares $\{s_i\}_{i\notin\mathcal{B}}$ corresponding to $S_\mathcal{B}, d_{pub}, d$, and the adversary's view of the simulation $\mathsf{SIM}_{\mathsf{TSign}}$ on inputs m, N, e, d_{pub}, signature $\sigma = m^d \bmod N$, and shares $S_\mathcal{B}$, is at most $n2^{-\tau_{zk}}$.*

SECURITY OF PROACTIVE UPDATE. We show a simulator $\mathsf{SIM}_{\mathsf{Update}}$ for the proactive update protocol which is similar to the simulator for TKeyDist. Recall that $\mathcal{B}$ is the set of corrupt players and $\mathcal{G}$ is the set of correct players. During an execution of Update, the adversary sees the following values: $\{d_{i,j}\}_{i\in\mathcal{G},j\in\mathcal{B}}$, $\{d_{i,pub}\}_{i\in\mathcal{G}}$, $\{w_{i,j}\}_{i\in\mathcal{G},j\in[1...n]}$, $\{s_j^{(i)}\}_{i\in\mathcal{G},j\in\mathcal{B}}$, and $\{b_k^{(i)}\}_{i\in\mathcal{G},k\in[1...t]}$. The simulator proceeds on input (N, e) and all information created by $\mathsf{SIM}_{\mathsf{TKeyDist}}$ as follows:

1. For each $i \in \mathcal{G}, j \in [1 \ldots n]$, choose $\hat{d}_{i,j} \xleftarrow{\$} [R']$ and set $\hat{d}_{i,pub} \leftarrow \hat{d}_i - \sum_{j=1}^n \hat{d}_{i,j}$ (over integers).

2. Set $\hat{w}_{i,j} \leftarrow g^{\hat{d}_{i,j}} \bmod N$ for each $i \in \mathcal{G}\backslash\{n\}, j \in [1 \ldots n]$, and set $\hat{w}_{n,j} \leftarrow g^{\hat{d}_{n,j}} \bmod N$, but $\hat{w}_{n,n} \leftarrow \hat{w}_n/g^{\hat{d}_{n,pub}} \prod_{j=1}^{n-1} \hat{w}_{n,j} \bmod N$.

3. Set $\hat{d}_i \leftarrow \sum_{j=1}^n \hat{d}_{i,j}$. For $i \in \mathcal{G} \setminus \{n\}$, create a Feldman-$Z_N$-VSS sharing of $\hat{d}_i$. To simulate the sharing of $\hat{d}_n$, follow the same procedure as in step 4 of SIM$_{\mathsf{TKeyDist}}$, i.e. generate $\{\hat{s}_i^{(n)}\}_{i \in \mathcal{B}}$ via the sharing procedure of Feldman-Z_N-VSS, and generate the matching verification values via Lemma 2.

4. If the adversary triggers any reconstructions, then follow the reconstruction procedure as in the protocol. Note that the reconstruction will only involve Feldman-Z_N-VSS shares distributed by the adversary, since only corrupt players can have their additive shares reconstructed in this manner.

We now argue that the above simulation procedure, along with the simulation of TKeyDist (presented and argued earlier) imply that the statistical difference between a simulation and an execution of TKeyDist followed in each case by r rounds of Update is upper-bounded $2^{-\tau}$. The Update simulator takes as input the values created by SIM$_{\mathsf{TKeyDist}}$, and we argued above that the outputs of SIM$_{\mathsf{TKeyDist}}$ have statistical distance at most $N/R + 2^{-\hat{\tau}}$, where $R = n(r+1)2^{\tau+1}$ and $\hat{\tau} = \tau + \log r + 2$, from the same values created in an execution of TKeyDist.

Note that the additive shares $\hat{d}_{i,j}$ which the simulator sends to the adversary are distributed identically to the corresponding values in the real execution. However, for the one player P_n on which the simulation diverges from the execution, even though the adversary does not see values $\{d_{n,i}\}_{i \notin \mathcal{B}}$, and in particular it does not see $d_{n,n}$, the revealed value $d_{n,pub}$ can be seen as result of an application of an imperfect one-time pad to d_n (imperfect because computed over integers). However, since the difference between d and $\hat{d}$ is at most N, and the additive shares in this re-sharing protocol are chosen from range $[R']$, the total statistical distance introduced by revealing $d_{i,pub}$ values for $i \notin \mathcal{B}$ in this additive re-sharing of d is upper-bounded by N/R'. In step 3, the fact that the Feldman-Z_N-VSS sharing for player P_n has to be simulated contributes additional statistical distance of at most $2^{-\hat{\tau}}$, by Lemma 1. Therefore, the total statistical distance between the real and simulated executions of TKeyDist and r rounds of Update is $N/R + 2^{-\hat{\tau}} + r(N/R' + 2^{-\hat{\tau}})$, which is upper-bounded by $2^{-\tau}$. This implies the following lemma:

Lemma 4. *For RSA instance (N, e, d), a security parameter τ, any sequence of t sets of players $\mathcal{B}_1, ..., \mathcal{B}_r$ corrupted in r rounds of the proactive scheme, there is at most $2^{-\tau}$ statistical difference between the adversary's view of an execution of the TKeyDist on inputs (N, e, d) and τ, followed by r executions of procedure Update on the resulting outputs, and the adversary's view of an execution of the SIM$_{\mathsf{TKeyDist}}$ on inputs (N, e) and τ, followed by r executions of SIM$_{\mathsf{Update}}$.*

References

1. Shoup, V.: Practical Threshold Signatures. In: Preneel, B. (ed.) EUROCRYPT 2000. LNCS, vol. 1807, pp. 207–220. Springer, Heidelberg (2000)
2. Rabin, T.: A simplified approach to threshold and proactive RSA. In: Krawczyk, H. (ed.) CRYPTO 1998. LNCS, vol. 1462, pp. 89–104. Springer, Heidelberg (1998)
3. Jarecki, S., Saxena, N.: Further simplifications in proactive RSA signatures. In: Kilian, J. (ed.) TCC 2005. LNCS, vol. 3378, pp. 510–528. Springer, Heidelberg (2005)

4. Desmedt, Y., Frankel, Y.: Threshold Cryptosystems. In: Brassard, G. (ed.) CRYPTO 1989. LNCS, vol. 435, pp. 307–315. Springer, Heidelberg (1990)
5. Herzberg, A., Jarecki, S., Krawczyk, H., Yung, M.: Proactive secret sharing or: How to cope with perpetual leakage. In: Coppersmith, D. (ed.) CRYPTO 1995. LNCS, vol. 963, pp. 339–352. Springer, Heidelberg (1995)
6. Herzberg, A., Jakobsson, M., Jarecki, S., Krawczyk, H., Yung, M.: Proactive Public Key and Signature Systems. In: Proc. ACM CCS 1997, pp. 100–110 (1997)
7. Ostrovsky, R., Yung, M.: How to Withstand Mobile Virus Attacks. In: 10th ACM Symp.on the Principles of Distributed Computing (PODC), pp. 51–61 (1991)
8. Amir, Y., Danilov, C., Dolev, D., Kirsch, J., Lane, J., Nita-Rotaru, C., Olsen, J., Zage, D.: STEWARD: Scaling byzantine fault-tolerant replication to wide area networks. Technical Report CNDS-2006-2, Johns Hopkins University (2006)
9. Saxena, N., Tsudik, G., Yi, J.H.: Admission Control in Peer-to-Peer: Design and Performance Evaluation. In: ACM Workshop on Security of Ad Hoc and Sensor Networks (SASN), pp. 104–114 (October 2003)
10. Frankel, Y., Desmedt, Y.: Parallel Reliable Threshold Multisignature. Technical Report TR-92-04-02, Dept.of EE and CS, U.of Winsconsin (April 1992)
11. De Santis, A., Desmedt, Y., Frankel, Y., Yung, M.: How to share a function securely. In: Proc. 26th STOC, pp. 522–533. ACM, New York (1994)
12. Frankel, Y., Gemmell, P., Yung, M.: Witness-based Cryptographic Program Checking and Robust Function Sharing. In: Proc. 28th STOC, pp. 499–508. ACM, New York (1996)
13. Gennaro, R., Jarecki, S., Krawczyk, H., Rabin, T.: Robust and efficient sharing of RSA functions. Journal of Cryptology 13(2), 273–300 (2000)
14. Damgård, I., Koprowski, M.: Practical threshold RSA signatures without a trusted dealer. In: Pfitzmann, B. (ed.) EUROCRYPT 2001. LNCS, vol. 2045, pp. 152–165. Springer, Heidelberg (2001)
15. Damgård, I., Dupont, K.: Efficient threshold RSA signatures with general moduli and no extra assumptions. In: Vaudenay, S. (ed.) PKC 2005. LNCS, vol. 3386, pp. 346–361. Springer, Heidelberg (2005)
16. Frankel, Y., Gemmell, P., MacKenzie, P.D., Yung, M.: Proactive RSA. In: Kaliski Jr., B.S. (ed.) CRYPTO 1997. LNCS, vol. 1294, pp. 440–454. Springer, Heidelberg (1997)
17. Frankel, Y., Gemmell, P., MacKenzie, P.D., Yung, M.: Optimal-Resilience Proactive Public-Key Cryptosystems. In: 38th FOCS, pp. 384–393. ACM, New York (1997)
18. Canetti, R., Gennaro, R., Jarecki, S., Krawczyk, H., Rabin, T.: Adaptive security for threshold cryptosystems. In: Wiener, M.J. (ed.) CRYPTO 1999. LNCS, vol. 1666, pp. 98–115. Springer, Heidelberg (1999)
19. Frankel, Y., MacKenzie, P.D., Yung, M.: Adaptive security for the additive-sharing based proactive RSA. In PKC 2001 (PKC 2001). In: Kim, K.-c. (ed.) PKC 2001. LNCS, vol. 1992, pp. 240–263. Springer, Heidelberg (2001)
20. Almansa, J.F., Damgård, I., Nielsen, J.B.: Simplified threshold RSA with adaptive and proactive security. In: Vaudenay, S. (ed.) EUROCRYPT 2006. LNCS, vol. 4004, pp. 593–611. Springer, Heidelberg (2006)
21. Damgård, I., Fujisaki, E.: A statistically-hiding integer commitment scheme based on groups with hidden order. In: Zheng, Y. (ed.) ASIACRYPT 2002. LNCS, vol. 2501, pp. 125–142. Springer, Heidelberg (2002)
22. Bellare, M., Rogaway, P.: The exact security of digital signatures - how to sign with RSA and Rabin. In: Maurer, U.M. (ed.) EUROCRYPT 1996. LNCS, vol. 1070, pp. 399–416. Springer, Heidelberg (1996)

23. Chaum, D., Antwerpen, H.V.: Undeniable signatures. In: Brassard, G. (ed.) CRYPTO 1989. LNCS, vol. 435, pp. 212–216. Springer, Heidelberg (1990)
24. Chaum, D.: Zero-knowledge undeniable signatures. In: Damgård, I.B. (ed.) EUROCRYPT 1990. LNCS, vol. 473, pp. 458–464. Springer, Heidelberg (1991)
25. Boyar, J., Chaum, D., Damgård, I., Pedersen, T.P.: Convertible undeniable signatures. In: Menezes, A., Vanstone, S.A. (eds.) CRYPTO 1990. LNCS, vol. 537, pp. 189–205. Springer, Heidelberg (1991)
26. Chaum, D., Pedersen, T.P.: Wallet databases with observers. In: Brickell, E.F. (ed.) CRYPTO 1992. LNCS, vol. 740, pp. 89–105. Springer, Heidelberg (1993)

Fair Traceable Multi-Group Signatures

Vicente Benjumea[1,*], Seung Geol Choi[2], Javier Lopez[1,*], and Moti Yung[3]

[1] Computer Science Dept. University of Malaga, Spain
{benjumea,jlm}@lcc.uma.es
[2] Computer Science Dept. Columbia University, USA
sgchoi@cs.columbia.edu
[3] Google Inc. & Computer Science Dept. Columbia University, USA
moti@cs.columbia.edu

Abstract. This paper presents fair traceable multi-group signatures (FTMGS), which have enhanced capabilities, compared to group and traceable signatures, that are important in real world scenarios combining accountability and anonymity. The main goal of the primitive is to allow multiple groups that are managed separately (managers are not even aware of the other ones), yet allowing users (in the spirit of the Identity 2.0 initiative) to manage what they reveal about their identity with respect to these groups by themselves. This new primitive incorporates the following additional features.

- While considering multiple groups it discourages users from sharing their private membership keys through two orthogonal and complementary approaches. In fact, it merges functionality similar to credential systems with anonymous type of signing with revocation.
- The group manager now mainly manages joining procedures, and new entities (called fairness authorities and consisting of various representatives, possibly) are involved in opening and revealing procedures. In many systems scenario assuring fairness in anonymity revocation is required.

We specify the notion and implement it in the random oracle model.

1 Introduction

Group signatures. Group signatures, introduced by Chaum and Van Heyst [12], and later studied and improved [10,2,24,26], were a major step in designing cryptographic primitives supporting anonymity. In these schemes, users join groups and issue signatures on behalf of the group. When these signatures are verified, we learn that some member of the group generated them, but not which one. It is also impossible to link two signatures generated by the same member of the group. However, the *group manager* has the capability of opening a signature and trace its signer among the members of the group (in [24] managing join of users and tracing by separate authorities was suggested).

---

* This work has been partially supported by the project CRISIS (TIN2006-09242) and Consolider project ARES (CSD2007-00004), funded by the Spanish Ministry of Education and Science.

G. Tsudik (Ed.): FC 2008, LNCS 5143, pp. 231–246, 2008.

Multi-group signatures and sharing private keys. Ateniese et al. [3] extended group signatures to deal with the case where a single anonymous user has to prove that she is simultaneously a member of several groups. In this scenario, a multi-group membership is proved by zero-knowledge proof of equality on some discrete logarithms in the signatures from different groups. Though multi-group signatures are based on the ability of linking some designated group signatures (via equality proofs), such a fact does not affect the main properties of group signatures such as anonymity and unlinkability for other signatures. Note that the multi-group feature is very interesting in anonymous authorization scenarios, since in these environments it is quite common for a user to prove simultaneous possession of some properties in order to be authorized to carry out some transaction. However, the scheme due to [3], as mentioned in the paper, presents some problems when linking signatures from groups that are managed separately with unrelated group keys.

Also, if a user is able to share some of the private keys with other users in a multi-group anonymous environment, it is a severe handicap in a system where privileges depend upon membership to some groups, since this sharing of private keys would undermine the whole system assumptions.

Embedding some valuable information into sensitive data is a commonly used method to dissuade users from sharing their private key. Dwork et al. [13] embedded some user's valuable information, such as the credit card number, into a key in order to protect digital content from illegal redistribution. Also, Goldreich et al. [19] presented several schemes to deter propagation of secondary secret keys in the field of self-delegation of personalized rights. Moreover, Lysyanskaya et al. [25] embedded a user's master secret key into the secret that allows a user to prove possession of a credential on a pseudonym.

Traceable signatures. In group signatures, under critical circumstances such as dishonest behavior, the group manager is able to open a signature and identify the dishonest user. If a user is under suspicion, a judge may decide to identify which transactions were performed by such user. In this latter case, the group manager has to open all selected signatures to identify which ones were issued by the user under suspicion. This approach has two main disadvantages: (i) it discloses the identity of the issuers of the signatures, violating their privacy, even for honest members; and (ii) the group manager has to be involved in this heavy task, being a potential bottleneck for scalability.

Taking into account the above scenario, Kiayias et al. [23] introduced *traceable signatures* as a group signature scheme with further refinement of tracing under anonymity. This primitive incorporates a feature that enables the group manager to reveal a trapdoor for a given member of the group. The trapdoor allows the tracing agents to identify which signatures were issued by the member under suspicion without revealing any further information. This approach benefits us by removing the aforementioned disadvantages: (i) the privacy of non-involved members remains unaltered; and (ii) the group manager is relieved from this task, which can be performed by several tracing agents. Additionally, traceable signatures also incorporate a claiming facility, that allows a member to claim that a given signature was issued by herself.

Splitting roles of the group manager. It is usually accepted that the group manager is a trusted party with respect to joining new members to the group. However, in many scenarios the group manager is a party in interest, and therefore it can not be trusted with respect to user's privacy. For example, a company can manage a group for employees and a group for clients, and can be trusted with respect to joining users that are actually employees or clients respectively. However, the company does not offer any guarantee with respect to keep users' privacy, specially when they carry out anonymous transactions with the company itself.

We note that in group signatures, there have been several proposals to divide the duties of the group manager into two entities [24,26], one responsible for joining new members and the other one responsible for opening signatures. However, in the context of traceable signatures such splitting of duties has not been considered yet.

Our contribution. This paper presents Fair Traceable Multi-Group Signatures (FTMGS, pronounced: fat-mugs), a new primitive that supports anonymity with extended concerns that rise in realistic scenarios. It can be regarded as a primitive that has the flavor of anonymous signatures with various revocations but with a refined notion of access control (via multiple groups) and thus supporting anonymous activities in a fashion similar to anonymous credential systems [25,8]. The main issues that make this primitive suitable to various trust relationships are:

- It provides anonymous and unlinkable signatures in the way group and traceable signatures do.
- It includes multi-group features to guarantee that several signatures have been issued by the same anonymous user with no detriment of user's anonymity. This allows limited local linkability most useful in many cases (linking are user controlled).
- It includes a mechanism to dissuade the group members from sharing their private membership keys. This is very useful in increasing the incentive for better "access control" to anonymous credentials.
- It further splits the duties of the group manager into several authorities, allowing better control over opening and tracing operations. Now the group manager manages only joining. Newly introduced parties, whom we call *fairness authorities*, by cooperating with each other, manage opening signatures and revealing tracing trapdoors. A single fairness authority alone cannot do the opening or revealing. In this way, a user's sensitive information can be guaranteed only to be disclosed when there exist enough reasons.

Let us next further elaborate on some of the above characteristics of the primitive. With respect to multi-group features, as opposed to the scheme introduced in [3], group management is separate and groups are formed where group managers are not necessarily aware of each other. There is no coordination and group keys are solely under the control of its group manager (based on some accepted security parameters). At the user level, however, management of identity is up to herself; linking signatures and claiming identity are executed according to her desire. This latter approach is in concordance with the identity 2.0 [20] effort.

General scenario for this new primitive. The group manager creates a group with the collaboration of designated fairness authorities[1]. A user, that has been authorized by some external procedure, is able to join the group by engaging in an interactive protocol with the group manager. The external user's authentication can be based on her identity[2] or even an anonymous authentication supported by this new primitive. At the end of the procedure, the group manager gets some sensitive data regarding the new member (i.e. join transcript with authentication information), and the user gets a membership private key that enables her to issue signatures on behalf of the group.

When a user wants to carry out a transaction with a server, she sometimes has to generate a proof to show she has the required privilege. This proof usually implies that she belongs to several groups. In this case, she issues suitable signatures for the involved groups, and establishes a link among them to guarantee that they have been issued by the same single anonymous user.

Under critical circumstances, fairness authorities and the judge open a signature to identify a malicious user. If necessary, they may also reveal her tracing trapdoor so that tracing agents, using the trapdoor, trace all the transactions she issued.

2   A Model for Fair Traceable Multi-Group Signatures

In this section, we present our model for fair traceable multi-group signatures. We describe the types of entities and operations in the system. See Figure 1 for the notations used in the model.

Participating Entities. There are five types of participating entities: users, group managers, fairness authorities, tracing agents, and the judge.

- Users join groups and generate signatures, claims, link-claims, etc. Usually, users join groups if the group manager authorizes it.
- Each group has one group manager, which manages joining and the corresponding database.
- Each group has multiple fairness authorities. They cooperate together, under the judge's supervision, to either open a signature or to reveal a tracing key of a user under suspicion.
- Each group has multiple tracing agents. They trace the transaction databases and find out signatures related to the revealed tracing key.
- The judge manages opening and tracing operations with the help of the group manager, fairness authorities and tracing agents.
- It is assumed that an external PKI provides legal binding between users and public keys, such that users do not want to lend their corresponding private keys to any other user, since actions performed under these public keys entail legal responsibilities.

---

[1] Roughly Speaking, in order to split the roles, the group manager creates a part of group key related to joining procedure, and the fairness authorities create the other part related to opening and tracing procedures.

[2] A certified public key via PKI based on discrete logarithm (e.g., DSA, El-Gamal signatures, Schnorr signatures).

1. parameters
   ν: security parameter ζ: the number of fairness authorities
2. G^v: the group (i.e., service provider) with index v
3. participating entities
   GM^v: group manager of the group G^v U_i: user i J: judge
   $FA_j{}^v$: j-th fairness authority of G^v $TA_j{}^v$: j-th tracing agent of G^v
4. various keys and data
   gpk^v: group public key of G^v gsk^v: private key of GM^v
   $fgsk^v$: fairness private key of G^v $fgsk_j{}^v$: $FA_j{}^v$'s share for $fgsk^v$
   umk_i: master secret key of U_i. usk_i^v: signing key of U_i w.r.t. G^v
   $jlog_i^v$: join transcript generated while U_i joins the group G^v
   σ: signature $auth_i$: authentication string issued by U_i
   $\tau_i{}^v$: tracing key for U_i in G^v
   ω_σ: member reference (locator used to search for the corresponding join transcript)
5. predicates w.r.t $jlog_i^v$, usk_i^v and $auth_i$
   $mkey(usk_i^v$ or $auth_i)$: master secret key of usk_i^v or $auth_i$
   $mref(jlog_i^v$ or $usk_i^v)$: member reference of $jlog_i^v$ or usk_i^v
   $tkey(jlog_i^v$ or $usk_i^v)$: tracing key of $jlog_i^v$ or usk_i^v
6. etc
   acc: accept $\perp$: error m: message γ: challenge string

Fig. 1. Legends of our model for fair traceable multi-group signatures

Operations. A fair traceable multi-group signature scheme consists of the following operations. Two operations are newly added compared with original traceable signatures: CLAIMLINK and VERIFYLINK. The rest of the operations are slightly changed so that fairness authorities may be involved.

1. SETUP($1^\nu, \zeta$). This interactive procedure generates the group public key gpk^v, the secret key gsk^v for the group manager and the secret keys $\{fgsk_j{}^v\}_{j=1}^\zeta$ for the fairness authorities.
2. JOIN($gpk^v, [gsk^v], [umk_i]$). This interactive procedure is used when a user joins a group, where the group public key gpk^v is common input, and the group secret key gsk^v and user master key umk_i are private inputs of the group manager and the user respectively. As result, the group manager gets a join transcript $jlog_i^v$ and the user gets a membership private key usk_i^v.
3. JOINONAUTH($gpk^v, auth_i, [gsk^v], [umk_i]$). This interactive procedure is used when an authenticated user joins a group, where the group public key gpk^v and user authentication string $auth_i$ are common input, and the group secret key gsk^v and user master key umk_i are private inputs of the group manager and the user respectively. Depending on the situation, the authentication string $auth_i$ can be a public key, a digital signature, a traceable signature of another group or combination of them. We require that the key used to generate $auth_i$ should have umk_i as its part. As result, the group manager gets a join transcript $jlog_i^v$ and the user gets a membership private key usk_i^v.

4. SIGN(gpk^v, usk_i^v, m). With this algorithm, a member generates a group signature σ on message m.

5. VERIFY(gpk^v, m, σ). Any entity can verify a signature σ on a message m.

6. OPEN(gpk^v, σ, $[\{\text{fgsk}_j^v\}_{j=1}^\zeta]$). This interactive procedure opens a signature σ, generating a reference ω_σ to the member that issued it. It requires the private inputs of the fairness authorities' secret keys $\{\text{fgsk}_j^v\}_{j=1}^\zeta$.

7. REVEAL(gpk^v, jlog_i^v, $[\{\text{fgsk}_j^v\}_{j=1}^\zeta]$). This interactive procedure reveals the member tracing key τ_i^v from the join transcript jlog_i^v. It requires the private inputs of the fairness authorities' secret keys $\{\text{fgsk}_j^v\}_{j=1}^\zeta$.

8. TRACE(gpk^v, σ, τ_i^v). This tracing algorithm allows the tracing agents to check if the signature σ is associated with the tracing key τ_i^v.

9. CLAIM(gpk^v, usk_i^v, σ, γ). This algorithm generates an authorship proof π for a signature σ on the challenge γ.

10. VERIFYCLAIM(gpk^v, σ, γ, π). Any entity can verify an authorship proof π of a signature σ on a challenge γ.

11. CLAIMLINK(gpk^{v_1}, $\text{usk}_i^{v_1}$, σ^1, gpk^{v_2}, $\text{usk}_i^{v_2}$, σ^2, γ). This algorithm generates a link proof λ between two signatures σ^1, σ^2 on the challenge γ, if the two signatures have been issued with the same master key.

12. VERIFYLINK(gpk^{v_1}, σ^1, gpk^{v_2}, σ^2, γ, λ). Any entity can verify a link proof λ between two signatures σ^1, σ^2 on a challenge γ.

3 Preliminaries

Notation. We denote $\{0, \ldots, \ell - 1\}$ by $[\ell]$. Throughout the paper we work mostly in the group of quadratic residues modulo n, denoted by $QR(n)$, with $n = pq$, for safe primes p and q ($p = 2p' + 1$ and $q = 2q' + 1$). Let the security parameter $\nu := \lceil \log p'q' \rceil$. We define the following sets:

$$\Lambda = \{1, \ldots, 2^{\nu/4} - 1\}, \quad \text{M} = \{1, \ldots, 2^{\nu/2} - 1\},$$
$$\Gamma = \{2^{3\nu/4-1} + 1, \ldots, 2^{3\nu/4-1} + 2^{\nu/2} - 1\},$$
$$\Lambda_\epsilon^k = \{1 + \Delta_{\nu/4}, \ldots, 2^{\nu/4} - 1 - \Delta_{\nu/4}\}, \quad \text{M}_\epsilon^k = \{1 + \Delta_{\nu/2}, \ldots, 2^{\nu/2} - 1 - \Delta_{\nu/2}\},$$
$$\Gamma_\epsilon^k = \{2^{3\nu/4-1} + 1 + \Delta_{\nu/2}, \ldots, 2^{3\nu/4-1} + 2^{\nu/2} - 1 - \Delta_{\nu/2}\},$$

where $\Delta_\mu = 2^{\mu-1} - 2^{\frac{\mu-2}{\epsilon}-k}$ for $\epsilon > 1$ and $k > 128$. Sometimes we will call the sets $\Lambda, \text{M}, \Gamma$ spheres, and $\Lambda_\epsilon^k, \text{M}_\epsilon^k, \Gamma_\epsilon^k$ inner spheres.

Assumptions. Below are listed the assumptions we use in the paper.

Definition 1. (Strong-RSA [4]). *Given $n = pq$, where p and q are both safe primes, and $z \in QR(n)$, it is hard to find $u \in \mathbb{Z}_n$ and $e > 1$ such that $u^e = z \pmod{n}$.*

Definition 2. (Decision Composite Residuosity [27]) *n is as above. Consider the group $\mathbb{Z}_{n^2}$ and the subgroup $\mathbf{P}$ of $\mathbb{Z}_{n^2}^*$ consisting of all n-th powers of elements in $\mathbb{Z}_{n^2}^*$, it is hard to distinguish random elements of $\mathbb{Z}_{n^2}^*$ from random elements of $\mathbf{P}$.*

Definition 3. (Discrete-Logarithm) *Given two values a, b of a multiplicative group Z_n^* or $\mathbb{Z}_{n^2}^*$ it is hard to find x such that $a^x = b$ even if the factorization of n is known.*

Definition 4. (Decisional Diffie-Hellman [23]) *Given a generator g of a cyclic group $QR(n)$ where n is as above, define $\mathcal{D} := \{(g, g^x, g^y, g^{xy}) : x \in \mathcal{B}_1, y \in \mathcal{B}_2\}$ and $\mathcal{R} := \{(g, g^x, g^y, g^z) : x \in \mathcal{B}_1, y \in \mathcal{B}_2, z \in \mathcal{B}_3\}$, where $\mathcal{B}_i$ $(1 \le i \le 3)$ is Λ, M, Γ, or $[p'q']$. Define the DDH advantage of $\mathcal{A}$ as*

$$\mathsf{Adv}_{\mathcal{A}}^{\mathsf{DDH}}(\nu) = \Big| \mathrm{Pr}_{v \in \mathcal{D}}[\mathcal{A}(1^\nu, v) = 1] - \mathrm{Pr}_{v \in \mathcal{R}}[\mathcal{A}(1^\nu, v) = 1] \Big|.$$

Then for any PPT algorithm $\mathcal{A}$, we have $\mathsf{Adv}_{\mathcal{A}}^{\mathsf{DDH}}(\nu) = neg(\nu)$.
Kiayias et al. [24] showed that DDH over $QR(n)$ does not depend on the hardness of factoring, that is, if $\mathsf{Adv}_{\mathcal{A}}^{\mathsf{DDH}}(\nu) = neg(\nu)$ for a cyclic group modulo a safe prime, then $\mathsf{Adv}_{\mathcal{A}}^{\mathsf{DDH\text{-}KF}}(\nu) = neg(\nu)$ for the cyclic group of quadratic residues modulo a safe composite with known factorization.

Definition 5. (Cross Group DDH [21]) *Given generators g_1, g_2 of $QR(n_1)$ and $QR(n_2)$ where n_1 and n_2 are as above, $n_1 \neq n_2$, and $\nu_1 = \nu_2$, we define $\mathcal{D} := \{(g_1, g_1^x, g_2, g_2^x) : x \in \mathcal{B}_1 \cap \mathcal{B}_2\}$ and $\mathcal{R} := \{(g_1, g_1^x, g_2, g_2^y) : x, y \in \mathcal{B}_1 \cap \mathcal{B}_2\}$, where $\mathcal{B}_i$ $(1 \le i \le 2)$ is Λ_i, M_i, Γ_i, or $[p'_i q'_i]$. Define the advantage of $\mathcal{A}$ as*

$$\mathsf{Adv}_{\mathcal{A}}^{\mathsf{CG\text{-}DDH}}(\nu_1) = \Big| \mathrm{Pr}_{v \in \mathcal{D}}[\mathcal{A}(1^{\nu_1}, v) = 1] - \mathrm{Pr}_{v \in \mathcal{R}}[\mathcal{A}(1^{\nu_1}, v) = 1] \Big|.$$

Then for any PPT algorithm $\mathcal{A}$, we have $\mathsf{Adv}_{\mathcal{A}}^{\mathsf{CG\text{-}DDH}}(\nu_1) = neg(\nu_1)$.
We also assume that $\mathsf{Adv}_{\mathcal{A}}^{\mathsf{CG\text{-}DDH\text{-}KF}}(\nu_1) = neg(\nu_1)$ for the cyclic group of quadratic residues modulo a safe composite with known factorization.

In other words, the CG-DDH assumption states that it is infeasible to test equality of discrete logs across groups.

4 Building Blocks

Signature of Knowledge of Discrete Logarithm. We use the notation due to Camenisch and Stadler [10] for signatures of knowledge of discrete logarithms. For example, $SK\{(a, b) : y = g^a; z = h^a f^b\}(m)$ denotes a *signature of knowledge of integers a and b on m such that $y = g^a$ and $z = h^a f^b$ holds.*

Kiayias et al. [23] presented a scheme for signatures of knowledge in discrete-log relation sets and proved its security. Here we only briefly describe how it works by taking an example[3]. Consider the following signature of knowledge of a discrete logarithm: $SK\{ (x) : y = g^x \pmod{n} ; \gamma = \beta^x \pmod{\rho} \}(m)$. It can be represented as the following triangular discrete-log relation set:

$$\begin{bmatrix} \text{Objects}: & y & g & \gamma & \beta & \\ \hline y = g^x : & -1 & x & 0 & 0 & (\bmod\ n) \\ \gamma = \beta^x : & 0 & 0 & -1 & x & (\bmod\ \rho) \end{bmatrix}.$$

The signature of knowledge for this relation is $\langle c, s_x \rangle$, where $B_1 = g^{t_x} \pmod{n}$ (t_x is chosen randomly), $B_2 = \beta^{t_x} \pmod{\rho}$, $c = \mathrm{Hash}(B_1, B_2, g, n, y, \beta, \rho, \gamma, \mathit{env\text{-}data}, m)$ and $s_x = t_x - cx$. Verification is done by computing $B'_1 = g^{s_x} y^c \pmod{n}$, $B'_2 = \beta^{s_x} \gamma^c \pmod{\rho}$ and checking if $c \overset{?}{=} \mathrm{Hash}(B'_1, B'_2, g, n, y, \beta, \rho, \gamma, \mathit{env\text{-}data}, m)$.

---

[3] For simplicity, we ignored details on range checking of discrete log variable. See [23] for more technical detail.

DL-Representations. In the exposition below we use some fixed values $a_0, a, b \in QR(n)$.

Definition 6. (DL-Representation [23]) *A discrete-log representation is a tuple $\langle A, e, x, x' \rangle$ such that $A^e = a^x b^{x'} a_0$ holds where $x \in M$, $x' \in \Lambda$ and $e \in \Gamma$.*

Note that we changed the range of x to M (originally the range was Λ) in order to ensure the hardness of the following problem in the adaptive setting.

Definition 7. (Adaptive One-More Representation Problem) *Let Q_{rep} be an oracle that, on input $x'_i \in \Lambda$, ouputs A_i, e_i, x_i such that $A_i^{e_i} = a^{x_i} b^{x'_i} a_0$ holds with $x_i \in M$, e_i is a prime number in Γ (i.e., $\langle A_i, e_i, x_i, x'_i \rangle$ is a DL-representation.) The "adaptive one-more representation problem" is to find another DL- representation where it is allowed to query to the Q_{rep} oracle K times adaptively.*

Lemma 1. *Under the Strong RSA assumption, the adaptive one-more representation problem is hard.*

Non-adaptive Drawing of Random Powers. Kiayias et al. [23] showed an efficient two-party protocol for the non-adaptive drawing of random powers, where n and $a \in QR(n)$ are the common input parameters to the protocol. As result one party gets a random secret x in a certain sphere, and the other party gets $a^x \in QR(n)$ with the guarantee that the unknown x was non-adaptively selected at random. See [23] for more details.

Threshold Cryptosystems. It is often dangerous for only one person to have the power of decryption. By distributing the decryption ability, threshold cryptosystems [29,11,16,1] avoid the risk. Following the notation due to [16], a (t, ζ)-threshold cryptosystem consists of the following components:

- A key generation algorithm $\langle pk, \{sk_j\}_{j=1}^{\zeta}, \{vk_j\}_{j=1}^{\zeta} \rangle \leftarrow K(1^{\nu}, t, \zeta)$, where 1^{ν} is a security parameter, ζ is the number of decryption servers, t is the threshold parameter, pk is the public key, and sk_j (resp. vk_j) is the secret key share (resp. the verification key) of the j-th decryption server.
- An encryption algorithm $c \leftarrow E(pk, m)$, where m is cleartext, and c is ciphertext.
- Partial decryption algorithms $\sigma_j \leftarrow D_j(sk_j, c)$, for $j \in [1, \zeta]$. Here, σ_j is called a decryption share, and it may include a verification part to achieve robustness.
- A recovery algorithm $m \leftarrow R(c, \{\sigma_j\}_{j=1}^{\zeta}, \{vk_j\}_{j=1}^{\zeta})$, which recovers the plaintext m from the ciphertext c.

The security of threshold cryptography must satisfy two properties: security of the underlying encryption (IND-CPA or IND-CCA2) and robustness. Robustness means that corrupted players should not be able to prevent uncorrupted servers from decrypting ciphertexts. In our scheme, we use two simplified $(\zeta - 1, \zeta)$ threshold IND-CPA cryptosystems by assuming all decryption servers do not abort.

ElGamal Cryptosystem. Consider the following ElGamal encryption scheme [14]:

Let $g \in QR(n)$ be a generator. Let $y = g^x$ be the public key for the secret key x. The encryption of a message m is $(g^r, m \cdot y^r)$ for $r \in_R [1, p'q']$. The decryption of a ciphertext (α, β) is β / α^x.

The threshold version is as follows [28,17,18,7]:

Let $g \in QR(n)$ be a generator. Let $y_j = g^{x_j}$ and x_j be the verification key and the secret key respectively for the j-th decryption server. Let $y = \prod_{j=1}^{\varsigma} y_j$ be the encryption public key. Encryption of a message m is as ElGamal above. To decrypt a ciphertext (α, β), each decryption server computes a decryption share $\alpha_j = \alpha^{x_j}$, and proves that $\log_g y_j = \log_\alpha \alpha_j$. The combiner gets the shares and computes $\alpha_\pi = \prod_{j=1}^{\varsigma} \alpha_j$. Finally, the combiner recovers the message by computing β / α_π.

Under the DDH assumption, this threshold ElGamal cryptosystem is semantically secure and robust.

Simplified Camenisch-Shoup (sCS) Cryptosystem. The Camenisch-Shoup encryption scheme [9] can be simplified into a semantically secure encryption scheme by removing the CCA checking tag.[4]

Let n be as above: $n = pq$, where p, q are safe primes. In this encryption scheme, multiplications and exponentiations are done in $\mathbb{Z}_{n^2}$. Let $g = g'^{2n}$ where $g' \in_R \mathbb{Z}_{n^2}$. Denote $h = 1 + n$. Then public key is $y = g^x$ and secret key is $x \in_R [1, n^2/4]$. The encryption of a message $m \in \mathbb{Z}_n$ is $(g^r, h^m y^r)$ for $r \in_R [1, n/4]$. To decrypt a ciphertext (α, β), compute $\hat{m} = (\beta / \alpha^x)^{2t}$ for $t = 2^{-1} \pmod{n}$; if $m = \frac{\hat{m}-1}{n}$ is an integer in $\mathbb{Z}_n$, then output m, otherwise output $\perp$.

The threshold version can be constructed by using the similar technique for the ElGamal encryption, but generating the modulus n, with unknown factorization is done by means of a suitable distributed key generation protocol [15] to guarantee that $QR(n)$ is cyclic and has large prime factors. Under the Decision Composite Residuosity assumption, this threshold sCS cryptosystem is semantically secure and robust.

5 Design of a FTMGS Scheme

Our scheme is based on the original traceable signature scheme from [23][5]; the main differences lie in the setup and join procedures. Here, in our scheme, the user owns a single master key (i.e., x_i'), and this key is embedded in every membership private key of hers. Because this master key is actually the private key corresponding to her public key (e.g., published via the PKI), she is dissuaded from sharing her membership private keys. Moreover, this binding also guarantees that different users have different master keys.

---

[4] Jarecki and Shmatikov [22] showed that this holds even when the length of the secret key is shortened. However, in the paper, we use a version with only the CCA checking tag removed.

[5] Which is in turn based on the state of the art in group signatures [2].

This master key provides a common nexus among all membership private keys that belong to each user, so that she can link any two signatures of hers by proving that the signatures have been issued by membership private keys into which the same master key is embedded. This capability of linking helps our scheme to enjoy multi-group features. Note that even when the user joins the group by means of an anonymous authentication, the join procedure forces her to use the same master key, so that the relationship between her master key and public key still holds.

The group is created by the collaboration among the group manager and the fairness authorities. The GM knows the factorization of n, and therefore is able to join new members. Fairness authorities are also involved in the setup process, in such a way that the keys related opening (o_j) and revealing ($\hat{o}_j$) are distributed among the fairness authorities. Therefore, opening a signature or revealing a member tracing key requires the participation of fariness authorities.

Opening a signature is a matter of the distributed decryption, by the fairness authorities (without GM), of part of the signature (i.e., encrypted A_i). Likewise, revealing a member tracing key is also a matter of the distributed decryption, by the fairness authorities (without GM), of the encrypted member tracing key (x_i). This key, however, has to be generated when a user joins the group and cannot be generated randomly without GM. Therefore, we employ a little more complicated mechanism: verifiable encryption. The user encrypts the member tracing key using the public key ($\hat{y} \in QR(\hat{n})$) of verifiable encryption scheme, where the corresponding private key is shared among fairness authorities ($\hat{o}_j$). Still, GM can verify the validity of the encryption without decryption. Later, if the user becomes under suspicion, then the fairness authorities collaborate to decrypt the encrypted form of her member's tracing key.

Finally, the join transcript (jlog_i) also holds some non-repudiable proofs that allow to verify the integrity of the record, making the scheme robust against some kind of database manipulation.

- **System Parameters.** $\epsilon \in \mathbb{R}$ such that $\epsilon > 1$, $k \in \mathbb{N}$, three spheres $\Lambda, \mathrm{M}, \Gamma$ as specified in Section 3, the inner spheres $\Lambda_\epsilon^k, \mathrm{M}_\epsilon^k, \Gamma_\epsilon^k$ and the security parameter ν.

- **FA$_0$–Setup.** Played by the fairness authorities to seed the computation of the public key. It generates a public modulus $\hat{n}$ with unknown factorization by using a suitable distributed key generation protocol [15] that guarantees that $QR(\hat{n})$ is cyclic and its order has no small prime factors. It also selects $\hat{g}' \in_R \mathbb{Z}_{\hat{n}^2}$ and sets $\hat{g} = \hat{g}'^{2\hat{n}}$. Denote the output of this procedure by $\mathrm{fpk}_0 = \langle \hat{n}, \hat{g} \rangle$.

- **FA$_j$–Setup.** Played by j-th fairness authority $\forall j \in \{1, \cdots, \zeta\}$ to compute the private and public key pair to manage membership tracing keys. Given $\mathrm{fpk}_0 = \langle \hat{n}, \hat{g} \rangle$, the j-th authority selects a random prime $\hat{o}_j \in \mathbb{Z}_{\hat{n}^2/4}$ and computes $\hat{y}_j = \hat{g}^{\hat{o}_j} \pmod{\hat{n}^2}$. Denote the private and public output by $\mathrm{fsk}_j = \langle \hat{o}_j \rangle$ and $\mathrm{fpk}_j = \langle \hat{y}_j \rangle$ respectively.

- **Group–Setup.** It is an interactive procedure composed of the following procedures: *GM–Init–Setup*, *FA$_j$–Group–Setup*, and *GM–Group–Setup*.

- **GM–Init–Setup.** Played by GM to seed the creation of the group. It generates the prime numbers p, p', q, q' such that $p = 2p' + 1$, $q = 2q' + 1$, and sets $n = pq$. It also selects $a_0, a, b, g \in_R QR(n)$. Let $\mathrm{gsk} = \langle p, q \rangle$ and $\mathrm{gdef} = \langle n, a_0, a, b, g \rangle$ be the private and public output respectively.

- **FA_j–Group–Setup.** Played by j-th fairness authority $\forall\, j \in \{1, \cdots, \zeta\}$ to compute the opening private and public key pair for the group. Given gdef $= \langle n, a_0, a, b, g \rangle$, it selects $h_j \in_R QR(n)$ and a random prime $o_j \in \mathbb{Z}_{\nu/2}$, then computes $y_j = g^{o_j} \pmod{n}$. Let $\mathsf{fgsk}_j = \langle o_j \rangle$ and $\langle h_j, \mathsf{fgpk}_j \rangle$ be the private and public output respectively, where $\mathsf{fgpk}_j = \langle y_j \rangle$.

- **GM–Group–Setup.** Played by GM to compute the group public key from previously computed public values. Given $\langle \mathsf{gdef}, \mathsf{fpk}_0, \{h_j, \mathsf{fgpk}_j, \mathsf{fpk}_j\}_{j=1}^{\zeta} \rangle$, it computes $h = \prod_{j=1}^{\zeta} h_j \pmod{n}$, $y = \prod_{j=1}^{\zeta} y_j \pmod{n}$ and $\hat{y} = \prod_{j=1}^{\zeta} \hat{y}_j \pmod{\hat{n}^2}$. Let $\mathsf{gpk} = \langle n, a, a_0, b, g, h, y, \hat{n}, \hat{g}, \hat{y} \rangle$ be the public output of the procedure.

- **JoinOnAuth.**[6] Interactive procedure played between a user and the GM when the user joins the group as a new member. Let $\langle \mathsf{gpk}, \mathsf{auth}_u \rangle$ be the common input of the procedure, and let gsk and umk_u be the GM's and the user's private inputs respectively, where auth_u may be $\langle \rho, \beta, \gamma \rangle$ (then $\gamma = \beta^{\mathsf{umk}_u} \pmod{\rho}$) or empty (then umk_u is empty). First, the user sets $x_i' = \mathsf{umk}_u$ (if umk_u is empty then chooses a random $x_i' \in \Lambda_e^k$). She computes $C_i = b^{x_i} \pmod{n}$ and send it to the GM. Second, the user and the GM engage in a protocol for non-adaptive drawing a random power, and as a result the user gets $x_i \in_R M_e^k$ and GM gets $X_i = a^{x_i} \pmod{n}$. The user encrypts x_i using sCS encryption scheme (see Section 4), i.e., $E_i = \langle U_i = \hat{g}^{\hat{r}}, V_i = \hat{y}^{\hat{r}} \cdot \hat{h}^{x_i} \rangle \pmod{\hat{n}^2}$, where $\hat{h} = 1 + \hat{n}$ and $\hat{r} \in_R \mathbb{Z}_{\hat{n}/4}$. Now, the user computes the following signatures of knowledge that guarantee that C_i and E_i are well formed[7].

$$E_i^{\wp} = SK\{(x', r, x) : C_i = b^{x'} \pmod{n}; \ \gamma = \beta^{x'} \pmod{\rho}; \ X_i = a^x \pmod{n};$$
$$U_i = \hat{g}^r \pmod{\hat{n}^2}; \ V_i = \hat{y}^r \hat{h}^x \pmod{\hat{n}^2}\}(\mathsf{auth}_u, C_i, X_i, U_i, V_i).$$

The GM, having received $E_i^{\wp}$ from the user, verifies $E_i^{\wp}$. Then GM selects a random prime $e_i \in \Gamma_e^k$, computes $A_i = (C_i X_i a_0)^{e_i^{-1}} \pmod{n}$, sends $\langle A_i, e_i \rangle$ to the user. Let $\mathsf{jlog}_i = \langle A_i, e_i, C_i, X_i, U_i, V_i, E_i^{\wp}, \mathsf{auth}_u \rangle$ and $\mathsf{usk}_i = \langle A_i, e_i, x_i, x_i' \rangle$ be the GM's and User's private outputs respectively.

- **Sign.** Played by a member of the group to issue signatures. Let $\langle m, \mathsf{gpk}, \mathsf{usk}_i \rangle$ be the input of the procedure, then it computes
$$T_1 = A_i y^r, \ T_2 = g^r, \ T_3 = g^{e_i} h^r, \ T_4 = g^{x_i k}, \ T_5 = g^k, \ T_6 = g^{x_i' k'}, \ T_7 = g^{k'}.$$
where $r, k, k' \in_R M$, and then computes the following signature of knowledge:
$$\sigma^{\wp} = SK\{(x, x', e, r, h') : T_2 = g^r ; \ T_3 = g^e h^r ; \ T_2^e = g^{h'} ; \ T_5^x = T_4 ;$$
$$T_7^{x'} = T_6 ; \ a_0 a^x b^{x'} y^{h'} = T_1^e \}(m).$$
Let $\sigma = \langle T_1, \cdots, T_7, \sigma^{\wp} \rangle$ be the public output of the procedure.

- **Verify.** Played by any entity that wants to verify a signature. Let $\langle m, \mathsf{gpk}, \sigma \rangle$ be the input of the procedure, then it verifies if $\sigma^{\wp}$ specified in the *Sign* procedure holds.

- **Open.** It is an interactive procedure composed of the following procedures: *OpenSigDShare, OpenSignature, OpenRefCheck.*

- **OpenSigDShare.** Played by j-th fairness authority $\forall\, j \in \{1, \cdots, \zeta\}$ to decrypt a share of the member reference from the signature. Let $\langle \sigma, \mathsf{gpk}, \mathsf{fgpk}_j, \mathsf{fgsk}_j \rangle$ be the input of the procedure, then computes $\hat{\omega}_{j\sigma} = T_2^{o_j} \pmod{n}$ and a signature of knowledge that the share is correct:

---

[6] The design of *Join* and *JoinOnAuth* have been merged due to space limitations.

[7] If auth_u is empty, the part $\gamma = \beta^{x'} \pmod{\rho}$ is ignored.

$$\hat{\omega}_{j\sigma}^{\wp} = \text{SK}\{(o) : y_j = g^o \ (\text{mod } n) \ ; \ \hat{\omega}_{j\sigma} = T_2^o \ (\text{mod } n)\}(\sigma) .$$

Let $\langle \hat{\omega}_{j\sigma}, \hat{\omega}_{j\sigma}^{\wp} \rangle$ be the public output of the procedure.

• **OpenSignature.** Played by Judge, combines the shares to compute a member reference. Let $\langle \sigma, \text{gpk}, \{\text{fgpk}_j, \hat{\omega}_{j\sigma}, \hat{\omega}_{j\sigma}^{\wp}\}_{j=1}^{\varsigma} \rangle$ be the input of the procedure, then it verifies if $\{\hat{\omega}_{j\sigma}^{\wp}\}_{j=1}^{\varsigma}$ specified in the *OpenSigDShare* procedure holds. and computes $\omega_\sigma = T_1/(\prod_{j=1}^{\varsigma} \hat{\omega}_{j\sigma}) \ (\text{mod } n)$. Let ω_σ be the public output of the procedure.

• **OpenRefCheck.** Played by Judge or the GM to check the matching of the member reference with a given join transcript. Let $\langle \omega_\sigma, \text{jlog}_i \rangle$ be the input of the procedure, then it verifies the jlog_i integrity, by means of the *VerifyJoinLog* procedure (described later), and checks if ω_σ equals A_i from jlog_i.

• **Reveal.** It is an interactive procedure composed of the following procedures: *RevealDShare* and *RevealTKey*.

• **RevealDShare.** Played by j-th fairness authority $\forall \ j \in \{1, \cdots, \varsigma\}$ to decrypt a share of the member tracing key from the join transcript. Let $\langle \text{jlog}_i, \text{gpk}, \text{fpk}_j, \text{fsk}_j \rangle$ be the input of the procedure, then it verifies if $E_i^{\wp}$ specified in the *JoinOnAuth* procedure holds, and computes $\hat{\tau}_{ji} = U_i^{\hat{o}_j} \ (\text{mod } \hat{n}^2)$ and a signature of knowledge that the share is correct:

$$\hat{\tau}_{ji}^{\wp} = \text{SK}\{(o) : \hat{y}_j = \hat{g}^o \ (\text{mod } \hat{n}^2) \ ; \ \hat{\tau}_{ji} = U_i^o \ (\text{mod } \hat{n}^2)\}(\text{jlog}_i) .$$

Let $\langle \hat{\tau}_{ji}, \hat{\tau}_{ji}^{\wp} \rangle$ be the public output of the procedure.

• **RevealTKey.** Played by Judge, combines the shares to compute a member tracing key. Let $\langle \text{jlog}_i, \text{gpk}, \{\text{fpk}_j, \hat{\tau}_{ji}, \hat{\tau}_{ji}^{\wp}\}_{j=1}^{\varsigma} \rangle$ be the input of the procedure, then it verifies the jlog_i integrity by means of the *VerifyJoinLog* procedure, and if $\{\hat{\tau}_{ji}^{\wp}\}_{j=1}^{\varsigma}$ specified in the *RevealDShare* procedure hold, then computes $\hat{x}_i = (V_i/(\prod_{j=1}^{\varsigma} \hat{\tau}_{ji}))^{2t} \ (\text{mod } \hat{n}^2)$ with $t = 2^{-1} \ (\text{mod } \hat{n})$, and $\tau_i = (\hat{x}_i - 1)/\hat{n}$. Let τ_i be the public output of the procedure.

• **Trace.** Played by the Tracing Agents to identify if the member tracing key matches a signature. Let $\langle \text{gpk}, \tau_i, \sigma \rangle$ be the input of the procedure, then checks if T_4 equals $T_5^{\tau_i} \ (\text{mod } n)$.

• **Claim.** Played by a member of the group to prove that issued the signature. Let $\langle \text{gpk}, \sigma, \gamma, \text{usk} \rangle$ be the input of the procedure, where γ is a challenge string, then it computes a signature of knowledge:

$$\pi^{\wp} = \text{SK}\{(x') : T_6 = T_7^{x'} \ (\text{mod } n)\}(\sigma, \gamma) .$$

Let $\pi^{\wp}$ be the public output of the procedure.

• **VerifyClaim.** Played by any entity that wants to verify a claim. Let $\langle \text{gpk}, \sigma, \gamma, \pi^{\wp} \rangle$ be the input of the procedure, then it verifies if $\pi^{\wp}$ specified in the *Claim* procedure holds.

• **ClaimLink.** Played by a member of both groups to create a link between two signatures. Let $\langle \text{gpk}_1, \sigma_1, \text{gpk}_2, \sigma_2, \gamma, \text{usk}_1, \text{usk}_2 \rangle$ be the input of the procedure, such that $\text{mkey}(\text{usk}_1) = \text{mkey}(\text{usk}_2)$ and γ is a challenge string, then it computes a signature of knowledge:

$$\lambda^{\wp} = \text{SK}\{(x') : T_{6\sigma_1} = T_{7\sigma_1}^{x'} \ (\text{mod } n_{\sigma_1}) \ ; T_{6\sigma_2} = T_{7\sigma_2}^{x'} \ (\text{mod } n_{\sigma_2})\}(\sigma_1, \sigma_2, \gamma) .$$

Let $\lambda^{\wp}$ be the public output of the procedure.

- **VerifyLink.** Played by any entity that wants to verify a link between two signatures. Let $\langle \mathsf{gpk}_1, \sigma_1, \mathsf{gpk}_2, \sigma_2, \gamma, \lambda^\wp \rangle$ be the input of the procedure, then it verifies if $\lambda^\wp$ specified in the *ClaimLink* procedure holds.
- **VerifyJoinLog.** It checks that the integrity of the join transcript holds. Let $\langle \mathsf{gpk}, \mathsf{jlog}_i \rangle$ be the input of the procedure then it verifies if $A_i^{e_i}$ equals $a_0 X_i C_i \pmod{n}$ and if $E_i^\wp$ holds. Note that $E_i^\wp$ is a user's non-repudiable proof that binds $\langle \mathsf{auth}_u, C_i, X_i, E_i \rangle$.

Note 1. Note that the order of $QR(\hat{n})$ must be unknown because the security of the verifiable encryption scheme is based on the Decision Composite Residuosity assumption, which does not hold if the factorization of $\hat{n}$ is known.

Note also that h is computed by the fairness authorities because if $\mathrm{dlog}_g h$ is known by any party, then such party would be able to open and trace the signatures for this group.

Note 2. The *JoinOnAuth* procedure accepts both: (i) a string that identifies the user, in this case auth_u relates the user's public key, which in case of a DSA public key would be $\langle \rho, \beta, \gamma \rangle$, such that $\gamma = \beta^\alpha \pmod{\rho}$; and (ii) a string that anonymously authenticates the user, such as a FTMG–signature, and then auth_u takes the values $\langle n, T_7, T_6 \rangle$ from the signature.

In any case, the user master key is the private key (α) that corresponds with the user's public key ($\alpha = \mathrm{dlog}_\beta \gamma$ and $\alpha = \mathrm{dlog}_{T_7} T_6$ respectively), and remains unaltered even if a user joins a group, and then uses this group for being authenticated to join another group, an so on successively. Note that if a signature is opened or traced, the non-repudiable binding with the user holds even through multiple nested anonymous joins.

If the authentication string in *JoinOnAuth* is used in the aforementioned way, then different users have different master keys, and therefore it is not possible to link signatures issued by different users.

Note 3. For security of our scheme, refer to the full version [6].

6 Performance Analysis

This section analyzes the performance of the proposed scheme and compares it with related works, considering the features provided by each one.

Table 1 shows the performance for the proposed scheme (FTMGS) and compares it with the state of the art in group signatures (ACJT00 [2]), and a anonymous credential systems (CL01 [8]). In this analysis, joining to a group and sign/verify[8] in both ACJT00 and FTMGS are compared with credential issuance and showing a credential under a pseudonym with revocation in CL01 respectively.

In this table, the *member-size* row refers to the size[9] of data (in bytes) the group manager (organization) has to keep for each member of the group (credential issued).

---

[8] In FTMGS, the overhead of linking signatures is included in the signature analysis.

[9] In the measures, the elements of $QR(n)$, the free variable witnesses, and the hashed challenges are 1024, 512 and 128 bits long respectively.

Table 1. Performance Analysis			
	ACJT00	CL01	FTMGS
Member-Size	1280	608	1488
Sign-Size	656	1728	1312
Sign-Exp	12	28	21
Vrfy-Exp	11	30	21

Table 2. Summary of Features			
	ACJT00	CL01	FTMGS
Anonymous	+	+	+
Unlinkable	+	$-^{(\star)}$	+
Reversible	+	+	+
Traceable	−	−	+
Revocable	−	$-^{(\ddagger)}$	+
MultiGroup	−	$+^{(\star)}$	+
DeterSharing	−	+	+
Fairness	−	+	+
Non-Repudiation	$+^{(\dagger)}$	+	+

The *sign-size* row shows the length (in bytes) of a signature (credential show). Moreover, the *sign-exp* and *vrfy-exp* rows show the number of exponentiations required to generate and verify a signature (credential show).

Additionally, Table 2 shows a summary of the main features that the proposed scheme (FTMGS) exhibits, and compares it with the above schemes. In this case, ACJT00$^{(\dagger)}$ assumes that during the join phase, the user signs some binding term. Also, CL01$^{(\ddagger)}$ calls revocation to what we call reversibility, and by revocability we means the ability to remove a member from the group, or in the CL01 case, the ability to make sure that a given user can not succeed in showing a credential if the given credential has been revoked (without breaking the anonymity of non-revoked users). Additionally, when a user shows several credentials to an organization in CL01$^{(\star)}$, she guarantees that the credentials belong to the same person by exposing the pseudonym under which the organization knows that user. In this case the scheme exhibits multi-group features, but then protocols showing credentials are linkable. Otherwise, if the pseudonym is not exposed, then the protocols showing credentials are unlinkable, but then they do not enjoy the multi-group feature.

Finally, both ACJT00 and FTMGS can be incorporated into standard frameworks [5] to provide support, with very interesting features, for anonymous authentication and authorization inside standard infrastructures.

References

1. Aditya, R., Peng, K., Boyd, C., Dawson, E., Lee, B.: Batch verification for equality of discrete logarithms and threshold decryptions. In: Jakobsson, M., Yung, M., Zhou, J. (eds.) ACNS 2004. LNCS, vol. 3089, pp. 494–508. Springer, Heidelberg (2004)
2. Ateniese, G., Camenish, J., Joye, M., Tsudik, G.: A practical and provably secure coalition-resistant group signature scheme. In: Bellare, M. (ed.) CRYPTO 2000. LNCS, vol. 1880, pp. 255–270. Springer, Heidelberg (2000)
3. Ateniese, G., Tsudik, G.: Some open issues and new directions in group signatures. In: Financial Cryptography, pp. 196–211 (1999)
4. Bari, N., Pfitzmann, B.: Collision-free accumulators and fail-stop signature schemes without trees. In: Fumy, W. (ed.) EUROCRYPT 1997. LNCS, vol. 1233, pp. 480–494. Springer, Heidelberg (1997)

5. Benjumea, V., Choi, S.G., Lopez, J., Yung, M.: Anonymity 2.0: X.509 extensions supporting privacy-friendly authentication. In: CANS 2007, pp. 265–281 (2007)
6. Benjumea, V., Choi, S.G., Lopez, J., Yung, M.: Fair traceable multi-group signatures. Cryptology ePrint Archive, Report, 2008/047 (2008), http://eprint.iacr.org/
7. Brandt, F.: Efficient cryptographic protocol design based on distributed ElGamal encryption. In: Won, D.H., Kim, S. (eds.) ICISC 2005. LNCS, vol. 3935, pp. 32–47. Springer, Heidelberg (2006)
8. Camenisch, J., Lysyanskaya, A.: An efficient system for non-transferable anonymous credentials with optional anonymity revocation. In: Pfitzmann, B. (ed.) EUROCRYPT 2001. LNCS, vol. 2045, pp. 93–118. Springer, Heidelberg (2001)
9. Camenish, J., Shoup, V.: Practical verifiable encryption and decryption of discrete logarithms. In: Boneh, D. (ed.) CRYPTO 2003. LNCS, vol. 2729, pp. 126–144. Springer, Heidelberg (2003)
10. Camenish, J., Stadler, M.: Efficient group signature schemes for large groups. In: Kaliski Jr., B.S. (ed.) CRYPTO 1997. LNCS, vol. 1294, pp. 410–424. Springer, Heidelberg (1997)
11. Canetti, R., Goldwasser, S.: An efficient threshold public key cryptosystem secure against adaptive chosen ciphertext attack. In: Stern, J. (ed.) EUROCRYPT 1999. LNCS, vol. 1592, pp. 90–106. Springer, Heidelberg (1999)
12. Chaum, D., van Heyst, E.: Group signatures. In: Davies, D.W. (ed.) EUROCRYPT 1991. LNCS, vol. 547, pp. 257–265. Springer, Heidelberg (1991)
13. Dwork, C., Lotspiech, J.B., Naor, M.: Digital signets: Self-enforcing protection of digital information (preliminary version). In: STOC, pp. 489–498 (1996)
14. ElGamal, T.: A public key cryptosystem and a signature scheme based on discrete logarithms. In: CRYPTO, pp. 10–18 (1985)
15. Fouque, P., Stern, J.: Fully distributed threshold RSA under standard assumptions. In: Boyd, C. (ed.) ASIACRYPT 2001. LNCS, vol. 2248. Springer, Heidelberg (2001)
16. Fouque, P.-A., Pointcheval, D.: Threshold cryptosystems secure against chosen-ciphertext attacks. In: Boyd, C. (ed.) ASIACRYPT 2001. LNCS, vol. 2248, pp. 351–368. Springer, Heidelberg (2001)
17. Gennaro, R., Jarecki, S., Krawczyk, H., Rabin, T.: Secure distributed key generation for discrete-log based cryptosystems. In: Stern, J. (ed.) EUROCRYPT 1999. LNCS, vol. 1592, pp. 295–310. Springer, Heidelberg (1999)
18. Gennaro, R., Jarecki, S., Krawczyk, H., Rabin, T.: Secure applications of pedersen's distributed key generation protocol. In: Joye, M. (ed.) CT-RSA 2003. LNCS, vol. 2612, pp. 373–390. Springer, Heidelberg (2003)
19. Goldreich, O., Pfitsmann, B., Rivest, R.L.: Self-delegation with controlled propagation - or - what if you lose your laptop. In: Krawczyk, H. (ed.) CRYPTO 1998. LNCS, vol. 1462, pp. 153–168. Springer, Heidelberg (1998)
20. Identity 2.0, http://www.identity20.com/
21. Jakobsson, M., Juels, A., Nguyen, P.Q.: Proprietary certificates. In: Preneel, B. (ed.) CT-RSA 2002. LNCS, vol. 2271, pp. 164–181. Springer, Heidelberg (2002)
22. Jarecki, S., Shmatikov, V.: Efficient two-party secure computation on committed inputs. In: Naor, M. (ed.) EUROCRYPT 2007. LNCS, vol. 4515, pp. 97–114. Springer, Heidelberg (2007)
23. Kiayias, A., Tsiounis, Y., Yung, M.: Traceable signatures. In: Cachin, C., Camenisch, J.L. (eds.) EUROCRYPT 2004. LNCS, vol. 3027, pp. 571–589. Springer, Heidelberg (2004), http://eprint.iacr.org/2004/007
24. Kiayias, A., Yung, M.: Group signatures: Provable security, efficient constructions and anonymity from trapdoor-holders. Cryptology ePrint Archive, Report 2004/076 (2004), http://eprint.iacr.org/

25. Lysyanskaya, A., Rivest, R., Sahai, A., Wolf, S.: Pseudonym systems. In: Selected Areas in Cryptography, pp. 184–199 (1999)
26. Nguyen, L., Safavi-Naini, R.: Efficient and provably secure trapdoor-free group signature schemes from bilinear pairings. In: Lee, P.J. (ed.) ASIACRYPT 2004. LNCS, vol. 3329, pp. 372–386. Springer, Heidelberg (2004)
27. Paillier, P.: Public-key cryptosystems based on composite degree residuosity classes. In: Stern, J. (ed.) EUROCRYPT 1999. LNCS, vol. 1592, pp. 223–238. Springer, Heidelberg (1999)
28. Pedersen, T.P.: Non-interactive and information-theoretic secure verifiable secret sharing. In: Feigenbaum, J. (ed.) CRYPTO 1991. LNCS, vol. 576, pp. 129–140. Springer, Heidelberg (1992)
29. Shoup, V., Gennaro, R.: Securing threshold cryptosystems against chosen ciphertext attack. In: Nyberg, K. (ed.) EUROCRYPT 1998. LNCS, vol. 1403, pp. 1–16. Springer, Heidelberg (1998)

Identity-Based Online/Offline Encryption[*]

Fuchun Guo[1], Yi Mu[2], and Zhide Chen[1]

[1] Key Lab of Network Security and Cryptology
School of Mathematics and Computer Science
Fujian Normal University, Fuzhou, China
fuchunguo1982@gmail.com, zhidechen@fjnu.edu.cn
[2] Centre for Computer and Information Security Research
School of Computer Science and Software Engineering
University of Wollongong, Wollongong NSW 2522, Australia
ymu@uow.edu.au

Abstract. We consider a scenario of identity-based encryption (IBE) where the encryption device (such as a smartcard) has low power. To improve the computation efficiency, it is desirable that part of computation can be done prior to knowing the message and the recipient (its identity or public key). The real encryption can be conducted efficiently once the message and the recipient's identity become available. We borrow the notion of online/offline signatures introduced by Even, Goldreich and Micali in 1990 and call this kind of encryption *identity-based online/offline encryption* (IBOOE), in the sense that the pre-computation is referred to as *offline phase* and the real encryption is considered as *online phase*. We found that this new notion is not trivial, since all previously proposed IBE schemes cannot be separated into online and offline phases so that the online phase is very efficient. However, we also found that with a proper transformation, some existing identity-based encryption schemes can be converted into IBOOE schemes with or without random oracles. We look into two schemes in our study: Boneh-Boyen IBE (Eurocrypt 2004), and Gentry IBE (Eurocrypt 2006).

1 Introduction

The notion of online/offline digital signature was introduced by Even, Goldreich and Micali [7,8]. With this notion, a signing process can be divided into two phases, the first phase is performed *offline* prior to the arrival of a message to be signed and the second phase is performed *online* after knowing the message. The online phase is typically very fast. Online/offline signatures are particularly useful for low-power devices such as smartcard applications. There exist several online/offline digital signatures in the literature [14,12,5]. Amongst those works, Shamir and Tauman [14] used a new paradigm, named "hash-sign-switch" to design an efficient online/offline signature schemes. A much more efficient scheme was proposed in [5] with the same idea.

---

[*] Supported by the Science and Technology grant of Fujian Province (2006F5036).

G. Tsudik (Ed.): FC 2008, LNCS 5143, pp. 247–261, 2008.

We notice that there exists no a parallel notion for public-key encryption. It could be due to the reason that the encryption scheme is not separable, i.e., RSA encryption, or it is trivial to separate it into online/offline parts, i.e., ElGamal encryption. The latter is suitable for the situation where the sender knows who will be the recipient of the encrypted message, since the offline phase requires the knowledge of the public key of the recipient. We are not interested in this scenario; instead, we consider a novel notion that is motivated by the following situation.

Suppose there are some sensitive data stored in a smartcard, which has limited computation power. In order to send a sensitive data item to a recipient in a secure way, it should be encrypted using the recipient's public key, based on a standard IBE system [1], for instance. To ensure timely delivery, it would be desirable that part of the encryption process could be performed prior to knowing the data item to be delivered and the public key (ID) of the recipient, so that the real encryption process is very quick once the data item and the ID are known. Suppose that recipients are much more powerful, so that they do not care about a reasonable increase of decryption overhead. Unfortunately, all previously published IBE schemes do not accommodate this feature, because the recipient's ID must be known for pre-computation.

We refer to such pre-computation based approach as *identity-based online/offline encryption* (IBOOE). In this paper, we describe how to construct IBOOE schemes where the public key is an arbitrary sting of user's identity. Our work is based on the two well-known IBE schemes: (1) Boneh-Boyen IBE [1], which was introduced by Boneh and Boyen in 2004 and is based on the selective-ID model, and (2) Gentry IBE [10], which shows an improvement over Waters' IBE scheme without random oracles [15] in terms of the size of public master parameters and security reduction. The Gentry IBE scheme is based on Cramer-Shoup's work [6]. In this paper, we show how to transform these two IBE schemes into online/offline encryption such that the online phase has a very low computational overhead. We prove that the proposed IBOOE schemes hold the same level of security as their original schemes.

Road Map: In Section 2, we will provide the definitions of IBE, including security requirements. In Sections 3 and 4, we present our IBOOE schemes from the Boneh-Boyen IBE and the Gentry IBE scheme. We give a comparison in Section 5 and conclude our paper in Section 6.

2   Definitions

2.1   Security Models

An IBE system consists of four algorithms : Setup, KeyGen, Encrypt, Decrypt for master *params* and master secret key generation, private key generation, encryption and decryption, respectively. In this section, we review two security models that will be applied to our schemes.

IND-sID-CCA Model

Initialization: The adversary outputs an identity ID^* to be challenged.

Setup: The challenger takes as input a security parameter 1^k, and then runs the algorithm Setup. It gives the adversary the resulting master public parameters denoted by *params* and keeps the master secret key for itself.

Phase 1: The adversary makes queries $q_1, q_2, \cdots, q_m$, where q_i is one of the following:

- Key generation query on ID_i. The challenger responds by running algorithm KeyGen to generate the private key d_{ID_i} and sending it to the adversary.
- Decryption query $\langle ID_i, C_i \rangle$. The challenger responds by running algorithm KeyGen to generate the private key d_{ID_i}, running algorithm Decrypt to decrypt the ciphertext $\langle ID_i, C_i \rangle$ and sending the result to the adversary.

These queries may be asked adaptively according to the replies of queries.

Challenge: Once the adversary decides that **Phase 1** is over, it outputs two plaintexts m_0, m_1 on which it wishes to be challenged. The challenger picks a random bit $c_r \in \{0, 1\}$ and sets $C_{ch} = \mathsf{Encrypt}(params, ID^*, m_{c_r})$. It sends C_{ch} as the challenge to the adversary.

Phase 2: It is the same as **Phase 1** but with a constraint that the adversary cannot make a key generation query on ID^* or decryption query on (ID^*, C_{ch}).

Guess: The adversary outputs a guess $c_g \in \{0, 1\}$ and wins the game if $c_g = c_r$.

We refer to such an adversary $\mathcal{A}$ as an IND-sID-CCA adversary. We define the advantage of adversary $\mathcal{A}$ in attacking the scheme $\mathcal{E}$ as

$$Adv_{\mathcal{E},\mathcal{A}}^{IND-sID-CCA} = \left| \Pr[c_g = c_r] - \frac{1}{2} \right|.$$

The probability is over the random bits used by the challenger and the adversary.

Definition 1. [1] *We say that an IBE system $\mathcal{E}$ is $(t, q_{ID}, q_C, \epsilon)$-adaptively chosen ciphertext secure if for any t-time IND-sID-CCA adversary $\mathcal{A}$ making at most q_{ID} chosen private key queries and at most q_C chosen decryption queries has advantage at most ϵ. As shorthand, we say that $\mathcal{E}$ is $(t, q_{ID}, q_C, \epsilon)$ IND-sID-CCA secure.*

ANON-IND-ID-CCA Model

Setup: as IND-sID-CCA.

Phase 1: as IND-sID-CCA.

Challenge: Once the adversary decides that **Phase 1** is over it outputs two plaintexts m_0, m_1 and two identities ID_0, ID_1 on which it wishes to be challenged. The challenger picks two random bits $b_r, c_r \in \{0, 1\}$ and sets $C_{ch} = \mathsf{Encrypt}(params, ID_{b_r}, m_{c_r})$. It sends C_{ch} as the challenge to the adversary.

Phase 2: It is the same as **Phase 1**, except the constraint that the adversary cannot make key generation queries on ID_0, ID_1 or decryption C_{ch} under either identity.

Guess: The adversary outputs two bits $b_g, c_g \in \{0, 1\}$ as the guess and wins the game if $b_g = b_r$ and $c_g = c_r$.

We refer to such an adversary $\mathcal{A}$ as an ANON-IND-ID-CCA adversary. We define the advantage of adversary $\mathcal{A}$ in attacking the scheme $\mathcal{E}$ as

$$Adv_{\mathcal{E},\mathcal{A}}^{ANON-IND-ID-CCA} = \left| \Pr[b_g = b_r, c_g = c_r] - \frac{1}{4} \right|.$$

The probability is over the random bits used by the challenger and the adversary.

Definition 2. [10] *We say that an IBE system $\mathcal{E}$ is $(t, q_{ID}, q_C, \epsilon)$-adaptively chosen ciphertext secure if for any t-time ANON-IND-ID-CCA adversary $\mathcal{A}$ making at most q_{ID} chosen private key queries and at most q_C chosen decryption queries has advantage at most ϵ. As shorthand, we say that $\mathcal{E}$ is $(t, q_{ID}, q_C, \epsilon)$ ANON-IND-ID-CCA secure.*

2.2   Bilinear Pairing

Let $\mathbb{G}$ and $\mathbb{G}_T$ be two cyclic groups of prime order p. Let g be a generator of $\mathbb{G}$. A map $e : \mathbb{G} \times \mathbb{G} \to \mathbb{G}_T$ is called a bilinear pairing (map) if this map satisfies the following properties:

- Bilinear: for all $u, v \in \mathbb{G}$ and $a, b \in \mathbb{Z}_p$, we have $e(u^a, v^b) = e(u, v)^{ab}$.
- Non-degeneracy: $e(g, g) \neq 1$. In other words, if g be a generator of $\mathbb{G}$, then $e(g, g)$ generates $\mathbb{G}_T$.
- Computability: It is efficient to compute $e(u, v)$ for all $u, v \in \mathbb{G}$.

2.3   Complexity Assumption

We review the Decisional Bilinear Diffie-Hellamn (DBDH) problem and truncated q-Decisional Augmented Bilinear Diffie-Hellman Exponent (q-DABDHE) problem [1,10].

Definition 3. *Given the group $\mathbb{G}$ of prime order p with generator g and elements $g, g^a, g^b, g^c \in \mathbb{G}^4$ where a, b, c are selected uniformly at random from $\mathbb{Z}_p$, the DBDH problem in $(\mathbb{G}, \mathbb{G}_T)$ is to decide whether a random value $Z \in \mathbb{G}_T$ is equal to $e(g, g)^{abc}$ or not.*

Definition 4. *We say that the (t, ϵ)-DBDH assumption holds in $(\mathbb{G}, \mathbb{G}_T)$ if no t-time algorithm has advantage at least ϵ in solving the DBDH problem in $(\mathbb{G}, \mathbb{G}_T)$.*

Definition 5. *Given the group $\mathbb{G}$ of prime order p with generators g, g' and a vector of $q + 3$ elements $g', g'^{a^{q+2}}, g, g^a, g^{a^2}, \cdots, g^{a^q} \in \mathbb{G}^{q+3}$ where a is selected uniformly at random from $\mathbb{Z}_p$, the q-DABDHE problem in $(\mathbb{G}, \mathbb{G}_T)$ is to decide whether a random value $Z \in \mathbb{G}_T$ is equal to $e(g, g')^{a^{q+1}}$ or not.*

Definition 6. *We say that the the (t, ϵ) q-DABDHE assumption holds in $(\mathbb{G}, \mathbb{G}_T)$ if no t-time algorithm has advantage at least ϵ in solving the q-DABDHE problem in $(\mathbb{G}, \mathbb{G}_T)$.*

3   IBOOE from the Boneh-Boyen IBE

3.1   Construction

Let $e : \mathbb{G} \times \mathbb{G} \to \mathbb{G}_T$ be the bilinear map, $\mathbb{G}, \mathbb{G}_T$ be two cyclic groups of order p and g be the corresponding generator in $\mathbb{G}$. Let $(\mathcal{G}, \mathcal{S}, \mathcal{V})$ be the three algorithms of a one-time strong signature scheme for key generation, signing, and signature verification, respectively. The verification key space is $\mathbb{Z}_p$ (or we can hash it into $\mathbb{Z}_p$). The signature σ can be naturally divided into online and offline phases. We denote by σ_{of} the offline signature and σ_{on} the online signature.

Setup
The system parameters are generated as follow. Choose at random a secret $a \in \mathbb{Z}_p$, choose g, g_2, h_1, h_2 randomly from $\mathbb{G}$, and set the value $g_1 = g^a$. The master public *params* and master secret key K are, respectively,

$$params = \left(g, g_1, g_2, h_1, h_2, \mathcal{G}, \mathcal{S}, \mathcal{V} \right), \qquad K = g_2^a.$$

KeyGen
To generate a private key for $ID \in \mathbb{Z}_p$, pick a random $r \in \mathbb{Z}_p$ and output

$$d_{ID} = (d_1, d_2) = \left(g_2^a (h_1 g_1^{ID})^r, g^r \right).$$

Encrypt

General Encryption: We refer to the original Boneh-Boyen IBE as *general encryption*. It is not required in our IBOOE, but since our IBOOE decryption is associated the Boneh-Boyen IBE, we outline the scheme as follows.

Given a message $m \in \mathbb{G}_T$ and the public key $ID \in \mathbb{Z}_p$, randomly choose $s \in \mathbb{Z}_p$, and generate one pair of signing/verification key (sk, vk) from $\mathcal{G}$ and output the ciphertext

$$C_\mu = \left((h_1 g_1^{ID})^s, (h_2 g_1^{vk})^s, g^s, e(g_1, g_2)^s \cdot m, \sigma, vk \right) = (c_1, c_2, c_3, c_4, c_5, c_6),$$

where $\sigma = \mathcal{S}_{sk}(c_1, c_2, c_3, c_4)$ is the signature on c_1, c_2, c_3, c_4, and $\mathcal{S}_{sk}$ denotes a one-time signature created using sk.

Online/offline Encryption: We now describe our IBOOE, which is divided into two phases:

– Offline encryption: randomly choose $\alpha, \beta, s \in \mathbb{Z}_p$ and (sk, vk) as the above, and output

$$C_{of} = \left((h_1 g_1^\alpha)^s, g_1^{s\beta}, (h_2 g_1^{vk})^s, g^s, e(g_1, g_2)^s, \sigma_{of} \right) = (c_1, c_2, c_4, c_5, c_6', c_7).$$

Store the offline parameters $C_{of}, \alpha, \beta^{-1}, sk, vk$ for the online phase.

- Online encryption: given a message $m \in \mathbb{G}_T$ and the public key $ID \in \mathbb{Z}_p$, and output

$$C_{on} = \left(\beta^{-1}(ID - \alpha), c_6' \cdot m, \sigma_{on} \right) = (c_3, c_6, c_8),$$

where $\sigma_{on} = \mathcal{S}_{sk}(c_1, c_2, c_3, c_4, c_5, c_6)$.
The ciphertext for ID is set as

$$C_\nu = (c_1, c_2, c_3, c_4, c_5, c_6, c_7, c_8, c_9)$$

$$= \left((h_1 g_1^\alpha)^s, g_1^{s\beta}, \beta^{-1}(ID - \alpha), (h_2 g_1^{vk})^s, g^s, e(g_1, g_2)^s \cdot m, \sigma_{of}, \sigma_{on}, vk \right).$$

Observe that the online phase has a very low computational complexity and the offline phase does not require the knowledge of the message and the public key (ID) of a recipient.

Decrypt

IBOOE Decryption: Let $C_\nu = (c_1, c_2, c_3, c_4, c_5, c_6, c_7, c_8, c_9)$ be a valid encryption for $ID \in \mathbb{Z}_p$. To decrypt C_ν with d_{ID}, test whether

$$\mathcal{V}_{c_9}(c_7, c_8) = TRUE,$$

where $\mathcal{V}_{c_9}$ denotes the verification function wrt vk. If the verification fails, reject. Otherwise, it outputs

$$c_0 = c_1 \cdot c_2^{c_3} = (h_1 g_1^\alpha)^s \cdot (g_1^{s\beta})^{\beta^{-1}(ID-\alpha)} = (h_1 g_1^{ID})^s.$$

We then have $(c_0, c_4, c_5, c_6) = \left((h_1 g_1^{ID})^s, (h_2 g_1^{vk})^s, g^s, e(g_1, g_2)^s \cdot m \right)$, which is the same as the output of the general encryption described earlier in this section and the message can be recovered with the general decryption procedure described below.

General Decryption: We refer to the decryption process of the original Boneh-Boyen IBE as *general decryption*, which is outlined as follows.

Let $C_\mu = (c_1, c_2, c_3, c_4, c_5, c_6)$ be a valid encryption tuple for $ID \in \mathbb{Z}_p$. To decrypt C_μ with d_{ID}, test whether

$$\mathcal{V}_{c_6}(c_5) = TRUE.$$

Then[1], test whether the ciphertext is indeed for ID using vk by

$$e(c_1, g) = e\left((h_1 g_1^{ID})^s, g \right) = e(h_1 g_1^{ID}, g^s) = e(h_1 g_1^{ID}, c_3)$$

$$e(c_2, g) = e\left((h_2 g_1^{vk})^s, g \right) = e(h_2 g_1^{vk}, g^s) = e(h_2 g_1^{vk}, c_3)$$

---

[1] The IBOOE continues the decryption from here.

If it fails, reject. Otherwise, the ciphertext to be decrypted is

$$C'_\mu = \left((h_1 g_1^{ID})^s, (h_2 g_1^{vk})^s, g^s, e(g_1, g_2)^s \cdot m \right),$$

and the decryption is as follows:

- Compute the 2-level private key of $d_{ID|vk}$ using a random value $r' \in \mathbb{Z}_p$ as

$$d_{ID|vk} = (d'_1, d'_2, d'_3) = \left(g_2^a (h_1 g_1^{ID})^r (h_2 g_1^{vk})^{r'}, g^r, g^{r'} \right);$$

- Output the message by

$$c_4 \cdot \frac{e(d'_2, c_1) e(d'_3, c_2)}{e(d'_1, c_3)} = (e(g_1, g_2)^s m) \cdot \frac{e\left(g^r, (h_1 g_1^{ID})^s \right) e\left(g^{r'}, (h_2 g_1^{vk})^s \right)}{e\left(g_2^a (h_1 g_1^{ID})^r (h_2 g_1^{vk})^{r'}, g^s \right)}$$

$$= (e(g_1, g_2)^s m) \cdot \frac{1}{e(g_1, g_2)^s}$$

$$= m.$$

3.2 Security

Theorem 1. *The IBOOE scheme from the Boneh-Boyen IBE construction is still IND-sID-CCA secure assuming the DBDH assumption holds.*

Proof. Suppose there exists a $(t, q_{ID}, q_C, \epsilon)$-adversary $\mathcal{A}$ against the BB-IBE scheme, Boneh and Boyen constructed an algorithm $\mathcal{B}_\mu$ that solves the DBDH problem, which is given as input a random tuple (g, g^a, g^b, g^c, Z) that Z is either $e(g, g)^{abc}$ or just a random value in $\mathbb{G}_T$. Suppose there exists the same $(t, q_{ID}, q_C, \epsilon)$-adversary $\mathcal{A}$ against the our IBOOE scheme, we construct an algorithm $\mathcal{B}_\nu$ that solves the DBDH problem with the same challenge tuple. To avoid repeating the simulation, we only show that $\mathcal{B}_\nu$ can be construed from $\mathcal{B}_\mu$ without any additional requirements.

Initialization. The adversary outputs an identity $ID^* \in \mathbb{Z}_p$ to be challenged.

Setup: To generate the master public *params*, $\mathcal{B}_\nu$ simulates the master public *params* as $\mathcal{B}_\mu$ completely, using the same public *params* in both BB-IBE and IBOOE schemes.

Phase 1: The adversary makes the following queries:

- The adversary makes key generation query on ID_i and $\mathcal{B}_\nu$ simulates the private key d_{ID_i} as $\mathcal{B}_\mu$ completely, using the same private key construction in both BB-IBE and IBOOE schemes.

- The adversary makes key generation query on $\langle ID_i, C_i \rangle$. To respond the decryption query, $\mathcal{B}_\nu$ first tests the correctness of signature according to the Decryption algorithm of IBOOE, and then simulates the following decryption as $\mathcal{B}_\mu$, using the same decryption algorithm in both BB-IBE and IBOOE schemes.

Challenge: When $\mathcal{A}$ decides that phase 1 is over, it outputs two messages $m_0, m_1 \in \mathbb{G}_T$ on which it wishes to be challenged. $\mathcal{B}_\mu$ picks a random bit $c_r \in \{0, 1\}$ and generates its challenge ciphertext $C_{\mu, ch}$ for the BB-IBE scheme, where

$$C_{\mu, ch} = \left((h_1 g_1^{ID^*})^s, (h_2 g_1^{vk^*})^s, g^s, e(g_1, g_2)^s \cdot m_{c_r}, \sigma^*, vk^* \right),$$

and $\mathcal{B}_\mu$ still holds the signing key sk^* of vk^*. Using the challenge ciphertext $C_{\mu, ch}$ and sk^* without any additional simulation, $\mathcal{B}_\nu$ generates the challenge ciphertext as follows:

- Draw the elements $(h_1 g_1^{ID^*})^s, (h_2 g_1^{vk^*})^s, g^s, e(g_1, g_2)^s \cdot m_{c_r}$ from $C_{\mu, ch}$;
- Randomly choose k_1, k_2, and output

$$C' = \left((h_1 g_1^{ID^*})^s g^{-k_1 k_2}, g^{k_1}, k_2, (h_2 g_1^{vk^*})^s, g^s, e(g_1, g_2)^s \cdot m_{c_r} \right);$$

- Sign the above ciphertext using sk^* and output $\sigma = \langle \sigma_{of}, \sigma_{on} \rangle$.

The challenge ciphertext for IBOOE is

$$C_{ch} = \left((h_1 g_1^{ID^*})^s g^{-k_1 k_2}, g^{k_1}, k_2, (h_2 g_1^{vk^*})^s, g^s, e(g_1, g_2)^s \cdot m_{c_r}, \sigma_{of}, \sigma_{on}, vk^* \right).$$

Let $\alpha = ID^* - \frac{k_1 k_2}{as}, \beta = \frac{k_1}{as}$, we have

$$(h_1 g_1^{ID^*})^s g^{-k_1 k_2} = (h_1 g_1^{\alpha})^s$$
$$g^{k_1} = g_1^{s\beta}$$
$$k_2 = \beta^{-1}(ID^* - \alpha).$$

Then, it has that

$$C_{ch} = \left((h_1 g_1^{\alpha})^s, g_1^{s\beta}, \beta^{-1}(ID^* - \alpha), (h_2 g_1^{vk^*})^s, g^s, e(g_1, g_2)^s \cdot m_{c_r}, \sigma_{of}, \sigma_{on}, vk^* \right)$$

is a valid online/offline challenge ciphertext for ID^*.

Phase 2: As phase 1.

Guess: Finally, $\mathcal{A}$ outputs c_g and $\mathcal{B}_\nu$ outputs 1 if $c_g = c_r$; outputs 0, otherwise.

This completes the description of $\mathcal{B}_\nu$ in the simulation. From the above, we know that both $\mathcal{B}_\nu$ and $\mathcal{B}_\mu$ will reject all invalid ciphertext queries in a similar way and then the private key simulation and decryption simulation are identical. The challenge ciphertext in both BB-IBE simulation and IBOOE simulation appear to be the same to the adversary; therefore, what the adversary outputs are the same guess. Therefore, the IBOOE scheme from the BB-IBE construction is still IND-sID-CCA secure.   □

4   IBOOE from the Gentry IBE

The Gentry IBE [10] proposed an IBE without random oracles. In comparison to Waters' encryption scheme [15], the Gentry IBE has much shorter public master parameters and offers a tighter reduction in security proofs.

4.1   Construction

Let $e : \mathbb{G} \times \mathbb{G} \to \mathbb{G}_T$ be the bilinear map, $\mathbb{G}, \mathbb{G}_T$ be two cyclic groups of order p and g be the corresponding generator in $\mathbb{G}$.

Setup

The system parameters are generated as follows. Choose at random a secret $a \in \mathbb{Z}_p$, choose g, h_1, h_2, h_3 randomly from $\mathbb{G}$, and set the value $g_1 = g^a \in \mathbb{G}$. Choose a hash function $H : \{0,1\}^* \to \mathbb{Z}_p$ from a family of universal one-way hash function. The master public *params* and the master secret key K are

$$params = \Big(g, g_1, h_1, h_2, h_3, H\Big), \quad K = a.$$

KeyGen

To generate a private key for $ID \in \mathbb{Z}_p$, pick random $r_{ID,i} \in \mathbb{Z}_p$ for $i = 1, 2, 3$, and output

$$d_{ID} = \Big\{(r_{ID,i}, h_{ID,i}) : i = 1, 2, 3\Big\}, \text{ where } h_{ID,i} = (h_i g^{-r_{ID,i}})^{\frac{1}{a-ID}}.$$

If $ID = a$, abort. It requires the same random values $r_{ID,i}$ for ID.

Encrypt

General Encryption. Again, we refer to the original Gentry IBE as *general encryption*, which is not required in our IBOOE. Since it is related to our IBOOE decryption procedure, we outline it as follows.

Given a message $m \in \mathbb{G}_T$ and the public key $ID \in \mathbb{Z}_p$, randomly choose $s \in \mathbb{Z}_p$ and output the ciphertext

$$C_\mu = \Big(g_1^s g^{-sID}, e(g,g)^s, e(g,h_1)^{-s} \cdot m, e(g,h_2)^s e(g,h_3)^{sH_c}\Big) = (c_1, c_2, c_3, c_4),$$

where $H_c = H(c_1, c_2, c_3) \in \mathbb{Z}_p$.

Online/Offline Encryption.

- Offline Encryption: Choose at random $\alpha, \beta, \gamma, \theta, s \in \mathbb{Z}_p$, and output

$$C_{of} = \Big(g_1^s g^{-s\alpha}, g^{s\beta}, e(g,g)^s, e(g,h_1)^{-s}, e(g,h_2)^s e(g,h_3)^{s\gamma}, e(g,h_3)^{s\theta}\Big)$$
$$= (c_1, c_2, c_4, c_5', c_6, c_7).$$

Store $C_{of}, \alpha, \beta^{-1}, \gamma, \theta^{-1}$ for the online computation.
- Online Encryption: Given a message $m \in \mathbb{G}_T$ and the public key $ID \in \mathbb{Z}_p$, output

$$C_{on} = \Big(\beta^{-1}(\alpha - ID), c_5' \cdot m, \theta^{-1}(H_c - \gamma)\Big) = (c_3, c_5, c_8),$$

where $H_c = H(c_1, c_2, c_3, c_4, c_5, c_6, c_7) \in \mathbb{Z}_p$.

The ciphertext for ID is $C_\nu = (c_1, c_2, c_3, c_4, c_5, c_6, c_7, c_8)$, and

$$C_\nu = \Big(g_1^s g^{-s\alpha}, g^{s\beta}, \beta^{-1}(\alpha - ID), e(g,g)^s, e(g,h_1)^{-s} \cdot m,$$
$$e(g,h_2)^s e(g,h_3)^{s\gamma}, e(g,h_3)^{s\theta}, \theta^{-1}(H_c - \gamma) \Big).$$

Decrypt

Online/Offline Decryption: Let $C_\nu = (c_1, c_2, c_3, c_4, c_5, c_6, c_7, c_8)$ be a valid encryption for $ID \in \mathbb{Z}_p$. To decrypt C_ν with d_{ID}, set $H_c = H(c_1, c_2, c_3, c_4, c_5, c_6, c_7)$ and compute

$$c_0 = c_1 c_2^{c_3} = g_1^s g^{-s\alpha} \cdot (g^{s\beta})^{\beta^{-1}(\alpha - ID)} = g_1^s g^{-sID},$$
$$c_9 = c_6 c_7^{c_8}$$
$$= e(g,h_2)^s e(g,h_3)^{s\gamma} \cdot \left(e(g,h_3)^{s\theta} \right)^{\theta^{-1}(H_c - \gamma)}$$
$$= e(g,h_2)^s e(g,h_3)^{sH_c}.$$

Then, check whether

$$c_9 = e\Big(c_0, h_{ID,2} h_{ID,3}^{H_c} \Big) c_4^{r_{ID,2} + r_{ID,3} H_c}.$$

If it fails, reject. Otherwise, we have

$$(c_0, c_3, c_4) = \Big(g_1^s g^{-sID}, e(g,g)^s, e(g,h_1)^{-s} \cdot m \Big),$$

which is te same as the output from a general encryption whose decryption process is referred to as *general decryption*, described below.

General Decryption: Let $C_\mu = (c_1, c_2, c_3, c_4)$ be a valid encryption tuple for $ID \in \mathbb{Z}_p$. To decrypt C_μ with d_{ID}, set $H_c = H(c_1, c_2, c_3)$ and check whether

$$c_4 = e\Big(c_1, h_{ID,2} h_{ID,3}^{H_c} \Big) c_2^{r_{ID,2} + r_{ID,3} H_c}.$$

If it fails, reject. Otherwise, output the ciphertext:

$$C_\mu' = \Big(g_1^s g^{-sID}, e(g,g)^s, e(g,h_1)^{-s} \cdot m \Big),$$

and the decryption is conducted by computing

$$m = c_3 \cdot e(c_1, h_{ID,1}) c_2^{r_{ID,1}}.$$

The correctness of the scheme can be easily verified:

$$e\left(c_1, h_{ID,2}h_{ID,3}{}^{H_c}\right)c_2^{r_{ID,2}+r_{ID,3}H_c}$$

$$= e\left(g^{s(a-ID)}, (h_2h_3^{H_c})^{\frac{1}{a-ID}}g^{\frac{-(r_{ID,2}+r_{ID,3}H_c)}{a-ID}}\right)\cdot e\left(g,g\right)^{s(r_{ID,2}+r_{ID,3}H_c)}$$

$$= e\left(g^{s(a-ID)}, (h_2h_3^{H_c})^{\frac{1}{a-ID}}\right)$$

$$= e(g, h_2)^s e(g, h_3)^{sH_c}.$$

$$e(c_1, h_{ID,1})c_2^{r_{ID,1}}$$

$$= e\left(g^{s(a-ID)}, h_1^{\frac{1}{a-ID}}g^{\frac{-r_{ID,1}}{a-ID}}\right)e(g,g)^{sr_{ID,1}} = e(g, h_1)^s.$$

4.2   Security

Theorem 2. *The IBOOE scheme from the Gentry IBE construction is still ANON-IND-ID-CCA secure assuming the q-DABDHE assumption holds.*

Proof. Suppose there exists a $(t, q_{ID}, q_C, \epsilon)$-adversary $\mathcal{A}$ against the Gentry IBE scheme, Gentry constructed an algorithm $\mathcal{B}_\mu$ that solves the q-DABDHE problem, where it is given as input a random tuple $(g', g'^{a^{q+2}}, g, g^a, g^{a^2}, \cdots, g^{a^q}, Z)$ that Z is either $e(g, g)^{a^{q+1}}$ or a random value in $\mathbb{G}_T$. Suppose there exists the same $(t, q_{ID}, q_C, \epsilon)$-adversary $\mathcal{A}$ against the our IBOOE scheme; we construct an algorithm $\mathcal{B}_\nu$ that solves the q-DABDHE problem with the same challenge tuple. To avoid repeating the simulation, we also only show that $\mathcal{B}_\nu$ can be construed from $\mathcal{B}_\mu$ without any additional requirements.

Setup: To generate the master public *params*, $\mathcal{B}_\nu$ simulates the master public *params* as $\mathcal{B}_\mu$ completely, due to same public *params* in both Gentry IBE and IBOOE scheme.

Phase 1: The adversary makes the following queries:

– The adversary makes key generation query on ID_i and $\mathcal{B}_\nu$ simulates the private key d_{ID_i} as $\mathcal{B}_\mu$ completely, using the same private key construction in both Gentry IBE and IBOOE schemes.

– The adversary makes key generation query on $\langle ID_i, C_i \rangle$. To respond the decryption query, $\mathcal{B}_\nu$ first tests the correctness of the ciphertext according to the Decryption algorithm of IBOOE, and then simulates the following decryption as $\mathcal{B}_\mu$, using the same decryption algorithm in both Gentry IBE and IBOOE schemes.

Challenge: When $\mathcal{A}$ decides that phase 1 is over, it outputs and identities ID_1, ID_2 and two messages $m_0, m_1 \in \mathbb{G}_T$ on which it wishes to be challenged.

$\mathcal{B}_\mu$ picks random bits $b_r, c_r \in \{0,1\}$ and generates its challenge ciphertext $C_{\mu,ch}$ for Gentry IBE scheme, where

$$C_{\mu,ch} = \left(g_1^s g^{-sID_{b_r}}, e(g,g)^s, e(g,h_1)^{-s} \cdot m_{c_r}, e(g,h_2)^s e(g,h_3)^{sH_c}\right),$$

and $\mathcal{B}_\mu$ still holds the elements of $e(g,h_2)^s$ and $e(g,h_3)^s$. Using the challenge ciphertext $C_{\mu,ch}$ and $e(g,h_2)^s, e(g,h_3)^s$ without any additional simulation, $\mathcal{B}_\nu$ generates the challenge ciphertext as follows:

- Draw the elements $g_1^s g^{-sID_{b_r}}, e(g,g)^s, e(g,h_1)^{-s} \cdot m_{c_r}$ from $C_{\mu,ch}$;
- Randomly choose $k_1, k_2 \in \mathbb{Z}_p$ and output

$$C' = \left((g_1^s g^{-sID_{b_r}})^{\frac{k_1}{k_1+k_2}}, (g_1^s g^{-sID_{b_r}})^{\frac{1}{k_1+k_2}}, k_2, e(g,g)^s, e(g,h_1)^{-s} \cdot m_{c_r}\right);$$

- Randomly choose $\gamma, \theta \in \mathbb{Z}_p$ and output

$$\left(e(g,h_2)^s e(g,h_3)^{s\gamma}, e(g,h_3)^{s\theta}, \theta^{-1}(H_c - \gamma)\right),$$

where H_c is the hash value of C' and $e(g,h_2)^s e(g,h_3)^{s\gamma}, e(g,h_3)^{s\theta}$.

The challenge ciphertext for IBOOE is

$$C_{ch} = \left((g_1^s g^{-sID_{b_r}})^{\frac{k_1}{k_1+k_2}}, (g_1^s g^{-sID_{b_r}})^{\frac{1}{k_1+k_2}}, k_2, e(g,g)^s, e(g,h_1)^{-s} \cdot m_{c_r},\right.$$
$$\left. e(g,h_2)^s e(g,h_3)^{s\gamma}, e(g,h_3)^{s\theta}, \theta^{-1}(H_c - \gamma)\right).$$

Let $\alpha = \frac{k_1 ID_{b_r} + k_2 a}{k_1 + k_2}$, $\beta = \frac{a - ID_{b_r}}{k_1 + k_2}$, we have

$$(g_1^s g^{-sID_{b_r}})^{\frac{k_1}{k_1+k_2}} = g_1^s g^{-s\alpha}$$
$$(g_1^s g^{-sID_{b_r}})^{\frac{1}{k_1+k_2}} = g^{s\beta}$$
$$k_2 = \beta^{-1}(\alpha - ID_{b_r}).$$

Then, it has that

$$C_{ch} = \left(g_1^s g^{-s\alpha}, g^{s\beta}, \beta^{-1}(\alpha - ID_{b_r}), e(g,g)^s, e(g,h_1)^{-s} \cdot m_{c_r},\right.$$
$$\left. e(g,h_2)^s e(g,h_3)^{s\gamma}, e(g,h_3)^{s\theta}, \theta^{-1}(H_c - \gamma)\right)$$

is a valid online/offline challenge ciphertext for ID_{b_r}.

Phase 2: as phase 1.

Guess: Finally, $\mathcal{A}$ outputs b_g, c_g and $\mathcal{B}_\nu$ outputs 1 if $b_g = b_r$ and $c_g = c_r$; outputs 0, otherwise.

This completes the description of $\mathcal{B}_\nu$ in the simulation. We know that both $\mathcal{B}_\nu$ and $\mathcal{B}_\mu$ will reject all invalid ciphertext queries in a similar way and then the private key simulation and decryption simulation are identical. The challenge ciphertext in both the Gentry IBE simulation and the IBOOE simulation appear to be the same to the adversary; therefore what the adversary outputs is the same guess. Therefore, the IBOOE scheme from the Gentry IBE construction is still ANON-IND-ID-CCA secure. $\qquad\square$

5   Comparison

We now justify our schemes by comparing them with the online/offline scheme based on *natural splitting*. In the following, we will utilize the keyword "natural" to denote natural splitting.

5.1   Natural IBOOE

It is not hard to "naturally" divide the encryption procedure into online/offline phases. Because the schemes are only different in algorithm **Encrypt**, we omit other algorithms.

Encrypt
Natural Online/offline Encryption from BB-IBE:

- Offline encryption: randomly choose $s \in \mathbb{Z}_p$ and one pair of signing/verification key (sk, vk) from $\mathcal{G}$, and output

$$C_{of} = \left(h_1^s, g_1^s, (h_2 g_1^{vk})^s, g^s, e(g_1, g_2)^s, \sigma_{of} \right) = (c_1, c_2, c_4, c_5, c_6', c_7).$$

  Store the offline parameters C_{of}, sk, vk for the online phase.
- Online encryption: given a message $m \in \mathbb{G}_T$ and the public key $ID \in \mathbb{Z}_p$, and output
$$C_{on} = \left(c_1 \cdot c_2^{ID}, c_6' \cdot m, \sigma_{on} \right) = (c_3, c_6, c_8),$$

  where $\sigma_{on} = \mathcal{S}_{sk}(c_3, c_4, c_5, c_6)$ is the signature signed with sk.
  The ciphertext for ID is $C_\nu = (c_3, c_4, c_5, c_6, c_7, c_8, c_9)$, and

$$C_\nu = \left((h_1 g_1^{ID})^s, (h_2 g_1^{vk})^s, g^s, e(g_1, g_2)^s \cdot m, \sigma_{of}, \sigma_{on}, vk \right).$$

Natural Online/offline Encryption from Gentry IBE:

- Offline encryption: randomly choose $s \in \mathbb{Z}_p$, and output

$$C_{of} = \left(g_1^s, g^{-s}, e(g, g)^s, e(g, h_1)^{-s}, e(g, h_2)^s, e(g, h_3)^s \right) = (c_1, c_2, c_4, c_5', c_6, c_7).$$

  Store the offline parameters C_{of} for the online phase.
- Online encryption: given a message $m \in \mathbb{G}_T$ and the public key $ID \in \mathbb{Z}_p$, and output

$$C_{on} = \left(c_1 \cdot c_2^{ID}, c_5' \cdot m, c_6 \cdot c_7^{H_c} \right) = (c_3, c_5, c_8),$$

  where $H_c = H(c_3, c_4, c_5)$.
  The ciphertext for ID is $C_\nu = (c_3, c_4, c_5, c_8)$, and

$$C_\nu = \left(g_1^s g^{-sID}, e(g, g)^s, e(g, h_1)^{-s} \cdot m, e(g, h_2)^s e(g, h_3)^{sH_c} \right).$$

5.2 Comparison

We provide a comparison of computational cost in Table 1. We denote, in the table, by "natural" a "natural split" and by "ours" our IBOOE scheme. We denote by E the exponentiation in $\mathbb{G}$, ME the multi-exponentiation in $\mathbb{G}$, M the multiplication in $\mathbb{G}$, m_c the modular computation in $\mathbb{Z}_p$, G the time in generating the pair of (sk, vk), and S the time in offline signing.

Table 1. This table presents a comparison of the related IBE schemes. The cost of an efficient online/offline signature [14] to achieve CCA secure in Boneh-Boyen IBE scheme is about $1G + 1S$ in offline phase result of $1\sigma_{of}$ length offline signature and $1m_c$ in online phase.

Scheme	Boneh-Boyen IBE[1]	Gentry IBE[10]
Security Model	Selective-ID model	Standard model
Assumption	DBDH	q-DABDHE
Reduction	Tight	Tight
Offline phase (natural)	4E+1ME+1G+1S	6E
Online phase (natural)	1E+2M+1m_c	2E+3M
Store in offline (natural)	5+1vk+1sk+1σ_{of}	6
Offline phase (ours)	3E+2ME+1G+1S	4E+2ME
Online phase (ours)	1M+2m_c	1M+2m_c
Store in offline (ours)	7+1vk+1sk+1σ_{of}	10

6   Conclusion

In this paper, we introduced a new notion of *identity-based online/offline encryption* (IBOOE). There is no doubt that IBOOE schemes are useful where the computational power of a device is limited. We presented two IBOOE schemes based on two existing IBE schemes: the Boneh-Boyen IBE [1] and the Gentry IBE [10]. The merits of the proposed schemes lie in the following two aspects. (1) The online encryption is extremely efficient. (2) The offline phase can be implemented without the need of the message to be encrypted and the public key (or ID) of a recipient.

Acknowledgement. The authors would like to thank the anonymous reviewers for their helpful comments on this work.

References

1. Boneh, D., Boyen, X.: Efficient selective-id secure identity based encryption without random oracles. In: Cachin, C., Camenisch, J.L. (eds.) EUROCRYPT 2004. LNCS, vol. 3027, pp. 223–238. Springer, Heidelberg (2004)
2. Boneh, D., Franklin, M.: Identity-Based Encryption from the Weil Pairing. In: Kilian, J. (ed.) CRYPTO 2001. LNCS, vol. 2139, pp. 213–229. Springer, Heidelberg (2001)

3. Boneh, D., Katz, J.: Improved efficiency for cca-secure cryptosystems built using identity based encryption. In: Proceedings of RSA-CT 2005 (2005)
4. Canetti, R., Halevi, S., Katz, J.: Chosen-ciphertext security from identity-based encryption. In: Cachin, C., Camenisch, J.L. (eds.) EUROCRYPT 2004. LNCS, vol. 3027, pp. 207–222. Springer, Heidelberg (2004)
5. Chen, X., Zhang, F., Susilo, W., Mu, Y.: Efficient Generic online/offline Signatures Without Key Exposure. In: Katz, J., Yung, M. (eds.) ACNS 2007. LNCS, vol. 4521, pp. 18–30. Springer, Heidelberg (2007)
6. Cramer, R., Shoup, V.: A Practical Public Key Cryptosystem Provably Secure Against Adaptive Chosen Ciphertext Attacks. In: Krawczyk, H. (ed.) CRYPTO 1998. LNCS, vol. 1462, pp. 13–25. Springer, Heidelberg (1998)
7. Even, S., Goldreich, O., Micali, S.: online/offline digital signatures. In: Brassard, G. (ed.) CRYPTO 1989. LNCS, vol. 435, pp. 263–275. Springer, Heidelberg (1990)
8. Even, S., Goldreich, O., Micali, S.: online/offline digital signatures. Journal of Cryptology 9(1), 35–67 (1996)
9. Horwitz, J., Lynn, B.: Toward hierarchical identity-based encryption. In: Knudsen, L.R. (ed.) EUROCRYPT 2002. LNCS, vol. 2332, pp. 466–481. Springer, Heidelberg (2002)
10. Gentry, C.: Practical Identity-Based Encryption Without Random Oracles. In: Vaudenay, S. (ed.) EUROCRYPT 2006. LNCS, vol. 4004, pp. 445–464. Springer, Heidelberg (2006)
11. Gentry, C., Silverberg, A.: Hierarchical id-based cryptography. In: Proceedings of the 8th International Conference on the Theory and Application of Cryptology and Information Security, pp. 548–566. Springer, Heidelberg (2002)
12. Kurosawa, K., Schmidt-Samoa, K.: New online/offline signature schemes without random oracles. In: Yung, M., Dodis, Y., Kiayias, A., Malkin, T.G. (eds.) PKC 2006. LNCS, vol. 3958, pp. 330–346. Springer, Heidelberg (2006)
13. Shamir, A.: Identity-based cryptosystems and signature schemes. In: Blakely, G.R., Chaum, D. (eds.) CRYPTO 1984. LNCS, vol. 196, pp. 47–53. Springer, Heidelberg (1985)
14. Shamir, A., Tauman, Y.: Improved online/offline signature schemes. In: Kilian, J. (ed.) CRYPTO 2001. LNCS, vol. 2139, pp. 355–367. Springer, Heidelberg (2001)
15. Waters, B.: Efficient Identity-Based Encryption without Random Oracles. In: Cramer, R.J.F. (ed.) EUROCRYPT 2005. LNCS, vol. 3494, pp. 114–127. Springer, Heidelberg (2005)

Countermeasures against
Government-Scale Monetary Forgery*

Alessandro Acquisti, Nicolas Christin, Bryan Parno, and Adrian Perrig**

Carnegie Mellon University

Abstract. Physical cash is vulnerable to rising threats, such as large-scale, government-mandated forgeries, that digital cash may protect against more effectively. We study mechanisms to combine physical cash with digital cash to remove their respective shortcomings and obtain their combined advantages. We discuss initial mechanisms and examine their cost and benefit trade-offs.

Keywords: Economics of security, Monetary forgeries, Secure payment systems.

1 Introduction

We consider the problem of monetary forgery by an extremely powerful adversary, such as a hostile government. Government-scale monetary forgery differs from traditional forgery perpetrated by organized crime in scale, motivation, and perception. A counterfeiting government has access to manufacturing resources and capabilities that can be considered equivalent to that of the national bank whose currency is being faked. Further, the forged bills may be used to finance hostile activities, such as weapons purchases or terrorism sponsorship. As a result, targeted countries may be willing to consider relatively expensive defenses against government-mandated forgeries.

The core contribution of this paper is to introduce and outline the main technical and economic challenges that stem from the design and deployment of possible countermeasures against government-scale monetary forgery.

An approach to preventing forgery of physical cash is to combine it with digital cash, yielding *physical digital cash*. Physical digital cash consists of regular bills in which the issuing government embeds an easily verifiable cryptographic value. The goal is to devise a monetary system resilient to forgery, which preserves the usability of existing cash and does not require drastic changes to the existing monetary infrastructure.

Physical digital cash presents a number of design trade-offs between the security properties achieved, the technological complexity involved, and the economic costs incurred. We explore these trade-offs by discussing security requirements, comparing different proposals, and examining possible attacks against physical digital cash.

2 Physical Digital Cash Requirements

The macroeconomic impact of monetary forgeries remains small: forged US dollar production would have to increase by a factor of 200 compared to the current amount of

---

* An extended version of this paper is available [1].
** Authors listed in alphabetical order.

G. Tsudik (Ed.): FC 2008, LNCS 5143, pp. 262–266, 2008.

forgeries in circulation to have a 1% impact on the US inflation rate [1]. Thus, to justify any drastic changes to the current approach of physical security combined with police intervention, the marginal cost of physical digital cash should be tightly constrained - that is, digital extensions required for physical bills should impose a negligible overhead over current production methods (*simple upgrade*). Moreover, people are generally conservative when it comes to currency, and tend to resist drastic changes when they do not perceive any added value. Hence, physical digital cash should present only a *minimal cost to the users* while at the same time providing tangible benefits.

In terms of usability, physical digital cash should provide the same *universal use* characteristics as current physical cash, offering extreme ruggedness and enabling exchange without any digital devices. A single physical digital cash bill should also be *reusable* once it is passed from one owner to another. This is in contrast to digital cash, which is used only once, then destroyed.

To be resistant to any type of counterfeit, physical digital cash should be *forgery-proof*, that is, it must be computationally infeasible to create bills with new denominations or serial numbers. Physical digital cash must also ensure *useless duplication*, that is, it must be impossible to duplicate an existing bill and successfully cash both bills.[1] In addition, bills must be *universally verifiable*, for instance by using a commodity electronic verification device, such as current camera-equipped smart phones. Finally, one of the most salient features of physical cash is *anonymity*. Even though banknotes do not ensure perfect anonymity [5], physical digital cash should provide a level of anonymity equivalent to that provided by physical cash.

3 Physical Digital Cash Techniques

We consider a number of techniques for designing physical digital cash, including novel proposals. We evaluate both the advantages and disadvantages of each system. While none of the techniques perfectly meets all requirements outlined in Section 2, they represent interesting and useful building blocks for future physical digital cash schemes.

Barcode signatures. To keep all the properties of existing physical cash while strengthening the design by cryptographic primitives to make forgery impossible, the issuing authority can sign the sequence number N and denomination D of the bill with its private key R_{gov}. To preserve the ruggedness of physical cash, we propose to embed the digital signature on the bill using a 2-D barcode, e.g., PDF417 [4]. Embedding such signatures maintains *universal use*, makes bills *forgery-proof*, and can be *universally verifiable*, using for instance smart phones with barcode reader software. The manufacturing technology for adding a barcode is trivial, making it a *simple upgrade* to the production process. Finally, a physical digital cash bill does not contain more information than a traditional bill: the signature itself can only be used to verify the authenticity of a bill. Thus, the proposed scheme satisfies our *reusability* and *anonymity* requirements. However, used alone, signatures cannot enforce the *useless duplication* property. Indeed, a duplicated bill would have the same serial number N and denomination D as the original (valid) bill, so that the signature $\{N, D\}_{R_{gov}}$ would remain valid.

---

[1] This property does not necessarily imply that duplicating a physical digital cash bill is impossible, but merely that the duplicated bill should be useless.

RFID-based protection.   An alternative solution, which was once considered for Euro bills [8], is to embed RFID chips in bills. Using an RFID chip offers two primary advantages over 2-D barcodes. First, an RFID chip can perform limited computations and can even interact with a reader. Second, while 2-D barcodes are read-only, some RFID chips have writable memory. Assuming tamper-resistant RFID chips (an assumption we cannot make given current technology), this solution can enforce all desired security properties, using a per-bill public/private key pair [1]. However, RFID chips are less tolerant of daily wear and tear and extreme environmental conditions than the original bill, and may not satisfy the *universal use* requirement. Also, RFID readers have yet not yet penetrated the consumer market, preventing *universal verifiability*, and embedding a computational device in each bill would significantly raise the cost per bill, preventing a *simple upgrade*. Last, RFIDs may be remotely read, which could raise numerous new vulnerabilities [1].

Physical one-way functions.   The useless duplication property can be enforced by making each bill structurally unique (physical one-way function). This can be done by randomly sprinkling bits of optical fiber in the fabric of each banknote [7], or by using magnetic polymers [3]. The issuing authority can numerically encode the bill's unique structure, digitally sign the resulting value, and print a machine-readable version of the signature on the bill. The unique physical structure prevents *duplication*, and the signature make bills *forgery-proof*.

Three important problems remain open, however, regardless of the physical one-way function used. First, the manufacturing cost of such bills is hard to assess, but probably does not satisfy our *simple upgrade* requirement. Second, fibers or polymers may break or get dirtied easily, resulting in genuine bills failing the verification process. Third, the equipment needed to verify such enhanced bills is likely to be too high an investment for most merchants, let alone individual users. However, as we discuss later, physical one-way functions may be useful in conjunction with other techniques.

Centralized verification.   To make duplication more costly for counterfeiters, the central issuing bank can keep a database of issued serial numbers. When a bank receives a note for deposit, it consults the database to verify that the serial number is legitimate and has not already been deposited elsewhere. Similarly, banks inform the central bank of the serial numbers of notes that leave their control. Since this approach can be applied to unmodified physical cash, it retains the benefits of existing cash. Even *anonymity* remains, since serial number data is already available at the member banks.

The major drawback of the method is that it imposes costs on the central bank, which must maintain the serial number database, as well as on the member banks that must constantly monitor and report on the serial numbers entering and leaving their control. In addition, forged and duplicated bills remain undetected until deposited.

Online verification.   Ideally, we could achieve instant detection of duplicates, such that no one would accept a duplicate bill. This could be done by an online verification scheme using a decentralized database that associates each bill's serial number with a cryptographic "lock bit". Once a bill is locked, only the current "owner" of the bill can unlock it. To transfer ownership of a locked bill, the current owner cryptographically unlocks it and allows the new owner to lock it. Participants can check the current state of a particular bill's lock bit and refuse to accept a locked bill.

We describe an online verification scheme that preserves anonymity and handles legacy users in our technical report [1]. The key idea is to allow the current owner of a bill to lock it using a one-time public/private key pair. Such a key pair may be generated by choosing a (private) random number and computing its (public) hash value. The bill is locked under the public value until the owner asks the bank to unlock the bill to pass it on to a different user. The unlock operation is authorized by providing the owner's private value. Because the cryptographic material is not reused across bills or transactions, tracing users is difficult, so that the scheme provides reasonable anonymity.

The whole exchange assumes that users are able to contact the bank during the transaction, using for instance a cellular phone. "Legacy" users unable (or unwilling) to be online can only use unlocked bills. The size of the database of locking materials is non-trivial, but it remains smaller than that of giant databases like web indexes, and therefore appears manageable. More importantly, the economic costs associated to the deployment and maintenance of such a online database warrant further investigation.

Such a scheme could achieve all of the desired properties, with one key assumption: the central bank has to be able to distinguish a duplicate from a real bill through some, possibly costly, secondary verification process. For instance, the physical one-way functions described above could assist in the verification process on the bank side. Used as a back-up verification system, physical one way functions do not need the same level of robustness as when used as the primary mechanism to prevent duplication.

4 Security Analysis

The various techniques outlined above for implementing physical digital cash raise a number of questions regarding possible vulnerabilities of physical digital cash.

Compromised private keys. If the private key R_{gov} used for signing the bills is compromised, then physical digital cash is no longer forgery-proof, and the security level degrades to that of physical cash. Replacing keys is easy, but recalling bills signed with the compromised key may be problematic. One approach is to use many different private keys, and only sign a relatively limited number of bills with a given private key. This can for instance be implemented with forward-secure digital signature schemes [2].

Fake signatures. Setting cryptographic attacks aside, fake bills may be produced with missing or incorrect digital signatures. A missing signature is easy to notice, but, in the absence of scanning equipment, there is no obvious visual distinction between a good and a bad signature. Worse, the visible presence of a digital signature (e.g., a 2-D barcode) may convince users that the bill is good, even though other physical indicators, e.g., the quality of the paper, or the absence of a watermark, may be questionable.

Rogue financial institutions. One whole class of attacks can be characterized as "money laundering," that is, in our context, exchanging fake bills for good bills. For instance, a dishonest merchant may try to pass on bad bills to customers. This type of attack already affects the existing physical cash network, and the defense for physical digital cash is identical: individuals should check bills they are given.

A more elaborate version of money laundering involves an attacker colluding with a rogue bank, which cashes counterfeited bills produced by the attacker without checking them. Then, the counterfeited bills are sent to the bank's currency exchange office, where they are exchanged for good foreign currency bills from unsuspecting tourists.

As long as bills are not verified, they may travel in the network. Monitoring banks is a plausible countermeasure against such an attack. Compared to the large number of bill users, there are relatively few banks in the world, so a centralized authority (e.g., a treasury department) could monitor them effectively. Recent events [6] indicate that such monitoring already exists in practice.

Localized injection. Massive, localized, injection of forged notes can cause serious economic problems if the forgeries cannot be immediately detected. For instance, an attacker using a plane to drop millions in fake currency over a metropolitan area could significantly damage the local economy, with a ripple effect on the national economy.

The only way to counter such an attack is to make the fake bills impossible to spend; that is, to ensure that bills can be immediately verified, and that useless duplication can be readily enforced. Conversely, any method requiring expensive verification devices will have the adverse effect of letting the fake money travel in the network for a longer time period, and possibly to be spent multiple times. Among the techniques we discussed in this paper, inexpensive online verification coupled with a 2-D barcode signature seems more robust against this type of attack than alternative proposals.

5 Conclusion

To significantly strengthen current bills against government-scale monetary forgery, we propose to augment bills with cryptographic material directly embedded in the bill. None of the techniques we investigate or propose, when used in isolation, satisfies all the properties we would like to enforce. However, a combination of these techniques – for instance, coupling our online verification protocol with barcode signatures (with physical one-way functions serving as back-up) – comes very close to implementing all of our requirements. By driving forgeries back to the banks quickly, an online system should work very effectively as a deterrent against counterfeiting, even in the absence of wide deployment. In that respect, a deeper consideration of the economics at stake in the deployment of counterfeit-resistant bills warrants further research.

References

1. Acquisti, A., Christin, N., Parno, B., Perrig, A.: Countermeasures against government-scale monetary forgery. CyLab TR-07-016, Carnegie Mellon University (December 2007)
2. Bellare, M., Miner, S.: A forward-secure digital signature scheme. In: Wiener, M.J. (ed.) CRYPTO 1999. LNCS, vol. 1666. Springer, Heidelberg (1999)
3. Hoshino, H., Takeuchi, I., Yoda, M., Komiya, M., Sugahara, T.: Object to be checked for authenticity and a method for manufacturing the same, US Patent nr. 5,601,931 (February 1997)
4. Itkin, S., Martell, J.: A PDF417 primer: a guide to understanding second generation bar codes and portable data files. Technical Report Monograph 8, Symbol Tech. (April 1992)
5. Kügler, D.: On the anonymity of banknotes. In: Martin, D., Serjantov, A. (eds.) PET 2004. LNCS, vol. 3424, pp. 108–120. Springer, Heidelberg (2005)
6. Mihm, S.: No Ordinary Counterfeit. New York Times Magazine (July 23, 2006)
7. Simmons, G.J.: Identification of data, devices, documents and individuals. In: Proc. IEEE CCST 1991, pp. 197–218, Taipei, Taiwan, ROC (October 1991)
8. Yoshida, J.: Euro bank notes to embed RFID chips by 2005. EE Times (December 2001), http://www.eetimes.com/story/OEG20011219S0016

OpenPGP-Based Financial Instruments and Dispute Arbitration

Daniel A. Nagy[1] and Nadzeya V. Shakel[2]

[1] Eötvös Lóránd University, Faculty of Science
Department of Computer Science,
ELTECRYPT Research Group,
Pázmány Péter sétány 1/C
H-1117 Budapest, Hungary
nagydani@epointsystem.org
[2] Belarusian State University, Faculty of International Relations
Department of Private and European Law,
Akademicheskaya ul., 25-602
220030 Minsk, Belarus
nshakel@gmail.com

Abstract. In this paper, we present some guidelines for implementing various financial instruments for the purposes of credit and payment, including protocols for commercial transactions, dispute resolution, and establishing credit reputation. We strive to employ only widely used, standardized cryptography and keep the proposed procedures as simple as possible on the conceptual level. Also, we want all the documents to resemble their paper-based counterparts as closely as possible and be readable by humans, while also facilitating automated processing by computers. The presented results are being actively implemented within the ePoint System framework.

1 Introduction

Electronic commerce is currently severely hampered by the lack of reliable financial and legal services matching the speed and convenience of on-line transactions. When online contracts are made by filling out and submitting web forms (with no customer copy beyond an easily forgeable confirmation email) and payment authorization is done by entering one's credit card details, all involved parties are highly vulnerable to fraud. In case of such fraud, especially in an international setting, legal proceedings are prohibitively slow and expensive and fraught with inconsistent rulings due to the lack of reliable evidence.

The problems resulting from the lack of common jurisdiction, ill-equipped central authorities and impracticality of coercive enforcement of contracts are nothing new; international trade has always been beset by such problems [4,5]. The body of laws and customs for international trade, commonly known as *Lex Mercatoria*[3,8], provides us with both inspiration and guidance for designing a set of on-line protocols for overcoming the above described difficulties in electronic commerce. In this paper, we describe some core techniques and procedures

G. Tsudik (Ed.): FC 2008, LNCS 5143, pp. 267–271, 2008.
© Springer-Verlag Berlin Heidelberg 2008

concerning financial instruments used for payment and credit that rely as much as possible on the existing infrastructure.

OpenPGP[1] is the IETF standard inspired by Phil Zimmerman's PGP program that, among other things, describes digitally signed documents and facilities for peer-to-peer certification of public keys. Over time, a distributed, decentralized, massively redundant network of so-called Public Key Servers (PKS) has been established, based on Mark Horowitz's web- and email-based protocol (HKP[2]). At the time of writing, the peer-to-peer certification facility and the PKS network is used solely for establishing bindings between public keys and identities and the trustworthiness of participants in such matters, forming the so-called PGP Web of Trust. However, as shown in this paper, this infrastructure can be leveraged for the purpose of the more general task of reputation tracking. In particular, for recording and disseminating arbitrator decisions and other information affecting credit reputation.

Our goal is to design procedures that can be easily understood by the Internet-using public. In particular, we would like to avoid relying on "exotic cryptography" that is conceptually difficult to grasp. Instead, we rely on third parties that require only very limited trust (e.g. PKS servers, time stampers, etc.). Also, we often forfeit the ability to prevent fraud by making it infeasible; instead, we deter it by reactive security measures made possible by strong evidence in the spirit of *Lex Mercatoria*.

2 Electronic Evidence

Unfortunately, *Lex Mercatoria* is often not applicable directly to electronic commerce, because many of its implicit assumptions break down on the Internet. Also, in many cases, contemporary telecommunications allow for short-cuts and considerable improvements in efficiency over customary practices.

Traditionally, documentary evidence is the result of marking paper with ink. Once the paper is marked, it is very difficult to remove these marks as if they have never been there and it is often also difficult to make an exact duplicate of the unmarked document. With electronic documents, this is not the case; any change to a document can be reversed with minimal effort, precisely by the way of keeping an exact duplicate of the unmarked version, which is practically free. This problem alone renders large parts of *Lex Mercatoria* inapplicable to electronic transactions, at least directly.

Instead, in the digital world, the irreversible operation is revealing information that was not previously known [11]. It is very costly to force someone to forget a piece of information and it is even more problematic to completely erase something from the public records. Conveniently, PKS infrastructure provides us with straightforward means to irreversibly publish pieces of information.

The above implies that digital signatures cannot, in a legal sense, be always treated as digital equivalents of pen-and-paper signatures[9] or even seals[10] (with which they actually have more in common, as a seal can be stolen just like a private key). There is a qualitative difference between the two, limiting the usefulness of the metaphor. Instead, digital signatures should be treated as an integrity protection mechanism; evidence witnessed by the signer that the document has not been altered by unauthorized parties.

3   Digital Representations of Debt and Credit Reputation

3.1   General Negotiable Financial Instrument

Traditionally, negotiable instrument is generally defined as a transferable, signed document that unconditionally promises to pay the bearer a sum of money at a future date or on demand. Negotiable instruments are commonly used in business transactions to finance the movement of goods and to secure and distribute loans. Examples include cheques, bills of exchange, and promissory notes. All of them have statutory requirements that define their main elements, and these should be strictly fulfilled. It is also important to emphasize that there is a number of similar financial instruments, such as letters of credit that are treated separately by law and custom, which, nevertheless, can be represented digitally in a very similar way[6,7].

In addition to their paper-based equivalents, digital instruments must include a cryptographic challenge corresponding to a secret known to the bearer of the instrument. Endorsements must include a proof of knowledge of this secret (typically, the secret itself) and a new challenge corresponding to a secret known to the new bearer. Technically, revealing such a secret invalidates the instrument; endorsements are, in fact, back-to-back instruments carrying the same promise. The exact legal interpretation will hopefully emerge from future precedents.

It is possible to turn these instruments into smart contracts[12], that are automatically processed by suitable machinery. We believe that this approach has some very important benefits over expressing smart contracts in universal programming languages (even specialized ones, such as E[14]), such as limiting the possibility of obfuscation and being generally readable to non-programmers.

3.2   General Reputation Record

A rarely used feature of OpenPGP called "notation data" embedded in signatures (only available since version 4) allows OpenPGP users to make elaborate statements about themselves and one another. It can be used in combination with another rarely used (and only partially implemented) feature: signatures made directly on the public key of the subject (tag 0x1F, see Section 5.2.1. of [1]), which make it impossible for the subjects to get rid of these statements without discarding their entire digital identity and reputation.

Such statements can be disseminated (reliably and irreversibly) using the existing PKS infrastructure. All the techniques that have been developed (and already implemented) for judging the reliability of statements about the identities corresponding to public keys can be directly applied to statements about their creditworthiness, with relevant information written into notation data.

4 Arbitration

In this section, we outline the arbitration protocol, with Alice being the claimant, Bob the respondent and Justin the arbitrator.

First, Alice sends a claim against Bob to Justin, *including* evidence supporting her claim and a digital invoice (payable by Bob) for the value claimed. After receiving it, Justin invoices Alice for the arbitration fee. This invoice refers to Alice's statement of claim by hash value.

Once the fee is paid, Justin notifies Bob, presenting him with Alice's claim and the supporting evidence. This is done automatically, without human intervention.

Bob, at this point, has four options:

1. He can *settle* by paying Alice the claimed amount; this would be evidenced by a signed transaction record containing the same cryptographic challenge and value as Alice's statement of claim.
2. He can *contest* Alice's claim. At this point, he should also present Justin with evidence proving Alice's claim wrongful. Justin acknowledges receiving Bob's documents in a signed receipt, referring to each document and Alice's statement of claim by hash value.
3. Bob may also *demur* at Alice's claim. This means that Bob is not contesting any of the factual statements, but informs Justin that in his view they do not imply that Bob should pay anything to Alice. It is the formal way of saying "so what?". The demurrer is a document signed by Bob referring to Alice's statement of claim by hash value. Justin acknowledges receiving Bob's demurrer in a signed receipt with the corresponding hash value.
4. Bob may *do nothing* within the time frame allotted for responding to Alice's claim.

The consequence of the first choice is that the case is closed. Clearly, from Justin's point of view, this is the most desirable outcome, as he ends up pocketing the arbitration fee, without using human resources.

In the second case, Justin proceeds with evaluating the available evidence. Depending on its nature, the process can be automated to some extent. In some cases it can be even fully automated. If Alice's claim does not stand up, both Alice and Bob get notified about the case being closed. If Justin finds Bob in the wrong, then Bob is invoiced for damages and arbitration. If he fails to pay this invoice on time, then Alice shall receive a demerit signature of Justin on Bob's key, which she is free to upload to the PKS network.

In the third case, Justin decides on the demurrer assuming that the factual statements in Alice's claim are true. Otherwise, however, the demurrer is *not* an admission of those facts by Bob. If the demurrer is sustained, both parties receive a signed statement to this effect from Justin and the case is closed. If not, the case proceeds as if Bob decided to do nothing. The reason for using the largely obsolete demurrer is that its use results in possibly crucial evidence for other arbitration procedures connected to the one in question, such as appeals or disputes further up the endorsement chain of some negotiable instrument.

The consequences of the fourth choice (doing nothing) also depend on the particular case. In general, Bob should not be encouraged to delay arbitration by doing nothing, but on the other hand Bob should be protected from harassment.

Acknowledgements and Final Remarks

The authors would like to thank Mihály Bárász, Ian Grigg, Ágnes Koltay, Nick Szabo and Janis Schuller for inspiration, encouragement and fruitful discussions.

A server program processing various financial instruments is described in detail in Janis Schuller's thesis [13]. This piece of software will be the basis for the reference implementation of the protocols and data formats used for procedures described above.

For a detailed discussion with examples, please see the full version of this paper available online at http://www.epointsystem.org/~nagydani/fc2008.pdf

References

1. Callas, J., Donnerhacke, L., Finney, H., Shaw, D., Thayer, R.: OpenPGP Message Format. RFC 4880, IETF (2007)
2. Horowitz, M.: A PGP Public Key Server. Master's Thesis. MIT, Cambridge (1997)
3. Lando, O.: The Lex Mercatoria in International Commercial Arbitration. The Int'l and Comparative Law Quarterly 34(4), 747–768 (1985)
4. Varady, T., Barcelo III, J.J., von Mehren, A.T.: International Commercial Arbitration. A Transnational Perspective, 2nd edn. West Group (2003)
5. Redfern, A., Hunter, M., Blackaby, N., Partasides, C.: Law & Practice of International Commercial Arbitration, 4th edn. Sweet & Maxwell (2004)
6. Uniform Customs and Practice for Documentary Credits (UCP 600) International Chamber of Commerce (2007)
7. Supplement to UCP 600 for Electronic Presentation (eUCP V1.1) International Chamber of Commerce (2007)
8. Berger, K.P.: The Creeping Codification of the Lex Mercatoria. Kluwer Law International, Dordrecht (1999)
9. Schneier, B.: Why Digital Signatures Are Not Signatures. Crypt-Gram Newsletter, http://www.schneier.com/crypto-gram-0011.html
10. Boudrez, F.: Digital signatures and electronic records, http://www.expertisecentrumdavid.be/docs/digitalsignatures.pdf
11. Nagy, D.A.: On Digital Cash-Like Payment Systems. In: Proceedings of the 2nd Int'l Conf. on E-Business and Telecom. Networks. ICETE, pp. 66–73 (2005)
12. Szabo, N.: Smart Contracts, http://szabo.best.vwh.net/smart.contracts.html
13. Schuller, J.: Designing and Implementing a System for Digital Cash, Master's Thesis, University of Bremen (2007)
14. The E Language, http://erights.org/elang

An Efficient Anonymous Credential System

Norio Akagi[1], Yoshifumi Manabe[1,2], and Tatsuaki Okamoto[1,2]

[1] Department of Social Informatics, Graduate School of Informatics, Kyoto University
akagi@ai.soc.i.kyoto-u.ac.jp
[2] NTT Laboratories, Nippon Telegraph and Telephone Corporation
{manabe.yoshifumi,okamoto.tatsuaki}@lab.ntt.co.jp

Abstract. This paper presents an efficient anonymous credential system that includes two variants. One is a system that lacks a credential revoking protocol, but provides perfect anonymity-unlinkability and computational unforgeability under the strong Diffie-Hellman assumption. It is more efficient than existing credential systems with no revocation. The other is a system that provides revocation as well as computational anonymity-unlinkability and unforgeability under the strong Diffie-Hellman and decision linear Diffie-Hellman assumptions. This system provides two types of revocation simultaneously: one is to blacklist a user who acted wrong so that he can no longer use his credential, and the other is identifying a user who acted wrong from his usage of credential. Both systems are provably secure under the above-mentioned assumptions in the standard model.

1 Introduction

1.1 Background

The concept of anonymous credential systems was introduced by Chaum [1], and many anonymous credential systems since then have been proposed.

The basic properties of any anonymous credential system are as follows: It should be hard for a user to forge a credential. Credentials also should be anonymous and unlinkable, thus, a verifier cannot learn anything about the user when it proves its credential to the verifier. Finally, the system is expected to be efficient. The details of the history and motivation behind anonymous credentials can be found in [2].

One of the most efficient existing anonymous credential systems is the Camenisch-Lysyanskaya system [3] that is secure under the LRSW assumption for groups with bilinear maps [4]. However, this system lacks a credential revoking protocol.

There are roughly two types of revocations in anonymous credential systems. One is to reveal the user's identity if the user misbehaves, and the other enables a verifier to reject blacklisted users when they show their credentials to the verifier.

One of the most efficient existing anonymous credential systems with revocation of revealing the misbehaved user's identity is [5], which is secure under the strong RSA (SRSA) and decisional Diffie-Hellman (DDH) assumptions. The only existing anonymous credential system with revocation of blacklisting users is [6], which is secure under the strong Diffie-Hellman (SDH) and DDH assumptions in the random oracle model.

No efficient anonymous credential system with two types of revocation simultaneously has been proposed.

G. Tsudik (Ed.): FC 2008, LNCS 5143, pp. 272–286, 2008.

1.2 Our Result

This paper proposes two variants of a anonymous credential system.

One is an anonymous credential system without revocation (called a "basic anonymous credential system") that is more efficient than the most efficient existing protocol without revocation [3]. It is unforgeable under the SDH assumption, and perfectly (information theoretically) anonymous-and-unlinkable.

The other is the first efficient anonymous credential system that provides two types of revocation (blacklisting and revealing an identity) simultaneously. Our system is unforgeable under the SDH assumption, and anonymous-and-unlinkable under the decision linear Diffie-Hellman assumption (the decision linear assumption).

Both systems are provably secure under the above-mentioned assumptions in the standard model.

2 Preliminaries

2.1 Notation

We will use notation PK as follows: $PK\{(\alpha, \beta) : y = g^\alpha h^\beta\}$ denotes a "zero-knowledge proof of Knowledge of integers α and β such that $y = g^\alpha h^\beta$ where y, g, and h are elements of some group $\mathbb{G} = \langle g \rangle = \langle h \rangle$.

2.2 Bilinear Groups

This paper follows the notation regarding bilinear groups given in [7,8]. Let $(\mathbb{G}_1, \mathbb{G}_2)$ be bilinear groups as follows:

1. $\mathbb{G}_1$ and $\mathbb{G}_2$ are two cyclic groups of prime order p, where possibly $\mathbb{G}_1 = \mathbb{G}_2$,
2. g_1 is a generator of $\mathbb{G}_1$ and g_2 is a generator of $\mathbb{G}_2$,
3. ψ is an isomorphism from $\mathbb{G}_2$ to $\mathbb{G}_1$, with $\psi(g_2) = g_1$.
4. e is a non-degenerate bilinear map $e : \mathbb{G}_1 \times \mathbb{G}_2 \to \mathbb{G}_T$, where $|\mathbb{G}_1| = |\mathbb{G}_2| = |\mathbb{G}_T| = p$, i.e.,
    - (Bilinear): for all $u \in \mathbb{G}_1$, $v \in \mathbb{G}_2$, for all $a, b \in \mathbb{Z}_p^*$, $e\left(u^a, v^b\right) = e(u, v)^{ab}$
    - (Non-degenerate): $e(g_1, g_2) \neq 1$ (i.e., $e(g_1, g_2)$ is a generator of $\mathbb{G}_T$),
    - (Efficient): e, ψ and the group in $\mathbb{G}_1$, $\mathbb{G}_2$ and $\mathbb{G}_T$ can be computed efficiently.

2.3 Anonymous Credential System

In this section, we outline the protocols and the security of anonymous credential systems. We first refer to the basic system, without the credential revoking protocol.

Definition of Basic Anonymous Credential System. A basic anonymous credential system consists of three parties users, an authority, and verifiers. An anonymous credential system performs the following operations.

Key Generation: Authority Auth, given security parameter 1^k, outputs a pair of public-key and secret-key, (pk, sk).

Credential Issuing Protocol: A user $\mathcal{U}$ has some kind of data m that $\mathcal{U}$ wants to obtain a certificate for. Examples of m are properties such as "belongs to some University", "is over the age of 20." or rights such as "can access the secure room". How Auth detects whether m is valid or not with regard to $\mathcal{U}$ is outside this protocol.

$\mathcal{U}$ executes the credential issuing protocol for m with Auth by using $\mathcal{U}$'s input m and Auth's secret-keys. At the end of the protocol, $\mathcal{U}$ obtains a credential Cred, corresponding to m.

Credential Proving Protocol: After $\mathcal{U}$ obtains the credential of m, $\mathcal{U}$ executes the credential proving protocol of m with a verifier $\mathcal{V}$, that proves $\mathcal{U}$'s possession of Cred. At the end of the protocol, $\mathcal{V}$ outputs accept if $\mathcal{U}$ really has a valid Cred, otherwise outputs reject.

Security of Basic Anonymous Credential System. In this section, we refer to the definition of the security of the basic anonymous credential system. The security of the basic anonymous credential system is defined as follows.

Unforgeability: $\mathcal{U}$ cannot forge a valid credential Cred on any value unless Cred was issued by Auth. We show a more formal definition: Let us consider the following game. Let Adv be an adversary. Adv runs in time at most τ. It first executes the credential issuing protocol with Auth at most q_{Auth} times, and obtains valid credentials of adaptively chosen messages. Finally, Adv and $\mathcal{V}$ execute the credential proving protocol for message m, which has not been chosen by Adv yet, and $\mathcal{V}$ outputs accept or reject. If the probability that $\mathcal{V}$ outputs accept at the end of the protocol is at most ϵ for any Adv, the anonymous credential system is $(\tau, q_{Auth}, \epsilon)$-unforgeable.

Anonymity and Unlinkability: An anonymous credential system should provide user privacy. It should be impossible for verifier $\mathcal{V}$ and authority Auth to find anything about user $\mathcal{U}$, except the fact that $\mathcal{U}$ has some set of credentials, even if $\mathcal{V}$ cooperates with other verifiers or the authority (this feature is called anonymity). In particular, two credentials belonging to the same user $\mathcal{U}$ cannot be linked by $\mathcal{V}$ and Auth (this feature is called unlinkability). We merge these two properties into one definition of security. Anonymous credential systems should have the property of (τ, ϵ)-anonymity-and-unlinkability.

The formal definition is as follows: There is an adversary Adv that plays the role of a verifier and an authority. Let us introduce the following game among Adv and two honest users $\mathcal{U}_0$ and $\mathcal{U}_1$.

1. Adv outputs its public-key (except some system parameters).
2. Adv engages in the credential issuing protocol of m with two users, $\mathcal{U}_0$ and $\mathcal{U}_1$. These two users employ the same data, m, to obtain credentials.
3. (a) Adv engages in the credential proving protocol with $\mathcal{U}_0$ and $\mathcal{U}_1$. Adv can execute this protocol a polynomial number of times.
   (b) $d \in \{0, 1\}$ is chosen randomly. $\mathcal{U}_d$ and Adv execute the credential proving protocol. Adv also can execute this a protocol polynomial number of times. Next, Adv can execute 3(a) again.
   (c) Adv outputs $d' \in \{0, 1\}$, which is supposed to be the Adv's guess of value d.

If the probability that $d' = d$ is $1/2 + \epsilon$, then the adversary's advantage is defined to be ϵ. The anonymous credential system is said to be (τ, ϵ)-anonymous-and-unlinkable if the advantage of any adversary, whose running time is at most τ, is at most ϵ.

We next refer to an anonymous credential system that has the credential revoking functions.

Definition of Anonymous Credential System with Revocation. In this paper, we provide two types of revocation functions, blacklisting and identity revealing. Blacklisting is where Auth creates a blacklist BL of unacceptable users, and $\mathcal{V}$ reads the list and can reject the listed users in the credential proving protocol. In the existing anonymous credential system with this type of revocation [6], $\mathcal{V}$ lists bad users to BL when $\mathcal{V}$ notices that they had done something wrong, by using the transcript which $\mathcal{V}$ obtained in the authentication protocol (corresponding to the credential proving protocol in this paper). In our system, the authority Auth creates BL, by listing users when Auth detects that they did something wrong. $\mathcal{V}$ can read but not write BL.

Identity revealing, where $\mathcal{V}$ can know the identity of some user whose transactions are illegal [5]. In order to achieve this property, an anonymous credential system needs another party, an opener O. O can reveal the identity of $\mathcal{U}$ for a successful credential proving transaction between $\mathcal{U}$ and $\mathcal{V}$. Auth also has a database DB to record the data used in the credential issuing protocol with users. O can read but not write DB.

In this system, not only Auth but also $\mathcal{U}$ and O generate a pair of public-key and secret-key. $\mathcal{U}$ then uses O's published data in the credential proving protocol.

Identity Revealing Protocol: This protocol is executed between $\mathcal{V}$ and O, and reveals the relations between Cred and the data $\mathcal{U}$ sends to $\mathcal{V}$ in the credential proving protocol, and that identifies the user.

Security of Anonymous Credential System with Revocation. In addition to **Unforgeability** and **Anonymity and Unlinkability**, the anonymous credential system with revocation needs the following security properties:

Traceability: Traceability demands that user $\mathcal{U}$ is unable to produce a credential such that either the honest opener O declares itself unable to identify the origin of the credential, or, O believes it has identified the origin but is unable to produce a correct proof of its claim.

The formal definition is as follows: Let Adv be an adversary, which runs in time at most τ, corrupts users, and interacts with Auth on their behalf. Now Adv obtains credential Cred on m from Auth, and proves the credential to $\mathcal{V}$. If the probability that O fails in the credential revoking protocol of Cred is at most ϵ for any Adv, the anonymous credential system with revocation is (τ, ϵ)-traceable.

Non-frameability: Opener O is unable to create a proof, accepted by $\mathcal{V}$, that an honest user produced a certain valid proof of the credential unless the user really did produce the proof of the credential.

The formal definition is as follows: Let Adv be an adversary, and $\mathcal{U}$ be an honest user that does not produce an accepted proof of the credential Cred to an honest verifier $\mathcal{V}$. Now Adv, who acts as a user, the authority, and the opener, whose running time is at most τ, first successfully executes the credential proving protocol to $\mathcal{V}$ in the credential proving protocol, and then tries to prove to $\mathcal{V}$ that honest $\mathcal{U}$ is the user of the credential proving protocol by the identity revealing protocol. If the probability of **Adv**'s success is at most ϵ for any **Adv**, the the anonymous credential system with revocation is (τ, ϵ)-non-frameable.

3   Assumptions and Basic Signature Scheme

3.1   Strong Diffie-Hellman (SDH) Assumption

Let $(\mathbb{G}_1, \mathbb{G}_2)$ be bilinear groups (introduced in Section 2.1). The problem in $(\mathbb{G}_1, \mathbb{G}_2)$ is defined as follows: given the $(q + 2)$-tuple $\left(g_1, g_2, g_2^x, ..., g_2^{x^q}\right)$ as input, output pair $\left(g_1^{\frac{1}{x+c}}, c\right)$ where $c \in \mathbb{Z}_p^*$. Algorithm $\mathcal{A}$ has advantage, $\mathbf{Adv}_{SDH}(q)$, in solving q-SDH in $(\mathbb{G}_1, \mathbb{G}_2)$ if $\mathbf{Adv}_{SDH}(q) \leftarrow Pr[\mathcal{A}\left(\mathbb{G}_1, \mathbb{G}_2, g_1, g_2, g_2^x, ..., g_2^{x^q}\right) = \left(g_1^{\frac{1}{x+c}}, c\right); g_2 \xleftarrow{U} \mathbb{G}_2, g_1 \xleftarrow{U} \mathbb{G}_1, x, y \xleftarrow{U} \mathbb{Z}_p^*]$.

Definition 1. *Adversary* **Adv** (τ, ϵ)-*breaks the q-SDH problem if* **Adv** *runs in time at most τ and* $\mathbf{Adv}_{SDH}(q)$ *is at least ϵ. The (q, τ, ϵ)-SDH assumption holds if no adversary* **Adv** (τ, ϵ)-*breaks the q-SDH problem.*

3.2   The Decision Linear Diffie-Hellman Assumption [9]

Let $\mathbb{G}$ be a cyclic group of prime order p. Let u, v, h be generators of $\mathbb{G}$. The problem in $\mathbb{G}$ is defined as follows: Given $u, v, h, u^a, v^b, h^c \in \mathbb{G}$ as input, output **yes** if $a + b = c$ and **no** otherwise.

Algorithm $\mathcal{A}$ has advantage, $\mathbf{Adv}_{Linear}$ in deciding the Decision Linear problem in $\mathbb{G}$ if $\mathbf{Adv}_{Linear} \leftarrow |Pr[\mathcal{A}\left(\mathbb{G}, u, v, h, u^a, v^b, h^{a+b}\right) = \mathbf{yes} : u, v, h \xleftarrow{U} \mathbb{G}, a, b \xleftarrow{U} \mathbb{Z}_p^*] - Pr[\mathcal{A}\left(\mathbb{G}, u, v, h, u^a, v^b, \eta\right) = \mathbf{yes} : u, v, h, \eta \xleftarrow{U} \mathbb{G}, a, b \xleftarrow{U} \mathbb{Z}_p^*]|$.

Definition 2. *The (τ, ϵ)-Decision Linear Diffie-Hellman Assumption (the Decision Linear Assumption) holds in $\mathbb{G}$ if no τ-time algorithm has advantage of at least ϵ in solving the Decision Linear Problem in $\mathbb{G}$.*

3.3   Basic Signature Scheme

We now describe a signature scheme [10] that is strongly existentially unforgeable against chosen plaintext attacks. This scheme is a fundamental element of the credential issuing protocol of our proposed anonymous credential systems.

Key Generation

Randomly select generators $g_2, u_2, v_2 \xleftarrow{U} \mathbb{G}_2$ and set $g_1 \leftarrow \psi(g_2)$, $u_1 \leftarrow \psi(u_2)$, and $v_1 \leftarrow \psi(v_2)$. Randomly select $x \xleftarrow{U} \mathbb{Z}_p^*$ and compute $w_2 \leftarrow g_2^x \in \mathbb{G}_2$. $(\mathbb{G}_1, \mathbb{G}_2, \mathbb{G}_T, \psi, e, g_1, g_2, u_2, v_2)$ is the system parameter, w_2 is the public-key, and x is the secret-key.

Signature Generation

Let $m \in \mathbb{Z}_p^*$ be the message to be signed. Signer $\mathcal{S}$ randomly selects $r, s \xleftarrow{U} \mathbb{Z}_p^*$, and computes $\sigma \leftarrow \left(g_1^m u_1 v_1^s\right)^{1/(x+r)}$. Here $1/(x+r) \bmod p$ (and $m/(x+r) \bmod p$ and $s/(x+r) \bmod p$) are computed. In the unlikely event that $x + r \equiv 0 \bmod p$, we try again with a different random r. (σ, r, s) is the signature of m.

Signature Verification

Given system parameters (g_1, g_2, u_2, v_2) and public-key w_2, message m, and signature (σ, r, s), check that $m, r, s \in \mathbb{Z}_p^*, \sigma \in \mathbb{G}_1, \sigma \neq 1$, and $e\left(\sigma, w_2 g_2^r\right) \stackrel{?}{=} e\left(g_1, g_2^m u_2 v_2^s\right)$. If they hold, the verification result is `valid`, otherwise `invalid`.

Proposition 1 (Security of the Basic Signature Scheme [10])
If the $(q_S + 1, \tau', \epsilon')$-SDH assumption holds in $\mathbb{G}_1$ and $\mathbb{G}_2$, the basic signature scheme is (τ, q_S, ϵ)-strongly existentially-unforgeable against adaptively chosen message attacks, provided that

$$\epsilon \geq 3q_S \epsilon', \tau \leq \tau' - \Theta\left(q_S^2 T\right),$$

where T is the maximum time for a single exponentiation in $\mathbb{G}_1$ and $\mathbb{G}_2$.

4   Proposed Basic Anonymous Credential System

In this section, we describe the construction of the proposed basic anonymous credential system. We use a bilinear group pair $(\mathbb{G}_1, \mathbb{G}_2)$ with a computable isomorphism ψ, as in Section 2.2. We assume the basic signature scheme is strongly existentially unforgeable against chosen message attacks and the Strong Diffie-Hellman assumption holds in $\mathbb{G}_2$. We use the basic signature scheme in the credential issuing protocol of our proposed system.

4.1   Key Generation

Authority `Auth` generates public-key w_2 and secret-key x in the same way as in the signature scheme in Section 3.3.

4.2   Credential Issuing Protocol

First, user $\mathcal{U}$ sends data m as a message, for which $\mathcal{U}$ wants to obtain a certificate, to authority `Auth`. When message m is received from $\mathcal{U}$, `Auth` signs m by using the signature scheme described in Section 3.3. $\mathcal{A}$ then sends triple signature (σ, r, s), to $\mathcal{U}$ as `Cred`, where $\sigma = \left(g_1^m u_1 v_1^s\right)^{1/(x+r)}$. $\mathcal{U}$ then verifies whether `Cred` is a valid signature on m. $\mathcal{U}$ calculates $\alpha \leftarrow w_2 g_2^r, \beta \leftarrow g_2^m u_2 v_2^s$ and verifies $e(\sigma, \alpha) \stackrel{?}{=} e(g_1, \beta)$.

4.3   Credential Proving Protocol

After getting its credential, $\mathcal{U}$ proves knowledge of the credential to verifier $\mathcal{V}$, instead of sending the credential directly to $\mathcal{V}$.

First, $\mathcal{U}$ randomises its credential, and sends the data including the randomised credential to $\mathcal{V}$ as follows: Prover $\mathcal{U}$ randomly selects $t, \theta \xleftarrow{\mathsf{U}} \mathbb{Z}_p^*$, and computes

$$\sigma' \leftarrow \sigma^{t/\theta} = \left(g_1^m u_1 v_1^s\right)^{t/\theta(x+r)}, \alpha' \leftarrow \left(w_2 g_2^r\right)^\theta, \beta' \leftarrow \left(g_2^m u_2 v_2^s\right)^t.$$

and sends $(\sigma', \alpha', \beta')$ to the verifier $\mathcal{V}$. $\mathcal{V}$ then checks the equation $e\left(\sigma', \alpha'\right) \overset{?}{=} e\left(g_1, \beta'\right)$.

Second, $\mathcal{U}$ has to prove to $\mathcal{V}$ that $\mathcal{U}$ fairly created $(\sigma', \alpha', \beta')$. Therefore $\mathcal{U}$ proves knowledge for the following statement:

$$PK\{(\theta, r\theta) : \alpha' = w_2^\theta g_2^{r\theta}, \theta \neq 0\}, \ PK\{(t, st) : \beta' = \left(g_2^m\right)^t u_2^t v_2^{st}, t \neq 0\}.$$

Details of this proof of knowledge are shown in **Figure.1**.

Common input: Public-key and α' **Prover's input:** $(\theta \neq 0, r\theta)$
Protocol:
Step1: $\mathcal{U}$ randomly selects $R_1, R_2, R_3 \xleftarrow{\mathsf{U}} \mathbb{Z}_p^*$, and computes $\gamma \leftarrow \alpha'^{R_1} g_2^{R_2} u_2^{R_3}, \delta \leftarrow \theta R_1 \bmod$
$p, \omega \leftarrow r\theta R_1 + R_2 \bmod p$ and sends (γ, δ) to $\mathcal{V}$. If $\delta \neq 0$ then $\mathcal{V}$ outputs reject. Otherwise, $\mathcal{U}$
and $\mathcal{V}$ executes

$$PK\{(R_1, R_2, R_3, \omega) : \gamma = \alpha'^{R_1} g_2^{R_2} u_2^{R_3}, \ \gamma/w_2^\delta = g_2^\omega u_2^{R_3}\}$$

as follows.
Step2: $\mathcal{U}$ picks random numbers $r_1, r_2, r_3, r_4 \xleftarrow{\mathsf{U}} \mathbb{Z}_p^*$, computes $A = \alpha'^{r_1} g_2^{r_2} u_2^{r_3}, B = g_2^{r_4} u_2^{r_3}$, and
sends (A, B) to $\mathcal{V}$.
Step3: $\mathcal{V}$ sends a random number $b \xleftarrow{\mathsf{U}} \mathbb{Z}_p^*$ to $\mathcal{U}$.
Step4: $\mathcal{U}$ sends (c_1, c_2, c_3, c_4) to $\mathcal{V}$ such that $c_1 \leftarrow r_1 + bR_1 \bmod p, c_2 \leftarrow r_2 + bR_2 \bmod p, c_3 \leftarrow$
$r_3 + bR_3 \bmod p, c_4 \leftarrow r_4 + b\omega \bmod p$.
Step5: $\mathcal{V}$ checks that $\alpha'^{c_1} g_2^{c_2} u_2^{c_3} \overset{?}{=} A\gamma^b, g_2^{c_4} u_2^{c_3} \overset{?}{=} B\left(\gamma/w_2^\delta\right)^b$.

Fig. 1. $PK\{(\theta, r\theta) : \alpha' = w_2^\theta g_2^{r\theta}, \theta \neq 0\}$

$PK\{(t, st) : \beta' = \left(g_2^m\right)^t u_2^t v_2^{st}, t \neq 0\}$ can be proved in the same way as above. If $\mathcal{V}$ succeeds in these two proofs of the knowledge, $\mathcal{V}$ outputs accept, otherwise outputs reject.

4.4 Security

Unforgeability

Theorem 1. *If the basic signature scheme is $(q_{Auth}, \tau, \epsilon)$-strongly existentially unforgeable against chosen message attacks, then our proposed basic anonymous credential system is $\left(\tau', q'_{Auth}, \epsilon'\right)$-unforgeable, provided that*

$$\frac{1}{2}\left(1 - 2e^{\frac{\epsilon'}{2(\epsilon'-1)}n}\right)\left(1 - 2e^{\frac{p\epsilon'-4}{2(p\epsilon'-4-2p)}n}\right) \geq \epsilon, \ 2n\tau' + \Theta(T) \leq \tau, \ q'_{Auth} \leq q_{Auth}.$$

Proof. Let us assume our system is not $\left(\tau', q'_{Auth}, \epsilon'\right)$-unforgeable. We will then show that the basic signature scheme is not $(\tau, q_{Auth}, \epsilon)$ -unforgeable. Under this assumption, adversary $\mathcal{U}$ can prove the two protocols in Section 4.3 as a prover with success probability greater than ϵ. We will then construct extractor $\mathcal{E}$ that outputs (σ, r, s).

Let us focus on protocol PK in **Figure.1**. $\mathcal{E}$ uses $\mathcal{U}$ as a black-box. After receiving (A, B), $\mathcal{V}$ sends $b \xleftarrow{U} \mathbb{Z}_p^*$ to $\mathcal{U}$ and receives (c_1, c_2, c_3, c_4). $\mathcal{E}$ then resets $\mathcal{U}$, and after receiving the same (A, B), $\mathcal{E}$ sends $b' \xleftarrow{U} \mathbb{Z}_p^*/\{b\}$ to $\mathcal{U}$ and receives $\left(c'_1, c'_2, c'_3, c'_4\right)$. If both runs of the protocols are accepted, $\mathcal{E}$ calculates $R_1 \leftarrow \frac{c'_1 - c_1}{b'-b} \bmod p, R_2 \leftarrow \frac{c'_2 - c_2}{b'-b} \bmod p, R_3 \leftarrow \frac{c'_3 - c_3}{b'-b} \bmod p, \omega \leftarrow \frac{c'_4 - c_4}{b'-b} \bmod p$. Note that (R_1, R_2, R_3, ω) satisfies $\gamma = \alpha'^{R_1} g_2^{R_2} u_2^{R_3}$ and $\gamma = g_2^\omega u_2^{R_3} w_2^\delta$. Now $\mathcal{E}$ succeeds in extracting (R_1, R_2, R_3). $\mathcal{E}$ then calculates $\theta \leftarrow \frac{\delta}{R_1} \bmod p, r \leftarrow \frac{\omega - R_2}{\theta R_1} \bmod p$. Note that $\alpha' = w_2^\theta g_2^{r\theta}$ and $\theta \neq 0$ since $\delta \neq 0$. In the same way, $\mathcal{E}$ computes the value (s, t) such that $\beta' = \left(g_2^m\right)^t u_2^t v_2^{st}$ and $t \neq 0$ from $PK\{(t, st) : \beta' = \left(g_2^m\right)^t u_2^t v_2^{st}, t \neq 0\}$, and then computes $\sigma \leftarrow \sigma'^{\frac{\theta}{t}}$. (σ, r, s) is a valid signature of the basic signature scheme.

Therefore, $\mathcal{E}$, using black-box $\mathcal{U}$, can forge the basic signature scheme (σ, r, s) with probability of at least ϵ' such that $\frac{1}{2}\left(1 - 2e^{\frac{\epsilon}{2(\epsilon'-1)}n}\right)\left(1 - 2e^{\frac{p\epsilon'-4}{2(p\epsilon'-4-2p)}n}\right) \geq \epsilon$ (by using the heavy row lemma and Chernoff bound). $2n$ is the number of times which $\mathcal{E}$ uses $\mathcal{U}$ as a black-box. The running time is at most $2n\tau' + \Theta(T)$, and the number of chosen message attack queries is at most q'_{Auth}. $\qquad\square$

Anonymity and Unlinkability

Theorem 2. *Our proposed basic anonymous system is information-theoretically anonymous-and-unlinkable.*

Proof. The game described in **Anonymity and Unlinkability** of Section 2.3 is used to assess our system. If the protocols of proving knowledge are witness-indistinguishable, the system is anonymous and unlinkable; that is, in this game, the view of Step.3(a) and that of Step.3(b) are information-theoretically independent. The Σ-protocol is witness-indistinguishable. We show that the distributions of $\left(\sigma'_0, \alpha'_0, \beta'_0\right)$ and $\left(\sigma'_1, \alpha'_1, \beta'_1\right)$ are the same.

Let $b \in \{0, 1\}$. Using some set of numbers (z_b, y_b, w_b), $\sigma'_b = \left(g_1^{z_b}\right)^{\frac{t_b}{\theta_b}}, \alpha'_b = \left(g_2^{y_b}\right)^{\theta_b}, \beta'_b = \left(g_2^{w_b}\right)^{t_b}$ holds. Since $e\left(\sigma'_b, \alpha'_b\right) = e\left(g_1, \beta'_b\right)$, $z_b y_b = w_b \bmod p$ is satisfied. Thus, when the values of σ'_b, α'_b are fixed, the value of β'_b can be uniquely decided. Therefore, there are two independent values in $\left(\sigma'_b, \alpha'_b, \beta'_b\right)$ and there are two random values t_b and θ_b. The distribution of $\left(\sigma'_b, \alpha'_b\right)$ is the same as the distribution of $\sigma'_b \xleftarrow{U} \mathbb{G}_1$ and $\alpha'_b \xleftarrow{U} \mathbb{G}_2$. Therefore, the distributions of $\left(\sigma'_0, \alpha'_0, \beta'_0\right)$ and $\left(\sigma'_1, \alpha'_1, \beta'_1\right)$ are the same. $\qquad\square$

5   Proposed Anonymous Credential System with Revocation

We next show our proposed anonymous credential system with revocation. In this section, we assume that the Decision Linear Diffie-Hellman assumption holds in $\mathbb{G}_2$.

5.1 Key Generation

In addition to the secret and public keys generated in our proposed basic anonymous credential system, randomly selected $h, \hat{h}, a_2 \xleftarrow{\text{U}} \mathbb{G}_2$ are also used as system parameters. Auth proves $PK\{x : w_2 = g_2^x\}$ to get a certificate.

Now, in our proposed system with revocation, user $\mathcal{U}$ and opener $\mathcal{O}$ also generate secret and public keys. $\mathcal{U}$ randomly selects its secret-key $q \xleftarrow{\text{U}} \mathbb{Z}_p^*$, and calculates g_2^q(thus $g_1^q = \psi\left(g_2^q\right)$). $\mathcal{U}$ also generates a pair (pk_U, sk_U) of public-key and secret-key for some signature scheme. $\mathcal{U}$ publishes pk_U as its public-key. $\mathcal{O}$ randomly selects $\xi_1, \xi_2 \xleftarrow{\text{U}} \mathbb{Z}_p^*$ as its secret-key and computes $U \leftarrow g_2^{\xi_1}, V \leftarrow g_2^{\xi_2}$. $\mathcal{O}$ also publishes (U, V) as its public-key.

5.2 Credential Issuing Protocol

First, user $\mathcal{U}$ creates signature of g_2^q, $sig_U\left(g_2^q\right)$, using sk_U. $\mathcal{U}$ then sends $g_2^q, sig_U\left(g_2^q\right)$, and m as a message, for which $\mathcal{U}$ wants to obtain a certificate, to authority Auth.

Upon receiving these data from $\mathcal{U}$, Auth verifies $sig_U\left(g_2^q\right)$ by using pk_U, then signs m together with q by using the signature scheme described in Section 3.3. Namely, Auth creates the following signature (σ, r, s), where $\sigma = \left(g_1^m g_1^q u_1 v_1^s\right)^{1/(x+r)}$. Auth then sends the signature to $\mathcal{U}$ as Cred.

$\mathcal{U}$ then verifies whether Cred is a valid signature on m and q, $\mathcal{U}$ calculates $\alpha \leftarrow w_2 g_2^r, \beta \leftarrow g_2^m g_2^q u_2 v_2^s$ and verifies $e(\sigma, \alpha) \overset{?}{=} e(g_1, \beta)$. Auth writes $\left(\sigma, r, s, m, g_2^q, sig_U\left(g_2^q\right)\right)$ in database DB whenever Auth engages in the credential issuing protocol with users.

5.3 Credential Proving Protocol

After getting its credential, $\mathcal{U}$ proves knowledge of the credential to verifier $\mathcal{V}$, instead of sending the credential directly to $\mathcal{V}$.

BL $= (b_1, b_2, \cdots, b_l)$ is $\mathcal{V}$'s current blacklist of users who did something wrong (Auth can write and read, while $\mathcal{V}$ can only read BL), where $b_i (1 \leq i \leq l) \leftarrow g_2^{q_i} (q_i$ is the i-th blacklisted user's secret-key). $\mathcal{U}$ encrypts its credential, and sends the data, including an encrypted credential, data unique to the user related to revocation to $\mathcal{V}$ as follows:

Step1: $\mathcal{U}$ randomly selects $t_1, t_2, \theta, \rho \xleftarrow{\text{U}} \mathbb{Z}_p^*, f, \hat{f} \xleftarrow{\text{U}} \mathbb{G}_1$, and computes $\sigma' \leftarrow \sigma \cdot g_1^{t_1+t_2} = \left(g_1^m g_1^q u_1 v_1^s\right)^{\frac{1}{x+r}} \cdot g_1^{t_1+t_2}, \alpha' \leftarrow \left(w_2 g_2^r\right)^\theta, \beta' \leftarrow \left(g_2^m g_2^q u_2 v_2^s\right)^\theta \cdot \alpha'^{t_1+t_2}, d_1 \leftarrow \psi(U)^{t_1}, d_2 \leftarrow \psi(V)^{t_2}, \chi \leftarrow f^q \hat{f}^\rho$ and sends $\left(\sigma', \alpha', \beta', d_1, d_2, \chi, f, \hat{f}, g_2^q\right)$ to $\mathcal{V}$.

Step2: Verifier $\mathcal{V}$ verifies $e(\sigma', \alpha') \overset{?}{=} e(g_1, \beta')$ and $e(\chi, g_2) \overset{?}{\neq} e(f, b_i) e\left(\hat{f}, g_2^\rho\right)$ for every $i (1 \leq i \leq l)$.

Step3: $\mathcal{U}$ has to prove to $\mathcal{V}$ that $\mathcal{U}$ fairly created $(\chi, \sigma', \alpha', \beta', d_1, d_2)$. Therefore, $\mathcal{U}$ proves knowledge for the following statement: $PK\{(q, \rho, \theta, r\theta, s\theta, t_1, t_2) : \chi = f^q \hat{f}^\rho, \alpha' = w_2^\theta g_2^{r\theta}, \beta' = \left(g_2^m\right)^\theta g_2^{q\theta} u_2^\theta v_2^{s\theta} \alpha'^{t_1+t_2}, d_1 = \psi(U)^{t_1}, d_2 = \psi(V)^{t_2}, \theta \neq 0\}$. We detail this proof of knowledge in **Figure.2.**

Step4: If all verifications in **step.2** hold and the proof of knowledge is accepted, $\mathcal{V}$ finally outputs `accept`, otherwise outputs `reject`. Because blacklisted users cannot satisfy the latter verification in **step.2** as well as succeed in the proof of knowledge in **Figure.2**, this protocol provides blacklisting.

Common input: $(\chi, \alpha', \beta', d_1, d_2)$ and public-key
Prover's input: $(q, \rho, \theta, r\theta, s\theta, t_1, t_2)$
Protocol:

Step1: $\mathcal{U}$ requests $\mathcal{V}$ to start the protocol. $\mathcal{V}$ then picks random numbers $b, \lambda \xleftarrow{U} \mathbb{Z}_p^*$ and computes $z \leftarrow h^b \hat{h}^\lambda$ (commitment of b) and sends z to $\mathcal{U}$.

Step2: $\mathcal{U}$ randomly selects $R_1, R_2, R_3, R_4 \xleftarrow{U} \mathbb{Z}_p^*$, computes $\gamma \leftarrow \alpha'^{R_1} g_2^{R_2} u_2^{R_3}$, $\delta \leftarrow \theta R_1 \bmod p$, $\omega \leftarrow r\theta R_1 + R_2 \bmod p$, $\xi \leftarrow \alpha'^{R_1} a_2^{R_4}$, and sends (γ, δ, ξ) to $\mathcal{V}$. If $\delta \neq 0$ then $\mathcal{V}$ outputs `reject`. Otherwise, $\mathcal{U}$ and $\mathcal{V}$ execute $PK\{(R_1, R_2, R_3, R_4, \omega, q, \rho, s, t_1, t_2, (t_1+t_2)R_1, (t_1+t_2)R_4) : \gamma = \alpha'^{R_1} g_2^{R_2} u_2^{R_3}, \gamma/w_2^\delta = g_2^\omega u_2^{R_3}, \chi = f^q \hat{f}^\rho, \xi = \alpha'^{R_1} a_2^{R_4}, g_2^{m\delta} u_2^\delta = \beta'^{R_1} g_2^{-\delta q} v_2^{\delta s} \xi^{-(t_1+t_2)} a_2^{(t_1+t_2)R_4}, g_2^{m\delta} u_2^\delta = \beta'^{R_1} g_2^{-\delta q} v_2^{\delta s} \alpha'^{-(t_1+t_2)R_1})\}$, as follows.

Step3: $\mathcal{U}$ picks random numbers $r_1, r_2, r_3, r_4, r_5, r_6, r_7, r_8, r_9, r_{10}, r_{11}, r_{12} \xleftarrow{U} \mathbb{Z}_p^*$, computes $A = \alpha'^{r_1} g_2^{r_2} u_2^{r_3}$, $B = g_2^{r_5} u_2^{r_3}$, $C = f^{r_6} \hat{f}^{r_7}$, $D = \alpha'^{r_1} a_2^{r_4}$, $E = \beta'^{r_1} g_2^{-\delta r_6} v_2^{r_9} \xi^{-(r_9+r_{10})} a_2^{r_{12}}$, $F = \beta'^{r_1} g_2^{-\delta r_6} v_2^{-\delta r_8} \alpha'^{-r_{11}}$, $G = \psi(U)^{r_9}$, $H = \psi(V)^{r_{10}}$, and sends (A, B, C, D, E, F, G, H) to $\mathcal{V}$.

Step4: $\mathcal{V}$ sends b, λ to $\mathcal{U}$ in order to open the commitment.

Step5: $\mathcal{U}$ sends $(c_1, c_2, c_3, c_4, c_5, c_6, c_7, c_8, c_9, c_{10}, c_{11}, c_{12})$ to $\mathcal{V}$ such that $c_1 \leftarrow r_1 + bR_1 \bmod p$, $c_2 \leftarrow r_2 + bR_2 \bmod p$, $c_3 \leftarrow r_3 + bR_3 \bmod p$, $c_4 \leftarrow r_4 + bR_4 \bmod p$, $c_5 \leftarrow r_5 + b\omega \bmod p$, $c_6 \leftarrow r_6 + bq \bmod p$, $c_7 \leftarrow r_7 + b\rho \bmod p$, $c_8 \leftarrow r_8 + bs \bmod p$, $c_9 \leftarrow r_9 + bt_1 \bmod p$, $c_{10} \leftarrow r_{10} + bt_2 \bmod p$, $c_{11} \leftarrow r_{11} + b(t_1+t_2)R_1 \bmod p$, $c_{12} \leftarrow r_{12} + b(t_1+t_2)R_4 \bmod p$.

Step6: $\mathcal{V}$ checks that $\alpha'^{c_1} g_2^{c_2} u_2^{c_3} \overset{?}{=} A\gamma^b$, $g_2^{c_5} u_2^{c_3} \overset{?}{=} B(\gamma/w_2^\delta)^b$, $f^{c_6} \hat{f}^{c_7} \overset{?}{=} C\chi^b$, $\alpha'^{c_1} a_2^{c_4} \overset{?}{=} D\xi^b$, $\beta'^{c_1} g_2^{-\delta c_6} v_2^{-\delta c_8} \xi^{-(c_9+c_{10})} a_2^{c_{12}} \overset{?}{=} E(g_2^{m\delta} u_2^\delta)^b$, $\beta'^{c_1} g_2^{-\delta c_6} v_2^{-\delta c_8} \alpha'^{-c_{11}} \overset{?}{=} F(g_2^{m\delta} u_2^\delta)^b$, $\psi(U)^{c_9} \overset{?}{=} Gd_1^b$, $\psi(U)^{c_{10}} \overset{?}{=} Hd_2^b$.

Fig. 2. $PK\{(q, \rho, \theta, r\theta, s\theta, t_1, t_2) : \chi = f^q \hat{f}^\rho, \alpha' = w_2^\theta g_2^{r\theta}, \beta' = (g_2^m)^\theta g_2^{q\theta} u_2^\theta v_2^{s\theta} \alpha'^{t_1+t_2}, d_1 = \psi(U)^{t_1}, d_2 = \psi(V)^{t_2}, \theta \neq 0\}$

If $\mathcal{V}$ succeeds in this proof of knowledge, $\mathcal{V}$ outputs `accept`, otherwise outputs `reject`.

5.4   Identity Revealing Protocol

If verifier $\mathcal{V}$ finds that a user has misused his credential, $\mathcal{V}$ informs O. O then reveals the credential of the user as follows:

Step1: $\mathcal{V}$ sends σ', d_1, and d_2 to O, and asks O to reveal the user who created σ'.
Step2: O computes $\sigma = \frac{\sigma'}{d_1^{1/\xi_1} d_2^{1/\xi_2}}$ and searches the database DB to identify the user $\mathcal{U}$. O then finds $\left(r, s, m, g_2^q, sig_U\left(g_2^q\right)\right)$ in DB (they are related to σ) and sends $\left(\sigma, r, s, m, g_2^q, sig_U\left(g_2^q\right)\right)$ to $\mathcal{V}$.

Step3: O proves knowledge for the following statement: $PK\{(\xi_1, \xi_2) : U = g_2^{\xi_1}, V = g_2^{\xi_2}, \sigma = \frac{\sigma'}{d_1^{1/\xi_1} d_2^{1/\xi_2}}\}$. We detail this proof of knowledge in **Figure.3**. $\mathcal{V}$ checks $e\left(\sigma, w_2 g_2^r\right) \stackrel{?}{=} e\left(g_1, g_2^m g_2^q u_2 v_2^s\right)$.

$\mathcal{V}$ then finally can find that σ' was created fairly by $\mathcal{U}$, by using pk_U and checking whether $sig_U\left(g_2^q\right)$ is a valid signature on g_2^q. This protocol provides the identity revealing.

Common input: Public key and $(d_1, d_2, \sigma, \sigma')$
Prover's input: (ξ_1, ξ_2)
Protocol:
Step1: O picks random numbers $R_1, R_2 \xleftarrow{U} \mathbb{Z}_p^*$, computes $Y_1 = g_1^{R_1}, Y_2 = g_1^{R_2}, X_1 = d_1^{1/\xi_1}, X_2 = d_2^{1/\xi_2}, Y_3 = X_1^{R_1}, Y_4 = X_2^{R_2}$, and sends these data to $\mathcal{V}$.
Step2: $\mathcal{V}$ sends a random number $b \xleftarrow{U} \mathbb{Z}_p^*$ to O.
Step3: O sends (c_1, c_2) to $\mathcal{V}$ such that $c_1 \leftarrow R_1 + b\xi_1 \bmod p, c_2 \leftarrow R_2 + b\xi_2 \bmod p$.
Step4: $\mathcal{V}$ checks that $g_1^{c_1} \stackrel{?}{=} Y_1 U^b, g_2^{c_2} \stackrel{?}{=} Y_2 V^b, X_1^{c_1} \stackrel{?}{=} Y_3 d_1^b, X_2^{c_2} \stackrel{?}{=} Y_4 d_2^b, \sigma \stackrel{?}{=} \sigma'/X_1 X_2$.
If it holds, $\mathcal{V}$ outputs accept, otherwise outputs reject.

Fig. 3. $PK\{(\xi_1, \xi_2) : U = g_1^{\xi_1}, V = g_2^{\xi_2}, \sigma = \sigma'/\left(d_1^{1/\xi_1} d_2^{1/\xi_2}\right)\}$.

Remark: If we require a stronger non-frameability where verifier $\mathcal{V}$ as well as an opener is dishonest, $\mathcal{V}$ should publish a transcript of the credential proving protocol in which $\mathcal{V}$'s challenge is a hashed value of prover's first message in a Σ-protocol. However, the protocol in **Figure.2** is not a Σ-protocol as challenge b is committed in **Step.1**. Hence, in order to guarantee the stronger non-frameability, we should change the protocol in **Figure.2** to a standard Σ-protocol, and challenge message, b, by $\mathcal{V}$ is a hash value of (A, B, C, D, E, F, G, H). Instead, to prove the anonymity-and-unlinkability, an oracle-linear assumption is needed (it will be shown in the full version of this paper).

5.5 Security

Unforgeability

Theorem 3. *If the basic signature scheme is $(q_{Auth}, \tau, \epsilon)$-strongly existentially unforgeable against chosen message attacks, our proposed anonymous credential system with revocation is $\left(\tau', q'_{Auth}, \epsilon'\right)$-unforgeable, provided that*

$$\frac{1}{2}\left(1 - 2e^{\frac{\epsilon'}{2(\epsilon'-1)}n}\right)\left(1 - 2e^{\frac{p\epsilon'-2}{2(p\epsilon'-2-2p)}n}\right) \geq \epsilon, \quad 2n\tau'' + \Theta(T) \leq \tau, \quad q'_{Auth} \leq q_{Auth}.$$

Proof. The proof follows the same approach used in our proposed basic system. Assuming our system is not $(\tau', q_{Auth}, \epsilon')$-unforgeable, $\mathcal{U}$ can forge $(\sigma', \alpha', \beta', d_1, d_2)$ that satisfies verifier $\mathcal{V}$'s equation in the credential proving protocol with $(\tau', q_{Auth}, \epsilon')$. We then construct extractor $\mathcal{E}$ that outputs the original credential (σ, r, s) (and U, V). $\qquad\square$

Anonymity and Unlinkability

Theorem 4. *If the (τ, ϵ)-Decision Linear Assumption holds in $\mathbb{G}_2$ then our proposed anonymous credential system with revocation is (τ', ϵ')-anonymous-and unlinkable, provided that $\epsilon' \geq \epsilon, \tau' \leq \tau$.*

Proof. Assume Adv is an adversary that (τ', ϵ')-breaks the anonymity and unlinkability of our proposed anonymous credential system with revocation. We construct an algorithm $\mathcal{A}$ that, by interacting with Adv, solves the Decision Linear Problem in time τ with advantage ϵ.

Algorithm $\mathcal{A}$ is given random instance $(\mathbb{G}_2, U, V, g_2, U^{t_1}, V^{t_2}, \eta)$ of the Decision Linear Problem. It randomly selects $u_2, v_2 \xleftarrow{\mathsf{U}} \mathbb{G}_2$ and gives $(\mathbb{G}_2, g_2, u_2, v_2)$ to Adv as a system parameter. Adv outputs public key w_2 and proves $PK\{x : w_2 = g_2^x\}$. $\mathcal{A}$ extracts x by using Adv as a black-box prover. $\mathcal{A}$ then generates two users' $(\mathcal{U}_0$ and $\mathcal{U}_1)$ secret-key i.e., selects random $q_0, q_1 \xleftarrow{\mathsf{U}} \mathbb{Z}_p^*$ and users' signature key pair $sk_{\mathcal{U}_0}, pk_{\mathcal{U}_0}, sk_{\mathcal{U}_1}, pk_{\mathcal{U}_1}$. It then sends $\left(g_2^{q_0}, g_2^{q_1}, pk_{\mathcal{U}_0}, pk_{\mathcal{U}_1}\right)$ to Adv and carries out the credential issuing protocol with Adv, as $\mathcal{U}_0$ and $\mathcal{U}_1$. $\mathcal{A}$ obtains (σ_0, r_0, s_0) and (σ_1, r_1, s_1), where $\sigma_0 = \left(g_1^m g_1^{q_0} u_1 v_1^{s_0}\right)^{1/(x+r_0)}$, and $\sigma_1 = \left(g_1^m g_1^{q_1} u_1 v_1^{s_1}\right)^{1/(x+r_1)}$.

Next, $\mathcal{A}$ can execute the credential proving protocol with $\mathcal{U}_0$ and $\mathcal{U}_1$ polynomial-times. When Adv queries $\mathcal{U}_{b'}$ $(b' \in \{0, 1\})$, $\mathcal{A}$ selects $\theta, r_1, r_2 \xleftarrow{\mathsf{U}} \mathbb{Z}_p^*$, and computes $\sigma' \leftarrow \sigma_{b'} \cdot \psi(\eta) \cdot g_1^{r_1+r_2}, \alpha' \leftarrow \left(w_2 g_2^{r_{b'}}\right)^\theta, \beta' \leftarrow \left(g_2^m g_2^{q_{b'}} u_2 v_2^{s_{b'}}\right)^\theta \cdot \eta^{\theta(x+r_d)} g_2^{r_1+r_2}, d_1 \leftarrow \psi(U^{t_1}) g_2^{r_1}, d_2 \leftarrow \psi(V^{t_2}) g_2^{r_2}$. $\mathcal{A}$ randomly chooses $\rho_{b'} \xleftarrow{\mathsf{U}} \mathbb{Z}_p^*$ and $f_{b'}, \hat{f}_{b'} \xleftarrow{\mathsf{U}} \mathbb{G}_1$, and calculates $\chi_{b'} \leftarrow f_{b'}^{q_{b'}} \hat{f}_{b'}^{\rho_{b'}}$, and sends them to Adv as $\mathcal{U}_{b'}$. $\mathcal{A}$ first executes the protocol and obtains the value of b in **Step.3**, and resets Adv. $\mathcal{A}$ then re-executes the proof of knowledge protocol. Now $\mathcal{A}$ knows the value of b, so $\mathcal{A}$ can successfully finish the proof of knowledge protocol without knowing the witness. $\mathcal{A}$ and Adv then engage in the credential proving protocol. Adv now requests its anonymity challenge. $\mathcal{A}$ chooses uniformly random bit of $d \in \{0, 1\}$, selects random $\theta \xleftarrow{\mathsf{U}} \mathbb{Z}_p^*$ and computes $\sigma' \leftarrow \sigma_d \cdot \psi(\eta) \cdot g_1^{r_1+r_2}$, $\alpha' \leftarrow \left(w_2 g_2^{r_d}\right)^\theta, \beta' \leftarrow \left(g_2^m g_2^{q_d} u_2 v_2^{s_d}\right)^\theta \cdot \eta^{\theta(x+r_d)} g_2^{r_1+r_2}, d_1 \leftarrow \psi(U^{t_1}) g_2^{r_1}, d_2 \leftarrow \psi(V^{t_2}) g_2^{r_2}$. $\mathcal{A}$ and Adv then engage in the credential proving knowledge of σ_d. After this, Adv can query $\mathcal{U}_0$ and $\mathcal{U}_1$ polynomial-times. The procedure is just the same as the above.

Finally, Adv outputs bit d'. If $d' = d$, $\mathcal{A}$ outputs yes(guesses $\eta = g_2^{t_1+t_2}$). Else(if $d' \neq d$), $\mathcal{A}$ outputs no. If $\eta = g_2^{t_1+t_2}$, $Pr[\mathcal{A}\left(\mathbb{G}_2, U, V, g_2, U^{t_1}, V^{t_2}, g_2^{t_1+t_2}\right) = \mathsf{yes} : U, V, g_2, \xleftarrow{\mathsf{U}} \mathbb{G}_2, t_1, t_2 \xleftarrow{\mathsf{U}} \mathbb{Z}_p^*] = Pr[d' = d]$. If $\eta \neq g_2^{t_1+t_2}$, let $\eta = g_2^\zeta$. $\sigma' = \sigma_b \cdot g_1^\zeta$ holds. $\alpha' = \left(w_2 g_2^{r_b}\right)^\theta$ and $\beta' = \left(g_2^m g_2^{q_b} u_2 v_2^{s_b}\right)^\theta \cdot \alpha'^\zeta$ are satisfied. Since there are two independent elements in $(\sigma', \alpha', \beta')$ and these are randomised by θ and ζ, the distribution of (α', β') is just the same as the following distribution $\alpha' \xleftarrow{\mathsf{U}} \mathbb{G}_2, \beta' \xleftarrow{\mathsf{U}} \mathbb{G}_2$. Therefore, the distribution is independent of the value of d, thus $Pr[\mathcal{A}(\mathbb{G}_2, U, V, g_2, U^{t_1}, V^{t_2}, \eta) = \mathsf{yes} : U, V, g_2, \eta \xleftarrow{\mathsf{U}} \mathbb{G}_2, t_1, t_2 \xleftarrow{\mathsf{U}} \mathbb{Z}_p^*] = \frac{1}{2}$. $\square$

Traceability

Theorem 5. *If the basic signature scheme is* $(q_{Auth}, \tau, \epsilon)$*-strongly existentially unforgeable against chosen message attacks, our proposed anonymous credential system is* $\left(\tau', q'_{Auth}, \epsilon'\right)$*-traceable, provided that*

$$\frac{1}{2}\left(1 - 2e^{\frac{\epsilon'}{2(\epsilon'-1)}n}\right)\left(1 - 2e^{\frac{p\epsilon'-2}{2(p\epsilon'-2-2p)}n}\right) \geq \epsilon, \ 2n\tau'' + \Theta(T) \leq \tau, \ q_{Auth'} \leq q_{Auth}.$$

Proof. Assume Adv is an adversary that $\left(\tau', q'_{Auth}, \epsilon'\right)$-breaks the traceability of our proposed anonymous credential system with revocation. We construct an extractor $\mathcal{E}$ that, by interacting with Adv, can forge the basic signature scheme in time τ with advantage ϵ, where q'_{Auth} is the maximum number of queries made by Adv.

Adv succeeds in generating such $(\sigma', \alpha', \beta', d_1, d_2)$ that is accepted by $\mathcal{V}$, but O fails in revealing the original credential stored in DB. $\mathcal{E}$ then extracts (σ, r, s) by using Adv as a black-box in the same way as in the proof of **Unforgeability**. Since (σ, r, s) is not in DB, it is a forged signature of the basic signature scheme. $\square$

Non-frameability

Theorem 6. *If the user's signature scheme is* $(q_{Auth}, \tau, \epsilon)$*-existentially unforgeable against chosen message attacks and the discrete logarithm problem in* $\mathbb{G}_1$ *is* (τ', ϵ')*-hard, then our proposed anonymous credential system with revocation is* $\left(\tau'', q''_{Auth}, \epsilon''\right)$*-non-frameable, provided that*

$$\frac{1}{2}\left(1-2e^{\frac{\epsilon''}{2(\epsilon''-1)}n}\right)\left(1-2e^{\frac{p\epsilon''-2}{2(p\epsilon''-2-2p)}n}\right) \geq \epsilon', \ \epsilon'' \geq \epsilon, min\left(\frac{\tau'-\Theta(T)}{2n}, \tau\right) \geq \tau'', q_{Auth'} \leq q_{Auth}.$$

Proof. Assume Adv is an adversary that (τ', ϵ')-breaks the non-frameability of our proposed anonymous credential system with revocation. We then construct an algorithm $\mathcal{A}$ that, by interacting with Adv, breaks the unforgeability of the user's signature scheme or the discrete logarithm problem.

Algorithm $\mathcal{A}$ is given public-key pk_U of the user's signature scheme and instance $g_2, g_2^q \in \mathbb{G}_2$ of the discrete logarithm problem. $\mathcal{A}$ gives Adv $\mathbb{G}_2, g_2$ as a system parameter. Adv generates authority's public-keys and opener's public keys. Adv then generates its secret-key. $\mathcal{A}$ concurrently executes the following two procedures. The first one is breaking the unforgeability of the user's signature scheme. $\mathcal{A}$ generates a user $\mathcal{U}$ and registers pk_U as the public-key of $\mathcal{U}$. The second one is breaking the discrete logarithm problem. $\mathcal{A}$ generates a user $\mathcal{U}$, generates a new key $\left(pk'_U, sk'_U\right)$, and uses g_2^q as the value given to Adv (Auth) at credential issuing protocol.

Adv first generates its secret-key as a user, and creates its credential Cred_{Adv} on m. Adv then executes the credential proving protocol of σ_{Adv} with an honest verifier $\mathcal{V}$. Eventually, Adv employs the identity revealing protocol with $\mathcal{V}$, and creates accepted proof for $\mathcal{V}$ that $\mathcal{U}$, who is an honest user, produced the proof of Cred_{Adv}. This means Adv outputs $\left(\sigma, r, s, sig_U\left(g_2^q\right), g_2^q, m\right)$ that is accepted by $\mathcal{V}$ as $\mathcal{U}$'s proof of Cred_{Adv}.

If Adv outputs in the first procedure, $\left(g_2^q, sig_U\left(g_2^q\right)\right)$ is a forged signature of the user's signature scheme. If Adv outputs in the second procedure, $\mathcal{A}$ extracts q in the same manner as in the proof of **Unforgeability** by using `Adv` as a black-box. Thus, $\mathcal{A}$ can forge the signature scheme or break the discrete logarithm problem, with the maximum time $\tau' \geq 2n\tau'' + \Theta(T)$ and the advantage $\frac{1}{2}\left(1 - 2e^{\frac{\epsilon''}{2(\epsilon''-1)}n}\right)\left(1 - 2e^{\frac{p\epsilon''-2}{2(p\epsilon''-2-2p)}n}\right) \geq \epsilon'$.   □

5.6   Comparison

We turn now to the efficiency of our anonymous credential system. The upper table in **Table.1** is a comparison of our basic system and an existing system [3]. "pk" means the public-key specific to each user (excluding the system parameters), and "sk" means the secret-key. "Size of `Prov`" means communication complexity between $\mathcal{U}$ and $\mathcal{V}$ in the credential proving protocol (`Prov` denotes a credential proving protocol). "Ops" means the number of operations.

We show a comparison of our system with revocation and the existing system [5] in the lower table in **Table.1**. "Size of `Reveal`" means communication complexity between O and $\mathcal{V}$ in the identity revealing protocol (`Reveal` denotes an identity revealing protocol). N is the size of an RSA modulus. A number l means the number of blacklisted users.

Table 1. Comparison

	CL04 [3]	Our proposed basic system
Assumption	LRSW	SDH
Size of pk	3 elements in $\mathbb{G}_1$	1 element in $\mathbb{G}_1$
Size of sk	3 elements in $\mathbb{Z}_p$	1 element in $\mathbb{Z}_p$
Size of Cred	5 elements in $\mathbb{G}_1$	1 element in $\mathbb{G}_1$, 2 elements in $\mathbb{Z}_p$
Size of Prov	5 elements in $\mathbb{G}_1$, 1 element in $\mathbb{G}_T$, 4 elements in $\mathbb{Z}_p$	9 elements in $\mathbb{G}_1$, 12 elements in $\mathbb{Z}_p$
Ops to issue Cred	4.3 exps in $\mathbb{G}_1$	1.3 exps in $\mathbb{G}_1$
Ops to verify Cred	4.3 exps in $\mathbb{G}_1$, 8 pairings	2.6 exps in $\mathbb{G}_1$, 2 pairings
Ops to prove in Prov	4 pairings, 5 exps in $\mathbb{G}_1$, 1.3 exps in $\mathbb{G}_T$	11.4 exps in $\mathbb{G}_1$
Ops to verify in Prov	10 pairings, 1.3 exps in $\mathbb{G}_1$	2 pairings, 5.2 exps in $\mathbb{G}_1$
	CL01 [5]	Our proposed system with revocation
Assumption	strong RSA, DDH	SDH
Size of pk	10 elements in $\mathbb{Z}_N^*$	3 elements in $\mathbb{G}_1$, size of sk_U
Size of sk	7 elements in $\mathbb{Z}_N^*$	4 elements in $\mathbb{Z}_p$, size of pk_U
Size of Cred	3 elements in $\mathbb{Z}_N^*$	1 element in $\mathbb{G}_1$, 2 elements in $\mathbb{Z}_p$
Size of Prov	9 elements in $\mathbb{Z}_N^*$	20 elements in $\mathbb{G}_1$, 15 elements in $\mathbb{Z}_p$
Size of Reveal	15 elements in $\mathbb{Z}_N^*$	12 elements in $\mathbb{G}_1$, 3 elements in $\mathbb{Z}_p$
Ops to issue Cred	1 exp in $\mathbb{Z}_N^*$	1.3 exps in $\mathbb{G}_1$, Ops to issue $sig_U\left(g_2^q\right)$
Ops to verify Cred	1 exp in $\mathbb{Z}_N^*$	2.6 exps in $\mathbb{G}_1$, 2 pairings
Ops to prove in Prov	6.5 exps in $\mathbb{Z}_N^*$	20.6 exps in $\mathbb{G}_1$
Ops to verify in Prov	3.9 exps in $\mathbb{Z}_N^*$	$(3l + 2)$ pairings, 10.4 exps in $\mathbb{G}_1$
Ops to open in Reveal	10.2 exps in $\mathbb{Z}_N^*$	7.3 exps in $\mathbb{G}_1$, Ops to verify $sig_U\left(g_2^q\right)$
Ops to verify in Reveal	5.9 exps in $\mathbb{Z}_N^*$	2 pairings, 7.5 exps in $\mathbb{G}_1$
Blacklisting	Not available	Available
Identity revealing	Available	Available

References

1. Chaum, D.: Security without identification: transaction systems to make big brother obsolete. Commun. ACM 28(10), 1030–1044 (1985)
2. Lysyanskaya, A.: Signature Schemes and Applications to Cryptographic Protocol Design. Ph.D thesis, Massachusetts Institute of Technology, Cambridge, MA, USA (2002)
3. Camenisch, J., Lysyanskaya, A.: Signature schemes and anonymous credentials from bilinear maps. In: Franklin, M. (ed.) CRYPTO 2004. LNCS, vol. 3152, pp. 56–72. Springer, Heidelberg (2004)
4. Lysyanskaya, A., Rivest, R.L., Sahai, A., Wolf, S.: Pseudonym Systems. In: Heys, H.M., Adams, C.M. (eds.) SAC 1999. LNCS, vol. 1758, pp. 184–199. Springer, Heidelberg (2000)
5. Camenisch, J., Lysyanskaya, A.: An efficient non-transferable anonymous multi-show credential system with optional anonymity revocation. In: Pfitzmann, B. (ed.) EUROCRYPT 2001. LNCS, vol. 2045, pp. 93–118. Springer, Heidelberg (2001)
6. Tsang, P., Au, M.H., Kapadia, A., Smith, S.: Blacklistable Anonymous Credentials: Blocking Misbehaving Users without TTPs. In: CCS 2007, 14th ACM conf. on computer and communications security, pp. 72–81 (2007)
7. Boneh, D., Boyen, X.: Short Signatures without Random Oracles. In: Cachin, C., Camenisch, J.L. (eds.) EUROCRYPT 2004. LNCS, vol. 3027, pp. 382–400. Springer, Heidelberg (2004)
8. Boneh, D., Lynn, B., Shacham, H.: Short Signatures from the Weil Pairing. In: Boyd, C. (ed.) ASIACRYPT 2001. LNCS, vol. 2248, pp. 514–532. Springer, Heidelberg (2001)
9. Boneh, D., Boyen, X., Shacham, H.: Short Group Signatures. In: Franklin, M. (ed.) CRYPTO 2004. LNCS, vol. 3152, pp. 41–55. Springer, Heidelberg (2004)
10. Okamoto, T.: Efficient Blind and Partially Blind Signatures Without Random Oracles. In: Halevi, S., Rabin, T. (eds.) TCC 2006. LNCS, vol. 3876, pp. 80–99. Springer, Heidelberg (2006)

Practical Anonymous Divisible E-Cash from Bounded Accumulators*

Man Ho Au, Willy Susilo, and Yi Mu

Centre for Computer and Information Security Research
School of Computer Science and Software Engineering
University of Wollongong, Australia
{mhaa456,wsusilo,ymu}@uow.edu.au

Abstract. We present an efficient off-line divisible e-cash scheme which is *truly anonymous* without a trusted third party. This is the second scheme in the literature which achieves full unlinkability and anonymity, after the seminal work proposed by Canard and Gouget. The main trick of our scheme is the use of a bounded accumulator in combination with the classical binary tree approach.

The aims of this paper are twofold. Firstly, we analyze Canard and Gouget's seminal work on the efficient off-line divisible e-cash. We point out some subtleties on the parameters generation of their scheme. Moreover, spending a coin of small value requires computation of several hundreds of multi-based exponentiations, which is very costly. In short, although this seminal work provides a new approach of achieving a truly anonymous divisible e-cash, unfortunately it is rather impractical. Secondly, we present our scheme that uses a novel approach of incorporating a bounded accumulator. In terms of time and space complexities, our scheme is 50 to 100 times more efficient than Canard and Gouget's work in the spend protocol at the cost of an 10 to 500 (the large range is due to whether pre-processing is taken into account and the probabilistic nature of our withdrawal protocol) times less efficient withdrawal protocol. We believe this trade-off between the withdrawal protocol and the spend protocol is reasonable as the former protocol is to be executed much less frequent than the latter. Nonetheless, while their scheme provides an affirmative answer to whether divisible e-cash can be *truly anonymous*, our result puts it a step further and we show that truly anonymous divisible e-cash can be *practical*.

1 Introduction

Electronic cash (e-cash) was introduced by Chaum [15] in 1982. In its simplest form, an *e-cash* system consists of three parties (the bank $\mathcal{B}$, the user $\mathcal{U}$ and the merchant $\mathcal{M}$) and four main procedures, namely, account establishment, withdrawal, spending and deposit. The user $\mathcal{U}$ first performs an account establishment protocol with the bank $\mathcal{B}$. The currency circulating around is quantized as

---

* This work is supported by ARC Linkage Project LP0667899 and ARC Discovery Grant DP0877123.

G. Tsudik (Ed.): FC 2008, LNCS 5143, pp. 287–301, 2008.

coins. $\mathcal{U}$ obtains a coin by performing a withdrawal protocol with $\mathcal{B}$ and spends the coin by participating in a spend protocol with $\mathcal{M}$. To deposit a coin, $\mathcal{S}$ performs a deposit protocol with $\mathcal{B}$.

A practical electronic cash system should be *secure*, *offline* and *anonymous*. An e-cash system is *offline* when the spend protocol does *not* require $\mathcal{B}$'s participation. In a *secure* e-cash system, only $\mathcal{B}$ can produce a valid electronic coin and users who double-spent the same coin should be identified. The problem of double-spending occurs in the electronic world due to the digital coins ease of duplication. Additionally, honest spenders cannot be slandered to have double-spent (*exculpability*), and when $\mathcal{M}$ deposits the money from the payee, $\mathcal{B}$ should not be able to trace who the actual spender is (*anonymity*). In a *truly anonymous* e-cash, $\mathcal{B}$, even with the help of $\mathcal{M}$, cannot obtain any information about the identity of the payee. In particular, spending of the same payee cannot be linked together (sometimes refer to as *unlinkability*).

High *efficiency* is also of key importance for practical *e-cash* systems. For efficiency, we look at: (1) the time and bandwidth needed for the withdrawal, spend and deposit protocols; (2) the size of an electronic coin; and (3) the size of the bank's database. In particular, it is desirable if several coins can be withdrawn or spent more efficiently than repeating several times a single withdrawal or spending protocol.

1.1 Related Results

In a compact e-cash system [9,4], users can withdraw efficiently a wallet $\mathcal{W}$ containing 2^L coins. However, these coins must be spent one by one. Users in a divisible e-cash system can efficiently withdraw a wallet $\mathcal{W}$ containing 2^L coins (à la compact e-cash). However, these 2^L coins can be spent together efficiently. In particular, spending $2^\ell, \ell \leq L$, coins together can be done more efficiently than repeating the spend protocol for 2^ℓ times.

A lot of divisible e-cash schemes exist in the literature [24,25,16,17,23,14,21,12]. Nonetheless, with the exception of [12], none of the above divisible e-cash system is *truly anonymous*. For instance, everyone can tell whether the spending in [23,14] is from the same wallet (i.e., linkable). In [21], there exists a trusted party who can revoke the identity of every spender (also known as fair e-cash [13]). Moreover, which part of the wallet that is being used is known. That is, if the payee of transaction one and the payee of transaction two are using the same part of a wallet, everyone can conclude that these two transactions are indeed performed with different wallets. We shall investigate the practicality of the only *truly anonymous* divisible e-cash scheme [12] in the next subsection. On the other hand, in contrast to the divisible e-cash schemes, existing compact e-cash schemes [9,4,3] are all *truly anonymous*.

1.2 On the Practicality of the Truly Anonymous Divisible E-Cash in [12]

We analyze the Canard and Gouget's scheme from [12]. To allow efficeint withdrawal of 2^L coins, the construction in [12] requires a series of $L+2$ cyclic groups

$(\mathbb{G} = \langle g \rangle, \mathbb{G}_1 = \langle g_1 \rangle, \ldots, \mathbb{G}_{L+1} = \langle g_{L+1} \rangle)$ such that $\mathbb{G}_i \subset \mathbb{Z}^*_{|\mathbb{G}_{i+1}|}$ for $i = 1$ to $L + 1$ and $\mathbb{G} \subset \mathbb{Z}^*_{|\mathbb{G}_1|}$[1] and the decisional discrete logarithm assumption (DDH) holds in all $\mathbb{G}_i$. However, whether such series of groups exists, for moderate L (say, $L = 10$), is unknown. The authors suggest using the same setting of groups in [21] which proposes to set $|\mathbb{G}_i|$, for $i = 1$ to $L+1$, to be of prime order and assume $|\mathbb{G}_{i+1}| = 2|\mathbb{G}_i| + 1$ for $i = 1$ to $L + 1$. This implies finding a series of primes $p_1, \ldots, p_{L+1}$ such that $p_{i+1} = 2p_i + 1$. Again, whether such series of primes exist, for moderate L, is unknown and it is also unknown how these series of primes can be efficiently generated. The authors in [21] propose using a brute-force approach. That is, randomly generate an odd number n (equals to order of group $\mathbb{G}$) and test if $p_1 := 2n + 1$ is a prime. If yes, compute and test if $p_2 := 2p_1 + 1$ is prime. Continue until $p_{L+1} := 2p_L + 1$ is also a prime. A well-known result, the prime number theory, states that the number of primes not exceeding m is approximately $\frac{m}{\ln(m)}$. Thus, probability that a k-bit odd number is a prime is about $\frac{2}{k \ln 2}$. For a randomly generated k-bit odd number n, probability that $(p_1, \ldots, p_{L+1})$ are primes such that $p_{i+1} := 2p_i + 1$ and $p_1 := 2n + 1$ is approximately $\frac{k! 2^L}{(k+L+1)!(\ln(2)^L)}$. Taking $k = 170$ and $L = 10$, probability of obtaining such series of prime numbers on a given k-bit odd number n is about 2^{-66}. In fact, in [21], n is taken to be an RSA-modulus (which is normally of 1024-bit), and the corresponding probability is 2^{-94}. Therefore, it is questionable whether the systems in [21] or [12] are in fact implementable.

The spend protocol in [12] is also quite inefficient. As mentioned in the same paper, the authors regard spending a single coin as quite an expensive operation. It is due to the need of L "1-out-of-2 zero-knowledge proof-of-knowledge of of double discrete logarithm". For a cheating probability of 2^{-t}, a single zero-knowledge proof-of-knowledge of double discrete logarithms requires t exponentiations. For a cheating probability of 2^{-40} and a moderate L (say 10), spending a single coin requires $2 * 40 * 10 = 800$ exponentiations. Moreover, it requires a commmunication cost of more than 800 group elements (each group element shall be of size greater than 1kb). Details analysis of the cost of each protocol can be found in Section 5. Nonetheless, while [12] provides an affirmative answer to whether divisible e-cash can be truly anonymous, it is fair to say constructing a *practical* divisible e-cash which is truly anonymous is not as easy.

1.3   Our Approach

The construction of our divisible e-cash is derived from the classical binary tree approach [23,21,14,12], in combination with the use of a bounded accumulator [4]. We make use of the bounded accumulator to make a trade-off between computational cost during the withdrawal protocol and the spend protocol. The cost (computational and bandwidth) of our withdrawal protocol and spend protocol is $O(L)$ and $O(1)$, respectively, while the corresponding figures for [12] is $O(1)$

---

[1] In [12], it was written as $\mathbb{G}_1 \subset \mathbb{Z}^*_{|\mathbb{G}|}$. However, according to their construction(as it involves computation of $g_1^{g^s}$ for some s in $\mathbb{Z}^*_{|\mathbb{G}|}$), $\mathbb{G} \subset \mathbb{Z}^*_{|\mathbb{G}_1|}$ should be the case.

and $O(Lt)$. Since the spending protocol is executed much more frequently than the withdrawal protocol, our system is much more desirable in practice.

The trade-off is achieved with the use of accumulators [7,5]. During the withdrawal protocol, the user computes the accumulation of the binary tree into $L+1$ accumulator values $(V_1, \ldots, V_{L+1})$ and obtains $L + 1$ signatures. In the spending protocol, if a node of level ℓ is to be used, the user only needs to compute a zero-knowledge proof-of-knowledge such that the node he is about to use is inside the accumulator V_ℓ. In this way, our spend protocol achieves a complexity of $O(1)$.

An obvious way to ensure the user honestly accumulates node values that form a binary tree, while maintaining anonymity, is to require the user to produce zero-knowledge proof-of-knowledge such that these set of accumulator values $(V_1, \ldots, V_{L+1})$ is correctly formed. This approach, however, is inefficient. Another approach is to apply the cut-and-choose method in a straight-forward manner. Specifically, the user prepares k sets of value, submits them all to the bank who requires the user to reveal $k - 1$ of them in random. The bank checks if these $k - 1$ sets of value are honestly generated and signs the remaining one if the check is successful. To ensure that a user cannot cheat, k has to be large. Thus, this approach is inefficient as well.

Luckily, bounded accumulator gives us the possibility of a third solution, which is a modification of the cut-and-choose method. Our approach is *statistical*, that is, a cheating user might spend more than what he withdraws for a particular withdrawal protocol but in a long run, the bank is guaranteed that users cannot spend more than they withdraw on average. The idea is derived from the following fact: since the accumulator we use is bounded, the user can only accumulate a predefined number of values regardless of whether they are cheating or not. Naturally, there is an upper bound for which a cheating user might gain. In our scheme, the cheating user can get at most a monetary value of $L2^L$, compared with a value of 2^L for an honest user. If the bank inspects the withdrawal protocol every two withdrawal requests and imposes a fine of monetary value $2L2^L$ if a user is found cheating, the bank is guaranteed it will not lost money on average. In Section 3, we will formally define the security model for divisible e-cash schemes that employ this kind of *statistical* approach. In particular, the gain of a cheater cannot be large; since if the gain is large, a cheater might not be able to pay the fine if he is caught. Secondly, a large gain gives extra incentive for people to cheat.

Our Contributions. We propose a practical offline divisible e-cash without a trusted third party which is truly anonymous (unlinkable). We formalize the security model of divisible e-cash scheme that employs a *statistical* approach and prove that our construction is secure under this model. We compare the efficiency of our construction to that of [12] and shows that our system can be more than 50 to 100 times more efficient, in terms of time and space, in the spending protocol.

Paper Outline. The rest of the paper is organized as follows. In Section 2 we present preliminary information on the various cryptographic tools and assumptions used in our construction. Security model of divisible e-cash is presented in Section 3. We present our construction in Section 4 and its efficiency analysis in Section 5. Finally we conclude in Section 6.

2 Preliminaries

2.1 Pairing

A pairing is a bilinear mapping from two group elements to a group element. Let $\hat{e}$ be a bilinear map such that $\hat{e} : \mathbb{G}_1 \times \mathbb{G}_2 \to \mathbb{G}_3$ and the following holds.

- $\mathbb{G}_1$ and $\mathbb{G}_2$ are cyclic multiplicative groups of prime order p.
- Each element of $\mathbb{G}_1$, $\mathbb{G}_2$ and $\mathbb{G}_3$ has unique binary representation.
- g, h are generators of $\mathbb{G}_1$ and $\mathbb{G}_2$ respectively.
- (*Bilinear*) $\forall x \in \mathbb{G}_1$, $y \in \mathbb{G}_2$ and $a, b \in \mathbb{Z}_p^*$, $\hat{e}(x^a, y^b) = \hat{e}(x, y)^{ab}$.
- (*Non-degenerate*)$\hat{e}(g, h) \neq 1$.

$\mathbb{G}_1$ and $\mathbb{G}_2$ can be the same or different groups. We say that two groups $(\mathbb{G}_1, \mathbb{G}_2)$ are a bilinear group pair if the group action in $\mathbb{G}_1$, $\mathbb{G}_2$ and the bilinear mapping e are all efficiently computable.

2.2 Mathematical Assumptions

Security of our construction depends on the following existing mathematical assumptions, namely, Decisional Diffie-Hellman, Symmetric External Diffie-Hellman [1], q-Strong Diffie-Hellman [8] and AWSM [4]. Their definitions can be found in the full version of the paper [2].

2.3 Useful Tools

Zero-Knowledge Proof of Knowledge. In zero-knowledge proof of knowledge [19], a prover proves to a verifier that a statement is true without revealing anything other than the veracity of the statement. Our construction involves statements related to knowledge of discrete logarithms constructed over a cyclic group $\mathbb{G}$ of prime order p. These proofs can also be used non-interactively by using the Fiat-Shamir heuristic [18]. The non-interactive counter part is referred to as signature proof of knowledge, or SPK for short. They are secure in the random oracle model [6]. Following the notation introduced by Camenisch and Stadler [11], $PK\{(x) : y = g^x\}$ denotes a zero-knowledge proof of knowledge protocol between a prover and a verifier such that the prover knows some $x \in \mathbb{Z}_p$ such that $y = g^x \in \mathbb{G}$. Construction of this proof first appeared in the Schnorr Identification[26]. The corresponding non-interactive signature proof of knowledge shall be denoted as $SPK\{(x) : y = g^x\}(M)$.

ESS+ Signature. Extended special signature (ESS) was introduced in [4]. It allows signing a block of messages, one of which being an element in a cyclic group $\mathbb{G}$. The authors also proposed two protocols, namely, signature generation protocol and signature possession protocol. The signature generation protocol allows a user to obtain a signature from the signer on message M in $\mathbb{G}$, together with a block of messages $m_1, \ldots, m_L$ in a commitment. The signer learns nothing about $m_1, \ldots, m_L$ while he knows M. The signature possession protocol allows a user to conduct a zero-knowledge proof of knowledge on a message signature pair. ESS scheme is uf-cma secure[20] under the AWSM assumption. We modify the signing protocol of ESS so that the signer learns nothing on the block of messages to be signed as well. We refer this modified signature scheme as ESS+ Signature, which is outlined in the full version of the paper [2].

ESS+ signature is uf-cma secure in the standard model under the AWSM assumption. We would like to remark that AWSM is a strong assumption, as it requires bilinear group pair where the SXDH assumption [1] holds.

Bounded Accumulator. The notion, bounded accumulator was introduced in [4] as an accumulator with a limit q as the maximum number of elements that can be accumulated. We briefly review their construction here.

Let $\mathbb{G}_1, \mathbb{G}_2$ be a bilinear group pair. Let u_0 be a random element in $\mathbb{G}_1$ and v_0 be a random element in $\mathbb{G}_2$. Let q be the bound of the accumulator. The generation algorithm randomly selects $\alpha \in \mathbb{Z}_p^*$ and computes $u_i = u_0^{\alpha^i}$ for $i = 1 \ldots, q$. Compute $v_1 = v_0^\alpha$. The public parameters is $(u_0, \ldots, u_q, v_0, v_1)$.

To accumulate a set of q values $(e_1, \ldots, e_k)$, the evaluation algorithm computes the accumulator value $V = u_0^{\prod_{k=1}^{k=q}(e_k + \alpha)}$. This operation does not require knowledge of α since the u_i's are published. A witness w_i such that value e_i is accumulated in the accumulator V is computed by $w_i = u_0^{\prod_{k=1, k \neq i}^{k=q}(e_k + \alpha)}$. The witness-value pair shall satisfy $\hat{e}(w_i, v_1 v_0^{e_i}) = \hat{e}(u_0, v_0)$. Construction of Zero-knowledge proof of knowledge on a value-witness pair can be found in [22].

3 Syntax

A (statistical) divisible e-cash is a tuple (BankSetup, UserSetup, WithdrawalProtocol, SpendProtocol, DepositProtocol, RevokeDoubleSpender, VerifyGuilt) of seven polynomial time algorithms/protocols between three entities the bank $\mathcal{B}$, the merchant $\mathcal{M}$ and the user $\mathcal{U}$.

- BankSetup. On input an unary string 1^λ, where λ is the security parameter, the algorithm outputs $\mathcal{B}$'s key pair bpk, bsk, which includes wallet size L, punishment P if a user is found cheating in Inspection Routine(to be discussed) and frequency of which Inspection Routine is carried out K.
- UserSetup. On input bpk, the algorithm outputs a key pair $(pk_\mathcal{U}, sk_\mathcal{U})$ (resp. $(pk_\mathcal{M}, sk_\mathcal{M})$) for $\mathcal{U}$ (resp. $\mathcal{M}$).
- WithdrawalProtocol. $\mathcal{U}$ with input $(pk_\mathcal{U}, sk_\mathcal{U})$ wishes to withdraws a wallet $\mathcal{W}$ of 2^L coins from $\mathcal{B}$ (with input (bpk, bsk)). This protocol consists of two routines, namely, Withdrawal Routine and Inspection Routine, respectively. These

two routines share the same steps in the beginning such that the user is not aware which routine the bank selects. At a particular point in the protocol, the bank chooses one of these two routines.

- Withdrawal Routine. With probability $\frac{K-1}{K}$, Withdrawal Routine is executed. The user obtains a wallet $\mathcal{W}$ after executing the protocol, while the bank (possibly) retains certain information τ_w, called the trace information.
- Inspection Routine. With probability $\frac{1}{K}$, Inspection Routine is executed. Inspection Routine outputs pass/cheat. If the output is cheat, a fine of P shall be deducted from the user account. If the output is pass, the user is asked to restart WithdrawalProtocol from the beginning.

- SpendProtocol. This is the protocol when $\mathcal{U}$(with input $\mathcal{W}$, $pk_{\mathcal{M}}$) spends a divisible coin of value 2^ℓ ($\ell \leq L$ and is decided by the user) to $\mathcal{M}$. After the protocol, $\mathcal{M}$ obtains a coin serial number S_ℓ, a proof of validity π_S, and possibly some auxiliary information aux, and outputs 0/1, depending whether the payment is accepted. $\mathcal{U}$'s output is an updated wallet $\mathcal{W}'$.
- DepositProtocol. $\mathcal{M}$ submits (S_ℓ, π_S, aux) to $\mathcal{B}$ for deposit in this protocol. $\mathcal{B}$ outputs 0/1, indicating whether the deposit is accepted. $\mathcal{B}$ computes, from S_ℓ, 2^ℓ serial numbers $\tilde{S}_1, \ldots, \tilde{S}_{2^\ell}$. If any of the serial numbers $\tilde{S}_i$ already belongs to $\mathcal{L}$ (the database of spent coins), $\mathcal{B}$ invokes the RevokeDoubleSpender algorithm to find out the double-spender. Otherwise, it adds $\tilde{S}_i, S_\ell, \pi_S, aux$ to $\mathcal{L}$.
- RevokeDoubleSpender. Formally, on input two spending protocol transcripts involving the same coin, the algorithm outputs the public key pk of the double-spender.
- VerifyGuilt. This algorithm allows the public to verify that the user with public key pk is guilty of double-spending. In particular, when the bank uses RevokeDoubleSpender and outputs π_D and pk of the double-spender, everyone can check if the bank is honest.

Requirements:

- (Correctness for User.) It is required whenever an honest user obtains $\mathcal{W}$ from the bank *who might be dishonest*, an honest merchant shall output 1 when the user engage with the merchant in SpendProtocol.
- (Correctness for Merchant.) It is required whenever an honest merchant obtains (S_ℓ, π_S, aux) from some execution of SpendProtocol with some user *who might be dishonest*, there is a guarantee that this transaction will be accepted by the honest bank.[2]
- (Practicality.) It is required that P should be small enough so that the fine is payable. For example, if $P = (2^L)^2$, it is very likely that even when a user is found cheating in Inspection Routine, he is unable to pay the fine. In practice, we suggest $P \leq KL2^L$.

---

[2] It can be seen that it is the bank's responsibility to identify the double-spender. The rationale behind is that a user can always spend the same coin to different merchants in an offline e-cash system and the merchant have no way to detect such a double-spending.

3.1   Security Notions

We describe informally the security requirements of a statistical divisible e-cash system. A *secure* statistical divisible e-cash scheme should possess, *statistical balance, IdentificationOfDoubleSpender, anonymity* and *exculpability*, introduced as follows. The reader may refer to the full version [2] for the formal version of these definitions.

- *Statistical Balance.* This is the most important requirement from the bank's point of view. Roughly speaking, *balance* means that no collusion of users and merchants together can deposit more than they withdraw without being identified. *Statistical Balance* means that, in a long run, the *balance* property is guaranteed. *Statistical Balance* is a relaxation of *balance* since it does not rule out the possibility that a user might cheat without being detected and gain a certain advantage within a small number of times. However, in a long run, no successful strategy would allow collusion of users and merchants to deposit more than they withdraw without being identified.

  In particular, what we wish to model is the following situation. The bank does not check every withdrawal request. However, if the user cheats during the withdrawal, at most he can gain a monetary value P. If the bank only checks once every K transactions and imposes a fine of KP for each caught cheating, the *Statistical Balance* property will be achieved. It turns out that this relaxation greatly increase the efficiency of our system.
- *Anonymity.* It is required that no collusion of users, merchants and the bank can ever learn the spending habit of an honest user. In particular, spending of the same user *cannot* be linked.
- *Exculpability.* It is required that an honest user cannot be proven to have double-spent, even all other users, merchants and the bank collude.

A statistical divisible e-cash is said to be *secure* if it has Statistical Balance, Anonymity and Exculpability.

4   Construction

In this section, we describe our cryptographic construction in detail and assess its security, after giving a high level description.

4.1   High Level Description

Following the terminology of [9,12], spending a single electronic coin consists of generating a serial number S, which is used to detect double-spending, a security tag T, which is used to reveal identity of the double-spender should the underlying coin is being spent twice. The spender has to prove to the merchant that the pair (S, T) is well-formed. Nonetheless, we provide an overview of our system as follows.

The Setup Procedure. The bank $\mathcal{B}$ generates **ESS+**.pk, **ESS+**.sk pair of the ESS+ Signature. The bank also generates the public parameters of the bounded accumulator as $\mathbf{Acc}_1, \ldots, \mathbf{Acc}_{L+1}$. Let LF, RF be two secure cryptographic hash functions. Let H be another secure cryptographic hash function. Let $\mathbb{G} = \langle g \rangle$ be a cyclic group of prime order p such that DDH assumption holds. Let g_U, h be additional generators of $\mathbb{G}$.

The Account Establishment Procedure. User Alice establishes an account with the bank $\mathcal{B}$ by selecting $x \in \mathbb{Z}_p^*$ and computes $PK_{Alice} := g_U^x$. She sends PK_{Alice} to $\mathcal{B}$, along with a zero-knowledge proof-of-knowledge of the corresponding secret key x.

The Withdrawal Procedure. Suppose user Alice, who has already established an account with the bank, wishes to withdraw a wallet containing 2^L coins. She first randomly chooses a wallet secret w and computes a binary tree of $L + 1$ level as follows. The root note $N_{0,0}$ is assigned the node key value $k_{0,0} := w$. For all nodes $N_{i,j}$, the left children, $N_{i+1,2j}$, is assigned a node key value $k_{i+1,2j} := LF(g^{k_{i,j}})$. Similarly, the right children, $N_{i+1,2j+1}$, is assigned a node key value $k_{i+1,2j+1} := RF(g^{k_{i,j}})$. Let T_w be the resulting binary tree computed by Alice.

For $i = 0$ to L, compute $V_i := \mathbf{Acc}_i.\text{Accumulate}(k_{i,0}, \ldots, k_{i,2^i-1})$. Alice then tries to obtain $L + 1$ ESS+ Signature on block of messages (V_i, x) using the signature generation protocol of ESS+ Signature.

$\mathcal{B}$ flips a fair coin b and if $b == 1$, $\mathcal{B}$ generates signatures $\sigma_i = \mathbf{ESS+}.\text{Sign}(V_i, x)$ using the signature generation protocol of ESS+ Signature (so that $\mathcal{B}$ learns nothing about V_i, x as discussed.) $\mathcal{B}$ sends $\sigma := \{\sigma_0, \ldots, \sigma_L\}$ back to Alice. Alice stores (σ, T_w) as her wallet $\mathcal{W}$.

Otherwise if $b == 0$, $\mathcal{B}$ asks Alice to reveal her binary tree. $\mathcal{B}$ tests if the V_i's are honestly generated (that is, checks whether V_i is the accumulation of $k_{i,0}, \ldots, k_{i,2^i-1}$). If yes, $\mathcal{B}$ asks Alice to restart the withdrawal procedure. Otherwise, a fine of $2L2^L$ is deducted from Alice's account.

The Spending Procedure. Suppose user Alice with wallet $\mathcal{W}$ wishes to spend to merchant Bob 2^ℓ dollar where $\ell \leq L$. Alice and Bob agree on certain transaction information I which contains identity of Bob and the monetary value 2^ℓ. Bob also sends Alice a random challenge R.

She first chooses a node from the binary tree T_w at level $L - \ell$ which has not been marked as used. Let $N_{i,j}$ be the node chosen (that is, $i = L - \ell$). Compute serial number $S = g^{k_{i,j}}$. Compute security tag $T = g_U^x h^{k_{i,j}R}$.

Alice sends to Bob S, T together with a proof π which is a non-interactive zero-knowledge proof-of-knowledge of the following statement:

Alice is in possession of quantities V_i, $k_{i,j}$, x, σ_i which satisfy the following relationship:

1. $\mathbf{ESS+}.\text{Verify}(\sigma_i, V_i, x) = 1$ (using the signature possession algorithm of ESS+ Signature.)
2. $k_{i,j}$ is a value inside the accumulator V_i

3. $S = g^{k_{i,j}}$
4. $T = g_U^x h^{k_{i,j}R}$

Bob verifies if π is a valid proof. It accepts the payment if the proof is valid. If Bob accepts the payment, Alice marked down $N_{i,j}$ and all its children, as well as ancestors, from T_w as used node.

The Deposit Procedure. Bob sends (S, T, π, R, ℓ) to the bank for deposit. The bank checks if R is fresh (that is, if R has been used before by Bob). If the check is successful, then credit Bob's account.

The bank then tries to detect if the coin S has been double-spent. Let S be the serial number of a coin of monetary value 2^ℓ. Let $N_{i,j}$ be the corresponding node of the binary tree. From S, the bank computes the 2^ℓ serial numbers corresponding to the leaves of subtree of node $N_{i,j}$ by repeatedly applying the functions $LF(\cdot)$, $RF(\cdot)$ and $g^{(\cdot)}$.

For each serial number S_i, the bank checks if it exists in the database. If not, it stores (S_i, S, T, R, π) in its database. Suppose there exists another entry in the database (S_i', S', T', R', π'), the bank runs the identify procedure discussed in the following subsection.

The Identify (Double-Spender) Procedure. On input two entries (S_i, S, T, R, π) and (S_i', S', T', R', π'), the bank computes the identity of the double-spender as follows. If S and S' are the same, compute $PK_{\text{cheater}} := (\frac{T^{R'}}{T'^R})^{\frac{1}{R'-R}}$.

On the other hand, if S and S' are different, S and S' must be of different monetary value. Without loss of generality, assume the monetary value of coin with serial number S is greater than that of S'. The bank can compute the node key $k_{i,j}$ such that $S' = g^{k_{i,j}}$ from S by repeatedly applying the $LF(\cdot)$, $RF(\cdot)$, $g^{(\cdot)}$ in suitable order. From $k_{i,j}$, the bank computes $pk_{\text{cheater}} = \frac{T'}{h^{R'k_{i,j}}}$ and obtains identity of the double-spender.

This completes the high-level description of our system.

4.2   System Construction

Bank's Setup. Let 2^L be the size of a wallet in the system. Let λ be a security parameter. On input λ, generate a λ-bit prime p. Generate a bilinear group pair of order p. That is, $\hat{e} : \mathbb{G}_1 \times \mathbb{G}_2 \to \mathbb{G}_3$ is a bilinear map such that $|\mathbb{G}_1| = |\mathbb{G}_2| = |\mathbb{G}_3| = p$. Let $g, g_A, g_B, g_0, g_1, g_2, g_3, g_4, u_0, g_U, g_S, g_T$ be random elements in $\mathbb{G}_1$, h, h_1, h_2, h_3, v be random elements in $\mathbb{G}_2$. Since $\mathbb{G}_1$, $\mathbb{G}_2$ are of prime orders, all the above random elements are generators. Let $H : \{0,1\}^* \to \mathbb{Z}_p^*$ be a secure cryptographic hash function. Let $H_0 : \{0,1\}^* \to \mathbb{Z}_p^*$, $H_1 : \{0,1\}^* \to \mathbb{Z}_p^*$ be two other secure cryptographic hash function.

The bank randomly chooses $X \in \mathbb{G}_1$, $y, \alpha_0, \ldots, \alpha_L \in \mathbb{Z}_p^*$. Compute $Y = h^y$ and $Z = \hat{e}(X, h)$. For $i = 0$ to L and for $j = 1$ to 2^i, compute $u_{i,j} = u_0^{\alpha_i^j}$. Compute $v_i = v^{\alpha_i}$ for $i = 0$ to L.

The public key of the bank is $bpk := \left(\lambda,\ \hat{e},\ \mathbb{G}_1,\ \mathbb{G}_2,\ \mathbb{G}_3,\ p,\ H,\ H_1,\ L\ ,\ g,\ g_A,\right.$
$g_B,\ g_0,\ g_1,\ g_2,\ g_3,\ g_4,\ u_0,\ g_U,\ g_T,\ [u_{i,1},\ \ldots,\ u_{i,2^i}]_{i=0}^{i=L} \in \mathbb{G}_1,\ Y,\ h,\ h_1,\ h_2,\ h_3,\ v,\ v_0,$
$\left.\ldots,\ v_L \in \mathbb{G}_2,\ Z \in \mathbb{G}_3\ \right)$. The private key of the bank is $bsk := \left(X \in \mathbb{G}_1, y \in \mathbb{G}_2\right)$.
Remarks: The α_i's are no longer needed and the bank shall delete them. Later
we shall see knowledge of α_i helps breaking the balance property of the scheme,
while, it does not help breaking anonymity or exculpability. Thus, we shall believe the bank to delete those values since keeping them is exactly against its
interest.

User Account Establishment. User Alice chooses x as her private key and
computes $PK_{Alice} = \{g_U^x\}$. She sends PK_{Alice} to the bank, along with the proof
of correctness. The bank stores PK_{Alice} as the identity of Alice in its database.
Alice stores (PK_{Alice}, x) as her key pair.

Withdrawal Protocol. To withdraw a wallet $\mathcal{W}$ from the bank, Alice first
prepares a binary tree T_w as follows. Randomly chooses $w \in \mathbb{Z}_p^*$. Set $k_{0,0} := w$
and obtain all node key $k_{i,j}$ of the binary tree T_w. The algorithm, denoted as
ComputeAllNodeKey, can be found in the full version of the paper[2]. Then, she
computes the accumulation of the node keys of each levels as follows. For $i = 0$
to L, she computes $V_{w,i} = u_0^{\prod_{j=0}^{2^i-1}(\alpha_i+k_{i,j})_3}$. She computes the commitment of
the binary tree T_w and her private key x. This is done by randomly choosing
$a_i, b_i' \in \mathbb{Z}_p^*$, computes $C_{w,i} = V_{w,i}g_A^{a_i}$, $D_{w,i} = g_0^{b_i'}g_B^{a_i}$. She sends $\left[C_{w,i}, D_{w,i}\right]_{i=0}^{i=L}$
to the bank.

With probability $1/2$, the bank will ask Alice to execute Inspection Routine.
Alice has to reveal T_w, a_i, b_i' for $i = 0,\ldots,L$ to the bank. The bank checks
if Alice computes the values $V_{w,i}$'s honestly. If Alice is found dishonest, a fine
of $2L2^L$ is deducted from Alice account. Otherwise, the withdrawal protocol is
repeated from the beginning.

If Inspection Routine is not chosen to be carried out, Alice is required to send
a proof of knowledge of representation of $D_{w,i}$ to the bank. The bank verifies the proof, randomly chooses $b_i'', c_i \in \mathbb{Z}_p^*$ for $i = 0$ to L and computes
$A_i = X(C_{w,i})^{c_i}$, $B_i = (gg_0^{b_i''}PK_{Alice}D_{w,i})^{\frac{1}{y+c_i}}$, $C_i = h^{c_i}$. Then bank sends
$[(A_i, B_i, C_i, a_i, b_i'')]_{i=0}^{i=L}$ to Alice.
Alice computes $b_i = b_i' + b_i''$ for $i = 0$ to L, checks, for $i = 0$ to L, if

$$\hat{e}(A_i, h) \stackrel{?}{=} Z_i\hat{e}(V_{w,i}g_A^{a_i}, C_i),$$

$$\hat{e}(B_i, C_iY) \stackrel{?}{=} \hat{e}(g, h)\hat{e}(g_B, h)^{a_i}\hat{e}(g_0, h)^{b_i}\hat{e}(g_U, h)^x,$$

and set $\mathcal{W} := \left(T_w, \left[(A_i, B_i, C_i, a_i, b_i)\right]_{i=0}^{i=L}\right)$.

---

[3] This computation does not require knowledge of α_i. It can be computed using
$u_0^{\alpha_i}, \ldots, u_0^{\alpha_i^{2^i}}$.

Spend Protocol. Alice with wallet $\mathcal{W}$ wishes to pay merchant Bob with 2^ℓ $(\ell < L)$ dollar in the spend protocol. Alice and Bob first agree on the transaction information I which includes ℓ and Bob's identity. Alice chooses an unused node key of level $i := L - \ell$. Let $k_{i,j}$ be the node key being chosen.

1. Bob sends to Alice a random challenge m.
2. Alice computes $M = H(I, m)$. She computes serial number of the coin $S = g_S^{k_{i,j}}$ and security tag $T = PK_{Alice}g_T^{Mk_{i,j}}$. She also computes a proof of correctness Π_S such that S, T are correctly formed as follows:

$$SPK_{Spend}\Big\{ (A_i, B_i, C_i, a_i, b_i, x, k_{i,j}, V_{w,i}, W_{i,j}) :$$

$$\hat{e}(A_i, h) = Z_i\hat{e}(V_{w,i}g_A^{a_i}, C_i) \ \wedge\ \hat{e}(B_i, C_iY) = \hat{e}(gg_B^{a_i}g_0^{b_i}g_U^x, h) \ \wedge$$

$$S = g_S^{k_{i,j}} \ \wedge\ T = g_U^x g_T^{Mk_{i,j}} \ \wedge\ \hat{e}(W_{i,j}, v_iv^{k_{i,j}}) = \hat{e}(V_{w,i}, v) \Big\}(M),$$

where $W_{i,j} = u_0^{\prod_{k=0,k\neq j}^{k=2^i-1}(\alpha_i + k_{i,k})}$. She sends $\$:= (S, T, \Pi_S, I, m)$ to Bob.
3. Bob accepts the payment $\$$ if Π_S is a valid proof statement.
4. Alice marks the node $N_{i,j}$, its ancestors and all its children in T_w as used nodes.

Remarks: Instantiation of SPK Π_S is shown in the full version[2].

Deposit Protocol. Bob with $\$$ from Alice approaches the bank in the deposit protocol. He submits $\$$ to the bank, who checks if I matches the merchant identity and checks if m has been used before. The bank credits Bob if both checks passes.

Let 2^ℓ be the value of the coin and $i := L - \ell$. The bank compute all serial numbers accompanying S and obtains $S_{L,0}, \ldots, S_{L,2^\ell}$. The algorithm, denoted as ComputeAllSerials, can be found in the full version of the paper[2]. The bank then checks if $S_{L,0}$, $S_{L,2^\ell}$ is in its database of spent-coin serial numbers. If yes, it runs the RevokeDoubleSpender algorithm described below. Otherwise, it stores $S_{L,0}, S_{L,2^\ell}$, together with $\$$ in its database of spent-coin serial numbers.

RevokeDoubleSpender. Let $\$:= (S, T, \Pi_S, I, m)$ and $\$' := (S', T', \Pi_{S'}, I', m')$ be two coins such that one of the output from algorithm ComputeAllSerials is the same. Denote $M := H(I, m)$ and $M' := H(I', M')$. If both coins are of the same value, compute $PK := (\frac{T^{M'}}{T'^M})^{\frac{1}{M'-M}}$ and output PK as the identity of the double-spender.

Without loss of generality, assume value of coin $\$$ is 2^ℓ and value of coin $\$'$ is $2^{\ell'}$ such that $\ell > \ell'$. Let $S_{L,\alpha}$, $0 \le \alpha \le 2^\ell - 1$, be the output from ComputeAllSerials on (S, L, ℓ) such that $S_{L,\alpha}$ equals to one of the output serial numbers from ComputeAllSerials on (S', L, ℓ'). Compute K by applying H_0 or H_1 suitably such that $S = g_S^K$. The algorithm, denoted as GetNodeKey can be found in the full version of the paper[2]. Compute $PK := \frac{T'}{h^{M'k}}$ and output PK as the identity of the double-spender.

Table 1. Time and Space Complexities of this paper and [12]

		Time Complexities			
		This paper		Canard *et. al.*[12]	
WithdrawalProtocol	User		Bank	User	Bank
	w/o Preproc.	w/ Preproc.			
multi-EXP	$2^{L+1} + 9L + 5$	$2L + 2$	$2^{L+1} + 8L + 6$	2	3
Pairing	$2L + 2$	$2L + 2$	0	0	0
SpendProtocol	User		Merchant	User	Merchant
(coin of value 2^{L-i})	w/o Preproc.	w/ Preproc.			
multi-EXP	21	1	13	$6 + 2ti + i$	$2ti + i + t + 7$
Pairing	6	0	8	0	0
		Space Complexities			
WithdrawalProtocol	Total Bandwidth Required			Total Bandwidth Required	
$\mathbb{G}$ element	$7L + 7$			3	
$\mathbb{Z}^*_{|\mathbb{G}|}$ element	$7L + 8$			2	
SpendProtocol	Total Bandwidth Required			Total Bandwidth Required	
(coin of value 2^{L-i})					
$\mathbb{G}$ element	9			$2(i + 1) + 6$	
$\mathbb{Z}^*_{|\mathbb{G}|}$ element	21			$2ti + 4t + i + 11$	

VerifyGuilt. The algorithm RevokeDoubleSpender can be executed by the public. Thus, a proof that the bank is outputting the double-spender honestly is to publish two double-spent transcript.

4.3 Security Analysis

Regarding the security of our construction, we have the follow theorem whose proof can be found in the full version of the paper[2].

Theorem 1. *Our construction is secure under the q-SDH assumption and the AWSM assumption in the random oracle model.*

5 Efficiency Analysis

Table 1 summarizes the complexities of different protocols of our scheme and the scheme in [12]. The cost of the protocol with pre-processing of our scheme is listed as a reference. It is somehow hard to quantify the exact cost of the spend protocol in [12] as the instantiation of the SPK is very complex. Furthermore, it involves $L + 1$ cyclic groups of different orders. We simplify the comparison by stating the total number of group elements needed. If the Strong RSA-based CL signature [10] is used, as stated in [12], the group $\mathbb{G}$ in the paper would be the group of quadratic residue modulus a safe-prime product n, which would be of 1024-bit. t is the security parameter controlling the cheating probability of the proof-of-knowledge of double-discrete logarithm. For example, $t = 80$ would give the protocol a cheating probability of 2^{-80}.

For a moderate value $L = 10$ and $t = 40$, spending a coin of monetary value 1 in [12] requires 816 and 857 multi-based exponentiations from the user and the merchant respectively, and a total bandwidth of 981 elements in $\mathbb{Z}^*_{|\mathbb{G}|}$ and 28 elements in $\mathbb{G}$. If the base group is of order n which is 1024-bit, each of the above elements is at least 1024-bit in size. On a contrary, spending a coin of any monetary value in our scheme requires a constant cost of 21 and 13 multi-based exponentiations from the user and the merchant respectively. And a total bandwidth of 9 elements in $\mathbb{G}$ and 21 elements in $\mathbb{Z}^*_{|\mathbb{G}|}$ is needed.

6   Conclusion

We presented an efficient off-line divisible e-cash scheme which is *truly anonymous*. While [12] shows that *truly anonymous* off-line divisible e-cash can be constructed, in this paper, we provided one step further by providing an affirmative answer whether a practical and efficient off-line divisible e-cash can be constructed. Our scheme is very efficient and practical (c.f. [12]).

Acknowledgments

We would like to thank Qiong Huang and the anonymous reviewers of FC 2008 for their helpful comments and suggestions.

References

1. Ateniese, G., Camenisch, J., de Medeiros, B.: Untraceable rfid tags via insubvertible encryption. In: ACM Conference on Computer and Communications Security, pp. 92–101 (2005)
2. Au, M.H., Susilo, W., Mu, Y.: Practical anonymous divisible e-cash from bounded accumulators. Cryptology ePrint Archive, Report, 2007/459 (2007), http://eprint.iacr.org/
3. Au, M.H., Susilo, W., Mu, Y.: Practical compact e-cash. In: Pieprzyk, J., Ghodosi, H., Dawson, E. (eds.) ACISP 2007. LNCS, vol. 4586, pp. 431–445. Springer, Heidelberg (2007)
4. Au, M.H., Wu, Q., Susilo, W., Mu, Y.: Compact e-cash from bounded accumulator. In: Abe, M. (ed.) CT-RSA 2007. LNCS, vol. 4377, pp. 178–195. Springer, Heidelberg (2006)
5. Bari, N., Pfitzmann, B.: Collision-free accumulators and fail-stop signature schemes without trees. In: Fumy, W. (ed.) EUROCRYPT 1997. LNCS, vol. 1233, pp. 480–494. Springer, Heidelberg (1997)
6. Bellare, M., Rogaway, P.: Random oracles are practical: A paradigm for designing efficient protocols. In: ACM Conference on Computer and Communications Security, pp. 62–73 (1993)
7. Benaloh, J.C., de Mare, M.: One-way accumulators: A decentralized alternative to digital sinatures (extended abstract). In: EUROCRYPT, pp. 274–285 (1993)
8. Boneh, D., Boyen, X.: Short signatures without random oracles. In: Cachin, C., Camenisch, J.L. (eds.) EUROCRYPT 2004. LNCS, vol. 3027, pp. 56–73. Springer, Heidelberg (2004)

9. Camenisch, J., Hohenberger, S., Lysyanskaya, A.: Compact e-cash. In: Cramer, R.J.F. (ed.) EUROCRYPT 2005. LNCS, vol. 3494, pp. 302–321. Springer, Heidelberg (2005)

10. Camenisch, J., Lysyanskaya, A.: A Signature Scheme with Efficient Protocols. In: Cimato, S., Galdi, C., Persiano, G. (eds.) SCN 2002. LNCS, vol. 2576, pp. 268–289. Springer, Heidelberg (2003)

11. Camenisch, J., Stadler, M.: Efficient group signature schemes for large groups (extended abstract). In: CRYPTO, pp. 410–424 (1997)

12. Canard, S., Gouget, A.: Divisible e-cash systems can be truly anonymous. In: Naor, M. (ed.) EUROCRYPT 2007. LNCS, vol. 4515, pp. 482–497. Springer, Heidelberg (2007)

13. Canard, S., Traoré, J.: On fair e-cash systems based on group signature schemes. In: Safavi-Naini, R., Seberry, J. (eds.) ACISP 2003. LNCS, vol. 2727, pp. 237–248. Springer, Heidelberg (2003)

14. Chan, A.H., Frankel, Y., Tsiounis, Y.: Easy come - easy go divisible cash. In: Nyberg, K. (ed.) EUROCRYPT 1998. LNCS, vol. 1403, pp. 561–575. Springer, Heidelberg (1998)

15. Chaum, D.: Blind Signatures for Untraceable Payments. In: McCurley, K.S., Ziegler, C.D. (eds.) Advances in Cryptology 1981 - 1997. LNCS, vol. 1440, pp. 199–203. Springer, Heidelberg (1999)

16. D'Amiano, S., Crescenzo, G.D.: Methodology for digital money based on general cryptographic tools. In: De Santis, A. (ed.) EUROCRYPT 1994. LNCS, vol. 950, pp. 156–170. Springer, Heidelberg (1995)

17. Eng, T., Okamoto, T.: Single-term divisible electronic coins. In: De Santis, A. (ed.) EUROCRYPT 1994. LNCS, vol. 950, pp. 306–319. Springer, Heidelberg (1995)

18. Fiat, A., Shamir, A.: How to prove yourself: Practical solutions to identification and signature problems. In: Odlyzko, A.M. (ed.) CRYPTO 1986. LNCS, vol. 263, pp. 186–194. Springer, Heidelberg (1987)

19. Goldwasser, S., Micali, S., Rackoff, C.: The knowledge complexity of interactive proof-systems (extended abstract). In: STOC, pp. 291–304 (1985)

20. Goldwasser, S., Micali, S., Rivest, R.L.: A digital signature scheme secure against adaptive chosen-message attacks. SIAM J. Comput. 17(2), 281–308 (1988)

21. Nakanishi, T., Sugiyama, Y.: Unlinkable divisible electronic cash. In: Okamoto, E., Pieprzyk, J.P., Seberry, J. (eds.) ISW 2000. LNCS, vol. 1975, pp. 121–134. Springer, Heidelberg (2000)

22. Nguyen, L.: Accumulators from Bilinear Pairings and Applications. In: Menezes, A. (ed.) CT-RSA 2005. LNCS, vol. 3376, pp. 275–292. Springer, Heidelberg (2005)

23. Okamoto, T.: An efficient divisible electronic cash scheme. In: Coppersmith, D. (ed.) CRYPTO 1995. LNCS, vol. 963, pp. 438–451. Springer, Heidelberg (1995)

24. Okamoto, T., Ohta, K.: Universal electronic cash. In: Feigenbaum, J. (ed.) CRYPTO 1991. LNCS, vol. 576, pp. 324–337. Springer, Heidelberg (1992)

25. Pailles, J.C.: New protocols for electronic money. In: ASIACRYPT, pp. 263–274 (1992)

26. Schnorr, C.-P.: Efficient signature generation by smart cards. J. Cryptology 4(3), 161–174 (1991)

Panel: Usable Cryptography:
Manifest Destiny or Oxymoron?

Mary Ellen Zurko[1] and Andrew S. Patrick[2]

[1] IBM, Westford, Massachusetts, USA
mzurko@us.ibm.com
[2] Institute for Information Technology, National Research Council of Canada
Andrew.Patrick@nrc-cnrc.gc.ca

Abstract. Outside of SSL, Notes/Domino, and federal PKIs, PK cryptography hasn't caught on. SSL is hugely successful in providing network protection. But its server authentication feature is currently useless in phishing attacks, and its client authentication is largely unused. A number of user studies indicate that while some subset of users know about and notice "the padlock", few know what it really is, and none use it to protect them from phishing. This panel posits that the points where the cryptographic system meets the user are where its success has been blocked (e.g. key mgmt, password for protecting keys, understanding risk, threat, and assurance). We explore that assumption, and the past, present, and future of usable cryptography.

Keywords: User-centered security, cryptography.

1 Introduction

As a conference and a community, the "financial cryptography" conference (which this panel was part of) is obviously dedicated (at least in part) to the practical utility of cryptography in financial applications. A straw poll of the attendees found that the majority believed the notion of "usable cryptography" to be a manifest destiny. Many cryptographic breakthroughs have been targeted at the promise of practical use. Part of the allure of public key cryptography is the promise of deployability and usability. We all get one key pair (or the number we like), and use them with each other. More recently, Identity Based Encryption makes it easier to find or know someone's public key (another deployability and usability concern). Examples of successful use of cryptography include SSL, Notes/Domino, federal PKIs, virtual private networks (VPNs) and wireless protocols.

These examples fall short of the hope and promise of public key (and other sorts of) cryptography. "Why Johnny Can't Encrypt" [1] was foundational usable security research in 1999, covering email encryption. While there has been much follow on research, cryptographically protected email is still not widely deployed. SSL is hugely successful in providing network protection. But its server authentication feature is currently useless in phishing attacks, and its client authentication is largely unused

G. Tsudik (Ed.): FC 2008, LNCS 5143, pp. 302–306, 2008.
© Springer-Verlag Berlin Heidelberg 2008

and even unknown. A number of user studies indicate that while some subset of users know about and notice "the padlock" (browser indications of when SSL protection is being provided on a page), few know what it really is, and none use it to protect them from phishing [2]. Digital Rights Management (DRM) seems largely stalled, and many big players are actively looking for alternative economic approaches.

This panel posits that the points where the cryptographic system meets the user are where its success has been blocked. These include key management and distribution, passwords for protecting keys, deciding what keys to trust and understanding the risks in trust, understanding threats to the cryptographic protocols, and assurance. The panel (and conference participants) explored that assumption, and the past, present, and future of usable cryptography.

The panelists were Andrew Patrick (NRC Canada & Carleton University), Phil Hallam-Baker (Verisign) and Gene Tsudik (UC Irvine). Below, Mary Ellen Zurko summarizes the positions of Phil Hallam-Baker and Gene Tsudik, and Andrew Patrick outlines his own position on this topic

2 You Can't Make Them Drink

Phil Hallam-Baker's position was, "you can give a user crypto but you can't make them drink". He sees unusable software as insecure shelfware. The way to change this is to not make mistakes, a daunting task. While science generally asks "Did I make a mistake?", Engineering produces rules which, if followed, are meant to minimize mistakes. Phil posits two laws of usable secure interfaces to help minimize mistakes. The first is to avoid providing insufficient information for the user to be usably secure. He sees violating this law as a prime reason for phishing. An example that provides sufficient information to the user to authenticate a bank is Secure Internet Letterhead, which uses cryptography to provide the assurance behind a display of company origin in email. A second law is to minimize complexity. A cryptographic example of that is the encryption of email. Encrypting some, but not all email, or only some of the time, increases complexity, by introducing additional user choice and additional error cases. For example, if the user chooses to encrypt, but the system cannot, due to the system's inability to find a key to use, the user is generally asked if they want to send unencrypted or not send the email. This additional complexity can be done away with by the use of promiscuous encryption; always encrypting email sent.

3 Usable Cryptography: What Is It Good for?

Gene Tsudik asks, "usable cryptography, what is it good for?". He suggests that perhaps we need to strive for useful cryptography, and states that they are not the same (usable <.> useful). He chooses neither manifest destiny nor oxymoron for the notion of usable cryptography, but that it is too early to say. The examples of protected pipes (SSL) and walled gardens (Notes/Domino) are successful because they are either unobtrusive or imposed on users. He outlines two curses. The first is that security is not a service, but an enabler. Security and privacy are not **useful** to the average user. Instant messaging, social networking, web searching and browsing are useful. Even backups are useful. But we have not convinced users that security is useful. Since it's not **useful**, making it **usable** is **useless**. Our second curse is abbreviations and jargon. Security professionals use the terms "authenticate" and "authentication", but not in the same way it's used in the more common notion to "authenticate a document". Our technical use of "repudiate" and "repudiation" is not the same as the natural language notion, "repudiate this statement by so-and-so". When we use "certificate" and "certification", we don't' mean "course completion" or "quality", as in ISO 9000. And we don't use "revoke" or "revoked" in the same sense as "your authority is revoked". Abbreviations that an average user might encounter include SSL, TLS, HTTPS, CA, CRL, OCSP, PKC, WEP, WPA, IEEE 802.1x, VPN, IPSEC, and IKE. Some jargon makes sense, perhaps accidentally, including "firewall", "spam", and "virus". Gene posits that the curse of abbreviations and jargon can be overcome, perhaps the same way that automotive jargon is coped with. However, the curse of security as an enabler, not a service, is here to stay, and we need to figure out what usable cryptography might mean within that context.

4 "Usable Cryptography" as an Impossible State

When the topic of this panel, "usable cryptography", was proposed, I immediately thought it was a curious choice of words. To me, usability and cryptography don't go together, not because it is hard to make usable cryptography, but because they are really terms from two different domains. It is the usual case of comparing "apples" and "oranges" or worse, it is really talking about an impossible state. Saying "usable cryptography" is equivalent to saying "usable osmosis" or "usable photosynthesis" – it just doesn't make any sense.

Wanting to re-assure myself that my first reactions were correct, I consulted an all-powerful, non-random oracle. I did a Google search on the term "usable cryptography", and Google returned 12 hits. One of the hits was a description of this panel. Another was a paper at the 2004 Swiss Unix Conference on disk encryption that actually said little about usability. Other uses of the term included cryptography that was usable in the real-world and therefore always susceptible to attacks, and cryptography that was freely usable (free as in beer). One corporate site described "usable cryptography" as cryptography that could be defeated by their password recovery and forensic tools, and one patent application used the term to describe any cryptography that was currently available. None of the Google results used the term "usable cryptography" in the sense of information hiding that is easy for people to use.

The reason why "usable cryptography" is an impossible state is that cryptography is a process or method, while users interact with products or services. Rarely is cryptography a product or service of interest. Cryptography and usability occur at different levels in a hierarchy of human-technology interaction, as is shown in Figure 1. At the top level of this scheme are the products and services that users care about, for example banking or shopping or communicating. At lower levels are various technologies that enable these top-level services, and these lower levels provide key functions or features for the applications above (e.g., integrity, transaction security). This hierarchical model of end-user services and enabling technologies was developed as an extension of the traditional 7-layer OSI model by Bauer and Patrick [3] and applied in a number of areas. In the model, three new human-computer interaction layers are proposed on top of the traditional OSI layers: human needs (10), human performance (9), and display (8).

Users don't want cryptography, they want products and services. Some of these products and services may employ cryptographic methods, and they might even need cryptography to fulfill the users' needs, but rarely do users want cryptography directly. Users value product and services based on their "usefulness", where usefulness is determined by utility and usability. Utility and usability does not happen at the level of "cryptography", but instead at the level of products and services.

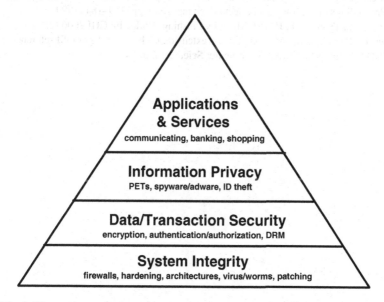

Fig. 1. Hierarchical scheme of human-technology interaction as it relates to security

How does one address, then, the issue of "usable cryptography"? The answer is to think in terms of products and services, and not in terms of processes and methods. What is needed is a top-down approach that begins by understanding users' tasks and goals. From there, we can determine the users' needs and requirements. Only then can we think about particular methods and technologies that can meet those requirements. The process becomes one of product design rather than technology development.

Good products don't just happen. Product design (or industrial design) is a well-established discipline that has developed its own methods for gathering information about people and the things they interact with. Most great products have large product design teams behind them. These teams identify human needs and establish target specifications in terms of utility and usability. Designers develop product concepts, which can be realized in prototypes and tested in a laboratory. Product designers often continue to test their products once they are in the marketplace, to gauge acceptance and assess the competition. Product designers use a variety of methods for gathering data, including ethnography, interviews, surveys, focus groups, usability tests, and secret shoppers. What is needed to build "usable cryptography" is for more people to adopt a product design perspective. This is in addition to the talented people who are currently developing new, improved cryptographic methods and procedures.

Acknowledgments. Thank you to the FC08 organizers who accepted this panel, and particularly to Ray Hirschfeld, for his hard work and support.

References

1. Whitten, A., Tygar, J.D.: Why Johnny Can't Encrypt: A Usability Evaluation of PGP 5.0. In: Proceedings of the 8th Usenix Security Symposium, pp. 169–184 (1999)
2. Dhamija, R., Tygar, J.D., Hearst, M.: Why Phishing Works. In: CHI 2006 (2006)
3. Bauer, B., Patrick, A.S.: A human factors extension to the seven-layer OSI reference model. IAENG International Journal of Computer Science (in press)

Real Electronic Cash Versus Academic Electronic Cash Versus Paper Cash (Panel Report)

Jon Callas[1], Yvo Desmedt[2,*], Daniel Nagy[3], Akira Otsuka[4],
Jean-Jacques Quisquater[5], and Moti Yung[6,7]

[1] PGP Corporation, USA
[2] Dept. of Computer Science, University College London, UK
[3] ELTECRYPT research group, Eötvös Lóránd University, Budapest, Hungary
[4] RICS, AIST, 1-18-13 Sotokanda, Chiyoda-ku, Tokyo 101-0021, Japan
a-otsuka@aist.go.jp
[5] UCL Crypto Group, Louvain-la-Neuve, Belgium
[6] Google Inc., USA
[7] Computer Science, Columbia University, USA

Abstract. Most electronic cash systems being deployed look very different from what academics have been envisioning over the last 3 decades. Experts on the panel gave different definitions for electronic cash, surveyed systems deployed in some countries, discussed reliability, privacy and security concerns. Moreover, electronic cash and advertisements were linked together.

Keywords: anonymity, availability, advertising, cash, chip card, credit card, deployed systems, electronic cash, fraud, hacking, reliability.

1 Introduction

Electronic cash is replacing paper cash and (metal) coins. We encounter different types (see Section 2). In different countries different systems have been deployed (see, e.g., Sections 2, 4, 5). Several issues related to reliability, privacy and security, have been described (see, e.g., Sections 2 and 3). Implementations are quite different, as explained in Sections 2, 4, and 6. Finally a link is made between e-advertisements and e-cash (see Section 7).

2 Different Types of Electronic Payment Systems (by Jon Callas)

"Classical" eCash is a virtual artifact, made out of bits. It may use signatures (blinded or ordinary), collision-based, or just tracked in a database (no intrinsic security). It is like physical cash, having a bearer certificate that can

---

* Moderator of the panel. A part of this research was funded by EPSRC EP/C538285/1. Yvo Desmedt is BT Chair of Information Security.

G. Tsudik (Ed.): FC 2008, LNCS 5143, pp. 307–313, 2008.

be spent and respent. It can be more or less untraceable. Unlike physical cash it is a digital artifact. So, it can easily be copied or cloned. Unless the holder is the entity that got it from the mint, the holder can never be completely assured that the eCash is good. The eCash mint always gains some information about the use, even if it is fully blinded.

A nosy mint can learn a lot about blinded cash, but a blithe one can keep even the simplest system reasonably untrackable. A coin's holder must always consider the trustworthiness of the last holder, even if that was the mint.

It is often used for bimodal values, either very small sums, where the risks of the system matter little, or very large sums, where the system contains other safeguards.

Book-Entry Micropayments systems include payment via mobile phone, credit cards, traditional cheques, Internet systems such as PayPal, and so on. These are not like cash. They are tracked, traced, analyzed, and reported upon and similar to cheques. The user experience of these systems is often similar to cash, and can even be better than cash. Indeed, credit cards often offer insurance, loyalty points, or rebates.

Physical Cash security problems are inherent to its being a physical artifact that is a bearer certificate. They contain physical and data-oriented mechanisms to make counterfeiting hard. Since cash is usable by the bearer, much security revolves around the secure transport of it. There are user experience issues (torn notes, the weight of coins, the lack of any user protection).

Hybrid Systems: So-called e-stamps are digital artifacts that have been printed on paper. Scrip, coupons, and limited-scope cash/cards (e.g. London Underground's Oyster Card, or Atlanta MARTA's Breeze Card) are local currencies. Convenience and security are each both raised and lowered because of their limits. The limited scope can advantage some populations over others (e.g., favor the native population over visiting travelers).

They can provide some combination of convenience and untraceability. For example, the Oyster Card can be "registered" which gives protection and convenience to the holder, or "unregistered" which gives some limited untraceability — all the rides are in a database, but not connected to a specific identity.

2.1   Edge Conditions

Virtual artifacts such as Linden Dollars can be converted into and out of other currencies with ease. Loyalty program benefits, such as airline miles can often be given to other people, or used to buy tickets for other people.

Large-denomination banknotes are often difficult to use as cash, since not all businesses accept them (see [7]). Similarly, small-denomination coins may be hard to spend in large quantities. Special-purpose credit cards may function exactly as a credit card, but only at one store. Lastly, the most interesting edge condition of all is barter. Barter is the oldest way to transfer value, and can be used in any of these systems. A person might trade a subway card for eStamps.

3 Incompatibility, Reliability and Security (by Yvo Desmedt)

Any payment method involving electronics will be viewed in this section as electronic cash. Today paper cash is getting untenderable. Indeed, e.g., parking fees in Westminster City (London, UK) and the Sydney Harbor Tunnel (Australia) can no longer be paid in paper cash[1]! When we are switching to e-cash we better understand the impact before we regret this! Our society should be aware of, at least, the following issues:

Lack of reliability: e.g., the earthquake that hit near Hawaii on October 15, 2006 knocked out ATM systems. During a large scale catastrophe, one wants to avoid a lawless society. When e-cash no longer works, this will worsen the situation! History has shown the importance of having cash available after the 1906 earthquake in San Francisco [3, pp. 21–32].

Incompatibility: phone cards from different countries are incompatible, the Roam Express Visitor's e-PASS that can be used to pay the Lane Cove Tunnel in Sydney (Australia) cannot be used on the Sydney Harbor Tunnel, etc. A similar incompatibility occurred with paper cash. Indeed, in the middle of the 19th century there existed 7,000 varieties of US paper cash!

Barriers: no longer being able to pay except with credit cards has economic and social barriers. Other barriers come from user unfriendly interface, etc.

Legal: since cash is tenderable, is, e.g., the Westminster parking solution legal?

Longlivity: many forms of e-cash expire, e.g., some phone cards after 1 year.

Research focused heavily on anonymity (privacy), but only a fraction of e-cash systems deployed take this concern into account. Few payment systems studied by researchers are widely deployed. Most research does not address compatibility, exchangeability, reliability, etc. Many of these aspects, such as reliability, can be considered as being much more important than anonymity! One also needs to wonder whether is it time for an international electronic cash standard which allows electronic cash which is exchangeable, reliable, universal, etc?

A possible solution to achieve reliability is to have paper cash, which already has RFID chips today, be usable as e-cash. When futuristic money is being used as e-cash, the RFID chip could trigger the paper money to change its face value displaying a "Void" text. When the electronics is down, this type of paper cash can be continued to be used.

Finally, should scientists warn the Treasuries of different countries that e-cash is displacing "paper" cash and what the potential consequences might be?

4 Academic vs. Real E-Cash in the Developing World and the Shadow Economy (by Daniel Nagy)

Academic research has highlighted several attractive properties of cash that might be worth implementing for the purpose of electronic commerce. Most

---

[1] This was pointed out to the author by Ron Steinfeld.

of these properties, in addition to those of all payment systems, are related to issues of privacy in general and those of anonymity and untraceability in particular. Outside of academia, almost any electronic payment system is considered a competitor to cash. Arguably in order to successfully compete and eventually replace cash, an electronic payment system should satisfy a wide range of requirements and strike the right balance between contradicting ones. A good benchmark for being cash-like for a payment system is its suitability for the purpose of paying bribes. However, that does not imply that the availability of such an electronic payment system will have a positive or a negative effect on bribery or corruption.

It is very difficult to design a payment system which strikes the right balance between requirements of issuer governance (accountability), user privacy, security against fraud, etc. Getting the priorities right is one of the toughest challenges for which current academic research provides little guidance. Finding a market niche which a new electronic payment system could fill is another difficult task.

Two such niche markets are provided by the developing world: remittance payments from diaspora (friends and family members living and working in rich countries) and international phonecalls. While there is much ad-hoc innovation happening in these two important fields of electronic payment, it would be interesting to see some scientific research addressing the specific needs of these markets.

Also of interest is the fact that cellular operators in many cases act in many ways similarly to banks and not being subject to banking regulation, indeed act as banks for the needs of the shadow economy. On one hand, one can buy pre-paid plans (so-called pay-as-you-go), where one can make (anonymous) deposits onto an account which can be used for making phone calls. On the other hand, it is not difficult to set up premium rate services, through which such deposits can be withdrawn, with the service provider taking its cut. Additionally, there is a large demand for (anonymous) mobile communication within the shadow economy, so top-up codes or SIM cards corresponding to topped-up accounts, which are often used as vehicles of payment for illegitimate business, are not fully converted into cash either.

The recent work by Genkin [2] on private money with an emphasis on electronic money, is one of the first comprehensive scientific studies of real-world e-cash. In particular, the author draws on the experience of WebMoney, an e-cash system that started in the remittance business in 1997, but gained enormous popularity after the financial meltdown in 1998, having proved to be more reliable than the Russian banking industry including the Central Bank.

5   Interoperability of e-Cash Systems in Japan (by Akira Otsuka)

In this section, we quickly review incompatibility issues of e-cash systems in Japan and how they try to solve it.

Felica[2], the most successful e-cash platform in Japan, was first launched in 2001 in two "currencies": one is for transportation, called "Suica" [4] and the other is for general-purpose payments, called "Edy". Three years after the first deployment, Sony and DoCoMo launched Mobile Felica[1] which is an e-cash platform implemented in a mobile phone so that e-cash can be charged and sent over a network, and its payment history is viewable through an LCD display. As other carriers also followed later, the number of Mobile-Felica capable mobile-phones rapidly increased to 40 million out of 102 million mobile phones during the last four years. Observing this success, many retailers rushed to install Felica readers to accept e-cash. In order to avoid a monopoly by Sony-DoCoMo e-cash, the two largest retailers, IY Group and Ion Group, launched their own currency, called "Nanaco" and "Waon" respectively. Now there are four major e-cash currencies, and surprisingly, they are all incompatible! One reason for the incompatibility came from the mechanism used to get profit from the e-cash systems. E-cash issuers, especially in the early deployment stage, took the partial risk of deploying Felica readers to shops. As a reward of taking this risk, E-cash issuers asked the retailers a percentage of the e-cash revenue. As a consequence of this deployment-risk sharing strategy, retailers were required to be loyal to some particular e-cash issuer.

The consequence of four incompatible e-cash systems was that (1) even at shops equipped with Felica readers, consumers often cannot make e-cash pay-ment because of a currency mismatch, (2) in order to reduce the loss due to a possible currency mismatch, retailers had to facilitate multiple Felica readers around their POS terminals where space is very tight. Quite recently they recog-nized this issue and developed solutions as the number of e-cash consumers hit the critical mass. One approach is that recent versions of Mobile Felica became capable of accommodating multiple e-cash currencies due to expanded memory space. Moreover, manufactures of Felica readers started to ship multiple-currency Felica readers[5]. Consumers have to press a currency-logo button before making an e-cash payment, but it reduced the number of Felica readers scattered around the POS terminal.

Fortunately, the above incompatibility issue appeared only on the same de-facto standard Felica platform, thus the development of solutions was relatively easy. They still have incompatibility issues among different payment systems such as at Electronic Toll Collection points. Future extensions of Mobile Fel-ica may, hopefully, include (1) offline person-to-person payment, (2) real-time currency exchange, and (3) anonymity.

6   Reflections on Real Electronic Cash (by Jean-Jacques Quisquater)

Electronic cash is coming for everyday transactions and it is not the way David Chaum invented. From chips (RFID) inside paper cash to signed numbers

---

[2] Felica is a registered trademark of Sony Corporation.

(SWIFT) everything is electronic, under the protection of cryptography and under the control of authorities. Privacy is also evaporating, because anonymity is less and less easy to achieve.

7   Implicit eCash: Embed e-Payment Indirectly in Your e-Processes (by Moti Yung)

One may ask what is the major difference between e-money and other ways of payments? My answer is the fact that *in the electronic domain things are easy to change and so is the way money is represented*. So, e-cash can be made in many ways, and be embedded in various indirect methods as part of the transaction. The thesis I put forth is that *e-cash can be built implicitly in the e-transaction flow and not necessarily as a direct payment*.

The case of micropayments: These forms of payment were designed as methods for buying small information goods by paying small fraction of a coin amounts. They were positioned as computationally cheap and thus different from off-line e-cash systems requiring costly public-key cryptographic operations. The various systems designed suggest some notions. The first being the one of *aggregation*. Since payments are done in fraction of a coin amount, some entity aggregates the cash spent over time by a user and to a merchant, since it is really hard and costly to manage financial books based on small fractions of a coin. The aggregator may be a company providing the service and taking some *service fee* for its role (similar to credit cards). In *statistical payments*, the basic idea is that a user, based on a coin flip, pays with some probability. Say the average cost is $1/10$ of a cent, then a user flips a coin and with probability $1/10$ pays a cent and otherwise gets the content for free. However, managing fractions and stochastic payments is hard to understand or manage within financial systems (say, how will it be justified legally if a user over-pays and is unhappy about it and goes to court).

Rather than paying directly, perhaps some beneficiary will pay to the service provider the "service fee." Now, allow an aggregator of payments to provide some special service on-line, perhaps with some content of its own or as a content distributor. This looks like and it is, in fact, on-line advertisements (ads). The aggregator is the ads placement company, it gives ads as content or in association with content as part of its own service, namely search or content display (that now is for free to consumers). At the same time it gives a service to another merchant who gets the benefit of the ad (whose goods and services can be well associated with the content). Some consumers will use the ad to buy and will be paying in some statistical fashion to that benefited merchant who will move some money to the ads placement company (which aggregates the payment to itself and perhaps pays some of it to content providers or ad providers). The content itself is free of DRM or payment, but the ads pay for it in some statistical fashion from the market of the beneficiaries of the ads and to an aggregator who may share it with content providers. This configuration incentivizes the ads placement company to match good content to the ads. These benefitted merchants, in turn, indirectly collect money from end consumers for the ads, by having the price for their goods include the cost of ads (through their ad budget).

Under the above analysis, in some sense, advertisement is the dual method to micropayments assuming the existence of the merchants who can associate content with their ads. The above analogy between advertisement as a way to realize micropayments in a larger market, but for a specific service (matching merchants to consumer), and using it effectively to otherwise allow free content (i.e., free search, free displays of relevant related content, etc.), raises a few questions. Is the analogy above complete? Of course not, since micropayments may find other uses besides financing content display, and cases where ads are not possible. So what does this imply? I believe it means that the nature of micropayments may change since it becomes hard for them to penetrate their original content market.

The position analyzed above may provoke an enhanced view of payments and e-cash in particular, and will help in merging business models and implicit e-payments when new ways for e-commerce and e-finance are designed in cyberspace.

References

1. Felica Networks Inc. Mobile Felica,
   http://www.felicanetworks.co.jp/company/domain/en/summary.html
2. Genkin, A.S.: Realization of economic interests in private and national monetary systems. D.Sc.thesis Financial Academy under the Government of Russian Federation (2006)
3. James, M., James, B.R.: Biography of a Bank: The Story of the Bank of America. Harper & Brothers, New York (1954)
4. JR East. Mobile Suica,
   http://www.jreast.co.jp/e/press/20071201/index.html
5. Sony Corp. Felica product information,
   http://www.sony.net/Products/felica/pdt/index.html
6. The Economist. The End of the Cash Era (February 17, 2007)
7. U. S. D. of the Treasury, Legal tender status,
   http://www.ustreas.gov/education/faq/currency/legal-tender.shtml

Securing Web Banking Applications

Antonio San Martino and Xavier Perramon

Universitat Pompeu Fabra, Pg. Circumval·lació 8, 08003 Barcelona, Spain
asm@dp-security.com, xavier.perramon@upf.edu

Abstract. This paper presents the main results of a PhD thesis work aimed at defining a model for secure operation of an Internet Banking environment, even in the presence of malware on the client side. Its goal is to be resistant to the nowadays too frequent phishing and pharming attacks, and also to more classical ones like social engineering or man-in-the-middle attacks, and those exploiting technical flaws like buffer overflows, SQL injection, cross site scripting, etc. The key point of this model is the need for mutual authentication, instead of simply basing the security on the digital certificate of the financial entity.

1 Introduction

A number of techniques and standards have been developed for providing information security in different applications [1], but currently there is no official standard for a methodological approach to web banking security. However, there are an increasing number of new attacks and viruses against web pages of financial entities, such as "phishing" and "pharming" frauds, that must be addressed in order to guarantee customers' trust in web banking services.

The goal of this work, which has been conducted in collaboration with several financial entities in Spain and Italy, is to specify a methodology for defining security policies in Internet-based banking applications. In the development of this work a number of different Internet Banking scenarios have been considered, and specific Internet Banking threats have been included in the risk analysis.

2 Logical Model

Our approach to web banking security is based on a logical model comprising the following elements:

- Web browser and customer network
- Internet
- Bank server and private network

Our model focuses on the following aspects of web banking service deployment: web application security (which includes authentication, authorization, session management, data validation, error handling and logging [2]), platform security, password policy, backup, business continuity plan, and support.

G. Tsudik (Ed.): FC 2008, LNCS 5143, pp. 314–315, 2008.

The goal is to provide security in the abovementioned environments: customer bank network, Internet, and bank server, and to be immune to threats, such as viruses and Trojan horses, which affect the customer's network.

3 Internet Banking Mutual Authentication Process

The best authentication method is mutual authentication as it avoids, when carried out properly, phishing and pharming attacks. Such authentication process comprises key interchange, server authentication, and user authentication.

The goal of any authentication method is to work reliably under adverse security conditions in a hostile environment, and in particular it must be resistant to "man-in-the-middle" attacks.

Figure 1 shows the sequence diagram for accomplishing the mutual authentication process.

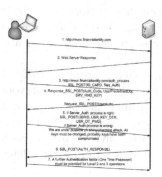

Fig. 1. Mutual authentication sequence

4 Conclusions

The goal has been reached by defining an exhaustive list of security policies, and in particular by basing the protection on the mutual authentication process, of which each detail has been accurately studied. The main proposed novelty is this mutual authentication process, which is responsible for making the financial entity system highly invulnerable and immune to phishing and pharming attacks, and obviously also to identity theft, man-in-the-middle attacks. A simulation of this model is being developed in order to demonstrate its robustness.

References

1. ISO/IEC 27001: Information technology — Security techniques — Information security management systems — Requirements (2005)
2. The Open Web application Security Project, http://www.owasp.org/

Privacy Threats in Online Stock Quotes

Peter Williams

Stony Brook University, Stony Brook, NY 11794
petertw@cs.stonybrook.edu

Abstract. Stock traders reveal information about their pending trades by their selection of stock performance data to retrieve from the web. Potentially malicious quote publishers have access to this information, and can use it to profit at the trader's expense. This poster examines several potential methods to prevent this type of behavior.

Providing online stock quotes and performance history is a lucrative business. Many web sites provide this valuable information, especially targeted to individual independent traders, who are not working for a larger firms that maintain their own databases.

These online repositories offer a great deal of information that evens out the trading field for an independent investor; everyone now has quick access to detailed stock performance history and projections. This compilation of information was previously only easily accessible by large investment firms, but with the arrival of the web, any casual investor has access to much of the same information, increasing his or her ability to make intelligent decisions about market futures.

1 Privacy Issues

What a casual trader may not know is that the companies providing this information are also observing the users of this information. In the days when investors relied primarily on stock tickers and newspaper listings, there was nobody to watch an independent investor as he researched stocks and made decisions. On the Internet, every stock view is tracked; the companies providing this information now accumulate precise information about what individual investors are interested in.

This information about a stock trader's future investment plans is very sensitive. Any investor revealing his or her future stock purchases or sell-offs to another party loses all investment advantage. Moreover, if a trader's information access pattern correlates even slightly with the trader's pending purchases, the observer can generate revenue at the trader's expense, by bumping up the prices right before purchases. The fundamental issue is that knowledge of the accesses to stock performance data creates an artificial boost in the value on popular stocks. Effectively, potential investors are penalized simply for researching stock information.

G. Tsudik (Ed.): FC 2008, LNCS 5143, pp. 316–317, 2008.

2   Potential Solutions

Disguising the browsing pattern. An investor concerned that the stock information provider is using his or her access patterns to preempt transactions can reduce the publisher's ability to do so by disguising his or her browsing pattern. By examining many potential stocks, including ones that the investor has no intention to purchase, the investor does not reveal as much about which stocks he intends to purchase.

The access pattern must also be chosen carefully, so that the publisher cannot sort the fake accesses from the real ones. And even with a carefully chosen access pattern, the investor can only reduce the publisher's ability to predict his or her buying patterns; some correlation ability is still present, unless every investor maintains identical browsing patterns for *every* potential stock.

Detecting or tricking corrupt publishers. Insider trading laws may apply to stock information publishers using browsing patterns to predict purchases. If this malicious behavior is done intermittently through third parties, however, and over a large set of individuals, this behavior can be very difficult to detect, and just as profitable.

If a trader believes the information publisher is acting based on stock information viewing patterns, the trader can attempt to profit by sending false signals to the publisher, then selling stock when the publisher expects a purchase instead. The trader thereby obtains a small boost to his or her stocks before a sell-off, creating a disincentive to the publisher for abusing the access pattern. The publisher can mitigate this risk, however, if it has knowledge of the existing holdings of such clients, by avoiding the purchase races on stocks for which the clients can initiate a large sell-off.

Mix network. An investor can avoid being targeted individually by accessing the stock database via an anonimizing network. If all investors use such a network to view stock information, this can hide the source of each information request. This may reduce the provider's ability to profit off of specific profitable individuals, but they may still be able to analyze global trends. The conflict, that examining a stock can make it more valuable, still applies.

Private Information Retrieval. One final approach is to use a Private Information Retrieval algorithm to transfer stock information. Private Information Retrieval allows a client to request information from the server, without revealing to the server which information is requested.

One possible implementation requires a stock information provider to maintain an encrypted database with a secure CPU, such as the IBM 4764. The secure CPU then accesses database records without revealing to the provider which records are accessed, responding over an encrypted link to the browser. Moreover, with code verification on the secure CPU, it can be guaranteed to the trader that the provider has no knowledge of which stocks have been researched.

The downsides to this approach are a decrease in the throughput the stock information provider can support, and requiring the information provider to use specialized hardware. This is, however, a provably secure method of obtaining information without revealing which information is being obtained.

A Platform for OnBoard Credentials

N. Asokan and Jan-Erik Ekberg

Nokia Research Center, Helsinki, Finland
{n.asokan,jan-erik.ekberg}@nokia.com

Securely storing and using credentials for authentication is an essential part of protecting financial applications like on-line banking and other distributed applications. Existing approaches fall short: Requiring users to memorize credentials suffers from bad usability and is vulnerable to phishing. "Password managers" ease the usability problem somewhat, but are open to software attacks, like Trojans that steal passwords. At the other extreme, dedicated hardware tokens provide high levels of security, but are expensive and not very flexible. We observe that general-purpose secure hardware are becoming widely available and use them to develop a platform for "OnBoard Credentials" (ObCs) which combine the flexibility of virtual credentials with the higher levels of protection due to the use of secure hardware.

Several types of general-purpose secure hardware are starting to be deployed: e.g., Trusted Platform Modules (TPM) and Mobile Trusted Modules [2] specified by the Trusted Computing Group and other platforms like M-Shield [4] and ARM TrustZone. All these platforms enable, to different degrees, a strongly isolated secure environment, consisting of secure storage, and supporting secure execution where processing and memory are isolated from the rest of the system. TPMs are already available on many high-end personal computers. Several high-end Nokia phones are based on hardware security features of the M-Shield platform.

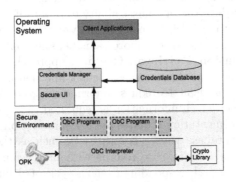

Fig. 1. OnBoard Credentials Platform

Fig. 1 shows a high-level overview of the ObC platform architecture. The primary component is the ObC interpreter which runs in the secure environment. Credential logic can be implemented in the form of "credential programs"(aka

"ObC programs") which are scripts that can execute on the interpreter. Ideally, the secure environment should provide strongly isolated run-time memory for the interpreter, such as System-on-Chip memory. Typically the amount of such strongly isolated run-time memory available is very small. For this reason, it is important to keep the memory and code footprint of the interpreter as well as the credential programs very compact. In our current implementation, we use a subset of Lua[1] as the scripting language. Our custom Lua interpreter has a code footprint of about 6kB when compiled for ARM 11 processors. Of course the architecture does not mandate the use of Lua – it is possible to use any suitable scripting language as long as any constraints from the target secure environment are satisfied. In addition to simple language constructs, our interpreter also provides an interface for commonly used cryptographic primitives.

The interpreter has exclusive access to a device-specific master key called the ObC platform key (OPK). OPK is the only secret protected by the secure storage in the secure environment. The interpreter provides sealing and unsealing functions using which credential programs can protect credentials for persistent storage. The key used by the sealing/unsealing function depends on OPK and a digest of the code of the credential program which invokes the function, thereby inherently isolating persistently stored data among credential programs.

Client applications use ObCs via a Credentials Manager (CM). CM has a simple "secure UI" which the user can recognize by customizing its appearance. It also manages a credential database where secret credential data sealed by the credential programs can be stored persistently. A strong point of our architecture is that anyone can be allowed to write and provision credential programs for the ObC platform because the platform isolates credential programs from one another. By using device-specific keypairs, we also enable anyone to provision secret credential data securely to any given set of credential programs. The same provisioning mechanism can also be used to support encrypted credential programs which are decrypted and executed within the secure environment.

We have implemented the platform on Linux on top of TPMs [3] and on Symbian OS running on a hardware secure environment based on M-Shield [1]. We have also implemented some credential programs and modified client applications to use them. For example we have extended a web browser and a SIP client to use ObCs based on a credential program implementing HTTP Digest authentication. A forthcoming report [1] provides a more in-depth description of the design and implementation of our ObC platform.

References

1. Asokan, N., et al.: On-board credentials platform: design and implementation, NRC report NRC-TR-2008-001 (to appear) (January 2008),
   http://research.nokia.com/files/NRCTR2008001.pdf
2. Ekberg, J.-E., Kylänpää, M.: Mobile trusted module. NRC report NRCTR- 2007-015 (2007), http://research.nokia.com/files/NRCTR2007015.pdf

---

[1] http://www.lua.org

3. Sharma, A.: On-board credentials: Hardware-assisted secure storage of credentials. Master's thesis, Helsinki University of Technology (2007), http://asokan.org/asokan/research/Aish-Thesis-final.pdf
4. Srage, J., Azema, J.: M-shield mobile security technology, TI White paper (2005), http://focus.ti.com/pdfs/wtbu/ti_mshield_whitepaper.pdf

ST&E Is the Most Cost Effective Measure for Comply with Payment Card Industry (PCI) Data Security Standard

Ken Huang and Paul Douthit

CGI, 12601 Fair Lakes Circle
Fairfax, VA, 22033
Ken.huang@cgifederal.com, paul.douthit@cgifederal.com

In September of 2006, the five leading payment brands formed an independent council to manage the Payment Card Industry (PCI) Data Security Standard (DSS). American Express, Discover Financial Services, JCB, MasterCard Worldwide and Visa International saw the need to secure payment account data in a globally consistent manner. As such, the financial institutions which store, process and transact the credit card must comply with the PCI/DSS. The Non-compliance fines can reach up to US $500,000 per incident including the public disclosure of breaches. Financial Institution can implement very broad security controls to comply with the PCI/DSS standard. The cost can be prohibitive. This poster argues that the most cost effective security measure is to conduct a Security Testing and Evaluation (ST&E) project before the expensive auditing performed by a PCI DSS Qualified Security Assessor (QSA) Company. We have proposed 5 distinct phases of ST&E, and what it means to the CIO/CTO of the financial institutions.

The five phases of ST&E are 1) Planning, 2) Develop Evaluation Methods and Tool Selection, 3) Test Execution and Reporting, 4) Corrective Measures Recommendation and 5) Re-Testing.

During the Planning Phase, the scope and rule of engagement is defined, and the requirement of the ST&E is signed off. The scope depends on identifying the mission critical applications which host or process the credit card data. For example, the web server, the application server and database can all be used for processing or storing the credit card information. And the application may have dependency on other applications. So the communication channels between different applications could be the crucial components and are in scope. The rule of engagement identity all stakeholders of the ST&E project, and define the responsibilities of each part involved. A poorly defined rule of engagement would be fatal for the ST&E project.

During the second phase, the testing and evaluation method is defined and agreed upon by all stakeholder involved in the ST&E. The testing method could be black box testing, meaning that the tester has no knowledge of the systems and try different ways to find the security vulnerabilities. Another testing method is the white box testing. During the white box testing, the tester reviews the code and different configuration files, and then constructs the attack methods which could hack into the system. This method is more cost effective and should be used to find the majority of the securities holes in the system.

The third phase is the Testing Execution and Reporting, the testers could use both manual ethnic hacking methods or automated tool to find the security vulnerabilities in the system. Keep in mind that the automated tool can only find

G. Tsudik (Ed.): FC 2008, LNCS 5143, pp. 321–322, 2008.

very small portion of the vulnerabilities. Thus, the advanced manual ethnic hacking skills are crucial to the success of the ST&E project. After the testing execution, the tester needs to analyze the results to identity the false positives and then produce the report which will be the input to the next phase of the ST&E.

The forth phase is the Corrective Measures Recommendation. If the application impacted is developed in house, the corrective measure could be applied by working with the developers in house. Otherwise, the tester can work with stakeholders of ST&E project to find the appropriate patches from the vendor or report the bug with the vendor if the patch is not available.

The final phase is the Re-testing phase. We emphasize that security testing is not a once and done evaluation. In order to maintain an acceptable level of security, the system must be retested periodically, as well as when the developers make any changes to the system. By developing a reoccurring phase of retesting, Phase Five depends upon the system passing its first ST&E evaluation. Once the system is deemed secure after the initial ST&E, a summation of the results can then be presented to the stakeholders. At that point, the frequency for which the system will be retested can be established.

In this poster presentation, we will demo some common vulnerabilities in the financial applications, such as cross site script attack, SQL injection, weak session management, improver exception handling, and weak encryption. After the demo, we will present in detail the ST&E methodology and how the CTO/CIO can benefit by implementing the ST&E in house, and how ST&E can benefit organizations to achieve the PCI/DSS compliance.

Making Quantitative Measurements of Privacy/Analysis Tradeoffs Inherent to Packet Trace Anonymization

William Yurcik, Clay Woolam, Greg Hellings, Latifur Khan,
and Bhavani Thuraisingham

University of Texas at Dallas
byurcik@gmail.com
{cpw021000,gsh062000,lkhan,bhavani.thuraisingham}@utd.edu

Abstract. Anonymization provides a mechanism for sharing data while obscuring private/sensitive values within the shared data. However, anonymization for sharing also sets up a fundamental tradeoff – the stronger the anonymization protection, the less information remains for analysis. This privacy/analysis tradeoff has been descriptively acknowledged by many researchers but no one has yet attempted to quantify this tradeoff. We perform anonymization options on network packet traces and make empirical measurements using IDS alarms as an indicator for security analysis capability. Preliminary results show most packet fields have unexpected complex tradeoffs while only two fields exhibiting the classic zero sum tradeoff.

Keywords: anonymization, privacy-preserving, data sharing, privacy/utility tradeoff, log anonymization, network intrusion detection systems.

1 A Quantitative Approach to a Qualitative Tradeoff

Researchers have conjectured qualitatively for the last decade about the tradeoff between anonymization protection and utility of resultant data [4,2,3]. To more fully understand this tradeoff in the context of sharing network data for security analysis, we perform experiments for a specific example (network packet traces) using a *tcpdump* anonymizer and IDS alarms as a security analysis metric. Preliminary results in [5,6] report privacy/analysis tradeoffs on packet fields are complex, with only two fields (transport protocol and packet length fields) displaying a zero sum tradeoff. We seek feedback from FC'08 participants on our experimental design and the unexpected empirical results.

2 Experimental Design

Our experimental design aims to compare the security analysis content of data to be shared *before* and *after* anonymization has been applied. We select network packet trace data to be studied since it is a worst case scenario containing the most private/sensitive information of any potential data source and is a commonly shared

G. Tsudik (Ed.): FC 2008, LNCS 5143, pp. 323–324, 2008.

dataset for collaborative security analysis. We experiment with the largest publicly available packet trace dataset [1]. We use the *SCRUB-tcpdump* [5] network packet trace anonymizer due to its flexibility to anonymize all fields and options that provide for different levels of anonymization within each field.

We use scripts to feed the packet trace dataset to an IDS, both *with* and *without* anonymization applied to each field, and then observe alarm counts as a proxy for security analysis. With a dataset consisting of over 100 separate files which vary in size, content, and when the packet traces were captured, we developed a uniform way to compare IDS alarm results from different files by first establishing a benchmark number of IDS alarms for each file *without* anonymization. Then for each experiment *with* anonymization, we measure the deviation from the corresponding file benchmark with standard statistical measures and visual scatter plots.

We are aware that IDS alarms are not a perfect proxy for security analysis. While less IDS alarms map to lower levels of security analysis, the relationship of more IDS alarms to security analysis is non-linear. With more IDS alarms, more security analysis may have taken place if *new* information is revealed by the *new* IDS alarms. However, more IDS alarms may also decrease security analysis if additional alarms are inaccurate or redundant. Despite this additional complexity, IDS alarms do provide an objective, replicable, quantitative metric for comparing security analysis with careful examination of IDS alarm output.

3 Conclusions and Future Work

Intuition is that data anonymization results in a zero sum tradeoff between privacy protection and analysis capability. We have been able to show with empirical data [5,6] that for the specific instance of packet trace, anonymization for data sharing is not simply a zero sum tradeoff but actually consists of complex tradeoffs. Future work will continue to characterize anonymization privacy/analysis tradeoffs in packet traces, first single field then emergent tradeoffs from multiple field interactions.

References

1. LBNL/ICSI Enterprise Tracing Project, http://www.icir.org/enterprise-tracing/
2. Lundin, R., Jonsson, E.: Privacy vs Intrusion Detection Analysis. In: International Symposium on Recent Advances in Intrusion Detection (RAID) (1999)
3. Rastogi, V., Suciu, D., Hong, S.: The Boundary Between Privacy and Utility in Data Publishing. In: Very Large Data Bases (VLDB) Conference (2007)
4. Sobirey, M., Fischer-Hubner, S., Rannenberg, K.: Pseudonymous Audit for Privacy Enhanced Intrusion Detection. In: 13th International Information Security Conference (1997)
5. Yurcik, W., et al.: SCRUB-tcpdump: A Multi-Level Packet Anonymizer Demonstrating Privacy/Analysis Tradeoffs. In: 3rd IEEE International Workshop on the Value of Security through Collaboration (SECOVAL) (2007)
6. Yurcik, W., et al.: Toward Trusted Sharing of Network Packet Traces Using Anonymization: Single-Field Privacy/Analysis Tradeoffs. ACM Computing Research Repository (CoRR) Technical Report cs.CR/0710.3979v1 (2007)

Author Index

Lecture Notes in Computer Science

Sublibrary 4: Security and Cryptology

For information about Vols. 1– 3958
please contact your bookseller or Springer

Vol. 5155: R. Safavi-Naini (Ed.), Information Theoretic Security. XI, 249 pages. 2008.

Vol. 5154: E. Oswald, P. Rohatgi (Eds.), Cryptographic Hardware and Embedded Systems – CHES 2008. XIII, 445 pages. 2008.

Vol. 5143: G. Tsudik (Ed.), Financial Cryptography and Data Security. XIII, 326 pages. 2008.

Vol. 5137: D. Zamboni (Ed.), Detection of Intrusions and Malware, and Vulnerability Assessment. X, 279 pages. 2008.

Vol. 5134: N. Borisov, I. Goldberg (Eds.), Privacy Enhancing Technologies. X, 237 pages. 2008.

Vol. 5107: Y. Mu, W. Susilo, J. Seberry (Eds.), Information Security and Privacy. XIII, 480 pages. 2008.

Vol. 5086: K. Nyberg (Ed.), Fast Software Encryption. XI, 489 pages. 2008.

Vol. 5057: S.F. Mjølsnes, S. Mauw, S.K. Katsikas (Eds.), Public Key Infrastructure. X, 239 pages. 2008.

Vol. 5037: S.M. Bellovin, R. Gennaro, A.D. Keromytis, M. Yung (Eds.), Applied Cryptography and Network Security. XI, 508 pages. 2008.

Vol. 5023: S. Vaudenay (Ed.), Progress in Cryptology – AFRICACRYPT 2008. XI, 415 pages. 2008.

Vol. 5019: J.A. Onieva, D. Sauveron, S. Chaumette, D. Gollmann, K. Markantonakis (Eds.), Information Security Theory and Practices. XII, 151 pages. 2008.

Vol. 4991: L. Chen, Y. Mu, W. Susilo (Eds.), Information Security Practice and Experience. XIII, 420 pages. 2008.

Vol. 4990: D. Pei, M. Yung, D. Lin, C. Wu (Eds.), Information Security and Cryptology. XII, 534 pages. 2008.

Vol. 4986: M. Robshaw, O. Billet (Eds.), New Stream Cipher Designs. VIII, 295 pages. 2008.

Vol. 4965: N. Smart (Ed.), Advances in Cryptology – EUROCRYPT 2008. XIII, 564 pages. 2008.

Vol. 4964: T. Malkin (Ed.), Topics in Cryptology – CT-RSA 2008. XI, 437 pages. 2008.

Vol. 4948: R. Canetti (Ed.), Theory of Cryptography. XII, 645 pages. 2008.

Vol. 4939: R. Cramer (Ed.), Public Key Cryptography – PKC 2008. XIII, 397 pages. 2008.

Vol. 4920: Y.Q. Shi (Ed.), Transactions on Data Hiding and Multimedia Security III. IX, 91 pages. 2008.

Vol. 4896: A. Alkassar, M. Volkamer (Eds.), E-Voting and Identity. XII, 189 pages. 2007.

Vol. 4893: S.W. Golomb, G. Gong, T. Helleseth, H.-Y. Song (Eds.), Sequences, Subsequences, and Consequences. X, 219 pages. 2007.

Vol. 4890: F. Bonchi, E. Ferrari, B. Malin, Y. Saygin (Eds.), Privacy, Security, and Trust in KDD. IX, 173 pages. 2008.

Vol. 4887: S.D. Galbraith (Ed.), Cryptography and Coding. XI, 423 pages. 2007.

Vol. 4886: S. Dietrich, R. Dhamija (Eds.), Financial Cryptography and Data Security. XII, 390 pages. 2007.

Vol. 4876: C. Adams, A. Miri, M. Wiener (Eds.), Selected Areas in Cryptography. X, 409 pages. 2007.

Vol. 4867: S. Kim, M. Yung, H.-W. Lee (Eds.), Information Security Applications. XIII, 388 pages. 2008.

Vol. 4861: S. Qing, H. Imai, G. Wang (Eds.), Information and Communications Security. XIV, 508 pages. 2007.

Vol. 4859: K. Srinathan, C.P. Rangan, M. Yung (Eds.), Progress in Cryptology – INDOCRYPT 2007. XI, 426 pages. 2007.

Vol. 4856: F. Bao, S. Ling, T. Okamoto, H. Wang, C. Xing (Eds.), Cryptology and Network Security. XII, 283 pages. 2007.

Vol. 4833: K. Kurosawa (Ed.), Advances in Cryptology – ASIACRYPT 2007. XIV, 583 pages. 2007.

Vol. 4817: K.-H. Nam, G. Rhee (Eds.), Information Security and Cryptology - ICISC 2007. XIII, 367 pages. 2007.

Vol. 4812: P. McDaniel, S.K. Gupta (Eds.), Information Systems Security. XIII, 322 pages. 2007.

Vol. 4784: W. Susilo, J.K. Liu, Y. Mu (Eds.), Provable Security. X, 237 pages. 2007.

Vol. 4779: J.A. Garay, A.K. Lenstra, M. Mambo, R. Peralta (Eds.), Information Security. XIII, 437 pages. 2007.

Vol. 4776: N. Borisov, P. Golle (Eds.), Privacy Enhancing Technologies. X, 273 pages. 2007.

Vol. 4752: A. Miyaji, H. Kikuchi, K. Rannenberg (Eds.), Advances in Information and Computer Security. XIII, 460 pages. 2007.

Vol. 4734: J. Biskup, J. López (Eds.), Computer Security – ESORICS 2007. XIV, 628 pages. 2007.

Vol. 4727: P. Paillier, I. Verbauwhede (Eds.), Cryptographic Hardware and Embedded Systems - CHES 2007. XIV, 468 pages. 2007.

Vol. 4691: T. Dimitrakos, F. Martinelli, P.Y.A. Ryan, S. Schneider (Eds.), Formal Aspects in Security and Trust. VIII, 285 pages. 2007.

Vol. 4677: A. Aldini, R. Gorrieri (Eds.), Foundations of Security Analysis and Design IV. VII, 325 pages. 2007.

Vol. 4657: C. Lambrinoudakis, G. Pernul, A.M. Tjoa (Eds.), Trust, Privacy and Security in Digital Business. XIII, 291 pages. 2007.